MACROMEDIA
Flash MX
DESIGN & APPLICATION

Denise Seguin
Fanshawe College • London, Ontario

Developmental Editor	James Patterson
Cover and Text Designer	Jennifer Wreisner
Desktop Production	Desktop Solutions
Proofreader	Susan Capecchi
Copy Editor	Desiree Faulkner
Indexer	Donald Glassman

Publishing Team: George Provol, Publisher; Janice Johnson, Director of Product Development; Tony Galvin, Acquisitions Editor; Lori Landwer, Marketing Manager; Shelley Clubb, Electronic Design and Production Manager.

Acknowledgments: The author and publisher wish to thank the following reviewers for their technical and academic assistance in testing exercises and assessing instruction: Janet Blum, Fanshawe College, London, Ontario and Desiree Faulkner.

Text and CD: ISBN 0-7638-1940-9
Text and CD Order Number: 41599
C/N 01599

© 2003 by Paradigm Publishing Inc.
 Published by **EMC**Paradigm
 875 Montreal Way
 St. Paul, MN 55102

 (800) 535-6865
 E-mail: educate@emcp.com
 Web Site: www.emcp.com

Care has been taken to verify the accuracy of information presented in this book. However, the author, editor, and publisher cannot accept any responsibility for Web, e-mail, newsgroup, or chat room subject matter or content, or for consequences from application of the information in this book, and make no warranty, express or implied, with respect to its content.

Trademarks: Macromedia® Flash™ MX Copyright © 1996-2002. Macromedia, Inc., 600 Townsend Street, San Francisco, CA 94103 USA. All rights reserved. Macromedia and Flash MX are trademarks or registered trademarks of Macromedia, Inc. in the United States and/or other countries.

Some of the product names and company names included in this book have been used for identification purposes only and may be trademarks or registered trademarks of their respective manufacturers and sellers. The author, editor, and publisher disclaim any affiliation, association, or connection with, or sponsorship or endorsement by, such owners.

All rights reserved. No part of this book may be reproduced, stored in a retrieval system, or transmitted, in any form or by any means, electronic, mechanical, photocopying, recording, or otherwise, without prior written permission of Paradigm Publishing Inc.

Printed in the United States of America
10 9 8 7 6 5 4 3 2 1

CONTENTS

Preface	**vi**

Chapter 1
Drawing Fundamentals — 3

Uses of Flash	4
Advantages of Using Flash	5
Vector Graphics	5
Bitmapped Graphics	6
Streaming Technology	7
Ease of Use	7
Compatibility	7
Starting Flash	7
The Flash Environment	8
The Stage	9
The Workspace	9
Toolbox	9
Timeline	10
Panels	10
Property Inspector	10
Working with Panels	10
Drawing Basic Shapes	12
Saving in Flash	16
File Types	16
Starting a New Document	16
Templates	16
Drawing Lines, Freehand, and Brush Strokes	17
Brush Tool	17
Pen Tool	19
Rulers, Grid, and Guides	20
Grid	21
Snapping	22
Moving, Copying, and Deleting Objects	28
Selecting Objects	28
Lasso Tool	28
Subselection Tool	29
Creating a Basic Animation Using Frames	32
Exploring the Timeline	32
Using Help	36
Chapter Summary	*41*
Commands Review	*43*
Concepts Check	*43*
Skills Check	*44*

Chapter 2
Working with Text and Editing Drawn Objects — 49

Using the Text Tool	50
Editing Text	51
Moving, Deleting, and Copying a Text Block	51
Resizing a Text Block	51
Text Properties	53
Font and Font Attributes	53
Font Size	54
Vertical Text Blocks	55
Alignment and Format Options Dialog Box	57
Character Spacing and Kerning	59
Superscripts and Subscripts	59
Text Menu	60
Breaking Text Apart	60
Document Properties	62
Changing Fill and Stroke Colors for Existing Objects	63
Ink Bottle Tool	64
Eye Dropper Tool	64
Viewing the Stage	66
Zoom Tool	67
Hand Tool	67
Using the Eraser Tool	67
Drawing Curved Lines	71
Editing Objects with the Free Transform Tool	75
Rotate and Skew	75
Scale	76
Distort	76
Envelope	76
Editing Stroke Lines	79
Lengthening Line Segments, Shortening Line Segments, and Adjusting the Shape	80
Editing Fills	82
Segmenting Fills within Shapes	83
Breaking a Shape Apart	83
Using the Lasso Tool to Select Fills	84
Intersecting Lines to Create Segments	85
Grouping Shapes	86
Grouping Multiple Shapes	87
Working with Colors	89
Color Swatches Panel	91
Applying a Gradient Fill Color	91
Creating a Gradient	92
Fill Transform	93
Chapter Summary	*95*
Commands Review	*97*
Concepts Check	*97*
Skills Check	*98*

Chapter 3
Working with Layers, Libraries, and Importing Graphics — 103

Organizing Content with Layers	104

Inserting and Renaming Layers	106
Moving and Copying Objects to a Layer Using the Clipboard	106
Moving a Layer	108
Deleting a Layer	108
Hiding and Locking Layers	109
Viewing Objects as Outlines	110
Distributing Objects to Layers	112
Creating a Mask Layer	113
Creating a Guide Layer	116
Layer Properties Dialog Box	118
Creating a Layer Folder	119
Moving Layers to a Layer Folder	120
Resizing the Timeline Panel	120
Libraries, Symbols, and Instances	120
Creating a Symbol	121
Inserting and Modifying an Instance of a Symbol	122
Editing a Symbol	124
Converting an Existing Object to a Symbol	125
Inserting Symbols from Another Movie's Library File	127
Inserting Symbols from Common Libraries	127
Creating Your Own Common Library	128
Library Management	130
Importing Graphics from Other Sources	131
Bitmap Properties	134
Breaking Apart and Editing Colors in a Bitmap	138
Using a Bitmap as a Fill	140
Converting a Bitmap to a Vector Graphic	142
Importing Bitmaps Directly to the Library	144
Copying and Pasting Images Using the Clipboard	145
Importing a Freehand Vector Graphic	145
Importing Other Vector Graphics Files	148
Importing a Fireworks Drawing into Flash	148
Reducing File Size and Increasing Efficiency by Optimizing Graphics	151
Sources of Artwork for Flash	153
Chapter Summary	*154*
Commands Review	*156*
Concepts Check	*156*
Skills Check	*157*

Chapter 4
Creating Animation and Guidelines for Flash Project Design — 163

Techniques for Creating Animation	164
Creating a Motion Tweened Animation	165
Rotating and Scaling a Motion Tween	167
Slowing Down or Speeding Up a Motion Tween	168
Creating a Motion Path for an Object to Follow During Animation	169
Orienting the Object to the Path	172
Creating a Tween to Change the Color of the Instance	172
Inserting a Keyframe in a Motion Tween	174
Working with Frames	174
Inserting and Removing Frames	174
Clearing Frames	175
Moving Frames	175
Copying Frames	176
Previewing Animations	179
Scrubbing	179
Using the Controller	179
Creating a Shape Tweened Animation	181
Using Shape Hints	184
Adding a Shape Hint	185
Viewing Shape Hints	185
Removing Shape Hints	185
Adjusting the Frame Rate for Animations	187
Creating Frame-by-Frame Animations	189
Working with Keyframes	189
Converting a Regular Frame to a Keyframe	190
Onion Skin View	192
Viewing Onion Skinned Frames as Outlines	193
Editing in Onion Skin View	194
Changing Frame View Options	196
Centering a Frame within the Timeline Panel	198
Organizing Animations Using Scenes	198
Navigating Scenes	199
Guidelines for Flash Project Design	201
The Role of Communication	202
Defining the Goals and Limiting Factors for a Flash Project	202
Determining the Audience for the Movie	203
Researching Best Practices for Flash	203
Creating a Flow Chart and Storyboard for the Movie	203
Chapter Summary	*205*
Commands Review	*207*
Concepts Check	*208*
Skills Check	*209*

Chapter 5
Adding Sound, Video, and Basic Interactivity with Buttons — 215

Adding Sound to a Movie	216
Importing a Sound File	216
Adding Sound to Animation	217
Synchronizing Sound to the Animation	219
Looping a Sound Instance	221
Applying Sound Effects	221
Editing the Sound Envelope	221

Defining Sound Properties	224
Compressing Sound Files	226
Using Sounds from the Common Library	228
Increasing Layer Height to Display Sound in Frames	230
Finding Sound on the Internet	230
Importing Video	231
Choosing the Import Video Settings	232
Importing Video Directly to the Library	236
Embedded Video Properties	236
Modifying a Video Instance	237
Importing Video in a Movie Clip Symbol	237
Creating Buttons	240
Inserting an Instance of a Button	244
Testing a Button	244
Adding Sound to a Button	245
Adding an Action to a Button	246
Using the Actions Panel	247
Creating Animated Buttons	253
Chapter Summary	*255*
Commands Review	*257*
Concepts Check	*258*
Skills Check	*259*

Chapter 6
Animating Using Symbols and Masks and Publishing Flash Movies — 263

Creating Animations Using Symbols	264
Animating Using a Graphic Symbol	266
Duplicating Symbols	269
Stopping Playback of a Movie Clip Symbol Animation	269
Converting an Existing Animation to a Movie Clip Symbol	274
Animating Using a Mask Layer	277
Using the Test Environment Before Publishing a Movie	278
Viewing the Movie in the Testing Environment	279
Using the Bandwidth Profiler	279
Testing Using Download Speed Statistics	281
Optimizing the Movie	284
Simulating the Internet Connection Speed	287
Publishing a Movie	287
Choosing Publish Settings for a Flash Player File	288
Choosing HTML Settings for a Flash Player File	290
Previewing the Movie in the Browser Window	293
Publishing the Movie	294
Viewing the HTML Code	297
Using HTML Templates	298

Publishing in Other Formats	298
Exporting in Other Formats	302
Exporting the Current Frame as an Image	302
Chapter Summary	*304*
Commands Review	*306*
Concepts Check	*307*
Skills Check	*308*

Chapter 7
Using ActionScript and Creating Templates — 313

Understanding ActionScript Concepts and Terms	314
Object-Oriented Programming	314
Actions	315
Events	315
Parameters	315
General Guidelines for Writing ActionScript	315
Using Normal Mode and Expert Mode in the Actions Panel	316
Controlling Movie Playback	319
Goto	319
On	320
Play	320
Stop	320
StopAllSounds	320
Assigning Labels and Comments to a Keyframe	321
Adding a Comment to a Keyframe	322
Creating a Preloader Animation	326
Performing a Conditional Test	326
Adding an Else Statement	326
Nesting If Statements	327
Testing for Status of Frames Loaded	327
Using Buttons to Toggle the Playing of a Soundtrack On and Off	331
With Statement	332
Using the getURL Action to Open a Web Page During a Movie	336
Using the fscommand to Control the Player Window	339
Creating and Using a Template	343
Using a Template	344
Using the Movie Explorer Panel	346
Finding Information About Flash on the Web	348
Go to the Source	349
Flashkit.com Flash Developer Resource Site	349
Flash Magazine	350
Chapter Summary	*351*
Commands Review	*353*
Concepts Check	*353*
Skills Check	*354*

PREFACE

Macromedia Flash MX by Denise Seguin teaches the essential skills and creative applications of Macromedia Flash MX. Using this book, students will become proficient in creating images and animations for Web sites. Developers familiar with earlier software releases can use this text to improve their skills and become familiar with the latest features of the software.

This text gives students hands-on experience with Macromedia Flash MX as used in a typical Web design environment. After mastering the basics of drawing and creating animations (both frame-by-frame and tweened), students learn how to manage assets using the library, organize projects in scenes, create interactive buttons, add sound, publish movies, and apply basic ActionScript statements.

Design principles and best practices are demonstrated through comprehensive, hands-on practice. A variety of exercise types teach Flash skills using authentic context and guided practice techniques. Step-by-step exercises are rich with illustrative screen captures and guided instructions.

Exercises and projects explore a variety of business applications for Flash movies. A number of projects require students to integrate graphics from other sources including Macromedia Fireworks and FreeHand.

Chapters 1 and 2 teach drawing fundamentals as students create original artwork in Flash. In Chapter 3, students import and use images from resources outside of Flash. Once students have learned how to create and edit images, Chapter 4 teaches animation techniques. A section on design principles and project management in Flash is included at the end of Chapter 4 to promote an awareness of the scope of Flash project development. In Chapter 5, students add sound and video, and create buttons. Chapter 6 teaches students how to implement intermediate-level animation techniques such as animating using symbols and masks. In addition, Chapter 6 teaches the testing, previewing, and publishing process for Flash movies. Chapter 7 introduces the use of ActionScript statements to control movie playback and demonstrates how to use templates.

Performance assessments at the end of each chapter provide opportunities for students to demonstrate their creativity and to design novel solutions to problems. Using a wide range of project cases, the performance assessments require students to demonstrate how proficient they are with the skills learned in the chapter. In these assessments, students create Flash projects from scratch and also work with project source files.

Resources for the Student

Extensive example files provide learners with a rich and imaginative learning environment by simulating a variety of businesses. Student files are available on the student CD-ROM and also can be downloaded from the Internet Resource Center (IRC) at www.emcp.com/.

In addition, a free, full-featured, 30-day trial version of Macromedia Flash MX is included on the student CD-ROM. The learner can load the software on a Windows-based computer once and enjoy the convenience of practicing and perfecting Flash MX skills at home for 30 days.

Resources for the Instructor

Instructor's resources include teaching hints, model answers in *fla* and *swf* formats (where applicable), supplementary performance projects, and a test bank of objective items. All instructor resources are furnished on both the password-protected instructor's IRC and on the Instructor's Guide CD-ROM.

About the Author

Denise Seguin has been teaching at Fanshawe College in London, Ontario since 1986. She has taught a variety of software applications to adult learners in Continuing Education courses and learners in postsecondary Information Technology diploma programs. In addition to *Macromedia Flash MX*, she has authored *Microsoft Outlook 2000* and *Microsoft Outlook 2002* and has co-authored *Office 2000* and *Office XP* for Paradigm Publishing.

CHAPTER 1

DRAWING FUNDAMENTALS

PERFORMANCE OBJECTIVES

Upon successful completion of Chapter 1, you will be able to:
- Describe applications for Flash for Web sites and other multimedia projects.
- List advantages of using Flash for creating graphics and animation.
- Define streaming, bitmap graphics, and vector graphics.
- Start Flash MX and identify components in the working environment.
- Expand and collapse panels.
- Open and close panels.
- Draw basic shapes.
- Choose stroke colors, fill colors, line thickness, and line styles for shapes.
- Save a Flash project.
- Explain the difference between *fla* and *swf* files.
- Start a new Flash document.
- Draw lines, freehand, and brush strokes.
- Turn on rulers, grids, and guides to assist with drawing shapes.
- Choose appropriate modifiers in the Options section of the toolbox for a tool.
- Create a custom fill color.
- Move, copy, and delete drawn objects.
- Close a Flash document.
- Create a basic animation by inserting keyframes.
- Describe the difference between ordinary frames and keyframes.
- Use Flash help.

There are no student data files to copy for this chapter.

Macromedia Flash MX is a software application used to create rich content for Web sites or other multimedia devices such as CD-ROMs. Using Flash, a developer creates eye-catching graphics and other components such as buttons for a user interface. The graphics or other elements can be animated to produce stimulating effects and interactivity can be added to components to enrich a user's experience.

Within Flash, a developer creates the sequence of images or imports images and then applies animation or other special effects such as sound or video. This process is referred to as *authoring*. When a project is complete, the content has to be converted to a format that can be viewed by others in an application called the Flash Player.

Drawing Fundamentals 3

The converted output is referred to as a *movie*. A user must have the Flash Player installed on his or her computer in order to view the movie. The Flash Player is distributed to Web users free of charge, and, in most cases, it is included with the Web browser software. When the Web browser accesses a site containing a Flash movie, the player is automatically launched and the movie begins playing. In this instance, the user would not even be aware that the player has loaded. Alternatively, the player can be downloaded and installed from the Macromedia Web site. As of June 2002, there were over 454 million computers worldwide that have the Flash Player.

Uses of Flash

If you have viewed a Web site where you saw images moving across the page in a sequence, or menus appear when you move the mouse over text or an icon, you have probably viewed a Flash movie. The uses of Flash are limited only by a developer's imagination. In the first exercise you will look at some content on the Web that incorporates Flash.

exercise 1

VIEWING FLASH CONTENT ON THE WEB

(Note: Web sites chage in appearance and functionality. If links in this exercise do not appear as instructed, look elsewhere on the site or substitute using other instructions as provided by your instructor.)

1. Make sure that you are connected to the Internet.
2. Start Internet Explorer or Netscape. *(Note: Screen images shown in this textbook were created using Internet Explorer version 6.0 operating in Windows XP.)*
3. Click over the current URL in the A̲ddress text box, key **www.macromedia.com**, and then press Enter.
4. Watch the Flash movie that plays on the Macromedia home page. When the movie is finished, move the mouse pointer over the word PRODUCTS at the top left of the page. Notice that the background color behind the word changes as the mouse rolls over it and the word SHORT CUTS with a right-pointing arrow appears. This example shows how Flash can be used for interactivity with the user.
5. Click SHORT CUTS. The images at the right side of the page are replaced with new content.
6. Click Macromedia Flash MX in the Products list and then click read more below the Macromedia Flash MX title.
7. Watch the Flash movie that plays as the Macromedia Flash MX page loads. When the movie is finished, click Showcase at the right of the completed Flash movie to expand the Showcase list and then click Case Studies.

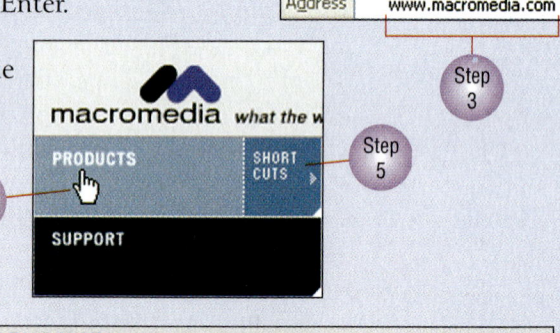

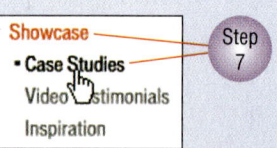

Chapter One

8. The Macromedia Showcase page includes links to organizations that use Flash MX to provide dynamic and enriching Web content. A brief description is included for each organization that describes the site's purpose and includes the Macromedia products used to create the site. Click the icon next to the United States Air Force link.
9. Read the information presented on the next page and then click the link to Airforce.com below the sample Web page.
10. Watch the opening movie that plays as the U.S. Air Force home page loads and then explore the page to see how Flash has been used to enhance the site. When you are finished browsing the site, close the Internet Explorer window to return to the Macromedia Web site. *(Note: If the U.S. Air Force page did not launch in a separate window, click Back on the browser's toolbar until you return to the Macromedia Web site.)*
11. At the Macromedia Showcase page for the United States Air Force, click Back on the browser's toolbar to return to the Showcase page listing all of the featured organizations. Choose two or three other organizations on the Showcase page and view their Web sites to see the different ways in which Flash is incorporated.
12. Close Internet Explorer or Netscape.

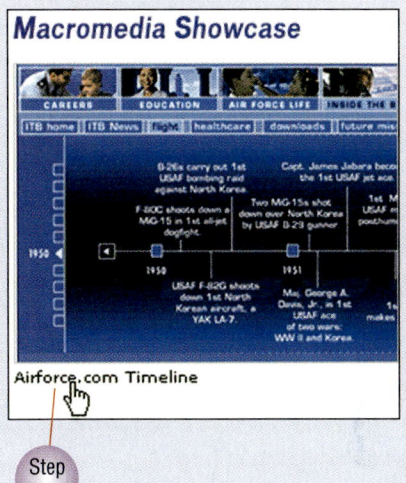

Advantages of Using Flash

Everyone who has browsed the Web has experienced visiting a Web site that contained several graphics that seemed to take forever to load. A few seconds in Internet time can mean the difference between staying to browse the site or moving to another site. An organization that is building a Web site to inform, promote, educate, or entertain the audience wants powerful graphics at the fastest speed. Graphic images are generally one of two types: *vector* or *bitmaps*. Flash has become the market leader due to its use of vector graphics.

Vector Graphics

Vector graphics use geometrical formulas to define all of the shapes representing the graphic object. For example, a straight line would be represented mathematically with the start point, end point, and included would be additional information about the line between the points such as color, thickness, and line style. File sizes for vector graphics are small, resulting in extremely fast download time for Web pages. Also, a vector graphic can be resized without becoming distorted or causing the file size to enlarge. Graphics created in Flash are stored as vectors by default.

Since vector graphic files contain mathematical equations, vector graphics generally have to be viewed within a special program such as Flash. The Flash Player is needed to view movies.

Drawing Fundamentals 5

Bitmapped Graphics

Bitmapped graphics are represented by a grid of rows and columns of dots, called *pixels*, that are numerous in quantity and densely positioned so as to blend together to form the image. Each dot requires one or more bits of data to instruct the computer as to its display state. For a simple black and white graphic, one bit can accurately describe each dot. Images with multiple colors or various shades of gray require more than one bit of data in which to accurately describe each dot. As you can imagine, file sizes for bitmapped graphics become very large in order to store all of the information about each pixel.

The house shown in Figure 1.1 was created in Microsoft Paint, which stores files as bitmaps, and then duplicated in Flash, which stores files as vectors. Notice the significant difference in file sizes between the two programs for the same image.

FIGURE 1.1 *House image created in Microsoft Paint used 503KB in disk space. Image duplicated in Flash used only 16 KB – a difference of 487 KB!*

Not only does the larger file size cause the download time to increase but bitmapped graphics, because of their construction method, do not resize well. If you enlarge a bitmapped graphic, some distortion may occur and the quality of the image deteriorates as the pixels become evident. The roof of the house shown in Figure 1.1 is shown in Figure 1.2 at 200% magnification. Notice the diagonal lines forming the roof are becoming jagged. This is referred to as being *pixelated*.

FIGURE 1.2 *Roof at 200% magnification showing pixelated lines.*

Bitmapped graphics are also called *raster graphics*. Graphic files ending with the file extension *.bmp, .gif, .jpeg, .png,* or *.tif* are bitmapped files. In some cases you will need to use a bitmapped graphic within Flash because vectors are not suitable to describe some images, such as a photograph. Flash supports bitmapped graphics as well as vector graphics and uses file compression technology to reduce the file to its smallest possible size.

Streaming Technology

Prior to the advent of streaming technology, a user had to wait until an entire file was downloaded before he or she could watch a movie. You may have experienced this in the past where you wanted to view a video or listen to an audio clip on the Internet. When you clicked the link, an audio and/or video player opened and then you waited patiently until the file downloaded, at which time it started playing. If you were using a dial-up connection with a modem and the multimedia file you requested was large, you ended up waiting several minutes before the file was completely sent.

Streaming is a technology in which a multimedia file can begin playing almost immediately while data is still being transferred from the Web server in the background. The computer at the receiving end stores the data in a buffer (a temporary storage area) and sends it to the audio/video player application in such a way that a continuous stream of content can be played without interruption. Flash streams content so that movies with graphics, sound, animation, and video can begin playing as soon as they are launched.

Ease of Use

As you will soon experience for yourself, Flash is relatively easy to learn. For someone who has only used standard applications such as word processing or e-mail, the Flash interface will take some getting used to. However, with a little practice you will quickly be able to create innovative content for a Web site. The drawing tools are similar to those used in other applications and Flash provides assistance for beginners with adding animation and interactivity.

When it is time to publish your content to the Web, Flash automatically generates the HTML code required for the Web page to start the Flash movie. You can also choose to publish the Flash movie in various other formats if the content is not destined for the Web.

Compatibility

Since Flash movies are viewed within the Flash Player, incompatibilities between Web browsers or operating systems are not issues of concern as they were in the past when a Web page had to be tested within multiple browsers to ensure it worked in all cases. The movie will display consistently no matter what environment the user is operating within.

Starting Flash

To start Flash in Windows XP:
- Click Start.
- Point to *All Programs*.
- Point to *Macromedia*.
- Click *Macromedia Flash MX*.

In Windows XP, a two-column menu appears when you click the Start button. By default, the first or leftmost column displays the last six opened applications. Get in the habit of scanning the list of recently used programs once you have used Flash for the first time; you can reopen it later after clicking the Start button with a single click on Macromedia Flash MX in the first column.

If you are using a computer with Windows 2000 or an earlier version of Windows, follow similar steps as above to start Flash, with the exception that earlier versions of Windows display *Programs* instead of *All Programs* after clicking Start.

Alternatively, if a shortcut exists on the desktop, double-click the shortcut to launch Flash. Depending on your system configuration, the steps to start Flash on the computer you are using may differ. If necessary, check with your instructor.

The Flash Environment

The first time Macromedia Flash MX is loaded, the screen shown in Figure 1.3 appears. This screen may appear daunting to a first-time Flash user. In the remainder of this chapter you will focus on the components required to create simple drawings and animations. You will close or collapse those elements that are not needed. This will alter the appearance of the screen shown in Figure 1.3 by removing distractions. In later sections and chapters, additional tools will be introduced as they are needed and explained in detail.

FIGURE 1.3 **The Flash Screen**

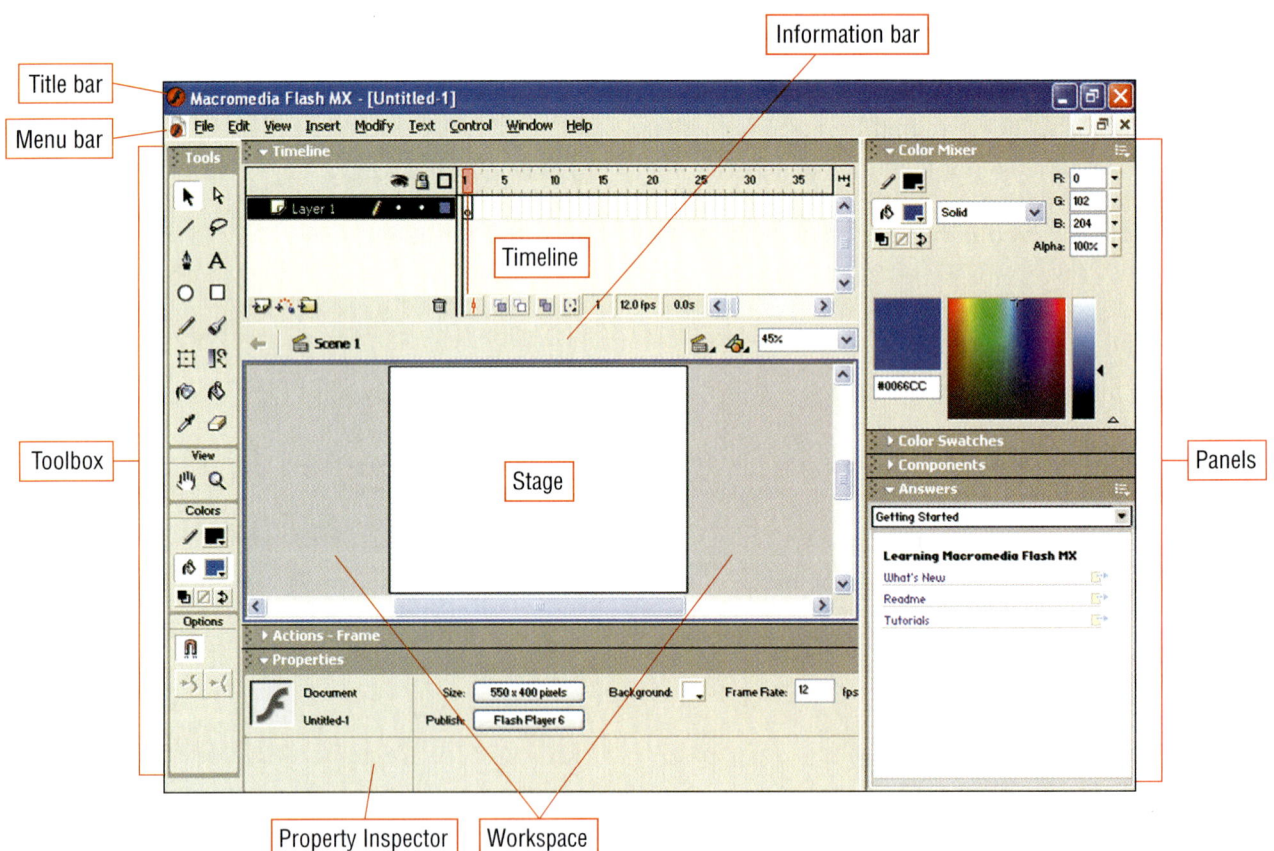

Very quickly you will understand that the authoring process in Flash is like being the director and producer of a film. In fact, Flash uses terminology analogous to the movie industry such as *stage, frames,* and *scene*. If you consider that you are creating a movie that is designed to capture your audience you will be able to relate to the director metaphor.

The Flash window contains elements standard to Windows-based applications such as the Title bar and Menu bar. The Title bar contains the standard buttons to minimize, restore, or close Flash. Options are accessed from the Menu bar using the same techniques as any other Windows program – click the option on the Menu bar and then click the desired command or feature from the drop-down list. Keyboard shortcuts are displayed next to the items on the menus for which a shortcut exists. Throughout this book, options will be accessed using the menus. As you become familiar with Flash, you may prefer to use some of the shortcut keys to access frequently used options.

Screen images shown throughout this book display menus with the shortcut keys underscored. If you are using Flash MX on a computer that uses Windows 2000 or Windows XP, press the Alt key before clicking a menu to view the shortcut key. Earlier versions of the Windows operating system display the underscored character by default. To access a menu using the keyboard, press Alt plus the underscored character. At the drop-down menus, press the underscored character to choose an option, or use the up and down arrow keys to move to the desired option and then press Enter.

The Stage

The white rectangle in the middle of the screen is called the *stage*. The stage is the place in which you will draw objects and/or place items that you want to appear in your movie. Regard the stage as the screen for your movie; items that you want the audience to see must appear on the stage.

The Workspace

To the left and right of the stage are gray areas called the *workspace*. Items in the workspace are not included when the Flash file is converted to a movie. From time to time as you are creating your Flash project, you will place objects in the workspace temporarily while you are building something or use this space to practice drawing with a new tool.

When creating animations you can also use the workspace for objects that you want to animate on or off the stage as the movie plays.

Toolbox

Using tools in the *toolbox* is how you will draw, edit, or otherwise work with objects on the stage or workspace. The toolbox can also be referred to as the *tools panel*. By default, the toolbox is docked at the left edge of the screen. By dragging its Title bar, the toolbox can move around the screen and float over the stage or workspace, or you may prefer to dock it at the right side of the screen. As you can see, there are several tools in the toolbox. Tools will be introduced as you use them.

Timeline

A Flash movie is segmented into *layers* with each layer containing *frames* that are controlled through the *Timeline*. Layers are used to organize and control the content in the movie and frames control the animations. Objects in one layer act independently from objects in another layer, allowing you to work with an object in the current layer without affecting objects in another layer. Layers are stacked on top of each other. You will learn how to create and use layers in Chapter 3.

Each layer has a sequence of frames associated with it. The frames for each layer display horizontally next to the layer name. By using frames, you will control what objects appear in the movie at which point in time and for how long they will remain visible. Think of the Timeline as the script for your movie.

Panels

Flash includes numerous *panels* that allow you to work with objects in your movie. The panels are organized by functions and are similar to Windows-based dialog boxes without the OK and Cancel buttons. Several panels are visible when Flash is launched in the default layout. The panels can be expanded, collapsed, or closed to remove them from the screen.

When you start Flash MX for the first time, the Answers panel is open at the bottom right corner with options for learning Flash.

Property Inspector

The *property inspector* is a context-sensitive panel that displays information about the currently selected object and includes options for modifying the object's attributes. When no object is selected, the property inspector provides information about the current document. You will use the property inspector frequently as you create Flash movies. Throughout this textbook the property inspector will be referred to as the *Properties panel* as this is the name displayed in the panel title bar.

Working with Panels

Each panel in Flash contains the buttons identified in Figure 1.4. In Exercise 2 you will learn how to manipulate panels using these buttons.

FIGURE 1.4 Panel Buttons

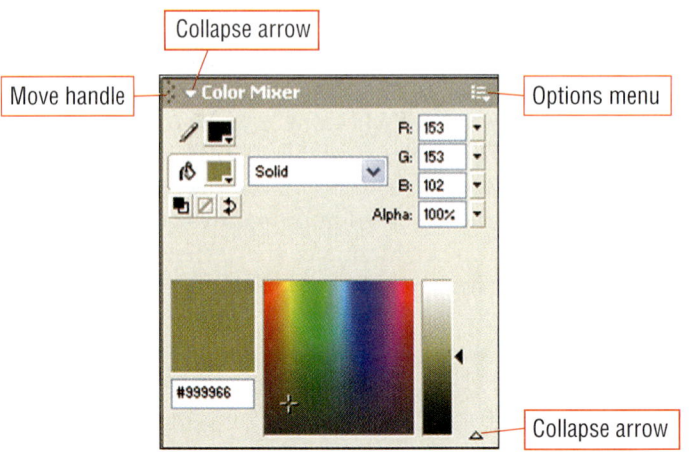

Click Window on the Menu bar to view a list of panels. Panels that are checked are currently open. Clicking a checked panel name removes it from the screen or collapses it. Clicking a panel name that is not checked will open the panel or expand it if it is already open. A group of panels that you use frequently can be customized and saved as a panel set.

exercise 2

OPENING, EXPANDING, COLLAPSING, AND CLOSING PANELS

1. Click Start, point to *All Programs* (Windows XP) or *Programs*, point to *Macromedia*, and then click *Macromedia Flash MX*; or click the Macromedia Flash MX icon on the Desktop to start Flash.
2. Open and move a panel by completing the following steps:
   a. Click Window on the Menu bar and then click Scene. The Scene panel opens in the middle of the screen.

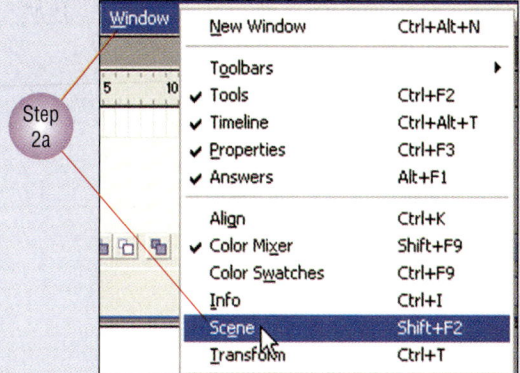

   b. Point to the Move handle (displays as 5 dots) in the Scene panel title bar until the four-headed arrow move icon appears.
   c. Hold down the left mouse button and then drag the panel to the bottom right corner of the screen. As you drag the panel, a dimmed image of the panel moves with the mouse and thick black borders appear to indicate the position the panel will be placed when you release the mouse.
3. Collapse, expand, and close a panel by completing the following steps:
   a. Click the collapse arrow (displays as a down-pointing triangle) in the Scene panel title bar. The Title bar is now the only visible element of the Scene panel.

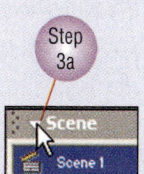

   b. Click the collapse arrow again (now displays as a right-pointing triangle) to expand the panel.

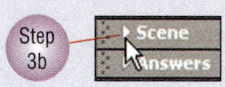

FLASH MX

Drawing Fundamentals 11

c. Click the Options menu button on the Scene panel title bar. *(Note: The Options button does not appear on the Title bar of a collapsed panel.)*
d. Click Close Panel. *(Note: Options menus contain different choices depending on the panel.)*
4. Close all panels along the right edge of the screen and close the Actions panel if it is visible above the Properties panel so that your Flash screen resembles the one shown below.

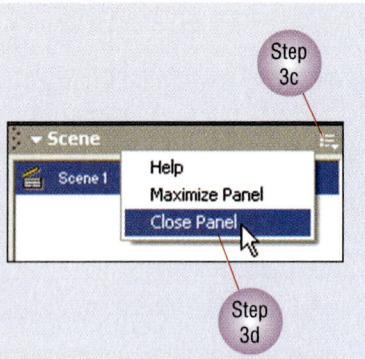

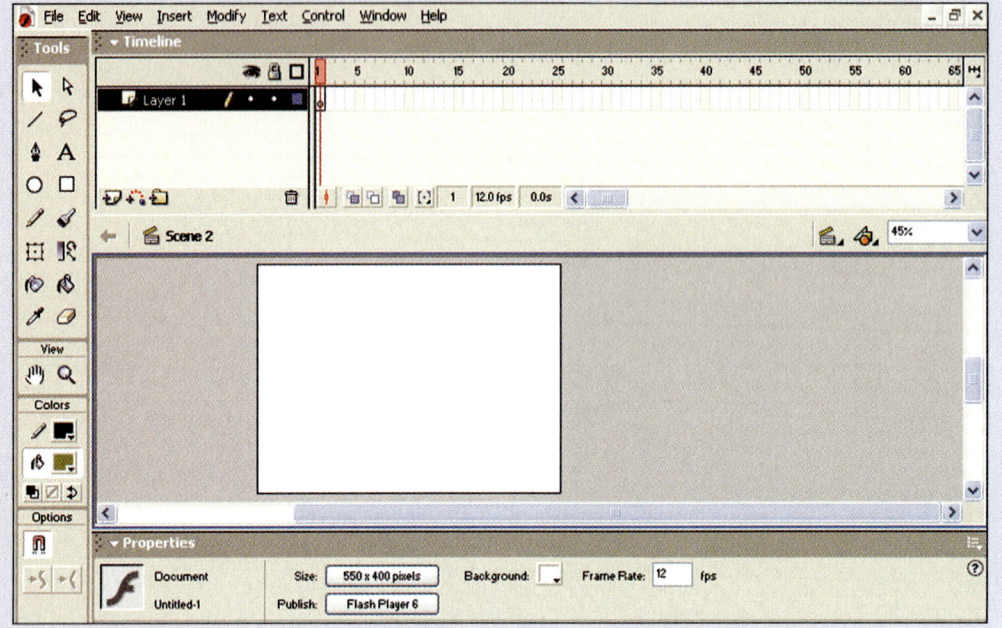

Drawing Basic Shapes

Objects are drawn on the stage using the drawing tools in the toolbox. Each button in the toolbox is identified in Figure 1.5. Do not worry about remembering each tool's name since Flash displays a tooltip when you point the mouse at a button in the toolbox. The keystroke equivalents are displayed in parentheses after each name in the tooltip.

FIGURE 1.5 Toolbox

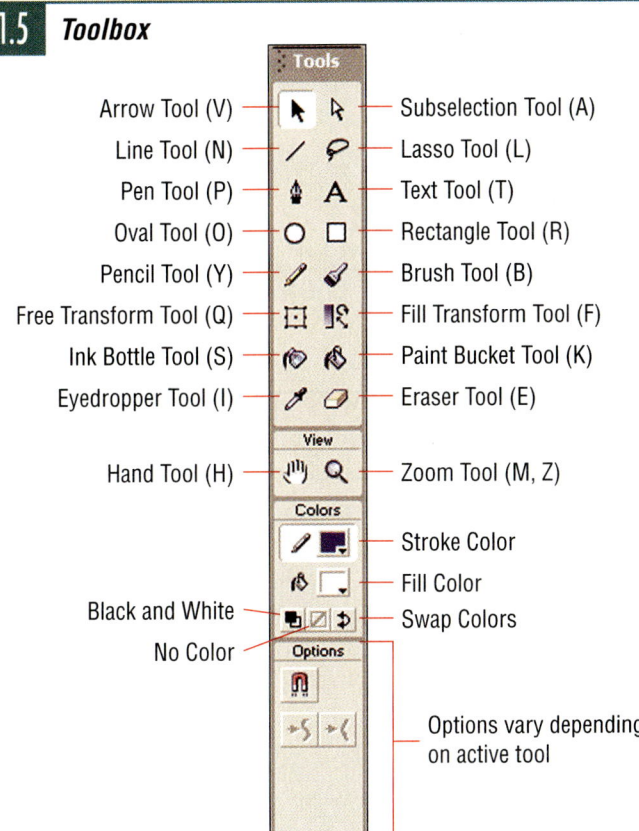

The process of drawing one of the shapes described in Table 1.1 generally involves the following steps:

- Click the tool in the Toolbox for the shape that you want to draw.
- Choose the attributes that you want to use for the shape such a line colors, fill colors, line thickness, line styles, and so on.
- Draw the shape by positioning the crosshair pointer on the stage at the starting point, drag the crosshair to the desired ending point, and then release the mouse button.

TABLE 1.1 Basic Drawing Tools

Icon	Function
/	Draw horizontal, vertical, or diagonal lines. Holding down the Shift key while drawing creates straight lines or lines at 45 degree angles.
♠	Draw straight-edged shapes or curved lines. Flash creates Bézier curves which are lines with selection handles that you drag to control the shape of the curve.

Continued on next page

Drawing Fundamentals

Icon	Function
○	Draw oval shapes. Holding down the Shift key while drawing creates a circle.
✎	Draw freehand.
□	Draw rectangle shapes. Holding down the Shift key while drawing creates squares. Rectangles with rounded corners can be created using the Round Rectangle Radius button in the Options section of the toolbox.
🖌	Draw brush strokes similar to painting with a paint brush. Several options for controlling the brush strokes are available using the Brush Mode, Brush Size, and Brush Shape buttons in the Options section of the toolbox.

The best way to learn how to draw is through practice. In Exercises 3, 4, 5, and 6 you will create graphics using each of the drawing tools described in Table 1.1.

DRAWING OVALS, CIRCLES, RECTANGLES, AND SQUARES

(Note: If you skipped Exercise 2, refer to the image of the Flash screen in Exercise 2, Step 4, and close all of the panels not shown in the image before starting this exercise.)

1. With Flash open, make sure the current magnification is set to 100% by clicking View, pointing to Magnification, and then clicking 100%. Draw ovals and circles by completing the following steps:
   a. If you have been experimenting with drawing prior to starting this exercise, click File and then click New to clear the stage.
   b. Click the Oval tool in the toolbox.
   c. Click the Stroke color button in the Properties panel to display the color palette. Flash uses the term *stroke* for the line that outlines a shape.
   d. Click the bright blue color in the first column of the palette as shown.

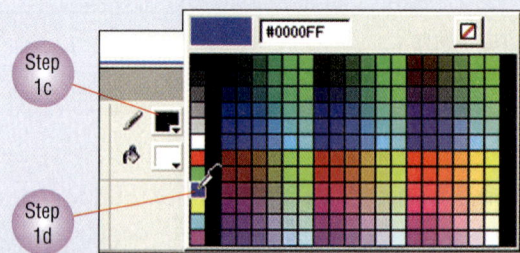

Step 1c
Step 1d

   e. Click the Fill color button in the Properties panel and then click the turquoise color in the first column of the palette as shown. Notice that the stroke color and fill color selections made in the Properties panel have also changed in the Colors section of the toolbox; you can use either set of buttons to change the colors.

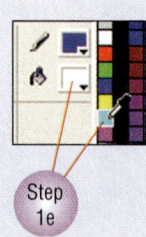

Step 1e

14 Chapter One

f. Position the crosshair pointer near the top left edge of the stage, hold down the left mouse button, drag down and right so that the outline of the oval shape is approximately 1.5 inches wide and 1 inch tall as shown, and then release the mouse. The oval shape is drawn with the bright blue outline and turquoise fill. *(Note: Dimensions provided for shapes are only approximations. Do not be overly concerned with exact height and width at this point.)*
g. Position the crosshair pointer near the left edge of the stage below the oval drawn in step 1f, hold down the Shift key, drag down and right so that the outline of the circle shape is approximately 1.5 inches wide and tall, and then release the mouse and the Shift key.

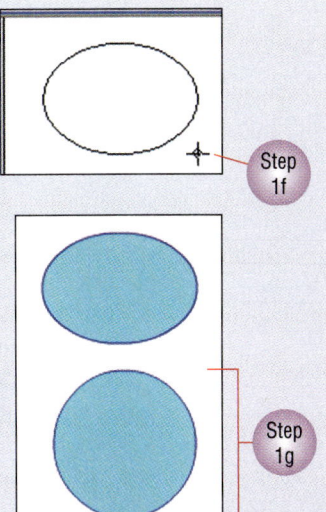

2. Draw rectangles and squares by completing the following steps:
    a. Click the Rectangle tool in the toolbox. Notice that the color selections made in the Properties panel in Step 1 remain in effect for the rectangle.
    b. Click the Stroke color button in the Properties panel and then click Black in the palette.
    c. Click the Fill color button in the Properties panel and then click the red color in the first column of the palette.
    d. Double-click over the current value in the Stroke height text box in the Properties panel and then key **4**.
    e. Click the down arrow next to the Stroke style list box and then click the hatched line in the pop-up list.
    f. Draw a rectangle to the right of the oval that is approximately 2 inches wide and 1-inch tall.
    g. Hold down the Shift key and draw a square to the right of the circle that is approximately 1.5 inches wide and tall.

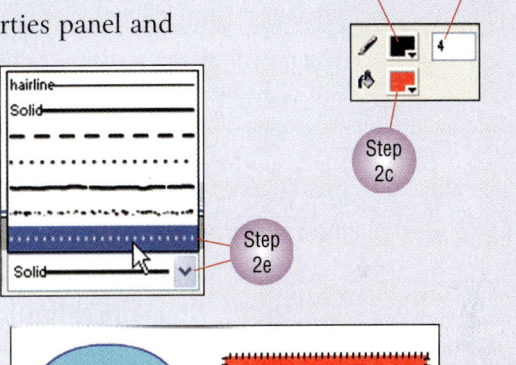

3. Save the Flash document by completing the following steps:
    a. Click File on the Menu bar and then click Save As.
    b. With *Untitled-1.fla* (your number may vary) selected in the File name text box, key **Ch1Ex03**.
    c. If necessary, change the drive and or folder in the Save in list box to the location where student files are to be stored. Check with your instructor if necessary.
    d. Click the Save button.
4. Click File and then click New to clear the stage.

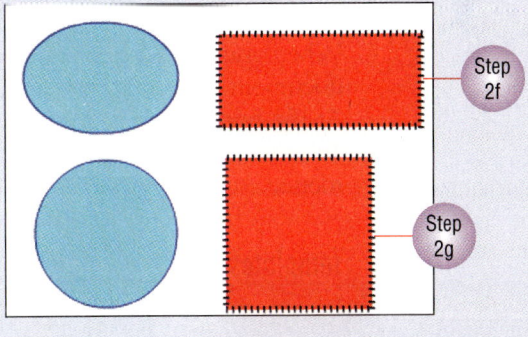

Drawing Fundamentals

Saving in Flash

In Exercise 3, Step 3, you clicked File and then Save As to save the Flash drawing. You could also have clicked File and then Save. Since the project was untitled, clicking Save would cause Flash to open the Save As dialog box so that you could assign a file name to the document.

Once the file name is assigned, use the Save As feature to change the name so that you can keep multiple versions of a project. For example, assume you are working on creating a new logo for a client. You create the first drawing and save it with the name Logo1Draft. After saving, you make alterations to the drawing. You want to keep the original drawing and the revised drawing so that you can show both versions to the client. In this case you would use Save As to save the revised drawing with a different name such as Logo2Draft.

As you are creating a drawing, it is a good idea to use File and then Save after each modification or addition to the drawing. By doing this, if you modify the drawing or add something that cannot be undone, you can use the Revert feature to return to the last saved version of the file. To do this, click File and then click Revert.

File Types

Flash files have the extension *.fla* automatically assigned to the end of the file name. The *fla* file is the authored document in which you created your movie. The *fla* file can only be opened in Flash.

When you convert the movie to the format recognized by the Flash Player, the file is copied and the extension is changed to *.swf*. The *swf* file can be viewed in any Web browser that includes the Flash Player. Users can view the *swf* file only; modifications to content have to be done in the *fla* file and then re-exported.

Starting a New Document

When you clicked File and then New to clear the stage in Exercise 3, Step 4, a new document was created. The Ch1Ex03 document was moved to the background. At the bottom of the Window menu, the open documents are listed by file name. To switch to another open document, click the document name at the Window menu.

Templates

Included with Flash are several templates which include predefined document properties, objects, and so on. Complete the following steps to start a new document using one of the Flash templates:

- Click File and then New from Template.
- Click a category name from the Category list box in the New Document dialog box.
- Click a document name from the Category Items list box.
- Use the Preview window to view the template and read the description below it.
- Click Create when you have chosen the template you want to use.

Drawing Lines, Freehand, and Brush Strokes

As described in Table 1.1, the Line tool draws horizontal, vertical, or diagonal lines. Use the Pencil tool when you want to draw freehand by dragging the mouse on the stage. With the Pencil tool active, the Options section of the toolbox displays the Pencil Mode modifier. Three modes are available for drawing with the pencil as shown in Figure 1.6.

Line Tool

Pencil Tool

FIGURE 1.6 *Pencil Modes*

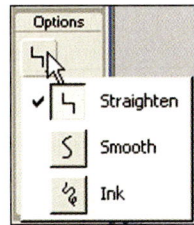

Straighten mode will cause Flash to create straight connected lines from the lines that you draw. For example, if you draw a rough outline of a rectangle, Flash will convert the shape to a rectangle when you release the mouse.

Smooth mode causes Flash to convert the lines you draw into smoother curves than you have made, and *Ink* mode will cause the least amount of smoothing possible so that the shape is as close to your actual dragging actions as possible. In Figure 1.7, each of the three modes is illustrated using the Pencil tool to draw the letter *S*.

FIGURE 1.7 *Letter S Drawn in Each Pencil Mode*

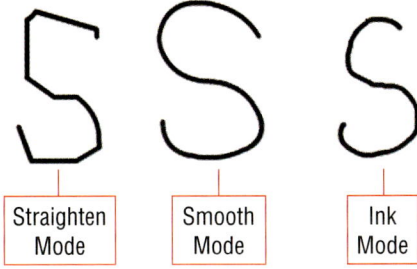

Brush Tool

The Brush tool can also be used to draw freehand when you want an effect similar to painting on a wall with a paint brush where the stroke is filled with a solid color or gradient but has no line outlining it. Three modifiers appear in the Options section of the toolbox when the Brush tool has been selected: Brush Mode, Brush Size, and Brush Shape. The five brush modes are described in Table 1.2 and each mode is illustrated in Figure 1.8.

Brush Tool

TABLE 1.2 Brush Modes

Icon	Mode	Function
	Paint Normal	The brush strokes will paint over any area on the stage including any drawn objects.
	Paint Fills	The brush strokes do not cover the stroke lines around filled objects.
	Paint Behind	The brush strokes appear in the background behind existing drawn objects.
	Paint Selection	The brush strokes appear only inside currently selected objects.
	Paint Inside	The brush strokes are drawn inside one filled object only, which is the object that you begin drawing in. Other filled objects in the stage remain unaffected.

FIGURE 1.8 Illustrated Brush Modes

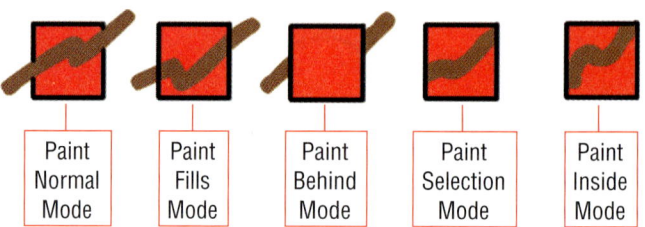

Paint Normal Mode | Paint Fills Mode | Paint Behind Mode | Paint Selection Mode | Paint Inside Mode

Click Brush Size in the Options section of the toolbox to choose the size of stroke that you want to create as shown in Figure 1.9. Click Brush Shape to choose the shape of the stroke that you want to create as shown in Figure 1.10.

FIGURE 1.9 **Brush Sizes**

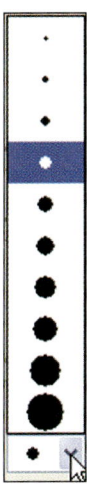

FIGURE 1.10 **Brush Shapes**

Pen Tool

The Pen tool can be used to create closed shapes, straight lines, or curved lines. With the Pen tool active in the toolbox and the desired stroke and fill options selected, click once on the stage to set the starting point for the closed shape. Click the other points needed to create the shape that you want. Lines connect the points as you go. Double-clicking the final point at the same position as the starting point closes the object and automatically fills the enclosed shape.

Pen Tool

To draw a shape comprised of straight lines, follow the steps in the previous paragraph. Double-clicking the last point ends the shape. If the final point does not meet the starting point, no fill is added to the shape.

A curved line known as a Bézier curve is drawn by completing the following steps:

- With the Pen tool active, position the mouse pointer with the Pen icon attached on the stage where you want the first curve to begin.
- Drag the pointer in the direction that you want a curve to follow. Flash will also extend a line with a point in the opposite direction that you drag so

Drawing Fundamentals 19

that the line that you see created on the stage has a point where you started, a point at the end of the line in the direction you dragged the mouse, and another point at the opposite end of the line. These points, called *handles* can be used later to modify the curve with the Subselection tool.

- Draw a second line starting at the position where you want the first curve to end. Drag a line the length and angle of the desired direction and curvature of the line. As you drag, the curve will appear between the two lines; keep dragging up or down as required to achieve the desired angle.
- Continue adding more lines as needed to create additional curves.
- Click the Arrow tool (solid black arrow) to complete the curved shape.

Figure 1.11 illustrates a closed shape, a straight line shape, and a curved shape created with the Pen tool. Curves can be complex to create and require practice. Do not be discouraged if your first curves require several attempts. You will practice creating curves in Chapter 2.

FIGURE 1.11 **Shapes Drawn with Pen Tool**

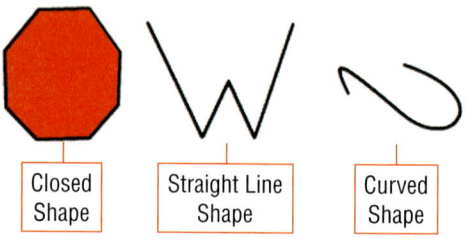

Rulers, Grid, and Guides

The View menu contains options to assist with the placement and sizing of shapes as you are drawing. Rulers can be toggled on or off by clicking View and then Rulers. By default, the unit of measure for the horizontal and vertical rulers are pixels. Pixel is the short form for *Picture Element*, which is a single point in a graphic image. Graphics monitors display images by dividing the screen into thousands (or millions) of pixels in a grid-like fashion. The units of measurement can be changed to inches, points, centimeters, or millimeters. To do this, display the Document Properties dialog box by clicking Modify and then Document or by clicking the Size button in the Properties panel with no objects selected. Click the down arrow next to Ruler Units and then choose the desired option.

When the rulers are visible, you can drag horizontal or vertical guides from the ruler to the stage. These guidelines help you place objects on the stage. They are not visible to the user when the output is converted to a movie. By default, Show Guides is turned on from the View menu, meaning that if you drag a guideline from a ruler, the line appears on the Stage. Click View, point to Guides, and then click Show Guides to turn off the display of the guidelines. To remove a guideline from the stage once the objects are drawn, with the Arrow tool active, point to the guide and then drag it back to the ruler. By default, green guidelines are displayed. Click View, point to Guides, and then click Edit Guides to change the color. Figure 1.12 illustrates the stage with the rulers and a horizontal and vertical guideline.

FIGURE 1.12 Rulers and Guide Lines Displayed on the Stage

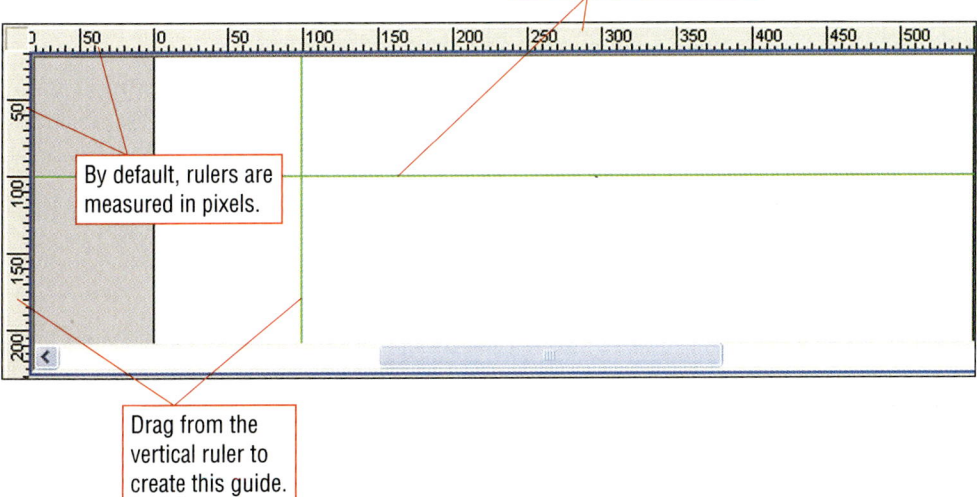

Grid

Turning on the display of the grid is another method to assist with placing objects on the stage. The grid places horizontal and vertical lines on the stage similar to a piece of graph paper as shown in Figure 1.13.

FIGURE 1.13 Grid Displayed on the Stage

Click View, point to Grid, and then click Show Grid to toggle the grid on or off. Click View, point to Grid, and then click Edit Grid to display the Grid dialog box where you can change the color of the gridlines or increase or decrease the width and height between gridlines.

Snapping

Flash will pull a line or object to another object, a grid point, or guideline as you draw. This feature is called *snapping*. Think of the grid and guidelines as magnets that attract objects to them. When you drag near a grid point or guideline, you will notice a circle attached to the crosshair pointer to indicate a snap point that the object can be snapped to. The circle appears small when you are away from a snap point and then enlarges when you are near a snap point.

In some cases, the snapping feature may interfere with your drawing if you are trying to move a precise distance. If you notice that you are attempting to draw a line or object or drag an existing line or object to a specific point and you cannot seem to get to the right position, you need to turn the snap feature off.

To turn on or off the snap feature for guides:
- Click View.
- Point to Guides.
- Click Snap to Guides to insert or remove a check mark. *(Note: By default, Snap to Guides is turned on as indicated by a check mark next to the option.)*

To turn on or off the snap feature for the grid:
- Click View.
- Point to Grid.
- Click Snap to Grid to insert or remove a check mark.

To turn on or off the snap to objects feature:
- Click View.
- Click Snap to Objects.

exercise 4
DISPLAYING RULERS, GUIDES, AND DRAWING LINES

1. With Flash open at a clear stage, turn on the display of the rulers and create horizontal and vertical guides by completing the following steps:
   a. Click View and then click Rulers.
   b. Position the mouse pointer anywhere on the vertical ruler bar, hold down the left mouse button, drag right to 100 pixels on the horizontal ruler, and then release the mouse button. A black line moves with the pointer so that you can see the guideline as you drag. A directional arrow is attached to the pointer. When you are positioned on an exact pixel position on the horizontal ruler, the black ruler tick mark changes to white.
   c. Position the mouse pointer anywhere on the horizontal ruler bar, hold down the left mouse button, drag down to 100 pixels on the vertical ruler, and then release the left mouse button.

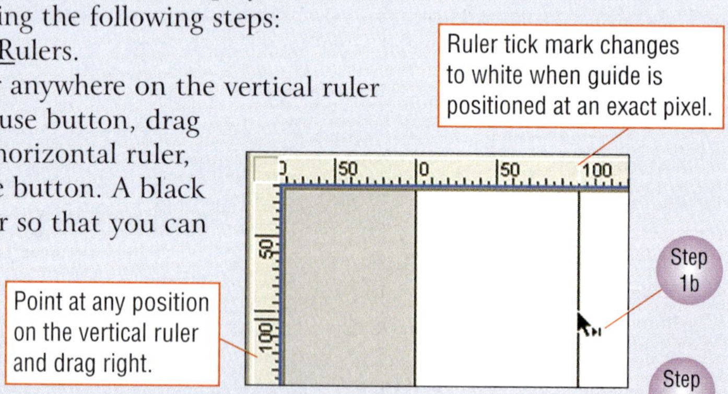

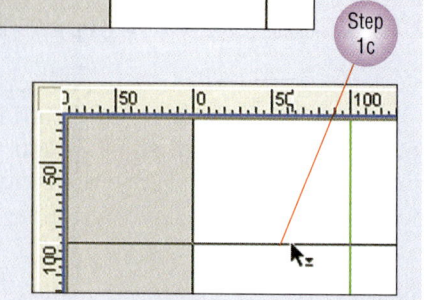

Ruler tick mark changes to white when guide is positioned at an exact pixel.

Point at any position on the vertical ruler and drag right.

Step 1b

Step 1c

d. Position the mouse pointer on the vertical ruler bar and then drag a guide right to 250 pixels on the horizontal ruler.
e. Position the mouse pointer on the horizontal ruler bar and then drag a guide down to 200 pixels on the vertical ruler.

2. Draw lines using the Line tool by completing the following steps:
    a. Click the Line tool in the toolbox.
    b. Click the down arrow next to the Stroke style list box and then click Solid at the pop-up list.
    c. Click the down arrow next to the Stroke height text box, drag the slider down to 2.5, and then click in the Properties panel anywhere outside the slider bar to close it.
    d. Position the crosshair pointer at the intersection of the vertical and horizontal guides at 100 pixels. The crosshair changes color to purple when it is positioned exactly on the guidelines and the ruler tick marks change to white.
    e. Hold down the left mouse button, drag right to the intersection of the vertical guide at 250 pixels and the horizontal guide at 100 pixels, and then release the left mouse button. As you drag, the line displays purple across the horizontal guideline. A circle appears attached to the crosshair to indicate the snap point.
    f. Position the crosshair pointer at the intersection of the vertical guide at 100 pixels and the horizontal guide at 200 pixels and then drag right to the intersection of the vertical guide at 250 pixels and the horizontal guide at 200 pixels.
    g. Position the crosshair pointer at the intersection of the vertical guide and horizontal guide at 100 pixels and then drag down and to the right to snap to the right end of the bottom line. *(Note: The shape appears as a backward Z.)*
    h. Draw another diagonal line starting at the right end of the top line and snapping to the left end of the bottom line.

3. Click File and then click Save As. Key **Ch1Ex04** in the File name text box and then click Save.

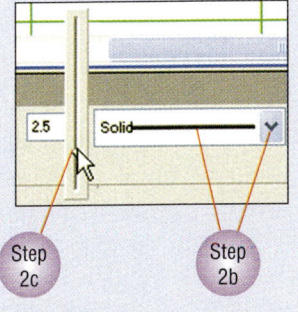
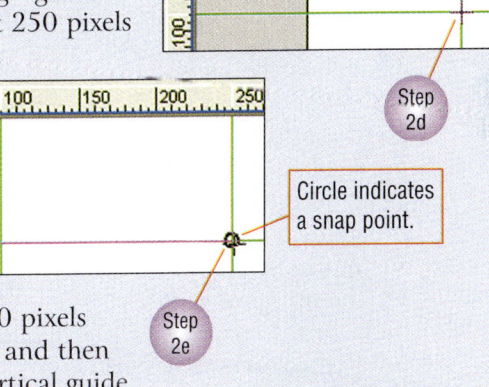
Circle indicates a snap point.
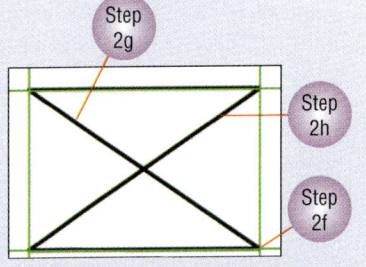

Drawing Fundamentals 23

exercise 5

REMOVING GUIDES AND RULERS, CREATING A CUSTOM FILL COLOR, AND DRAWING FREEHAND WITH THE BRUSH TOOL

1. With Ch1Ex04 open, remove the guidelines by completing the following steps:
   a. Click the Arrow tool (solid black arrow).
   b. Point at the vertical guideline at 100 pixels in a white area of the stage.
   c. Hold down the left mouse button, drag the guide to the vertical ruler bar, and then release the mouse. The guideline is removed from the stage.
   d. Remove the remaining three guides by completing steps similar to those in 1b and 1c.

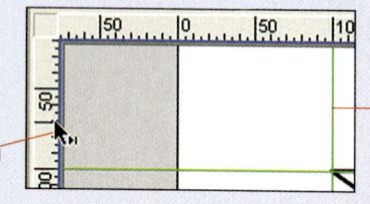

Step 1c

Point anywhere in white area on the vertical guide and then drag left to ruler.

2. Click View and then click Rulers to remove the horizontal and vertical ruler bars.
3. Create a custom fill color by completing the following steps:

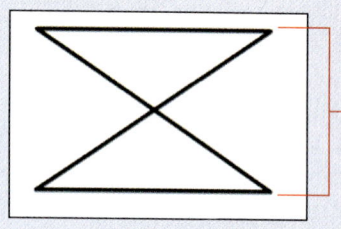

All guide lines removed

   a. Click the Brush tool.
   b. Click Fill Color in the Colors section of the toolbox.
   c. Click the color wheel at the top right of the color palette.
   d. Click the third color swatch from the left in the bottom row of the Basic colors section in the Color dialog box. This step moves the four-pronged pointer in the Color box at the right to a position closer to the base color from which you want to customize. If you did not see the four-pronged pointer move in the color box, click the Red color swatch and then repeat this step.

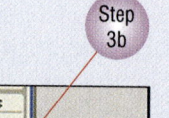

Step 3b

Step 3c

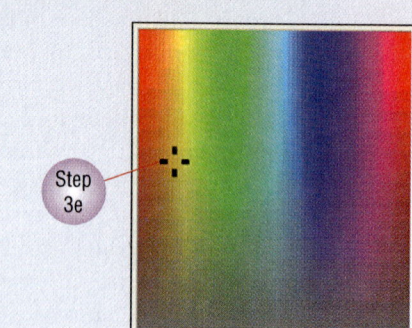

Step 3d

Step 3e

   e. Drag the four-pronged pointer up and slightly to the left to add more yellow and red to the base color until it is at the approximate location shown.
   f. Drag the brightness slider at the right of the color box up until the color is approximately the color shown.
   g. Click Add to Custom Colors. The customized color is added to the first color swatch in the Custom colors section. You can create up to 16 custom colors. This is only one method of creating custom fill colors. In Chapter 2 you will learn how to use the Color Mixer panel to create a custom stroke and fill color.
   h. Click OK to close the Color dialog box. The custom color is automatically selected as the Fill Color.

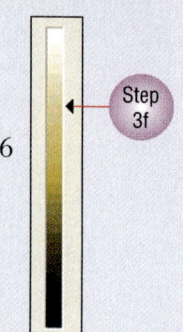

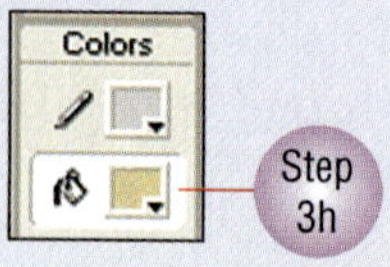

Step 3f

Step 3h

24 Chapter One

4. Change the brush mode, brush size, and draw freehand with brush strokes by completing the following steps:
   a. Click Brush Mode in the Options section of the toolbox.
   b. Click Paint Inside.
   c. Click the down arrow next to Brush Size in the Options section of the toolbox.
   d. Click the fourth brush size from the top.
   e. Practice freehand drawing in the workspace at the left of the stage by dragging the mouse to create strokes in a similar fashion as shown. *(Note: If necessary, click the left scroll button a few times to get more workspace to the left of the stage.)*
   f. Continue practicing in the workspace until you are comfortable drawing freehand with the brush tool. Use the workspace at the right of the stage if you need more room.

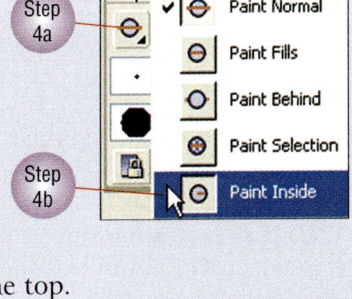
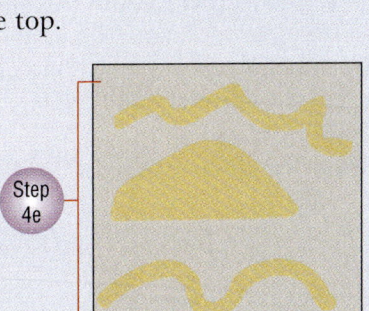
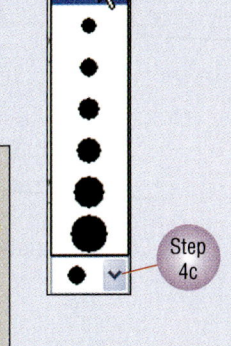

   g. Once you are comfortable using the Brush tool, draw inside the top and bottom triangles as shown. Do not worry if you spill into the lines creating the shape as you drag; the Paint Inside modifier means that the fill will not cover any lines once you release the mouse. If you need to make another attempt, click the Arrow tool and then click inside the triangle over the fill. This will select the fill as indicated by small black dots covering the fill area. Press Delete and then start again.
   h. Click Fill Color in the Colors section of the toolbox and then click a black color swatch.
   i. Change the Brush Size to the smallest possible size.
   j. Click four brush strokes in the bottom triangle as shown.
   k. Change the Fill Color back to the custom color created earlier in this exercise.
   l. Click four brush strokes in the bottom triangle as shown to resemble sand particles.

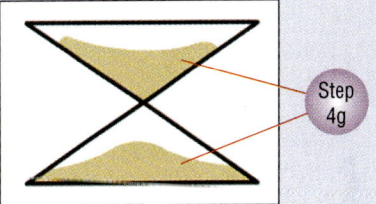
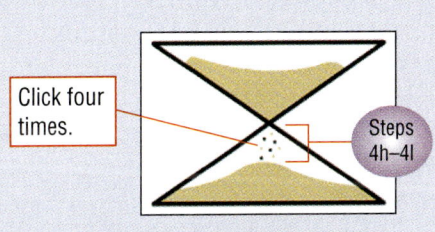

5. Click the Arrow tool, draw a box around the practice drawing you did in the workspace to select all of the brush strokes you created in Step 4e, and then press Delete. If necessary, repeat this step for any practice drawing in the workspace at the right of the stage.
6. Click File and then click Save to save the revised file using the same name (Ch1Ex04).
7. Click File and then click New to clear the stage.

DISPLAYING AND EDITING THE GRID, DRAWING WITH THE PEN TOOL, AND DRAWING FREEHAND WITH THE PENCIL TOOL

1. With Flash open at a clear stage, turn on the display of the grid by clicking View, pointing to Grid, and then clicking Show Grid.
2. Turn on the snapping feature, edit the space between gridlines, and turn on the rulers by completing the following steps:
   a. Click View, point to Grid, and then click Snap to Grid. *(Note: Skip this step if Snap to Grid already has a check mark next to it.)*
   b. Click View, point to Grid, and then click Edit Grid.
   c. Drag across the current value *(default width is 18 pixels)* in the width text box and then key **25**.
   d. Drag across the current value *(default height is 18 pixels)* in the height text box and then key **25**.

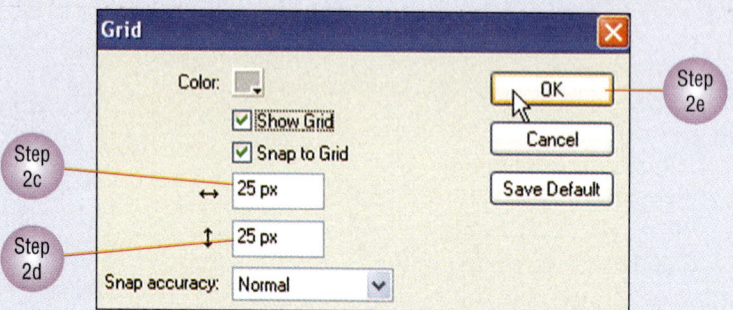

   e. Click OK to close the Grid dialog box.
   f. Click View and then click Rulers.
3. Draw the outline of a house using the Pen tool by completing the following steps:
   a. Click the Pen tool in the toolbox.
   b. In the Properties panel for the Pen tool change the following options:
      1) Choose a dark green color swatch for the stroke color.
      2) Change the stroke height to 1.5.
   c. With Fill Color active in the Colors section of the toolbox, click the No Color button.
   d. Position the mouse pointer at the vertical gridline at 150 pixels and the horizontal gridline at approximately 25 pixels. *(Note: You may need to scroll the stage up to see the 0 pixel point on the vertical ruler.)* The pointer displays the Pen icon with a small × attached. The × indicates this will be the first point in the drawing.

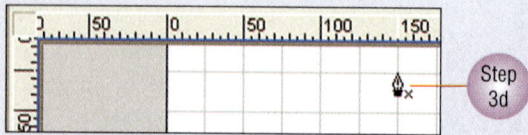

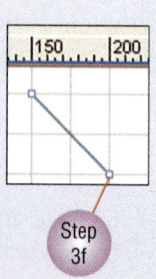

   e. Click the left mouse button. A small blue dot appears at the first point.
   f. Position the mouse pointer at the vertical gridline at 200 pixels and the horizontal gridline at approximately 75 pixels and then click the left mouse button. A diagonal line is drawn from the first point to the second point.

g. Click the third horizontal gridline below the second point.
h. Click the fourth vertical gridline to the left of the third point.
i. Click the third horizontal gridline above the fourth point.
j. Double-click at the starting point to complete the shape. The Pen icon displays with a circle to indicate you are closing a path.

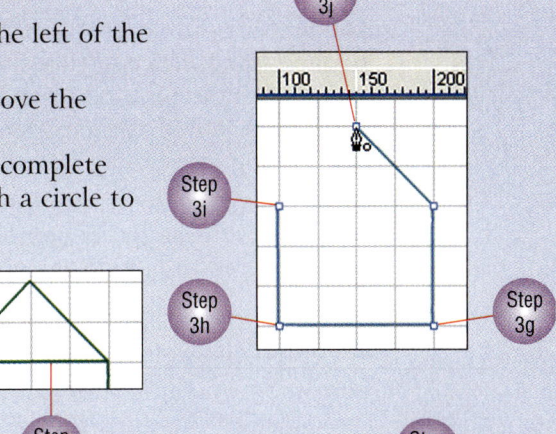

4. Save the current document and name it Ch1Ex06.
5. Use the Line tool to draw the roofline as shown.
6. Use the Line tool to draw the chimney as shown. *(Hints: Draw three separate lines. Remember that holding down the Shift key while dragging creates a straight line. Click Edit and then click Undo after drawing a line if you want to redo it.)*

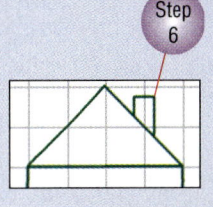

7. Draw smoke curling from the chimney and clouds using the Pencil tool by completing the following steps:
   a. Click the Pencil tool in the toolbox.
   b. In the Properties panel for the Pencil tool change the following options:
      1) Choose a dark gray color swatch for the stroke color.
      2) Change the stroke height to 1.
   c. Click Pencil Mode in the Options section of the toolbox and then click Ink.
   d. Click View, point to Grid, and then click Snap to Grid to turn the snapping feature off.
   e. If necessary, scroll the stage up so that you can see the top of the stage.
   f. Position the mouse pointer (displays as a pencil icon) in the middle of the top of the chimney, hold down the left mouse button, and then drag to create the curling smoke as shown. *(Hint: Remember to use the Undo feature if you want to redo the line.)*
   g. Change the Pencil Mode to Smooth and then draw the clouds as shown. *(Hint: Use the workspace to practice first.)*

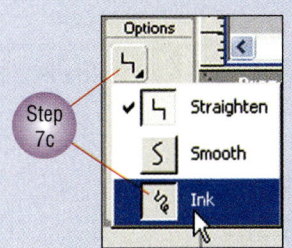

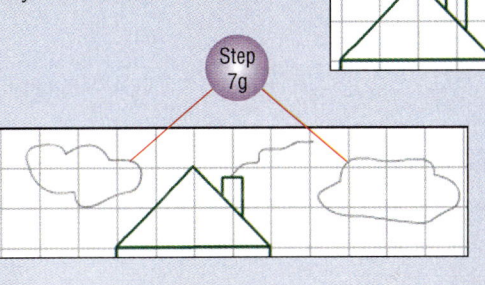

8. Turn off the display of the grid by clicking View, pointing to Grid, and then clicking Show Grid.
9. Turn off the display of the rulers by clicking View and then Rulers.
10. Save the revised document using the same name (Ch1Ex06).

Drawing Fundamentals 27

Moving, Copying, and Deleting Objects

Arrow Tool

As you learned in Step 5 of Exercise 5, the Arrow tool can be used to draw a box around shapes. Drawing a box around shapes selects all of the objects within the box. Flash indicates a selection by blanketing the area with dots of a contrasting color. Make sure that the correct objects or portions of objects are selected before you perform any editing operation.

To move an object, point over the selection and then drag to the desired position on the stage. To copy a selected object, hold down the Ctrl key while dragging. Pressing the Delete key will delete the selected object.

Selecting Objects

With the Arrow tool active, pointing at the line that outlines the object causes Flash to select the stroke line only. The inside fill, if any, is not selected. Conversely, pointing at the inside fill of an object and clicking with the Arrow tool selects only the fill and not the stroke line. This is beneficial in some cases if you want to work with the stroke or fill independently. Double-clicking an object with the Arrow tool selects both the stroke line and the fill. Figure 1.14 depicts three ovals, the left one with the stroke line only selected, the middle one with the fill only selected, and the right one with both the stroke line and the fill selected.

FIGURE 1.14 *Ovals Selected Using Arrow Tool*

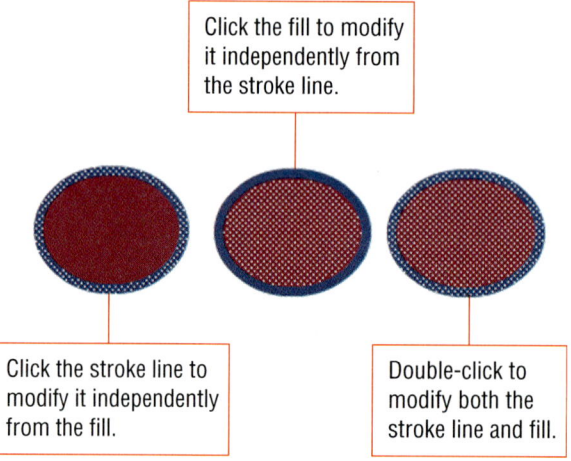

Multiple nonadjacent objects can be selected in Flash by holding down the Shift key while clicking with the Arrow tool.

Lasso Tool

Lasso Tool

Use the Lasso tool if the area to be selected is in a location in which drawing a box with the Arrow tool is not possible or might cause elements to be included that you do not want selected. The word *Sale* shown in Figure 1.15 was drawn using the Brush tool. To select *ale* so that the letters could be deleted and then redrawn would be cumbersome using the Arrow tool. With the Lasso tool, you are able to draw freehand around the area to be selected. When the mouse is released, anything within the shape drawn with the lasso is selected.

FIGURE 1.15 *Letters Selected Using Lasso Tool*

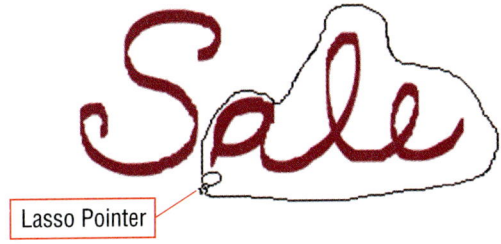

Lasso Pointer

Subselection Tool

Clicking the outline of an object with the Subselection tool displays the points that define the object. An individual point of an object can then be manipulated. For example, in Figure 1.16, a star was drawn with the Pen tool. Clicking the outline of the star with the Subselection tool caused the 10 points that comprise the object to be displayed as shown by the white handles. Dragging the top point of the star allows the top point to be lengthened while the remainder of the object is unaffected.

Subselection Tool

FIGURE 1.16 *Star Object Selected Using Subselection Tool*

Before you manipulate a selected object with the Subselection tool, look at the square that is attached to the white pointer. A filled square means that any action will affect the entire object while an empty square indicates the action will affect only the desired point as shown in Figure 1.17.

FIGURE 1.17 *Subselection Tool Pointers*

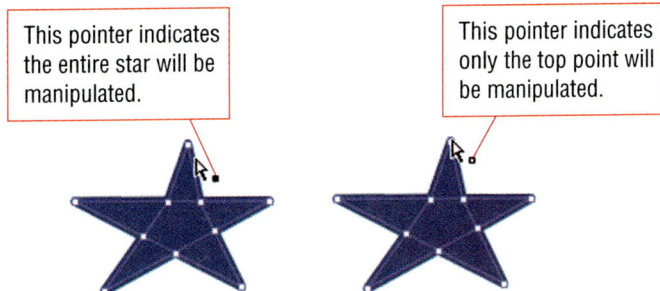

This pointer indicates the entire star will be manipulated.

This pointer indicates only the top point will be manipulated.

Drawing Fundamentals

exercise 7
SELECTING, MOVING, COPYING, AND DELETING OBJECTS USING THE ARROW TOOL

1. With Ch1Ex06 open, switch to the document created in Exercise 3 by completing the following steps:
   a. Click <u>W</u>indow on the Menu bar.
   b. Click Ch1Ex03.fla at the drop-down menu. All open Flash files are listed at the bottom of the menu below the Cascade and Tile options. A check mark next to a file name indicates it is the active project.

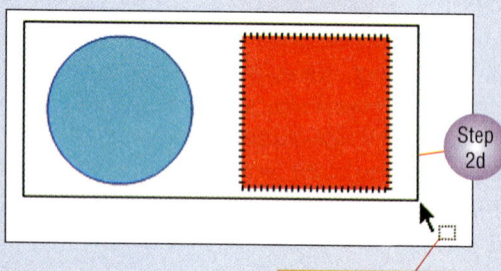
Step 1b

2. Select and delete objects by completing the following steps:
   a. Click the Arrow tool in the toolbox.
   b. Double-click the red rectangle at the top right of the stage. Double-clicking selects both the stroke lines and the fill.
   c. Press Backspace or Delete. The rectangle is deleted.
   d. With the Arrow tool still selected, draw a selection box around the turquoise circle and red square at the bottom of the stage.
   e. Click <u>E</u>dit on the Menu bar and then click Cl<u>e</u>ar.

Step 2b

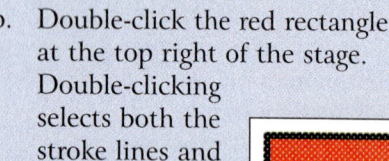
Step 2d

Pointer indicates selection box

3. Select and copy the oval and then move the duplicate oval by completing the following steps:
   a. Point to the stroke line surrounding the remaining oval and then click the left mouse button. This selects the stroke line only.

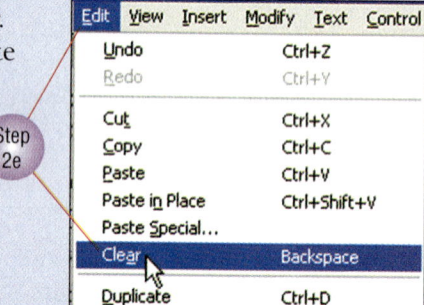
Step 2e

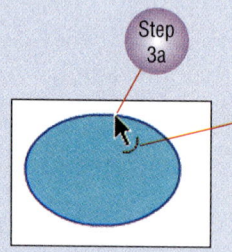
Step 3a

Click when you see this icon. The curved line attached to the pointer indicates you can manipulate a line or curve.

   b. Hold down the Shift key and then click inside the oval over the turquoise fill. Holding down the Shift key allows you to select multiple objects.
   c. Click <u>E</u>dit on the Menu bar and then click <u>C</u>opy.
   d. Click <u>E</u>dit on the Menu bar and then click <u>P</u>aste. A duplicate copy of the oval is dropped on the stage and is automatically selected with the original oval now deselected.

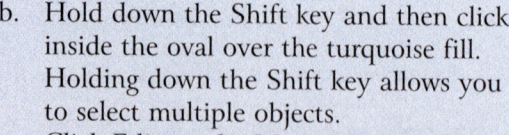
Step 3b

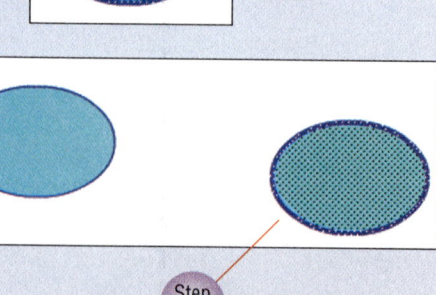
Step 3d

30 Chapter One

FLASH MX

e. Position the mouse pointer over the duplicate selected oval until you see the four-headed arrow move icon attached to the pointer, hold down the left mouse button, drag the oval until it is next to the first oval, and then release the mouse. As you drag, the outline of the object moves with the pointer so that you can see how it will be positioned when you release the mouse.

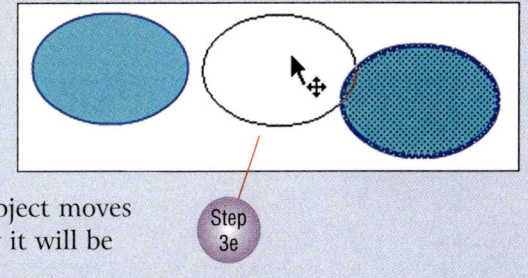

Step 3e

f. Click anywhere in a white area of the stage to deselect the oval.
4. Save the revised document using the same name (Ch1Ex03).
5. Click File and then click Close the close the document.

exercise 8 — SELECTING, MOVING, AND MODIFYING OBJECTS USING THE SUBSELECTION TOOL

1. With Ch1Ex06 open, switch to the Ch1Ex04 document.
2. Click the Subselection tool in the toolbox.
3. Practice selecting and moving an object with the Subselection tool by completing the following steps:
   a. With the Subselection tool active, point to the top line in the top triangle until the pointer displays with a filled black box attached to it and then click the left mouse button. All of the anchor points for the object are displayed as white handles. *(Note: The selection handles on the inside fills for your object may be in different positions from the illustration depending on how you painted the fill with the brush strokes.)*

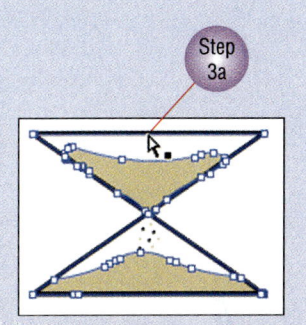

   Step 3a

   b. With the pointer still displaying with a filled black box attached to it drag the object to the right approximately 2 inches. Notice the individual sand particles drawn inside the hourglass did not move as they are not included in the path (stroke lines or inside fill) of the larger object.

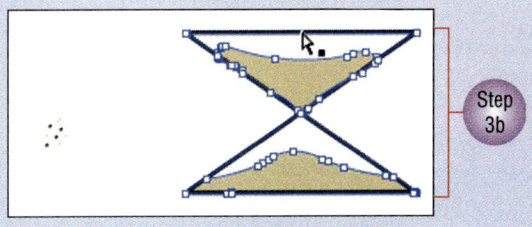

   Step 3b

   c. Click Edit and then click Undo to restore the object to its original position. The selection handles are removed from the object.
4. Modify an individual point within an object using the Subselection tool by completing the following steps:
   a. With the Subselection tool active, point to the bottom line in the bottom triangle until the pointer displays with a filled black box attached to it and then click the left mouse button.
   b. Turn the Snap to Objects feature off so that you can move a point more precisely by completing the following steps:
      1) Click View.
      2) Click Snap to Objects at the drop-down menu to remove the check mark.
      (Note: Skip this step if Snap to Objects is already deselected.)

FLASH MX   Drawing Fundamentals   31

c. Position the pointer on one of the selection handles for the fill inside the bottom triangle until the pointer displays with an empty box attached to it, hold down the left mouse button, drag the point up towards the edge of the triangle, and then release the mouse. As you drag the point, the modified fill will be outlined in blue so that you can see how the fill is being changed. 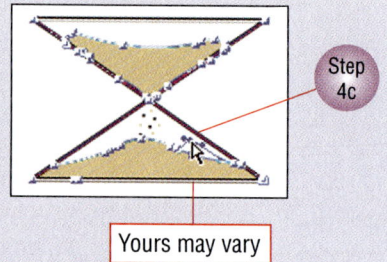
d. Click in a white area of the stage to deselect the object.
e. Click View and then click Snap to Objects to turn the snapping feature back on.
5. Save the revised document using the same name (Ch1Ex04).
6. Click File and then click Close.

Creating a Basic Animation Using Frames

In Exercise 1 you viewed Flash content on the Web and saw that one of the primary methods of grabbing a user's attention is through the use of moving images. *Animation* is the simulation of movement created by showing a series of graphics over a period of time where each graphic is slightly different from the previous graphic. When these graphics are played at a fast speed, one after the other, the illusion of progressive movement occurs.

Animation is one of the main reasons developers use Flash to create Web content. Chapter 4 deals extensively with animation principles and methods; however, now that you have experimented with drawing some basic shapes, creating a simple animation will get you motivated to learn more!

Exploring the Timeline

As previously stated, you should think of the Timeline as the script for your movie. The Timeline contains frames in which you control what objects appear in the movie at which point in time and how long they remain visible. Creating animations involves working extensively within the Timeline; therefore, an understanding of the Timeline and how it works is essential. Figure 1.18 shows the Timeline and identifies the key elements needed for our basic animation. Other components of the Timeline will be introduced later as needed.

FIGURE 1.18 **The Timeline**

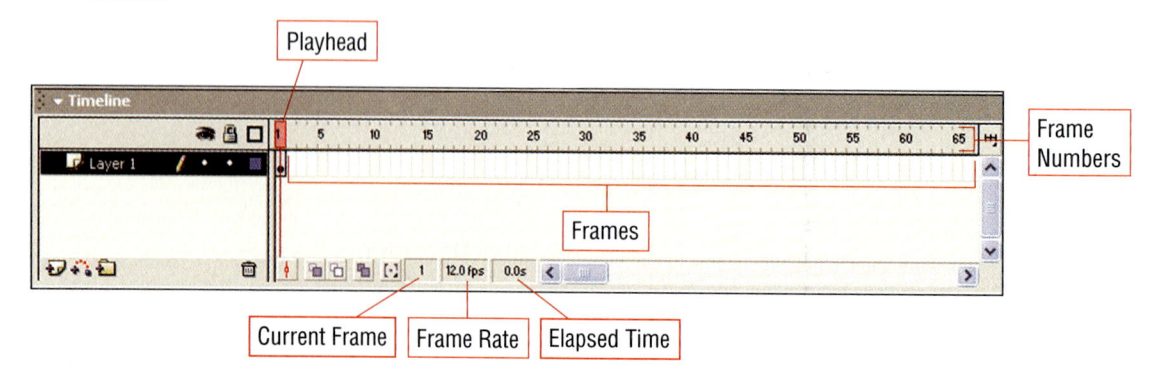

A *frame* controls what the user sees at a particular point in time when the movie is played. Associating a frame with a different graphic at a different point in the Timeline is how you animate using frames. The default *frame rate* for movies is 12 frames per second, meaning that 12 images are viewed each second. For example, assume you have an image of a person driving a sports car in frames 1 through 12, then at frames 13 through 25 the person is standing beside the car looking at a flat tire, and then at frames 26 through 38 the person is walking away from the car down the street. When the movie is played, the user would see the person driving the sports car for 1 second, then the person standing beside the car looking at the flat tire for 1 second, and finally the person walking away for 1 second.

Two types of frames display in the Timeline: *ordinary frames* and *keyframes*. As the author of a Flash movie, you work only in keyframes and Flash creates for you the frames between the keyframes, which are called ordinary frames. To follow the example in the previous paragraph, you would insert keyframes at frames 13 and 26 and then modify the images (frame 1 is automatically considered a keyframe since it is the starting point of the movie.) Flash would automatically generate the copies of the images in ordinary frames in frames 2 through 12, 14 through 25, and 27 through 38.

Keyframes are identified in the Timeline by a dot inside the frame. A solid dot indicates the keyframe contains content and an empty dot means the keyframe is currently blank.

The red *playhead* illustrates the current frame in the timeline. As the movie is played back, the playhead moves along the timeline to show the frames as they are played.

Complete the following basic steps to create an animation using frames:

1. Since frame 1 is automatically a keyframe, create the images and/or other content on the stage for the first portion of the movie.
2. Click on the Timeline below the frame number where you want the image in the movie to change to simulate movement. This selects the frame in the Timeline.
3. Insert a keyframe.
4. Modify the content on the stage for the second portion of the movie. For example, modify the drawing, add a new picture, or otherwise change the image.
5. Repeats Steps 2–4 for each area where you want to change the images to create the illusion of movement in the movie.
6. View the movie.

exercise 9

CREATING ANIMATION USING FRAMES

1. With Ch1Ex06 open, save the document using Save As and name it Ch1Ex09.
2. Click the Arrow tool in the toolbox.
3. Create the first change in the movie images by completing the following steps:
   a. Click in the Timeline below frame number 18. Flash indicates frame 18 is selected by filling the frame box with blue.

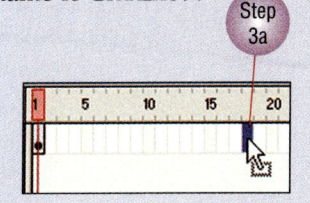

Step 3a

Drawing Fundamentals 33

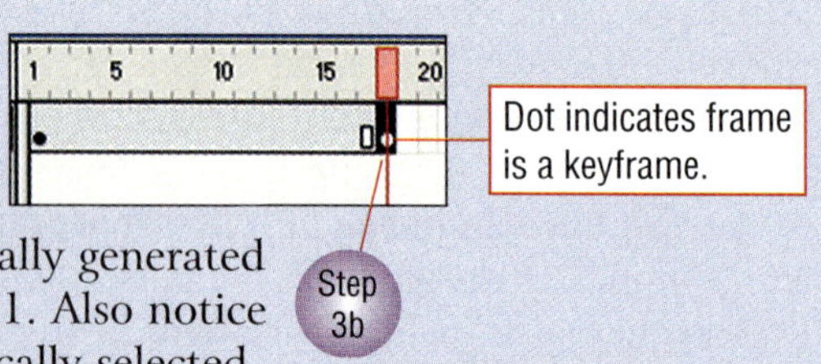

b. Click <u>I</u>nsert on the Menu bar and then click <u>K</u>eyframe. Flash displays a dot in frame 18 indicating the frame is a keyframe, the playhead moves to frame 18, and frames 2 through 17 are automatically generated with copies of the image that was in frame 1. Also notice that the graphics on the stage are automatically selected.

c. Click in any white area of the stage to deselect the images. You want rain to appear falling from the clouds in the second portion of the movie so you do not want to delete any of the existing images.

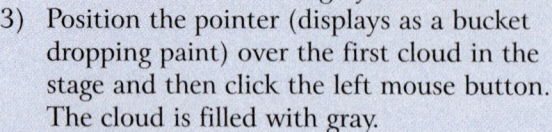

d. Darken the clouds and draw rain falling from the clouds on the stage by completing the following steps: 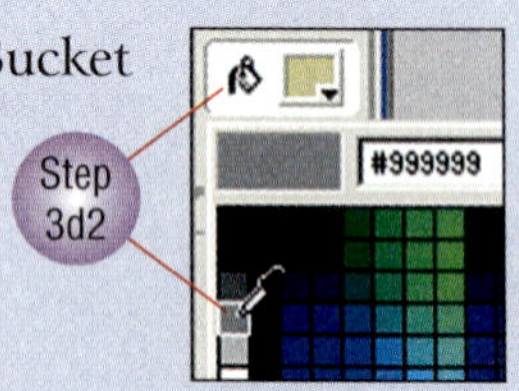
   1) Click the Paint Bucket tool in the toolbox. The Paint Bucket is used to add fill to images after they have been drawn.
   2) Click Fill Color in the Colors section of the toolbox and then choose a medium gray color swatch.
   3) Position the pointer (displays as a bucket dropping paint) over the first cloud in the stage and then click the left mouse button. The cloud is filled with gray. 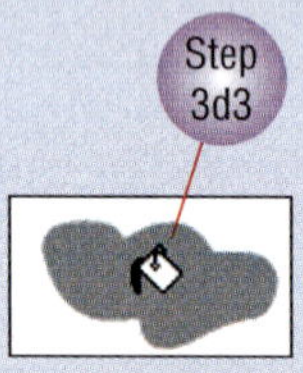 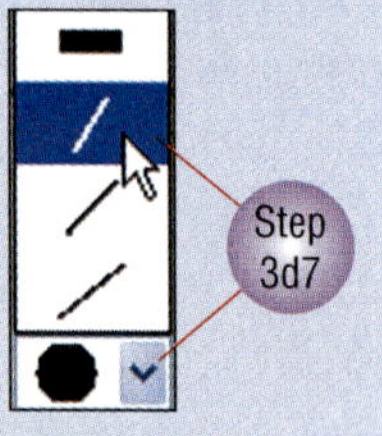
   4) Repeat Step 3d3 for the second cloud.
   5) Click the Brush tool.
   6) Choose the smallest brush size.
   7) Click the down arrow next to Brush Shape and then click the third shape from the bottom of the pop-up list.
   8) Practice a few brush strokes in the workspace to get a feel for drawing raindrops before drawing on the stage. When you are comfortable with your technique, select and delete the practice raindrops. 
   9) Draw several raindrops falling from each cloud by creating brush strokes similar to those shown.

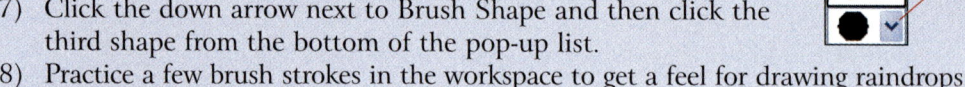

4. Create the second change in the movie images by completing the following steps:
   a. Click in the Timeline below frame number 30.
   b. Click <u>I</u>nsert and then <u>K</u>eyframe.
   c. Click the Arrow tool and then click in any white area of the stage to deselect the images. Again, you do not want to change the existing images, but add to them by adding more raindrops below the existing raindrops and thickening them.
   d. Click the Brush tool and then draw more raindrops falling to the ground level beside the house similar to the image shown.

34 Chapter One

FLASH MX

e. Click the Lasso tool in the toolbox and then draw a lasso around all of the rain drops falling from the first cloud. This selects all of the raindrops inside the lasso.
f. Click Fill Color in the toolbox and then click the darkest gray color swatch (almost black). The selected raindrops appear thicker with the darker color selected.
g. With the Lasso tool still selected, draw a lasso around all of the raindrops falling from the second cloud. Click the Fill Color button in the toolbox, and then click the same dark gray color swatch used in Step 4f.

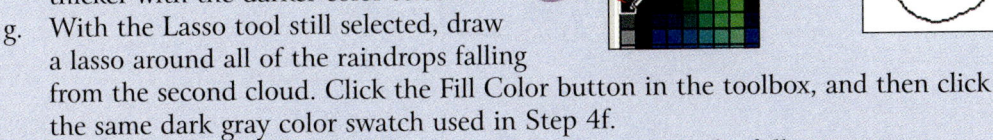

5. Create the third change in the movie images by completing the following steps:
    a. Click in the timeline below frame number 42.
    b. Click Insert and then Keyframe.
    c. Click the Arrow tool and then click in any white area of the stage to deselect the images. In this next change in the movie, you will delete the smoke, clouds, and rain, and then draw a sun.
    d. With the Arrow tool still selected, double-click the smoke curling from the chimney to select the line and then press Backspace or Delete.
    e. Using the Arrow tool, the Lasso tool, or a combination of both tools, delete the two clouds and all of the raindrops. All that should remain on the stage is the house.
    f. Draw a sun at the top left of the house by completing the following steps:
        1) Click the Oval tool.
        2) Change the stroke and fill colors to bright yellow.
        3) Draw a circle at the top left of the house.
        4) Click the Brush tool.
        5) Change the brush size to the second smallest size.
        6) Draw sun rays similar to those shown.

6. Create the final change in the movie images by completing the following steps:
    a. Click in the Timeline below frame number 54.
    b. Click Insert and then Blank Keyframe. A blank stage appears; do not worry about the other images as they are stored in the previous frames.
    c. Draw the words "The End" by completing the following steps:
        1) Turn on the display of the grid. *(Note: Refer to Exercise 6 if you need help with Steps 6c1-6c3.)*
        2) Turn off the Snap to Objects feature and then turn on the Snap to Grid feature.
        3) Change the grid's width and height pixels from 25 to 18 in the Grid dialog box.
        4) Click the Line tool.
        5) Change the stroke color to the green as shown.
        6) Change the stroke height to 4.
        7) Draw the letters as shown.
        8) Turn off the Snap to Grid feature.
        9) Draw the remainder of the *H* and the two *E*'s.
        10) Select the Pencil tool and make sure the selected Pencil Mode is Ink.
        11) Draw the curve for the letter *D*.
        12) Turn off the display of the grid.

13) Click the Arrow tool.
14) Draw a selection box around the first *E* and then move it closer to *H*.
15) Repeat Step 6c14 to move *N* and *D* closer to *E*.

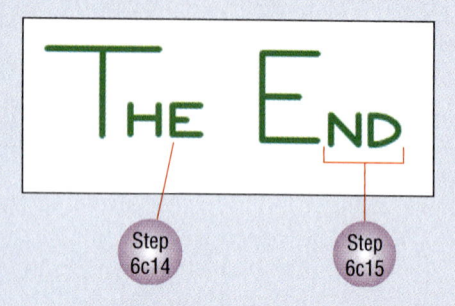

Step 6c14
Step 6c15

7. Save the revised document using the same name (Ch1Ex09).
8. Watch the movie play back by pressing the Enter key. Watch it a few times and notice how the playhead moves across the Timeline as the movie plays. When the movie is finished, compare your Timeline with the one shown.

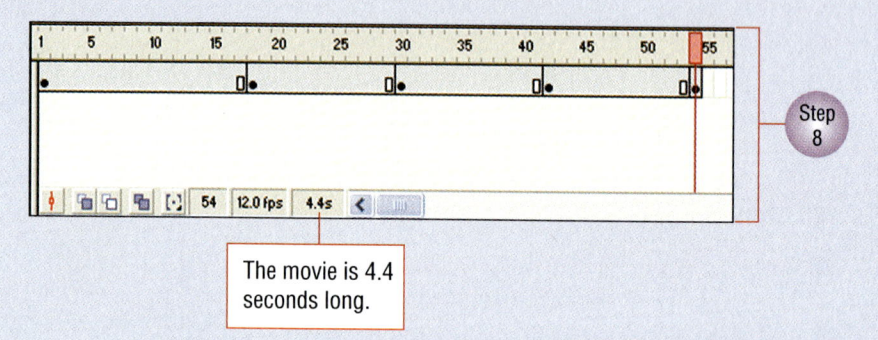

Step 8

The movie is 4.4 seconds long.

9. Click a frame on the Timeline between each keyframe to see how the stage changes to show the images stored in the frame.
10. Turn the Snap to Objects feature back on.
11. Close Ch1Ex09. Click Yes if prompted to save changes.

Using Help

A context-sensitive help resource system is available in Flash that operates through your Web browser. If you are working on something in Flash and need assistance, click F1 or click Help and then Using Flash. Flash presents a help screen for the object, tool, feature, or panel that is currently active. If nothing is active, the screen shown in Figure 1.19 displays.

FIGURE
1.19 *Flash Help*

[Screenshot of Flash Help window in Microsoft Internet Explorer showing CONTENTS, INDEX, SEARCH tabs with Using Flash, ActionScript Dictionary, and Tutorials listed, and the Macromedia Flash MX logo.]

Since Flash Help opens in a separate browser window, you can leave the Help window open while working in Flash and switch back and forth between Help and Flash as needed. Another advantage to working in a browser window is that the interface is easy to use since it is based on standard Web browsing methods with which you are familiar. You can print Help topics from the browser window to keep as reference for future use.

With CONTENTS selected, click Using Flash to expand the topic list. Each topic has further subtopics associated with it, which can also be expanded. Clicking a topic displays the help information in the right frame. Tutorials are included in the Help system which include step-by-step instructions on how to complete Flash tasks.

Click INDEX to scroll an alphabetical list of Help topics by clicking a letter in the alphabet as shown in Figure 1.20. For example, to view Help topics associated with animation you would click the letter *A* and then scroll through the topic list.

FIGURE
1.20 *Flash Help Index*

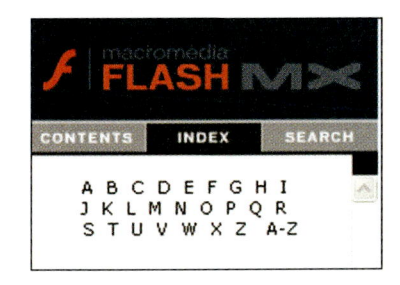

[Screenshot of Flash Help Index panel showing CONTENTS, INDEX, SEARCH tabs and alphabet letters A B C D E F G H I J K L M N O P Q R S T U V W X Y Z A-Z.]

Drawing Fundamentals   37

Click SEARCH to open the Search applet shown in Figure 1.21. Key a word or phrase that describes the feature with which you need assistance and then press Enter. Choose a topic in the topic list and then click Display to view the associated information in the Help window. The Search applet remains open so that you can click other topics to view or conduct a new search. Close the Search window when you have found the information you need. Close the browser window when you are finished using the Help system.

FIGURE 1.21 *Flash Help Search Applet*

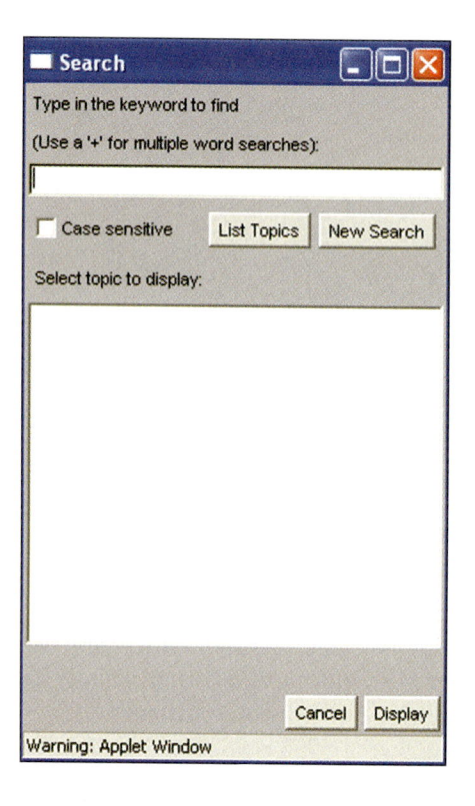

If the information you need was not found in Flash Help, try the Macromedia Flash Support Center, which includes searchable TechNotes and online tutorials. To do this, make sure you are connected to the Internet, click Help, and then click Flash Support Center to access the Macromedia Web site shown in Figure 1.22.

FIGURE 1.22 Macromedia Flash Support Center

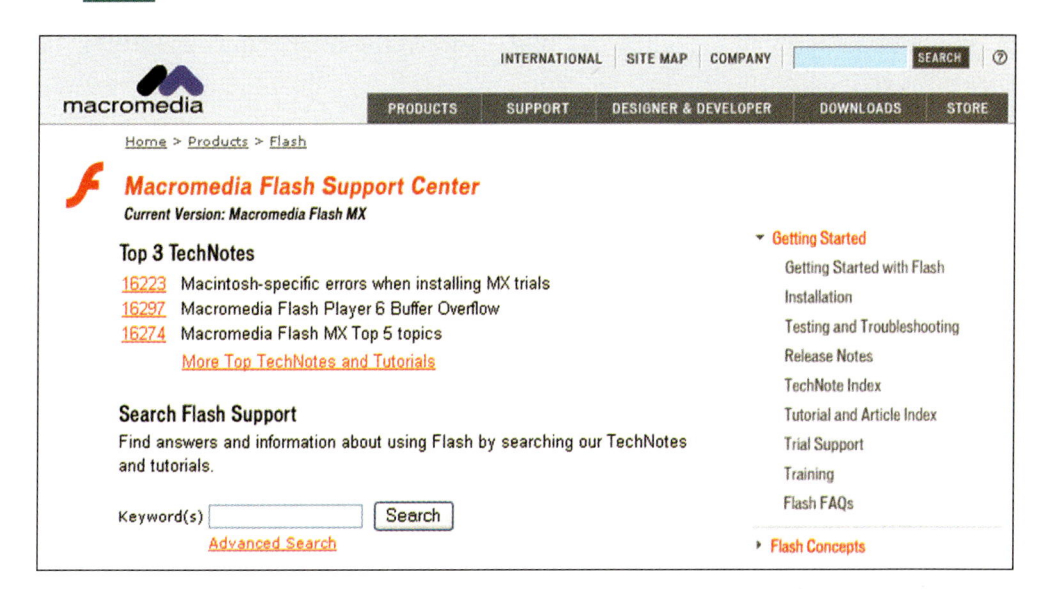

exercise 10

USING FLASH HELP

1. With the Flash window open and no documents displayed, click <u>H</u>elp on the Menu bar and then click Using <u>F</u>lash. Flash Help opens in a separate browser window.
2. Find information about how shapes overlap in Flash by completing the following steps:
   a. With CONTENTS already selected in the Flash Help window, click Using Flash to expand the topic list.
   b. Review the Using Flash topics by scrolling down the topic list.
   c. Scroll up as necessary to Drawing and then click the topic to expand the Drawing topic list.
   d. Click the topic About overlapping shapes in Flash.

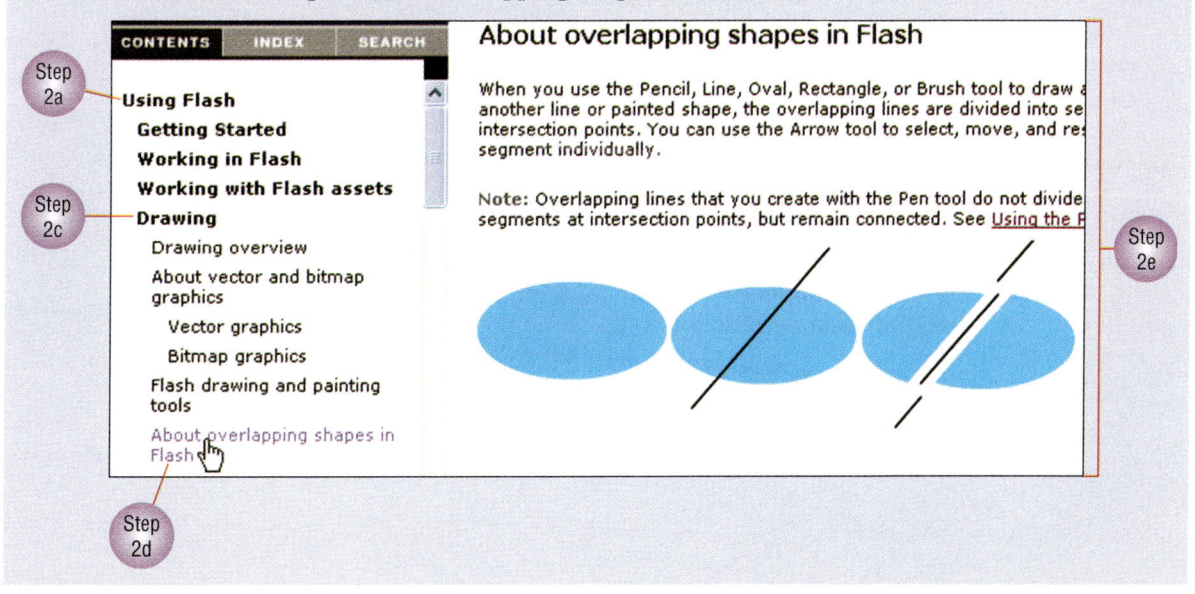

FLASH MX

Drawing Fundamentals   39

e. Read the information presented in the Help window.
   f. Print the Help page using the Print button on the browser toolbar if you want to keep the information for later reference.
3. Find information about using the Ink Bottle tool in the toolbox by completing the following steps:
   a. Click INDEX.
   b. Click the letter I in the alphabet list.
   c. Scroll down the list of topics beginning with the letter I and then click Ink Bottle tool.
   d. Read the information presented in the Help window.

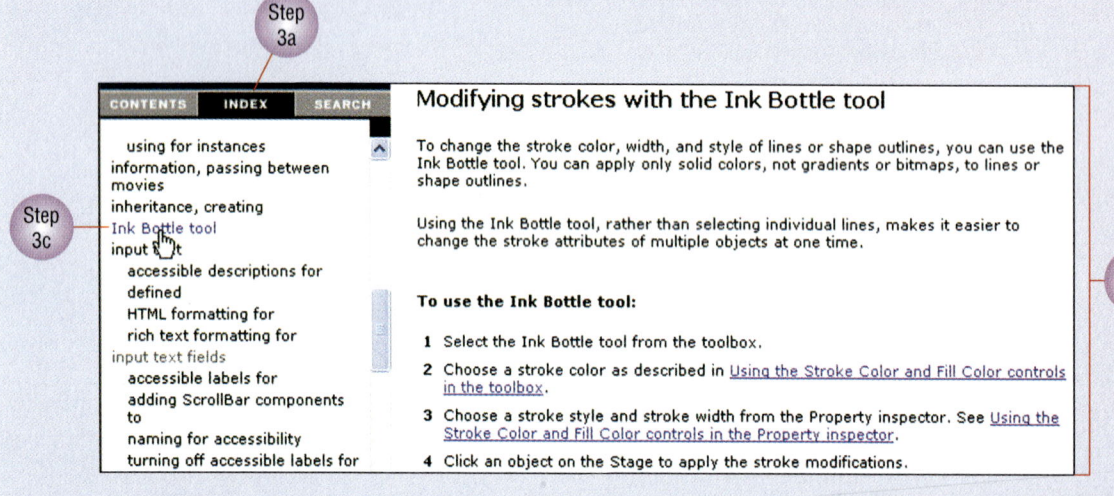

4. Find information on using the Eyedropper tool in the toolbox by completing the following steps:
   a. Click SEARCH.
   b. Key **Eyedropper tool** in the Type in the keyword to find text box and then press Enter.
   c. Double-click *Copying strokes and fills with the Eyedropper tool* in the Select topic to display list box. The associated help information for the topic displays in the browser window behind the Search window.
   d. If necessary, drag the Search window's title bar to the left of the screen to move it out of the way and then read the information presented in the Help window.
   e. Close the Search window.
5. Close the browser window.
6. Click File and then click Exit to close Flash.

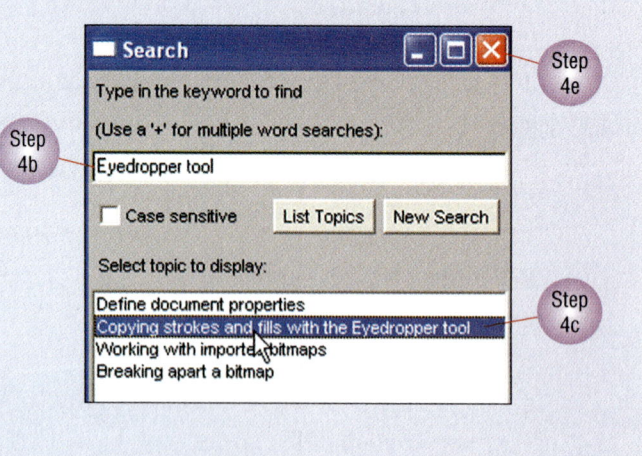

40 Chapter One

CHAPTER summary

- *Authoring* is the term given to the process of creating a sequence of images or importing images and then applying animation or other special effects in Flash.
- Content created in Flash has to be converted to a format that can be viewed by others using the Flash Player.
- The Flash Player is a plug-in that is distributed by Macromedia free of charge. It is included in most Web browsers.
- Graphics drawn in Flash are stored by default as vector files which describe images using mathematical equations.
- Bitmapped images are comprised of a grid of rows and columns of dots, or pixels, that are densely populated so as to blend together to form the image.
- Bitmapped graphics require much more storage space than vector images and tend to degrade in quality as they are resized.
- Streaming technology means that multimedia files begin playing instantaneously as data is being transferred from the Web server in the background.
- To start Flash click Start, point to *All Programs* (Windows XP) or *Programs*, point to *Macromedia*, and then click *Macromedia Flash MX*; or click the Macromedia Flash MX icon on the Desktop.
- The *stage* is the white rectangle in the middle of the Flash screen upon which you draw images or place imported objects.
- To the left and right of the stage are gray areas called the *workspace* in which you can practice drawing techniques or place objects that will be animated on or off the stage during a movie.
- The toolbox contains the tools needed to draw and modify objects on the stage.
- A movie is segmented into frames which are controlled in the timeline.
- *Panels*, available from the Window menu, contain options for controlling or manipulating the objects on the stage and can be moved or closed as needed.
- The *property inspector*, also called the Properties panel, is a context-sensitive panel that displays information and options for the active object.
- Draw horizontal, vertical, or diagonal lines using the Line tool.
- Ovals and circles are created using the Oval tool.
- The Rectangle tool is used to draw rectangles or squares.
- The line that outlines a shape is called the *stroke* line.
- The color that shades the inside of an object is called the *fill*.
- Straight-edged shapes, such as an octagon, can be drawn with the Pen tool by clicking anchor points on the stage.
- Bézier curves are drawn using the Pen tool.
- Freehand drawing can be done using the Pencil tool or Brush tool.
- The Pencil tool has three Pencil modes: Straighten, Smooth, and Ink.
- The Brush tool has five Brush modes: Paint Normal, Paint Fills, Paint Behind, Paint Selection, and Paint Inside.

- Two other modifiers for the Brush tool are Brush Size and Brush Shape.
- Save a Flash project by clicking File and then Save, or File and then Save As.
- The Revert option on the File menu will restore the Flash project to its last saved state.
- Flash files have the file extension *.fla* and movie files viewable in the Flash Player have the file extension *.swf*.
- Click File and then click New to open a new Flash document.
- Included with Flash are several templates which can be used to create a movie.
- Use rulers, grids, and guides from the View menu to assist with the placement and sizing of shapes as you are drawing.
- The width and height of the gridlines can be adjusted in the Grid dialog box.
- With the snapping feature turned on for grids and guides, Flash will pull an object to a gridline or guideline as you draw.
- Use the Arrow tool to select objects by clicking the object or drawing a selection box around a group of objects.
- Double-clicking an object with the Arrow tool selects both the stroke line and the fill.
- Hold down the Shift key while clicking the mouse to select multiple objects.
- The Lasso tool can be used to draw a lasso around an irregular group of objects that cannot be selected using the Arrow tool.
- Click the outline of an object with the Subselection tool to display the points that define the object.
- Animation is the simulation of movement that is created by playing a series of slightly different graphics over a period of time at a fast rate.
- The sequence of images for a movie is stored in *frames* which are controlled through the Timeline.
- The default *frame rate* is 12 frames per second.
- Images and other content are created in *keyframes* and Flash automatically generates the copies in the frames between the keyframes.
- Keyframes are identified by a solid black dot (keyframe with content) or an empty dot in the Timeline (blank keyframe).
- The *playhead* identifies the current frame and moves along the Timeline as the movie is being played.
- Animation using frames is done by changing the contents of the stage at various keyframes along the Timeline.
- Pressing Enter allows you to view the movie's animation.
- Web-based context-sensitive help is available in Flash by pressing F1 or by clicking Help, and then Using Flash.
- Macromedia maintains a Flash Support Center Web site where a user can search Tech Notes or complete online tutorials.

COMMANDS review

Command or Feature	Mouse/Keyboard	Shortcut Keys
Change magnification setting	View, Magnification	
Close a document	File, Close	Ctrl + W
Copy selected objects	Edit, Copy	Ctrl + C
Delete selected objects	Edit, Clear	Backspace/Delete
Display grid	View, Grid, Show Grid	Ctrl + '
Display rulers	View, Rulers	Ctrl + Alt + Shift + R
Display panels	Window, click panel name	
Edit grid settings	View, Grid, Edit Grid	Ctrl + Alt + G
Exit Flash	File, Exit	Ctrl + Q
Help	Help, Using Flash	F1
Insert a blank keyframe	Insert, Blank keyframe	
Insert a keyframe	Insert, Keyframe	
New Flash document	File, New	Ctrl + N
Paste copied or cut objects	Edit, Paste	Ctrl + V
Save Flash document using existing file name	File, Save	Ctrl + S
Save Flash document for the first time or change existing file name	File Save As	Ctrl + Shift + S
Snap to Objects feature	View, Snap to Objects	Ctrl + Shift + /
Snap to Grid feature	View, Grid, Snap to Grid	Ctrl + Shift + '
Snap to Guides feature	View, Guides, Snap to Guides	Ctrl + Shift + ;
Undo	Edit, Undo	Ctrl + Z

CONCEPTS check

Indicate the correct term or command for each item.

1. What is the name of the application in which people view the movies that you have created in Flash?
2. This type of image is comprised of densely populated rows and columns of pixels.

Drawing Fundamentals

3. This is the default format for storing images drawn in Flash.
4. This area is where the movie is segmented into frames.
5. These are similar to Windows-based dialog boxes in which you can control or manipulate the objects on the stage.
6. This is the name given to the line that outlines a shape.
7. Bézier curves are drawn using this tool.
8. Use this tool to draw freehand when you want an effect that is similar to painting.
9. This is the extension assigned to Flash files.
10. Turn on the display of this screen element in order to create guides.
11. This is the name of the feature in which objects are pulled to existing objects, gridlines, or guidelines as you draw.
12. Use this tool to draw a selection box around a group of objects.
13. Use this tool to display the anchor points for an object.
14. Use this tool to select an irregularly shaped group of objects that cannot be selected by drawing a box.
15. This is the term for a sequence of images, each of which is slightly different, played back at a fast rate to create the illusion of movement.
16. This is the default number of frames that are played in one second during a movie.
17. Insert this type of frame to change the image that is currently on the stage for a later portion of the movie.
18. This element of the Timeline indicates the current frame.
19. Press this key on the keyboard to watch a movie.
20. Flash Help opens in this application window.

SKILLS check

Assessment 1

FIGURE 1.23 *Assessment 1*

1. Start Flash MX.
2. Create the balloons shown in Figure 1.23 as follows:
   a. Draw the first three balloons using colored ovals with the stroke and fill colors as shown: red, bright blue, and purple.
   b. Draw the strings from the balloons using the Pencil tool with the following settings:

- Dark gray stroke color
- Stroke height at 1.5
- Smooth Pencil mode

3. Select and copy the first three balloons, positioning the duplicates to the right of the existing three.
4. Change the stroke and fill colors for the copied balloons as shown: dark green, turquoise, and orange.
5. Save the document and name it Ch1SA1.
6. Close Ch1SA1.

Assessment 2

FIGURE 1.24 Assessment 2

1. Start a new document.
2. Create the jack-o-lantern shown in Figure 1.24 as follows:
   a. Use the Pencil tool with a stroke color of orange and a stroke height of 2 to draw the pumpkin shape. *(Note: Make sure the Pencil Mode is still set to Smooth.)*
   b. Use the Paint Bucket tool to fill the pumpkin shape with the same orange color.
   c. Draw the stem using the Pencil tool, changing the stroke color to green, and then use the Paint Bucket to fill the stem with green.
   d. Use the Pen tool to draw the triangles that make up the jack-o-lantern's face as follows:
      - Change the stroke and fill colors to white.
      - Draw the first triangle in the workspace.
      - Turn off the Snap to Objects feature.
      - Select, copy and paste the triangle. Move the duplicate triangle to the inside of the pumpkin where you want the left eye positioned. Repeat this step to create the remainder of the pumpkin's face.
3. Save the document and name it Ch1SA2.
4. Close Ch1SA2.

Assessment 3

FIGURE 1.25 Assessment 3

Drawing Fundamentals 45

1. Start a new document.
2. Create the bicycle shown in Figure 1.25 as follows:
   a. Turn on the display of the grid to assist you with drawing the shapes.
   b. Create the first wheel using the Oval tool with the following attributes:
      - Stroke height set to 2
      - Black stroke color
      - No fill
   c. Copy and paste the first oval to create the second wheel of the bicycle.
   d. Use either the Pen tool or the Line tool to create the remaining shapes that are straight lines.
   e. Use the Brush tool to draw the seat of the bicycle. You determine the Brush settings.
   f. Use the Pencil tool to draw the bicycle handles. You determine the Pencil mode.
3. Save the document and name it Ch1SA3.
4. Turn off the display of the grid.
5. Close Ch1SA3.

Assessment 4

FIGURE 1.26 Assessment 4

1. Start a new document and then create the beach scene shown in Figure 1.26 as follows:
   a. Draw the shapes for the entire image (except the sand) freehand using the Pencil tool, changing stroke colors as required. You determine the Pencil settings. *(Hint: If you draw a shape and then realize the stroke color is wrong, use the Ink Bottle tool to change the color.)*
   b. Use the Paint Bucket tool to fill the enclosed shapes with the colors indicated. *(Hint: The hotspot for the Paint Bucket tool is the black paint flowing from the can.)*
   c. Use the Brush tool to draw the sand. You determine the brush settings.
2. Set the background color for the document to make the sky appear blue as follows:
   a. Click Modify and then click Document.
   b. Click the Background color swatch in the Document Properties dialog box.
   c. Click a color swatch similar to the one shown in Figure 1.26.
   d. Click OK.
3. Save the document and name it Ch1SA4.
4. Close Ch1SA4.

Assessment 5

FIGURE 1.27 *Assessment 5*

1. Start a new document and then create the robot shown in Figure 1.27 as follows:
   a. Draw the body, neck, arms, legs, and feet as rectangles. Change stroke and fill colors as required. If necessary, collapse the Properties panel to provide more space on the stage for drawing.
   b. Complete the following steps to create rounded rectangles:
      • Click the rectangle tool.
      • Click the Rounded Rectangle Radius button in the Options section of the toolbox.
      • Key a value in the Corner Radius text box in which to round the corners and then click OK. The values entered are points. A setting of 18 points was used to draw the image shown.
      • To return to square corners, key **0** (zero) in the Corner Radius text box.
   c. Draw the hands using the Pencil tool in Straighten Pencil mode and then fill the shape with black.
   d. Draw the head as an oval slightly overlapping the rectangle drawn for the neck and then draw the eyes.
   e. Draw small rectangles for the antennae.
2. Save the document and name it Ch1SA5.
3. Close Ch1SA5.

Assessment 6

1. Create an animation that will give the illusion that the balloons have flown away one-by-one in Ch1SA1 as follows:
   a. Click File, click Open, and then double-click Ch1SA1.fla.
   b. Insert a keyframe at frame 12.
   c. Delete the green balloon from the stage.
   d. Insert a keyframe at frame 18 and then delete the red balloon.
   e. Insert a keyframe at frame 24 and then delete the purple balloon.
   f. Insert a keyframe at frame 30 and then delete the orange balloon.
   g. Insert a keyframe at frame 36 and then delete the turquoise balloon.
   h. Insert a keyframe at frame 40 and then reposition the remaining blue balloon near the top center of the stage.

i. Insert a keyframe at frame 44 and then reposition the remaining blue balloon at the top right of the stage with the top portion of the balloon in the workspace.
   j. Insert a blank keyframe at frame 50.
2. Save the revised document and name it Ch1SA6.
3. Watch the movie a few times and make any adjustments that you deem necessary to improve the flow.
4. Close Ch1SA6. Click Yes if prompted to save changes.

Assessment 7

1. Create an animation that will give the illusion that the robot is working by changing the colors of its eyes and buttons in Ch1SA5 as follows:
   a. Open Ch1SA5.fla.
   b. Insert a keyframe at frame 12 and then change the fill color for both eyes to orange.
   c. Insert a keyframe at frame 16 and then change the fill colors of the buttons on the body of the robot as follows:
      - Change the two orange buttons to light green.
      - Change the red button to bright yellow.
      - Change the green button to black.
   d. Insert a keyframe at frame 19 and then change the fill colors for one eye to light purple and the other eye to light blue.
   e. Insert a keyframe at frame 23 and then change the fill colors of the buttons on the body of the robot as follows:
      - Change the two light green buttons to brown.
      - Change the bright yellow button to red.
      - Change the black button to green.
   f. Insert a keyframe at frame 27 and then change the fill colors for both eyes and all of the buttons on the body of the robot to red.
2. Save the revised document and name it Ch1SA7.
3. Watch the movie a few times and make any adjustments that you deem necessary to improve the flow or colors.
4. Close Ch1SA7. Click Yes if prompted to save changes.

Assessment 8

1. Choose the jack-o-lantern (Ch1SA2), the bicycle (Ch1SA3), or the beach scene (Ch1SA4) and create an animation using frames that will simulate some movement or otherwise change content.
2. Save the revised document and name it Ch1SA8.
3. Watch the movie a few times and then show the movie to another classmate.
4. Have the classmate give you a suggestion for improving the movie and then modify the required keyframes to incorporate the suggestion.
5. Save the revised document and name it Ch1SA8-Modified.
6. Close Ch1SA8-Modified.
7. Exit Flash.

CHAPTER 2

WORKING WITH TEXT AND EDITING DRAWN OBJECTS

PERFORMANCE OBJECTIVES

Upon successful completion of Chapter 2, you will be able to:
- Use the Text tool to insert a text block into a Flash document.
- Move, delete, copy, and resize a text block.
- Change the font, font size, and text color of selected text and text blocks.
- Create a vertical text block.
- Change alignment, line spacing, and margins within text blocks.
- Adjust tracking of letters in a text block.
- Break text apart into separate objects.
- Change document properties.
- Use the Paint Bucket and Ink Bottle tools to modify drawn objects.
- Use the Eye Dropper tool to copy attributes from one object to another object.
- Use the Hand and Zoom tools to view objects on the stage.
- Erase portions of a drawing using the Eraser tool.
- Draw and edit curved lines.
- Use the Free Transform tool to rotate, skew, scale, distort, or envelope an object.
- Adjust stroke length, smooth, and straighten strokes.
- Adjust a stroke line to change a shape's appearance.
- Edit fills, divide shapes into segments, and split a shape apart.
- Group and ungroup related shapes.
- Change colors using the Color Mixer panel and the Color Swatches panel.
- Apply and create gradient color to objects.
- Use the Fill Transform tool to modify a gradient fill.

Flash MX Chapter 02

There are eight student data files to copy for this chapter.

In Chapter 1 you learned the basics of creating objects in Flash and animating those objects using frames. In this chapter you will learn the rest of the tools in the toolbox with which you will add text to artwork and edit existing drawn objects. Increasing the magnification, zooming in, zooming out, and moving the stage assists with editing objects more precisely. Working with colors is made easier through the Color Mixer panel and the Color Swatches panel. Understanding how Flash works with objects on a single layer is important in order to edit and overlap objects.

Using the Text Tool

Text Tool

With the Text tool you can create two types of text blocks in a Flash document: an *extending text block* and a *fixed text block*. The extending text block automatically increases in width to accommodate the amount of the text that you key. Press Enter in an extending text block to key a second or third line as word wrap will not occur in this type of block. To create an extending text block, click the Text tool. As you move the pointer to the stage, the pointer appears as a crosshair with the letter *A* attached to it indicating you are creating a text block. Click in the stage where you want the text block to be positioned. An insertion point appears inside a small box with a circle handle at the top right. As you key text, the box automatically extends to accommodate the width of the keyed text as shown in Figure 2.1. Click outside the text block or choose another tool in the toolbox to complete the block.

FIGURE 2.1 Extending Text Block

All Items at 25% Off Lowest Ticketed Price!

Circle handle indicates extending text block with no word wrap.

A fixed text block is a block that has been defined to be a specific width. Text keyed inside the block will automatically wrap to the next line. The height of the block increases to accommodate the amount of keyed text. To create a fixed text block, click the Text tool and then drag the crosshair in the stage the width of the text block that you want to create. An insertion point appears inside the box with a square handle at the top right. Key the required text and then click outside the text block or choose another tool in the toolbox to complete the block. Text will automatically wrap to as many lines as needed to fit within the width that has been defined as shown in Figure 2.2.

FIGURE 2.2 Fixed Text Block

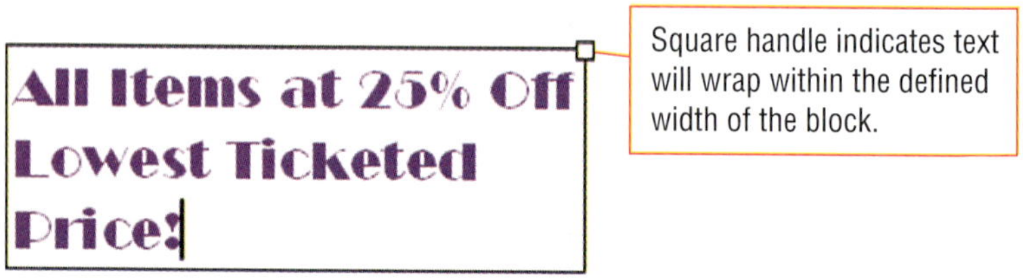

All Items at 25% Off Lowest Ticketed Price!

Square handle indicates text will wrap within the defined width of the block.

An extending text block can be converted to a fixed text block. To do this, click with the Text tool over the text box and then drag the circle handle to the width that you want for the block. The circle handle changes to a square, the existing text is wrapped inside the new width, and the height is automatically expanded to accommodate all of the text.

Editing Text

Flash does not have the capability to spell check text as many users will be used to with a word processor. For this reason it is wise to proofread the text in the block carefully. A stunning Flash movie will quickly be discredited by users if it contains spelling or grammatical errors. Many times it is useful to have someone else proofread after you have corrected what you think are all of the errors. A fresh pair of eyes will often spot an error that you missed.

If you spot a keying error after the text block has been created, click the Text tool and then position the pointer over the existing text block in the location where the error exists. The pointer appears as the I-beam pointer I indicating that a text entry is expected. Click the I-beam and then use the Backspace or Delete keys as required and key the correct text.

Moving, Deleting, and Copying a Text Block

Use the Arrow tool to select and then move, delete, or copy a text block. With the Arrow tool active, position the pointer over the text. The pointer appears with the four-headed arrow move icon attached indicating you can drag the block to a new location. To delete or copy a block, click the block while the four-headed arrow move icon is displayed attached to the pointer. A blue box surrounds the text indicating the block has been selected as shown in Figure 2.3.

FIGURE 2.3 *Selected Text Block*

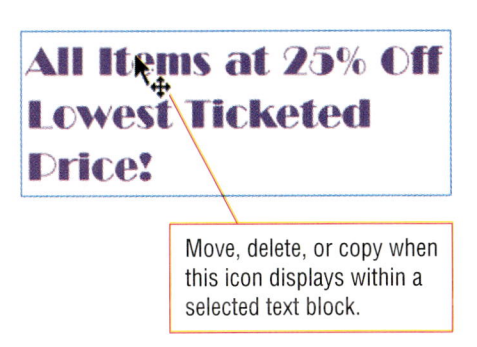

All Items at 25% Off Lowest Ticketed Price!

Move, delete, or copy when this icon displays within a selected text block.

Press Delete to delete the block or use the Copy and Paste commands to create a duplicate copy of the block in another location.

Resizing a Text Block

To change the width of a text block, click the Text tool and then click over the text block. Position the pointer over the square handle at the top right of the block. The pointer displays as a left- and right-pointing arrow. Drag left or right to decrease or increase the width as shown in Figure 2.4. The height of the block automatically adjusts as you drag the handle; this is indicated by the dashed box so that you can see the effect on the text of the new width.

FIGURE 2.4 **Resizing a Text Block**

> All Items at 25% Off
> Lowest Ticketed
> Price!

Height automatically adjusts as you resize the width.

exercise 1

CREATING, MOVING, AND RESIZING TEXT BLOCKS

1. Start Flash.
2. Collapse the Properties panel to provide a larger stage with which to work. Click <u>V</u>iew, point to <u>M</u>agnification, and then click <u>1</u>00%, or key **100** and then press Enter in the Zoom text box just above the stage at the right. *(Note: Skip this step if the stage is already set at 100% magnification.)*
3. Create an extending text block by completing the following steps:
   a. Click the Text tool, and then change the Fill Color to a blue color swatch similar to the color of the text shown.
   b. Position the crosshair pointer in the middle of the stage and then click the left mouse button.
   c. Key **Web Art Production Partners Limited**.
   d. Click in the stage outside the text box.
4. Create a fixed text block by completing the following steps:
   a. With the Text tool still active, position the crosshair pointer approximately 0.5 inch below the letter *P* in Production in the first text block, hold down the left mouse button, drag the block width to align it with the end of the block above it as shown, and then release the mouse button.
   b. Key the following text:

   > Specialists in original art work for your organization's Web site. Our team of graphic artists design and produce award winning logos and art work for publishing on your Web site or other multimedia devices.

   c. Click in the stage outside the text block.
5. Move and resize the text block by completing the following steps:
   a. Click the Arrow tool.

52 Chapter Two

b. Position the pointer over the text inside the fixed text block until the pointer displays with the four-headed arrow move icon, hold down the left mouse button, drag the text block to the left side of the stage as shown, and then release the mouse.
c. Click the Text tool.
d. Click the crosshair pointer over the fixed text block.
e. Position the pointer over the square handle until the pointer displays as a left- and right-pointing arrow, drag right to increase the width as shown, and then release the mouse button.
f. Click in the stage outside the text block.
6. Save the document and name it Ch2Ex01.

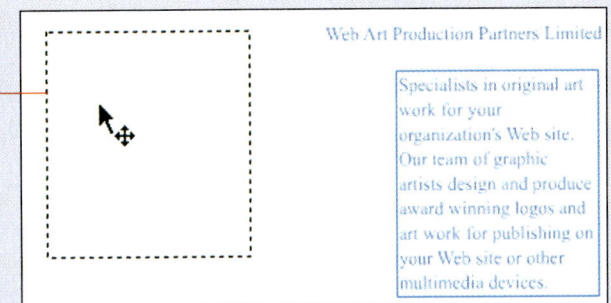

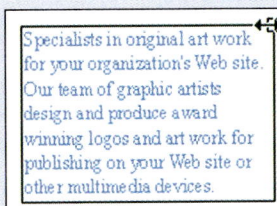

Text Properties

Flash saves the last changes made to font, font size, and text color. Until changed, the default font, font size, and color of text in a text block is Times New Roman, 12 points, and blue. Text properties can be changed before or after the text block is created. To change text properties for existing text blocks, select the block using the Arrow tool and then change the required options in the Properties panel. Use the Shift key to select multiple text blocks. As with drawn objects, any changes made to text properties remain in effect for future text blocks.

Font and Font Attributes

Click the down arrow next to the Font list box in the Properties panel to display a pop-up list of fonts. As you roll the mouse over the font names in the list, a preview of the highlighted font appears in the Font Preview window as shown in Figure 2.5. Click the desired font name in the font list.

FIGURE 2.5 *Font Preview Window*

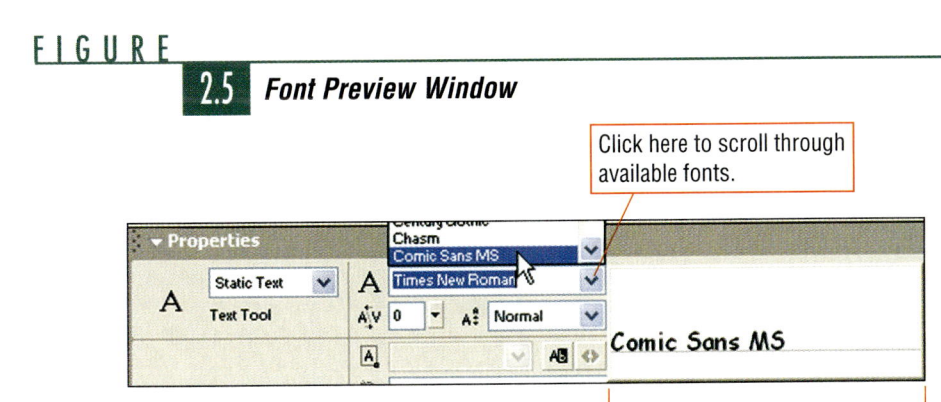

Bold **Italic**

A portion of text within a text block can have a different font applied to it by dragging the I-beam over the portion of the text for which you want a different font applied. Click the Bold or Italic buttons in the Properties panel to apply bold and/or italic attributes to the text block or selected text within the block. Click the Text (fill) color button to change the color of the text by selecting a color swatch in the palette. Clicking the color wheel, referred to as the *Color Picker*, at the top right of the palette opens the Color dialog box where you can create a custom font color.

Font Size

Change the font size in the Properties panel by double-clicking the existing value in the Font Size text box and then keying the desired size, which is measured in points. Text is defined in points, a measurement system that refers to the height of the characters. One point is approximately 1/72 of an inch. The higher the point size, the larger the characters.

Clicking the down-pointing triangle next to the Font Size text box in the Properties panel displays a slider bar in which you drag the font size up or down as needed. Click in the Properties panel outside the slider bar when you have chosen the desired size. If you are changing the font size using the slider bar after the text block has been created, the selected text block in the stage will display with the new font so that you can immediately see the effect of the new font size on the block as shown in Figure 2.6.

FIGURE 2.6 *Adjusting Font Size for Existing Text Block using Slider Bar*

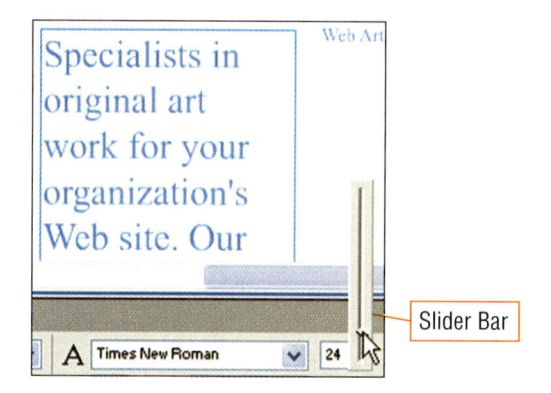

Slider Bar

exercise 2

CHANGING FONT, FONT SIZE, AND FONT COLOR

1. With Ch2Ex01 open and the Text tool active, change the font and font size of the extending text block by completing the following steps:
    a. Click the Arrow tool.
    b. Click on the extending text block. This selects the block as indicated by the blue border surrounding the text.
    c. Expand the Properties panel.
    d. Click the down arrow next to the Font list box in the Properties panel, scroll up the list box, and then click Impact. *(Note: Choose a different font if Impact is not in the font list on the computer you are using.)*

Step 1d

e. With the extending text block still selected, double-click the current value in the Font Size text box in the Properties panel, key **24**, and then press Enter.

f. Move the extending text block above the fixed text block as shown.

2. Change the font color of both text blocks by completing the following steps:
   a. With the extending text block still selected, hold down the Shift key and then click over the fixed text block. Both text blocks are now selected.
   b. Click the Text (fill) color button in the Properties panel and then click the maroon color swatch shown. Notice for the multiple selected text blocks, the Font and Font Size text boxes display with three dashes since the two blocks have different settings for these options.
   c. Click in the stage outside the selected text blocks.

3. Save the document using the same name (Ch2Ex01).

Vertical Text Blocks

Extending and fixed text blocks that display text vertically in columns can be created. In a vertical text block, only one character displays per line. Click the Change direction of text button in the Properties panel to define a vertical text block. Three options appear in the drop-down menu as shown in Figure 2.7: Horizontal, Vertical, Left to Right, and Vertical, Right to Left. Click the desired option and then create the extending text block or fixed text block using the same steps as for a horizontal text block. When you create a fixed vertical text block, drag down to the desired height. The insertion point inside a vertical text block is rotated 90 degrees in the text block indicating that the text will be displayed in a vertical column. Pressing Enter in an extending vertical text block creates a new column. In a fixed text block, a new column is created when the text fills the defined height.

Change direction of text

FIGURE 2.7 *Change Direction of Text Menu Options*

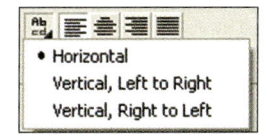

Rotation

In a vertical text block, the Rotation button below the Change direction of text button becomes active. Text or selected characters within the vertical block can be rotated 90 degrees by clicking the Rotation button. Figure 2.8 illustrates a vertical text block with no rotation in the first column. The middle column displays the entire text block rotated 90 degrees, and the right column displays the same text block with only the first character rotated 90 degrees.

FIGURE

2.8 *Rotated Characters in Vertical Text Blocks*

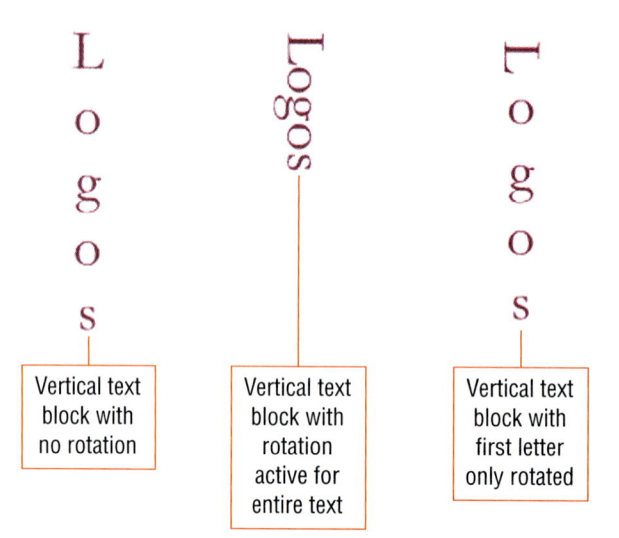

Vertical text block with no rotation

Vertical text block with rotation active for entire text

Vertical text block with first letter only rotated

exercise 3

CREATING A VERTICAL TEXT BLOCK

1. With Ch2Ex01 open and the Arrow tool active, create an extending vertical text block by completing the following steps:
   a. Click the Text tool.
   b. In the Properties panel, make sure the font selected is still Impact, change the font size to 14, and the Text (fill) color to navy blue.
   c. Click the Change direction of text button in the Properties panel and then click Vertical, Left to Right.
   d. Collapse the Properties panel.
   e. Position the crosshair pointer with the *A* attached at the right side of the stage below the letter *T* in Partners and then click the left mouse button.
   f. Key **Web-based** and then press Enter.
   g. Key **Outstanding** and then press Enter.
   h. Key **Work**.
   i. Click in the stage outside the vertical text block.
2. Move the vertical text block and change the color of single characters by completing the following steps:

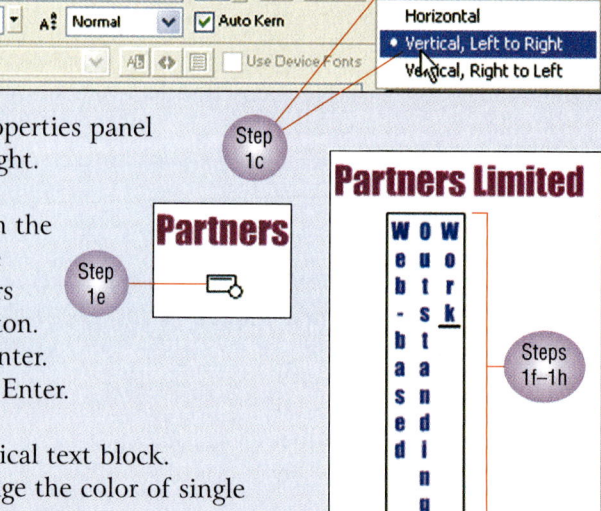

56 Chapter Two

a. Click the Arrow tool.
   b. Position the pointer over the vertical text block until the four-headed arrow move icon appears and then drag the text block to align it with the end of the text block above it.
   c. Double-click the text block. This positions an insertion point at the end of the text block and automatically selects the Text tool.
   d. Drag the I-beam over the letter *W* in the word Web-based.
   e. Expand the Properties panel.
   f. Click the Text (fill) color button and then click a green color swatch similar to the one shown.
   g. Drag the I-beam over the letter *O* in the word Outstanding, click the Text (fill) color button, and then click the same green color swatch selected in Step 2f.
   h. Drag the I-beam over the letter *W* in the word Work, click the Text (fill) color button, and then click the same green color swatch selected in Step 2f.
   i. Click in the stage outside the text block.
   j. Collapse the Properties panel.
3. Save the document using the same name (Ch2Ex01).

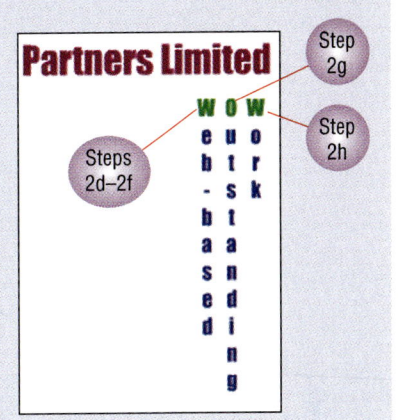

Alignment and Format Options Dialog Box

Text within a horizontal text block is aligned at the left edge of the text block's boundary. The Properties panel includes buttons to align the text in the center, at the right boundary, or fully justified between the left and right boundaries as shown in Figure 2.9. When the text block is defined as a vertical text block these buttons change to align at the top, center, bottom, or fully justify. Select the text block or text within the block and then click the desired alignment button in the Properties panel.

FIGURE 2.9 **Text Alignment Buttons**

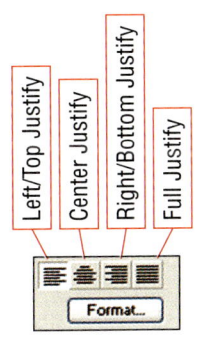

Click the Format button below the text alignment buttons in the Properties panel to open the Format Options dialog box shown in Figure 2.10. Open this dialog box to set a first line indent for each paragraph, change the spacing between lines, or change the left and right margins for the text block. The Indent, Left Margin, and Right Margin values are set in pixels by default while the Line Spacing value is set in points. The units of measurement can be changed to inches, points, centimeters, or millimeters at the Document Properties dialog box.

Working with Text and Editing Drawn Objects 57

FIGURE 2.10 Format Options Dialog Box

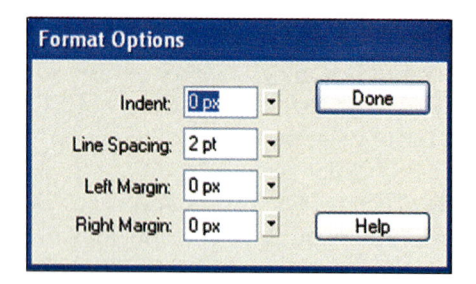

Each option can be changed by keying a value directly in the text box for the individual item, or by clicking the down-pointing triangle next to the option to drag a slider to increase or decrease the value. Click Done when you have finished making changes to the options.

exercise 4

CHANGING ALIGNMENT AND FORMAT OPTIONS

1. With Ch2Ex01 open and the Text tool active, click the Arrow tool and expand the Properties panel.
2. Change the alignment for the fixed text block, increase the spacing between lines, and change the right margin by completing the following steps:
   a. Click the fixed text block. (Text block that begins *Specialists in original…*).
   b. Click the Right/Bottom Justify alignment button in the Properties panel. The text in the block shifts to align at the right boundary for the text block as shown. 
   c. With the fixed text block still selected, click the Format button in the Properties panel.
   d. With 0 px selected in the Indent text box, press Tab to move to the Line Spacing text box.
   e. Key **6** and then press Tab twice to move to the Right Margin text box.
   f. Key **5** in the Right Margin text box and then click Done.
   g. Click in the stage outside the text block to deselect it.
   h. Collapse the Properties panel.
3. Save the document using the same name (Ch2Ex01).

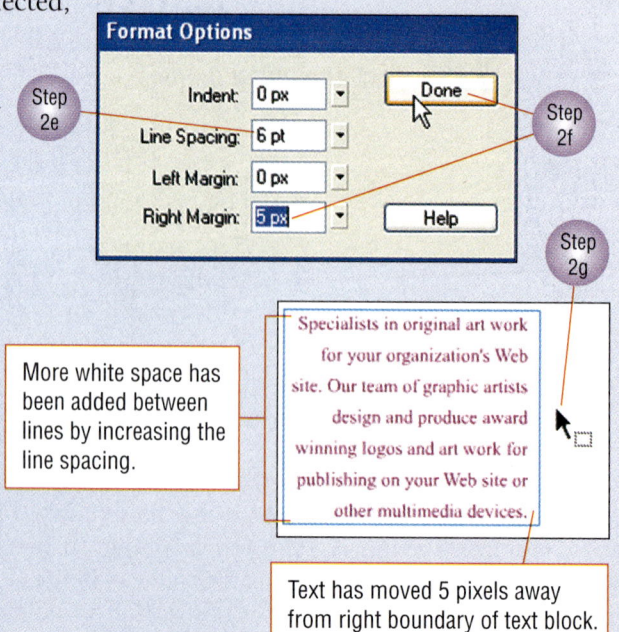

58 Chapter Two

Character Spacing and Kerning

The amount of horizontal white space between characters is called *tracking*. Flash inserts a uniform amount of space between characters. You can adjust the character spacing value to increase or decrease this amount of space. Key a negative value to tighten the space bringing the letters closer together or key a positive value to spread them further apart. In a vertical text block, character spacing refers to the amount of white space between the bottom of the one character and the top of the next character.

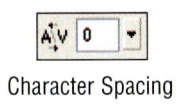

Kerning refers to the spacing between certain pairs of letters. Some letters are wider than others and when a wide letter appears next to a narrow letter, it may appear that there is extra white space between the two. For example, *W* requires more space on the page than *i*. Many fonts have information built into the system font file that instructs the computer on how to display and print certain troublesome letter pairs. By default, AutoKern is selected in the Properties panel. It is a good idea to use the font's built-in kerning information and leave this check box selected.

Character Spacing

exercise 5

ADJUSTING TRACKING

1. With Ch2Ex01 open and the Arrow tool active, expand the Properties panel.
2. Adjust the amount of white space between letters in the vertical text block by completing the following steps:
    a. Click the vertical text block.
    b. Double-click the value 0 in the Character spacing text box, key **-5**, and then press Enter. The characters in the vertical text block now appear closer together.
    c. Click in the stage outside the text block to deselect it.
    d. Collapse the Properties panel.
3. Save the document using the same name (Ch2Ex01).

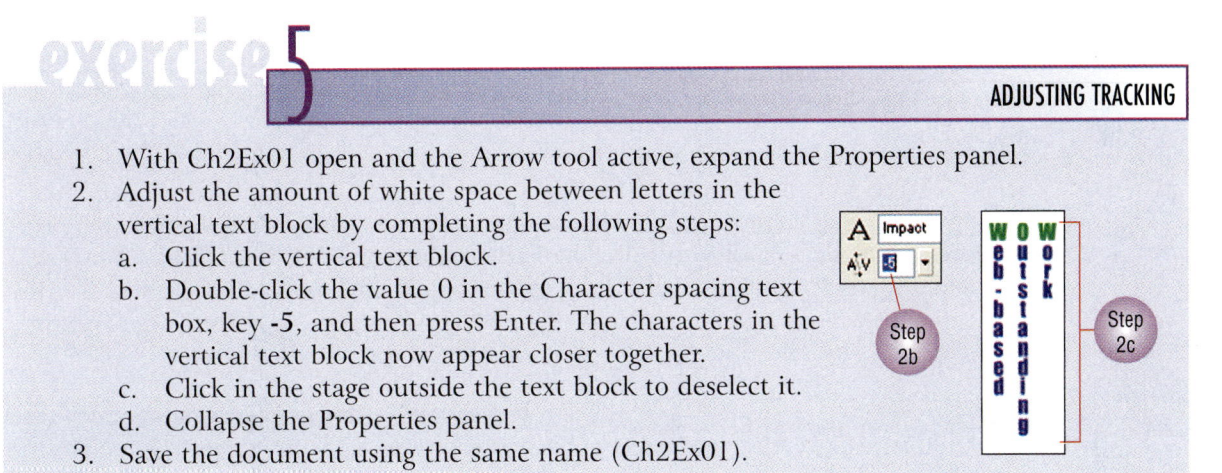

Superscripts and Subscripts

You can key *superscript* text (characters elevated slightly above the normal position for the text) or *subscript* text (characters placed slightly below the normal position for the text) as shown in the text blocks in Figure 2.11. To do this, key text in the text block to the point where you need to superscript or subscript, click the down arrow next to the Character position list box in the Properties panel, click Superscript or Subscript at the drop-down menu, and then key the character or characters. To return text to the baseline position in the block, click Normal at the Character position drop-down list.

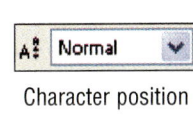

Character position

FIGURE 2.11 **Superscript and Subscript Characters**

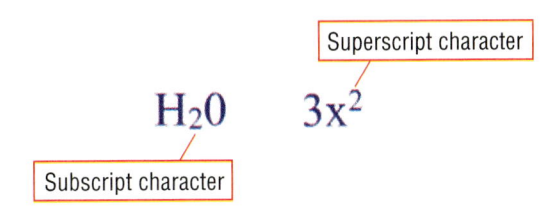

Superscript character

H_2O $3x^2$

Subscript character

Working with Text and Editing Drawn Objects

You may find it easier to key all of the text in the text block and perform the superscript or subscript formatting afterwards by dragging to select the character or characters and then applying the appropriate character position.

Text Menu

In the preceding exercises, the changes made to the text blocks were done in the Properties panel. The same options are also available from the Text option on the Menu bar as shown in Figure 2.12.

FIGURE 2.12 *Text Menu*

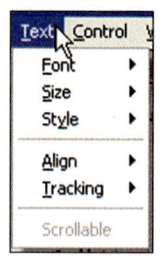

Point to Font to view a side menu listing the available fonts on the computer you are using. Point to Size to choose a point size in a side menu listing commonly used point sizes from 8 to 120. The Style option provides Bold, Italic, Subscript, and Superscript options. Point to Align to change the paragraph alignment for the active text block and use the Tracking option to increase or decrease the current character spacing.

Breaking Text Apart

The *Break Apart* feature in Flash allows you to convert an existing text block into multiple text blocks so that each character becomes its own block. By breaking a text block apart in this way you can control each character separately. For example, you can move, resize, change colors, distort, or animate the letters individually. To disassemble a text block, select the text block, click Modify on the Menu bar, and then click Break Apart. The letters are converted into individual blocks as shown in Figure 2.13.

Executing the Break Apart command a second time will transform the individual text blocks into individual graphic objects. The letters can be moved, resized, distorted, scaled, rotated, and changed in color, but they no longer have the features in the Text Properties panel available to them. Text blocks that have been converted to graphic objects cannot be converted back to text blocks.

FIGURE 2.13 *Text Block Broken Apart*

Sale on Now! — Original text block

Sale on Now! — Text block broken apart. Each character is now in its own block.

Sale on Now! — Broken Apart command issued a second time converts the text to graphics. In this example, a Stroke line was added to each letter using the Ink Bottle tool which is not possible in text blocks.

exercise 6

CREATING AND BREAKING APART A TEXT BLOCK

1. With Ch2Ex01 open and the Arrow tool active, expand the Properties panel.
2. Create an extending text block by completing the following steps:
   a. Click the Text tool, click the Change direction of text button, and then click Horizontal.
   b. Make sure the Font is Impact, the Font Size is 14, and the Text (fill) color is green.
   c. Double-click -5 in the Character Spacing text box and then key **0**.
   d. Click the Center Justify button.
   e. Click the crosshair pointer in the center of the stage below the letter *P* in Partners as shown.
   f. Key **Call** and then press Enter.
   g. Key **612 555 1234** and then click in the stage outside the text block.
3. Break the text block created in Step 2 into individual blocks by completing the following steps:
   a. Click the Arrow tool.
   b. Click over the text block created in Step 2.
   c. Click Modify.
   d. Click Break Apart. Each letter in the block is now in its own text block.
   e. Click outside the text blocks to deselect them.
4. Point over the letter *C* in Call until the four-headed arrow move icon appears, drag the letter *C* to another area on the stage, and then release the mouse.
5. Click Edit and then click Undo to move *C* back to its original position.
6. Save the document using the same name (Ch2Ex01).
7. Close Ch2Ex01.

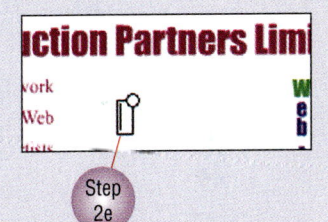

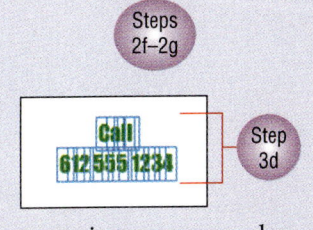

Step 2e

Steps 2f–2g

Step 3d

Working with Text and Editing Drawn Objects   61

Document Properties

In Chapter 1, Assessment 4, you used the Document Properties dialog box shown in Figure 2.14 to change the background color from white to blue to create the sky in the beach scene. Document Properties also contains options to set the size of the stage, the frame rate for animations, and the units of measurement for rulers and dialog box options where changes are made to settings that affect the size of objects.

FIGURE 2.14 Document Properties Dialog Box

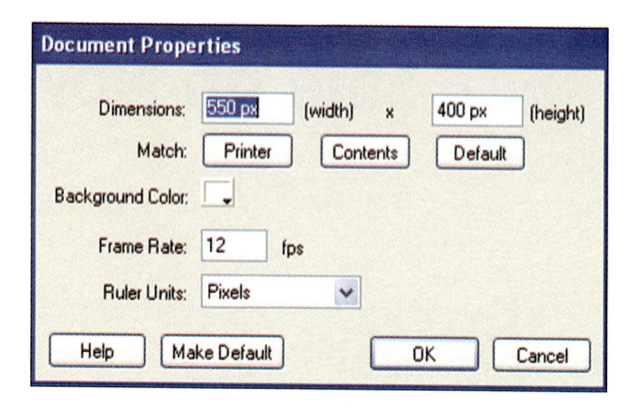

Display the Document Properties dialog box by doing any of the following actions:

- Click Modify on the Menu bar and then click Document.
- Right-click in any unused area of the stage and then click Document Properties at the shortcut menu.
- Click the Size button in the Properties panel with no objects selected.

The stage is initially set to 550 pixels wide by 400 pixels high which is approximately 7.5 inches wide by 5.5 inches high. Pixel is the standard unit of measurement for working on the Web since graphics cards for monitors calculate screen size in pixels. If you are using Flash to create a graphic for a Web site and have been given the dimensions in inches, you can set the stage size using inches as the units of measurement by clicking the down arrow next to Ruler Units. The drop-down menu shown in Figure 2.15 appears. Click Inches and then click OK to close the Document Properties dialog box. Other units of measurement are Inches (decimal), Points, Centimeters, and Millimeters.

FIGURE

2.15 *Ruler Units Drop-Down Menu*

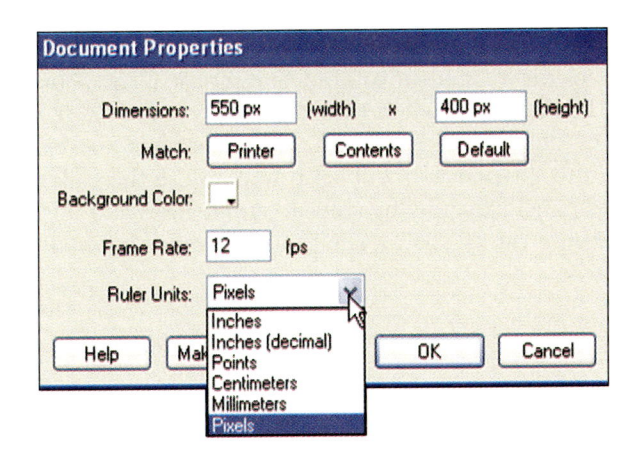

When no object is selected in the stage, the Properties panel displays Document Properties providing quick access to frequently used options such as Background and Frame Rate.

Changing Fill and Stroke Colors for Existing Objects

In Chapter 1, Exercise 9, you used the Paint Bucket tool to add gray fill color to two enclosed objects (clouds) that had been drawn with the Pencil tool. Closed objects drawn with the Oval tool, the Rectangle tool, or the Pen tool automatically have fill color applied. Enclosed shapes drawn using the Line tool or drawn freehand using the Pencil tool do not have fill color applied. Use the Paint Bucket tool to apply the currently selected Fill Color in the toolbox to a closed shape drawn with the Pencil or Line tools. When the Paint Bucket tool is active, the Options section of the toolbox displays the Gap Size modifier button. Click the button to instruct Flash on how to fill gaps that may be present in the stroke line of the shape you are trying to fill as shown in Figure 2.16. The default option of Close Small Gaps can be changed to Don't Close Gaps, Close Medium Gaps, or Close Large Gaps.

Paint Bucket Tool

FIGURE

2.16 *Gap Size Options for Paint Bucket*

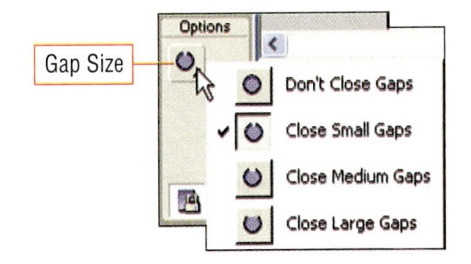

Working with Text and Editing Drawn Objects   63

The Paint Bucket can also be used to change the fill color of a closed shape drawn with the Oval tool, Rectangle tool, or Pen tool. Using the Paint Bucket is more efficient for an existing object as it requires one less mouse click. For example, to change the fill color of an existing rectangle, click the Arrow tool, click the fill inside the rectangle, click Fill Color, click the desired color swatch, and then click outside the object to deselect it—a total of five mouse clicks. You can achieve the same result with the Paint Bucket in four clicks. Click the Paint Bucket tool, click Fill Color, click the desired color swatch, and then click the existing fill in the rectangle. Later in this chapter you will learn how to use the Color Mixer panel and the Color Swatches panel for applying color to stroke lines and fills. If you are doing a lot of recoloring in a movie, using the panels is more efficient than using the Paint Bucket.

Ink Bottle Tool

The Ink Bottle tool is used to achieve a similar result as the Paint Bucket with the exception that the Ink Bottle changes the stroke height and color of existing objects. Click the Ink Bottle tool, change the stroke height and stroke color to the desired value and color, and then click the stroke line of the object to which you want the new settings applied. A shape drawn with the Brush tool contains fill color with no stroke color. Using the Ink Bottle tool you can add a stroke line to the brush shape. As seen in Figure 2.13, the Ink Bottle can also add stroke lines to outline the characters within a text block that has been converted to a graphic.

Eye Dropper Tool

An existing object's stroke or fill color can be copied to another object using the Eye Dropper tool. To do this, click the Eye Dropper tool, click the stroke or fill of the existing object from which you want the color copied, and then click the stroke or fill of the object to which you want the color applied. When the Eye Dropper is active and you click a stroke line, the Ink Bottle tool automatically becomes active and when you click a fill, the Paint Bucket automatically becomes active. Figure 2.17 illustrates the two icons that you will see when the Eye Dropper is active and you are pointing to a stroke line and a fill.

FIGURE 2.17 *Eye Dropper Icons*

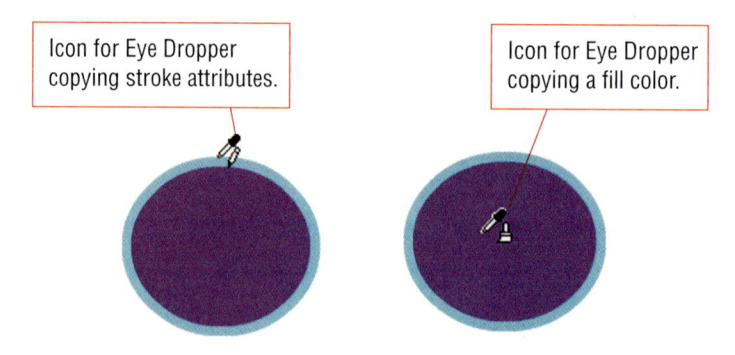

Icon for Eye Dropper copying stroke attributes.

Icon for Eye Dropper copying a fill color.

exercise 7

CHANGING STROKE AND FILL COLORS OF EXISTING OBJECTS

1. Open Ch1SA1.
2. Save the document with Save As and name it Ch2Ex07.
3. Change the fill color for three of the balloons to the same shade of yellow by completing the following steps:
   a. Click the Paint Bucket tool.
   b. Click Fill Color and then click the bright yellow color swatch shown in the first column of the color palette.
   c. Position the Paint Bucket over the second balloon from the left which is currently bright blue and then click the left mouse button. The balloon's fill is changed to yellow. Notice the stroke line remains the original bright blue color.
   d. Click the Paint Bucket over the fourth balloon from the left which is currently green.
   e. Click the Paint Bucket over the last balloon which is currently orange.
4. Change the stroke color on the balloons that were changed in Step 3 by completing the following steps:
   a. Click the Ink Bottle tool.
   b. Change the stroke color to the same yellow color swatch used for the Paint Bucket in Step 3.
   c. If necessary, change the stroke height to 1.
   d. Position the tip of the ink flow from the Ink Bottle pointer, called the *hotspot*, over the stroke line for the second balloon from the left which is currently bright blue and then click the left mouse button.
   e. Repeat Step 4d for the other two balloons to which the fill was changed in Step 3.
5. Copy the stroke and fill attributes from the purple balloon to the last balloon that was changed to yellow by completing the following steps:
   a. Click the Eye Dropper tool.

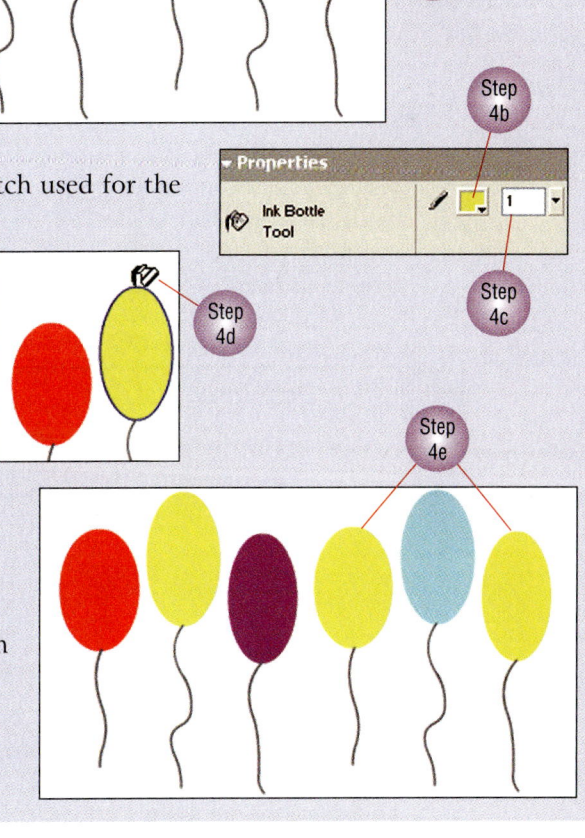

FLASH MX

Working with Text and Editing Drawn Objects 65

b. Point to the stroke color for the purple balloon and then click the left mouse button when the icon displays the eye dropper with the pencil attached. The stroke attributes are copied and the Ink Bottle tool automatically becomes active.
c. Click the Ink Bottle over the stroke line for the last balloon.
d. Click the Eye Dropper tool.
e. Point to the fill in the purple balloon and then click the left mouse button when the icon displays the eye dropper with the paint brush attached. The fill color is copied and the Paint Bucket tool automatically becomes active.
f. Click the Paint Bucket over the fill in the last balloon.
6. Save the revised document using the same name (Ch2Ex07).

Viewing the Stage

In Chapter 1, Exercise 3, and Exercise 1 of this chapter you used the View menu to change the magnification of the stage to 100%. Changing the magnification to higher percentages is often necessary when drawing or editing a document in order to precisely move, resize, or transform objects.

Zoom Text Box

The magnification setting can also be changed in the Zoom text box at the top right of the stage. Click the down arrow next to the Zoom text box to display the drop-down list shown in Figure 2.18. Click Show Frame to make the entire stage visible within the window. Show All ensures all objects in both the stage and the workspace are visible. You can also click the mouse in the text box over the current magnification setting, key a percentage value, and then press Enter to enlarge or reduce the viewing area by a percentage not shown in the drop-down list box.

FIGURE 2.18 **Zoom Drop-Down List Box**

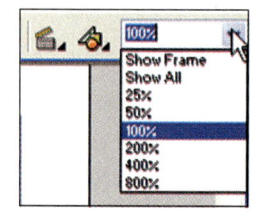

In addition to changing magnification settings on the View menu or in the Zoom text box, Flash provides the Zoom Tool and the Hand Tool in the toolbox. Use all of these tools in conjunction with each other to scroll and zoom to edit objects more precisely.

Zoom Tool

Clicking the Zoom tool (displays as a magnifying glass) in the toolbox displays the Enlarge and Reduce modifier buttons in the Options section as shown in Figure 2.19. Click the Zoom tool and then click over an object to enlarge or reduce its view. The pointer displays as a magnifying glass with a + or – sign inside depending on the current modifier.

Zoom Tool

FIGURE 2.19 Zoom Tool Modifier Buttons

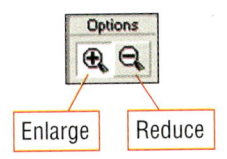

Each time you click the mouse, the magnification setting is doubled or halved. For example, if the current magnification setting is 100%, clicking the Zoom tool over an object with the Enlarge modifier selected enlarges the view to 200% or to 50% with the Reduce modifier active. Clicking the same object a second time enlarges the view to 400% or reduces it to 25%. Draw a selection box around an object with the Zoom tool and Flash calculates the required magnification percentage to enlarge the object so that it fits within the window.

Hand Tool

When the stage is enlarged you can scroll to various parts of the movie using the horizontal and vertical scroll bars. The Hand tool provides an alternative method of moving the stage and can be used to move to the required area more quickly than using the scroll bars. Click the Hand tool, move the pointer (displays as a hand) to the area on the stage in which you want navigate, and then drag the stage left, right, up, or down to scroll the stage.

Hand Tool

Using the Eraser Tool

Erasing is a valuable editing tool not only to do the obvious task of rubbing out unwanted portions of strokes, fills, or shapes, but it can also be used as a drawing tool. For example, assume you have drawn an apple and want to draw a worm hole in the apple. You can use the eraser tool in a similar manner as you would the brush tool to draw the hole. Once the hole is drawn by erasing the fill area where you want the hole to appear, you can then use the Paint Bucket and/or Ink Bottle tools to fill the erased portion with a different color or stroke.

Eraser Tool

The Eraser Mode, Faucet, and Eraser Shape modifier buttons shown in Figure 2.20 appear in the Options section with the Eraser tool active. The Faucet button allows you to erase an entire stroke line or fill just by clicking the eraser (displays as a faucet icon) anywhere on the stroke or fill. Clicking the down arrow next to Eraser Shape displays a pop-up list with various sizes and shapes for the eraser pointer. The five eraser modes shown in Figure 2.21 are described in Table 2.1. The active eraser mode controls what the eraser will do when it encounters stroke lines and fills as you drag on the stage.

Working with Text and Editing Drawn Objects 67

FIGURE 2.20 *Eraser Modifier Buttons*

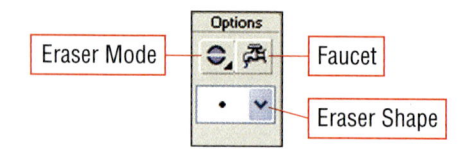

FIGURE 2.21 *Eraser Modes*

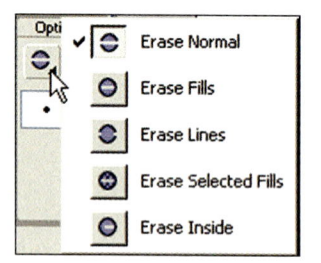

TABLE 2.1 *Eraser Modes*

Erase Normal	Erases stroke lines and fills that you drag the eraser over.
Erase Fills	Eraser will not remove the stroke lines that you drag over.
Erase Lines	Eraser will not remove any fills that you drag over.
Erase Selected Fills	Eraser removes only the currently selected fills and leaves stroke lines intact.
Erase Inside	Erasing is constrained to one filled object only—the object in which you begin erasing. Other filled objects in the stage remain unaffected.

As you drag the eraser it may appear that you are rubbing out a stroke line or fill even though you know you have selected the correct mode. Do not be overly concerned as Flash does not redraw the objects until you release the mouse button. If you choose a mode that you realize was incorrect after erasing, use the Undo feature to restore the object and then reselect the eraser mode. Figure 2.22 illustrates the effects of each eraser mode on an object. In each star shown in Figure 2.22 the eraser mode was changed as indicated and then erasing was done over both stroke lines and fills. The star was redrawn as illustrated upon release of the mouse.

FIGURE 2.22 Eraser Mode Effects

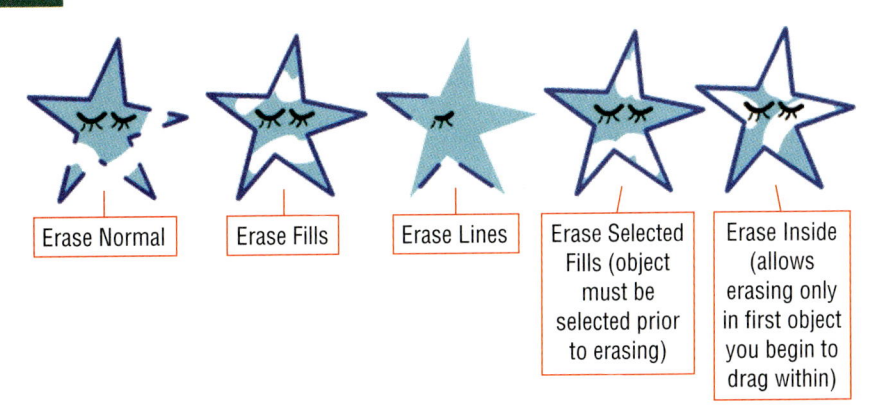

Erase Normal | Erase Fills | Erase Lines | Erase Selected Fills (object must be selected prior to erasing) | Erase Inside (allows erasing only in first object you begin to drag within)

exercise 8

CHANGING THE BACKGROUND, ZOOMING IN AND OUT OF THE STAGE, AND ERASING

1. With Ch2Ex07 open, change the background to light purple by completing the following steps:
   a. Make sure the Properties panel is expanded.
   b. Click the white color swatch next to Background in the Properties panel to open the color palette.
   c. Click the light purple color swatch as shown. 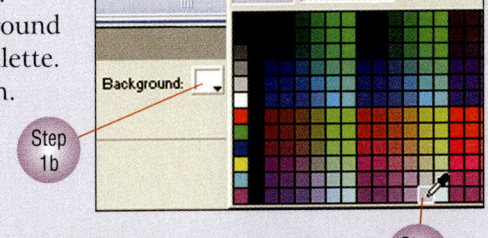
2. Decrease the magnification for the stage, zoom in and out, and use the Hand tool to move the stage by completing the following steps:
   a. Click the down arrow next to the Zoom text box and then click 50% at the drop-down list.
   b. Click the Zoom tool in the toolbox.
   c. Click the Reduce button in the Options section of the toolbox.
   d. Click the magnifying glass pointer with the minus sign over the second yellow balloon from the left. The stage is reduced to 25%.
   e. Click the Enlarge button in the Options section of the toolbox.
   f. Click the magnifying glass pointer with the plus sign over the red balloon. The stage is enlarged to 50%.
   g. Click the magnifying glass pointer with the plus sign over the turquoise balloon. The stage is now at 100%.
   h. Click the magnifying glass pointer with the plus sign over the last purple balloon. The stage is now at 200%.
   i. Click the magnifying glass pointer with the plus sign over the last purple balloon again. The stage is now at 400%.

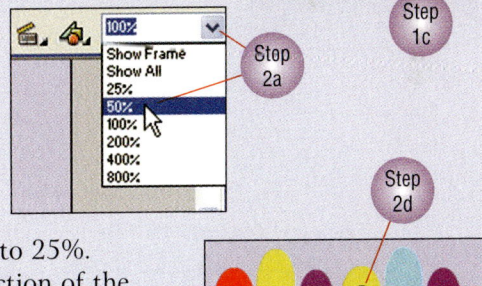

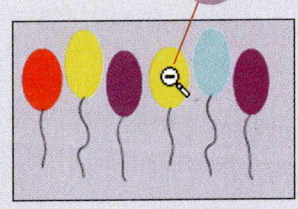

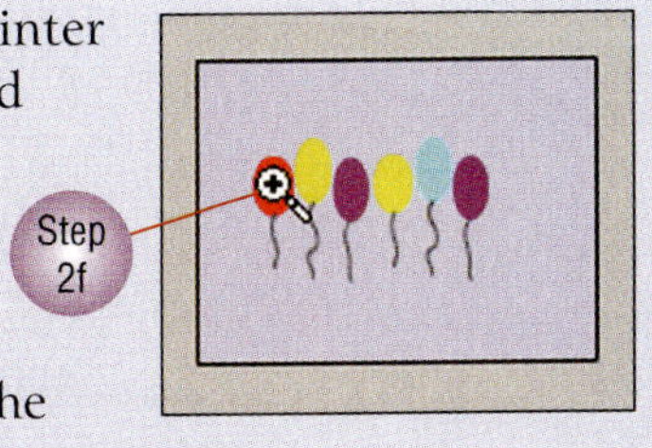

FLASH MX Working with Text and Editing Drawn Objects

j. Click the Hand tool in the toolbox.
k. Position the hand pointer approximately over the center of the purple balloon that is visible within the stage. 
l. Hold down the left mouse button and drag to the top right of the stage. Notice the horizontal and vertical scroll boxes adjust as you move the stage.

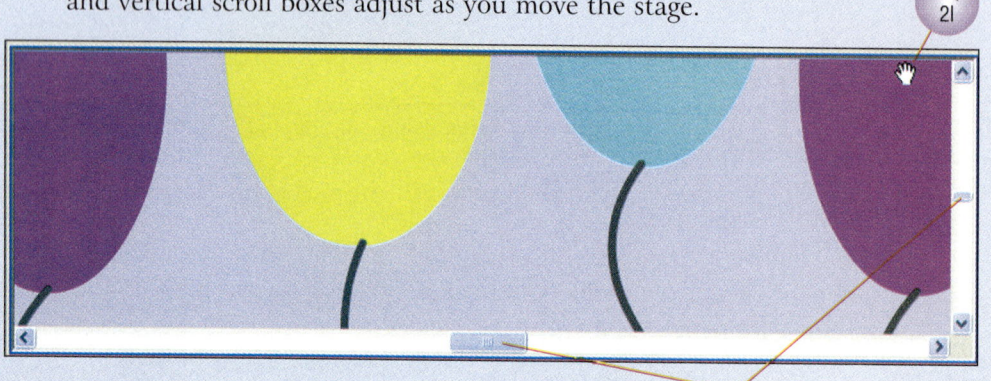

Step 2k

Step 2l

Scroll boxes move in conjunction with hand to show position of stage.

m. Drag the hand pointer into the Timeline area. Notice that you can drag the hand pointer outside the stage area and the stage continues moving. Continue practicing with the Hand tool until you are comfortable with the technique.
n. Click in the Zoom text box, key **175**, and then press Enter.
o. With the Hand tool still active, move the stage so that all of the balloons are visible.

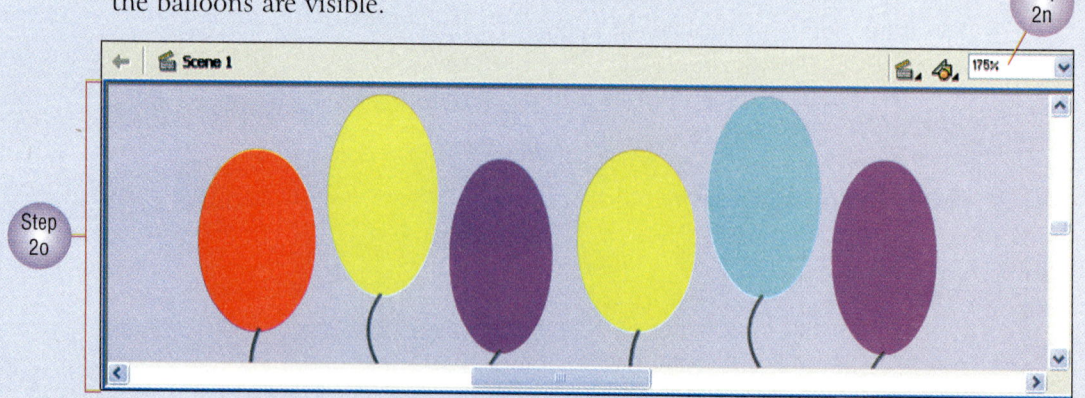

Step 2n

Step 2o

3. Use the Eraser tool to draw a hole in one of the balloons and shorten a string by completing the following steps:

70 Chapter Two

FLASH MX

a. Click the Eraser tool in the toolbox.
b. Click the down arrow next to Eraser Shape in the Options section of the toolbox and then click the smallest eraser shape in the pop-up list.
c. Erase the fill by dragging the eraser near the top right of the red balloon to create a small hole similar to the one shown.
d. Change the magnification to 100% and then scroll the stage if necessary so that you can see all of the strings hanging down from the balloons.
e. Erase approximately one-third of the string at the bottom of the turquoise balloon. The erasing will appear to leave a white trail until you release the mouse button at which point Flash redraws the object.
4. Save the revised document using the same name (Ch2Ex07).
5. Close Ch2Ex07.
6. Start a new document.

Drawing Curved Lines

As discussed in Chapter 1, curved lines known as Bézier curves are drawn using the Pen tool. In Chapter 1, you used the Pen tool to create straight-line shapes by clicking anchor points on the stage. Double-clicking the final anchor point completed the shape. Drawing a curved line requires a more complex process. The following steps describe how to draw the curved line shown in Figure 2.23. Each step is identified in Figure 2.23 so that you can see how the curve was created.

FIGURE 2.23 **Steps to Create a Bézier Curve**

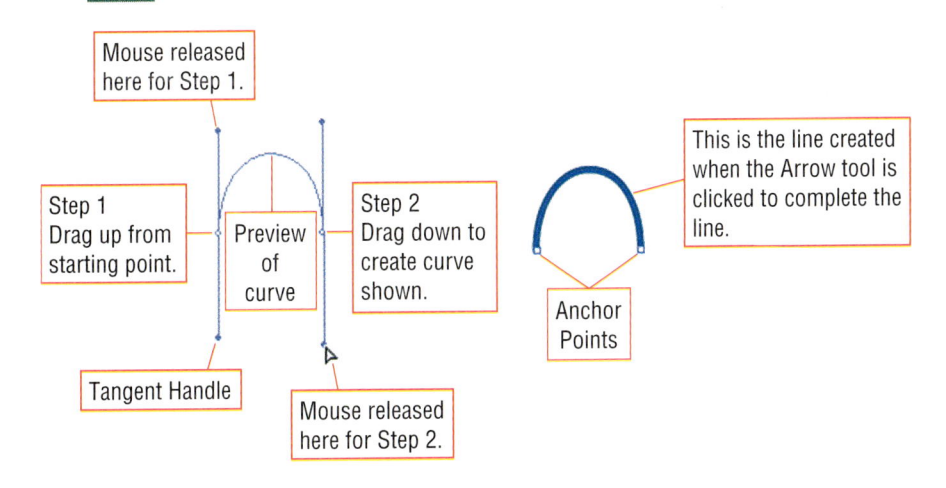

Working with Text and Editing Drawn Objects 71

1. With the Pen tool active, click in the stage where you want the anchor point for the first segment of the curved line, drag in the direction that you want the curve to go and then release the mouse. This creates a straight blue line on the stage with the anchor point where you began dragging the pen and a tangent handle at each end. The tangent handles define the size of the curved path and the shape of the curve. The curved line will begin at the first anchor point.

2. Move the Pen tool to the position where you want the curve to end, click, and drag a line the length and angle that you want the direction and curvature of the line. As you drag the pointer, a preview of the curve will appear between the two lines. Keep dragging up or down as required to achieve the desired angle.

3. Click the Arrow tool (solid black arrow) to complete the curved shape.

The curved line drawn in Figure 2.23 had only one curve. To create additional curves to the line you would not click the Arrow tool as Step 3 indicates. You would continue moving the Pen tool to the position of the next curve and then drag another segment line. Creating curved lines takes a lot of practice. To make the task easier, draw the curve in the approximate shape that you would like and then edit the curve using the anchor point handles.

With the Subselection tool active, click a curved line to reveal its anchor points. Dragging an anchor point allows you to modify the shape or length of the curve as shown in Figure 2.24.

FIGURE 2.24 Editing a Curved Line

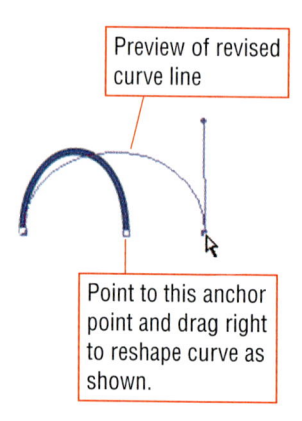

Preview of revised curve line

Point to this anchor point and drag right to reshape curve as shown.

exercise 9   DRAWING A SINGLE CURVED LINE

1. At a clear stage, draw a Bézier curve similar to the one shown in Figure 2.23 by completing the following steps:
    a. Turn on the display of the grid and change the magnification to 100%. While the grid was not shown in Figure 2.23 it is helpful to use the grid's intersection points to assist with the placement of anchor points.
    b. Click the Pen tool.
    c. Change the stroke height to 3.
    d. Change the stroke color to a shade of blue similar to the one shown.

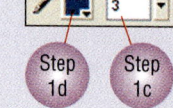

Step 1d   Step 1c

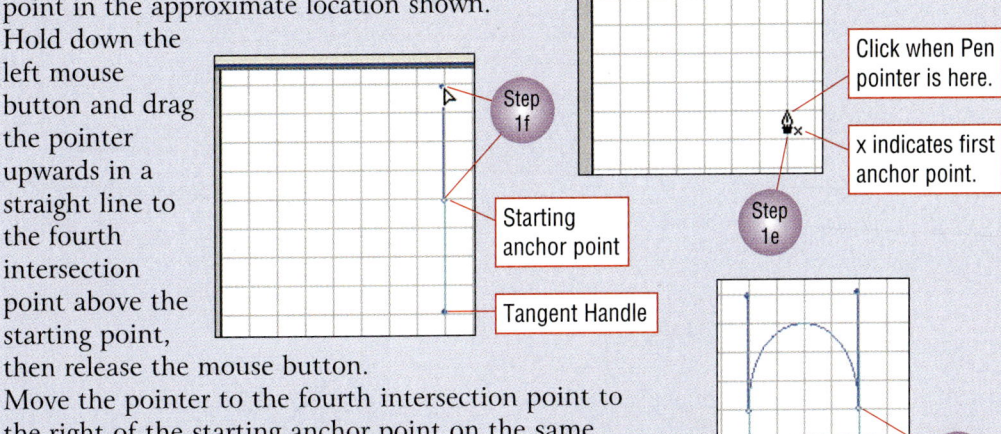

e. Position the Pen pointer at a grid intersection point in the approximate location shown.
f. Hold down the left mouse button and drag the pointer upwards in a straight line to the fourth intersection point above the starting point, then release the mouse button.
g. Move the pointer to the fourth intersection point to the right of the starting anchor point on the same horizontal gridline, hold down the left mouse button, drag down to end the segment line at the same tangent point as the first line, and then release the mouse.
h. Click the Arrow tool to complete the curved line.
2. Save the document and name it Ch2Ex09.
3. Close Ch2Ex09.
4. Start a new document.

exercise 10 — DRAWING A LINE WITH TWO CURVES

1. At a clear stage, turn on the display of the grid and increase magnification to 125%.
2. Draw a waved line with two curves by completing the following steps:
   a. Click the Pen tool.
   b. Position the Pen pointer at an intersection point in the grid at the approximate location shown and then drag a segment line angled right towards the next vertical gridline, three intersection points above the starting point as shown. 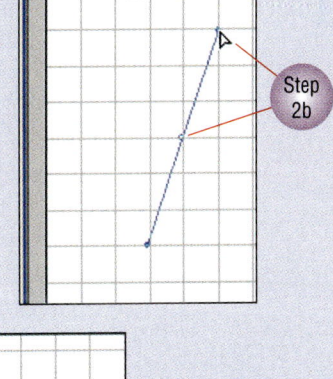
   c. Position the pointer four intersection points to the right of the starting point on the same horizontal gridline and then drag the second segment line the same direction and length as the first segment line.

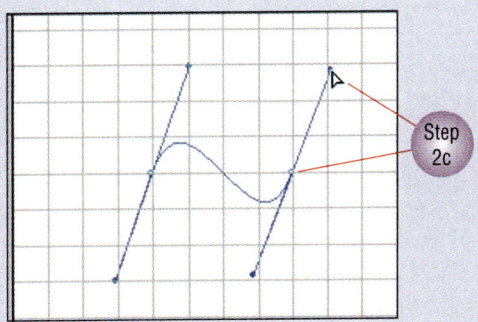

FLASH MX Working with Text and Editing Drawn Objects 73

d. Position the pointer four intersection points to the right of the second anchor point on the same horizontal gridline and then drag the third segment line the same direction and length as the first and second segment lines.
e. Click the Arrow tool to complete the curved line.
f. Turn off the display of the grid.
3. Save the document and name it Ch2Ex10.

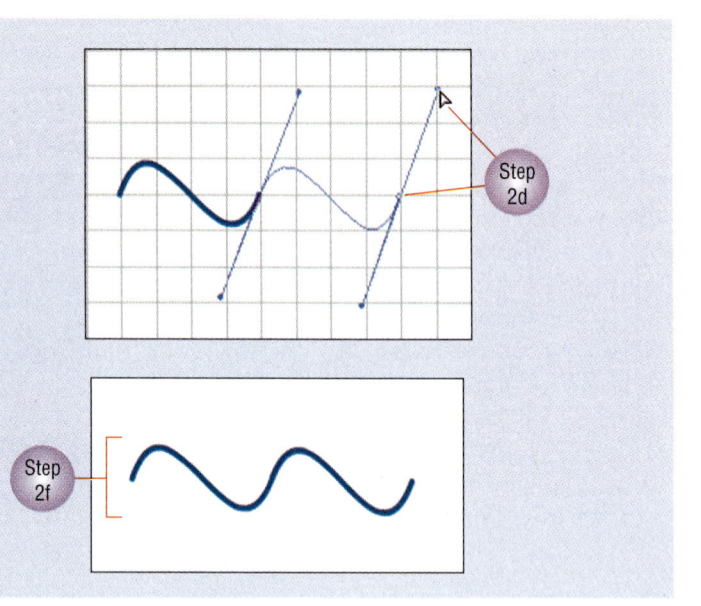

exercise 11

EDITING A CURVED LINE

1. With Ch2Ex10 open, edit the curved line by completing the following steps:
   a. Click the Subselection tool.
   b. Click the white pointer with the solid box attached over the curved line to display the anchor points. Recall from Chapter 1 that when the subselection pointer displays with a solid box it means the entire line will be selected.
   c. Position the white pointer on the second anchor point until the pointer displays with an empty box attached, hold down the left mouse button, drag down and slightly right as shown, and then release the mouse. The empty box attached to the pointer indicates you are editing the anchor point only as opposed to changing the entire line.
   d. Position the white pointer on the third anchor point and then drag the anchor point down and slightly right as shown.
   e. Click in the stage to deselect the curved line.
2. Save the document with Save As and name it Ch2Ex11.
3. Close Ch2Ex11.

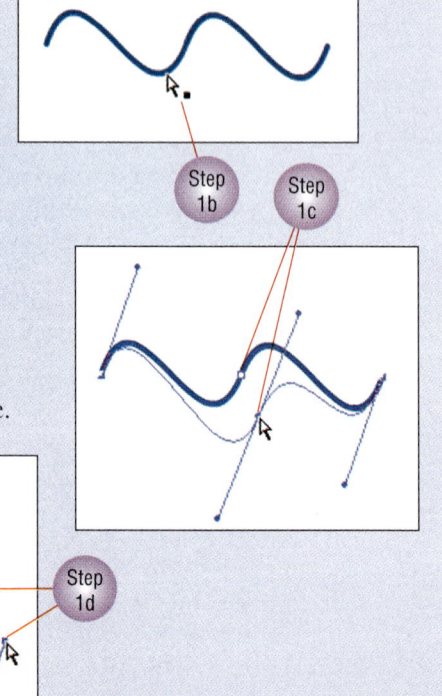

74 Chapter Two

Editing Objects with the Free Transform Tool

Click the Free Transform tool in the toolbox to select an object and rotate, skew, scale, distort, or modify a shape's envelope. With the Free Transform tool active, select the object that you want to edit as you would select an object with the Arrow tool. For example, double-click the Free Transform pointer over the object to select both the stroke line and the fill. With the Free Transform tool active in the toolbox, the modifier buttons shown in Figure 2.25 appear in the Options section. These modifiers are dimmed until an object is selected.

Free Transform Tool

A selected object displays with a white circle in the middle indicating the object's transformational point. This point can be dragged inside the object to change the point of reference for rotating or scaling. In addition, black handles display around the object's boundaries. To change the shape's appearance, drag the black handles in conjunction with the modifiers.

FIGURE 2.25 **Free Transform Modifier Options**

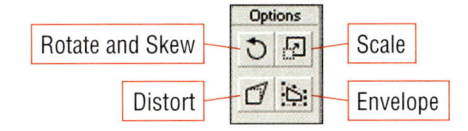

Rotate and Skew

With an object selected with the Free Transform tool and the Rotate and Skew modifier active, pointing to one of the object's corner handles displays the rotation arrow pointer. Drag the corner handle in the direction that you want the object to rotate as shown in Figure 2.26. Holding down the Shift key while dragging the rotation arrow causes the object to rotate in 45-degree increments.

Point to the object's boundary line between the handles to display the skew pointer and then drag the object in the direction in which you want the shape modified as shown in Figure 2.26.

FIGURE 2.26 **Rotating and Skewing an Object**

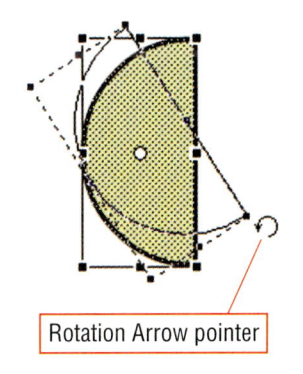

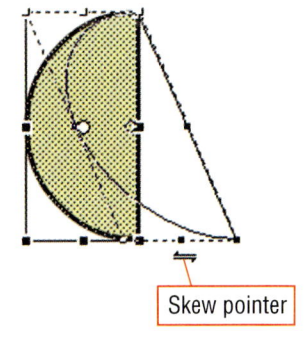

Display the Scale and Rotate dialog box shown in Figure 2.27 to key a scaling percentage value and/or the number of degrees in which you want to rotate a selected object. Click Modify, point to Transform, and then click Scale and Rotate. Key the required values in the Scale and Rotate text boxes and then click OK.

FIGURE 2.27 *Scale and Rotate Dialog Box*

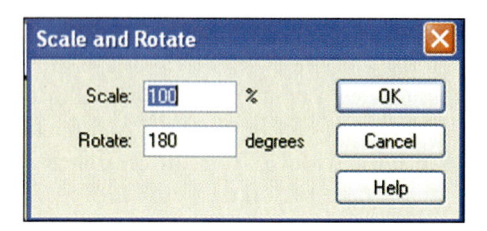

Scale

Scale an object by pointing to one of the black handles until a double-headed arrow pointer displays and then drag to enlarge or reduce the size of the object. Pointing to a corner handle displays a diagonally-shaped double-headed arrow pointer. Dragging the corner handle scales the object both horizontally and vertically at the same time.

Use the Scale and Rotate dialog box to scale the selected object by a percentage value. For example, to make the object 50% smaller, key **50** in the Scale text box in the Scale and Rotate dialog box shown in Figure 2.27.

Distort

The shape of the object can be altered by dragging the black handles with the Distort modifier active, as shown in Figure 2.28. The pointer displays as a white arrowhead when pointing at a handle in Distort mode.

FIGURE 2.28 *Distorting a Shape*

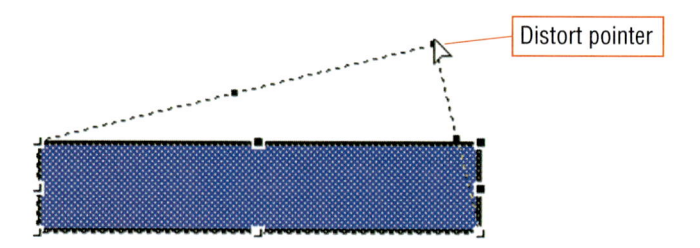

Envelope

Clicking the Envelope modifier displays additional handles around the selected object's boundaries as shown in Figure 2.29. Dragging the handles allows you to modify the shape's envelope, or boundary, which in effect warps or distorts the object inside the envelope. Dragging the handles bends the lines similar to the way the Subselection tool allows you to edit curved lines.

FIGURE

2.29 *Modifying a Shape's Envelope*

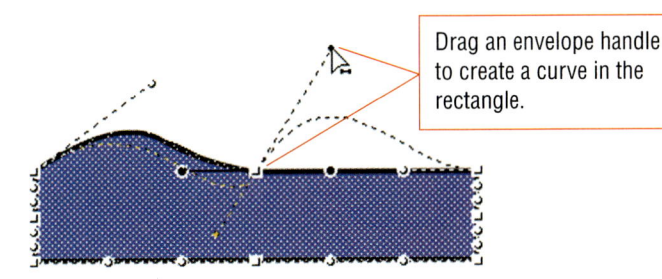

Drag an envelope handle to create a curve in the rectangle.

Text blocks can be distorted to create striking text shapes that are more interesting to look at than a traditional rectangular block. To distort a text block it must first be converted to a graphic object and then the block's envelope can be edited.

exercise 12

MODIFYING OBJECTS USING THE FREE TRANSFORM TOOL

(Note: Make sure you have copied the student data files from the CD-ROM or the IRC that accompanies this textbook before completing this exercise.)

1. Open the Flash document named TransformObjects.
2. Save the document with Save As and name it Ch2Ex12.
3. Free rotate the semicircle by completing the following steps:
   a. Click View and then click Snap to Objects to turn off the snapping feature. *(Note: Skip this step if Snap to Objects does not display with a check mark.)*
   b. Click the Free Transform tool in the toolbox.
   c. Double-click the semicircle to select the object.
   d. Click the Rotate and Skew modifier in the Options section of the toolbox.
   e. Point to the bottom right corner handle until the rotation arrow pointer appears, hold down the left mouse button, drag up until the outline of the semicircle displays as shown, and then release the mouse.
   f. Click outside the object to deselect it. 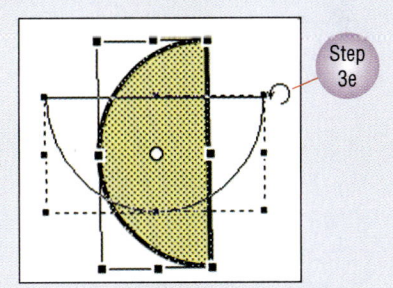
4. Scale the rectangle both horizontally and vertically by completing the following steps:
   a. With the Free Transform tool still active, drag a selection box around the rectangle.
   b. Click the Scale modifier in the Options section of the toolbox.
   c. Point to the bottom right corner handle until a diagonally-shaped double-headed arrow pointer displays, hold down the left mouse button, drag diagonally to the left until the outline of the rectangle is approximately the height and width shown, and then release the mouse button.
   d. Click outside the rectangle to deselect it.

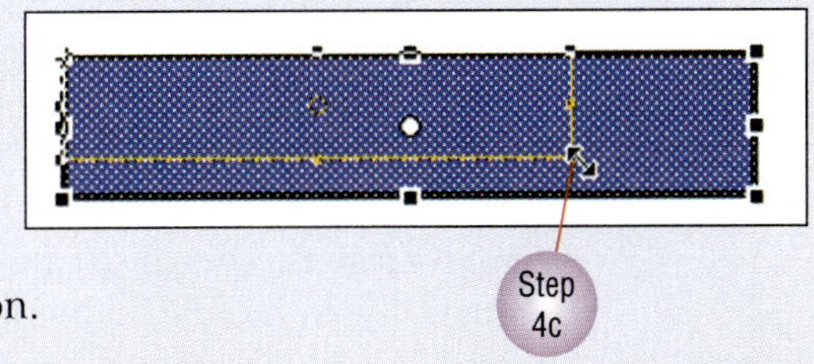

Step 3e

Step 4c

Working with Text and Editing Drawn Objects

5. Distort the rectangle to create a boat shape by completing the following steps:
   a. Click the Arrow tool.
   b. Double-click the rectangle.
   c. Click Modify on the Menu bar, point to Transform, and then click Distort. Notice that using the menus has caused the Free Transform tool and Distort buttons to become active in the toolbox.
   d. Position the arrowhead pointer on the bottom left corner handle, drag right as shown, and then release the mouse.
   e. Position the arrowhead pointer on the bottom right corner handle and drag left to create an effect similar to Step 5d.
   f. Click outside the rectangle to deselect it.
6. Using the techniques learned in Steps 3–5, rotate, scale, and move the semicircle to the rectangle as shown.
7. Change the appearance of the semicircle by changing its envelope by completing the following steps:
   a. With the Free Transform tool active, double-click the semicircle.
   b. Click the Envelope modifier in the Options section of the toolbox.
   c. Drag the handles along the top and middle of the semicircle to create the sail as shown. *(Note: Practice dragging a few handles to get a feel for how the semicircle is being modified to add the curves. Your sail does not have to appear exactly as shown. Use the Undo feature if you need to start over.)*

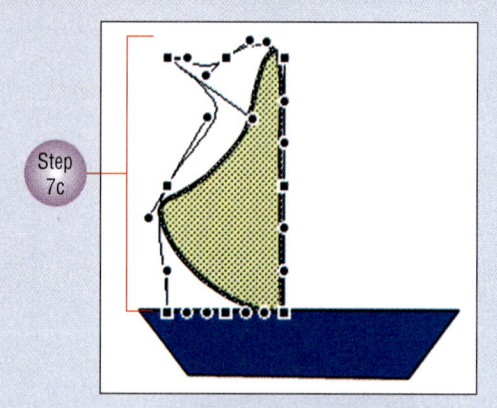

8. Save the revised document using the same name (Ch2Ex12).
9. Close the document.

In Step 5 of Exercise 12 you used the Transform side menu to distort the shape of the rectangle. Flash also includes a Transform panel, which can be opened by clicking Window and then Transform. The panel includes the scale, rotate, and skew options. Use this panel to scale an object by a percentage horizontally and/or vertically, rotate by keying a degree value, or skew by keying degree values.

78 Chapter Two

Editing Stroke Lines

With the Arrow tool selected, Flash includes the Smooth and Straighten modifiers in the Options section of the toolbox. These buttons are dimmed until a line segment is selected. Click the Smooth button over the selected line segment to smooth curves as shown in Figure 2.30. Continue clicking until the line reaches the desired shape. If you click one too many times and you do not like the effect on the shape, use the Undo feature to return to the shape before the last smooth command. Use the Straighten button to convert curved line segments into straight-line segments as shown in Figure 2.31.

Smooth Modifer   Straighten Modifer

FIGURE 2.30 *Lines Edited with Smooth Modifier*

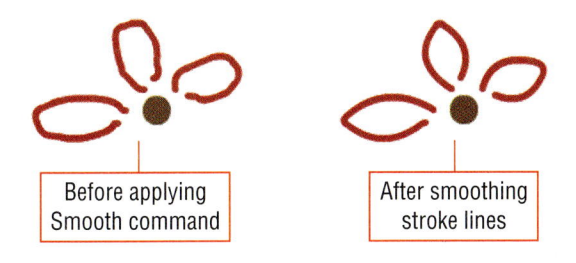

Before applying Smooth command

After smoothing stroke lines

FIGURE 2.31 *Lines Edited with Straighten Modifier*

Double-click a stroke line to select all points in the shape.

Before applying Straighten command

After straightening stroke lines

By default, the Recognize shapes feature in Flash is turned on at the Normal tolerance setting, which means Flash recognizes basic geometric shapes when using the Smooth and Straighten modifiers. For example, if you draw a shape that resembles a square but has rough edges to it, Flash converts the shape to a square when the Straighten modifier is applied. This feature can be turned off or its tolerance setting changed to Strict or Tolerant in the Preferences dialog box. The Strict and Tolerant options have different effects dependent on the computer's screen resolution and current magnification setting. Practice drawing and modifying a few shapes at each setting to find the tolerance level that works best for you. To do this, click Edit, click Preferences, and then click the Editing tab in the Preferences dialog box. Click the down arrow next to Recognize shapes and then choose the desired tolerance option.

Working with Text and Editing Drawn Objects

Lengthening Line Segments, Shortening Line Segments, and Adjusting the Shape

Each line segment has a starting point and an ending point, which can be used to lengthen or shorten the line or to adjust the appearance of the shape. To do this, simply point to the end of the line segment that you want to adjust, and then drag the end point in the direction necessary to lengthen or shorten the stroke or to adjust its position in the shape.

For this to work the line must not be selected. If you drag a line's starting or ending point and the line moves on the stage to another location, then you have dragged a selected line. Use Undo to put it back in its original position and then deselect the line before dragging. Watch the appearance of the pointer before dragging so that you do not inadvertently move it; the pointer always displays the four-headed arrow attached to it when the move command is active. The pointer displays with a shadowed box attached to it when you are adjusting an end point.

Stroke lines that have been drawn freehand are converted to a collection of individual line segments. Flash does this to convert the shape to a vector. For this reason, watch carefully when dragging a starting or ending point because what you thought was an entire line segment may be broken down into smaller segments. Figure 2.32 illustrates how to reshape an object by dragging a point and how to lengthen a line that was drawn too short.

FIGURE 2.32 *Edited Line Segments*

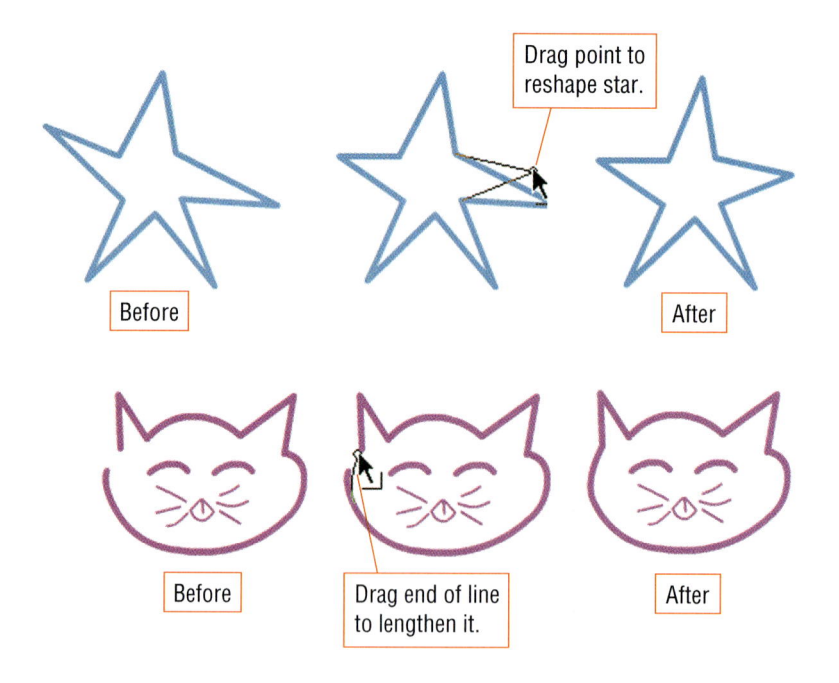

80 Chapter Two

exercise 13
SMOOTHING, STRAIGHTENING, AND SHORTENING LINE SEGMENTS AND RESHAPING OBJECTS

1. Open the Flash document named EditLines.
2. Save the document with Save As and name it Ch2Ex13.
3. Reshape and smoothen the line segments in the cloud by completing the following steps:
   a. Make sure the Arrow tool is active.
   b. Position the pointer over the curved line segment in the cloud at the approximate location shown. The pointer displays with a curved line attached to it indicating you can drag the point to reshape the curve.
   c. Hold down the left mouse button and drag up as shown. The curve is redrawn when you release the mouse.
   d. Double-click anywhere on the stroke line to select the entire cloud.
   e. Click the Smooth button twice in the Options section of the toolbox. Flash smooths all of the curves in the entire cloud in increments each time you click Smooth.
   f. Click Smooth a third time.
   g. Click Edit and then click Undo to restore the cloud to its shape in Step 3e.
   h. Click outside the cloud to deselect it. 
4. Straighten the line segments in the bottom middle object by completing the following steps:
   a. With the Arrow tool still active, draw a selection box around the bottom middle object to select the entire stroke line.
   b. Click the Straighten button once in the Options section of the toolbox. By default, Recognize Shapes is turned on in Flash and the shape is redrawn as an oval.
   c. Click outside the oval to deselect it. 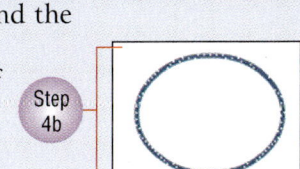
5. Shorten the straight line at the top of the stage by completing the following step: With the Arrow tool still active, position the arrow pointer over the right end of the line until the pointer displays with the shadow box attached to it, hold down the left mouse button, drag left until the line is approximately half its current size, and then release the mouse button. 
6. Reshape the diamond to make the top and bottom points more elongated by completing the following steps:
   a. With the Arrow tool still active, position the pointer on the top point in the diamond until the pointer displays with the shadow box attached to it and then drag up to the approximate location shown to elongate the top of the diamond.
   b. Repeat Step 6a on the bottom point to elongate the bottom of the diamond.
7. Save the revised document using the same name (Ch2Ex13).
8. Close the document.

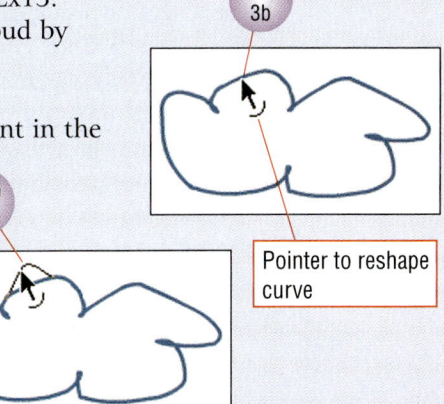

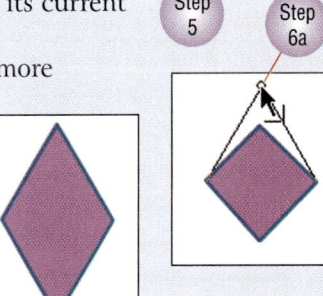

Editing Fills

The fill that shades an enclosed shape with color is treated separately from the stroke lines that surround it. As you have already learned, clicking the arrow pointer over the fill selects it as its own object. The fill can then be edited by moving it outside the object or reshaped by dragging the pointer over its edge using similar techniques as you learned for editing stroke lines. The Paint Bucket and Ink Bottle tools can be used to change the fill color and then surround the fill with a stroke line after it has been moved.

Editing the fill separately from the object can be used to create shadows or 3D effects. Consider the examples shown in Figure 2.33. Example A depicts two overlapping circles created from a single circle. In Step 1, a circle is drawn and then the fill is moved outside the circle. The area behind the fill and within the original stroke line is now treated as a separate object by Flash, which can be recolored as shown in Step 2.

In Example B, a three-dimensional open box is created by starting with a square object. In Step 1 a box is drawn and the fill is moved outside the square. In Step 2, the Paint Bucket and Ink Bottle tools are used to outline the fill with a black stroke line and recolor the fill white. Connecting line segments are drawn using the Line tool.

In Example C, a three-dimensional book is created originating from the diamond shape drawn in Step 1. The diamond's fill is moved outside the diamond in Step 2 and then the white area behind the fill is recolored in Step 3. The shape is rotated in Step 4 and connecting lines are drawn using the Line and Pencil tools.

FIGURE 2.33 **Edited Fill Examples**

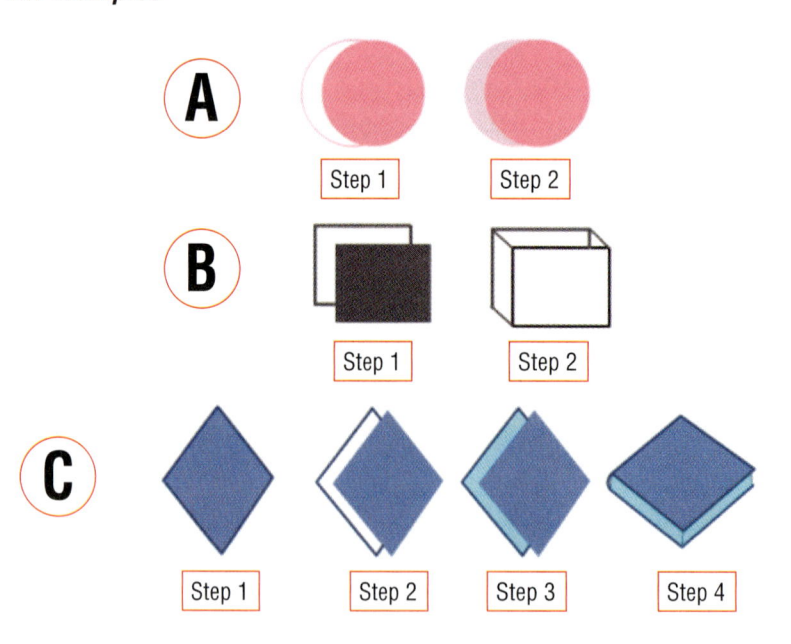

The possibilities for editing fills are limited only by your imagination. Experiment with drawing geometric shapes and moving, reshaping, and recoloring fills to achieve a variety of interesting objects and effects.

Segmenting Fills within Shapes

In Chapter 1, Exercise 10 you used Flash's help system to read about overlapped shapes being broken down into segments that can be manipulated individually. The examples in Figure 2.33 illustrate this concept of segmentation created by dragging the fill away from the stroke lines of an object.

A shape can also be segmented by drawing lines through it as shown in Figure 2.34, which depicts the steps to create the Italian flag. In Step 1, the rectangle is drawn with a black stroke line and white fill. In Step 2, the Line tool is used to draw two equidistant vertical lines inside the rectangle. In Step 3, the Paint Bucket tool is used to recolor the left- and right-segmented fills.

FIGURE 2.34 *Italian Flag Created by Breaking a Rectangle into Three Equal Parts*

Step 1 Draw rectangle.

Step 2 Draw two equidistant vertical lines inside rectangle.

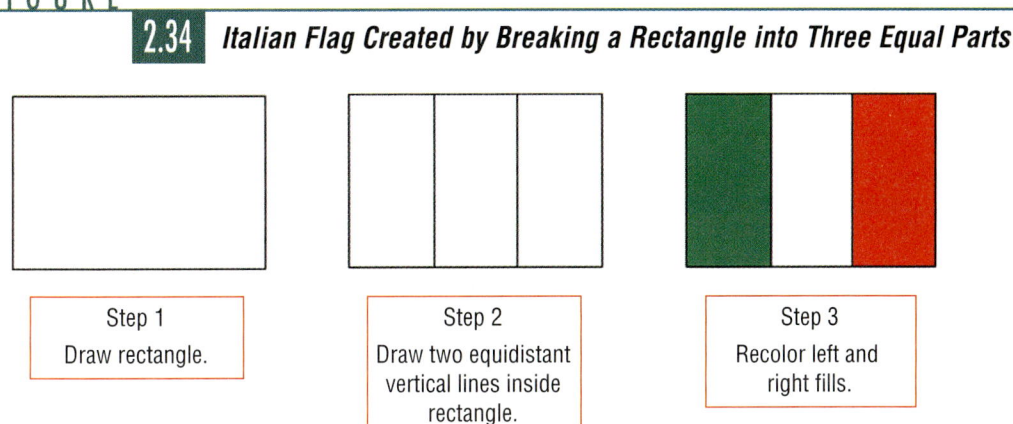

Step 3 Recolor left and right fills.

Breaking a Shape Apart

Using a similar technique as shown in Figure 2.34 you can split a shape apart by segmenting it with a line and then moving the segment away from the original shape. In Figure 2.35, a diamond is shown split into two triangles by drawing a horizontal line across the midsection and then dragging the top and bottom halves away from each other. In the final step, the Ink Bottle tool is used to add a stroke line to the bottom triangle after the shape has been split.

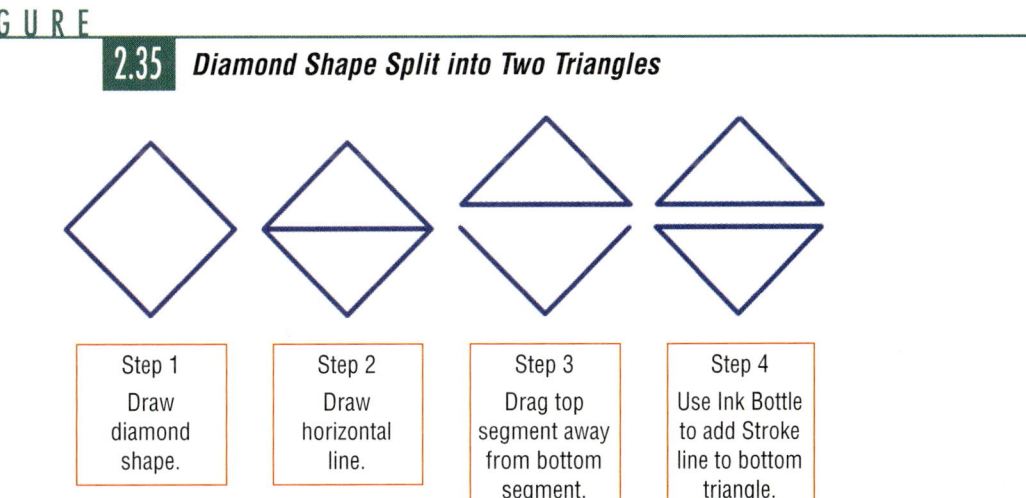

FIGURE 2.35 *Diamond Shape Split into Two Triangles*

Step 1 Draw diamond shape.

Step 2 Draw horizontal line.

Step 3 Drag top segment away from bottom segment.

Step 4 Use Ink Bottle to add Stroke line to bottom triangle.

Working with Text and Editing Drawn Objects

Using the Lasso Tool to Select Fills

Lasso Tool

Polygon Modifier

In Chapter 1 you learned to select objects or portions of objects using the Lasso tool to drag a selection area around an irregular shape. The Polygon modifier for the Lasso tool can also be used to select irregular shapes. With the Polygon modifier active, the Lasso tool draws straight line segments between points in a manner similar to drawing with the Pen tool. Click the Lasso tool, click the Polygon mode button in the Options section of the toolbox, and then click a sequence of points around the area to be selected as shown in Figure 2.36. Complete the selection by double-clicking. If you do not create an enclosed shape with the Lasso by double-clicking at the starting point, Flash will draw a straight line from the starting point to the point at which you double-clicked.

FIGURE 2.36 **Selecting with Lasso Tool in Polygon Mode**

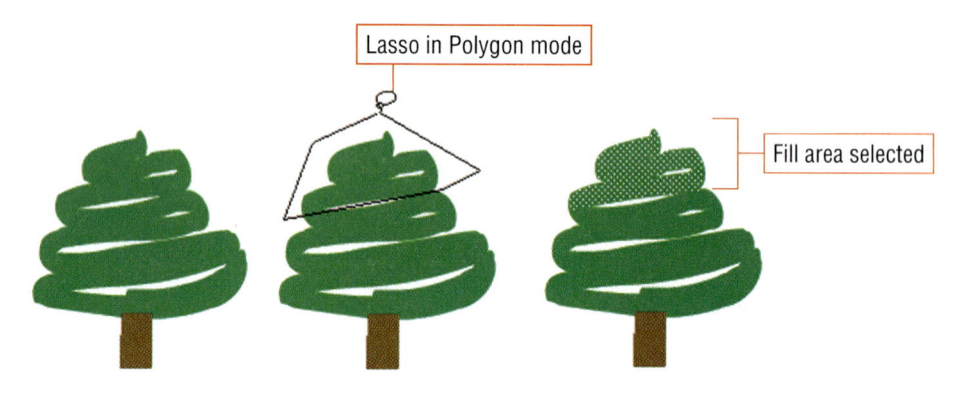

Lasso in Polygon mode

Fill area selected

exercise 14 — DISTORTING AND ROTATING SHAPES, SMOOTHING AND EDITING LINES, AND EDITING FILLS

1. Open the Flash document named RectangleToGlass.
2. Save the document with Save As and name it Ch2Ex14.
3. Distort the rectangle shape so that it resembles a water glass by completing the following steps:
    a. Click the Free Transform tool.
    b. Draw a selection box around the rectangle.
    c. Click the Distort modifier in the Options section of the toolbox.
    d. Drag the bottom right corner of the rectangle towards the center to create an angle as shown.
    e. Drag the bottom left corner of the bucket towards the center to create the left angle and then click outside the shape to deselect it.
4. Draw a line at the top of the glass, smooth the line, and then edit the top line of the rectangle to create a curve by completing the following steps:
    a. Click the Pencil tool.
    b. Set the stroke height to 3.5 and the stroke color to black.
    c. Draw a curved line from the top left corner to the top right corner of the glass as shown.

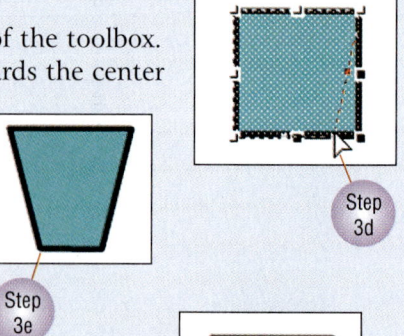

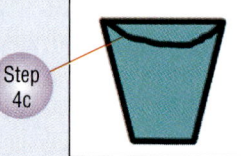

Step 3d

Step 3e

Step 4c

84 Chapter Two

d. Click the Arrow tool and then click the line you drew in Step 4c.
e. Click the Smooth button in the Options section of the toolbox until the line is curved as shown. 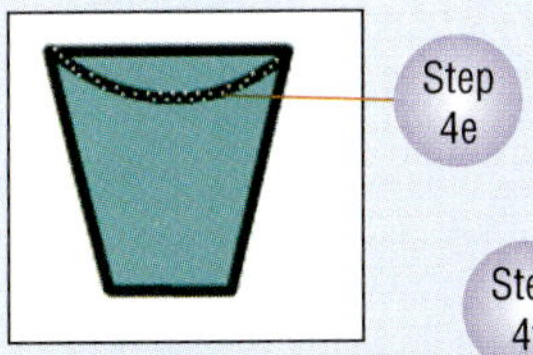
f. Point at the top stroke line for the glass until the pointer displays with the curved line attached and then drag the top to create a curved line similar to the one shown.

5. Rotate the glass to make it lie on its side by completing the following steps:
   a. Click the Free Transform tool.
   b. Draw a selection box around the glass.
   c. Click the Rotate and Skew modifier in the Options section of the toolbox.
   d. Point at the bottom right corner handle until the pointer displays with the rotation arrow, hold down the Shift key, and then drag up until the glass is rotated as shown. (*Note: Holding down the Shift key while rotating causes Flash to rotate the object in 45 degree increments.*)
   e. Click outside the glass to deselect it. 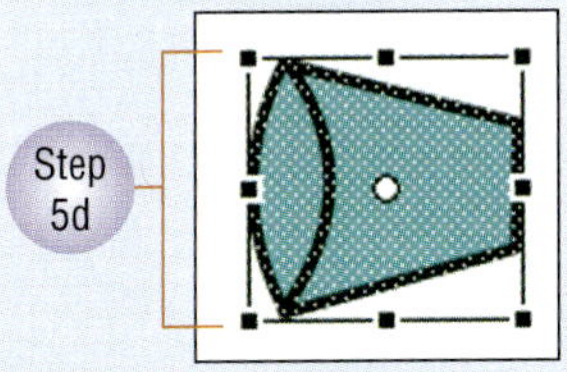

6. Distort the fill to make it appear as though water has spilled from the overturned glass by completing the following steps:
   a. Click the Arrow tool and then click the fill inside the glass.
   b. Drag the fill outside the glass as shown. 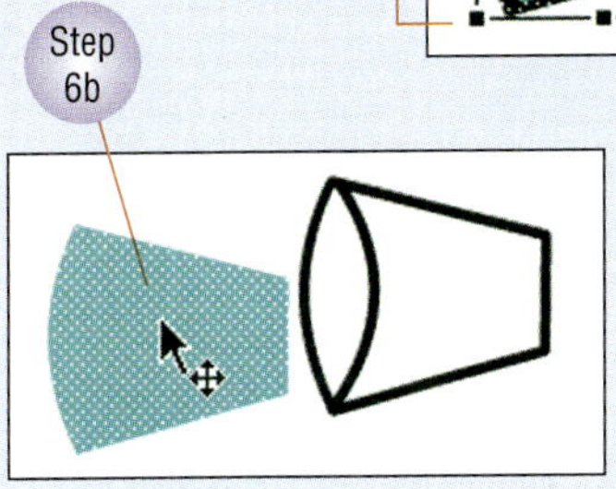
   c. Click outside the fill to deselect it.
   d. Point near the middle of the left curved edge of the fill until the pointer displays with a curve attached to it, hold down the left mouse button, and then drag left to distort the fill as shown.
   e. Continue dragging curves and points along the top of the fill to flatten the shape until it is similar to the one shown resembling spilled water.
   f. Drag the fill back towards the glass as shown to make it appear that the water is flowing from the overturned glass.

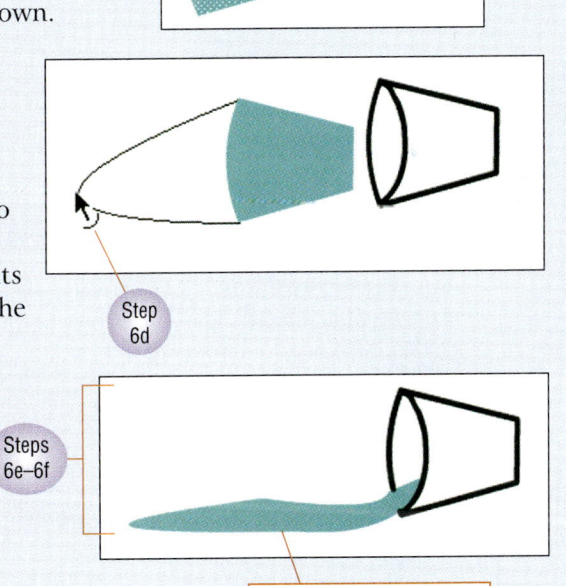

7. Save the revised document using the same name (Ch2Ex14).
8. Close Ch2Ex14.

Your fill shape may vary.

Intersecting Lines to Create Segments

In Exercise 14, Step 4 you might have expected the fill to become segmented when the curved line was drawn inside the glass. In Step 6 when you dragged the fill outside the glass, it would have been more difficult to distort the shape to resemble spilled water if the fill had been segmented.

Working with Text and Editing Drawn Objects

In Figure 2.37 the steps to segment the fill inside the glass are shown. The key to segmenting fill using curved lines is to start drawing the curve outside the glass and extend it past the glass on the other side so that the two sets of lines intersect each other as shown. When curved lines intersect, Flash creates line segments and fill inside the segmented lines also becomes a separate segment.

With this technique, the fill inside the glass is segmented and can then be recolored using the Paint Bucket tool and then the lines extending beyond the glass can be deleted.

FIGURE 2.37 *Segmenting the Fill Inside the Glass with Intersecting Lines*

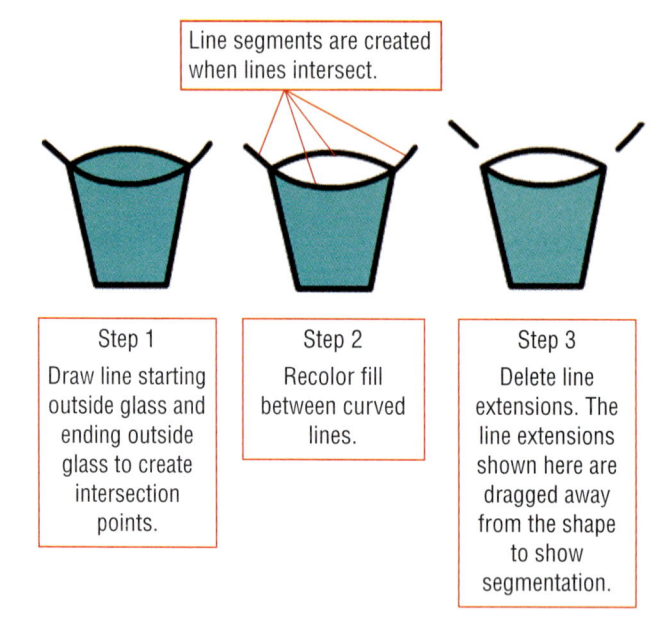

Line segments are created when lines intersect.

Step 1
Draw line starting outside glass and ending outside glass to create intersection points.

Step 2
Recolor fill between curved lines.

Step 3
Delete line extensions. The line extensions shown here are dragged away from the shape to show segmentation.

Grouping Shapes

Flash combines shapes that overlap, which can cause difficulty when combined shapes need to be edited independently from each other. In Figure 2.38 this problem is illustrated when the circle is moved away from the square it overlapped. The portion of the square that was hidden behind the circle has disappeared because the two shapes had become combined.

FIGURE 2.38 *Ungrouped Shape Interaction*

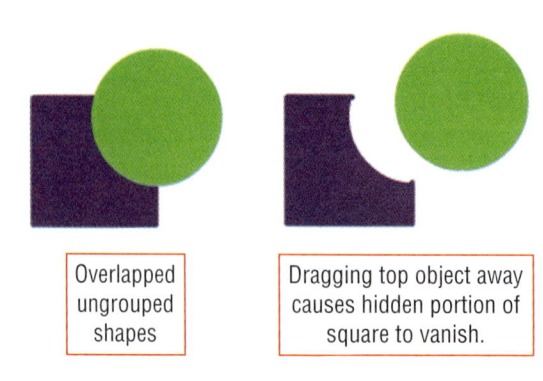

Overlapped ungrouped shapes

Dragging top object away causes hidden portion of square to vanish.

86 Chapter Two

It is also easy to accidentally drag the wrong line segment in a combined shape, causing you frustration when you try to edit the shape. Grouping objects can solve these two problems. Figure 2.39 illustrates the same two objects as Figure 2.38, however, in this case, each object was grouped separately before the circle overlapped the square. Flash now treats the square, including stroke lines and fill, as a distinct entity. When the circle is dragged away from the square, the portion that was hidden becomes visible.

FIGURE

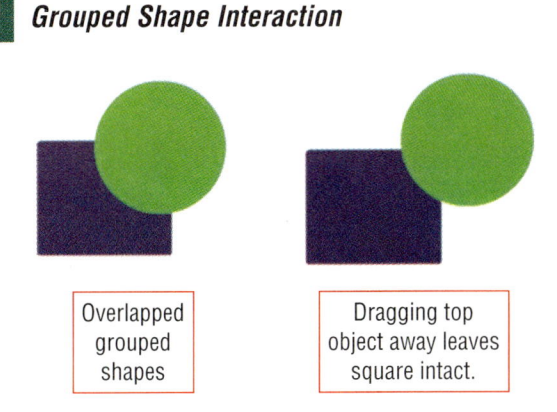

2.39 *Grouped Shape Interaction*

Overlapped grouped shapes

Dragging top object away leaves square intact.

To group an object, select both the stroke line and fill, click Modify, and then click Group. Clicking a grouped object displays a blue box surrounding the shape. If you need to change the fill or stroke color after the object has been grouped, you will have to ungroup it first. To do this, select the grouped object, click Modify, and then click Ungroup.

The order in which you group shapes is important. Flash refers to this as the *stacking order*. For example, in Figure 2.39, the purple square was grouped first and then the circle grouped second. The object grouped last *stacks* on top of the object(s) grouped before it. If you mix up the order of grouped shapes, an object you are attempting to overlap onto another object may keep popping into the foreground. To correct this situation, click the object that you are trying to place on top, click Modify, point to Arrange, and then click Bring to Front. The Arrange menu also contains options to Bring Forward, Send Backward, and Send to Back.

Grouping Multiple Shapes

Multiple shapes can be grouped and treated as a single unit as shown in Figure 2.40. If a group of shapes are related to each other, grouping them together will make editing tasks such as moving, copying, and rotating easier since the entire group resides within a single boundary. To group multiple shapes, draw a selection box around the group of shapes, or individually select all of the objects to be included in the group, click Modify, and then click Group.

FIGURE 2.40 Group Containing Multiple Shapes

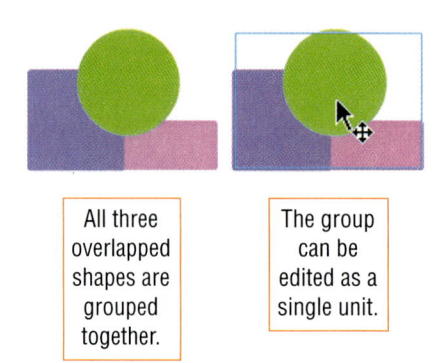

All three overlapped shapes are grouped together.

The group can be edited as a single unit.

exercise 15
GROUPING AND COPYING SHAPES

1. Open Ch2Ex07.
2. Save the document with Save As and name it Ch2Ex15.
3. Group the first three balloons individually by completing the following steps:
   a. With the Arrow tool active, draw a selection box around the first balloon including the string as shown.
   b. With all elements of the first balloon selected, click Modify and then click Group. A blue box surrounds the objects to indicate the group.
   c. Click outside the selected group to deselect it.
   d. Repeat Steps 3a–3c for the second balloon from the left.
   e. Repeat Steps 3a–3c for the third balloon from the left.
4. Overlap and edit the first three balloons by completing the following steps:
   a. Drag the second balloon left so that it covers the hole in the red balloon as shown.
   b. Drag the third balloon left so that it is overlapping the first two balloons as shown.
5. Create a group consisting of the three overlapping balloons and then copy the group by completing the following steps:
   a. Draw a selection box around the three overlapping balloons.
   b. Click Modify and then click Group. A single blue boundary line appears around the three selected objects indicating all three can be edited as a single unit.

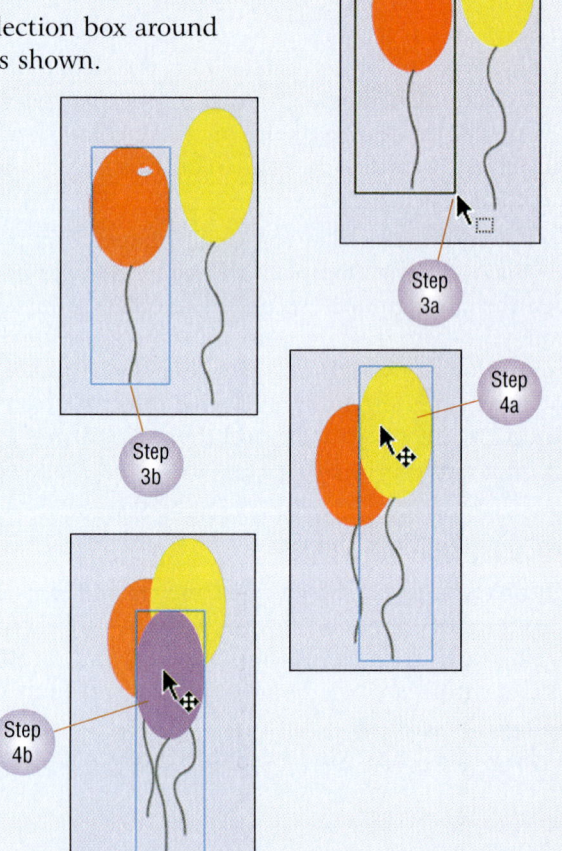

88 Chapter Two

c. Position the pointer over the grouped balloons until the pointer displays with the four-headed arrow icon attached, hold down the Ctrl key, and then drag the group to the space between the balloons as shown. This creates a copy of the group.
d. Click outside the group to deselect it.
6. Save the revised document using the same name (Ch2Ex15).
7. Close Ch2Ex15.

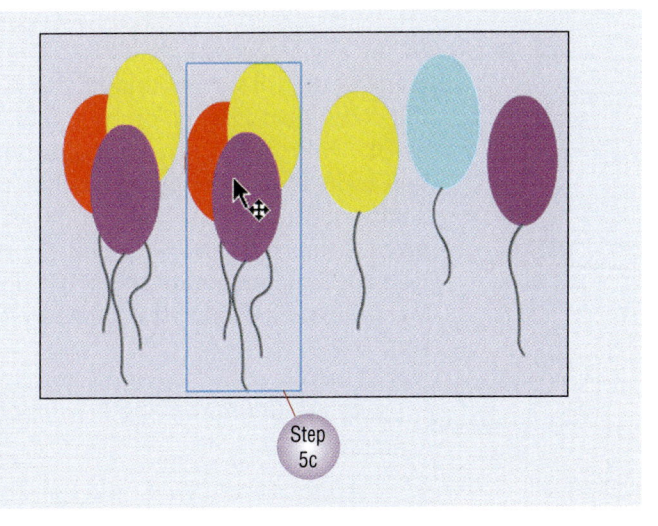

Step 5c

Working with Colors

Flash includes the Color Mixer panel and the Color Swatches panel to assist with adding colors to objects. To open the Color Mixer panel, click Window and then click Color Mixer. The panel displays as shown in Figure 2.41.

FIGURE 2.41 **Color Mixer Panel**

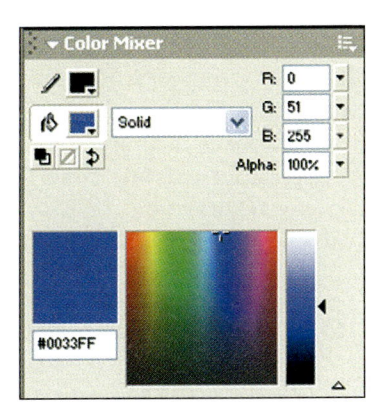

As you have already seen, changes to stroke or fill colors can be made from the appropriate buttons in the Colors section of the toolbox or in the Properties panel when a tool is active that requires a stroke and/or a fill color. Changing a color swatch in the toolbox causes the corresponding color swatch in the Properties panel to change and vice versa. Changes made to color swatches if an object is selected cause that object's color to update, and, if no object is selected, the change affects future drawing objects. All of these relationships hold true when the Color Mixer panel is open.

Changing colors for the stroke or fill is no different using the Color Mixer panel. Click the Stroke color swatch or Fill color swatch to display the same color palette as you saw using the other tools. Move the Eye Dropper to the desired color swatch and then click the mouse.

Working with Text and Editing Drawn Objects 89

The steps to create your own color swatch in the Color Mixer panel are similar to the steps you completed in Chapter 1, Exercise 5, where you created a custom color to the fill in the hourglass. Change the color swatch in the Stroke color or Fill color box to the color upon which you want to base your new color or click the Stroke color button or Fill color button (not the swatch) to select the color box you want to change and then click the crosshair pointer in the color box over the color you want to use. As you did in Chapter 1, you can drag the crosshair pointer around the color box until you see the color you need in the color preview box. If desired, drag the luminosity slider up or down to increase or decrease the brightness level. Figure 2.42 illustrates the steps described here.

FIGURE 2.42 *Using the Color Box and Luminosity Slider to Choose a Color in the Color Mixer Panel*

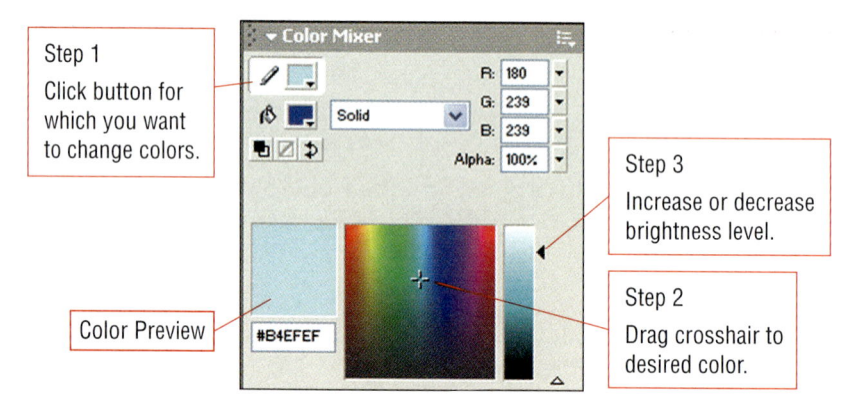

Another method to choosing a color in the Color Mixer panel is to adjust the selected color's red, green, and blue composition. To do this, click the crosshair pointer over the color you want to use in the color box. Click the down-pointing triangle next to the R, G, or B text boxes to drag a slider up or down. As you drag, watch the color preview box display the existing color and your revised color. Also watch the crosshair pointer move to show you the new color position in the color box. Figure 2.43 illustrates this method for choosing colors.

FIGURE 2.43 *Adjusting the Color's Red, Green, and Blue Composition in the Color Mixer Panel*

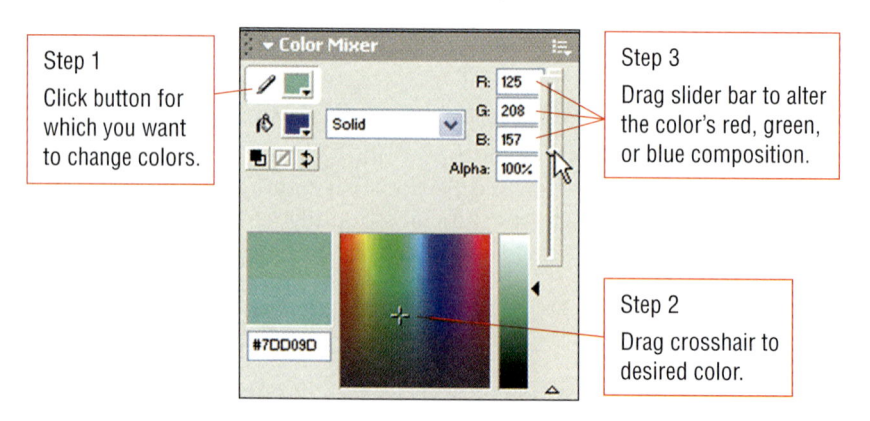

Finally, if you know the R, G, and B values for the color you want, key them directly into the R, G, and B text boxes in the Color Mixer panel. Use the Options menu for the Color Mixer panel to change from displaying the R, G, and B text boxes to the H, S, and B text boxes, which define colors with Hue, Saturation, and Brightness values. Key a percentage value or drag the Alpha Slider to apply a transparency effect to the selected color.

Color Swatches Panel

Click Window and then click Color Swatches to open the Color Swatches panel shown in Figure 2.44. With this panel open in the Flash window, you can change colors easily by clicking the Stroke color or Fill color button in the toolbox and then simply clicking the color swatch for the color you want in the Color Swatches panel. The toolbox button updates to the color swatch chosen.

The Color Swatches panel contains the color wheel at the top right of the panel, called the Color Picker, which you can click to open the Color dialog box and create a custom color as you did in Chapter 1, Exercise 5.

FIGURE 2.44 *Color Swatches Panel*

Applying a Gradient Fill Color

A gradient is a gradual change in the fill color of an object. The change in color is based upon a set of gradient pointers, of which there must be at least two, which make up the group of colors that will comprise the fill. The colors in the group blend together gradually in either a linear or radial fashion.

Gradients are often used to make an object appear affected by a light source that is causing a part of the object to appear shaded or brightened. To apply a gradient to the fill of a selected object, click the Fill Color button in the toolbox, the Color Mixer panel, or the Color Swatches panel, and then click the Eye Dropper over the color of gradient you want to use in the bottom row of the color palette. Figure 2.45 shows the Eye Dropper pointing to a red-to-black radial gradient. Figure 2.46 illustrates the difference between a radial and a linear gradient.

Working with Text and Editing Drawn Objects

FIGURE 2.45   **Choosing a Gradient Fill Color**

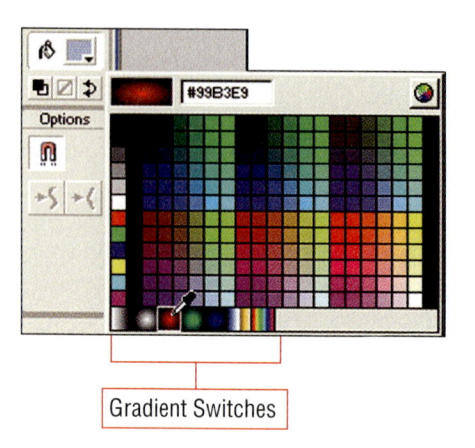

Gradient Switches

FIGURE 2.46   **Radial and Linear Gradients**

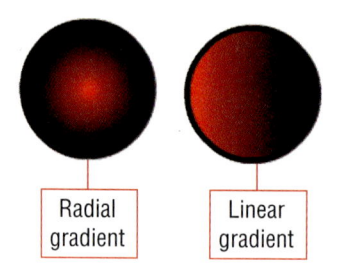

Radial gradient   Linear gradient

Creating a Gradient

You are not limited to the gradients available in the color palette. To create your own gradient, open the Color Mixer panel and then complete the following steps:

1. Click the down arrow next to Fill style (currently reads Solid) and then choose Linear or Radial. A color band with two pointers, one at each end, appears in the middle of the panel. Choose a color for each pointer and then Flash creates the gradient by blending the two colors together based upon the setting of Radial or Linear.
2. Click the pointer at the left end of the color band.
3. Click the color swatch above the color band and then choose the desired color swatch. For example, if you want to create a red-to-black linear gradient, you would choose red as the color at the left end of the color band.
4. Click the pointer at the right end of the color band.
5. Change the color swatch above the color band to the color for which you want the first color to blend into. For example, choose black at the right end of the color band to create a red-to-black linear gradient. The gradient displays in the color preview box.
6. The gradient is now active in the Fill Color button in the toolbox and can be applied to objects. If objects were selected when the gradient was created, the fill is automatically updated.

7. To make the gradient available for future objects that you might create in the file, click the Options menu in the Color Mixer title bar and then click Add Swatch. Flash adds the gradient you created to the gradient list in the color palette.

Figure 2.47 displays the Color Mixer panel with the Fill style set to Linear for creating a custom gradient.

FIGURE 2.47 Color Mixer Panel for Gradients

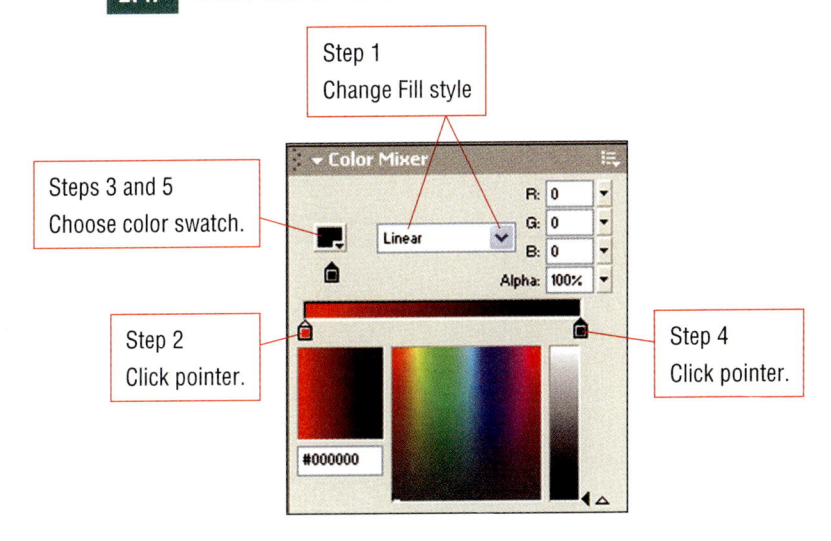

Fill Transform

An object filled with a gradient contains a center point, which can be moved with the Fill Transform tool to adjust the point at which the second color begins to blend with the first. To do this, select the Fill Transform tool in the toolbox and then click over the gradient fill. The center point and handles display as shown in Figure 2.48.

Fill Transform Tool

FIGURE 2.48 Gradient Fill Selected with Fill Transform Tool

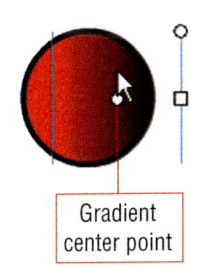

The white circle in the middle of the fill is the gradient center point. Drag this point to any location inside the fill to alter the gradient's direction or center point. The gradient in Figure 2.48 shows the center point being shifted to the right side of the object. This causes the gradient to blend the red color over a larger area of the object than the black, as shown in Figure 2.49.

Working with Text and Editing Drawn Objects   93

FIGURE
2.49 **Gradient with Modified Center Point**

Original fill

Fill with adjusted gradient center point

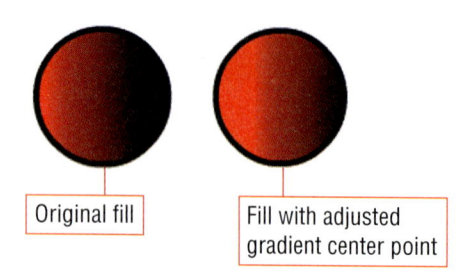

exercise 16

CHANGING COLORS USING THE COLOR SWATCH PANEL AND APPLYING AND MODIFYING A GRADIENT

1. Open Ch1SA1.
2. Save the document with Save As and name it Ch2Ex16.
3. Change balloon colors using the Color Swatches panel by completing the following steps:
   a. Click Window and then click Color Swatches to open the Color Swatches panel.
   b. With the Arrow tool active, double-click over the fill for the Turquoise balloon to select both the stroke line and fill color.
   c. If necessary, click the Stroke Color button in the toolbox to make it active. (*Note: Do not click on the color swatch, as this will open the color palette.*)
   d. Click the Eye Dropper over the bright pink color swatch in the Color Swatches panel as shown. Since an object's stroke color was selected in the stage, the new color is automatically applied to the turquoise balloon.
   e. Click the Fill Color button in the toolbox and then click the same pink color swatch in the Color Swatches panel that you selected in Step 3d.
   f. Click outside the selected balloon to deselect it.
   g. Change the color of the orange balloon to black by completing steps similar to those in Steps 3c–3f.
4. Apply and then modify a gradient to the black balloon by completing the following steps:
   a. Click the fill in the black balloon to select it.
   b. With the Fill Color button active in the toolbox, click the Eye Dropper over the white-to-black linear gradient (first button from left) in the gradient swatches in the Color Swatches panel.
   c. Click outside the selected balloon to deselect it and view the gradient effect.
   d. Click the Fill Transform tool.

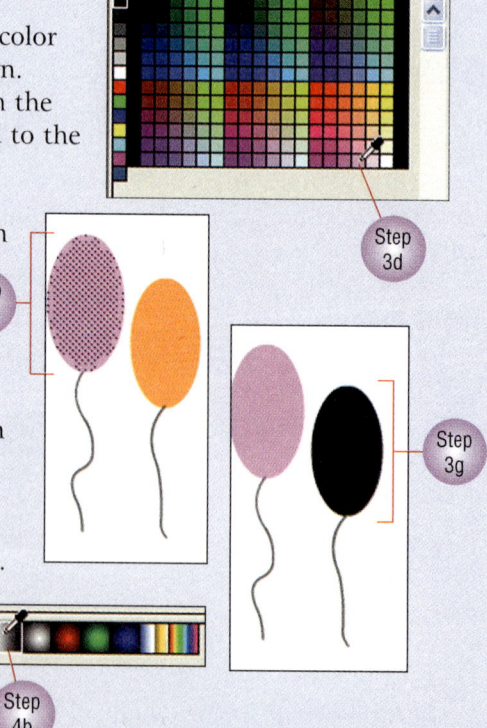

94   Chapter Two

e. Click over the balloon with the gradient applied to display the gradient's center point.
f. Drag the center point left as shown to show more black than white in the fill.
g. Click outside the selected balloon to deselect it.
5. Save the revised document using the same name (Ch2Ex16).
6. Click the Options menu button on the Color Swatches panel title bar and then click Close Panel at the drop-down menu.
7. Close Ch2Ex16.

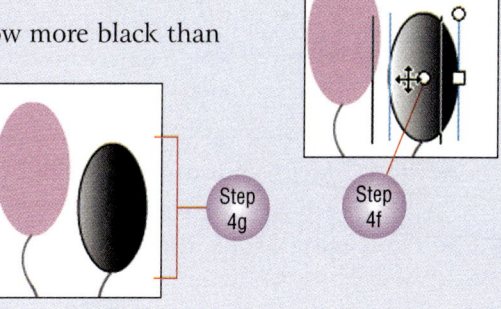

CHAPTER summary

- An *extending text block* expands automatically to the width of the text that you key inside the block.
- A *fixed text block* wraps the text within the defined width of the block.
- An extending text block can be converted to a fixed text block by dragging the block's circle handle to the width that you want.
- With the Text tool active, click a text block to place an insertion point inside the block in order to insert or delete text.
- Use the Arrow tool to select and then move, delete, or copy a text block.
- Resize a text block by selecting the block with the Text tool and then dragging the square handle left or right to decrease or increase its width.
- The Properties panel for a text block contains options to change the font, font size, font color, font attributes, alignment, format options, character spacing, kerning, or to create subscript and superscript characters.
- Create a vertical text block using the Change direction of text button in the Properties panel.
- The Break Apart feature converts each letter in a text block to an individual text block.
- Text blocks can be converted to graphic objects, which can then be manipulated similarly to drawn objects.
- The Document Properties dialog box contains options to set the size of the stage, change the background color, set the frame rate for animations, and change the units of measurement for rulers.
- Change colors of existing fills in objects using the Paint Bucket tool.
- Change colors of existing stroke lines in objects using the Ink Bottle tool.
- The Eye Dropper tool is used to copy a stroke's attributes or fill color from one object to another.

- The stage can be enlarged or reduced by choosing a magnification setting in the Zoom text box drop-down list, or by keying your own percentage in the text box.
- Click the Zoom tool in the toolbox and then click the Enlarge or Reduce modifier to zoom in or out on an object on the stage by doubling (enlarging) or halving (reducing) the magnification setting each time you click the pointer over an object.
- Scroll the stage using the Hand tool in the toolbox.
- The Eraser tool is used to rub out unwanted portions of strokes, fills, or shapes, or it can be used as a drawing tool.
- The Eraser Mode, Faucet, and Eraser Shape modifiers appear in the Options section when the Eraser tool is active.
- Draw curved lines using the Pen tool and then dragging the pointer starting at the anchor points for the curve and dragging a line the length and direction of the curve.
- Modify the shape of a curved line by dragging its anchor points. Use the Subselection tool to display anchor points for a curved line drawn with the Pen tool.
- The Free Transform tool is used to rotate and skew, scale, distort, or change the envelope for a selected shape.
- A selected line can be smoothed or straightened successively by clicking the Smooth or Straighten buttons in the Options section of the toolbox until the line is the desired shape.
- By default, the Recognize shapes feature is turned on which means Flash will convert shapes to geometric objects when the Smooth or Straighten button is clicked on a selected line.
- Lengthen or shorten a line segment by dragging an end point when you see the pointer with a shadow box attached to it.
- Reshape a curved line by dragging the pointer when you see the curve attached to it while pointing at a line.
- Fills can be dragged away from objects to create shadows or three-dimensional images.
- Draw lines inside a closed shape to segment the fill and edit each segment separately.
- The Lasso tool can be operated in Polygon mode which allows you to create a selection area inside a fill by clicking points to form a closed shape.
- Segment fill with curved lines by ensuring the curved lines intersect each other.
- Group shapes to have Flash treat the group as a single entity to facilitate editing tasks.
- The order in which you group objects within a document creates a *stacking order*.
- Stroke and fill colors can be changed using the Color Mixer panel or Color Swatches panel.
- A gradient is a gradual blending of two colors in a fill in either a radial or linear direction.
- You can create your own radial or linear gradient in the Color Mixer panel.
- A gradient has a center point which can be dragged with the Fill Transform tool to adjust the point at which the first color blends with the second color.

COMMANDS review

Command or Feature	Mouse/Keyboard	Shortcut Keys
Break apart a text block	Modify, Break Apart	Ctrl + B
Change magnification setting	View, Magnification, click desired option	
Change stacking order of an object	Modify, Arrange, click desired option	
Change text properties	Text, point to option, click desired setting	
Display Color Mixer panel	Window, Color Mixer	Shift + F9
Display Color Swatches panel	Window, Color Swatches	Ctrl + F9
Document properties	Modify, Document	Ctrl + J
Group select objects	Modify, Group	Ctrl + G
Transform an object	Modify, Transform, click desired option	
Ungroup objects	Modify, Ungroup	Ctrl + Shift + G

CONCEPTS check

Indicate the correct term or command for each item.

1. In this text block you have to press Enter to key a second line of text.
2. This is the pointer that appears when the Text tool is active and positioned over an existing text block.
3. A vertical text box displays this number of characters on each line.
4. The line spacing for text in a text block is changed at this dialog box.
5. This is the term used to define the horizontal white space between characters.
6. This is how you convert a text block to a graphic object.
7. The size of the stage is set in this dialog box.
8. Use this tool to copy the stroke height and color from one object to another.
9. These are the two modifier buttons that appear in the Options section of the toolbox when the Zoom tool is active.
10. This Eraser tool modifier erases an entire stroke segment or fill with one click.
11. Flash redraws an image that is being erased when you do this action.
12. This the name of the handle that appears at each end of the anchor point's straight line that Flash draws as you create curves.
13. Click this tool to complete a curved line that has been drawn with the Pen tool.

Working with Text and Editing Drawn Objects

14. What does it mean when the Subselection pointer displays with a solid box attached to it?
15. Holding down this key while dragging an object with the rotation arrow causes the object to rotate in 45-degree increments.
16. These are the four modifier buttons when Free Transform is active for a selected object.
17. Use this modifier when the Arrow tool is active for a selected line to convert curved line segments into straight-line segments.
18. A line segment can be lengthened or shortened when the pointer displays with this attached to it.
19. A shape can be segmented in order to split it apart by doing this.
20. The order in which you group shapes is referred to as this.
21. A custom gradient can be created in this panel.
22. Change the Fill Style to either of these two options to create a gradient.
23. Use this tool to adjust a gradient's center point.

SKILLS check

Assessment 1

1. With Flash open at a clear stage, create the following text blocks:
   a. An extending text block positioned at the top center of the stage set in 24-point bright blue Verdana containing the following text:

      Web Artworks Inc.

   b. A fixed width text block approximately 2 inches wide, starting below the *I* in Inc., set in 13-point bright blue Verdana, aligned at the right, containing the following text:

      15-349 Workaway Lane
      Cyberspace, USA 90909

   c. An extending vertical text block positioned at the left side of the stage approximately 2 inches in from its left edge and aligned horizontally with the text block created in 1b, set in 14 point bright red Verdana, containing the following text:

      888 555 9678

2. Create the image shown in Figure 2.40 on Page 88 in the center of the stage as follows:
   - Turn off the Snap to Objects feature.
   - Draw and then group each shape individually in separate areas of the stage in the following order: pink rectangle first, purple square second, green circle third.
   - Overlap the objects as shown.
   - Group the three overlapped objects.
   - Move the group so that the image is centered within the three text blocks.
3. Change the background color of the stage to light yellow.
4. Change the color of the text in the vertical text block to bright blue and adjust the tracking to bring the numbers closer together.
5. Reposition the objects on the stage to achieve a balanced look.
6. Save the document and name it Ch2SA1.
7. Close Ch2SA1.

Assessment 2

FIGURE 2.50 Assessment 2

Marquee Web Productions

1. Open the Flash document named Marquee. *(Note: If you receive a Missing Font Warning message box, click Use Default.)*
2. Save the document and name it Ch2SA2.
3. Convert the text block to a graphic.
4. Apply the red-to-black gradient fill to the text graphic.
5. Use the Envelope modifier with the Free Transform tool to warp the text graphic as shown in Figure 2.50.
6. Save the revised document using the same name (Ch2SA2).
7. Close Ch2SA2.

Assessment 3

FIGURE 2.51 Assessment 3

1. Open the Flash document named Owl.
2. Save the document and name it Ch2SA3.
3. The Owl document contains the beginnings of the owl shown in Figure 2.51. Only the outline of the Owl's face has been drawn, the hat is complete, and the feet are drawn but are missing the talons. Complete the drawing so that your copy matches as closely as possible with the drawing shown in Figure 2.51.
4. Save the revised document using the same name (Ch2SA2).
5. Close Ch2SA2.

Assessment 4

FIGURE 2.52 Assessment 4

1. Open the Flash document named Ladybug.
2. Save the document and name it Ch2SA4.
3. Create a group from all of the individual elements that make up the ladybug image.
4. Make two copies of the ladybug and position them side-by-side across the stage.
5. Rotate the middle ladybug 270 degrees.
6. Rotate the third ladybug 90 degrees.
7. Reposition the ladybugs at the left side of the stage in the pattern shown in Figure 2.52.
8. At the right side of the stage create a text block containing the following text. You determine the text properties.

    emcp.net/Beneficial Insects
    All you need to know about chemical-free gardening!

9. Change the background color of the stage to light green.
10. Save the revised document using the same name (Ch2SA4).
11. Close Ch2SA4.

Assessment 5

FIGURE 2.53 Assessment 5

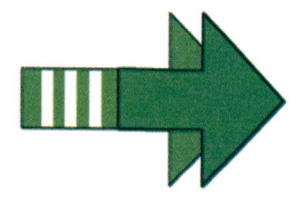

1. Open the Flash document named Arrow.
2. Save the document and name it Ch2SA5.
3. Modify the arrow so that it resembles the arrow shown in Figure 2.53 as closely as possible. *(Hint: The white lines were drawn using the Eraser tool.)*
4. Save the revised document using the same name (Ch2SA5).
5. Close Ch2SA5.

Assessment 6

FIGURE 2.54 *Assessment 6*

1. At a clear stage, look at the strawberries shown in Figure 2.54.
2. Recreate the image as closely as possible. *(Hints: You only need to draw one strawberry. The pits on the strawberry can be drawn by clicking with the Brush tool. Make good use of the smooth and straighten modifiers!)*
3. Save the document and name it Ch2SA6.
4. Close Ch2SA6.

Assessment 7

FIGURE 2.55 *Assessment 7*

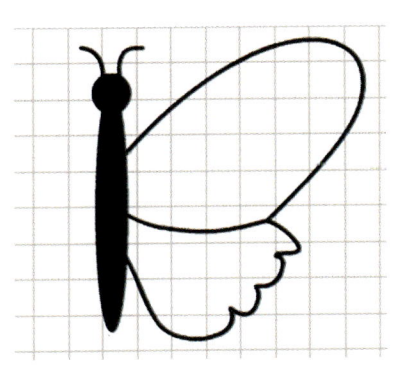

1. Open the Flash document named Butterfly.
2. Save the document and name it Ch2SA7.
3. The butterfly graphic has been started for you and appears as shown in Figure 2.55.
4. Using the Internet, look up pictures of butterflies and then complete the image by drawing and filling the right wing with color to resemble a picture that you find.
5. The left wing can be created by completing the following process:
    - Select all of the segments that make up the right wing.
    - Copy and paste the wing.
    - Drag the copy to the left side of the butterfly.
    - Use the Flip Horizontal option on the Transform menu to flip the wing around and then drag it to the butterfly's body.
6. Save the revised document using the same name (Ch2SA7).
7. Close Ch2SA7.

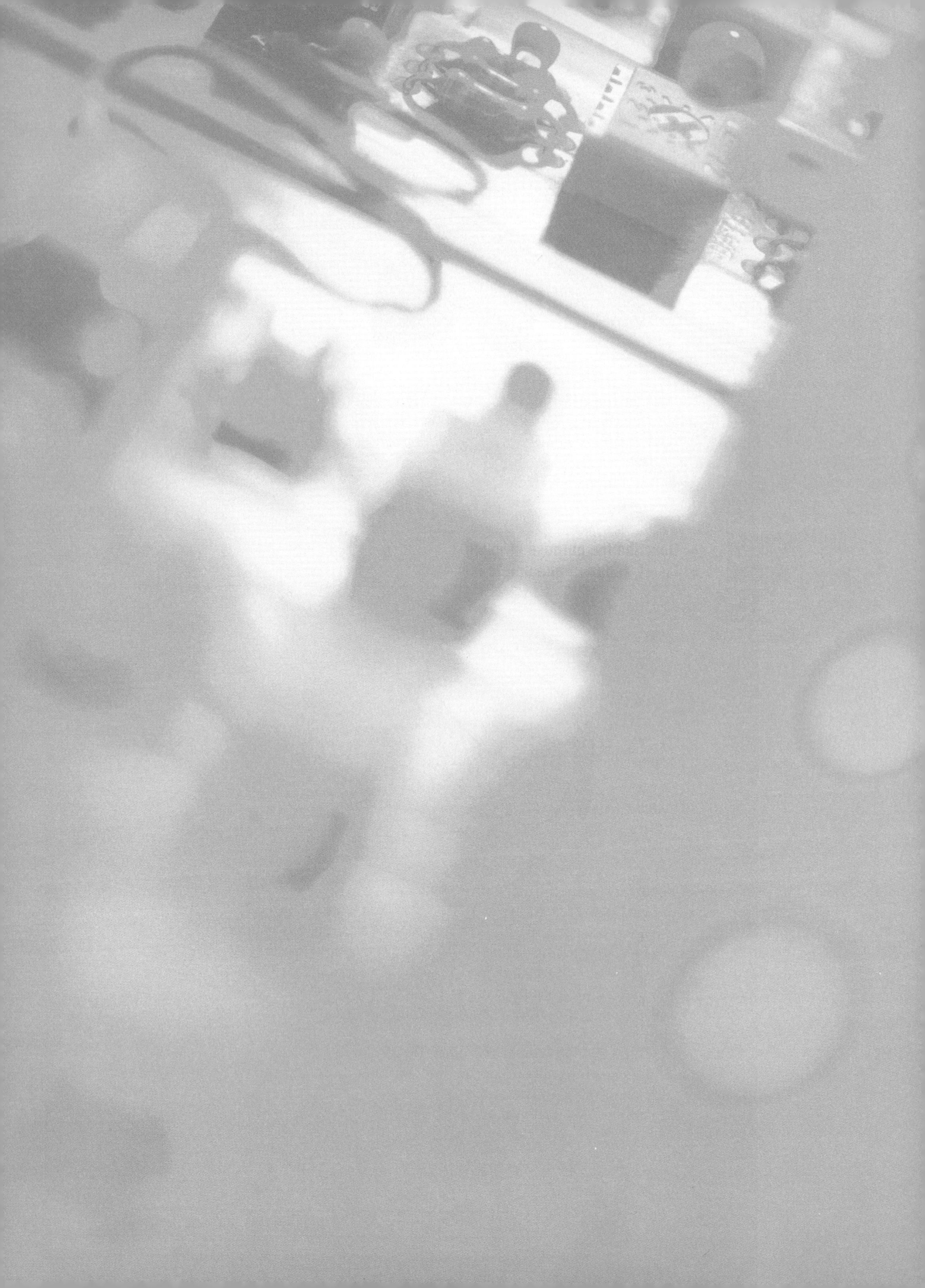

CHAPTER 3

WORKING WITH LAYERS, LIBRARIES, AND IMPORTING GRAPHICS

PERFORMANCE OBJECTIVES

Upon successful completion of Chapter 3, you will be able to:
- Describe the purpose of using layers in a Flash movie.
- Insert, rename, and delete layers.
- Move layers to change the stacking order.
- Hide and lock layers.
- View objects on a layer as outlines.
- Distribute objects to layers.
- Create a mask layer.
- Create a guide layer.
- Create a layer folder.
- Describe the role of libraries, symbols, and instances.
- Create and modify symbols.
- Create and modify instances of a symbol.
- Convert an existing graphic to a symbol.
- Insert symbols from another movie's library and from a common library.
- Create a library file with your own reusable objects.
- Import a bitmapped image to Flash and adjust the bitmap properties.
- Break up and edit a bitmapped image.
- Use a bitmapped image as a fill for a closed shape.
- Convert a bitmap image into a vector graphic.
- Copy and paste graphics from other sources to Flash using the Clipboard.
- Import a FreeHand vector image and a Fireworks bitmap image to Flash.
- Optimize a vector object.
- Describe sources of images for importing to Flash.

Flash MX Chapter 03

There are 23 student data files to copy for this chapter.

In Chapters 1 and 2 you learned how to create and edit content using the various tools in the toolbox. In both of these chapters the content you created existed in a single layer named *Layer 1*. Complex Flash movies containing many objects that may interact with each other during animations should be organized into multiple layers. Objects on a layer are manipulated independently from objects on other layers, making drawing and editing tasks much easier. A special type of layer called a *guide layer* can be used to position objects or make editing objects easier. Guide layers are also used in animations to define the motion path for an object. A *mask layer* is used to produce a special effect whereby the layer immediately below the mask layer is partially concealed. The overlapped filled objects in the mask layer allow content from the lower layer to filter through the stage. For example, a mask layer containing a circle object positioned just above a layer containing a large picture would screen out the picture so that the user would only see the portion of the picture that is overlapping the fill of the circle.

Content that will be reused in a movie, such as a button or graphic, can be created as a *symbol* and stored in a library. The symbol can then be inserted from the library whenever it is needed in the movie and is called an *instance*. Minor variations of the symbol, such as changing the text that appears on a button or changing the color of a fill, can be made to instances.

Files containing pictures or other images in either bitmapped or vector format can be imported into a Flash movie. A bitmapped image can be converted to a vector graphic and then edited in Flash.

Organizing Content with Layers

Layers are used in Flash to organize images, sounds, videos, animations, or any other elements contained in the Flash movie. A Flash document initially contains one layer. Additional layers are added as needed. Complex movies with many layers can also be organized with layer folders where related layers are grouped together to make finding and managing the content easier and more efficient. Layer management in Flash is similar to the process you use to organize the data files on your computer: creating layers and layer folders, renaming layers and folders, moving items to a layer or folder, and deleting layers and folders. The number of layers and folders you can create is limited only by the amount of memory on the computer you are using. However, adding layers does not cause the file size of your published movie to increase since Flash levels everything to a single layer in the player file.

To understand how layers operate in Flash, consider the analogy of a teacher presenting a lesson using multiple transparencies that he or she stacks on an overhead projector to demonstrate a complex concept. For example, to explain the solution for a math problem, a teacher might first project a transparency that presents the problem. After discussing the problem with the class, the teacher then places another transparency over the first one with the relevant mathematical equation needed to solve the problem. The equation is positioned on the second transparency so that it appears below the problem. Finally, the teacher places a third transparency over the second transparency with the working solution positioned below the equation.

Layers in Flash operate in a similar manner as stacked transparencies on an overhead projector. Placing objects on separate layers allows a developer to manipulate the objects independently from each other. Layers are managed in the Timeline as shown in Figure 3.1. Notice that each layer is named with a descriptive title to facilitate finding and editing content.

FIGURE

3.1 Multiple Layers in Flash

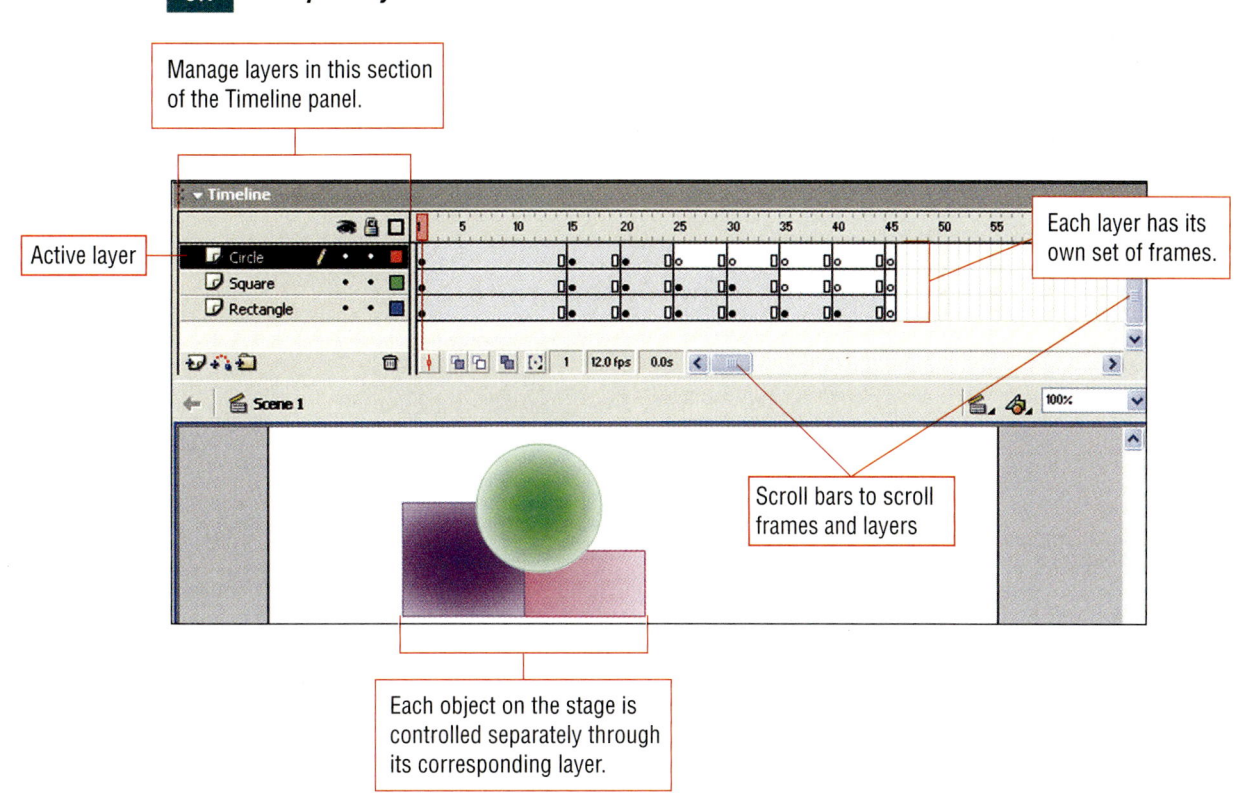

Manage layers in this section of the Timeline panel.

Active layer

Each layer has its own set of frames.

Scroll bars to scroll frames and layers

Each object on the stage is controlled separately through its corresponding layer.

The circle, square, and rectangle shown in Figure 3.1 each contain a set of frames in the Timeline so that each object's animation can be controlled separately in the movie. While each layer has its own set of frames, the same frame numbers for each layer are played simultaneously. For example, when the playhead reaches frame 15 of *Layer 1*, it also plays the content in frame 15 of all of the other layers in the movie.

In Chapter 2 you learned about grouped objects where the stroke and fill of one object can be grouped so that it is treated as a separate entity from other objects which it overlaps. Objects placed in a separate layer are also treated as separate entities. As with grouped objects, the order in which the layers are organized in the Timeline is also important. Layers in Flash are stacked with the topmost layer in the Timeline overlapping objects in layers below it. In Figure 3.1, *Circle* is the topmost layer, meaning the circle object overlaps both the square and rectangle below it. *Square* is next in the layer hierarchy, meaning it overlaps the rectangle which is the bottom layer. The layer hierarchy is referred to as the *stacking order*.

Figure 3.2 depicts the tools Flash provides in the Timeline panel to manage layers. Each tool is discussed as you learn to work with layers in the next sections.

FIGURE 3.2 Layer Management Tools

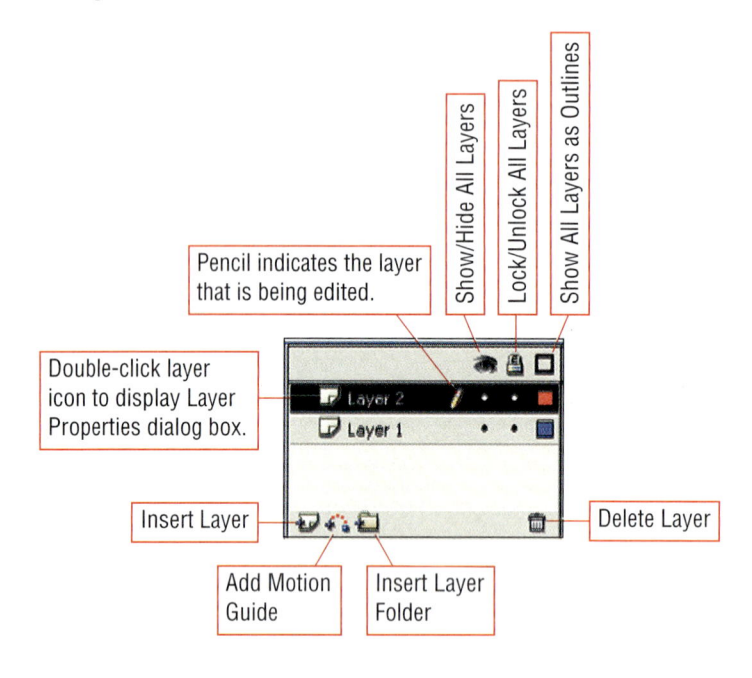

Pencil indicates the layer that is being edited.
Show/Hide All Layers
Lock/Unlock All Layers
Show All Layers as Outlines
Double-click layer icon to display Layer Properties dialog box.
Insert Layer
Add Motion Guide
Insert Layer Folder
Delete Layer

Inserting and Renaming Layers

Insert Layer

Each new Flash document contains one layer named *Layer 1*. Complete any of the following actions to add a new layer above the active layer in a Flash document:

- Click the Insert Layer button.
- Click Insert, and then click Layer.
- Right-click the active layer and then click Insert Layer at the shortcut menu.

As shown in Figure 3.2, Flash inserts a new layer above the active layer and names it *Layer #* where # represents the next sequential layer number in the movie. The new layer is automatically made the active layer as indicated by the black highlighting and the *pencil* icon to the right of the layer name. The pencil appears next to the layer name that is currently being edited. It is a good idea to get in the habit of looking for the pencil when editing complex movies as it is often easy to become confused as to which layer you are currently working within.

Layers should be renamed with a title that is descriptive of the layer's content. To rename a layer, double-click the current layer name, key the new layer name, and then press Enter.

Moving and Copying Objects to a Layer Using the Clipboard

Objects can be cut or copied and then pasted to layers using the Windows Clipboard. For example, to move an object from one layer to another, select the object, click Edit, and then click Cut. Click the layer in the Timeline in which you want to place the object, click Edit, and then click Paste.

To copy an object to another layer, select the object, click Edit, and then click Copy. Click the layer in the Timeline in which you want a duplicate copy of the object, click Edit, and then click Paste.

If you are doing several copy and paste operations, consider using the shortcut keys, Ctrl + X to Cut, Ctrl + C to Copy, and Ctrl + V to Paste. In a later section you will learn how to use Flash's Distribute to Layers command to automatically create and move objects from a single layer to multiple layers.

exercise 1

INSERTING AND RENAMING LAYERS AND COPYING AND PASTING OBJECTS TO OTHER LAYERS

1. Open the Flash document named Diamond.
2. Save the document with Save As and name it Ch3Ex01.
3. Make sure the Properties panel is collapsed and that the current magnification is set to 100%.
4. Rename the current layer by completing the following steps:
   a. Double-click the name *Layer 1* in the Timeline panel.
   b. Key **Blue Diamond** and then press Enter. 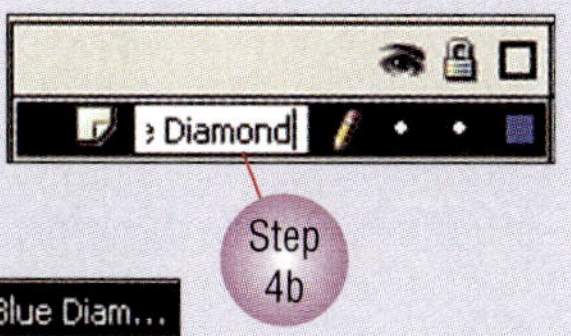
5. Insert a new layer above the current layer, rename the layer, and then copy the diamond to the new layer by completing the following steps:
   a. Click the Insert Layer button in the Timeline panel.
   b. Double-click the name *Layer 2* in the Timeline.
   c. Key **Red Diamond** and then press Enter.
   d. With the Arrow tool active, double-click the diamond object on the stage. Notice that *Blue Diamond* becomes the active layer in the Timeline. Since the diamond object is associated with the first layer in the movie, selecting the object automatically makes *Blue Diamond* the active layer.
   e. Click Edit and then click Copy.
   f. Click *Red Diamond* in the Timeline panel.
   g. Click Edit and then Paste. A copy of the diamond object is placed on the stage. 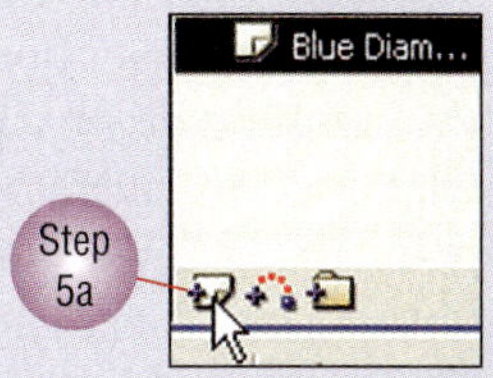  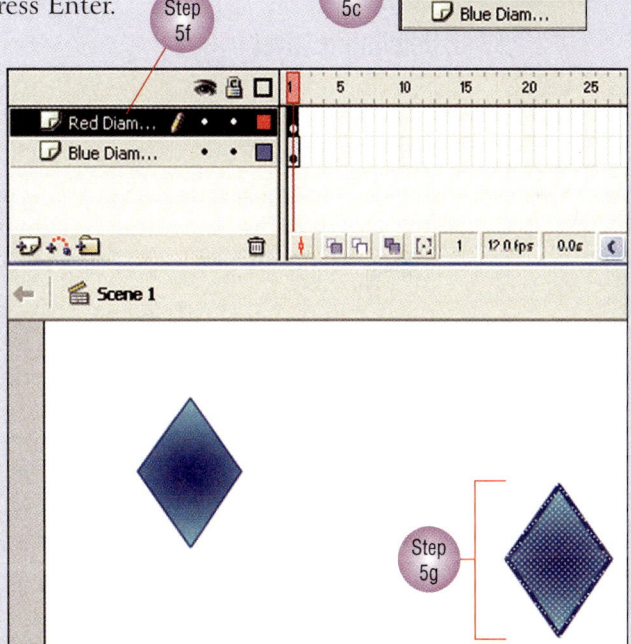
6. Edit the colors and then reposition the pasted diamond object by completing the following steps:
   a. With the pasted diamond object still selected, click Stroke Color in the toolbox and then click the bright red color swatch in the first column of the palette.
   b. With the pasted diamond object still selected, click Fill Color in the toolbox and then click the red-to-black color swatch in the gradient row of the palette.

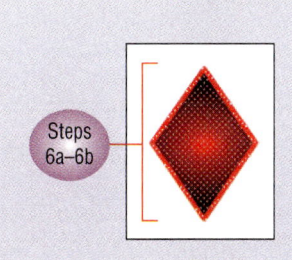

Working with Layers, Libraries, and Importing Graphics 107

c. Click <u>V</u>iew and then click Snap to O<u>b</u>jects to turn off the snapping feature. (*Note: Skip this step if Snap to Objects does not display with a check mark as the feature is already turned off.*)
d. With the copied diamond object still selected, position the pointer over the red diamond until the pointer displays with the four-headed arrow move icon and then drag the red diamond until it is overlapping the blue diamond as shown.
e. Click in the stage outside the red diamond to deselect it. 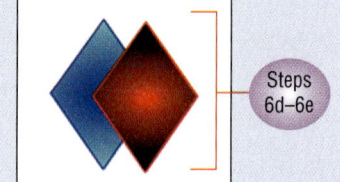
7. Save the revised document using the same name (Ch3Ex01).
8. Close Ch3Ex01.

Steps 6d–6e

Moving a Layer

As previously mentioned, the order in which layers appear in the Timeline determines the stacking order with the topmost layer overlapping objects on the stage that are contained in layers below it. To move a layer to a different position in the hierarchy, point to the layer name or layer icon and then drag the layer to the desired location in the Timeline. A gray bar appears between existing layer names as you drag the mouse up or down indicating where the layer will be repositioned when the mouse is released.

Deleting a Layer

Delete Layer

Deleting a layer removes the layer from the Timeline as well as any content on the stage that is associated with the layer. Complete either of the following actions to remove a layer from the movie:

- Make active the layer that you want to remove and then click the Delete Layer button in the Timeline panel.
- Right-click the layer and then click Delete Layer at the shortcut menu.

If you delete the wrong layer by mistake, use the Undo feature to restore the content to the stage.

exercise 2
DELETING AND MOVING LAYERS

1. Open the Flash document named FourDiamonds.
2. Save the document with Save As and name it Ch3Ex02.
3. Delete the yellow diamond from the stage by completing the following steps:
   a. Click the layer named *Yellow Diamond*.
   b. Click the Delete Layer button in the Timeline panel. 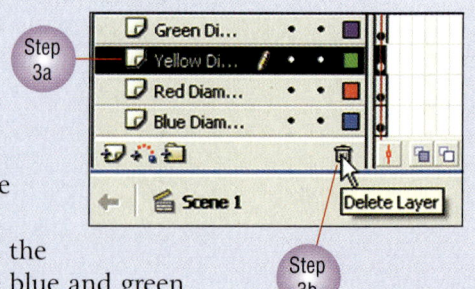
4. Rearrange the stacking order of the layers so that the red diamond is in the foreground overlapping the blue and green diamonds by completing the following steps:

Step 3a

Step 3b

a. Position the pointer over the layer named *Red Diamond*, hold down the left mouse button, drag the layer up above the layer named *Green Diamond*, and then release the mouse. As you drag the layer up, a gray bar appears indicating the position in the hierarchy where the layer will be placed when the mouse is released. Notice the red diamond is now in the foreground overlapping the blue and green diamonds which are in the layers below it.
b. With the red diamond still selected, position the pointer over the diamond until the pointer displays with the four-headed arrow move icon and then drag the diamond right to center it over the blue and green diamonds as shown.
c. Click in the stage outside the red diamond to deselect it.
5. Save the revised document using the same name (Ch3Ex02).

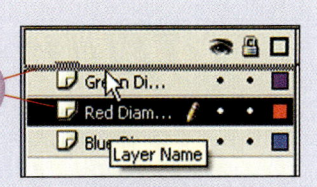

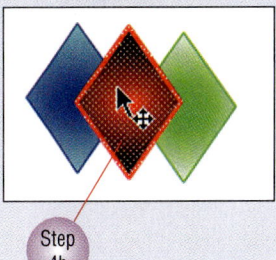

Hiding and Locking Layers

As you have seen in Exercises 1 and 2, the stage displays all of the objects from all of the layers in the stacked order. Objects are not always placed in separate layers in order to overlap but are also placed in layers to facilitate drawing and editing or to control animation. When a movie contains many objects in multiple layers, editing can be made easier by hiding the objects in the layers with which you are not working. Clicking the Show/Hide All Layers button at the top of the Timeline panel will hide all of the layers in the movie. In the column below the *eye* icon in the Timeline panel, a red *X* will appear next to each layer name. Click in the Show/Hide All Layers column next to the layer in which you want to edit, and the object or objects in the layer will reappear on the stage. Layers that are not hidden display with a solid black dot next to the layer name as shown in Figure 3.3.

To hide an individual layer, click the solid black dot in the Show/Hide All Layers column next to the layer name that you want to hide. Each Show/Hide is a toggle, meaning clicking it once hides the layer and clicking it again redisplays the layer.

Once you are satisfied with an object on the stage, it is a good idea to lock the layer to prevent further editing. It is easy to click an object by mistake when there are many objects on the stage while editing. Objects within a locked layer cannot be selected. Clicking the Lock/Unlock All Layers button at the top of the Timeline panel will lock all layers in the movie. A *closed padlock* icon appears in the column next to each layer name to indicate the layer is locked. Click in the Lock/Unlock All Layers column next to the layer in which you need to make a change to unlock the objects within the layer. Unlocked layers display with a solid black dot in the column as shown in Figure 3.3.

To lock an individual layer, click the solid black dot in the Lock/Unlock All Layers column next to the layer name for which you want to prevent changes. Each Lock/Unlock is a toggle.

FIGURE 3.3 Hidden and Locked Layers

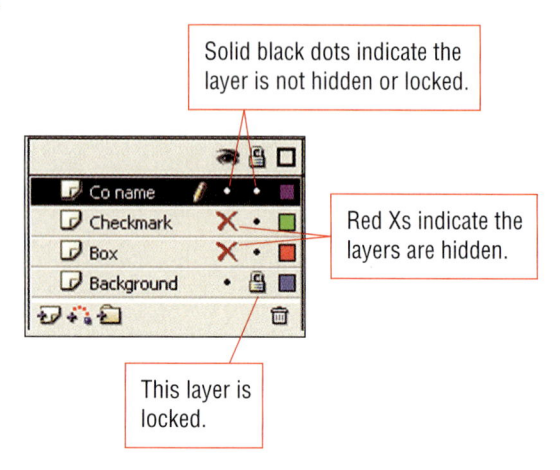

Solid black dots indicate the layer is not hidden or locked.

Red Xs indicate the layers are hidden.

This layer is locked.

Viewing Objects as Outlines

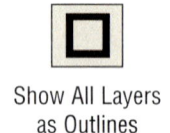

Show All Layers as Outlines

The Show All Layers as Outlines button at the top of the Timeline panel will display all objects on the stage in Outline mode color-coded to the layer in which each object is associated. Objects displayed in Outline mode are shown in Figure 3.4. As each new layer is added to a movie, Flash inserts a different colored filled box in the Show All Layers as Outlines column of the Timeline. Clicking the filled box next to a layer name will cause Flash to display the objects within the layer in Outline mode. The filled box changes to an empty box to indicate the layer is in Outline mode. Clicking the empty box will return the objects to their normal state.

Displaying a layer in Outline mode allows you to see which objects are associated with the layer if you cannot remember. Another method to determine which objects are associated with a layer is to click an object on the stage and then look in the Timeline to see which layer has become the active layer.

FIGURE 3.4 Objects in Outline Mode

This layer is not in Outline mode.

These layers are displayed as outlines.

Objects in Outline mode

110 Chapter Three

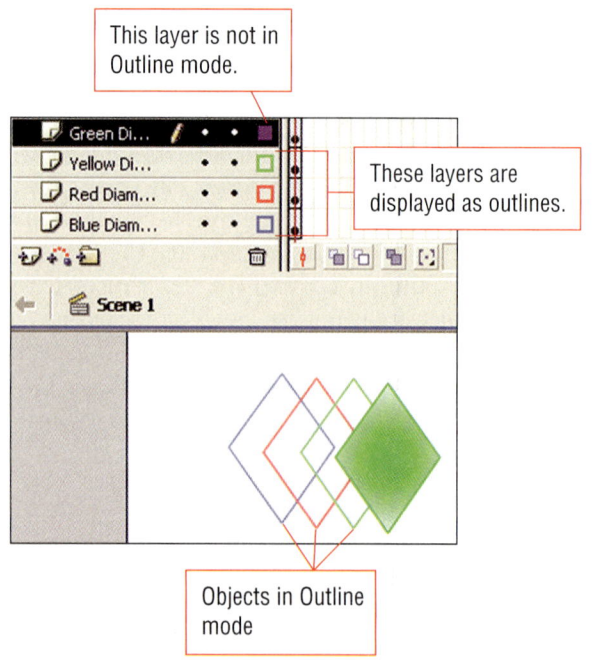

exercise 3
HIDING AND LOCKING LAYERS, AND DISPLAYING LAYERS AS OUTLINES

1. With Ch3Ex02 open, hide the blue and green diamond layers by completing the following steps: 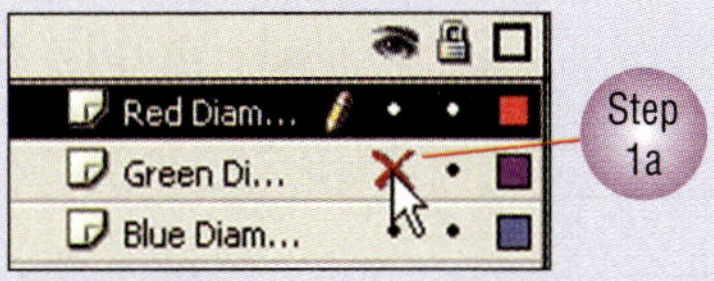
    a. Click the solid black dot next to the layer named *Green Diamond* in the Show/Hide All Layers column in the Timeline. The solid black dot changes to a red *X* and the diamond disappears from the stage.
    b. Click the solid black dot next to the layer named *Blue Diamond* in the Show/Hide All Layers column in the Timeline. Only the red diamond is left on the stage. 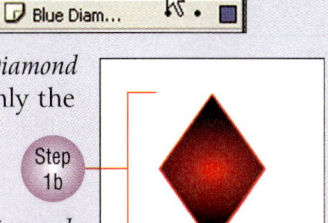
2. Lock the red diamond to prevent editing the object by completing the following steps:
    a. Click the solid black dot next to the layer named *Red Diamond* in the Lock/Unlock All Layers column in the Timeline. A closed padlock displays in the column and a red line is drawn through the pencil indicating the object cannot be selected. 
    b. With the Arrow tool active, try to select the red diamond object on the stage by clicking over it. Notice you cannot select the object.
3. Redisplay and unlock the diamond objects by completing the following steps:
    a. Click the red *X* in the Show/Hide All Layers column next to the layer named *Green Diamond*. The green diamond object reappears on the stage.
    b. Click the red *X* in the Show/Hide All Layers column next to the layer named *Blue Diamond*. The blue diamond object reappears on the stage.
    c. Click the closed padlock in the Lock/Unlock All Layers column next to the layer named *Red Diamond*. The red diamond object can now be selected with the Arrow tool. 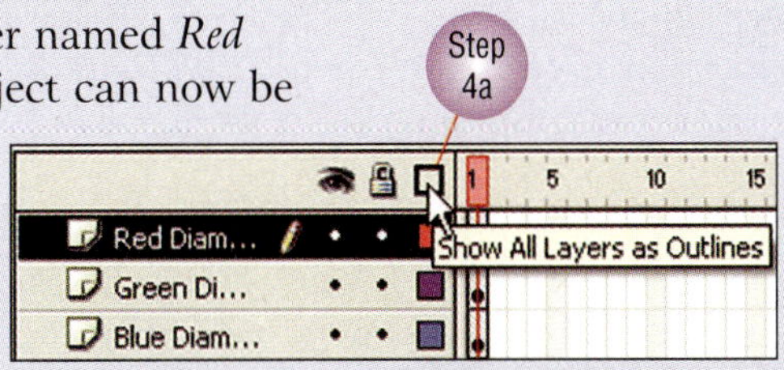
4. Display the diamond objects in Outline mode by completing the following steps:
    a. Click the Show All Layers as Outlines button at the top of the Timeline panel. Notice that each diamond is now represented as an outline in the color of the outline box for its associated layer in the Timeline. 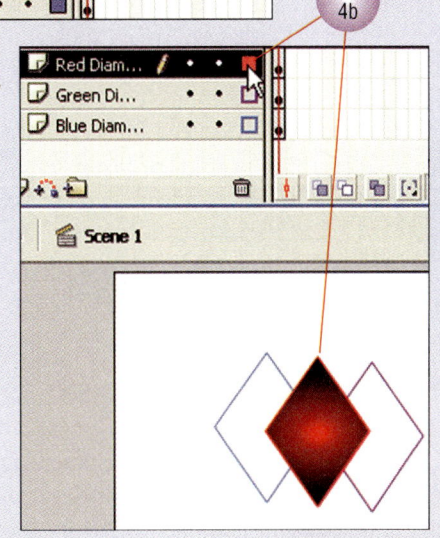
    b. Click the empty box in the Show All Layers as Outlines column next to the layer named *Red Diamond*. The red diamond displays in its normal state.
    c. Click the empty box in the Show All Layers as Outlines column next to the layer named *Green Diamond*.
    d. Click the empty box in the Show All Layers as Outlines column next to the layer named *Blue Diamond*.
5. Close Ch3Ex02. Click No when prompted to save changes.

Distributing Objects to Layers

Cutting and pasting objects to layers using the Clipboard can become tedious if a movie contains many objects on a single layer that you decide need to be split into individual layers. Flash includes the Distribute to Layers feature to facilitate this process. Select the objects on the layer that you wish to split into individual layers, click Modify, and then click Distribute to Layers. Flash will create a new layer for each separate object. Each new layer is named *Layer #* where # is the next layer number in sequence.

Select each new layer and then rename it after distribution is complete. The object that has been associated with the new layer will display on the stage with a blue box surrounding it called the *bounding box*. A text object selected to be distributed is automatically named with the text inside the object.

exercise 4

DISTRIBUTING OBJECTS TO LAYERS AND RENAMING LAYERS

1. Open the Flash document named Balloons.
2. Save the document with Save As and name it Ch3Ex04.
3. The Distribute to Layers command will create a new layer for each separate object in *Layer 1* of the Ch3Ex04 document. To distribute the three balloons with the strings attached to them as single objects you must first group the objects that you do not want split into separate layers. Group each balloon and its corresponding string by completing the following steps:
    a. Use the Arrow or Lasso tool to select the red balloon and the string below it.
    b. Press Ctrl + G. *(Note: Ctrl + G is the shortcut command to group the objects.)*
    c. Select and then group the blue balloon and the string below it by completing steps similar to those in Steps 3a–3b.
    d. Select and then group the purple balloon and the string below it by completing steps similar to those in Steps 3a–3b.

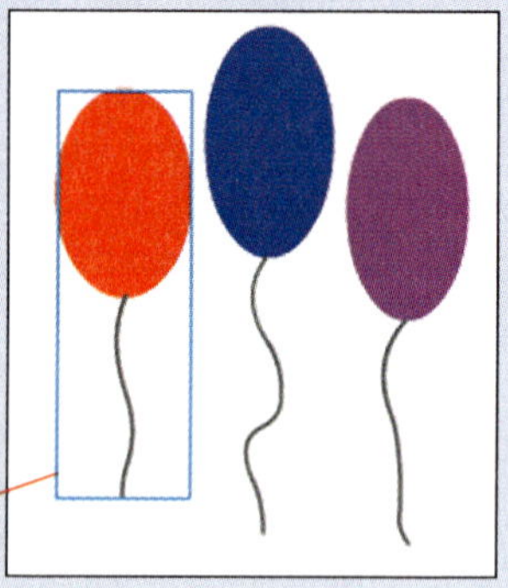

    Steps 3a–3b

4. Distribute the three balloons to individual layers by completing the following steps:
    a. With the Arrow tool active, click the red balloon group.
    b. Hold down the Shift key and then click the blue balloon group.
    c. Hold down the Shift key and then click the purple balloon group.
    d. Click Modify on the Menu bar and then click Distribute to Layers. The three balloon groups remain selected on the stage and the Timeline now displays four layers as shown. Each balloon group has been moved to a separate layer. *Layer 1* has been moved to the top of the stacking order.

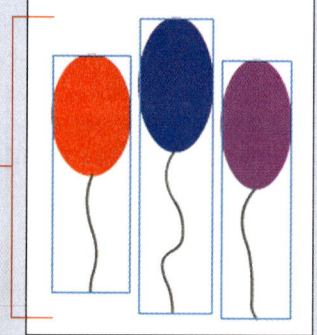

    Steps 4a–4c

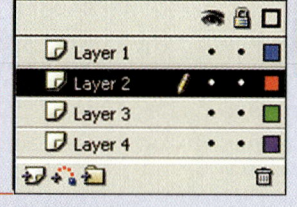

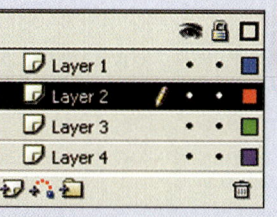

    Step 4d

5. Rename the layers to describe which balloon they represent by completing the following steps:

112 Chapter Three

a. Click in the stage outside the selected balloons to deselect them.
b. Click the red balloon and then look in the Timeline at the layer that has become the active layer.
c. Double-click *Layer 4*, key **Red Balloon**, and then press Enter.
d. Click the blue balloon on the stage and then rename the corresponding layer *Blue Balloon*.
e. Click the purple balloon on the stage and then rename the corresponding layer *Purple Balloon*. 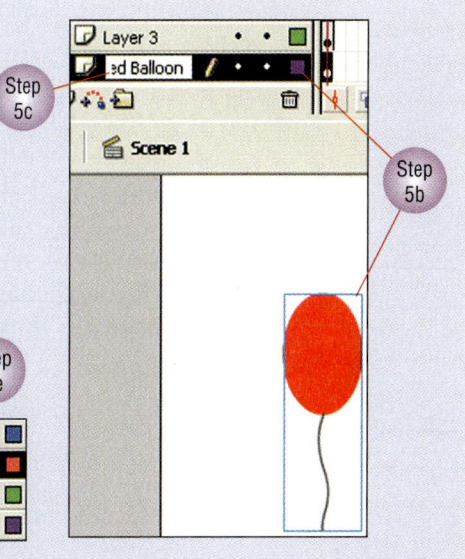 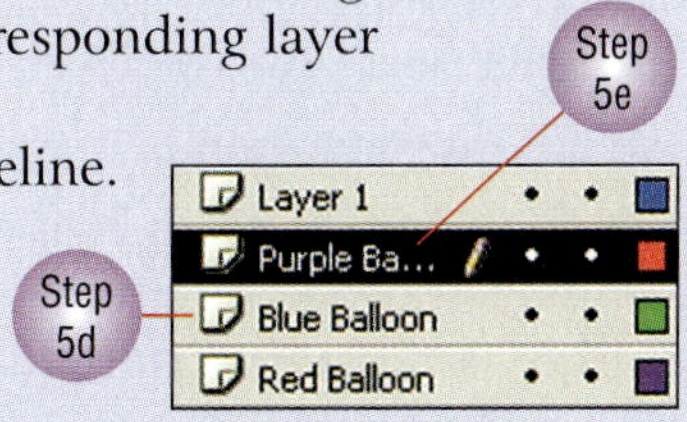
6. Click *Layer 1* in the Timeline. Notice that no objects on the stage are selected since the pre-existing *Layer 1* objects were distributed to new layers. Click the Delete Layer button in the Timeline panel.
7. Save the revised document using the same name (Ch3Ex04).
8. Close Ch3Ex04.

Creating a Mask Layer

As previously stated, a *mask layer* is used to create special effects in a movie. A masked layer partially conceals the layer immediately below it to which a link has been established. When a mask is created, the layer name for the layer that is linked to the mask appears indented and both the mask and the linked layer are locked.

A filled object is drawn on the mask layer over the area in the linked layer's content that you want to allow viewers to see. Filled areas within the mask layer allow the overlapping content from the linked layer to filter through the stage. All content outside masked filled objects is concealed in the lower layer. An example of the end result of a mask is shown in Figure 3.5.

FIGURE 3.5 **Mask Layer Special Effect**

Layer immediately below mask layer

When mask is created this layer becomes linked to the mask.

Mask layer

Draw a filled object over the area which you want viewers to see.

When the mask is created, this is what appears on the stage.

Complete the following steps to create an effect similar to the one shown in Figure 3.5:

1. Insert a picture, draw objects, or otherwise create the content on the lower layer that you want to partially screen out.
2. Insert a new layer positioned above the layer created in Step 1.
3. Draw filled objects overlapping the content in the lower layer where the size of the fill represents the amount of the content you want viewers to see. Think of the fill as the window to the lower layer. The bigger the fill, the bigger the window displays allowing viewers to see more of what lies beneath.
4. Right-click the layer name for the layer created in Step 3.
5. Click Mask at the shortcut menu.

Layer properties for the mask shown in Figure 3.5 are shown in Figure 3.6. Notice the two layers are locked; the lower layer is shown indented below the mask layer and mask icons display next to the layer names.

FIGURE 3.6 Timeline Showing Masked Layer and Linked Layer

Mask icons

Both the mask layer and the lower layer are automatically locked.

Unlock the layers to edit the objects on the mask layer or the linked lower layer. Applying animation to masks can create dynamic special effects. In Exercise 5 you will learn how to use a mask to fill text.

exercise 5

CREATING AND EDITING A TEXT MASK

1. Open the Flash document named TextMask.
2. Save the document with Save As and name it Ch3Ex05.
3. Make sure the Properties panel is expanded and the current magnification is set to 100%.
4. The stage contains a picture of a sailboat on a lake with a rolling hillside in the background. (You will learn how to import graphics later in this chapter.) Create a text mask by completing the following steps:
   a. Rename Layer 1 *Sailboat*.
   b. Click the Insert Layer button in the Timeline panel.
   c. With *Layer 2* the active layer, click the Text tool.
   d. Make the following changes to the text properties in the Properties panel:
      1) Change the font to 60-point Franklin Gothic Heavy Bold. If Franklin Gothic Heavy is not in your font list, choose a font that is similar to the font shown.
      2) Change the font color to bright red to make it easier to see on the stage over the picture.
      3) Change the alignment to Center.
      4) Collapse the Properties panel.

e. Drag a fixed text block the width of the picture in the approximate location shown.

Step 4e

f. Key the text **First Choice Travel** in the text block.
g. Click in the stage outside the text block to deselect it.
h. Move the text block so that it is positioned over the picture as shown.

Steps 4f–4h

i. Rename Layer 2 *Text*.
j. Right-click the layer named *Text* in the Timeline and then click Mask at the shortcut menu.
k. The filled characters in the text block become the mask to the picture below it. Look at the layers in the Timeline to see how Flash has locked the two layers and displayed mask icons next to the layer names.

Step 4j

Step 4k

5. Edit the text mask to reposition the text block lower in the picture to show more of the water through the characters by completing the following steps:
   a. Click the *padlock* icon in the Lock/Unlock column next to the layer named *Text*. The text block reappears with the linked picture below it.

Working with Layers, Libraries, and Importing Graphics 115

b. With the Arrow tool active, drag the text block lower in the picture as shown.

Step 5b

c. Click the solid black dot in the Lock/Unlock column next to the layer named *Text* to relock the layer.
d. Observe that the text mask shows more of the water through the letters as shown.

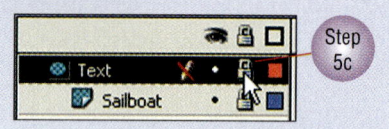

Step 5c

Step 5d

6. Save the revised document using the same name (Ch3Ex05).
7. Close Ch3Ex05.

Creating a Guide Layer

Flash includes two types of layers that can assist with the placement of objects called *guides* and *motion guides*. Objects drawn on a guide layer are not exported when the movie is published. They are only visible during the authoring process and are useful for aligning objects while creating the movie's content. For example, if your movie includes a series of text blocks that will transition onto the stage at various points and you want the text to appear in the same place each time, draw a rectangle on a guide layer the size and location where you want the text blocks to appear. Use the rectangle to align each text block at the right location as you create them. Shapes drawn using a guide layer in conjunction with activating the Snap to Guides feature can make the authoring process go more smoothly.

Motion guides are layers that are included in the exported movie but are not visible to the user when the movie is played. A motion guide layer contains a line that is connected to an object on another layer that will be animated across the stage. The motion guide determines the path the object will follow during its movement. Creating a motion guide layer will be discussed in the next chapter.

Creating a guide layer involves inserting a new layer, drawing the lines or shapes that will be used for alignment purposes, and then designating the layer as a guide. To do this, right-click the layer name in the Timeline panel, and then click Guide at the shortcut menu.

exercise 6

CREATING AND USING A GUIDE LAYER

1. Open the Flash document named PoisonIvy.
2. Save the document with Save As and name it Ch3Ex06.
3. The stage contains a drawing of a poison ivy plant that you have determined is too large for the allocated graphic space in the final movie. To make sure the drawing fits within your existing space in the movie plan, you decide to use a guide layer to resize the graphic. Draw a rectangle the size that is available for the graphic in the final movie in a new layer that will be designated as a guide layer by completing the following steps:
   a. Turn on the display of the rulers.
   b. Insert a new layer and rename the layer *Guide*.
   c. Rename Layer 1 *Poison Ivy*.
   d. Drag the layer named *Guide* below the layer named *Poison Ivy*. (Note: Guide layers are usually positioned at the bottom of the stacking order.) 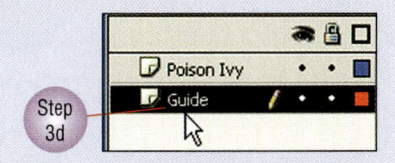
   e. Hide the layer named *Poison Ivy*. The graphic disappears from the stage. This will make it easier to draw the rectangle on the stage.
   f. Select the Rectangle tool in the toolbox, change the Stroke Color to bright red, and then change the Fill Color to White.
   g. Position the crosshair pointer on the stage with the horizontal ruler at 50 pixels and the vertical ruler at 150 pixels, drag right and down until the horizontal ruler is at 300 pixels and the vertical ruler is a 350 pixels, and then release the mouse.

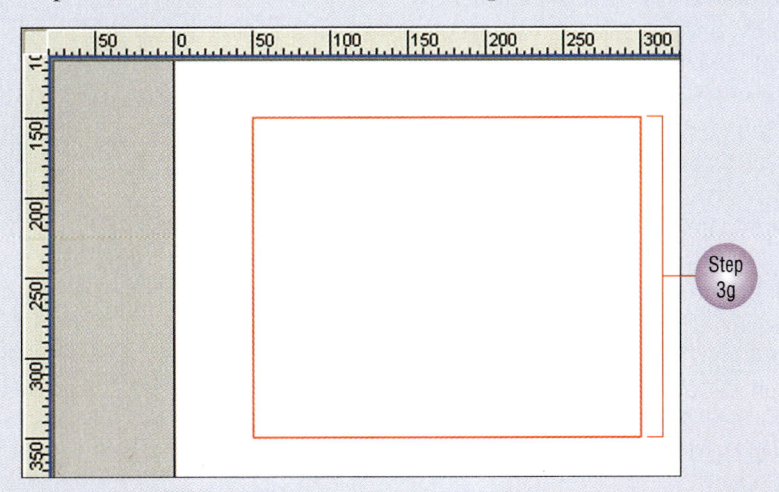

   h. Turn off the display of the rulers.
   i. Right-click the layer named *Guide* and then click Guide at the shortcut menu. Flash changes the layer to a guide layer as indicated by the *guide* icon next to the layer name in the Timeline.
   j. Lock the Guide layer.
   k. Make active the layer named *Poison Ivy*.
4. Resize the poison ivy graphic to fit within the rectangle on the guide layer by completing the following steps: 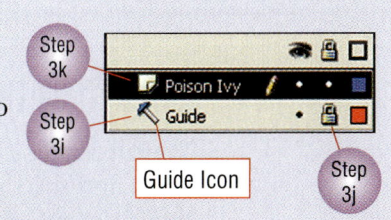
   a. Unhide the layer named *Poison Ivy*.
   b. Click View, point to Guides, and then click Snap to Guides to activate the feature. (*Note: Skip this step if Snap to Guides displays with a check mark.*)

Working with Layers, Libraries, and Importing Graphics 117

c. Select the Arrow tool and then draw a selection box that encompasses all of the elements in the poison ivy plant. The graphic is currently made up of several individually drawn objects. You want to group the objects so that you can resize it as one entity.

Steps 4c–4d

d. Press Ctrl + G.
e. With the blue bounding box displayed around the graphic, click the Free Transform tool in the toolbox.
f. Click the Scale modifier in the Options section of the toolbox. This will ensure that the graphic is resized horizontally and vertically maintaining its current height and width proportions.
g. Resize the graphic by dragging the black resizing handles until the poison ivy plant fits within the red rectangle guide below it. As you resize diagonally, horizontally, or vertically, you may have to move the graphic inside the rectangle to shift its position so that you can resize to the boundaries of the rectangle.
h. Click in the stage outside the graphic to deselect it.
i. Lock the *Poison Ivy* layer.

Steps 4g–4h

5. Save the revised document using the same name (Ch3Ex06).
6. Close Ch3Ex06.

Layer Properties Dialog Box

In the preceding sections you have used the layer management tools in the Timeline panel and the shortcut menus to change layer properties. Alternatively, the Layer Properties dialog box shown in Figure 3.7 can be used to rename, show or hide, lock or unlock, designate a mask or guide, change the color of the outline and switch to Outline mode for the active layer. To display the Layer Properties dialog box for the active layer, click Modify and then click Layer.

FIGURE 3.7 Layer Properties Dialog Box

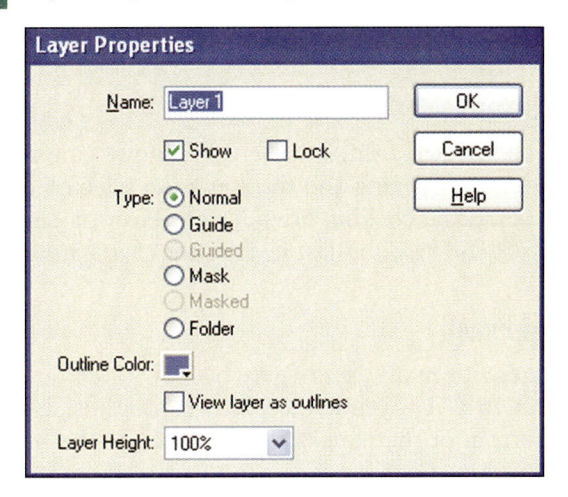

The Layer Height option at the bottom of the Layer Properties dialog box is used to increase the height of the layers in the Timeline from 100% to 200% or 300%. This option is often used when working with sound in a movie. Sounds will be discussed in Chapter 5.

Creating a Layer Folder

When the Timeline becomes filled with several layers you may want to consider grouping a set of related layers together in a layer folder. Figure 3.8 illustrates a Timeline with a layer folder named *Graphics*. Three layers relating to graphic objects are grouped within the layer folder. Layers grouped within a folder are shown indented below the folder name in the Timeline panel. Click the down-pointing triangle next to a layer name to collapse the folder's layers. The down-pointing triangle changes to a right-pointing triangle for a collapsed layer folder. Click the right-pointing triangle to expand the layer folder.

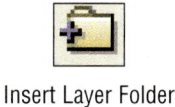

Insert Layer Folder

FIGURE 3.8 Layer Folder in the Timeline

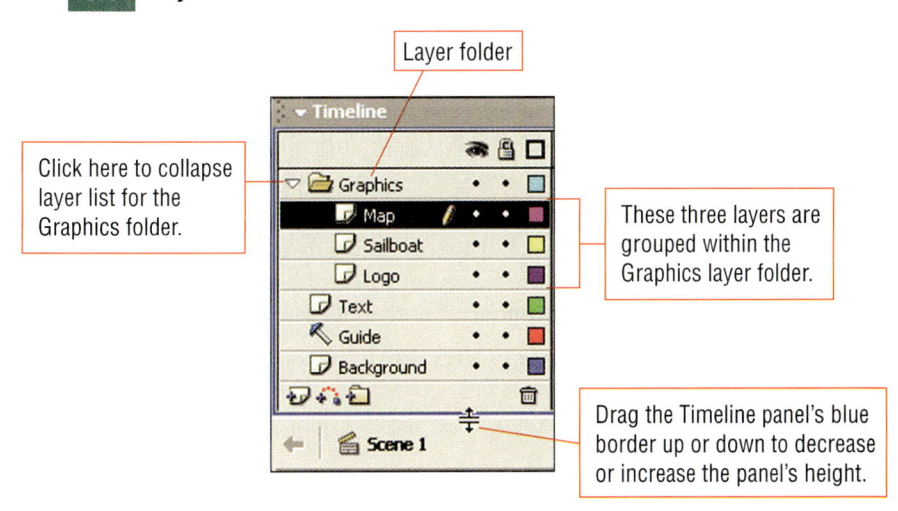

Layer folder

Click here to collapse layer list for the Graphics folder.

These three layers are grouped within the Graphics layer folder.

Drag the Timeline panel's blue border up or down to decrease or increase the panel's height.

Working with Layers, Libraries, and Importing Graphics

Click the Insert Layer Folder button in the Timeline panel, or click <u>I</u>nsert and then Layer F<u>o</u>lder to create a new layer folder. Layers are not automatically placed within a layer folder even if the active layer is a folder when a new layer is inserted. Layers are repositioned into a folder by moving them.

Moving Layers to a Layer Folder

Multiple layers can be selected using standard Windows conventions and then moved to a layer folder by dragging and dropping the selected layers. For example, hold down the Ctrl key while clicking nonadjacent layer names, or hold down the Shift key and then click the first and last layer names for a group of adjacent layers.

Resizing the Timeline Panel

Scrolling the Timeline with many layers may become a tedious process if you are changing layers frequently. The Timeline panel can be resized by dragging the blue border at the bottom of the panel down to increase the height as shown in Figure 3.8. Click inside the Timeline panel to display the blue border if it is not currently active. As an alternative you may want to consider undocking the Timeline panel by moving the panel inside the Flash window. The undocked Timeline panel can be resized as any other Window by dragging the panel's borders. Re-dock the panel by dragging the Timeline panel's title bar back to the top of the Flash window.

Libraries, Symbols, and Instances

In Chapters 1 and 2 you copied and pasted objects when you wanted to reuse shapes. For example, in Chapter 1, Assessment 1, you created three different colored balloons, copied them next to the first three on the stage, and then changed the stroke and fill colors of the duplicates. In this section you will learn how to make use of a library to reduce this workload, and, at the same time, reduce the size of your Flash movie file.

Every Flash document includes a library that is part of the project's *fla* file. The library is a repository in which you place symbols, imported bitmaps, and sound files. A *symbol* is any object that you want to reuse either in the current movie file or a different movie file. Examples of a symbol could be a drawn object, a text block, a button, a movie clip, or an imported logo. Symbols are placed in the library either by creating the symbol from scratch or by converting an existing object to a symbol. Once in the library, the symbol becomes the *master copy* of the object. When you want to use the graphic in your movie, you insert the symbol onto the stage from the Library panel. Each symbol insertion is referred to as an *instance*. An instance can be modified. For example, a balloon graphic stored as a symbol can be inserted as an instance on the stage and then the stroke and fill colors can be changed from those used in the master copy of the symbol. Advantages to creating symbols in the library and then inserting symbols as instances include:

- Once a symbol is created, it can be reused many times simply by dragging the symbol from the Library panel to the stage. This is more time efficient than copying and pasting.
- A symbol can be reused in other movie files in addition to the one in which it was created.

- File size is greatly reduced since Flash only needs to store information about the master copy of the symbol once. Instances are direct links to the symbol in the library. Flash simply needs to store each instance's location in the movie and also keep track of any modifications made to the instance such as a different color or size. This uses much less space than copied and pasted objects where Flash would store each object separately in the movie file.
- A change made to the master copy of the symbol causes Flash to automatically update each instance. This not only reduces time spent editing but ensures consistency in the movie and reduces the potential for errors if you had to edit each object individually.

In Chapter 1 you learned that Flash's use of vector graphics has contributed to making Flash the market leader for Web content due to the speed with which Flash files download. In addition to vector graphics, making use of symbols in libraries is a contributing factor in keeping file sizes as small as possible. Whenever you need to reuse an object, consider creating it as a symbol.

Click Window and then click Library to open the Library panel and view the symbols stored within the movie.

Creating a Symbol

To create a symbol from scratch, click Insert and then click New Symbol. The Create New Symbol dialog box shown in Figure 3.9 appears.

FIGURE 3.9 **Create New Symbol Dialog Box**

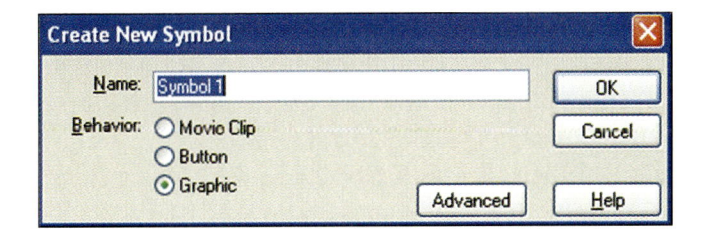

Key a descriptive name for the object in the Name text box. By default Flash names each symbol *Symbol#* where # represents the next sequential symbol. Three types of symbols, referred to as *behaviors*, can be created: Movie Clip, Button, or Graphic. A movie clip is an animation that you want to treat independently from the other animations in the file and has its own timeline; in essence it is a movie within a movie. A button is an interactive object, usually a button but it can also be any graphic that reacts differently depending on the user's action with the mouse. Graphics are images that you create or import that you want to reuse a number of times in the movie.

Click OK when you have named the symbol and selected its behavior type. The dialog box closes and you are now in symbol editing mode on the stage. You will notice that the workspace is gone and a plus symbol appears in the center of the stage as shown in Figure 3.10. The plus symbol represents the *registration point*, which is the point Flash uses as the center of the object when transforming it by rotating or scaling. Generally, you draw around the plus sign, keeping it in the center of your object as much as possible. A technique that you can use to make sure a drawn object is centered on the registration point is to draw the object anywhere on the stage, select, cut, and then paste the object. Flash pastes objects in the center of the stage.

FIGURE 3.10 **Stage in Symbol Editing Mode**

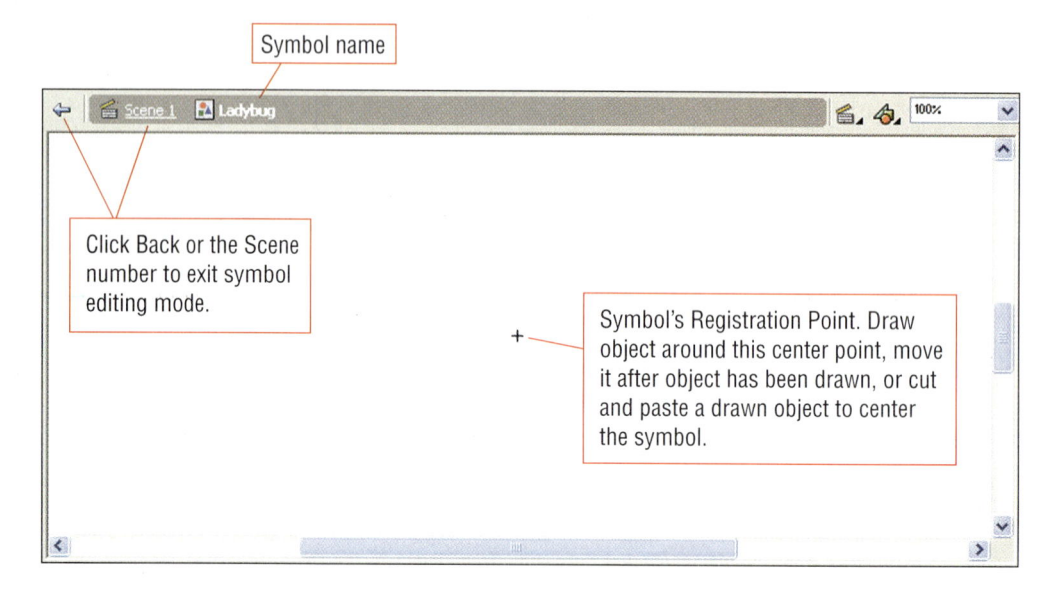

Symbol name

Click Back or the Scene number to exit symbol editing mode.

Symbol's Registration Point. Draw object around this center point, move it after object has been drawn, or cut and paste a drawn object to center the symbol.

When you have completed the drawn object, exit symbol editing mode by any of the following methods:

- Click the Back button in the Information bar at the top of the stage.
- Click the Scene number in the Information bar at the top of the stage. (The scene number appears as a hyperlink.)
- Click Edit and then click Edit Document.

The symbol you have drawn disappears from the stage when you exit symbol editing mode. The symbol has been placed in the library and can be viewed in the Library panel.

Inserting and Modifying an Instance of a Symbol

Display the Library panel to place instances of symbols within a movie by clicking Window and then Library. Click the desired symbol name in the bottom pane of the Library panel. A preview of the symbol appears in the top pane. Position the pointer over the symbol in the Preview pane and then drag to the location on the stage where you want the instance placed.

Once an instance has been inserted on the stage, you can use the Free Transform tool to rotate or scale the instance. To adjust the brightness or tint of the colors in the instance you must use the Properties panel.

exercise 7

CREATING A SYMBOL AND INSERTING AND EDITING INSTANCES

1. Start a new Flash document and make sure the magnification is set to 100%.
2. Create a symbol from scratch in symbol editing mode by completing the following steps:
   a. Click Insert and then click New Symbol.
   b. Key **Bamboo** in the Name text box in the Create New Symbol dialog box.
   c. If necessary, click Graphic in the Behavior section and then click OK. 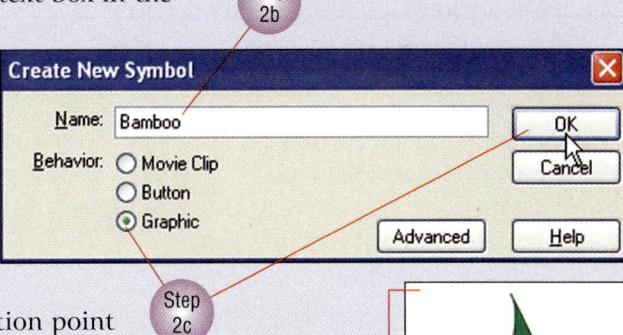
   d. Use the drawing tools to draw a graphic of a bamboo shoot similar to the one shown. Do not be concerned with the registration point as you draw as you will center the object in the next step. *(Hints: Draw a 3-point rounded corner rectangle as the main stalk, draw small ovals to create the joints, and then use the Arrow tool to create the curves between the joints. You need only draw one leaf which can then be copied and transformed to make the other two leaves.)*
   e. With the Arrow tool active, draw a selection box around the bamboo shoot, press Ctrl + X to cut the image, press Ctrl + V to paste the image in the center of the stage, and then click outside the image to deselect it. *(Note: If Flash does not center the image over the plus symbol, drag the selected object until the plus symbol is in the approximate center of the bamboo.)* 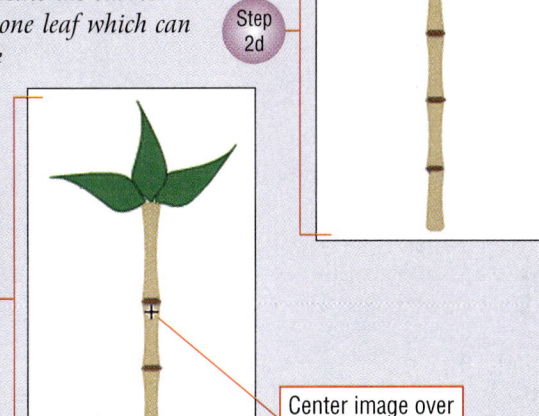 
   f. Click the Back button in the Information bar at the top of the stage. 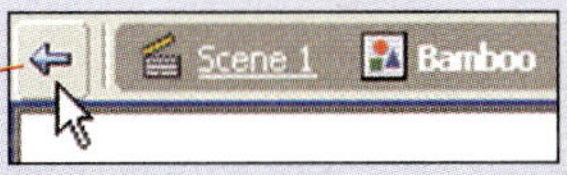
3. Save the document and name it Ch3Ex07.
4. Insert instances of the bamboo symbol and then modify instances by completing the following steps:
   a. Click Window and then click Library to open the Library panel.
   b. Drag the Library panel title bar to the left side of the stage.
   c. Click *Bamboo* in the Name column of the bottom pane in the Library panel. The graphic appears in the Preview pane above the symbol list.

Working with Layers, Libraries, and Importing Graphics 123

d. With the Arrow tool active, position the pointer over the symbol in the Preview pane of the Library panel and then drag the symbol to the stage as shown. An instance of the symbol is placed on the stage.
e. Drag two more instances of the symbol to the stage next to the first instance.
f. Close the Library panel.
g. Click to select the first instance of the Bamboo symbol.
h. Using the Free Transform tool and the Rotate and Scale modifiers in the Options section of the toolbox, resize, rotate, and then move the bamboo as shown.
i. Modify the third instance of the symbol as shown by completing steps similar to those in Steps 4g–4h.

5. Save the revised document using the same name (Ch3Ex07).

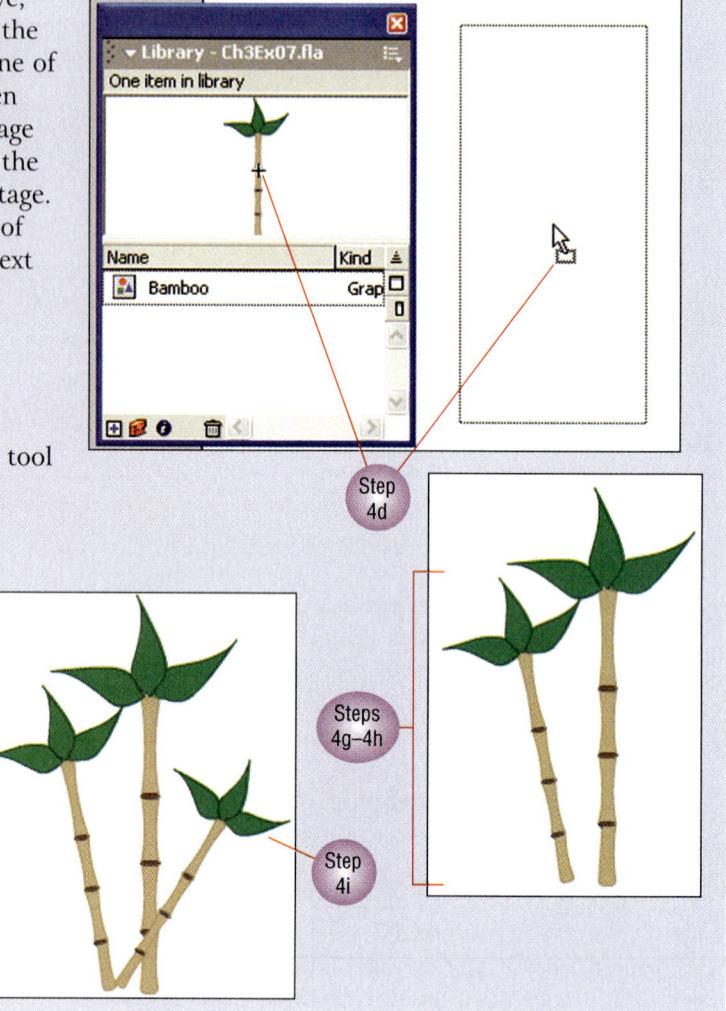

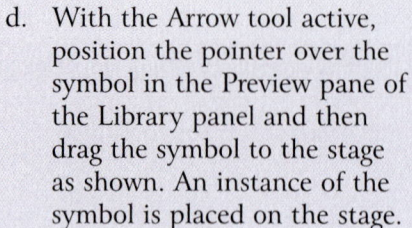

Editing a Symbol

To change the master copy of the symbol in the library, double-click any of the instances of the symbol on the stage. Flash opens the symbol in editing mode. Any other instances of the symbol on the stage will be dimmed and cannot be accessed. Make the required changes to the symbol and then exit symbol editing mode. As you are making changes to the master copy of the symbol, the other dimmed instances on the stage will be automatically updated as well to reflect your changes. If you accidentally double-click an instance and make changes to a symbol by mistake, use the Undo feature to return the symbol to its original state and then click the Back button on the Information bar to exit editing mode.

To edit a symbol using the Library panel, right-click the symbol name and then click Edit at the shortcut menu. Make the changes as required and then exit symbol editing mode.

exercise 8

EDITING A SYMBOL

1. With Ch3Ex07 open, edit the master copy of the bamboo symbol by completing the following steps:
    a. Double-click the middle bamboo instance on the stage. The two remaining instances are dimmed. Notice the symbol name appears in the Information bar at the top of the stage. 
    b. Click the inside of one of the leaves to select the fill. Hold down the Shift key and then click the inside fills of the other two leaves.
    c. Click Fill Color in the toolbox and then click the green-to-black gradient color swatch in the gradient row of the palette. The fill in the three leaves changes to the gradient and the leaves in the dimmed instances also update.  
    d. Click the Back button on the Information bar at the top of the stage to exit symbol editing mode.
2. Verify that the updated symbol is stored in the library by completing the following steps:
    a. Click Window and then click Library to open the Library panel.
    b. Click Bamboo in the Name list. The revised symbol appears in the Preview pane.
    c. Close the Library panel. 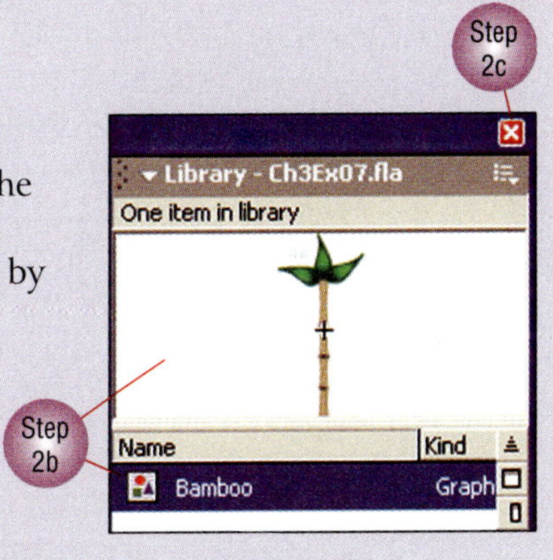
3. Save the revised document using the same name (Ch3Ex07).
4. Close Ch3Ex07.

Converting an Existing Object to a Symbol

If you have drawn an object on the stage and then realize afterwards that you want to reuse the object, convert it to a symbol by selecting the object, clicking Insert, and then Convert to Symbol. The Convert to Symbol dialog box shown in Figure 3.11 opens. Key a name for the symbol and then click OK.

FIGURE 3.11 Convert to Symbol Dialog Box

exercise 9

CONVERTING A DRAWN OBJECT TO A SYMBOL

1. Open the Flash document named Panda.
2. Save the document with Save As and name it Ch3Ex09.
3. Convert the panda graphic to a symbol by completing the following steps:
    a. With the Arrow tool active, click the panda graphic to select it. (*Note: The objects that make up the panda object have already been grouped.*)
    b. Click Insert and then click Convert to Symbol.
    c. Key **Panda** in the Name text box and then click OK.
    d. Click in the stage outside the panda to deselect it.
4. Insert two instances of the Panda symbol by completing the following steps:
    a. Display the Library panel.
    b. Click Panda and then drag two instances to the stage. Rotate and move the instances to position the pandas as shown.
    c. Close the Library panel.
5. Save the revised document using the same name (Ch3Ex09).
6. Close Ch3Ex09.

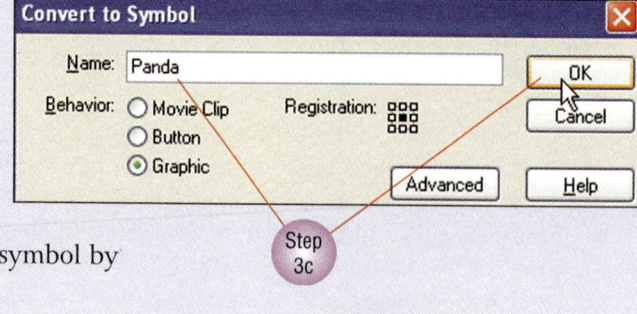

Step 3c

Step 4b

126 Chapter Three

Inserting Symbols from Another Movie's Library File

The library of another movie file can be opened in the current movie so that you can make use of the symbols stored within it. To do this, click File and then click Open as Library. Navigate to the location in which the Flash movie file is stored in the Open as Library dialog box and then double-click the file name in the file list box.

A library panel with the symbols from the selected movie file opens. The panel is differentiated from the Library panel of the current movie by a gray background as shown in Figure 3.12. When you drag an instance to the stage from the other movie file, Flash automatically inserts a copy of the symbol in the current movie's library. Close the library when you are finished inserting the required symbols.

FIGURE 3.12 *Opened Library Panel from Another Movie File*

Flash displays the background of another movie's library panel in gray.

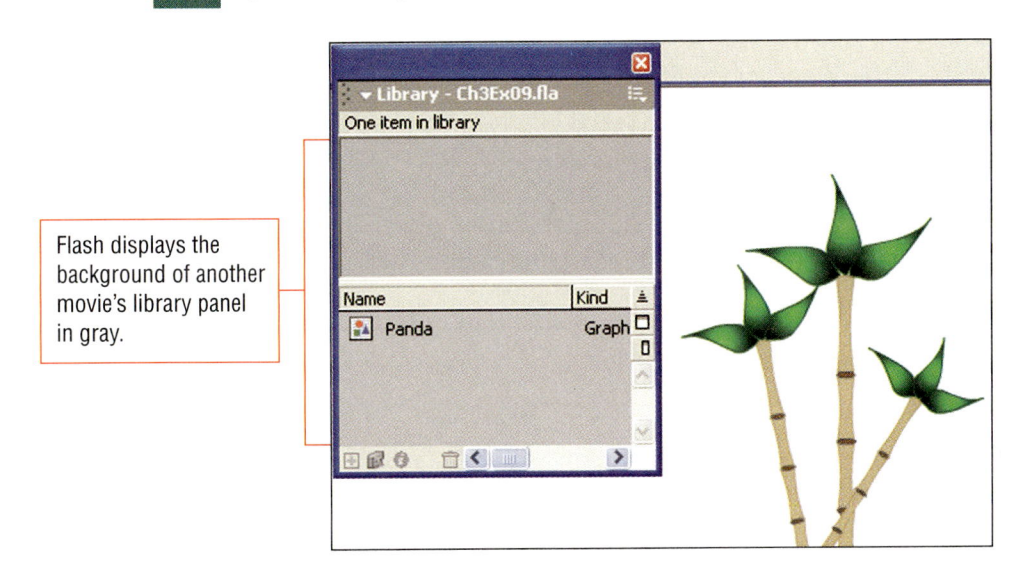

Inserting Symbols from Common Libraries

Included with Flash is a set of common libraries created by Macromedia containing objects that you are free to use without fear of copyright infringement in the movies that you create. These objects can add a professional look and feel to your movie without expending a lot of effort. To view the symbols in a common library, click Window, point to Common Libraries, and then click the name of the common library file that you want to use. The common library names are shown in Figure 3.13.

FIGURE 3.13 *Flash Common Libraries*

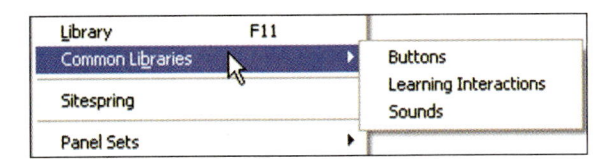

A library panel with the symbols in the selected common library opens in the current movie. As with an instance of a symbol selected from another movie's library, Flash creates a copy of the symbol in the current movie's library when an instance is inserted that originates from a common library.

Creating Your Own Common Library

The common library names that appear on the menu shown in Figure 3.13 are actually just Flash *fla* files stored in a special folder on the computer's hard drive. Complete the following steps to create your own common library:

1. At a new Flash document, create the symbols that you want to store in the common library.
2. If you create the symbols by drawing the objects on the stage and then using the Convert to Symbol command, make sure you delete the symbol from the stage after the conversion. Since the symbol will be stored in the library, leaving a copy on the stage uses unnecessary disk space.
3. Using the Save As command, save the Flash document using a descriptive file name and making sure to store the file in the following location:

    C:\Program Files\Macromedia\Flash MX\First Run\Libraries

4. Exit Flash.

When you restart Flash, the library saved in Step 3 will appear on the Common Libraries side menu as shown in Figure 3.14.

FIGURE 3.14 Common Library Added to Menu

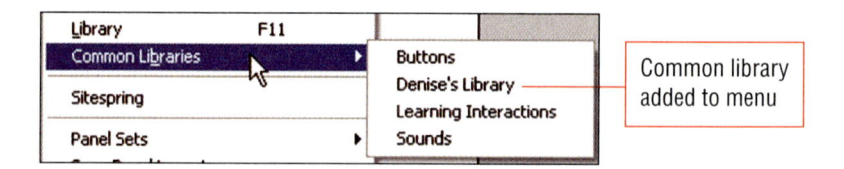

exercise 10

INSERTING A SYMBOL FROM ANOTHER MOVIE

1. Open the Flash document named Ch3Ex07.
2. Save the document with Save As and name it Ch3Ex10.
3. Change the background color for the document to light blue.
4. Rename Layer 1 *Bamboo*, insert a new layer above *Bamboo*, and then rename the new layer *Panda*.
5. Open the library from Ch3Ex09 and insert the panda symbol by completing the following steps:
    a. With the Panda layer active, click File and then Open as Library.
    b. Double-click Ch3Ex09.fla in the file list box.
    c. If necessary, drag the Library panel to the left side of the stage.
    d. Click Panda in the Library panel for Ch3Ex09.

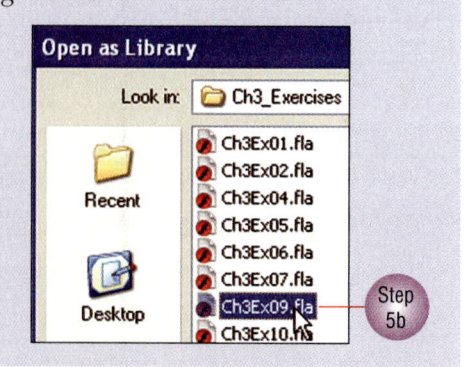

e. Drag an instance of the panda symbol to the stage as shown.
f. Close the Library panel for Ch3Ex09.
6. View the updated library panel for the current movie by completing the following steps:
   a. Press F11 to display the Library panel for the current movie file. The panel includes the symbol named *Panda* copied from Ch3Ex09.
   b. Close the Library panel.
7. Save the revised document using the same name (Ch3Ex10).
8. Close Ch3Ex10.

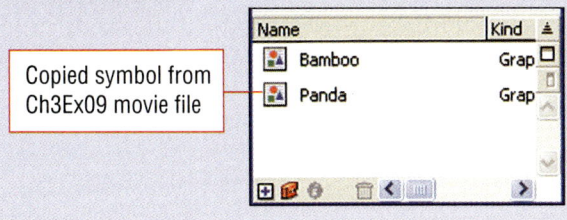

Step 5e

Copied symbol from Ch3Ex09 movie file

exercise 11

VIEWING SYMBOLS IN A COMMON LIBRARY

1. Start a new Flash document.
2. View the symbols in the common library named Buttons by completing the following steps:
   a. Click <u>W</u>indow, point to <u>C</u>ommon Li<u>b</u>raries, and then click Buttons.
   b. Notice the top of the Preview pane indicates that this library contains 122 Items.
   c. Click the Wide Library View button at the top of the vertical scroll bar in the bottom pane.
   d. If necessary, drag the Library pane so that it is centered within the Flash window.
   e. Double-click the folder icon next to the folder name *Arcade buttons*. This expands the folder list and displays the symbols grouped in the folder. Notice in Wide Library View that additional information about the symbol, such as the type of behavior for the symbol and the date the symbol was last modified, is displayed next to each symbol name.

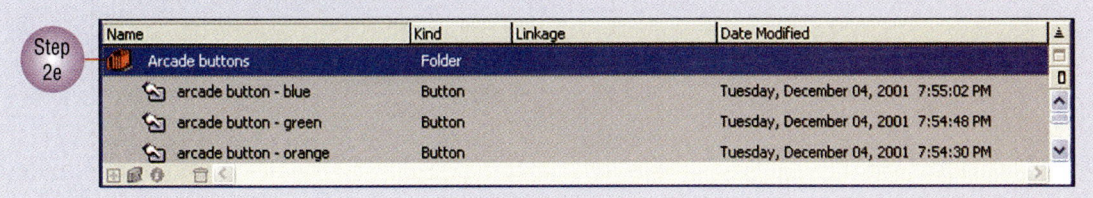

Step 2e

f. Click arcade button – blue in the symbol list to view the button in the Preview pane.

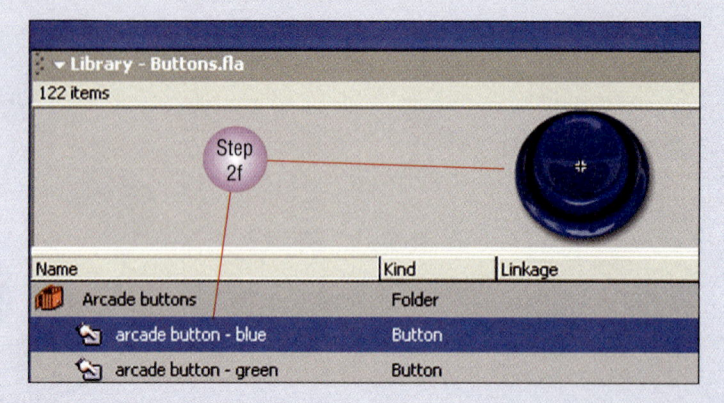

g. Scroll the names in the bottom pane and preview several other buttons by expanding other folders and selecting symbol names in the list. You may want to resize the Library panel to view more names in the bottom pane.

h. Close the panel when you have finished browsing the Buttons library.

Library Management

In the Buttons library viewed in Exercise 11, related symbols were grouped into folders. All of the techniques you learned earlier in this chapter to manage layers can be applied to managing symbols in a library. Create folders for related symbols and then drag and drop the symbols into the folder. Folders can be expanded and collapsed in the Library panel. Delete symbols using the Delete button at the bottom of the symbol list pane. The library management tools available in the Library pane are identified in Figure 3.15.

FIGURE 3.15 *Library Management Tools*

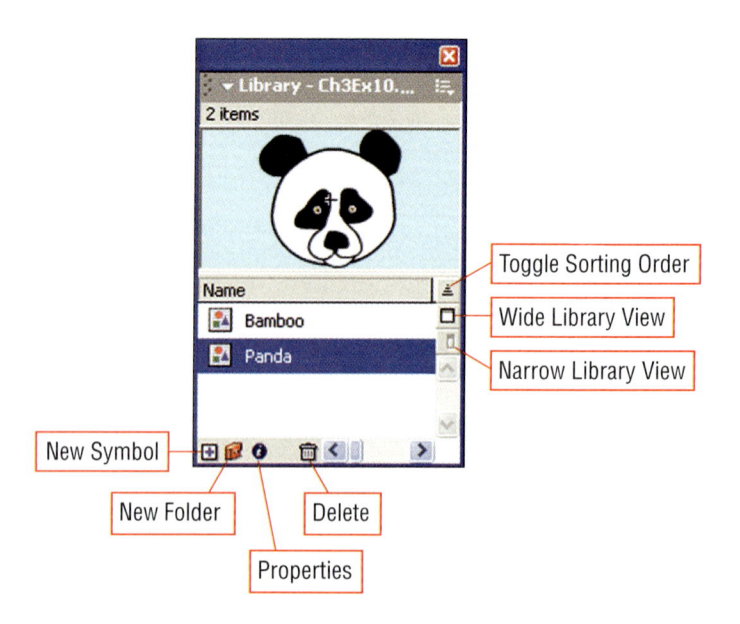

By default, symbols and folder names are displayed in the bottom pane in ascending alphanumeric order. Click the Toggle Sorting Order button to display the items in descending order. Click the Properties button to display the Symbol Properties dialog box for a selected symbol to view additional information about the item.

Right-clicking a symbol name in the Library panel displays the shortcut menu shown in Figure 3.16. Use this menu to perform management tasks such as renaming, duplicating, moving, deleting, and editing a symbol.

FIGURE 3.16 **Shortcut Menu for a Library Symbol**

Importing Graphics from Other Sources

In Chapter 1 you learned about the differences between vector graphics and bitmapped graphics and the advantages of using Flash's vector graphics format for file size minimization and graphic resizability. In some cases, however, you will need to import a graphic generated outside of Flash for use in a movie. For example, you may need to insert a company logo created in another graphics program, a picture taken with a digital camera, or a picture that has been scanned.

To import graphic files created outside Flash, click File and then click Import. Click the down arrow next to the Files of type list box and click the file format for the graphic which you want to insert into Flash. Figure 3.17 illustrates the Import dialog box with the Files of type pop-up list displayed. Notice the wide variety of images, sounds, and video that can be imported into a Flash movie.

Working with Layers, Libraries, and Importing Graphics — 131

FIGURE

3.17 *Import Dialog Box with Files of Type Pop-Up List*

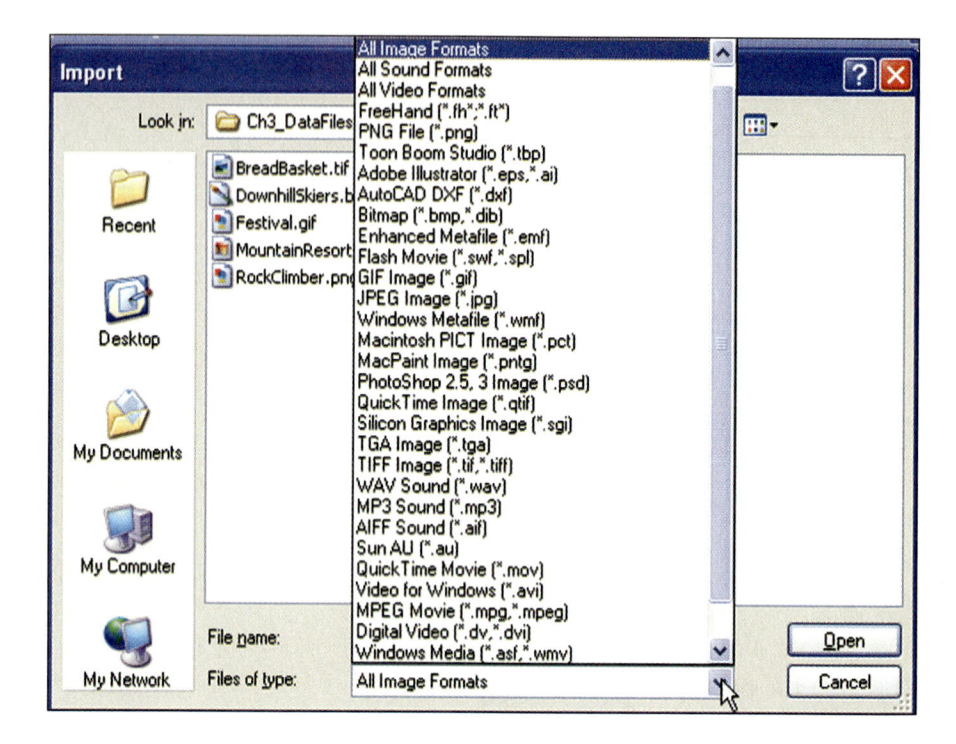

Navigate to the drive and/or folder in which the file is stored and then double-click the name of the graphic image in the file list. Imported bitmap images are automatically stored in the movie's library and a copy of the image is inserted in the active layer on the stage.

Flash recognizes vector file formats such as Macromedia FreeHand and Adobe Illustrator. FreeHand graphics can be imported with layers, pages, and text blocks maintained and Illustrator files can have the layers preserved in the Flash movie.

Commonly used bitmap formats *png, bmp, gif,* and *jpeg* are recognized by Flash and imported as objects in the active layer. By default, Flash compresses the bitmap using the *jpeg* or Lossless (*png/gif*) formats. Open the Bitmap Properties dialog box for the image to test a different compression format in order to achieve the smallest possible file size for the quality of image that you need to maintain. A bitmapped object in Flash can be rotated and scaled using the Free Transform tool. Since bitmapped graphics increase the file size of the published movie which causes download time on the Web to increase, it is a good idea to use pictures sparingly.

exercise 12

IMPORTING, MOVING, AND RESIZING A BITMAPPED GRAPHIC INTO FLASH

1. Open the Flash document named SummerFest.
2. Save the document with Save As and name it Ch3Ex12.
3. Import, move, and resize a bitmap of a summer festival picture in JPEG format by completing the following steps:
   a. Make active the layer named *Picture*.
   b. Click <u>F</u>ile and then click <u>I</u>mport.
   c. Click the down arrow next to the Files of <u>t</u>ype list box in the Import dialog box and then click JPEG Image (*.jpg) at the pop-up list.
   d. If necessary, change the Look in location to the drive and or folder where the data files are stored for Chapter 3.
   e. Double-click the file named SummerFest.jpg. Flash inserts a copy of the picture on the stage and imports the bitmap to the library.
   f. Change the magnification setting to 75%.
   g. With the picture selected on the stage, click the Free Transform tool.
   h. Move the picture to the top left of the stage as shown.
   i. Click Scale in the Options section of the toolbox.
   j. Drag the bottom right handle of the picture to enlarge it as shown.
   k. Click in the workspace to deselect the picture.

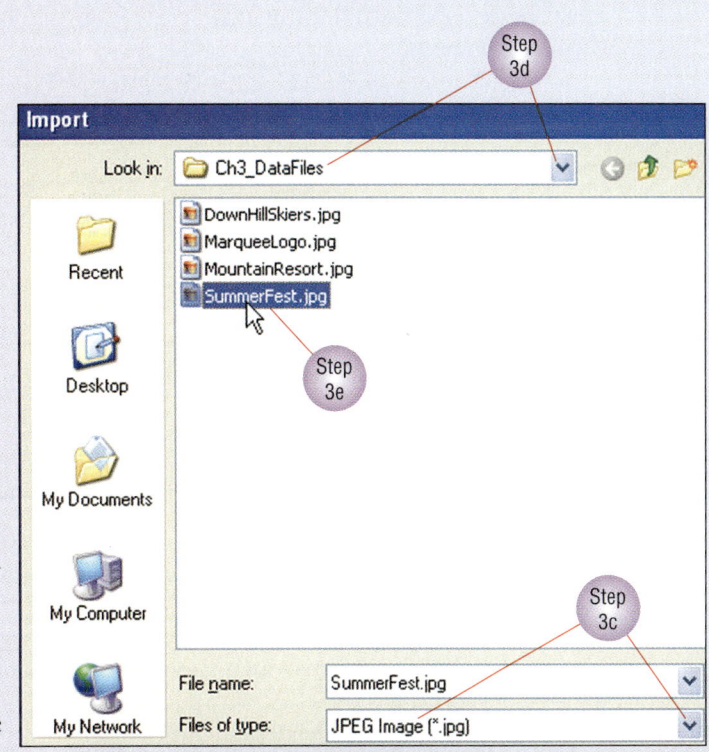

Working with Layers, Libraries, and Importing Graphics   133

4. Press F11 to open the Library panel. Notice the bitmap has been added to the library.
5. Close the Library panel.
6. Save the revised document using the same name (Ch3Ex12).

Step 5

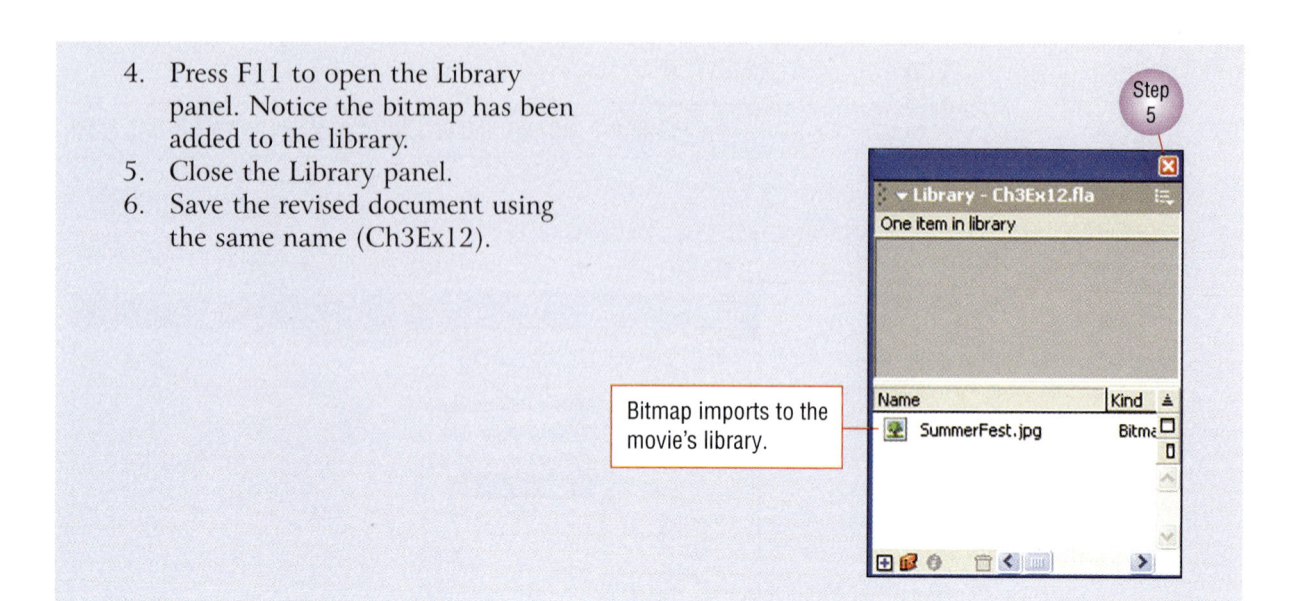

Bitmap imports to the movie's library.

Bitmap Properties

Each imported graphic has a set of properties associated with it that are displayed in the Bitmap Properties dialog box. Options such as smoothing and compression allow you to control the quality of the picture and the file size of the bitmap. The Bitmap Properties dialog box shown in Figure 3.18 displays the default settings for the picture inserted into the movie in Exercise 12.

FIGURE 3.18 *Bitmap Properties for Picture Inserted in Exercise 12*

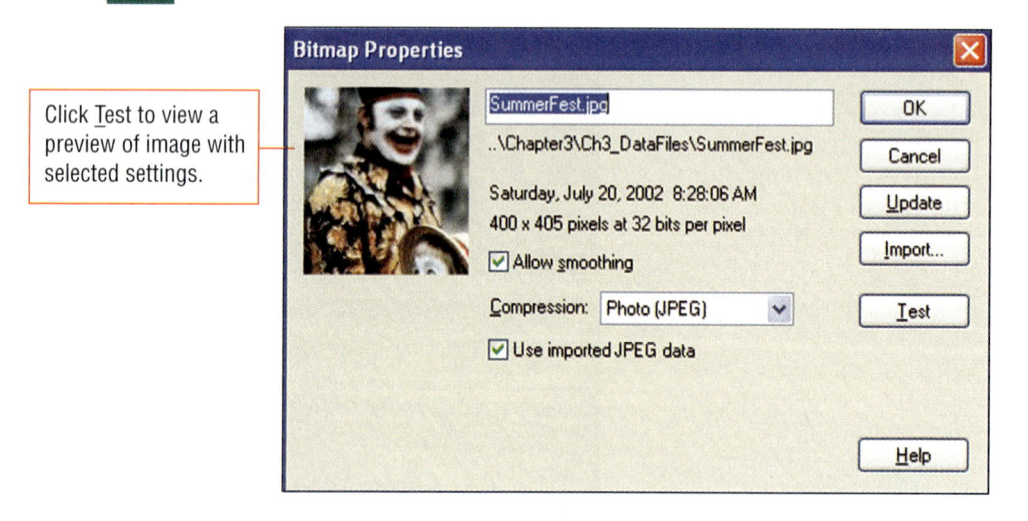

Click Test to view a preview of image with selected settings.

To display the Bitmap Properties dialog box, click the file name of the imported bitmap in the Library panel and then click the Properties button at the bottom of the window, or right-click the file name and then click Properties at the shortcut menu. The Preview window at the top left of the dialog box shows a portion of the image so that you can confirm you have selected the right graphic. In addition, the Preview window will update as you make changes to settings and click the Test button so that you can see the impact on the quality of the image.

134 Chapter Three

The file name of the imported bitmap displays in the name text box. Key a new name for the bitmap if you want to rename it. Below the name of the bitmap, the source location from which the bitmap was imported is displayed along with the pixel size and number of bits per pixel. By default, the Allow smoothing check box is turned on meaning the bitmap's edges will be smoothened or *antialiased*. Antialiasing is a term for a technique used in graphics software in which jagged edges are smoothened. Jagged edges occur when a monitor or printer does not have a high enough resolution to characterize a smooth line. Antialiasing reduces the appearance of these jagged edges by surrounding them with shades of gray or color. An example of a bitmap imported into Flash with Allow smoothing turned on and off is shown in Figure 3.19. The jaggedness is more evident in the word *Waterfront* in the bitmap on the right where anitaliasing has been turned off.

FIGURE 3.19 *Antialiasing a Bitmap*

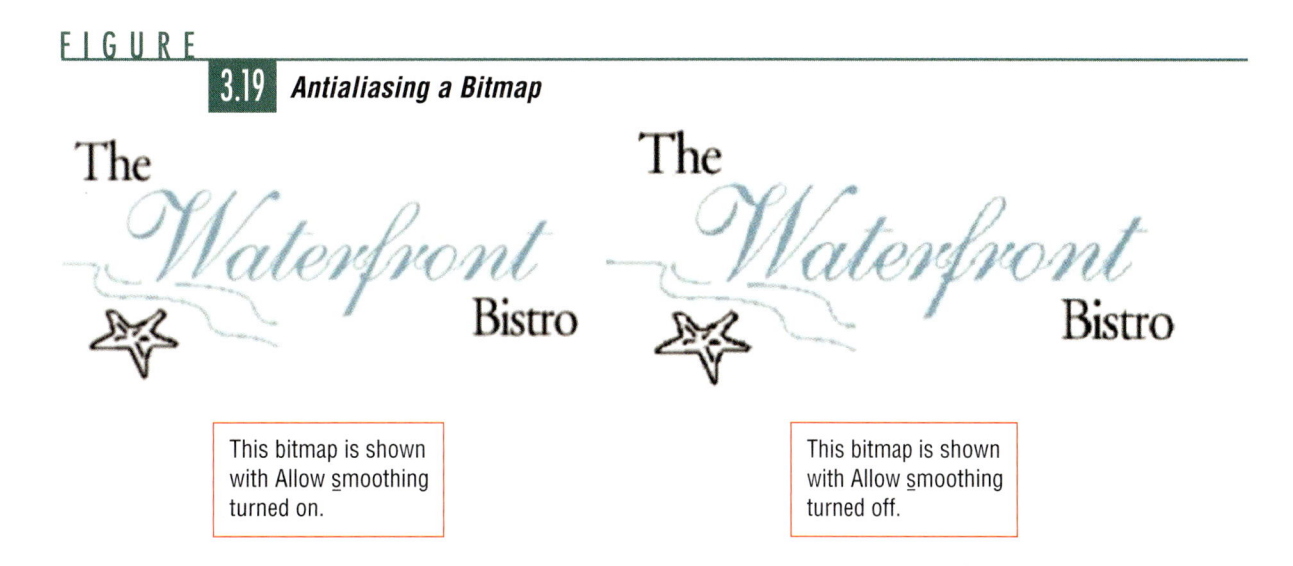

This bitmap is shown with Allow smoothing turned on.

This bitmap is shown with Allow smoothing turned off.

The Compression drop-down list contains two options: Photo (JPEG) or Lossless (PNG/GIF). It is recommended that you use Photo compression for bitmaps that are comprised of many different colors or colors in which a variety of tones have been used and use Lossless compression for bitmaps with uncomplicated objects and few color variations. By default the *Use imported JPEG data* check box is selected. Deselecting this option causes the Quality text box to appear below the check box as shown in Figure 3.20.

FIGURE 3.20 *Bitmap Properties Dialog Box with Use Imported JPEG Data Deselected*

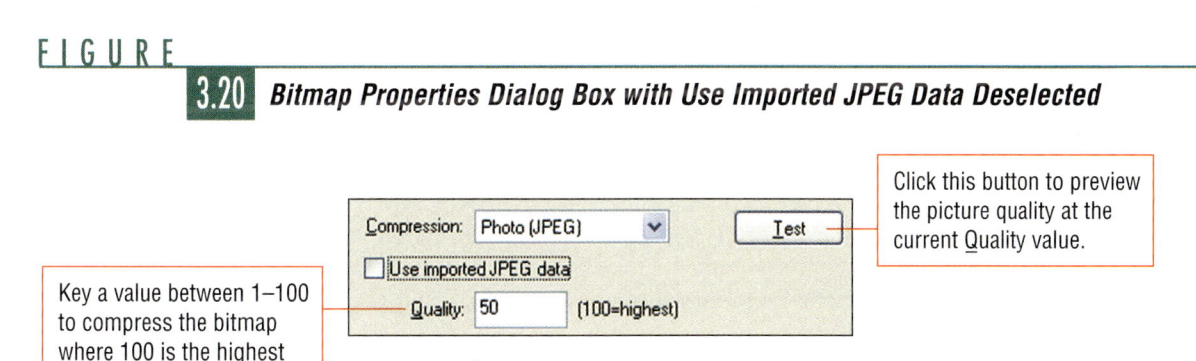

Click this button to preview the picture quality at the current Quality value.

Key a value between 1–100 to compress the bitmap where 100 is the highest possible quality.

Key a value between 1 and 100 to set the compression level for the image. The higher the value, the better the quality of the image; however, the consequence will be a larger file size. Flash provides the Test button in order to preview the image at various compression levels until you achieve the point at which the quality of image is sufficient for your needs at the lowest possible file size.

Click the Update button if you have edited the imported image in a program other than Flash and want Flash to incorporate the changes you have made. Make sure you have not moved the file from its original location from which it was imported to use the update feature. Click the Import button to change the image referenced in the library by selecting a new image in the Import Bitmap dialog box. Flash will update all instances of the bitmap in the Flash movie.

exercise 13

MODIFYING BITMAP PROPERTIES

1. With Ch3Ex12 open, preview the image at various compression settings by completing the following steps:
    a. Open the Library panel.
    b. Click SummerFest.jpg and then click the Properties button at the bottom of the panel window.
    c. Click the *Use imported JPEG data* check box to deselect it.
    d. Accept 50, which is the default value in the Quality text box, and then click Test to view the file size.

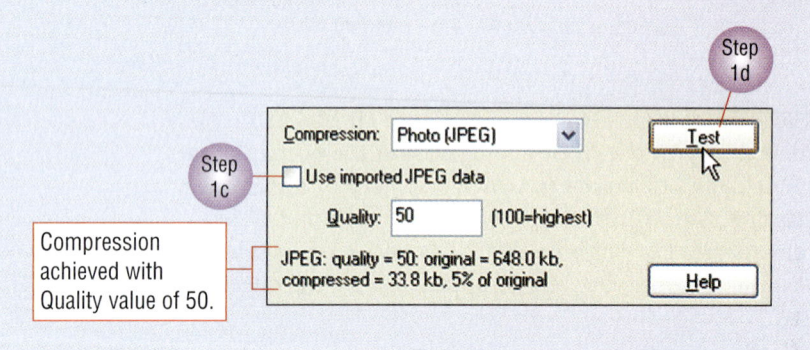

    Compression achieved with Quality value of 50.

    e. Look closely at the quality of the picture in the Preview window. Position the pointer over the picture until the pointer changes to an icon of a hand, hold down the left mouse button, and then drag the mouse up, down, left, and right to scroll to different parts of the picture. (*Note: You are not restricted to moving the mouse within the Preview area. Feel free to drag outside the Preview window and even outside the dialog box to scroll the various parts of the bitmap.*)
    f. Scroll the picture in the Preview window back to its original position of the top left corner of the bitmap.

136 Chapter Three

g. Drag across the value 50 in the Quality text box, key **25**, and then click the Test button. The file size has shrunk further from its original compressed size of 33.8 kb to 21.4 kb. Look at the picture in the Preview window to determine if this setting is acceptable.

h. Drag across the value 25 in the Quality text box, key **5**, and then click the Test button. Notice the file size has decreased to only 8.0 kb but the picture quality is now unacceptable.

i. Change the Quality value to 75 and test the compression level. File size increases to 44.1 kb and the picture is markedly improved.

j. Change the Quality value to 100 and test the compression level. File size has ballooned to 126.7 kb with only a slight improvement in quality from the previous setting.

k. Change the Quality value to 60 and test the compression level. Assume you want a better quality for the picture than the default value of 50 and have decided that 60 is a reasonable file size at 38.5 kb.

l. Click OK to close the Bitmap Properties dialog box.

m. Close the Library panel.

2. Save the revised document using the same name (Ch3Ex12).

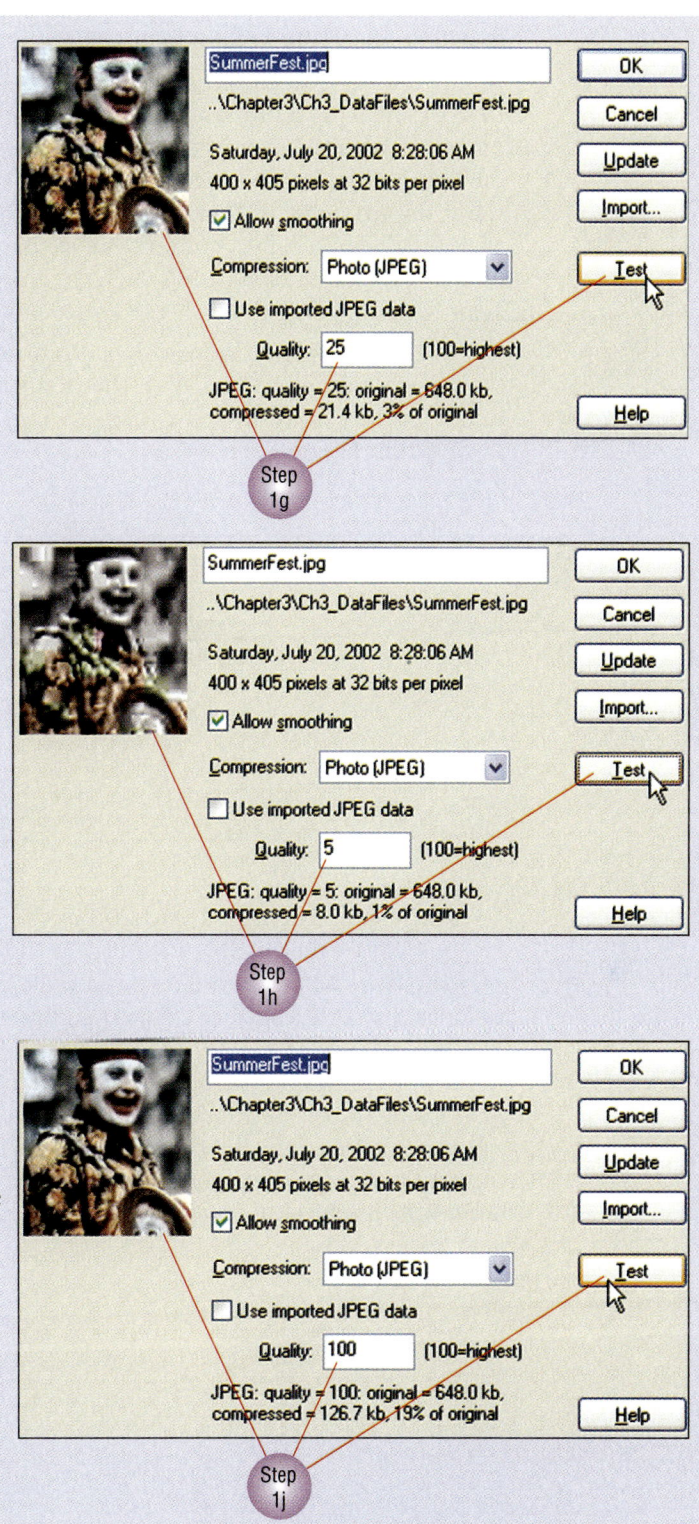

Breaking Apart and Editing Colors in a Bitmap

In Exercise 12 you edited a bitmap image by resizing it with the Free Transform tool. By breaking a bitmap image apart, portions of the bitmap can then be selected by colors within the image and then edited by changing fill colors, erasing, or moving portions of the bitmap's fill away from the rest of the image. To do this, select the instance of the bitmap which you want to edit, click Modify, and then click Break Apart. Flash converts the bitmap to an object similar to a closed shape drawn with the drawing tools such as a rectangle or oval. Changes made to the fill color for example, will cover the entire image.

Magic Wand

Magic Wand Properties

To edit the bitmap by selecting a color within the image, use the Lasso tool with the Magic Wand modifier. With the Lasso tool active, click Magic Wand Properties in the Options section of the toolbox. The Magic Wand Settings dialog box opens as shown in Figure 3.21.

FIGURE 3.21 *Magic Wand Settings Dialog Box*

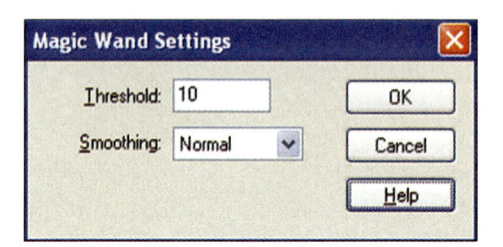

Key a value between 1 and 200 in the Threshold text box to determine the range of colors that will be included in the selection by how closely adjacent pixel colors match the color where you initially click the magic wand. A high number includes a wider breadth of colors than lower numbers. A threshold value of 0 means that pixels must be exactly the same color as the pixel where you click the magic wand in order to be included in the selection. Click the down arrow next to Smoothing to choose Pixels, Rough, Normal, or Smooth which defines how Flash will create a selection area by smoothening the edges around which you have clicked the magic wand. Experiment with different values for Threshold and a different option for Smoothing until Flash selects the fill colors that you want to edit.

exercise 14 — IMPORTING, BREAKING APART, AND EDITING A BITMAP

1. With Ch3Ex12 open, import a bitmap in JPEG format of a logo by completing the following steps:
   a. With *Picture* the active layer, click File and then click Import.
   b. Double-click the file named MarqueeLogo.jpg in the file list box.
   c. Press Ctrl + X to cut from the stage the copy of the image that Flash has inserted and put it in the Clipboard.
2. Position and then break apart the bitmap by completing the following steps:
   a. Make active the layer named *Logo*.
   b. Press Ctrl + V to insert the image from the Clipboard.

c. With the Arrow tool active, move the logo to the stage below the title *SummerFest 2004* as shown.
d. Click the Free Transform tool, click Scale in the Options section of the toolbox, resize, and then move the image as shown.  
e. With the image still selected, click Modify and then click Break Apart. The filled areas within the image are selected.
f. Click in the workspace to deselect the image.
3. Select and then delete the white fill color around the perimeter of the image by completing the following steps:
   a. Click the Lasso tool in the toolbox.
   b. Click Magic Wand Properties in the Options section of the toolbox.
   c. With 10 selected in the Threshold text box and Normal in the Smoothing list box, click OK. 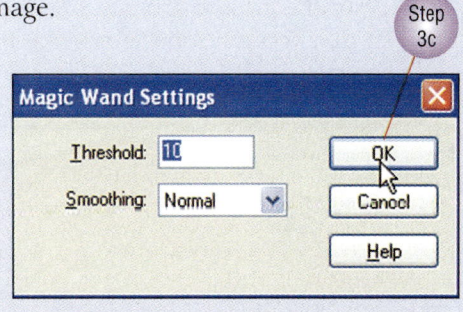
   d. Click Magic Wand in the Options section of the toolbox.
   e. Position the magic wand pointer over the white fill at the left edge of the logo as shown and then click the left mouse button. Flash will select the white area around the perimeter of the logo. You will not see the selection since the fill color is currently white and Flash displays a selected area with white dots. (*Note: The hotspot for the magic wand is in the center of the burst from the top of the wand.*) 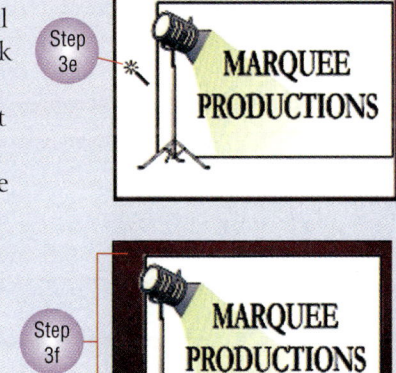
   f. Press Delete. The selected area is removed from the bitmap.
   g. Click the Arrow tool and then click in the workspace to deselect the logo.
4. Save the revised document using the same name (Ch3Ex12).
5. Close Ch3Ex12.

Using a Bitmap as a Fill

A bitmap that has been broken apart can be used as the fill for a closed shape. To do this, draw the shape on the stage for which you want the bitmapped image to fill. Import and then break apart the bitmapped image to be used as the shape's fill. Click the Eye Dropper tool in the toolbox and then click over the broken apart image. The Eye Dropper tool changes to the Paint Bucket tool and the Fill Color is automatically changed to the bitmap. Click the Paint Bucket over the shape to fill its background with the bitmapped image. Delete the broken apart bitmap from the stage after the shape has been filled with its image.

exercise 15

FILLING A SHAPE WITH A BITMAPPED IMAGE

1. Open the Flash document named Bread-2-Go.
2. Save the document with Save As and name it Ch3Ex15.
3. Import, move, and break apart a bitmap picture of a breadbasket in *gif* format by completing the following steps:
   a. Make active the layer named *ChefHat*.
   b. Press Ctrl + R to open the Import dialog box.
   c. Click the down arrow next to Files of type and then click GIF Image (*.gif) at the pop-up list.
   d. Double-click the file named BreadBasket.gif.
   e. With the imported image selected, move the graphic to the right side of the stage so that you can see the original file and the picture side-by-side. If necessary, scroll the stage right.

   Steps 3b–3e

   f. With the imported image still selected, click Modify and then click Break Apart.
4. Use the bitmap as the fill of the chef's hat by completing the following steps:
   a. With the broken apart image selected on the stage, click the Eye Dropper tool in the toolbox.

140 Chapter Three FLASH MX

b. Position the Eye Dropper over the broken apart bitmap and then click the left mouse button. The Eye Dropper changes to the Paint Bucket and Fill Color displays the bitmap in the color swatch in the toolbox.
c. Click over the fill in the top of the chef's hat with the Paint Bucket tool. The red fill is changed to the bitmapped image tiled within the closed shape.

d. With the Paint Bucket tool still selected, click over the fill in the bottom of the chef's hat.
e. Click the Arrow tool. With the broken apart bitmap at the right side of the stage still selected, press Delete.

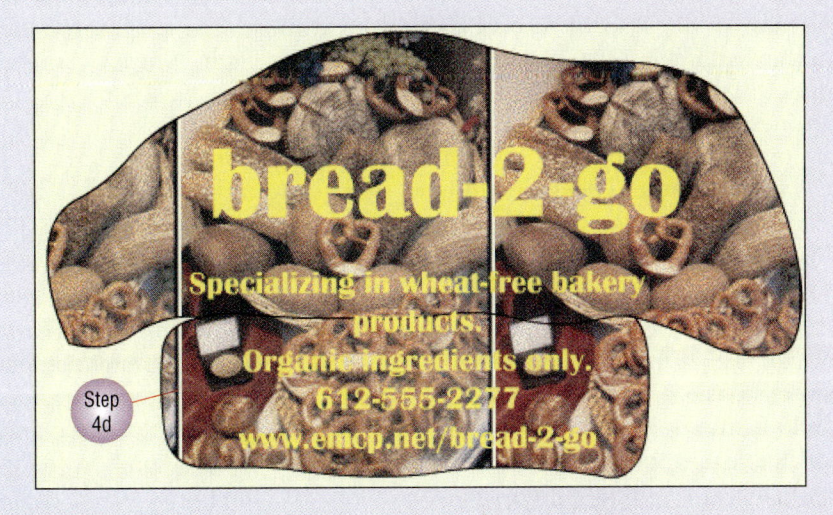

5. Save the revised document with the same name (Ch3Ex15).
6. Close Ch3Ex15.

A shape filled with a bitmap can be modified using the Fill Transform tool using the same techniques as you learned in Chapter 2 for modifying the fill of shapes drawn with the drawing tools.

Working with Layers, Libraries, and Importing Graphics

Converting a Bitmap to a Vector Graphic

Trace Bitmap on the Modify menu will convert a selected bitmap instance into a vector graphic. This feature will not work with a bitmap that has been broken apart. The vector graphic will be able to be edited as any other vector graphic within Flash. Use this feature to reduce file size and have the ability to edit separate areas within the image.

Flash analyzes the selected bitmap's pixels and then creates vector graphic shapes within the image based on the settings in the Trace Bitmap dialog box shown in Figure 3.22.

FIGURE 3.22 *Trace Bitmap Dialog Box*

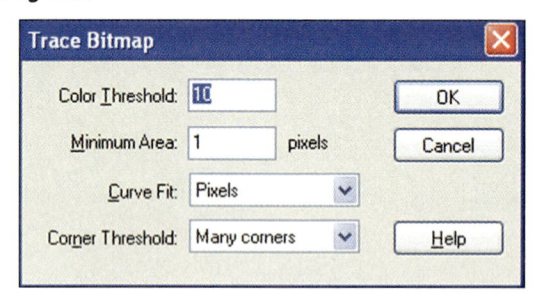

Key a value in the Color Threshold text box between 1 and 500. When Flash analyzes the bitmap, two pixels that reside next to each other with RGB color values less than the value in the Color Threshold text box will be considered the same color. Therefore, higher threshold values will decrease the number of colors in the converted vector graphic. Adjacent pixels considered the same color make up a vector shape in the converted graphic.

Key a value in the Minimum Area text box between 1 and 1000 representing the number of adjacent pixels Flash is to consider when assigning colors to make up the vector shapes. Choose Pixels, Very Tight, Tight, Normal, Smooth, or Very Smooth from the Curve Fit drop-down list to instruct Flash on how smoothly the outlines around the vector graphics should be created. Click the down arrow next to Corner Threshold to choose Many corners, Normal, or Few Corners. This setting tells Flash whether edges should have sharp or rounded corners.

The default settings in the Trace Bitmap dialog box shown in Figure 3.22 create a vector graphic that most resembles the original bitmap as recommended by Flash. A bitmap containing many colors in a series of complex shapes is not recommended to be traced to vectors since the resulting file size may end up larger than the original bitmap. Experiment with different settings in the Trace Bitmap dialog box until you reach the desired outcome for a bitmap that is converted to vectors. Use the Undo feature to restore the image back to a bitmap if the converted graphic is not acceptable and then try different trace options. Depending on how many times you have clicked the mouse after the conversion, you may have to Undo several times before the image is restored to the bitmap.

A progress bar displays inside the Tracing Bitmap dialog box (not shown) after clicking OK in the Trace Bitmap dialog box to indicate the progress of the bitmap conversion. A Cancel button is included in the dialog box in case you want to abort the bitmap conversion. When completed, the Tracing Bitmap dialog box closes and the image is displayed on the stage with the various shapes selected. The length of time for the bitmap conversion will depend on the complexity of the image and your system resources.

exercise 16
CONVERTING A BITMAP TO A VECTOR GRAPHIC

1. Open the Flash document named EuropeTravel.
2. Save the document with Save As and name it Ch3Ex16.
3. Import a bitmap of a logo by completing the following steps:
   a. Make active the layer named *Logo*.
   b. Press Ctrl + R to open the Import dialog box.
   c. With Files of type set to GIF Image (*.gif), double-click the file named FirstChoiceLogo.gif.
   d. With the imported image selected on the stage, click the Free Transform tool and the Scale modifier.
   e. Resize and move the image to the bottom right of the stage as shown. 
4. Convert the bitmapped logo to a vector graphic by completing the following steps:
   a. With the imported image still selected, click Modify and then click Trace Bitmap.
   b. Key **30** in the Color Threshold text box and then press Tab.
   c. Key **4** in the Minimum Area text box.
   d. Click the down arrow next to Curve Fit and then click Tight at the drop-down list.
   e. Click the down arrow next to Corner Threshold and then click Normal in the drop-down list.
   f. Click OK to close the Trace Bitmap dialog box and begin the conversion. A progress bar displays in the Tracing Bitmap dialog box as the conversion process takes place. Depending on the system resources on the computer you are using, the bitmap to vector conversion may take a few moments. When the conversion is complete, the Tracing Bitmap dialog box disappears.
   g. With the Arrow tool active, click in the workspace to deselect the converted image. 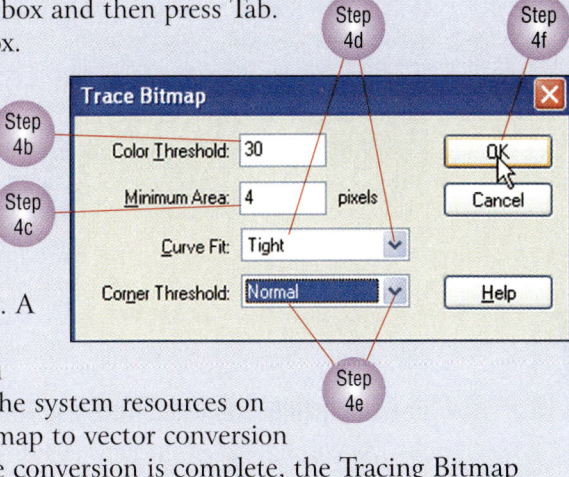
5. Modify the converted bitmap by completing the following steps:
   a. Increase magnification to 150% and scroll the stage so that the logo is prominently displayed.
   b. With the Arrow tool active, click over different colored areas of the converted graphic to see the selection area that is highlighted. Notice the various filled shapes that appear.
   c. Click over the white filled area of the image below the word *Travel*. Hold down the Shift key and then click the white filled area inside the handle of the suitcase. All white fills in the image should now be selected.
   d. Press Delete.

FLASH MX — Working with Layers, Libraries, and Importing Graphics

e. Click the Lasso tool in the toolbox.
f. Drag a selection area that surrounds the letters in the words *First Choice* at the top of the image. When you release the mouse, the letters appear selected as shown.
g. Press Delete.
h. Click the Arrow tool.
i. Change the magnification to 100% and then scroll the stage so that the document is centered within the Flash window.

6. Save the revised document using the same name (Ch3Ex16).
7. Close Ch3Ex16.

Importing Bitmaps Directly to the Library

As you have seen in the previous exercises, a bitmap that is imported using the menu sequence File and then Import causes Flash to place the bitmap in the library and also insert an instance of the bitmap on the active layer in the stage.

To import a bitmap directly into the library without a copy being placed on the stage, click File and then click Import to Library. Change the Files of type to the graphic's image format and then navigate to the drive and/or folder in which the file resides. Double-click the name of the graphic image in the file list. Open the Library panel to view the imported bitmap.

Copying and Pasting Images Using the Clipboard

Bitmaps can be added to a Flash movie via the Clipboard using the standard Windows copy and paste commands. Flash pastes a bitmap as a grouped object on the stage.

Open the source application containing the graphic that you want to duplicate and the Flash movie in which you want the graphic inserted. In the source application select the graphic, click Edit, and then Copy. Switch to Flash on the Windows Taskbar and then click Edit and Paste.

exercise 17

COPYING AND PASTING AN IMAGE USING THE CLIPBOARD

1. Open the Flash document named Easter.
2. Save the document with Save As and name it Ch3Ex17.
3. Start WordPad. (*Note: This application is available from the Accessories menu on all Windows installations.*)
4. Open the document named EasterSpecials.doc.
5. Copy and paste the picture of the bunny from WordPad to Flash by completing the following steps:
   a. Click the mouse pointer over the graphic image to select it.
   b. Click Edit on the Menu bar and then click Copy.
   c. Exit WordPad.
   d. With Flash the active application, insert a new layer and name the layer *Bunny*.
   e. With the *Bunny* layer active, click Edit and then click Paste.
   f. With the Arrow tool active, move the graphic to the left side of the stage as shown.

   Steps 5d–5f

   g. Click in the workspace to deselect the graphic.
6. Save the revised document using the same name (Ch3Ex17).
7. Close Ch3Ex17.

Importing a FreeHand Vector Graphic

Macromedia's FreeHand application is used to create more sophisticated vector drawings than is possible with Flash's drawing tools. FreeHand includes a wider array of drawing tools and options for creating graphics to be published in mediums beyond Flash's player format focus. A complex graphic may be easier for you to create in FreeHand and then import to a Flash movie. FreeHand and Flash are both included in Macromedia's Studio MX suite. Since both products are produced by Macromedia, importing a graphic from FreeHand to Flash is a smooth transition and includes more importing options than other vector drawing programs such as Adobe Illustrator.

Working with Layers, Libraries, and Importing Graphics 145

You use the same Import dialog box to import a FreeHand vector graphic as you use to import a bitmap graphic. Choose FreeHand (*.fh*,*.ft*) in the Files of type list box, navigate to the drive and/or folder in which the FreeHand drawing is stored, and then double-click the file name for the drawing in the list box. Flash displays the FreeHand Import dialog box shown in Figure 3.23.

FIGURE 3.23 **FreeHand Import Dialog Box**

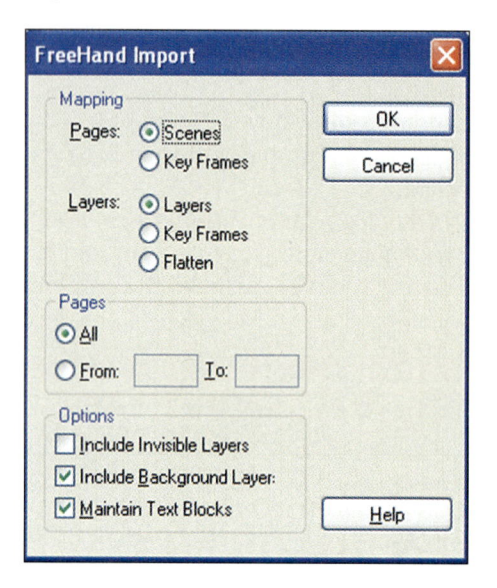

The Mapping section of the FreeHand Import dialog box allows you to control whether each new page in the FreeHand file is imported to Flash as a new scene or a new keyframe. FreeHand files containing multiple layers can be imported with the individual layers intact, with each layer converted to a new keyframe, or with all of the objects on the multiple layers flattened to a single layer.

The Pages section is used to specify all pages or a range of pages within the FreeHand file to be imported. The Options section contains three check boxes to include invisible and background layers and to maintain text blocks so that they can be edited within Flash.

Flash provides the following pointers to ensure a smooth FreeHand graphic import:

- Place multiple overlapping objects that you want to preserve as separate objects in Flash on separate layers in the FreeHand file and make sure you choose Layers in the Mapping section of the FreeHand Import dialog box.

- Flash supports up to eight colors in a gradient fill while FreeHand supports more than eight color changes. Restrict a graphic in FreeHand that you know will be imported to Flash to only eight color changes in a gradient to minimize the file size.

- An imported file containing grayscale images is converted to RGB images in Flash. This can cause the imported file's size to increase.

A graphic in a FreeHand Version 7 or higher file can also be inserted into Flash by dragging and dropping the object from the FreeHand window into the Flash window. Symbols created in FreeHand Versions 9 and higher are automatically added to the library in Flash when the file is imported.

exercise 18

IMPORTING A FREEHAND VECTOR GRAPHIC INTO FLASH

1. Open the Flash document named CheckList.
2. Save the document with Save As and name it Ch3Ex18.
3. Import a graphic of a stop sign drawn in FreeHand by completing the following steps:
   a. With *Text* the active layer, press Ctrl + R to open the Import dialog box.
   b. Click the down arrow next to Files of type and then click *FreeHand (*.fh*,*.ft*)* at the pop-up list. 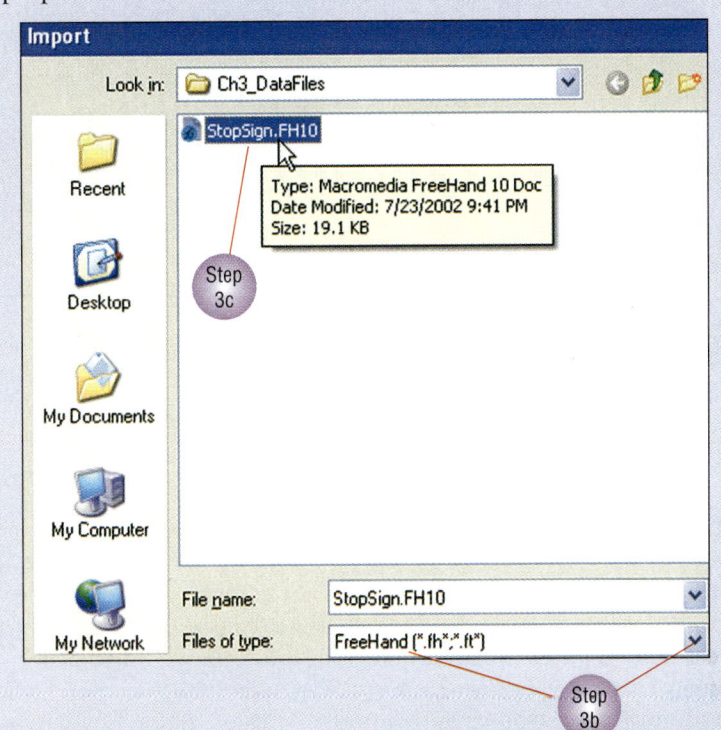
   c. Double-click the file named StopSign.FH10.
   d. If necessary, deselect the Include Background Layer: check box in the Options section of the FreeHand Import dialog box.
   e. Click OK. The imported graphic is inserted on the stage in a new layer that has been automatically added in the Timeline named *Foreground*.
4. Rename the Foreground layer *StopSign*.
5. Move and resize the stop sign graphic by completing the following steps:

Working with Layers, Libraries, and Importing Graphics 147

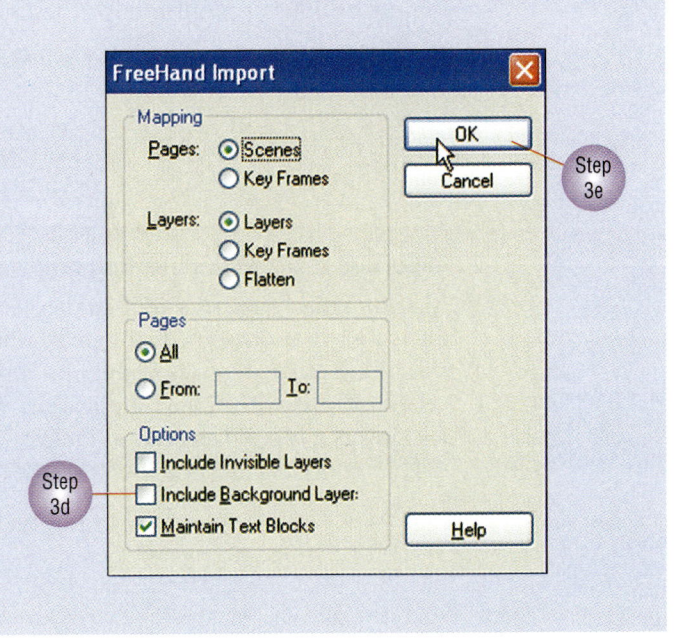

a. With *StopSign* the active layer and both the hexagon and the text block selected, press Ctrl + G to group the two objects.
b. Move and resize the graphic as shown.

Step 5b

6. Remove the guides and rulers.
7. Save the revised file using the same name (Ch3Ex18).
8. Close Ch3Ex18.

Importing Other Vector Graphics Files

Adobe Illustrator files in Version 8.0 format or earlier can be imported into Flash with layers preserved, converted to keyframes, or flattened to a single layer. After an Illustrator file has been imported into Flash, ungroup all of the objects on all of the layers in order to edit an object just as you would edit any other Flash drawing. When Files of type is set to *Adobe Illustrator (*.eps,*.ai)* and an Adobe file is opened, Flash displays the Illustrator Import Settings dialog box where you can select the import options appropriate for the image you are bringing into Flash.

If the vector graphic drawing program that you used to create an image does not appear in the Files of type pop-up list, it does not mean the graphic is not able to be recognized by Flash. Most of the drawing programs on the market today allow graphics to be exported in the Flash *swf* format. In the source program, export the file containing the graphic in *swf* format and then import the *swf* file into Flash.

Importing a Fireworks Drawing into Flash

Macromedia Fireworks MX is also part of the Macromedia Studio MX suite. Fireworks is an image editing program used to create interactive graphics for Web sites. One of the reasons Fireworks is popular is its ability to edit both bitmap and vector objects within one application. Fireworks files are saved in *png* format. Flash recognizes a *png* file created in Fireworks upon importing and presents the Fireworks PNG Import Settings dialog box shown in Figure 3.24.

FIGURE

3.24 *Fireworks PNG Import Settings Dialog Box*

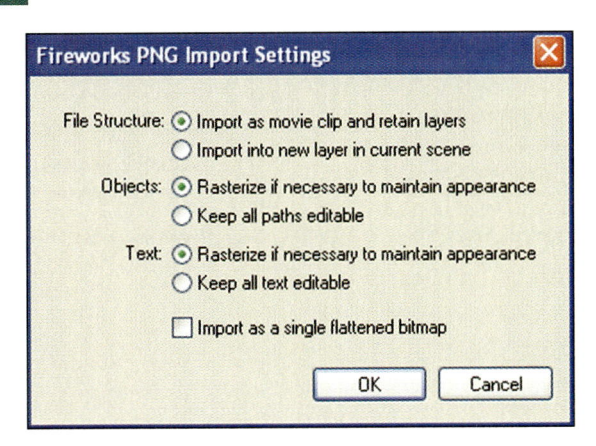

In the File Structure section, choose to import the file as a movie clip with layers preserved or as a new layer in the current scene. Graphic and text objects within the file can be rasterized (converted to a single bitmap image) or kept as separate editable objects with vectors retaining their format. Alternatively, you can choose to import the image as a single flattened bitmapped object. A Fireworks graphic imported into Flash as a flattened image can be edited by selecting the image, launching Fireworks within Flash, and then editing the object with the original *png* file.

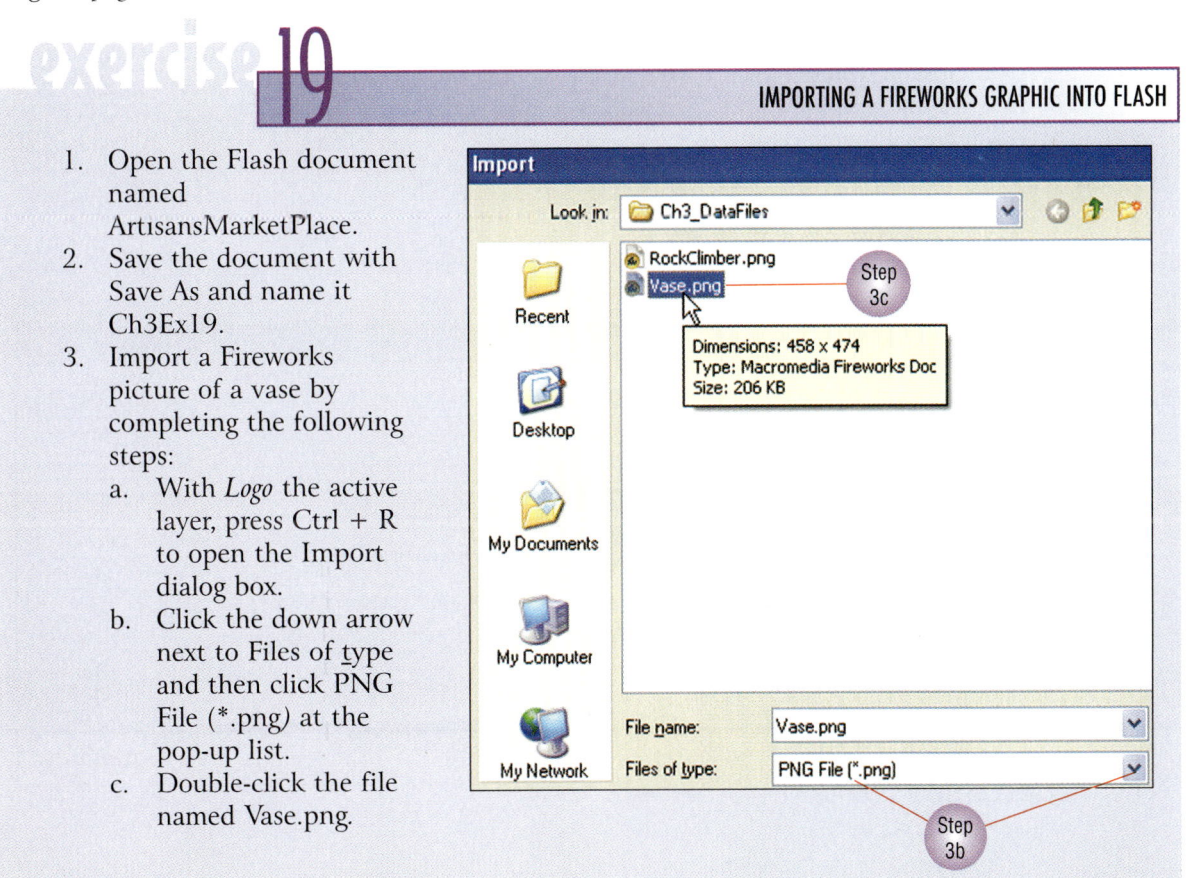

exercise 19 — IMPORTING A FIREWORKS GRAPHIC INTO FLASH

1. Open the Flash document named ArtisansMarketPlace.
2. Save the document with Save As and name it Ch3Ex19.
3. Import a Fireworks picture of a vase by completing the following steps:
   a. With *Logo* the active layer, press Ctrl + R to open the Import dialog box.
   b. Click the down arrow next to Files of type and then click PNG File (*.png) at the pop-up list.
   c. Double-click the file named Vase.png.

149

Working with Layers, Libraries, and Importing Graphics

d. If necessary, click *Import into new layer in current scene* in the File Structure section of the Fireworks PNG Import Settings dialog box.
e. If necessary, click *Keep all paths editable* in the Objects section of the Fireworks PNG Import Settings dialog box.
f. Click OK. The picture of the vase is added to the Flash movie in a new layer that has been automatically named *Fireworks PNG*. The vase picture is one of the sample graphics provided with Fireworks.

4. Decrease the magnification to 75%. Move the text blocks and logo, resize, and move the picture as shown.

5. Rename the bitmap in the Library and change the compression settings by completing the following steps:
   a. Press F11 to open the Library panel.
   b. Right-click Bitmap 1 and then click Properties at the shortcut menu.
   c. Key **Vase** in the name text box in the Bitmap Properties dialog box with Bitmap 1 selected.
   d. Click the down arrow next to <u>C</u>ompression and then click Lossless (PNG/GIF) at the drop-down list.
   e. Click <u>T</u>est to view the compressed file size.
   f. Click OK to close the Bitmap Properties dialog box.
   g. Close the Library panel.

6. Save the revised document using the same name (Ch3Ex19).

7. Close Ch3Ex19.

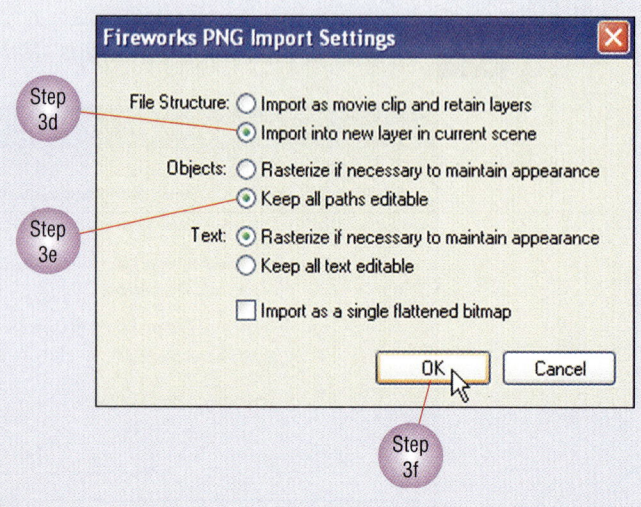

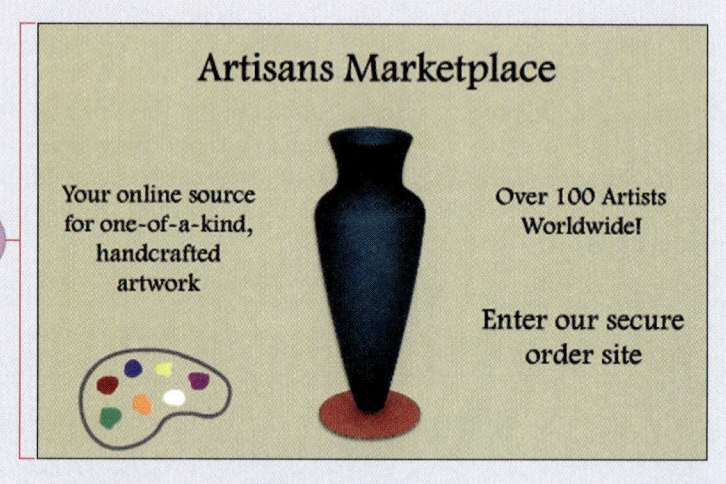

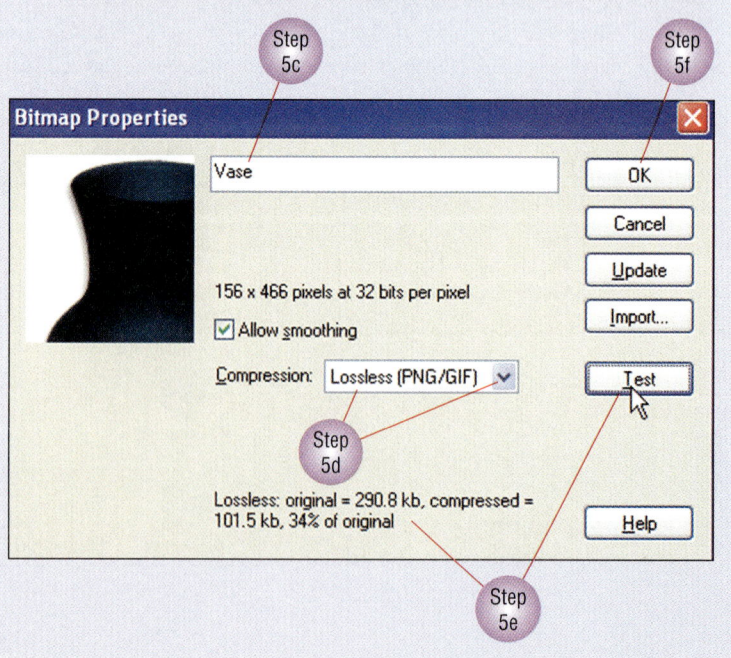

150 Chapter Three

Reducing File Size and Increasing Efficiency by Optimizing Graphics

When a Flash document contains imported graphics or graphics drawn within Flash with many vector curves, the file size and system processing required to display the movie increases. Reducing the number of curves within the file is a good idea to make the movie smaller and more efficient.

To do this, select the object in which you want to reduce curves, click Modify and then click Optimize to open the Optimize Curves dialog box shown in Figure 3.25. If the object to be optimized was drawn or imported as a group, ungroup the object before optimizing it.

FIGURE 3.25 *Optimize Curves Dialog Box*

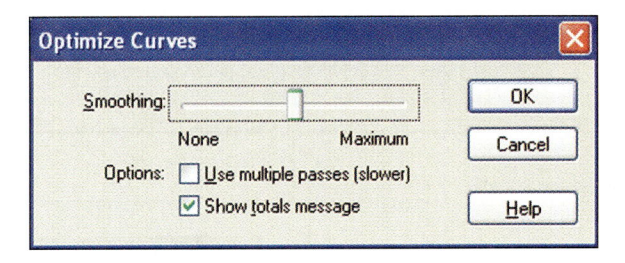

Drag the Smoothing slider to increase or decrease the amount by which you want Flash to optimize the object. Click the *Use multiple passes (slower)* check box in the Options section if you want Flash to continue optimizing the vector graphic until the curves cannot be further reduced. *Show totals message* displays a message similar to the one shown in Figure 3.26 indicating the amount of reduction that has taken place.

FIGURE 3.26 *Show Totals Message Box for Optimized Object*

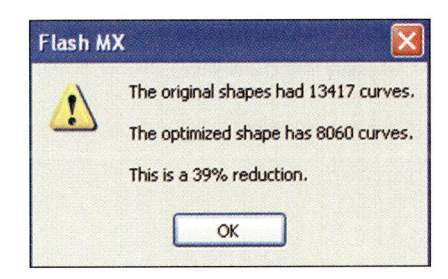

Working with Layers, Libraries, and Importing Graphics 151

exercise 20

OPTIMIZING A VECTOR GRAPHIC

1. Open Ch3Ex16.
2. Select and then optimize the logo at the bottom right of the movie by completing the following steps:
   a. With the Arrow tool active, draw a selection box around the travel logo at the bottom right of the stage. This selects all of the vector shapes in the converted graphic.
   b. Click <u>M</u>odify and then click <u>O</u>ptimize.
   c. Drag the <u>S</u>moothing slider left of the middle towards None as shown. Dragging the slider left reduces the number of smoothened curves in the optimized graphic.
   d. If necessary, click the *Show totals message* check box to select it.
   e. Click OK.
   f. Click OK at the Flash MX message box indicating the reduction that has been achieved. *(Note: The reduction values in your box may vary.)*
   g. Click in the workspace to deselect the image.
3. Optimize the picture of the canal at the top left of the stage by completing the following steps:
   a. Click over the picture of the canal to select it.
   b. Click <u>M</u>odify and then click <u>O</u>ptimize.
   c. Drag the <u>S</u>moothing slider to the middle between None and Maximum.
   d. Click OK.
   e. Click OK at the Flash MX message box indicating a 49% reduction has been achieved. Notice the curves around the edges of the picture have been smoothened out from their original shapes.
   f. Click in the workspace to deselect the picture.
4. Save the revised document using the same name (Ch3Ex16).
5. Close Ch3Ex16.

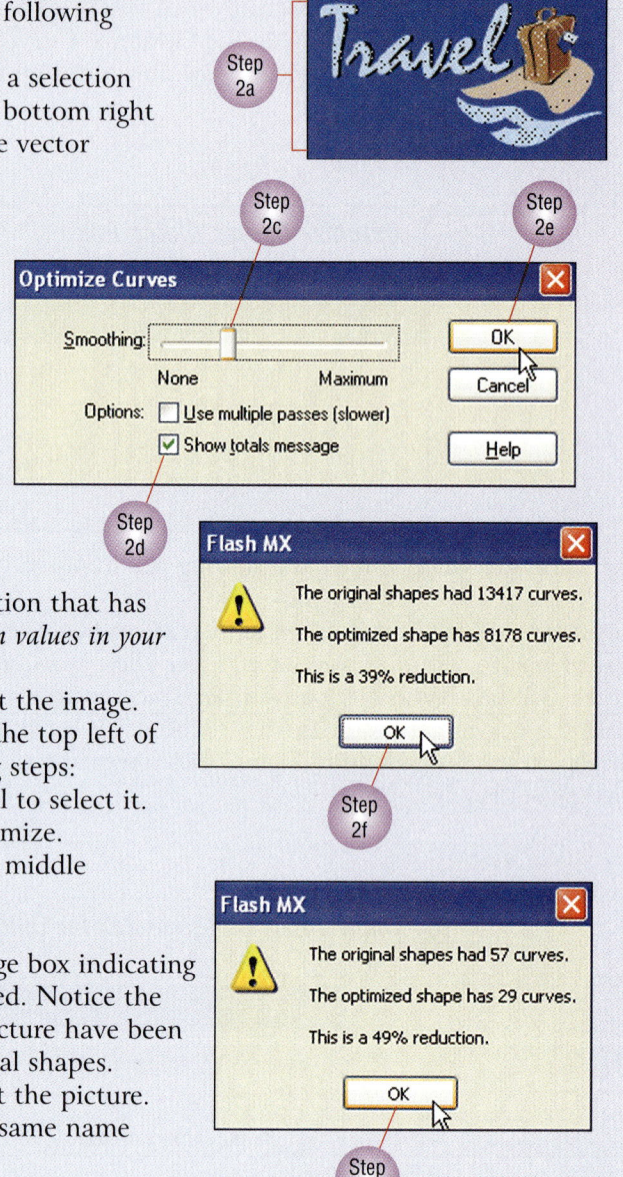

Depending on the settings in the Optimize Curves dialog box, an object's appearance can be noticeably changed after optimization. If the results are not acceptable use the Undo feature to restore the object to its original state and then experiment with a different <u>S</u>moothing setting.

152 Chapter Three

Sources of Artwork for Flash

While Flash and the companion applications FreeHand and Fireworks provide drawing tools with which you can create your own artwork, it is not always possible or feasible for you to create your own graphics. In this chapter you have learned how to import bitmaps and vectors from other applications. However, you may want to include a graphic in a Flash movie for which you do not have a bitmap or vector picture. In this case, use the Internet to find a graphic resource. Several sites offer downloadable graphics for free or for a small fee. Launch your favorite search engine and then use the keywords "free graphics" or "free clipart."

Some sites require that you register before downloading a graphic image. Be sure to read carefully the privacy policy of the site before providing any personal information in the registration form. If you find a graphic that you want to use, be sure to read the terms of use policy or look for some other restriction policy as the permitted uses vary greatly from site to site. If you are in doubt as to the usability of a graphic from a site, do not download and use it in your Flash movie.

Following is a list of Web sites that provide databases of graphics or maintain a portal of links to sites with free graphics:

- www.freegraphics.com
- www.clipart.com
- www.allfreeclipart.com

These sites are provided as a starting point only for your search: do not consider this list comprehensive nor consider these sites endorsed by the author or publisher. Free sites contain a lot of advertising and pop-up windows which allow the organization to generate revenue that pays for the free service. Be aware of these factors when using the Internet to find a free graphic.

CHAPTER summary

- Layers are used in Flash to organize images, sounds, videos, animations, or any other elements contained in the Flash movie.
- Layers are stacked with the topmost layer in the Timeline overlapping objects within the layers below it.
- New layers are inserted above the active layer.
- Rename a layer by double-clicking the layer name in the Timeline, keying the new name, and then pressing Enter.
- Objects in a single layer can be selected, cut or copied, and pasted to other layers.
- Drag a layer up or down in the Timeline to reposition it in the stacking order.
- Deleting a layer removes the layer from the Timeline and any associated content on the stage.
- Use the Show/Hide All Layers column in the Timeline to temporarily remove the display on the stage of all content or content on individual layers, or redisplay hidden content.
- Use the Lock/Unlock All Layers column in the Timeline to prevent changes to objects on all layers or individual layers, or unlock a locked layer.
- Display objects on all layers or on individual layers in Outline mode using the Show All Layers as Outlines column in the Timeline.
- The Distribute to Layers option on the Modify menu is used to split objects on a single layer into separate individual layers.
- A masked layer partially conceals objects in the linked layer immediately below the mask.
- Filled objects on the mask layer provide the window with which overlapped objects below the mask filter through to the stage.
- Flash automatically locks the mask layer and the linked layer when the mask is created.
- A guide layer is used to assist with the placement and alignment of objects in the authoring process. This type of guide layer is not exported when the movie is published.
- A motion guide layer is used to direct the path along which a connected object on another layer will travel during an animation. A motion guide layer is exported when the movie is published but is not visible to the end user.
- Related layers can be grouped together and displayed below a layer folder in the Timeline.
- Every Flash document includes a library which is used to store reusable objects.
- A *symbol* is a drawn object that you want to reuse in either the current movie or another movie.
- Each occurrence of a symbol on the stage is called an *instance*.
- Using symbols reduces file size and ensures consistency when editing objects.
- Click New Symbol on the Insert menu to create a new symbol from scratch in symbol editing mode.
- Display the Library panel to drag instances of a symbol to the stage.
- Instances of a symbol can be modified without affecting the master copy of the object.
- Double-click an instance or right-click a symbol name in the Library panel and then click Edit to make changes to the master copy of the symbol.

- An existing object can be converted to a symbol using the Convert to Symbol option on the Insert menu.
- Click File and then click Open as Library to open the library file of another movie and use a symbol.
- A copy of a symbol from another movie's library is automatically copied to the current movie's library when an instance is dragged to the stage.
- Flash includes common library files containing objects that you are free to use.
- Add your own common library to the menu by creating the symbols you want to share in a Flash document and then storing the fla file in the path *C:\Program Files\Macromedia\Flash MX\First Run\Libraries*.
- Group related symbols in folders that can be expanded and collapsed in the Library panel.
- Open the Import dialog box to insert pictures created outside Flash into the active layer in the current movie.
- Click the down arrow next to the Files of type list box in the Import dialog box to choose the file format of the graphic which you want to import.
- Imported bitmaps are automatically stored in the library.
- Each imported bitmap has a set of properties associated with it.
- Smoothing and compression options in the Bitmap Properties dialog box allow you to control the quality and file size of a selected image.
- Click the Test button in the Bitmap Properties dialog box to view the change in picture quality and file size before accepting changes.
- A bitmapped image can be broken apart and then edited by changing colors for a portion of the image using the Magic Wand modifier of the Lasso tool.
- A broken apart bitmap can become the fill of a closed shape.
- Click Modify and then Trace Bitmap to convert a bitmap to a vector graphic.
- Flash converts a bitmap to a vector graphic by analyzing the pixels in the bitmap and then creating vector shapes from adjacent pixels that are considered to be the same color based on the color threshold setting.
- Click File and then Import to Library to import a bitmap directly to the current movie's library.
- Images can be inserted into Flash using the standard Windows copy and paste commands.
- Import FreeHand vector graphics into Flash with control over how layers and pages are converted in the Flash movie.
- Adobe Illustrator vector graphics can be imported into Flash with control over the placement of layers.
- Other vector graphics can be imported by converting to the Flash *swf* player format in the source program.
- Fireworks graphics can be imported to Flash as *png* files with layers and editable objects intact or as a single flattened bitmapped object.
- Optimize vector graphics within Flash to reduce file size and increase processing efficiency.
- Artwork can be downloaded from the Internet for free or for a small fee if you do not have a current picture or graphic resource.

COMMANDS review

Command or Feature	Mouse/Keyboard	Shortcut Keys
Break apart a bitmap	Modify, Break Apart	Ctrl + B
Copy selected object	Edit, Copy	Ctrl + C
Convert bitmap to vector graphic	Modify, Trace Bitmap	
Convert object to symbol	Insert, Convert to Symbol	F8
Create new symbol	Insert, New Symbol	Ctrl + F8
Cut selected object	Edit, Cut	Ctrl + X
Display Common Library panel	Window, Common Libraries	
Display Library panel	Window, Library	F11
Distribute objects to layers	Modify, Distribute to Layers	Ctrl + Shift + D
Exit symbol editing mode	Edit, Edit Document	Ctrl + E
Import graphics	File, Import	Ctrl + R
Import graphics to library	File, Import to Library	
Insert layer	Insert, Layer	
Insert layer folder	Insert, Layer Folder	
Layer Properties	Modify, Layer	
Open library from another movie	File, Open as Library	Ctrl + Shift + O
Optimize selected object	Modify, Optimize	Ctrl + Alt + Shift + C
Paste object from Clipboard	Edit, Paste	Ctrl + V

CONCEPTS check

Indicate the correct term or command for each item.

1. This term refers to the hierarchy of layers.
2. A hidden layer displays with this indicator in the Show/Hide column next to the layer name.
3. This icon next to a layer name in the Lock/Unlock column indicates the contents of the layer cannot be edited.
4. Define a layer as this type to partially conceal content on the linked layer below the active layer.

5. Objects drawn on this type of layer are not exported in the published movie.
6. Group a set of related layers in this type of layer.
7. This is the term for an occurrence of a symbol on the stage.
8. The plus symbol in the center of the stage in symbol editing mode is called this.
9. Click the Back button or this in the Information bar to exit symbol editing mode.
10. Click this option on the File menu to open the library of another movie.
11. Click this option on the Window menu to view the libraries created by Macromedia that are available for all movies.
12. This view in the Library panel displays additional information about a symbol such as the date it was last modified.
13. Display this dialog box for an imported bitmap to test the file compression using different quality settings.
14. This is the term for the software technique where jagged edges in a bitmap are smoothened by surrounding the edges with shades of gray or color.
15. Colors within a broken apart bitmap can be selected using the Lasso tool with this modifier in the Options section of the toolbox.
16. Two adjacent pixels are considered the same color if their RGB values are less than the value in this text box in the Trace Bitmap dialog box.
17. Import a bitmap using this option on the File menu if you do not want a copy of the picture placed on the stage at the time of importing.
18. A FreeHand graphic file opened from the Import dialog box causes this additional dialog box to open with options for controlling the conversion in Flash.
19. A vector drawing for which the file format is not in the Files of type pop-up list in the Import dialog box can be imported to Flash by exporting the drawing in this format from the source program.
20. Fireworks files are saved in this format.
21. Open this dialog box to reduce the number of curves in a file in order to decrease file size and process the drawing more efficiently.
22. Read these policies carefully before downloading a free graphic from the Internet for use in a Flash movie.

SKILLS check

Assessment 1

1. Open the Flash document named Sailboat.
2. Save the document with Save As and name it Ch3SA1.
3. Use the Free Transform tool and the Scale modifier to resize the sailboat to approximately half of its current size and then move the object to the left side of the stage.
4. Rename Layer 1 *Sailboat1*.
5. Insert a new layer and name the new layer *Sailboat2*.
6. Copy and paste the sailboat graphic from *Sailboat1* to *Sailboat2* and then move the object on *Sailboat2* to the right side of the stage.
7. Save the document using the same name (Ch3SA1).

8. Select, ungroup the sailboat object on the *Sailboat2* layer, and then make the following changes to the graphic:
    - Change the stroke and fill colors of the sails.
    - Change the colors of the stripes on the second sail.
    - Open the Color Mixer panel and then create and apply a custom gradient fill to the bottom of the boat.
9. Regroup the sailboat object on the *Sailboat2* layer and then lock the layer.
10. Change the background color of the stage to a light blue color swatch.
11. Save the revised document using the same name (Ch3SA1).
12. Close Ch3SA1.

Assessment 2

1. Open Ch2SA4.
2. Save the document with Save As and name it Ch3SA2.
3. Select the three ladybugs and the text block.
4. Use the Distribute to Layers command to distribute each object to a separate layer.
5. Rename the layers as follows:
    - Rename the layer with the text block *OrgName*.
    - Rename the layer with the ladybug at the top facing downwards *TopBug*.
    - Rename the layer with the ladybug at the middle left *MiddleBug*.
    - Rename the layer with the ladybug at the bottom facing upwards *BottomBug*.
6. Create a new layer folder and name it *LadyBugs*.
7. Move the three layers *TopBug*, *MiddleBug*, and *BottomBug* into the layer folder LadyBugs.
8. Collapse the LadyBugs layer folder.
9. Delete the layer named *Layer1*.
10. Save the revised document using the same name (Ch3SA2).
11. Close Ch3SA2.

Assessment 3

FIGURE 3.27 *Mask Layer in Assessment 3*

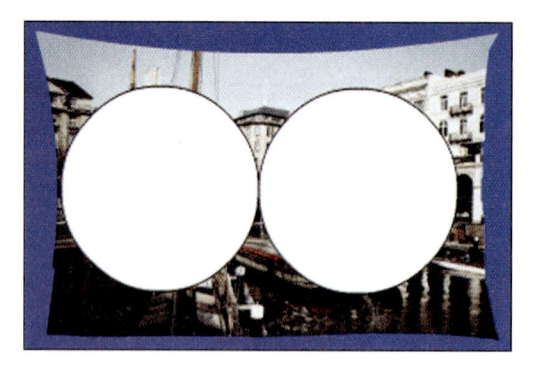

1. Open Ch3Ex16.
2. Save the document with Save As and name it Ch3SA3.
3. Insert a new layer above the layer named *Picture* and name the new layer *Mask*.
4. Hide the *Logo* and *Text* layers.
5. With *Mask* the active layer, draw two circles over the picture as shown in Figure 3.27.
6. Designate the layer named *Mask* as a mask layer.

7. Unhide the *Logo* and *Text* layers.
8. Save the revised document using the same name (Ch3SA3).
9. Close Ch3SA3.

Assessment 4

FIGURE 3.28 *Assessment 4*

1. Open Ch3Ex06.
2. Save the document with Save As and name it Ch3SA4.
3. Delete the guide layer from the stage.
4. Unlock the *Poison Ivy* layer.
5. Convert the Poison Ivy graphic object to a graphic symbol and name the symbol Poison Ivy.
6. Change the background color of the stage to a light green color swatch.
7. Rename the Poison Ivy layer *Ivy1*.
8. Insert five new layers above *Ivy1* and name each layer Ivy# where # represents the next sequence of Ivy.
9. Create a layer folder named Poison Ivy and then move *Ivy1* through *Ivy6* into the new folder. *(Hint: Resize the Timeline panel to facilitate the moving of the layers.)*
10. Display the Library panel and drag an instance of the Poison Ivy symbol to each Ivy layer.
11. Close the Library panel.
12. Move, resize, and rotate instances as shown in Figure 3.28 leaving enough space at the top, left, and right of the stage to add trees in Steps 13–16. *(Hint: Hide other layers as necessary while working with an instance.)*
13. Insert a new layer above the layer folder Poison Ivy and name it *Trees*.
14. Draw a tree at the left side of the stage next to the poison ivy and then group the tree shape.
15. Convert the tree to a graphic symbol and name the symbol Tree.
16. Open the Library panel, insert three instances of the tree across the stage on the *Trees* layer, and then move the *Trees* layer to the bottom of the stacking order.
17. Redisplay any hidden layers and then save the revised document using the same name (Ch3SA4).
18. Close Ch3SA4.

Assessment 5

FIGURE 3.29 *Assessment 5*

1. Start a new Flash document.
2. Change the background color of the stage to a light yellow color swatch.
3. Open the library from the document named Ch3Ex10.
4. Create the document shown in Figure 3.29 using the following information:
    - Insert a layer folder and name it Pandas.
    - Insert a layer folder and name it Bamboo.
    - Each instance of panda or bamboo should be inserted on a separate layer named *Panda#* and *Bamboo#* where # is the next in sequence and moved into the appropriate folder.
    - Lock the Panda and Bamboo layer folders once you have completed the graphics.
5. Create the text blocks on a new layer named *Text* at the top of the stacking order. You determine the text properties.
6. Save the document and name it Ch3SA5.
7. Close Ch3SA5.

Assessment 6

FIGURE 3.30 *Assessment 6*

1. Start a new Flash document.
2. Change the background color of the stage to a dark blue color swatch.
3. Create the document shown in Figure 3.30 using the following information:
    - The picture of the skiers is in *jpeg* format and is named DownHillSkiers.
    - The picture of the resort is in *jpeg* format and is named MountainResort.
    - Each picture should be imported on a separate layer.
    - Create the text blocks on a separate layer. You determine the text properties.
    - Break apart the picture of the skiers. Use the Lasso tool to delete the fill at the top of the picture above the mountain peaks and use the Eraser tool to delete the snow at the bottom.
    - Optimize the picture of the skiers with the smoothing slider set in the middle between None and Maximum.
    - Break apart the picture of the resort on top of the mountain and then use the Arrow tool to curve the edges.
    - Lock all of the layers when the document is complete.
    - Display the Bitmap Properties for MountainResort.jpg and then compress the file size. You determine the quality value to use to compress the picture as much as possible without sacrificing the quality.
4. Save the document and name it Ch3SA6.
5. Close Ch3SA6.

Assessment 7

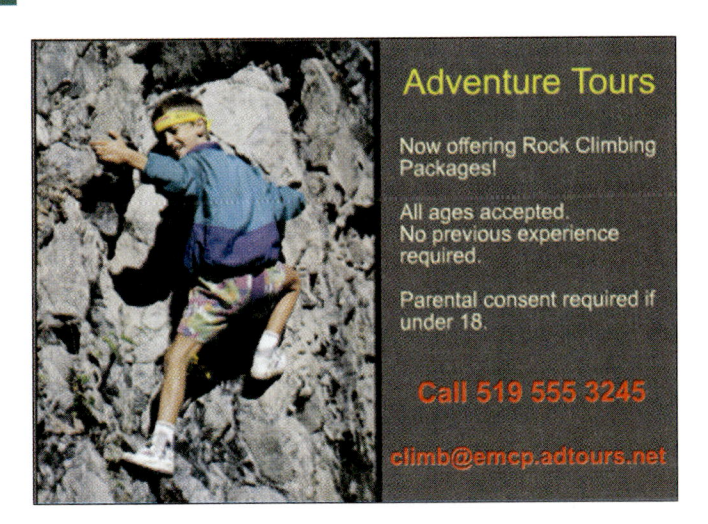

FIGURE 3.31 *Assessment 7*

1. Start a new Flash document.
2. Change the background color of the stage to a dark gray color swatch.
3. Create the document shown in Figure 3.31 using the following information:
    - Import the Fireworks file named RockClimber.png using the following options in the Fireworks PNG Import Settings dialog box:
        o Import into new layer in current scene.
        o Keep all paths editable.
        o Keep all text editable.

- Change the color of text in the text blocks and move the text blocks as shown.
- Rename the bitmap in the library Climber and then change the compression setting to Lossless PNG/GIF.

4. Save the document and name it Ch3SA7.
5. Close Ch3SA7.

CHAPTER 4

CREATING ANIMATION AND GUIDELINES FOR FLASH PROJECT DESIGN

PERFORMANCE OBJECTIVES

Upon successful completion of Chapter 4, you will be able to:
- Describe the difference between frame-by-frame animation and tweened animation.
- Create and edit a motion tweened animation.
- Distinguish between regular frames, keyframes, and tweened frames in the Timeline.
- Rotate and scale a motion tween.
- Ease in and Ease out a motion tween.
- Create a motion guide to move an object along a path other than a straight line.
- Change the color of an object in a motion tween.
- Add keyframes in a motion tween.
- Insert, move, copy, and delete frames and keyframes.
- Preview animations using scrubbing and looped techniques.
- Create and edit a shape tweened animation.
- Add shape hints to a shape tweened animation.
- Change the frame rate to slow down or speed up an animation.
- Create and edit a frame-by-frame animation.
- Use onion skin tools to view and edit multiple frames in an animation.
- Change frame view options.
- Describe the role of scenes in a Flash movie.
- Insert, rename, delete, duplicate, and rearrange scenes.
- Define a project's goals and limiting factors.
- Determine the audience for a Flash movie.
- Describe how to research best practices for Flash projects.
- List elements to be included in a flow chart and storyboard for a movie.

Flash MX Chapter 04

There are nine student data files to copy for this chapter.

In Chapter 1 you learned that animation is achieved by showing a series of images, each slightly different from each other, which when played back at a high speed create the illusion of movement. In Flash, this illusion is accomplished by inserting keyframes in the Timeline and then modifying the content on the stage. Recall the analogy of the Timeline being the script for your movie; the Timeline is comprised of a set of sequential frames for each layer along a time-based continuum where you control what the user will see at each point in time when the movie is played.

The animations created in Chapter 1 were designed to introduce the Timeline, frames, and keyframes. In this chapter, you will learn to work with the Timeline more extensively by managing frames and keyframes and how the Timeline's tools assist you with creating animations. You will also learn how Flash can do some of the work of generating frame content to reduce your workload. Flash is exciting and fun to use particularly when creating animations which bring Web pages and other CD-ROM-based content to life.

Once you have mastered the basic tools for drawing, importing graphics, and animation it is a good idea to step back from Flash and consider what you have learned and how it can be applied to basic design guidelines. For example, choosing appropriate colors or fonts for viewing on computer screens is just as important as the graphic or stunning animation that you spent hours perfecting in a movie. Managing a Flash project involves more than sitting at the computer drawing objects or creating animations. In fact, the time spent in Flash is dependent on how much time you spend *beforehand* on the planning and design considerations.

Techniques for Creating Animation

Animation can be created in Flash using either a frame-by-frame or tweened approach. *Frame-by-frame* animation is a technique in which you manually create each change in the movie in a separate frame. As you learned in Chapter 1, content is changed by inserting *keyframes* in the Timeline. Traditional animation employed the frame-by-frame technique where artists had to draw each change in a character and then the series of drawings were captured on film. Imagine the number of drawings required to create a classic movie such as Snow White or your favorite Saturday morning cartoon. In Flash, frame-by-frame animations are suited to movies where the images on the stage are complex, require quick movement, or need subtle changes. Each inserted keyframe adds to the file size of the published movie since Flash has to store the values for each complete frame. This factor combined with the tedium of drawing successive keyframes causes some people to avoid frame-by-frame animation whenever possible. You will learn techniques such as duplicating frames, converting to keyframes, and shortcut keys that will help make creating frame-by-frame animations more efficient.

In a *tweened* animation you create only two keyframes: the appearance of the stage at the beginning and at the end of the animation. Based upon the elapsed time from the start to finish keyframes, Flash creates the frames in between the keyframes called *interpolated frames*. Tweened animations are faster to create and use less file space since two complete frame values and only the changes in values between the two keyframes are stored. Use tweened animations for objects which move smoothly along a path.

Two types of tweened animations are available—motion and shape. *Motion tweens* move an object from one location on the stage to another and can change the object's position, size, rotation, or color as it moves. Motion tweens can be applied to a grouped object, instance, or text block and are limited to a single object in the keyframe; therefore, each object to be animated should reside in a separate layer. A grouped object included in a motion tween is automatically converted to a symbol named *Tween #* where # represents the next tweened object in sequence. For this reason, it is better to convert the object to a symbol before animating so that you can give it a name that more appropriately describes the symbol.

In a *shape tween*, the object is gradually transformed from one shape into another in a process known as *morphing*. For example, a rectangle in the first keyframe can be morphed into a hexagon in the ending keyframe. In shape tweens, the object cannot be a symbol or group for Flash to be able to create the morphing frames between the start and finish keyframes.

Creating a Motion Tweened Animation

A simple motion tween is fast and easy to create as seen by the following steps:

1. Create the object on the stage that you want to animate in the starting keyframe and convert the object to a symbol. Make sure the object resides in a separate layer from other objects on the stage.
2. Insert a keyframe in the Timeline where you want the object to end in the animation.
3. Move the instance to the ending location with the keyframe active that you created in Step 2.
4. Select the starting keyframe and change the frame properties to motion tween.
5. Preview the animation.

A new Flash document automatically has a keyframe created in frame 1 of *Layer 1*; therefore, to animate an object starting in frame 1, you need only insert a keyframe at the ending point in the Timeline.

Each layer has its own set of frames associated with it. In multi-layered movies, prior to inserting the keyframe for the motion tweened object in Step 2, you would first insert frames for all of the layers at the point in the Timeline that you want the tweened animation to end. This ensures that content from all other layers appears in the movie throughout the animation.

exercise 1

CREATING A MOTION TWEENED ANIMATION

1. Open the Flash document named Beachball.
2. Save the document with Save As and name it Ch4Ex01.
3. Make sure the Properties panel is collapsed and the current magnification is set to 100%.
4. Convert the beach ball graphic to a symbol by completing the following steps:
   a. With the Arrow tool active, click the beach ball object on the stage. The object has already been grouped.
   b. Press F8 to convert the object to a symbol.

c. Key **Beachball** in the Name text box of the Convert to Symbol dialog box.
d. If necessary, click Graphic in the Behavior section of the Convert to Symbol dialog box.
e. Click OK.

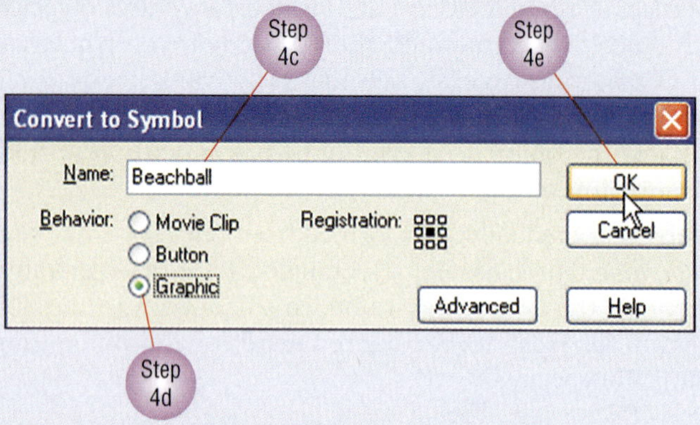

5. Create a motion tween animation to progressively move the ball from the left side of the stage to the right side by completing the following steps:
   a. Click in the Timeline below frame 24. At the default frame rate of 12 frames per second, this means the animation will last 2 seconds. A selected frame displays with blue highlighting in the frame box.
   b. Click Insert and then click Keyframe. Flash displays a hollow dot in frame 24 indicating the frame is a keyframe, the content of which is currently blank. The playhead moves to frame 24 indicating the current editing on the stage will be stored in frame 24 and frame boxes from frames 1 to 24 are shaded gray. 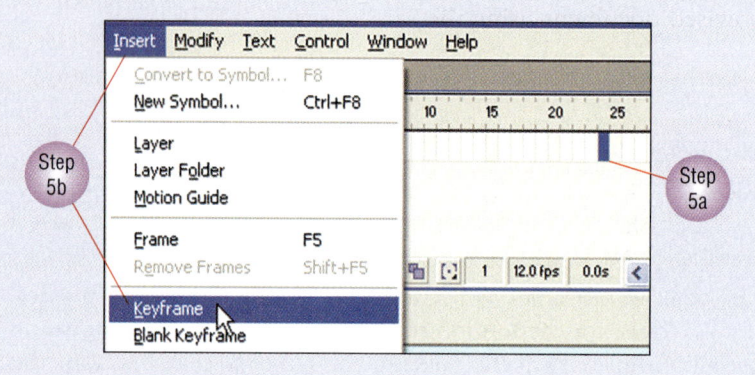
   c. With the beach ball currently selected, drag the object to the right side of the stage as shown.

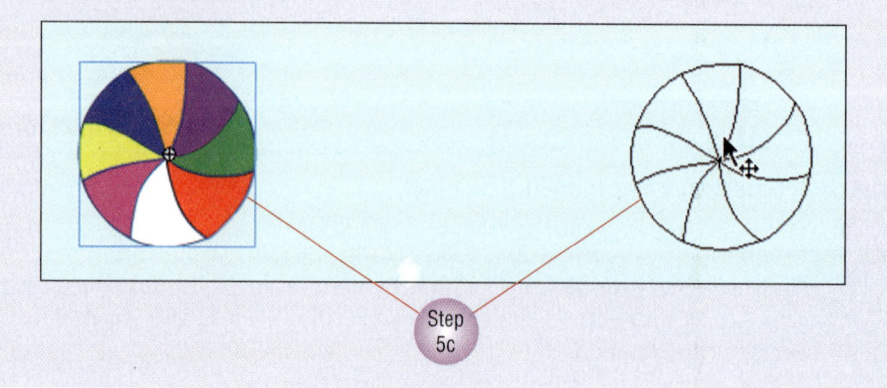

d. Click in the Timeline below frame 1. Notice the contents of the stage change to show you the position of the beach ball object at frame 1.
e. Click Insert and then click Create Motion Tween.
f. Look in the Timeline at the frame boxes between frames 1 through 24. Flash has shaded the background of the boxes light blue (almost light purple) and drawn a black arrow from frame 1 to frame 23. Moving the arrow pointer over any of these shaded frame boxes displays *Motion Tweening* in a tooltip. Also notice the keyframe in frame 24 now displays a filled dot indicating the keyframe now contains content.

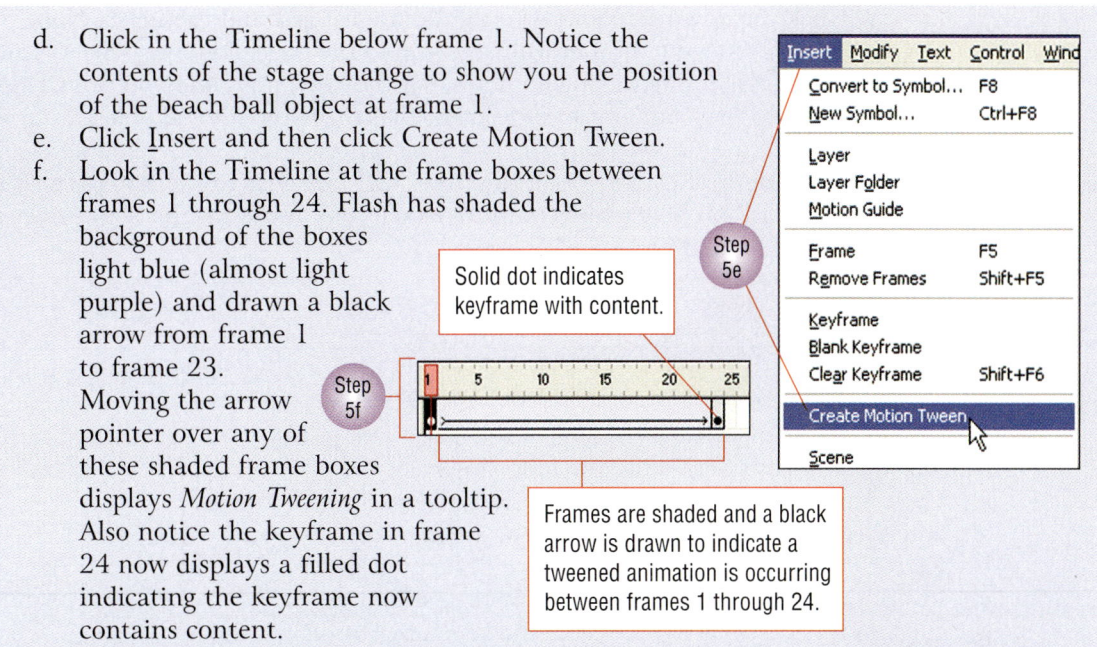

Solid dot indicates keyframe with content.

Step 5e

Step 5f

Frames are shaded and a black arrow is drawn to indicate a tweened animation is occurring between frames 1 through 24.

g. Click frame 12 in the Timeline. Notice the beach ball moves to the center of the stage between the starting and ending keyframes. Each position of the beach ball between frames 1 through 24 has been automatically calculated by Flash.
h. Click frame 1 to move the playhead back to the beginning of the animation.

6. Press Enter to preview the animation.
7. Save the revised document using the same name (Ch4Ex01).

Rotating and Scaling a Motion Tween

While moving the beach ball from the left side of the stage to the right was easy, it is not as impressive as if the ball spinned as it moved making it appear as if it were rolling across the stage. Also consider the effect of having a smaller sized beach ball at the left transform into a larger sized beach ball at the right. This could create an illusion of the ball being far away and moving closer.

With the starting keyframe in a motion tween active, expand the Properties panel to display the motion tween properties shown in Figure 4.1. By default the Scale check box is selected next to the Tween list box. This means that Flash will tween the size difference between a starting and ending keyframe in which an object has been made larger or smaller. Deselecting the Scale check box means Flash will keep the object the same size as the starting keyframe throughout the tween.

FIGURE 4.1 **Properties Panel for Motion Tween**

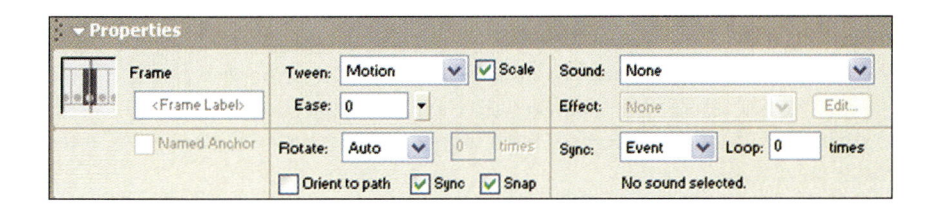

Creating Animation and Guidelines for Flash Project Design 167

Click the down arrow next to the Rotate list box and then click None, Auto, CW, or CCW at the drop-down list to rotate the tweened object. Select Auto if the object was rotated manually in one of the keyframes and you want Flash to calculate the least amount of movement to achieve the rotated object from start to finish. CW and CCW rotate the object in a clockwise (CW) or counterclockwise (CCW) motion. Key a value in the times text box next to the Rotate list box to instruct Flash on how many complete revolutions you want the object to complete during the animation.

exercise 2

SCALING AND ROTATING A TWEENED OBJECT

1. With Ch4Ex01 open, change the size of the beach ball in the starting keyframe by completing the following steps:
   a. Click frame 1 in the Timeline to activate the starting keyframe and select the beach ball object on the stage.
   b. Click the Free Transform tool and the Scale modifier.
   c. Resize the beach ball to the approximate size shown.
   d. Click in the workspace to deselect the beach ball and click the Arrow tool.
   e. Press Enter to preview the revised tweened animation. Since Scale is active by default Flash automatically tweens the object from smaller to larger throughout the animation.
2. Rotate the beach ball to make it appear as though the beach ball is rolling across the stage by completing the following steps:
   a. Click frame 1 in the Timeline to activate the starting keyframe and then expand the Properties panel.
   b. Click the down arrow next to the Rotate list box and then click CW at the drop-down list to rotate the beach ball in a clockwise direction.
   c. Drag across the value *1* in the times text box and then key **3**.
   d. Collapse the Properties panel.
   e. Press Enter to preview the revised animation.
3. Save the revised document using the same name (Ch4Ex01).

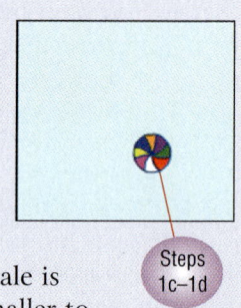

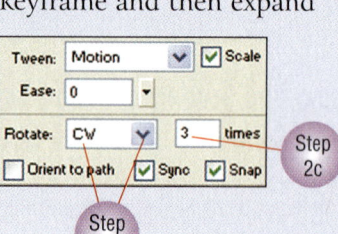

Slowing Down or Speeding Up a Motion Tween

By default, Flash evenly distributes the movements required to tween an object from the starting keyframe to the ending keyframe resulting in a constant rate of motion. Depending on the object being moved in the motion tween, you may want Flash to start off slow and then accelerate towards the end of the animation or vice versa. Click the down arrow next to Ease in the Properties panel for a motion tween to display a slider bar. Drag the slider up to enter a positive Ease value. Flash displays the word *Out* next to the Ease text box. Positive values mean the animation will start off fast and then gradually decelerate. Key a negative value in the Ease text box or drag the slider down to change the value to a negative and display the word *In* next to the Ease text box. Negative values cause the animation to start off slow and then gradually accelerate. Ease values should be in the range of 1 to 100, positive or negative.

exercise 3
CHANGING THE SPEED OF A MOTION TWEEN

1. With Ch4Ex01 open, slow down the speed at which the beach ball moves towards the end of the animation by completing the following steps:
    a. Click frame 1 in the Timeline to activate the starting keyframe and then expand the Properties panel.
    b. Click the down arrow next to Ease in the Properties panel and drag the slider up until the value *50* displays in the Ease text box and the word *Out* displays next to it.
    c. Click in the Properties panel in a blank area to close the Ease slider.
    d. With the Properties panel expanded, preview the animation. Did you notice the beach ball decelerate towards the end of the animation?
    e. Click frame 1 in the Timeline, drag across the value *50* in the Ease text box, key *100*, and then click in the stage area.
    f. Preview the animation. You should notice the speed slow down more noticeably towards the end making it appear as if the beach ball comes to more of a rolling stop.
2. Slow down the speed at which the beach ball moves at the beginning of the animation by completing the following steps:
    a. Click frame 1 in the Timeline.
    b. Drag across the value *100* in the Ease text box and then key *-100*.
    c. Click frame 1 in the Timeline. Notice the word *Out* changes to *In* next to the Ease text box.
    d. Click in the stage area and then collapse the Properties panel.
    e. Preview the animation. The beach ball appears to start off with a slow roll and then accelerates as it moves across the stage.
3. Save the document using the same name (Ch4Fx01).
4. Close Ch4Ex01.

Creating a Motion Path for an Object to Follow During Animation

By default, a tweened object moves in a straight line from the position at the starting keyframe to the position at the ending keyframe. In Chapter 3 you learned about guide layers and how to use a guide layer to position or align objects on the stage. A *motion guide* layer can be used to create a path connected to a tweened object on the layer immediately below the motion guide layer. The line or other object drawn on the motion guide layer determines the path the tweened object follows during its animation. The line is visible during the authoring process but is not visible when the movie is published for the end user.

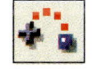

Add Motion Guide

Complete the following steps to create a motion guide path for a tweened object:
1. Make active the layer containing the tweened object.
2. Click Add Motion Guide in the Layer section of the Timeline panel.
3. Using the drawing tools, draw the path for which you want the object to follow.
4. Lock the motion guide layer to prevent accidental editing to the line.

5. Connect the tweened object to the beginning of the path by selecting the object and then dragging its center point to the beginning of the line.
6. Connect the tweened object to the end of the path by dragging its center point to the end of the line.

exercise 4 — CREATING A MOTION GUIDE FOR A TWEENED ANIMATION

1. Open the Flash document named Beachball-Guided.
2. Save the document with Save As and name it Ch4Ex04.
3. Make sure the Properties panel is collapsed and then set the Magnification to 75%. If necessary, scroll the stage so that it is centered within the window.
4. Create a motion guide layer containing a path for the beach ball to roll across the sand by completing the following steps:
   a. Make active the layer named *Beachball*.
   b. Click Add Motion Guide in the Timeline panel. Flash inserts a new layer above the *Beachball* layer, indents the *Beachball* layer below the motion guide layer, and displays the motion guide icon next to the layer name *Guide: Beachball*.
   c. Click the layer named *Guide: Beachball* to select it.
   d. Click the Pencil tool in the toolbox.
   e. Expand the Properties panel and set the following Pencil properties:
      1) Stroke color to Black.
      2) Stroke height to 3.
   f. With the Pencil tool and Smooth modifier active, draw a line following the curves in the sand similar to the one shown.

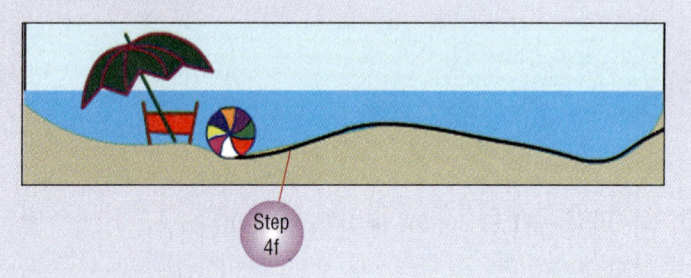

   g. Lock the *Guide: Beachball* layer.
5. Create a motion tween animation for the beach ball and connect the ball to the path on the motion guide layer by completing the following steps:
   a. Click in any frame box in the Timeline panel to activate the panel and then drag the bottom blue border of the panel down until you can see all five layer names in the Timeline. *(Note: Skip this step if you can already see all of the layers in the Timeline.)*

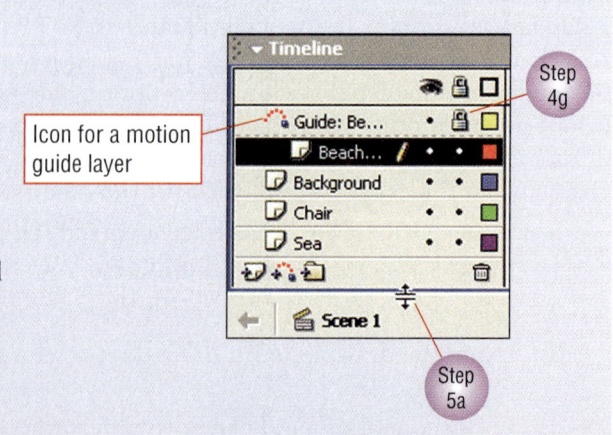

170 Chapter Four

b. Click frame 36 in the frame row next to the layer named *Guide: Beachball*.
c. Hold down the Shift key and then click frame 36 in the frame row next to the layer named *Sea*. This selects frame 36 in all five layers as indicated by the blue highlighting in all rows of the frame 36 column in the Timeline.
d. Right-click over any of the selected frames and then click Insert Frame at the shortcut menu. Frame boxes 1 through 36 are now shaded gray in all layers in the Timeline. This step is required to make sure that all objects in all layers are visible on the stage throughout the tweened animation.
e. Click frame 36 in the *Beachball* layer and then insert a keyframe.
f. With the beach ball object selected on the stage, click the Arrow tool and then drag the beach ball near the slope at the end of the line as shown. Position the beach ball so that its center point is on the line. If necessary, increase the magnification so that you can see the center point more clearly. Dragging an object's center point to a line on a motion guide layer connects the object to the path it is to follow.
g. Click frame 1 in *Beachball* layer and then drag the center point of the ball to the beginning of the line that you drew in Step 4f.
h. Right-click frame 1 in the *Beachball* layer and then click Create Motion Tween.
i. Expand the Properties panel and then make the following changes:
   1) Change the Rotate option to CW.
   2) Key **4** in the times text box.
   3) Change the Ease value to 100.
   4) Deselect the Scale check box.
j. Click in the stage to deselect the Properties panel, collapse the Properties panel, change the magnification to 70%, and then center the stage within the window.
6. Press Enter to preview the animation.
7. Click Control on the Menu bar and then click Test Movie to preview the animation in a Flash Player window within Flash. Notice the motion guide line is not displayed. If necessary, click View and then click Bandwidth Profiler to turn off the display of the movie statistics at the top of the window. The animation will continue to play over and over again until you press Enter or Esc. Click the Close button at the top of the Flash Player window (second Close button from the top right corner of the window) to return to the Flash movie.
8. In the Flash window, save the revised document using the same name (Ch4Ex04).
9. Close Ch4Ex04.

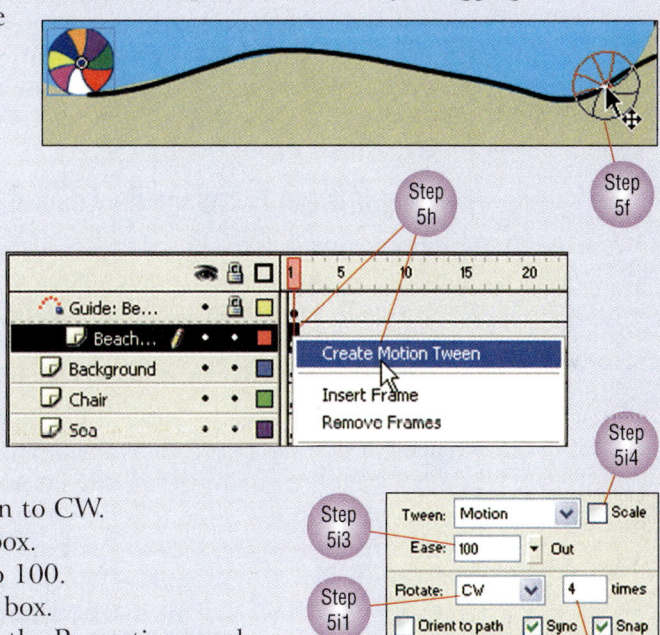

When you use <u>C</u>ontrol and then Test <u>M</u>ovie to preview an animation in a Flash Player window within Flash, your movie is exported in the player format. An additional file is created in the default file location with the same name as the movie file except the file extension is changed from *fla* to *swf*. In Exercise 4 this file is named Ch4Ex04.swf and is saved in the same folder in which you saved Ch4Ex04.fla. In Chapter 6 you will learn more about publishing, exporting, and using the Bandwidth Profiler.

Orienting the Object to the Path

In Exercise 4 the beach ball stayed at the same angle as it travelled along the curved motion path in the guide layer. By default the Orient to path check box in the Properties panel for a tweened animation is deselected. This means the object is oriented relative to the stage. In Exercise 4 it made sense for the beach ball to maintain its orientation to the stage during the animation. In other cases, however, you may want the tweened object to be oriented to the motion guide path. For example, a drawing of a roller coaster with a loop in the roller coaster would look unrealistic if, when animated, the cars maintained their orientation relative to the stage. In this case, you would want the cars to orient to the motion guide and when the cars enter the loop they would turn upside down when the loop curves. To do this, click the Orient to path check box to turn the feature on in the Properties panel for the motion tween.

Creating a Tween to Change the Color of the Instance

A motion tween can be used to gradually change an object's color throughout the animation. For example, a green banana at the beginning of a motion tween can gradually transform into a yellow banana by the end of the animation. Flash transitions the color gradually from the color of the first instance to the color of the second instance relative to the length of the animation.

As you have already learned, Flash creates a symbol for a grouped object when creating a motion tween if you have not already done so. To change colors of a symbol instance you must use the Properties panel since the Ink Bottle and Paint Bucket tools do not operate for a selected instance. Display the Properties panel for the instance in the second keyframe of the motion tween and then change the Color option to Tint. Figure 4.2 displays the additional options that appear in the Properties panel when Tint is selected in the Color list box.

FIGURE 4.2 *Tint Color Options for a Selected Instance*

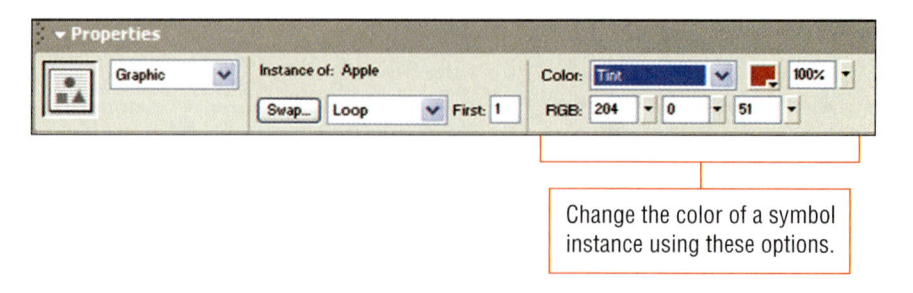

Change the color of a symbol instance using these options.

Click the color swatch next to the Color list box and then choose a new color for the tweened object in the color palette. Alternatively, you can key the RGB values in their respective text boxes below the Color list box. In the tint amount text box next to the tint color swatch, key a value between 1 and 100 representing the percentage amount that you want Flash to mix the old color with the new color. Leaving the default value of 100% means the old color is completely changed to the new color. A value less than 100% causes Flash to blend the original symbol color with the new color for the instance. For example, assume a master symbol color is yellow and you choose a red color swatch as the tint for a selected instance. Keying a value of 50% in the Percentage text box causes Flash to mix the yellow with the red and the instance would be recolored a shade of orange.

The Color drop-down list contains the options Brightness, Alpha, and Advanced in addition to Tint. Choose Brightness to key a value or drag the slider to determine the amount for which the color should be lightened or darkened. A value of 100 turns the color white and a value of –100 turns it black. Alpha determines the color's transparency percentage. A value of 0% creates a transparent color while a value of 100% creates an opague color. Click Advanced to adjust the red, green, blue, and transparency values of the color separately in the Advanced Effect dialog box.

exercise 5

CREATING A MOTION TWEEN TO RECOLOR AN OBJECT

1. Open the Flash document named Apple.
2. Save the document with Save As and name it Ch4Ex05.
3. The document contains a yellow apple that has been inserted as an instance from the symbol named *Apple* in the library. Notice in the Timeline that three layers exist in the movie. The apple stem and the worm hole are on separate layers because you want to change the color of the apple portion only and leave those elements at their original colors. Create a motion tween that will gradually transition the apple from yellow to red by completing the following steps:
   a. Frames 1–30 have already been created in each layer of the Timeline. Right-click frame 30 in the *Apple* layer and then click Insert Keyframe at the shortcut menu.
   b. Right-click frame 1 in the *Apple* layer and then click Create Motion Tween at the shortcut menu. 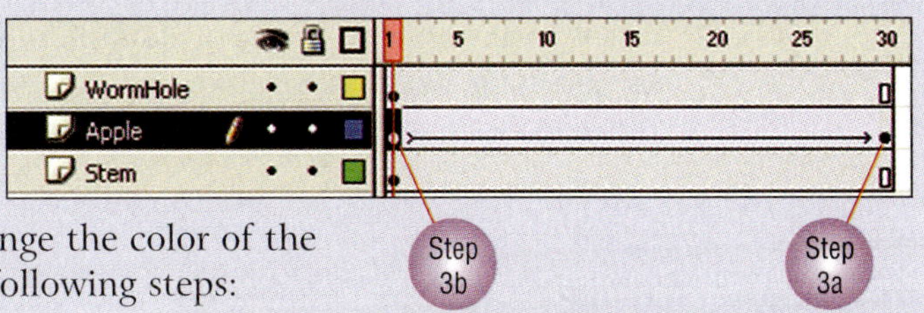
   c. Make active frame 30 in the *Apple* layer and then change the color of the instance by completing the following steps:
      1) Expand the Properties panel.
      2) Click the instance on the stage.
      3) Click the down arrow next to the Color list box and then click Tint at the drop-down list. 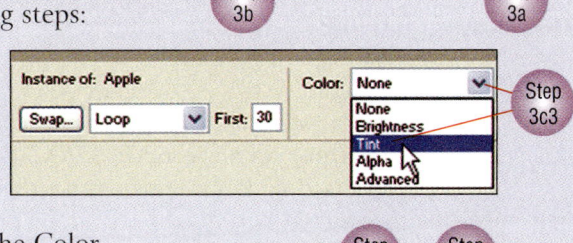
      4) Click the color swatch next to the Color list box and then choose a red color swatch similar to the one shown.
      5) Drag across the current value in the tint amount text box and then key 75.

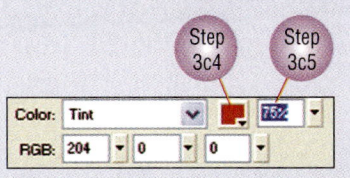

> 6) Click in the stage to deselect the Properties panel and then collapse the Properties panel.
> 4. Preview the animation.
> 5. Click frame 15 and look at the color of the apple on the stage. Click three or four other frames between frame 1 and frame 30 to view the progressive changes in the color of the apple as it moves from yellow in frame 1 to red in frame 30.
> 6. Save the revised document using the same name (Ch4Ex05).

Inserting a Keyframe in a Motion Tween

Inserting a keyframe between the starting and ending keyframes within an existing motion tween allows you to animate the object on more than two points. Flash automatically ends the first motion tween at the newly inserted keyframe. Existing frames between the newly inserted keyframe to the end of the original animation are automatically recalculated based on changes made to the content of the object. The revised animation consists of two back-to-back motion tweens.

To insert a new keyframe within an existing motion tweened animation, right-click the frame at which you want to change the object's motion and then click Insert Keyframe at the shortcut menu or select the frame and then click Insert Keyframe.

Working with Frames

In Exercise 4 you used a standard Windows multiple selection technique when you selected frame 36 for all five layers by clicking frame 36 in the first layer and then holding down the Shift key while clicking frame 36 in the last layer. All frames between the first selected frame and the last selected frame are selected when the Shift key is used. Use the Ctrl key to select multiple nonadjacent frames. Frames can also be selected by dragging the mouse across the selection area.

When selecting to insert, remove, move, or copy frames always keep in mind that all content on the stage associated with those frames will be adjusted by the action you perform. If you accidentally delete a frame and then realize an object on the stage has disappeared, use the Undo feature to restore it. Depending on the action, you may have to use Undo multiple times.

Inserting and Removing Frames

While previewing a movie you may decide you need to extend or decrease the duration of the movie to smooth the flow of the animation. One method to accomplish this is to add or delete frames between the starting and ending keyframes. For example, with the default setting of 12 frames-per-second, to reduce the movie's length by a half second, you would select and delete 6 frames between the starting and ending keyframes. Inserting 6 frames would lengthen the movie by a half second. When frames are added or deleted within a tweened range of frames, Flash automatically recalculates the frames in between the starting and ending keyframes.

To add or delete frames from the Timeline, select the range of frames, right-click over the selected area, and then click Insert Frame or Remove Frames at the shortcut menu, or click Insert on the Menu bar and then click Frame or Remove Frames. Figure 4.3 illustrates inserting 6 frames to all layers in the motion tweened animation created in Exercise 5 using the shortcut menu.

FIGURE

4.3 Inserting Frames Between Start and End Frames to Lengthen Animation

Selected frames within an existing animation display in black.

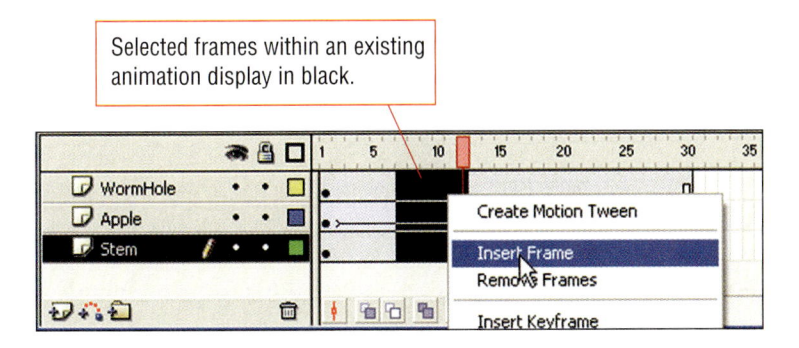

Clearing Frames

Click Edit and then Clear Frames (or Clear Frames from the shortcut menu) for a selected frame to clear the contents of the selected frame while leaving the frame intact within the Timeline. The result achieved is that content remains on the stage up to the point of the cleared frame, then the stage is blank during the cleared frame, and then content resumes after the cleared frame. Use this technique to insert blank space in an animation to create a blinking or flickering effect.

Clearing a frame within an existing frame-by-frame animation causes Flash to automatically convert the frame to a blank keyframe. The frame immediately following the cleared frame is also automatically converted to a keyframe. Clearing a frame within an existing motion tweened range of animated frames causes Flash to do the same action; however, the motion tween becomes broken from the first keyframe to the point at which the cleared frame exists. Flash displays a dashed line across a range of frames in a tween that has been broken or is otherwise incomplete.

Moving Frames

In the previous example, another method that can be used to extend the length of the movie is to move the ending keyframe further down the Timeline. Move a frame by dragging and dropping the frame box to another location on the Timeline. An ending keyframe in a motion tween can be dragged further down the Timeline and Flash will automatically recalculate the frames in between the starting and ending keyframes. If other layers exist in the movie be sure to select all of the frames in all of the layers at the ending keyframe of the tween and then drag the column of selected frames further down the Timeline. Figure 4.4 illustrates the ending frames in the motion tweened animation created in Exercise 5 being moved five frames right to extend the duration of the animation.

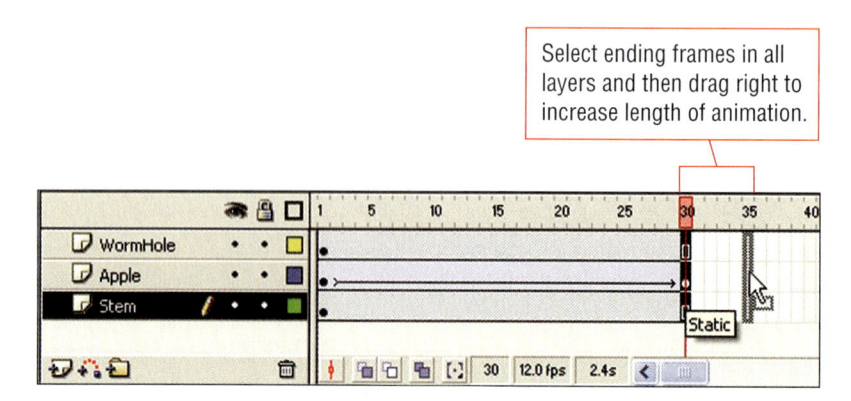

FIGURE 4.4 Extending Duration of Animation by Moving Ending Frames

Select ending frames in all layers and then drag right to increase length of animation.

If the ending keyframe of a motion tween is dragged left to shorten the duration of the animation, Flash converts the frames from the original ending keyframe position to the new keyframe position to regular frames. This means the shortened animation will play and then the content will remain on the stage for the remaining duration of the original animation. The frames beyond the new ending keyframe position would have to be removed if this is not the outcome that you wanted. For example, assume a movie's motion tween played for two seconds, ending at frame 24 and then the ending keyframe in frame 24 was dragged left to frame 12. The revised tweened animation would play for one second and then the content would remain static on the stage for an additional second since frames 13–24 were not removed.

Copying Frames

Frames can be copied and pasted in the Timeline to duplicate content within an animation. Using this technique can save a considerable amount of time in a frame-by-frame animation where a lot of content is the same and only minor editing is required to the pasted frames. Click Edit and then click Copy Frames or click Copy Frames from the shortcut menu for a selected frame. Click in the Timeline where you want the content duplicated, click Edit and then Paste Frames, or click Paste Frames from the shortcut menu. A frame between a starting and ending keyframe that is copied is automatically converted to a keyframe when pasted in the Timeline.

exercise 6 — COPYING AND MOVING KEYFRAMES

1. In Step 5 of Exercise 5 you viewed the gradual change in color from yellow to red by clicking frames between 1 and 30. The color transitioned from yellow to orange and then to red. Assume you want to show a more natural progression of an apple by editing the animation to change the color of the apple from green to yellow and then to red. With Ch4Ex05 open, edit the existing animation by copying and pasting a keyframe within the motion tween by completing the following steps:
    a. Click frame 1 in the *Apple* layer of the Timeline.

b. Click Edit and then click Copy Frames.
c. Click frame 12 in the *Apple* layer in the Timeline.
d. Click Edit and then click Paste Frames. Two motion tweens now appear in the Timeline at frames 1–12 and frames 13–30. The apple shown in the stage is now the same yellow apple instance as in frame 1.

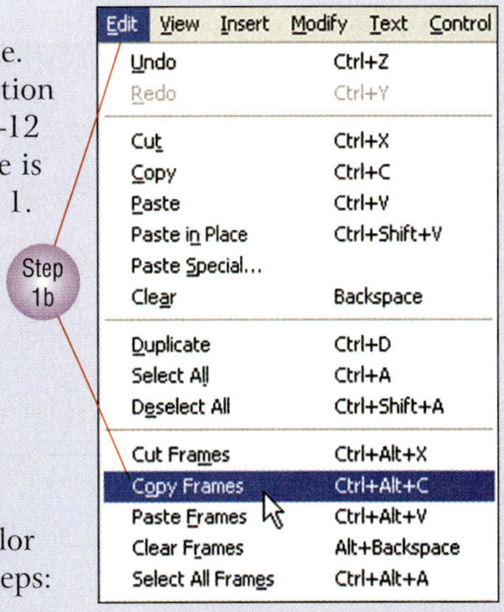

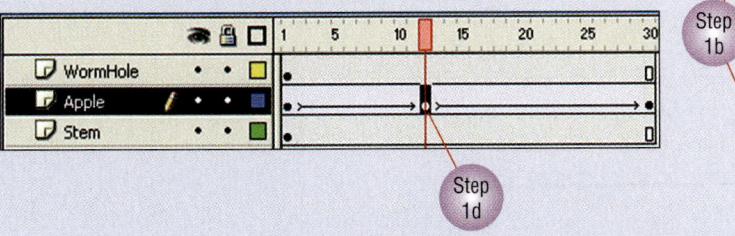

2. Edit the first instance of the apple to change the color from yellow to green by completing the following steps:
   a. Click frame 1 in the *Apple* layer in the Timeline.
   b. Expand the Properties panel.
   c. Click the instance on the stage.
   d. Click the down arrow next to the Color list box and then click Tint at the drop-down list.
   e. Click the color swatch next to the Color list box and then choose a green color swatch similar to the one shown.
   f. Drag across the current value in the tint amount text box and then key **40**.
   g. Click in the stage to deselect the Properties panel and then collapse the Properties panel.
3. Preview the animation. 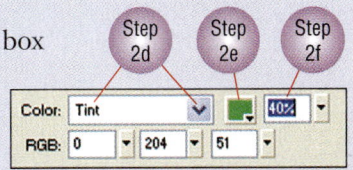
4. Save the revised document using the same name (Ch4Ex05).
5. Lengthen the duration of the animation to see if the colors transition more smoothly. Select and move frames by completing the following steps:
   a. Position the mouse pointer over frame 30 in the *WormHole* layer of the Timeline, hold down the left mouse button, and then drag to frame 30 in the *Stem* layer. This selects the three frames at the end of the animation.
   b. Position the mouse pointer over any of the selected frames and then drag right to frame 40. The pointer displays with a gray shaded box attached indicating you are completing a move operation. As you drag the pointer, a gray shaded box also appears in the Timeline's frame boxes to indicate the position to which the frames will be relocated when the mouse is released.
   c. Click frame 12 in the *Apple* layer.
   d. Position the mouse pointer over the selected frame and then drag right to frame 20.
6. Click frame 1 in any layer and then preview the animation. 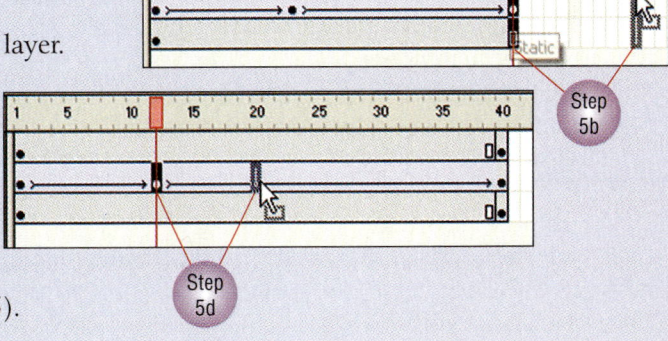 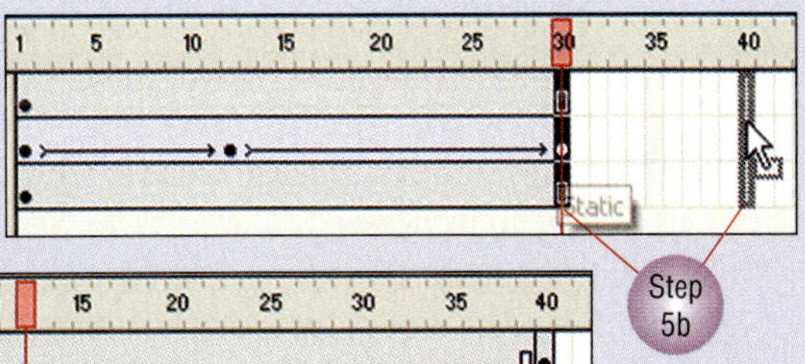
7. Save the revised document using the same name (Ch4Ex05).
8. Close Ch4Ex05.

exercise 7

INSERTING AND REMOVING FRAMES

1. Open Ch4Ex04.
2. Change the magnification to 70% and if necessary, center the stage within the Flash window.
3. Lengthen the duration of the animation by inserting frames between the starting and ending keyframes by completing the following steps:
   a. Position the mouse pointer over frame 10 in the *Guide: Beachball* layer, hold down the left mouse button, drag right and down to frame 25 in the *Sea* layer, and then release the mouse. If all layers are not currently visible, the Timeline will scroll down automatically as you drag down.

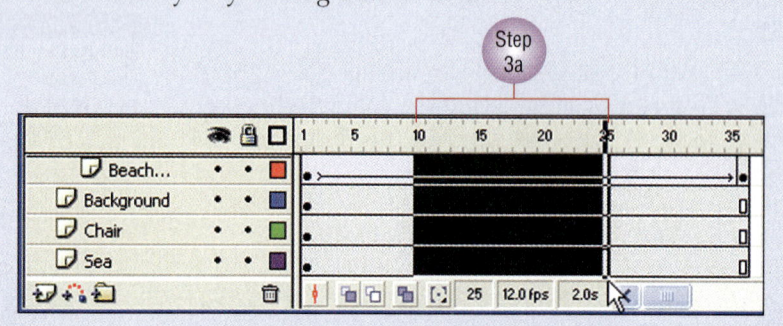

   Step 3a

   b. Position the mouse pointer over the selected block of frames, right-click, and then click Insert Frame at the shortcut menu. The duration of the animation has been lengthened by the amount of the inserted frames.

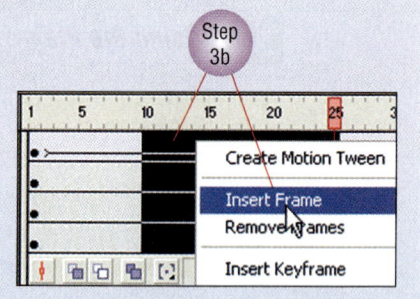

   Step 3b

4. Click <u>C</u>ontrol and then Test <u>M</u>ovie to preview the lengthened animation in the Flash Player window. Notice the ball moves more slowly along the sand and the easing out effect is more prominent.
5. Close the Flash Player window and then save the revised document using the same name (Ch4Ex04).
6. Shorten the duration of the animation by completing the following steps:
   a. If necessary, scroll up the Timeline to the first layer.
   b. Select frames 5–10 of all five layers.
   c. Right-click over the selected block of frames and then click Remove Frames at the shortcut menu. Notice the ending frames in the Timeline have shifted left by the number of deleted frames.

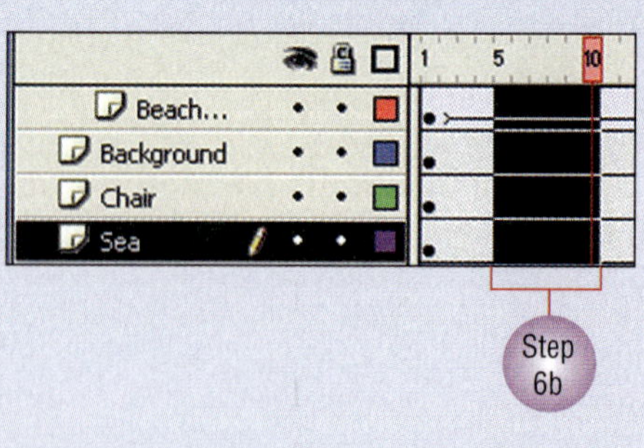

   Step 6b

7. Click <u>C</u>ontrol and then Test <u>M</u>ovie to preview the shortened animation in the Flash Player window.
8. Close the Flash Player window and then click in the workspace to deselect the frames in the Timeline.
9. Save the revised document using the same name (Ch4Ex04).

Previewing Animations

Pressing Enter when you preview an animation is the shortcut for the Play command from the Control menu. The animation plays once and then stops. Click Control and then Loop Playback to have the animation play continually until you issue the stop command. Loop playback is a toggle feature meaning once you click the option, it stays in effect until you click Control and then Loop Playback again to turn it off. When you want the animation to stop playing, press Enter or click Control and then Stop.

Viewing animations in the player format by clicking Control and then Test Movie plays the movie in looped playback mode by default. To turn off the loop playback feature in the Flash Player window, click Control and then click Loop.

Scrubbing

Dragging the box at the top of the playhead in the frame number area left and right across the Timeline as shown in Figure 4.5 is called *scrubbing*. This technique can be helpful to view an animation frame-by-frame in complex movies. Scrubbing slowly can provide a more thorough insight into the transitions in the movie. In addition, scrubbing left allows you to preview the animation in reverse.

FIGURE 4.5 **Using the Playhead to Scrub an Animation**

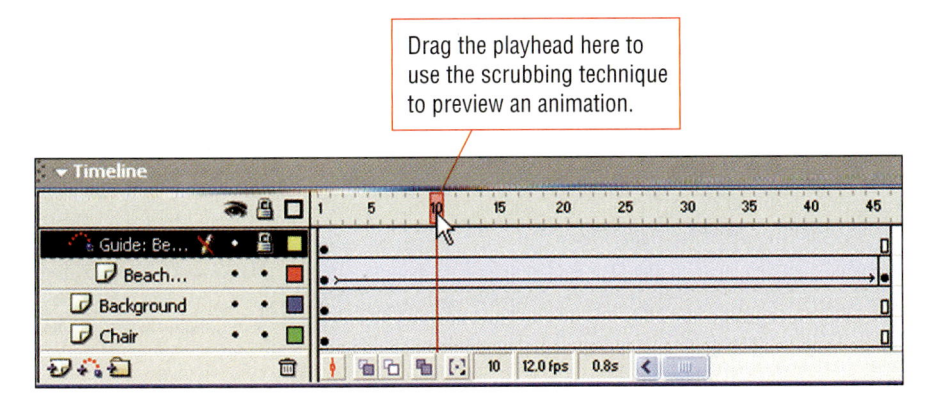

Drag the playhead here to use the scrubbing technique to preview an animation.

Using the Controller

Click Window, point to Toolbars, and then click Controller to open the Controller toolbar shown in Figure 4.6. Using the buttons in this window you can play, stop, rewind, and jump to the end of the animation. The Step Back and Step Forward buttons allow you to preview the animation forward or reverse frame-by-frame.

FIGURE 4.6 Controller Toolbar

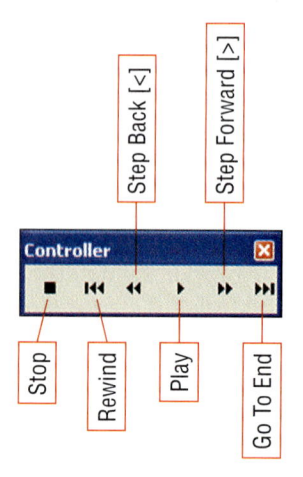

Labels on the Controller toolbar: Step Back [<], Step Forward [>], Stop, Rewind, Play, Go To End

exercise 8

PREVIEWING ANIMATIONS USING THE CONTROLLER AND SCRUBBING

1. With Ch4Ex04 open, display the Controller toolbar by clicking Window, pointing to Toolbars, and then clicking Controller. 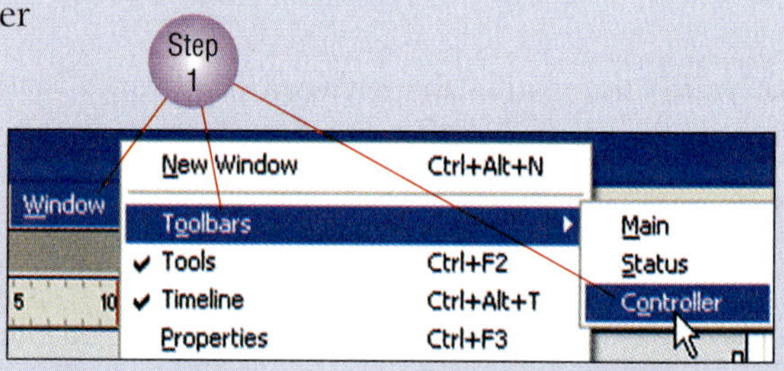
2. Preview the animation using the Controller buttons by completing the following steps:
   a. Drag the title bar of the Controller toolbar into the workspace at the top left of the stage.
   b. Click the Play button in the Controller toolbar to start the animation.
   c. When the animation is complete, click Rewind to return to the beginning of the animation.
   d. Click Play again and then click the Stop button when the animation is approximately halfway through the movie.
      (Hint: Watch the playhead and click Stop when it nears frame 22.)
   e. Click Step Forward several times to watch the remainder of the animation frame-by-frame. 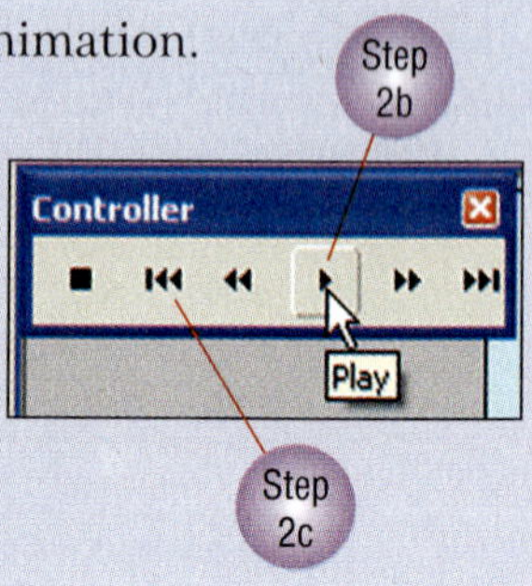
3. Preview the animation using the scrubbing technique by completing the following steps:
   a. Click Rewind in the Controller toolbar to return the playhead to frame 1.
   b. Position the mouse pointer on the red box at the top of the playhead in the frame numbers section of the Timeline, hold down the left mouse button, and then slowly drag the playhead right to the end of the animation. Watch the beach ball move as you drag across the frames.

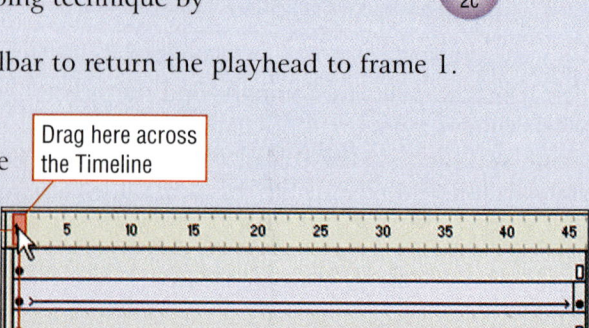

180 Chapter Four   FLASH MX

    c. Practice scrubbing the animation a few times by varying the speed with which you drag the mouse.
4. Click <u>W</u>indow, point to T<u>o</u>olbars, and then click <u>C</u>ontroller, or click the Close button on the Controller toolbar title bar to remove the Controller toolbar from the stage.
5. Close Ch4Ex04. Click <u>N</u>o if prompted to save changes.

Creating a Shape Tweened Animation

Constructing a shape tweened animation is very similar to the steps involved in creating a motion tweened animation. The difference resides in the object that is being tweened. In the ending keyframe, you draw the shape which you want the animation to morph into. In a motion tween, the object being animated is an instance of a symbol added to the library. You could also select a grouped object and Flash automatically creates the tween symbol in the library. In a shape tween the object being animated must be ungrouped so that Flash can calculate the vectors making up the incremental shapes as it morphs the object from the starting keyframe to the ending keyframe. As in a motion tween, Flash can change the shape's size, color, and location as it morphs the object.

Flash does not include an option on the Menu bar or the shortcut menu for a selected frame to create a shape tween. Expand the Properties panel for the starting keyframe to create a shape tween using the Interpolate drop-down list next to Tween as shown in Figure 4.7.

FIGURE 4.7 Creating a Shape Tween Using Properties Panel

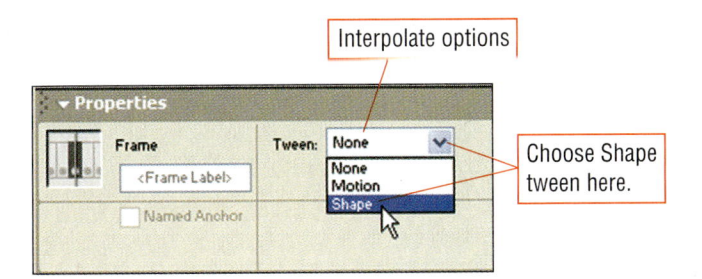

Interpolate options

Choose Shape tween here.

exercise 9

CREATING A SHAPE TWEENED ANIMATION

1. Open the Flash document named Sleeprite.
2. Save the document with Save As and name it Ch4Ex09.
3. Make sure the Properties panel is collapsed, set the magnification to 70%, and then center the stage within the window.
4. Create a shape tweened animation where the yellow half moon changes to a white full moon by completing the following steps:
    a. Click frame 40 in the *Text* layer.
    b. Hold down the Shift key and then click frame 40 in the *Background* layer. If necessary, scroll down or resize the Timeline to see the last layer.

Creating Animation and Guidelines for Flash Project Design   181

c. With frame 40 selected in all six layers, click Insert and then click Frame.

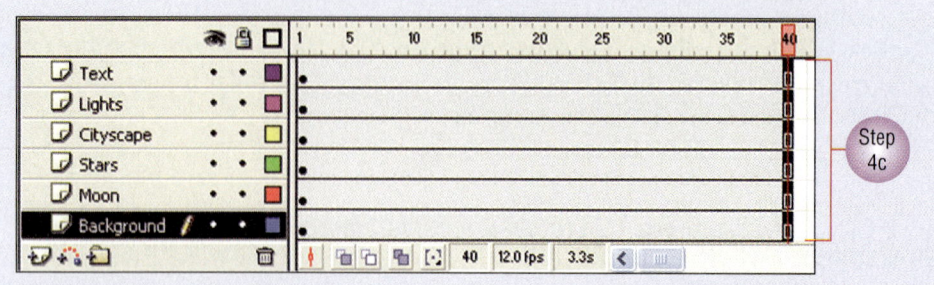

d. Click frame 40 in the *Moon* layer, click Insert and then click Keyframe.
e. With the moon currently selected in frame 40, click in the workspace to deselect the object. *(Note: Because of the light yellow color of the moon you might not see the fill color selection.)*
f. Position the pointer over the curved area at the left side of the moon until the pointer displays with the curve attached, hold down the left mouse button, and then drag left to create the circle shape as shown.
g. Make any other adjustments to the shape as you see fit until you are satisfied the object resembles a full moon.
h. Expand the Properties panel.
i. Change the Fill Color of the full moon to white.
j. Click frame 1 in the *Moon* layer.
k. Click the Interpolate down arrow next to Tween in the Properties panel and then click Shape at the drop-down list.

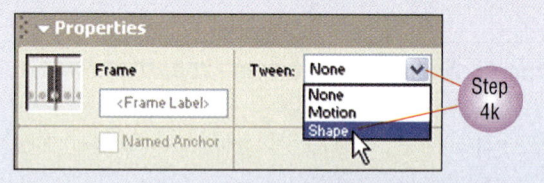

l. Collapse the Properties panel. Notice in the Timeline Flash has shaded the background of frames 1–39 light green and drawn the black arrow to indicate a shape tween has been created. Pointing to any of the light green shaded frames displays the tooltip *Shape Tweening*.

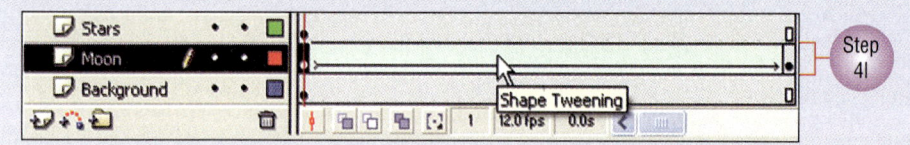

5. Preview the animation.
6. Save the document using the same name (Ch4Ex09).

In the Properties panel with shape tween selected as the Interpolate option, Flash displays the Ease and Blend properties as shown in Figure 4.8. Ease values function in the same manner for a shape tween as they do for a motion tween to accelerate or decelerate the tweened shape. Choose either Distributive or Angular from the Blend drop-down list. This setting refers to the method Flash uses to change the animated object's curves and/or corners from the starting shape to the ending shape. Choose Distributive to tween shapes in a smooth fashion and Angular to maintain corners and straight lines.

FIGURE 4.8 **Ease and Blend Properties for Shape Tween**

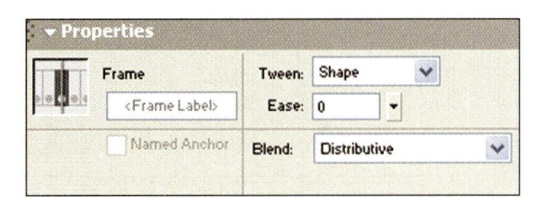

exercise 10

COMBINING A MOTION AND SHAPE TWEENED ANIMATION AND EDITING FRAMES

1. With Ch4Ex09 open, add a motion tween animation to the existing shape tween by completing the following steps:
   a. Insert a new layer above *Stars* and name it *FallingStar*.
   b. Click frame 1 in the *Stars* layer.
   c. Click in the workspace to deselect all of the selected stars on the layer and then click the star at the top right of the stage closest to the moon.
   d. Click Edit and then click Cut. The star is deleted from the *Stars* layer.
   e. Click frame 1 in the *FallingStar* layer, click Edit, and then click Paste in Place. The Paste in Place feature inserts the content of the Clipboard in the same location on the stage from which it was cut or copied. Paste in Place is a convenient tool for distributing objects drawn on a single layer to separate layers.
   f. Right-click frame 40 in the *FallingStar* layer, and then click Insert Keyframe at the shortcut menu.
   g. With the star object selected on the *FallingStar* layer, drag the star to the bottom of the stage as shown.
   h. Right-click frame 1 in the *FallingStar* layer and then click Create Motion Tween at the shortcut menu.
2. Preview the animation in the Flash Player window.
3. Close the Flash Player window and then save the revised document using the same name (Ch4Ex09).
4. After previewing the animation, you decide it would be better to have the falling star animation start after the full moon animation is complete. Edit the frames in the Timeline to reposition the falling star animation by completing the following steps:

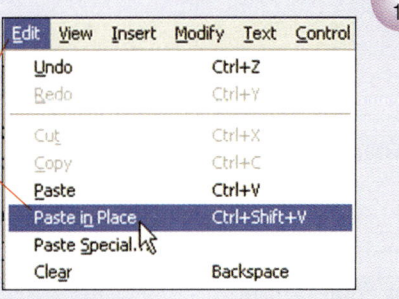

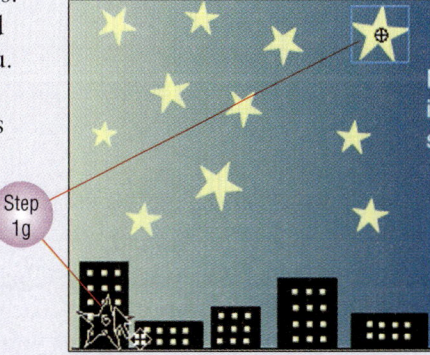

FLASH MX Creating Animation and Guidelines for Flash Project Design 183

a. Click frame 41 in the *Text* layer.
b. Hold down Shift and then click frame 60 in the *Background* layer. Frames 41–60 in all seven layers are selected.
c. Click Insert and then click Frame.
d. Click frame 40 in the *FallingStar* layer to select the ending keyframe in the motion tween and then drag right to frame 60.
e. Right-click frame 1 in the *FallingStar* layer and then click Copy Frames at the shortcut menu.
f. Right-click frame 40 in the *FallingStar* layer and then click Paste Frames at the shortcut menu.
g. Right-click frame 1 in the *FallingStar* layer and then click Remove Tween.
h. Compare your Timeline to the one shown. The shape tween occurs in frames 1–40 in the *Moon* layer and the motion tween has been repositioned to frames 40–60.

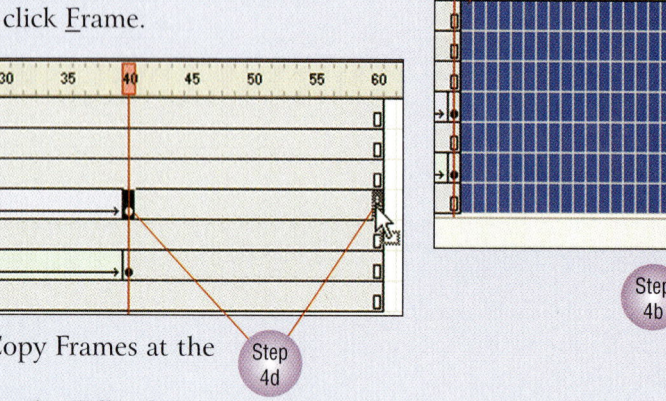

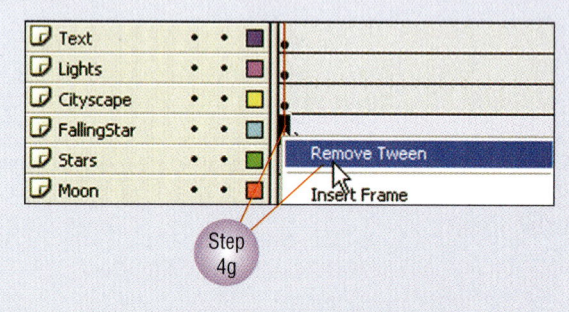

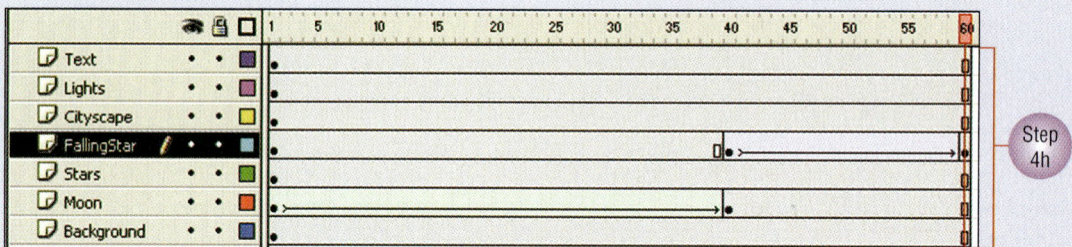

5. Preview the animation in the Flash Player window.
6. Close the Flash Player window and then save the document using the same name (Ch4Ex09).
7. Close Ch4Ex09.

Using Shape Hints

The shape tween created in Exercise 9 was easy for Flash to tween since the beginning and ending shapes had similar curvatures. Unexpected results can occur when morphing a beginning shape to an ending shape where the two objects are very dissimilar. If you create a shape tween and do not like the way in which Flash morphs the start to the end objects, you can give Flash additional information about how you want the objects tweened. This information is in the form of markers called *shape hints*.

A marker is placed on the start object and then a corresponding marker is inserted on the end object in the location in which you want Flash to treat the points as the same. This is referred to as *mapping*. Flash labels corresponding markers with lowercase alphabetic letters. Marker *a* on the starting object is matched to marker *a* on the ending object. You can add up to 26 shape hints to a tween.

Adding a Shape Hint

Shape hints are added beginning with the starting object in the tween. Select the keyframe for the beginning of the shape tween. With the tween object selected, click Modify, point to Shape, and then click Add Shape Hint. Flash inserts a red circle with the lowercase letter *a* in the middle of the object. Drag the marker to the location on the shape where you want to map your first point. Click the ending keyframe in the tween. A corresponding marker displays in the middle of the ending object. Drag the marker on the ending object to the point which you want to correlate with the marker on the starting object. Repeat the process until you have inserted all of the markers that you think are needed to improve the tween.

Markers need to be placed on the outside edges of a shape. Placing a marker inside the object will cause Flash to ignore it. To make sure the shape hints you have placed are valid, make sure the starting markers are yellow and the corresponding ending markers are green. A red shaded marker is not going to affect the tween's intermediate shapes. Reposition any red markers to the outer edges of the shape or drag them off the stage to remove them. Adding shape hints with the Snap to Object feature turned on will assist you with placing them at the outer perimeters of the shape.

Placing hints in order in an organized fashion will achieve better results than points mapped in random order. Try using a clockwise or counterclockwise direction around the edges of the starting and ending objects to achieve a smoother tween.

Viewing Shape Hints

By default, shape hints display on the objects. If you want to view the objects without the shape hints or if the shape hints disappear when editing an object and do not reappear, click View and then click Show Shape Hints. This feature toggles on or off the display of shape hints.

Removing Shape Hints

An individual shape hint can be dragged off the stage and its corresponding marker on the other shape will automatically be deleted. Click Modify, point to Shape, and then click Remove All Hints to delete all markers from the objects.

exercise 11

CREATING A SHAPE TWEEN AND ADDING SHAPE HINTS

1. Open the Flash document named Triangle-Arrow.
2. Save the document with Save As and name it Ch4Ex11.
3. The document contains a triangle object in frame 1 and a curved arrow in keyframe 30. Click frame 30 to view the end object.
4. Create a shape tween animation to morph the shapes in the frames between the starting and ending keyframes by completing the following steps:

a. Expand the Properties panel.
   b. Click frame 1.
   c. Click the Interpolate down arrow next to Tween in the Properties panel and then click Shape at the drop-down list.
   d. Collapse the Properties panel and then click in the workspace to deselect the triangle.
   e. Press Enter to preview the animation.
   f. Click frame 25 to view the intermediate shape. The shape you are viewing has less than a half second to complete the transformation to the end object. Notice the arrow tip is not yet properly aligned. 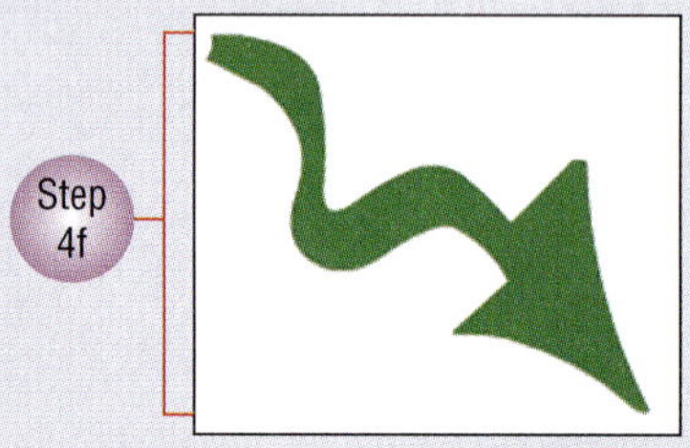
   g. Click a few frames before and after frame 25 to get a feel for the morphing process from the start to end object.

Step 4f

5. Change the shape tween properties and add shape hints to the animation by completing the following steps:
   a. Click frame 1 and expand the Properties panel.
   b. Click the down-pointing arrow for the Blend drop-down list and then click Angular at the drop-down list. 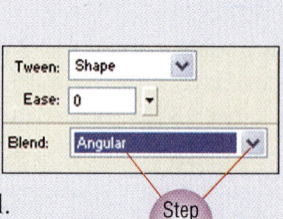
   c. Click in the stage area and then collapse the Properties panel.
   d. Click Modify, point to Shape, and then click Add Shape Hint. A red circle with the lowercase letter *a* is inserted in the middle of the triangle.

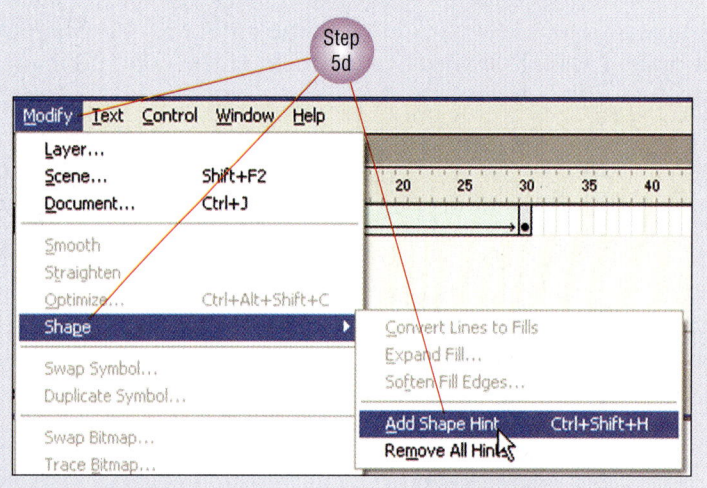

Step 5b

Step 5d

   e. Drag the shape marker to the top point of the triangle as shown. The marker will not change color to yellow until the corresponding marker on the end object is mapped to a valid point.

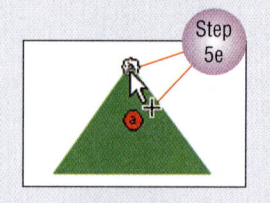

Step 5e

   f. Click frame 30. The corresponding red *a* marker is in the center of the curved arrow object. Drag the marker to the position shown. When you release the mouse, the marker changes color from red to green since it is now mapped to the marker created in Step 5e.
   g. Click frame 1. Notice the *a* marker has now changed color to yellow. 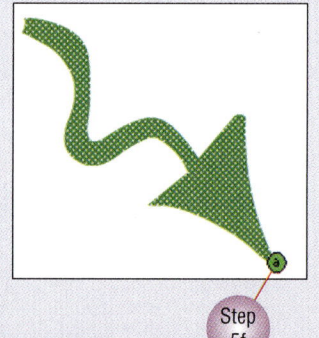

Step 5f

h. Click Modify, point to Shape, and then click Add Shape Hint. Continue dragging markers and adding shape hints on the objects in frames 1 and 30 until you have created the points as shown.

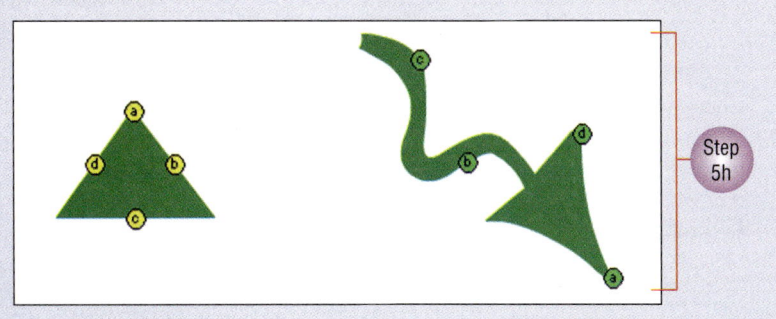

Step 5h

i. When you have finished adding the four shape hints, click frame 1 and then click in the workspace to deselect the object.
6. Press Enter to preview the revised animation.
7. Click frame 25 to view the intermediate shape. Notice with the addition of the shape hints and changing the tween property, with less than a half second left, the arrow tip is aligned almost perfectly.
8. Save the revised document using the same name (Ch4Ex11).

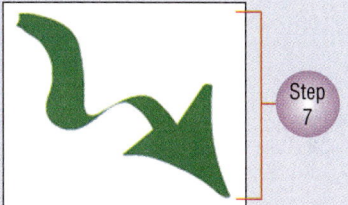

Step 7

Adjusting the Frame Rate for Animations

As you have already learned, the default frame rate for animations is 12 fps (frames per second.) This rate can be changed to increase or decrease the speed with which Flash plays the movie. Open the Document Properties dialog box shown in Figure 4.9 to adjust the frame rate by clicking Modify and then Document or by double-clicking the frame rate displayed in the Timeline panel.

FIGURE

4.9   *Changing Frame Rate in Document Properties Dialog Box*

Drag across current frame rate and then key desired value.

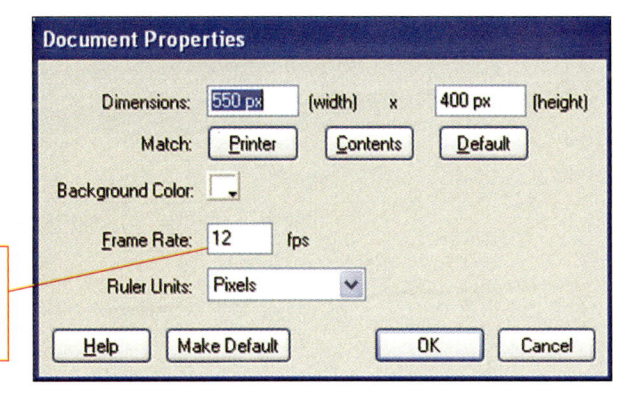

Frame rate is constant throughout the entire movie and is directly related to the number of frames that you have to include in the animation. For example, a 3-second movie at the default frame rate of 12 fps requires that you create 36

frames. Speeding up the movie to play at 15 fps means that you now have to create 45 frames for the same 3 seconds of animation. Another consequence of speeding up the frame rate is an increased file size since additional frames cause the file size to increase which also means longer download times.

To put the frame rate in perspective, consider that a Flash movie is a compilation of images stored in frames and that the animation is simply those images being drawn on the screen one after the other. At the default frame rate, each image is on the screen for one-fifth of a second and then is replaced with the next image in the next frame for another one-fifth of a second, and so on. In between the images the screen is blank however, this is not noticeable since our brains retain the last image we saw for an instant. In addition, the average person blinks approximately 7–9 times per minute while looking at a computer screen, but our perception provides us with a constant image. *(Note: People normally blink on average 10–15 times per minute; however, research has shown that this blink rate drops when using a computer.)*

At a larger fps setting, the images change more quickly which could result in a blurring effect. At a slower fps setting, the frames change more slowly which might make some movements appear disjointed. Flash has set the default frame rate of 12 fps since this rate generally provides the best quality on the Web factored with the shortest download time.

Complex animations can play back at variable rates depending on the processing speed of the computer upon which the movie is being viewed. For this reason, it is a good idea to test the speed of a movie on a variety of computers at the default fps setting. Based on the results of testing, you may then decide to adjust the frame rate.

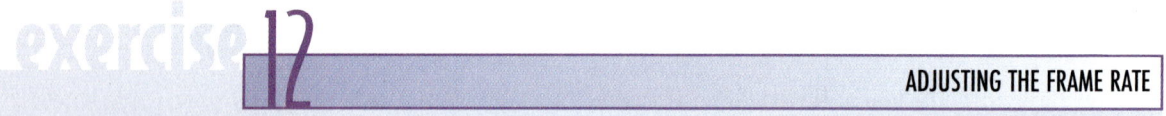

exercise 12

ADJUSTING THE FRAME RATE

1. With Ch4Ex11 open, adjust the speed with which the movie plays back by completing the following steps:
   a. Click frame 1 and then press Enter to preview the animation again at the default rate of 12 fps.
   b. Double-click the Frame Rate box (displays 12.0 fps) at the bottom of the Timeline panel.
   c. Drag across the current value *12* in the Frame Rate text box and then key **24**.
   d. Click OK to close the Document Properties dialog box.
2. Preview the animation at the increased speed.
3. Close Ch4Ex11. Click No when prompted to save changes.
4. Open Ch4Ex04.
5. Test the movie at different frame rates by completing the following steps:
   a. Click Modify and then click Document.

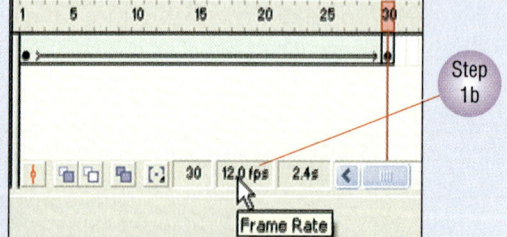

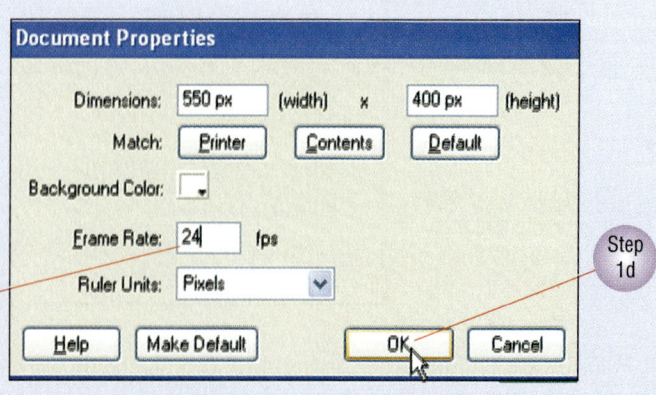

188   Chapter Four

b. Drag across *12* in the Frame Rate text box, key **30**, and then click OK.
c. Click Control and then click Test Movie to preview the animation in the Flash Player window.
d. Watch the animation a few times and then close the Flash Player window.
e. Change the frame rate to *10 fps*.
f. Preview the animation a few times in the Flash Player window and then close the window.
6. Close Ch4Ex04. Click No when prompted to save changes.

Creating Frame-by-Frame Animations

As you have previously learned, frame-by-frame animation is a technique in which each change in content is created by you in a keyframe. In many cases each frame in the Timeline is a keyframe.

In Chapter 1 you had the opportunity to create animations using frames by inserting keyframes and then editing the content on the stage. Using the techniques learned in this chapter to insert, remove, clear, move, and copy frames can assist with building a more complex frame-by-frame animation without the tedium of creating each frame from scratch.

Working with Keyframes

Right-clicking a keyframe in the Timeline displays the shortcut menu shown in Figure 4.10. You have already used the Insert Keyframe option to add a keyframe at the selected frame box in the Timeline. When you insert a new keyframe in the Timeline, the content from the previous keyframe is automatically copied to the new frame. You can edit the content as required and then move on to the next keyframe. Click Insert Blank Keyframe to clear from the stage objects in the previous keyframe. Blank keyframes are used to create new images from scratch or to display a blank stage within or at the end of a movie.

FIGURE 4.10 *Shortcut Menu for a Selected Keyframe*

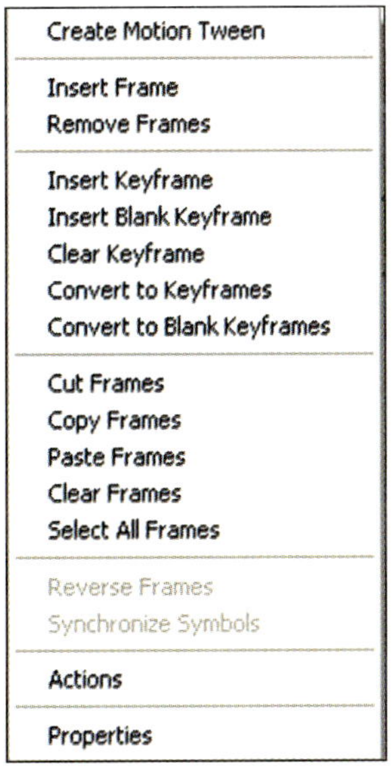

Click Clear Keyframe to remove the frame's keyframe status. Content associated with the keyframe is also removed from the stage. The frame that was previously identified as a keyframe is now a regular frame which displays objects from the previous keyframe in the Timeline.

Converting a Regular Frame to a Keyframe

As you saw in Chapter 1, frame 1 is automatically considered a keyframe. Inserting a keyframe in the Timeline causes Flash to automatically create frames between frame 1 and the frame at which a keyframe was inserted. For example, inserting a keyframe at frame 10 causes Flash to automatically generate frames 2 through 9. Frames 2 through 9 display the content from keyframe 1. The frames between keyframes are shaded gray in the Timeline and are referred to by a variety of terms such as regular frames, ordinary frames, or in-between frames. Flash treats all of the frames from one keyframe to the next keyframe as a *keyframe span*. Right-clicking a gray shaded regular frame and choosing Convert to Keyframes at the shortcut menu will convert the frame status to keyframe. Flash displays a hollow rectangle in the frame immediately left of the converted keyframe indicating the end of the keyframe span and then begins a new span at the converted keyframe. Edit the content in the converted keyframe as required.

Click Convert to Blank Keyframes to cause Flash to clear the stage of content from the blank keyframe to the end of the keyframe span. For example, in an animation with a keyframe at frames 1 and 10, right-clicking frame 6 and choosing Convert to Blank Keyframes would cause Flash to clear the objects from the stage in frame 1 for frames 6–9.

exercise 13 — CREATING AND EDITING A FRAME-BY-FRAME ANIMATION

1. Open the Flash document named Sailboats.
2. Save the document with Save As and name it Ch4Ex13.
3. Make sure the Properties panel is collapsed and the magnification is set to 100%.
4. Create a frame-by-frame animation in which the boats will pass each other in the water by completing the following steps:
   a. Click frame 2 in the *Water* layer.
   b. Hold down the Shift key and then click frame 7 in the *Sunset* layer.
   c. Click Insert and then click Frame.
   d. Rename the *Sailboat2* layer *RightSailboat*.
   e. Rename the *Sailboat1* layer *LeftSailboat*.

f. Turn on the display of the rulers.
g. Drag a vertical guide line to 50 pixels on the horizontal ruler. Continue dragging vertical guides every 50 pixels across the stage. You will have 10 guides when completed.

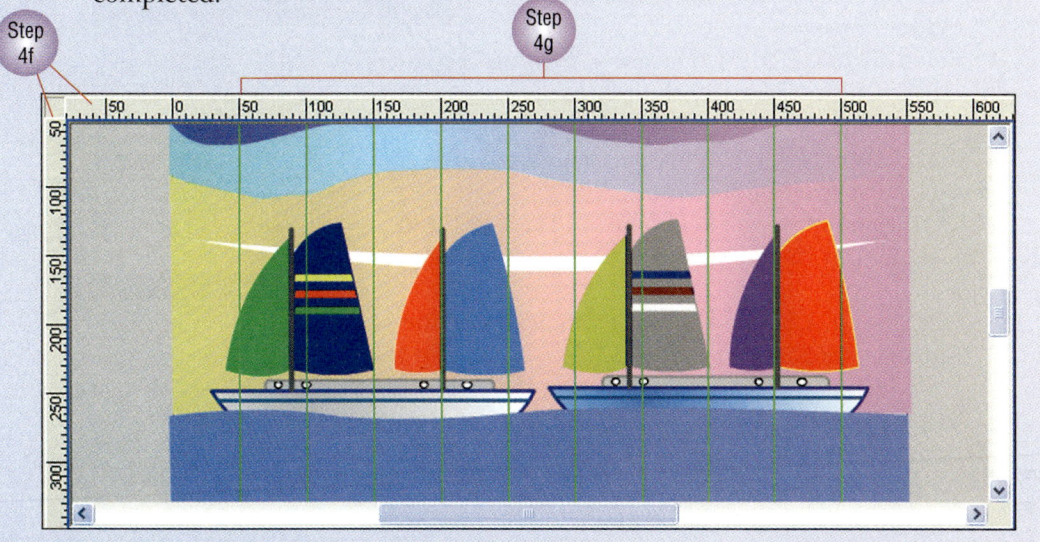

h. Right-click frame 2 in the *RightSailboat* layer and then click Insert Keyframe.
i. With the sailboat at the right side of the stage selected, drag the sailboat left to the guide at 250 pixels.

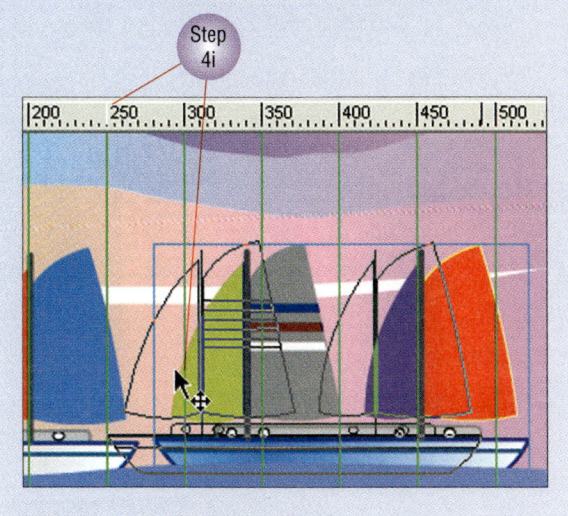

j. Insert a keyframe at frame 2 in the *LeftSailboat* layer.
k. With the sailboat at the left side of the stage selected, drag the sailboat right to the guide at 300 pixels.

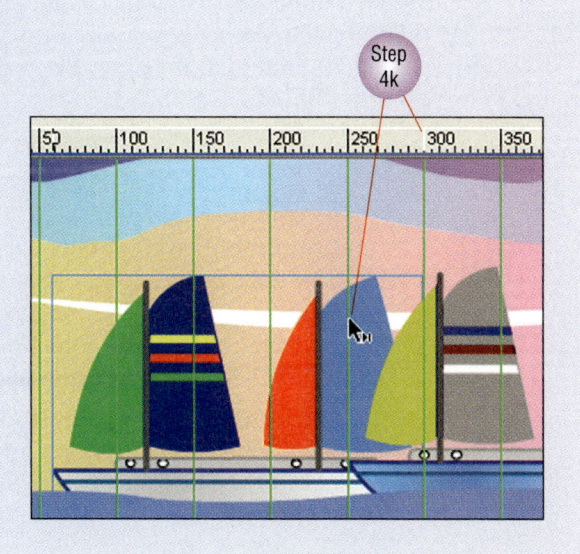

l. Continue inserting keyframes in frames 3–7 of the *RightSailboat* and *LeftSailboat* layers and then dragging the sailboats left and right to the nearest guide. When moving a sailboat, also drag up or down slightly. This will create a bobbing movement in the water during the animation.

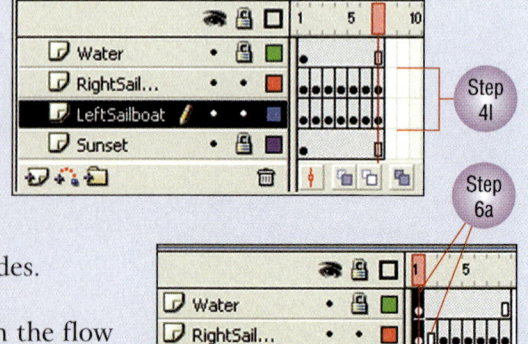

m. Turn off the display of the rulers and guides.

5. Preview the animation.
6. Add frames between the keyframes to smooth the flow of movement in the animation by completing the following steps:
   a. Click frame 1 in the *Water* layer, hold down the Shift key, click frame 1 in the *Sunset* layer, and then press F5, which is the shortcut key to the Insert Frame command. The new frames are inserted to the right of the selected frames. Notice the hollow rectangle displayed in the newly inserted frame 2 in the *RightSailboat* and *LeftSailboat* layers indicating the end of the keyframe span from keyframe 1.
   b. Click frame 4 in the *Water* layer, hold down the Shift key, click frame 6 in the *Sunset* layer, and then press F5. Selecting a block of frames in the Timeline allows you to insert more than one frame.
   c. Select frames 8–9 in all four layers and then insert frames.
   d. Select frames 11–13 in all four layers and then insert frames.
   e. Select frames 15–16 in all four layers and then insert frames.
   f. Click frame 1 in the *Water* layer and then preview the revised animation.
7. Change the frame rate to 10 fps and then preview the revised animation.
8. Save the revised animation using the same name (Ch4Ex13).

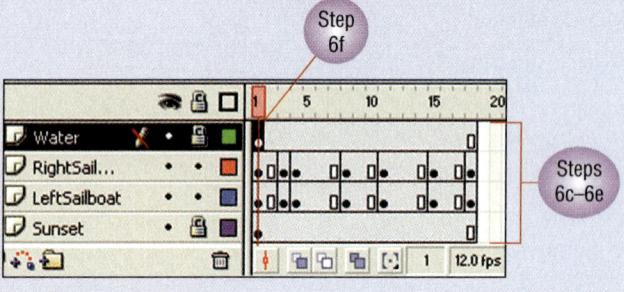

Onion Skin View

Traditional animation artists used tracing paper (sometimes referred to as onion skin) to draw frames which they could stack in order to see the effect of the current frame's change from the previous frames. Flash's Onion Skin view along with the Onion Skin tools in the Timeline panel provides you with a similar technique in which to view and edit frame-by-frame animations.

Click the Onion Skin button at the bottom of the Timeline panel to display a frame-by-frame animation in Onion Skin view. Figure 4.11 illustrates the animation created in Exercise 13 in Onion Skin view for all keyframes and with the *LeftSailboat* layer hidden.

FIGURE

4.11 Onion Skin View for a Frame-by-Frame Animation

   Displaying the movie in Onion Skin view provides you with a better insight into the movements in the animation since the flow of the object in each keyframe can be shown in one static image across the stage. Hidden or locked layers are not displayed when Onion Skin view is turned on. In an animation where multiple objects are being moved, hiding or locking layers allows you to focus on one object at a time. Several objects displayed in Onion Skin view can become confusing and detract from the purpose of the view.

   In Onion Skin view the object being animated is shown dimmed in each frame except the current frame. Dimmed frames cannot be selected. Clicking a keyframe in the Timeline causes Flash to remove the display of onion skinned frames left of the current keyframe in the Timeline. The position of the object in keyframes to the right of the active keyframe remain on the stage as dimmed onion skinned objects.

Viewing Onion Skinned Frames as Outlines

Clicking the Onion Skin Outlines button at the bottom of the Timeline panel displays the animation with outlined objects instead of dimmed objects. Figure 4.12 illustrates the animation created in Exercise 13 in Onion Skin Outlines view for all keyframes and with the *RightSailboat* layer hidden.

Onion Skin Outlines

FIGURE

4.12 Onion Skin Outlines View for a Frame-by-Frame Animation

FLASH MX

Creating Animation and Guidelines for Flash Project Design   193

Editing in Onion Skin View

Edit Multiple Frames

Viewing the position of an animated object in context with its position in later keyframes allows you to determine if the object needs to be edited. Click the Edit Multiple Frames button at the bottom of the Timeline panel if you decide to move an object once you have viewed the onion skinned frames. Figure 4.13 illustrates the animation created in Exercise 13 with Edit Multiple Frames turned on for five frames on either side of the current frame. Notice each object is displayed in full color indicating any of the frames can be selected and edited.

FIGURE 4.13 *Edit Multiple Frames View*

Start and End Onion Skin markers

The keyframe span for the object being moved is activated.

Any of the sailboats can be moved to a new position in Edit Multiple Frames.

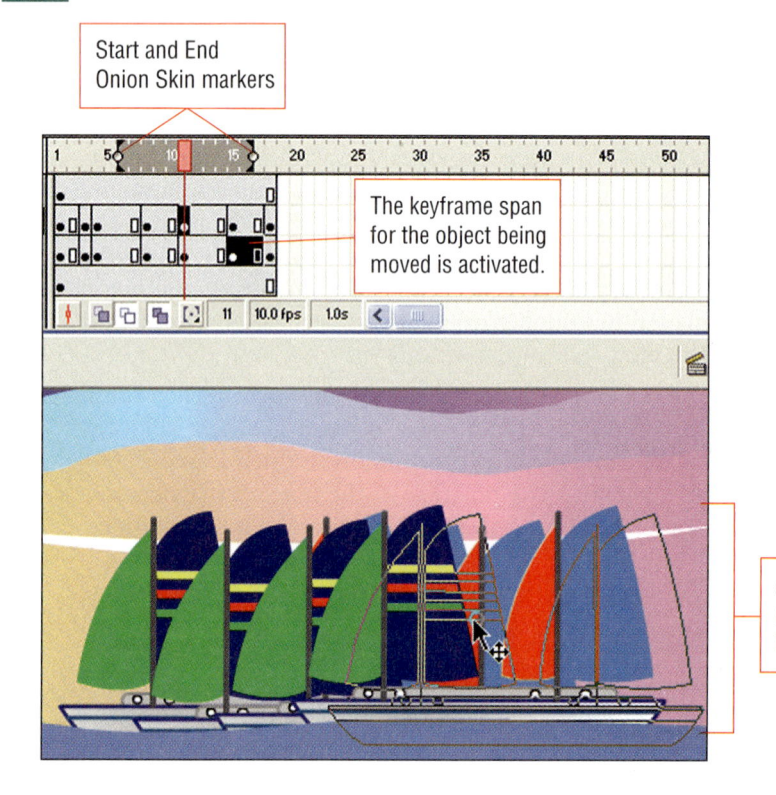

Modify Onion Markers

With Edit Multiple Frames active, you can drag the object in any of the frames to a new position. Flash automatically activates the keyframe span for the object being moved. The Start and End Onion Skin markers in the frame number row of the Timeline can be dragged left or right to increase or decrease the span of frames being viewed. In addition to dragging the onion skin markers, you can select options from the Modify Onion Markers menu shown in Figure 4.14.

FIGURE 4.14 *Modify Onion Markers Menu*

Always Show Markers
Anchor Onion

Onion 2
Onion 5
Onion All

194 Chapter Four

FLASH MX

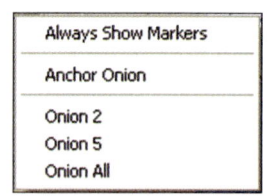

Click the Modify Onion Markers button at the bottom of the Timeline panel and then choose from the following options:

- Always Show Markers displays the onion skin markers in the frame number row of the Timeline whether or not Onion Skin view is currently turned on.
- Anchor Onion freezes the current location of the markers in the frame number row. This means that activating a frame outside the current range of markers will not cause the markers to move to the playhead position.
- Onion 2 sets the marker range to two frames on either side of the playhead position.
- Onion 5 sets the marker range to five frames on either side of the playhead position.
- Onion All sets the marker range to all frames.

exercise 14 — VIEWING AND EDITING AN ANIMATION USING ONION SKIN VIEWS

1. With Ch4Ex13 open, view the animation using various onion skin marker ranges and views by completing the following steps:
   a. If necessary, move the playhead to frame 1.
   b. Click the Onion Skin button at the bottom of the Timeline panel.
   c. Click Modify Onion Markers and then click Onion 5 at the drop-down list.
   d. Click frame 11 in the *RightSailboat* layer. Notice that with both animated sailboats displayed it is difficult to determine the movement path for either object.
   e. Hide the *LeftSailboat* layer.
   f. Click Modify Onion Markers and then click Onion 2 at the drop-down list.
   g. Drag the Start Onion Skin marker to frame 5 and the End Onion Skin marker to frame 15.
   h. Click Onion Skin Outlines to display the objects in Outline mode.
   i. Unhide the *LeftSailboat* layer and hide the *RightSailboat* layer.
2. Edit the animation using onion skins by completing the following steps:
   a. Click Edit Multiple Frames at the bottom of the Timeline panel.
   b. Click Modify Onion Markers and then click Onion All.

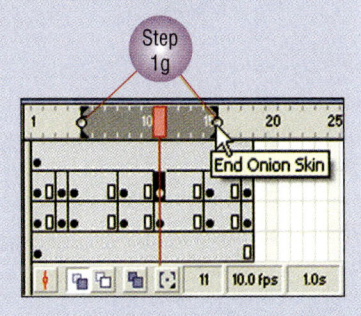

FLASH MX — Creating Animation and Guidelines for Flash Project Design

    c. Drag the sailboat in the last frame right until the entire first sail is in the workspace as shown. *(Note: What is visible on the stage is what the user will see in a published movie—if you were to publish this movie only the portion of the sailboat remaining on the stage would be visible.)*
    d. Unhide the *RightSailboat* layer and then hide the *LeftSailboat* layer.
    e. Drag the sailboat in the last frame until the entire first sail is in the workspace similar to Step 2c.
    f. Click Edit Multiple Frames to turn off the feature.
    g. Click Onion Skin Outlines to turn off the feature.
3. Unhide the *LeftSailboat* layer.
4. Click frame 1 and then preview the animation in the Flash Player window.
5. Save the revised document using the same name (Ch4Ex13).

Changing Frame View Options

Frame View

The frames in the Timeline can be changed to display in a different size or height, with or without the shading to indicate the type of tween, or as thumbnails. To change the appearance of the frame boxes, click the Frame View button located at the right end of the frame number row above the vertical scroll bar to display the menu shown in Figure 4.15.

FIGURE 4.15 *Frame View Options*

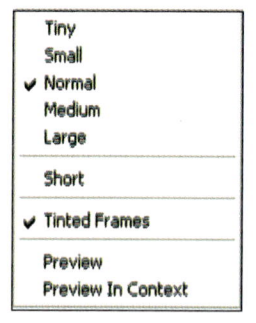

Tiny
Small
✓ Normal
Medium
Large

Short

✓ Tinted Frames

Preview
Preview In Context

    Depending on the number of frames and layers in the movie, changing the size of the frames or the height can alleviate some of the need to scroll through the Timeline. The width of frames can be set to Tiny, Small, Normal, Medium, or Large. Figure 4.16 illustrates examples of the various settings using the Timeline for the movie created in Exercise 13.

FIGURE 4.16 Frame View Width Options

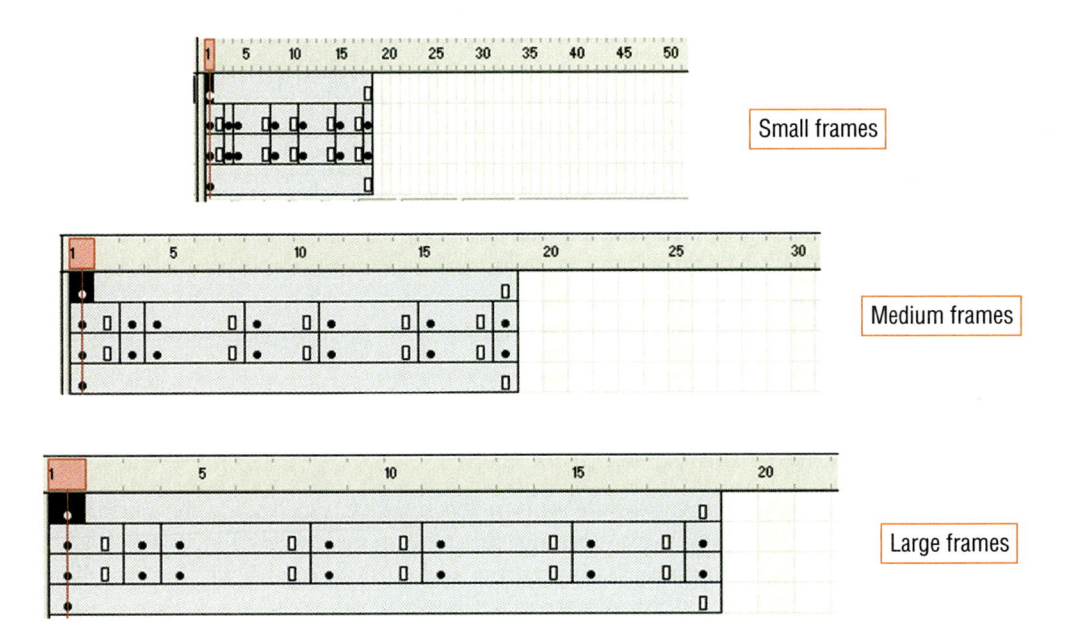

Small frames

Medium frames

Large frames

Click Short from the Frame View menu to decrease the height of frames. By default, Tinted Frames is turned on displaying shading in frame boxes indicating the type of tween in effect or inserted frame. Turning off tinting displays all frame boxes with a white background. Tweened frames are identified with filled dots and by different colored arrows from the start keyframe to the end keyframe.

Click Preview from the Frame View menu to display the objects in each frame scaled to fit (referred to as "thumbnails") within a large frame box. Preview In Context displays each frame's objects relative to the entire frame. Figure 4.17 illustrates the Timeline in Preview and Preview In Context view using the Timeline for the movie created in Exercise 13.

FIGURE 4.17 Preview and Preview In Context Frame View Options

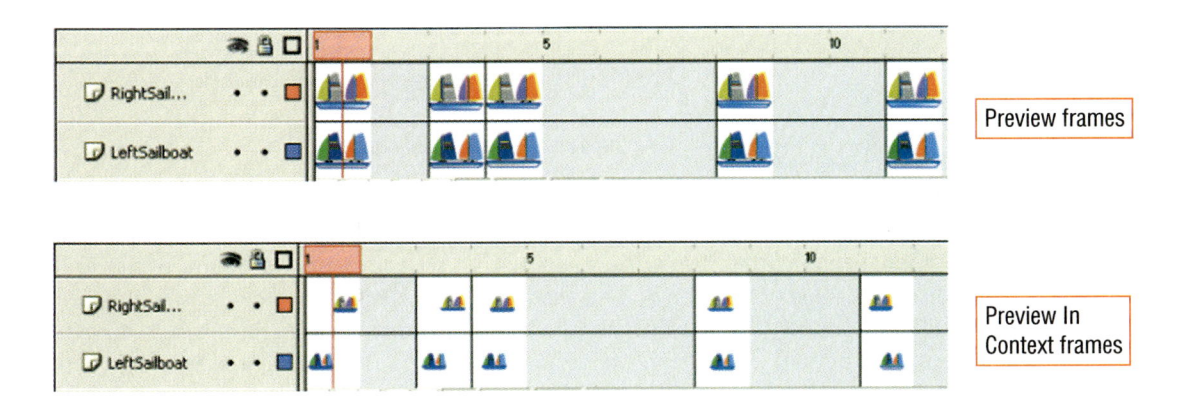

Preview frames

Preview In Context frames

FLASH MX
Creating Animation and Guidelines for Flash Project Design
197

Centering a Frame within the Timeline Panel

Center Frame

The animations that you have created in this chapter have not required any amount of scrolling left or right in the Timeline since all frames have fit within the current window. A large movie can contain hundreds of frames. The Center Frame button at the bottom left of the Timeline panel can be used to center the current frame in the Timeline panel window. Additionally, if you scroll left or right and the centered frame is no longer visible, clicking the Center Frame button returns the Timeline to the location where the centered frame is in the middle of the window. For example, assume you are currently editing frame 75 in a movie containing 600 frames. You want to quickly scroll to frame 500 to view the Timeline but then return back to frame 75. With frame 75 active, click the Center Frame button. Frame 75 moves to the center of the Timeline window. Scroll right to frame 500. Click the Center Frame button again to return the window back to frame 75 in the center with just one click.

Organizing Animations Using Scenes

You may have been wondering why in the Information bar for the Flash documents with which you have been working, *Scene 1* has displayed next to the Back button. The movies that you have been creating and editing so far have been small and have not necessitated a need to create additional scenes. Scenes are an organizational tool for larger, more complex movies.

Create scenes when you want to break down a movie into manageable sections for creating and editing purposes. Each scene's content and animation is viewed within a separate Timeline and stage. If you consider the Timeline the script for your movie, then scenes are the "acts." When the movie is previewed, scene one plays from start to finish, then scene two plays from start to finish, and so on until all scenes within the movie have been played. Click Window and then click Scene to open the Scene panel shown in Figure 4.18 in which scenes are created, renamed, deleted, and rearranged.

FIGURE 4.18 *Scene Panel*

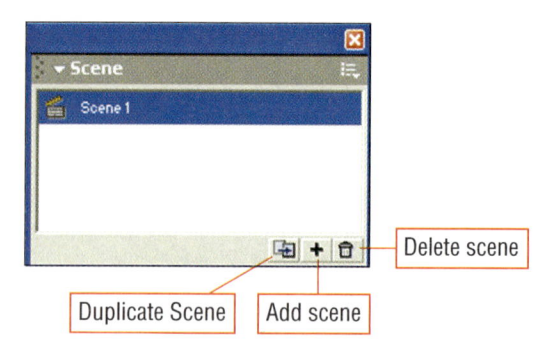

Click the Add scene button at the bottom of the Scene panel or click Insert and then Scene. *Scene 2* is added to the list of scenes in the Scene panel and automatically becomes active. The Flash window displays a new blank stage and Timeline. Looking at the scene number in the Information bar becomes important when working with a multiple-scene movie to keep track of where you are in the movie sequence. Although the first frame is numbered 1 at the beginning of the

Timeline, it is important to remember that the current scene will not begin until the previous scene has ended. Flash names scenes *Scene #* where # is the next in sequence in a similar manner as layers. Double-click the scene name in the Scene panel to key a more descriptive title.

Click the Delete scene button in the Scene panel or click Insert and then Remove Scene to delete a scene and all of its content from the movie. Since this will result in a destructive action that cannot be undone, Flash requires confirmation before the scene is deleted as shown in Figure 4.19.

FIGURE
4.19 **Delete Scene Confirmation Dialog Box**

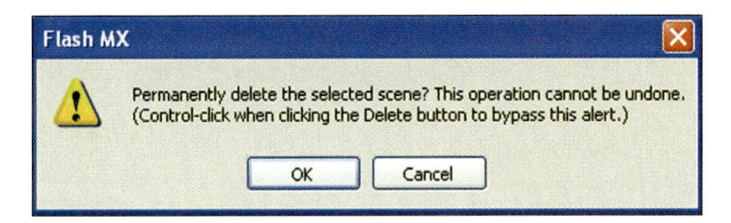

Click the Duplicate Scene button in the Scene panel to create an exact copy of the active scene. Flash adds the duplicated scene immediately below the source scene with the name *Scene # copy*. All content in all frames in the Timeline is copied to the new scene. This can be a useful tool if the next scene in the movie you are creating is similar to the current scene. Create a duplicate of the scene and then you only need to edit the objects and animation sequence that will be different in the next part of the movie.

Scenes can be reordered in the Scene panel by dragging and dropping the scene name in a similar manner to how you move layers in the Timeline.

Navigating Scenes

In a movie with multiple scenes, click a scene name in the Scene panel to display the content and Timeline of the scene in the Flash window. If the Scene panel is not currently open, click the Edit Scene button at the right end of the Information bar and then click the desired scene name in the drop-down list or click View, point to Go To, and then click the name of the scene at the side menu.

Edit Scene

exercise 15

CREATING AND EDITING SCENES

1. With Ch4Ex13 open, insert a new scene and rename scenes by completing the following steps:
   a. Click Window and then click Scene to open the Scene panel.
   b. Drag the Scene panel's title bar to the top right of the Timeline.
   c. Click the Add scene button at the bottom of the Scene panel. *Scene 2* is added to the scene list below Scene 1 and a clear stage and Timeline are displayed in the Flash window.

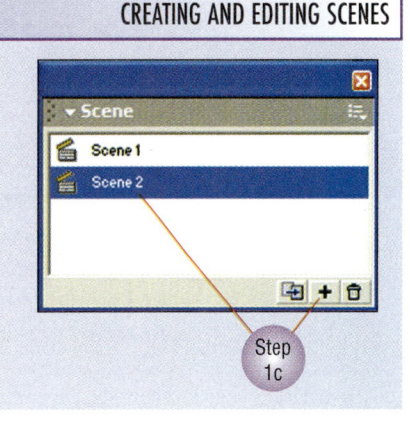

Step 1c

FLASH MX
Creating Animation and Guidelines for Flash Project Design
199

d. Double-click Scene 1 in the Scene panel, key **Sailboats**, and then press Enter. Notice the stage and Timeline for Scene 1 are redisplayed in the Flash window. 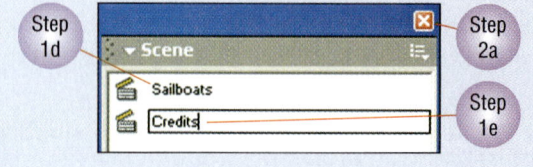
e. Double-click Scene 2 in the Scene panel, key **Credits**, and then press Enter.

2. Copy content from the existing scene to the new scene by completing the following steps:
    a. Close the Scene panel.
    b. Click the Edit Scene button at the right end of the Information bar and then click Sailboats at the drop-down list.
    c. With Sailboats the active scene in the Flash window, click the *Water* layer to select it, and then unlock the layer.
    d. With the water object selected on the stage, click *E*dit, click *C*opy, and then relock the *Water* layer.
    e. Click *V*iew, point to *G*o to, and then click Credits. 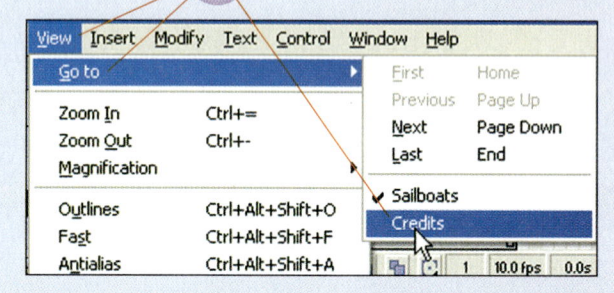 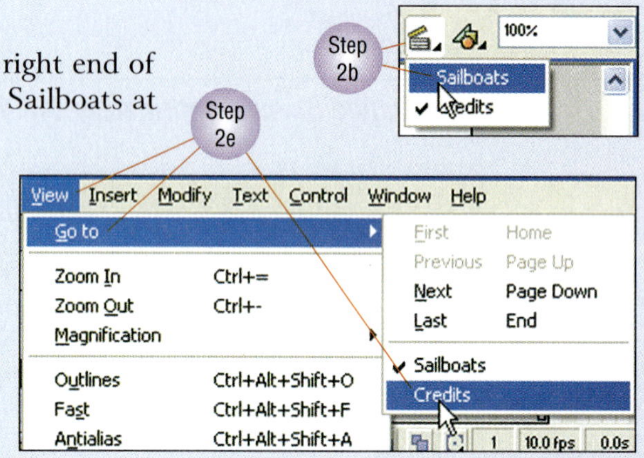
    f. With Credits the active scene, click *E*dit and then click Paste i*n* Place. The water is pasted to the stage in the same location as it resided in the Sailboats scene.
    g. Go to the Sailboats scene using either of the two methods learned in this exercise.
    h. Click the *Sunset* layer to select it and then unlock the layer.
    i. Press Ctrl + C to copy the selected content to the clipboard and then relock the *Sunset* layer.
    j. Go to the Credits scene and paste in place the copied content.

3. Create and animate new content in the Credits scene by completing the following steps:
    a. Rename Layer 1 *Background*.
    b. Insert a new layer and name it *Credits*.
    c. With *Credits* the active layer, click the Text tool.
    d. Set the following text properties:
        1) Font Comic Sans MS.
        2) Font size 36 points.

3) Choose a dark blue color swatch for the Text (fill) color.
4) Turn on bold.
5) Change alignment to Center.

   e. Create the text box containing the text shown in the approximate location on the stage. Substitute your first and last names for *Student Name*.

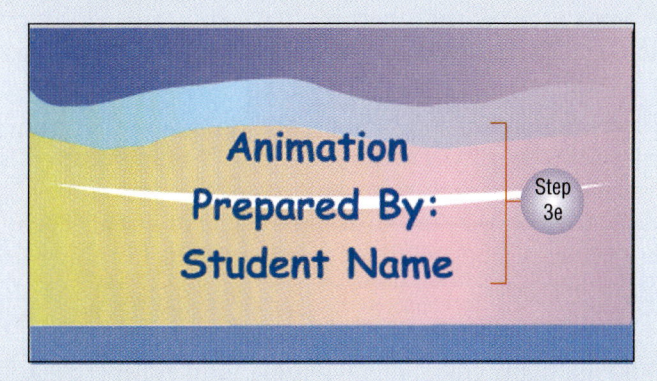

Animation
Prepared By:
Student Name — Step 3e

   f. Right-click frame 10 in the *Credits* layer and then click Insert Blank Keyframe at the shortcut menu.

   g. Right-click frame 10 in the *Background* layer and then click Insert Blank Keyframe at the shortcut menu.

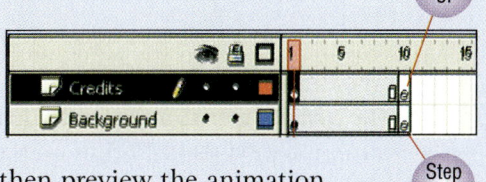

   h. Click frame 1 of either layer and then preview the animation.

4. Go to the Sailboats scene.
5. Click <u>C</u>ontrol and then click Test <u>M</u>ovie to preview the animation in the Flash Player window.
6. Close the Flash Player window and then save the revised document using the same name (Ch4Ex13).
7. Close Ch4Ex13.

Guidelines for Flash Project Design

At this point you have learned how to use the basic features of Flash with which you can draw your own pictures, create text blocks, import graphics, and create animations. Many more features in Flash are yet to be explored. In the following chapters you will learn how to incorporate sound, video, and buttons; how to prepare and publish a Flash movie; and how to add ActionScript statements.

   It is a good idea to explore the issues and processes involved in producing a Flash movie project since understanding the scope of the process will complement your technical skills and allow you to put the production process in perspective. Many times you will be part of a team of authors, designers, and developers where your contribution will be measured by how well you relate to others on the team and to the process. In the following sections you will be introduced to some of the preproduction concepts and procedures involved in the creation of a Flash movie.

The Role of Communication

The beginning of a Flash project is predominately concerned with finding the answers to several questions, as you will see in the following sections. The answers will drive the design of the project. Prior to commencing any work make sure you understand for whom the movie is being developed. If you are developing a Flash project for yourself then you have only yourself to answer to but if you are developing a Flash project for someone else, the needs of that person or organization must be clearly understood.

Clear communication between the client and the team, and within the team, must be a top priority. The importance of communication is often underestimated and yet poor communication can become the reason for a project running behind schedule, over budget, or outside the scope of intent. Each person involved in the process carries responsibility for communicating his or her needs and understanding the needs of others.

Defining the Goals and Limiting Factors for a Flash Project

Flash movies are incorporated in Web sites or as part of another multimedia product such as a training course delivered by CD-ROM. An understanding of the expected outcomes from the movie is the first step in the process. Ask the following questions:

- What is the movie's purpose?
- Is the movie intended to inform or entertain the end user?
- Should the movie promote a bias towards a product or service?
- What is the main message that is to be portrayed?

Once you have discussed and understand the project mission, you next need to determine if there are any limiting factors that will affect the project. Limiting factors can be technological, philosophical, or administrative in nature. Determine the answers to the following questions and whether they apply to the project:

- What is the project schedule?
- What is the project budget?
- How will the content be delivered?
- Are we starting from scratch or does the client have existing material that can be reused or re-engineered?
- Are graphics required that cannot be done in Flash?
- Is sound or video required?
- Has the client presented any design guidelines?
- What are the specifications for the Web site in which the movie will be incorporated?
- Are there any copyright issues that have to be resolved?

Many times a Flash project will be driven by the answers to the first three questions. Often in business, time and money become the critical factors. More than likely you will be required to deliver a movie in a short period of time for as little cost as possible. If the content will be delivered via the Web, then download time for the movie will be a considerable factor of concern. If, however, the content will be packaged in another medium, you may be able to incorporate more graphics, sounds, and/or video.

Determining the Audience for the Movie

Correctly defining the audience and then designing the Flash project to meet the needs of the target viewer will ensure the goals of the project are met. A movie to promote a retirement living community requires a totally different look and feel than a movie designed to inform postsecondary students on the latest job search strategies. Audience-centered design involves researching the following points:

- Demographics of expected audience.
- Audience expectations for a Web site or multimedia package for the product or service that is being represented.
- Presence of a bias or other preconception about the subject matter.

A popular strategy used at this stage is to assemble a focus group of members within the target audience and ask them what they like and don't like. Include questions on use of color, graphics, animations, sound, video, and interface design.

Researching Best Practices for Flash

Once you understand the audience you can use the Web to research sites targeted at those users. Consider the top Web sites used by your target audience and then spend a considerable amount of time surfing those sites. Find sites that have Flash incorporated and see how it has been used. At each site consider the following points:

- What was the element that held your interest?
- Was the surfing experience intuitive?
- How much interactivity was included?
- What colors were used and did the colors create a sense of harmony?
- What properties were used for the text?
- How much graphical content was incorporated and how was it used?
- Did the movie take too long to download?
- Was there a method with which users could turn the sound on or off?
- What would you improve at the site?

If possible, have focus group members visit the top two or three sites and provide you with feedback.

Creating a Flow Chart and Storyboard for the Movie

A flow chart provides you with a document that visually maps out the movie in sequence. It includes what the user will see first, then second, then third, and so on until the end. If the movie includes interactivity via buttons or other effects, then each action or effect must be considered and the sequences mapped. The flow-charting process causes you to organize the content in a logical manner and consider what each frame should include. The flow chart is a dynamic document. Often, as the project is being developed, changes are required as each segment is produced and tested.

A storyboard goes beyond the flow chart to include details and specifics on the document properties such as size, color, frame rate, background, graphics, text, sound, and video including colors, fonts, position of objects on the stage, and so on for each frame in the movie. Think of the storyboard as the master script describing each frame in each layer in the Timeline in enough detail so that any person who knows Flash could step in and create the movie by reading the script.

Once the storyboard is complete, the project is divided up among members of a production team. For example, the project may be divided by task specialists with one person responsible for graphics, another for sound, another for text, and another for programming. A project manager keeps track of the individuals and the progress of the movie.

The guidelines presented in this chapter are intended as an introduction to the process of larger Flash development work. Flash movies are usually part of an overall Web design strategy that may involve more comprehensive planning and specification.

CHAPTER summary

- Animation in Flash can be created using either a tweened approach or a frame-by-frame approach.
- In tweened animations only two keyframes are created and then Flash creates the frames between the start and end objects called *interpolated frames*.
- *Motion tweens* move a grouped object, instance, or text block from one location to another.
- *Shape tweens* morph an ungrouped object from one shape to another.
- By default, Flash scales the size difference between the starting and ending object in a motion tween.
- A motion tween can rotate the object clockwise or counterclockwise a set number of times between the starting and ending position on the stage.
- The speed with which an object moves in a tweened animation is constant.
- Key a positive or negative value between 1 and 100 in the Ease property of a motion or shape tween to accelerate or decelerate the speed of movement.
- A motion layer can be connected to a tweened object to direct its movement along a path other than a straight line.
- Orienting the tweened object to the motion path will cause the object to move relative to the angle of the line or shape on the guide layer.
- Clicking Control and then Test Movie exports the document in *swf* format and then previews the animation in a Flash Player window within the Flash window.
- A motion tween can be created that will gradually change the color of the tweened object by changing the instance's tint, brightness, or alpha settings.
- Inserting a keyframe between the starting and ending keyframes of an existing motion tween causes Flash to create back-to-back motion tweens.
- Holding down the Shift key and clicking the mouse selects the range of frames adjacent to the current frame.
- Holding down the Ctrl key and clicking the mouse selects nonadjacent frames.
- Frames can also be selected by dragging the mouse across the frame boxes.
- The duration of a movie can be lengthened by inserting frames or dragging the ending keyframe further down the Timeline.
- Remove Frames deletes the selected frames from the Timeline including all content associated with the frames.
- Use the Clear Frames command to remove a selected frame's content but leave the frame box intact.
- A cleared frame is converted to a blank keyframe.
- Move a frame by dragging the frame box to another location on the Timeline.
- The Copy Frame command is used to duplicate content within an animation.
- Press Enter to preview an animation using the Play command, which runs through the movie once and then stops.
- Click Loop Playback on the Control menu to preview animations using the Play command over and over again until a Stop command is issued.

- By default, animations in the Flash Player window within Flash play in looped playback mode.
- *Scrubbing* is a technique used to preview a movie by dragging the playhead back and forth.
- Display the Controller toolbar to preview animations using buttons to play, stop, rewind, step back, and step forward.
- Create a shape tweened animation from the Interpolate drop-down list for a selected frame in the Properties panel.
- Choose Distributive or Angular as the morph type in a shape tween to interpolate the frames in a smooth fashion or by maintaining corners and straight lines.
- Shape hints are corresponding markers placed on the start and end objects that control how the shape is interpolated.
- The default frame rate of 12 frames per second (fps) can be adjusted in the Document Properties dialog box to vary the speed with which the movie is played.
- A higher fps setting increases file size since more frames are required to achieve the same movie length as a lower fps setting.
- Complex animations can play back at variable rates dependent on the processing speed of the computer upon which the movie is being played.
- Frame-by-frame animations are built by inserting keyframes at each change in content.
- Inserting a blank keyframe clears the stage of content from the previous keyframe.
- Flash automatically creates a keyframe span which includes frames from the starting keyframe to the frame immediately left of the next keyframe.
- Frames between keyframes are shaded gray.
- Motion tweened frames are shaded light blue and shape tweened frames are shaded light green.
- Keyframes can be created by converting regular frames to keyframes.
- Onion Skin view displays the position of objects on more than one frame on the stage. This view can provide a better insight into an animation's movements.
- Hidden or locked layers do not display in Onion Skin view.
- Onion skinning displays the current frame in full color while adjacent frames are dimmed.
- Click Onion Skin Outlines to display objects within the dimmed frames in Outline mode.
- Onion skinned frames cannot be edited unless Edit Multiple Frames is turned on.
- The Start Onion Skin and End Onion Skin markers in the frame number row can be dragged left or right to increase or decrease the span of onion skinned frames.
- Click Modify Onion Markers to choose options controlling the number of frames displayed in Onion Skin view.
- Frames in the Timeline can be displayed with different width and height options by clicking the Frame View button at the top right of the Timeline panel.
- The Center Frame button in the Timeline panel centers the active frame within the Timeline window.
- Scenes are used in movies to organize content into manageable chunks.
- Each scene is created and edited in a separate Timeline and stage.
- Click Window and then Scene to open the Scene panel to insert, rename, duplicate, delete, and reorder scenes.
- Navigate to another scene in a movie by clicking the scene name from the Scene panel, the Edit Scene drop-down list from the Information bar, or by clicking View and then Go to, and then choosing the scene name at the side menu.

- The needs of the individual or organization for which a Flash project is being created must be clearly communicated and understood by all team members.
- Clear communication is essential for completion of a successful project.
- Begin a Flash project by defining the goals and limiting factors for the movie.
- Audience-centered design involves determining the audience for which a Flash movie is geared and then researching the demographics, expectations, needs, and bias of the target group.
- Research best practices for Flash design by spending a considerable amount of time surfing the Web sites of successful organizations who serve the target audience for your Flash project.
- A flow chart for a Flash project is a dynamic document that visually maps the movie in sequence and is designed to show the logical progression of the content.
- Storyboarding a project includes details and specifications on document properties, each individual frame and its objects including graphics, colors, fonts, position, sound, and video.
- The storyboard represents the master script for the movie with enough information so that anyone could take over the project and create the movie by reading the storyboard.
- Flash projects are usually divided up among group members based on expertise.
- A Flash project is usually part of a larger Web design strategy.

COMMANDS review

Command or Feature	Mouse/Keyboard	Shortcut Keys
Add scene	Insert, Scene	
Add shape hints	Modify, Shape, Add Shape Hint	Ctrl + Shift + H
Clear frames	Edit, Clear Frames	Alt + Backspace
Clear keyframe	Insert, Clear Keyframe	Shift + F6
Copy frames	Edit, Copy Frames	Ctrl + Alt + C
Controller toolbar	Window, Toolbars, Controller	
Create motion tween	Insert, Create Motion Tween	
Cut frames	Edit, Cut Frames	Ctrl + Alt + X
Document properties	Modify, Document	Ctrl + J
Insert blank keyframe	Insert, Blank keyframe	
Insert frame	Insert, Frame	F5
Insert keyframe	Insert, Keyframe	
Insert motion guide	Insert, Motion Guide	
Loop playback of movie	Control, Loop Playback	
Paste frames	Edit, Paste Frames	Ctrl + Alt + V

Paste in Place	Edit, Paste in Place	Ctrl + Shift + V
Play movie	Control, Play	Enter
Play movie in Flash Player format	Control, Test Movie	Ctrl + Enter
Remove frames	Insert, Remove Frames	Shift + F5
Remove scene	Insert, Remove Scene	
Remove shape hints	Modify, Shape, Remove All Hints	
Stop playback of a looped movie	Control, Stop	Enter
View shape hints	View, Show Shape Hints	Ctrl + Alt + H
Scene panel	Window, Scene	Shift + F2

CONCEPTS check

Indicate the correct term or command for each item.

1. This is the term used to describe the process where the shape of an object is gradually transformed into a different shape.
2. This type of frame is indicated by a hollow dot.
3. This is the term used to describe the frames between the starting keyframe and ending keyframe of a motion tween.
4. Selecting CCW from the Rotation options list box would cause Flash to do what action with the tweened object?
5. Keying a positive or negative value in the range 1–100 in this text box in the Properties panel for a motion or shape tween causes Flash to accelerate or decelerate the speed with which the object moves.
6. Insert this type of layer to move an object in a motion tween along a path other than a straight line.
7. Previewing an animation in the Flash Player window causes Flash to do this action with the movie.
8. Color styles for a selected instance are changed in this panel.
9. Use this key while clicking the mouse to select multiple nonadjacent frames.
10. Use this option to clear a frame of content but leave the frame box intact in the Timeline.
11. Extend the length of a motion tween by dragging this frame further down the Timeline.
12. Click this option from the Edit menu to paste objects to the stage in the same location from which they were copied.
13. With this option active a movie continually replays until a Stop command is issued.
14. This is the name of the preview technique where the playhead is dragged left and right across the Timeline.
15. Open this window to control the playback of movies using buttons to stop, rewind, step forward, and step backward.

16. The starting and ending objects in a shape tween must be in this state for the tween to create the vectors that transform the shape.
17. A shape hint marker on the starting object is displayed in this color.
18. Delete an individual shape hint marker by doing this action.
19. This is the default number of frames per second for animations.
20. This is the term used to describe all of the frames from a keyframe to the frame immediately left of the next keyframe.
21. In this view, all objects in frames except those in the current frame are dimmed and cannot be selected.
22. This Frame View option displays thumbnails of the frame content scaled to fit within a large frame box.
23. Add this to a movie to create content in a separate Timeline and stage.
24. This is the name for a dynamic document that visually maps the movie in sequence.
25. This document is the master script for the movie containing detailed information and specifics about the movie properties and each individual frame.

SKILLS check

Assessment 1

FIGURE 4.20 Assessment 1

1. Open the Flash document named Ladybug.
2. Save the document with Save As and name it Ch4SA1.
3. Create a motion tween that will move the bug from the left side of the stage to the right side using the following information:
   - Convert the ladybug graphic to a symbol named Ladybug.
   - Create the motion tween in frames 1–20.
   - End the tween with the ladybug at the position shown in Figure 4.20
4. Preview the animation.
5. Save the revised document using the same name (Ch4SA1).

Assessment 2

1. With Ch4SA1 open, save the document with Save As and name it Ch4SA2.
2. Edit the animation by adding two more motion tweens that will rotate the ladybug 165 degrees and then move the ladybug back to the starting position using the following information:
    - Create the second motion tween in frames 21–30.
    - In the ending keyframe of the second motion tween, rotate the graphic so that the ladybug is facing left instead of right. *(Hint: Display the Transform panel and then key -165 in the Rotate text box or use the Free Transform tool to rotate the ladybug.)*
    - Create the third motion tween in frames 31–50 and have the ladybug end in the same position (but facing the opposite direction) as the animation originally started.
3. Change the Ease value to –100 for the first motion tween.
4. Change the Ease value to 100 for the last motion tween.
5. Preview the animation.
6. Save the revised document using the same name (Ch4SA2).
7. Close Ch4SA2.

Assessment 3

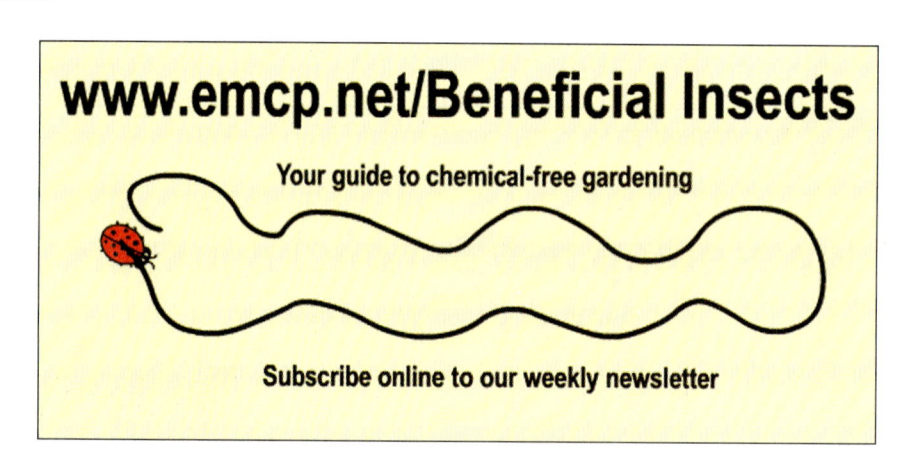

FIGURE 4.21 Assessment 3

1. Open Ch4SA1.
2. Save the document with Save As and name it Ch4SA3.
3. Use the Free Transform tool to resize, rotate, and then move the ladybug in the first keyframe as shown in Figure 4.21.
4. Create a motion guide layer above the *Bug* layer and draw a line for the bug to travel during the animation similar to the line shown in Figure 4.21.
5. Click frame 20 in the *Bug* layer and then resize the ladybug to the same size as the ladybug in Frame 1. Position the ladybug at the end of the motion guide line.
6. Preview the animation. Notice the ladybug does not turn around when the line curves to return back to the left side of the stage.
7. Display the motion tween properties and click the *Orient to Path* check box.
8. Preview the animation. This time the ladybug turns around on the path to return to the left side.
9. Lengthen the duration of the tween by adding 15 frames.

10. Change the frame rate to 10 fps.
11. Preview the animation in the Flash Player window so that you can see the ladybug move without the line visible on the stage.
12. Close the Flash Player window and then save the revised animation using the same name (Ch4SA3).
13. Close Ch4SA3.

Assessment 4

1. Open the Flash document named Bananas.
2. Save the document with Save As and name it Ch4SA4.
3. Create a motion tween that will gradually brighten the color of the bananas using the following information:
   - Create the motion tween in frames 1–25.
   - In the ending keyframe for the *Banana1* layer, change the brightness to 50%.
   - In the ending keyframe for the *Banana2* layer, change the tint to a bright yellow color swatch and set the tint amount to 50%.
   - In the ending keyframe for the *Banana3* layer, change the tint to a bright yellow color swatch and the tint amount to 65%.
4. Preview the animation.
5. Save the revised document using the same name (Ch4SA4).
6. Close Ch4SA4.

Assessment 5

FIGURE

4.22 **Assessment 5**

1. Start a new Flash document.
2. Change the background color of the stage to dark blue as shown in Figure 4.22.
3. Draw a octagon shape at the left side of the stage as shown in Figure 4.22 in frame 1.
4. Create a text block at the right side of the stage with the word *Stop* in frame 60 as shown in Figure 4.22. You determine the appropriate text properties.
5. Convert the text block to a graphic. *(Hint: Use the Break Apart command twice.)*
6. Create a shape tweened animation so that the octagon morphs into the word *Stop*.
7. Preview the animation using the scrubbing technique in slow motion so that you can see the intermediate shapes.
8. Add shape hints as you see fit to see if you can improve the tween.
9. Increase the frame rate to 20 fps.
10. Save the revised document using the same name (Ch4SA5).
11. Close Ch4SA5.

Assessment 6

FIGURE 4.23 *Assessment 6 First Movement of Spider Legs in Keyframe 3*

Drag the bottom section of each leg approximately this amount in keyframe 3.

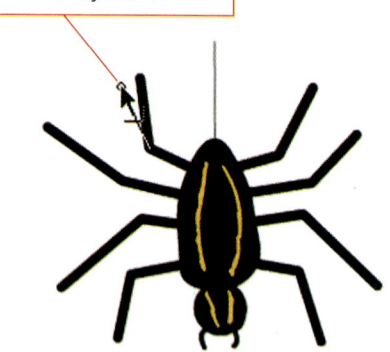

1. Open the Flash document named Spider.
2. Save the document with Save As and name it Ch4SA6.
3. Create a frame-by-frame animation that will move the spider's legs using the following information.
    - Insert a keyframe at frame 3 of the *Legs* layer and then deselect all 8 legs.
    - With the Arrow tool active, drag the bottom section of each leg by the amount shown in Figure 4.23. This first movement is small as shown by the last leg on the left side of the spider's body.
    - Copy keyframe 3, paste it to frame 6 in the *Legs* layer, and then move each leg individually by the same amount in the same direction as keyframe 3.
    - Copy keyframe 6, paste it to frame 10 in the *Legs* layer, and then move each leg individually backward by a small amount.
    - Copy keyframe 10, paste it to frame 12 in the *Legs* layer, and then move each leg individually backward by a small amount.
    - Copy keyframe 12, paste it to frame 15 in the *Legs* layer, and then move each leg individually forward by a small amount.
    - Make sure the other two layers have frames inserted to frame 15.
4. Open the Controller toolbar and then play the animation.
5. Use the Step Backward and Step Forward buttons to review the movement frame to frame. Rewind and then play the animation again.
6. Add four more leg movements to the animation by copying and pasting frames and then moving the legs forward and backward. The revised animation should end somewhere between frames 25–30.
7. Play the revised animation using the Controller buttons.
8. Save the revised document using the same name (Ch4SA6).

Assessment 7

1. With Ch4SA6 open, turn on Onion Skin view.
2. Choose Onion All from the Modify Onion Markers drop-down list.
3. Drag the Start Onion Skin and End Onion Skin markers so that the range of frames displayed is frames 1–15.
4. Change the Onion Skin view to display the frames as outlines.
5. Edit two or three leg movements in Onion Skin view.
6. Turn off Onion Skin view.
7. Play the revised animation using the Controller buttons.
8. Save the revised document using the same name (Ch4SA6).
9. Close the Controller toolbar.
10. Close Ch4SA6.

Assessment 8

1. Open Ch4SA3.
2. Save the document with Save As and name it Ch4SA8.
3. Add a new scene to the movie and name it *Credits*.
4. Rename Scene 1 Main and then close the Scene panel.
5. With Credits the active scene, create the following content:
    - Create a text block in the center of the stage horizontally and vertically containing the text *Animation by Student Name* where your first and last names are substituted for *Student Name*. You determine the text properties.
    - Select and then break apart the text block so that each character is in a separate block.
    - Distribute the text blocks to separate layers.
    - Delete *Layer 1*.
6. Animate each character by creating a motion tween that will show the letters entering from the top or bottom of the stage and ending at the center as follows:
    - Insert keyframes at frame 15 for each layer.
    - Click frame 1 of each layer and then drag the letter to the top or bottom of the stage depending on whether the text wraps to a second line. For example, if *Animation by* is on the first line, drag the letters in the words *Animation by* to the top of the stage. Drag the letters in the second line to the bottom of the stage.
    - Create a motion tween in each layer in the scene.
    - Play the animation in the Credits scene.
    - If necessary, adjust the starting position of some of the letters.
7. Go to the Main scene.
8. Preview the animation in the Flash Player window.
9. Close the Flash Player window.
10. Save the revised document using the same name (Ch4SA8).
11. Close Ch4SA8.

Assessment 9

1. Using the Internet, conduct a search using your favorite search engine for information on one of the following topics that interests you:
    - Web-safe Color Palette
    - Color Theory
    - Web Design
    - Storyboarding

2. Find at least three sites containing information about the topic that is as current as possible.
3. Work with another student in the class. If possible find a student who researched a topic different than the one you did.
4. Discuss with the other student what you learned from the Internet and have the other student explain his or her topic and research findings.
5. Create a document in Word or WordPerfect that briefly explains five main points that you learned from your research and then five main points from the other student's research.
6. Save the document and name it Ch4SA9.
7. Print and then close Ch4SA9. Exit Word or WordPerfect.

CHAPTER 5

ADDING SOUND, VIDEO, AND BASIC INTERACTIVITY WITH BUTTONS

PERFORMANCE OBJECTIVES

Upon successful completion of Chapter 5, you will be able to:
- List the audio formats supported in Flash.
- Import sound to a movie's library.
- Add sound to an animation in a keyframe.
- Change synchronization, sound effects, and loop sound.
- Edit the sound envelope to customize a sound effect and control volume.
- Specify the compression setting for the sound file.
- Describe how sampling rate and sample size affect a sound file.
- Use sounds from the common library.
- Increase the layer height to display sounds in frames.
- List the video formats supported in Flash.
- Import a video clip to a movie.
- Specify import video settings.
- Modify a video clip instance.
- Create a button symbol.
- Modify a button instance.
- Test the button in the authoring environment.
- Add sound to a button.
- Add an action statement to a button to control a movie using the Actions panel.
- Create a movie clip symbol.
- Create an animated button.

Flash MX Chapter 05

There are 15 data files to copy for this chapter.

Sound and video created in other programs are added to a movie by importing the source file and then defining at which point in the Timeline the sound or video will play. Flash recognizes the most popular sound and video file formats. Imported sound can be compressed in various formats to minimize the impact on file size. Video is compressed when importing and exporting using Sorenson Spark.

Interactivity with the user can be added to a movie through the addition of buttons. In this chapter you will learn how to create simple buttons that change in appearance when the mouse rolls over or clicks the button. You will add a sound effect to a button and add action statements with which a user can stop, play, or rewind a movie or stop sound. Inserting a movie clip symbol inside a button symbol creates an animated button.

Adding Sound to a Movie

While looking at examples of Flash on the Web you have probably viewed Flash movies that incorporated sound through the use of background music, as sound effects when an event happens to an object, when a button is clicked, or as a voice narrating during a movie. Sound, when used properly, adds another dimension to a movie that enriches the viewer's experience. You learned in Chapter 3 that a consequence of adding an imported picture to a movie is a larger file size that increases download time. The use of sound also causes the file size to increase, leading to longer download times. To minimize the impact on file size, consider adding sounds (music or sound effects) that are short in duration and playing the sound file looped only the number of times necessary to achieve the length you need in the movie.

Adding sound to a movie involves two steps: importing the sound file to the movie's library, and then adding the sound instance to a keyframe in the Timeline where you want the sound to begin playing.

Importing a Sound File

Since Flash does not have the capability to record sound, any audio that you want to add to a movie must already exist in a file. Flash recognizes the following sound file formats provided QuickTime 4 or later is installed on the computer you are using:

- *wav*
- *aif*
- *au*
- *mp3*

Without QuickTime 4 or later, you will not be able to import *aif* or *au* files on a Windows-based computer or *wav* files on a Macintosh computer. If the sound file you need to work with is not displayed in the Import files of type list, download a newer version of QuickTime from the Internet. QuickTime is available free of charge from **www.apple.com/quicktime**.

The same Import dialog box used to import pictures is used to import sounds. Click File and then Import to open the Import dialog box and then change the Files of type to the sound file format that you want to import. If necessary, change the drive and/or folder and then double-click the file name in the list box.

Flash imports sound files directly to the library. Open the Library panel to drag an instance of the sound to the stage. Flash displays Stop and Play buttons in the Preview pane of the library above the waveform as shown in Figure 5.1. Click the sound file name in the Library panel and then click Play to hear the audio file before inserting it into the current movie.

FIGURE 5.1 Sound File Imported to Library

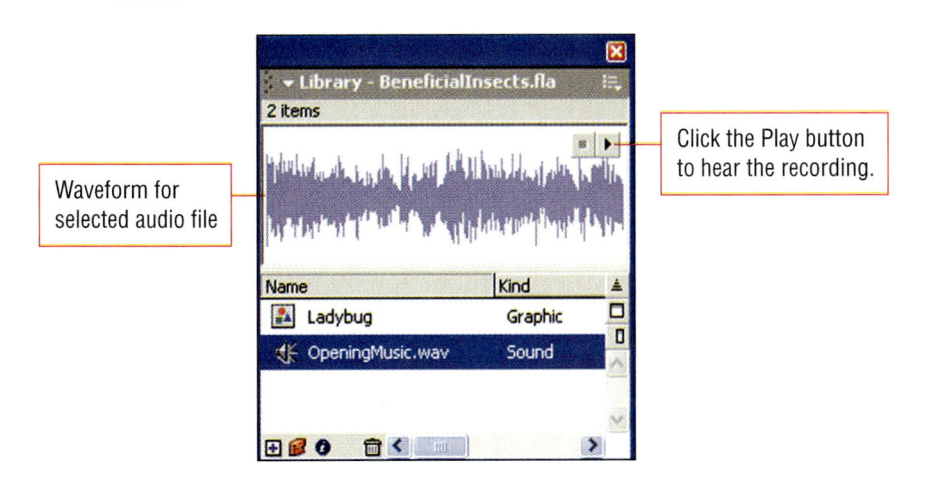

Waveform for selected audio file

Click the Play button to hear the recording.

Adding Sound to Animation

Once a sound file has been imported to the library, an instance of the sound can be inserted into a keyframe at the point in the Timeline at which you want the user to hear the audio recording. Complete the following steps to add the sound to the animation:

1. Insert a new layer in the Timeline. A new layer is not required to hold sound separately from the other objects in the movie but is recommended for ease of editing.
2. Insert a keyframe at the required frame in the Timeline.
3. With the keyframe active at which you want the sound to begin, open the Library panel, select the sound file, and then drag an instance of the sound to the stage, or open the Properties panel for the keyframe and choose the sound file name at the Sound name drop-down list.

Flash displays the waveform of the imported sound file in the frames in the Timeline. Positioning the mouse pointer over the waveform in the timeline displays a tooltip with the name of the sound file as shown in Figure 5.2.

FIGURE 5.2 Sound Waveform Displayed in Timeline

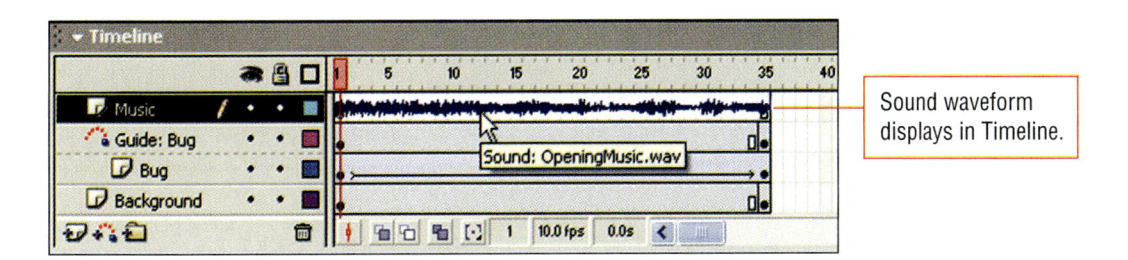

Sound waveform displays in Timeline.

FLASH MX

Adding Sound, Video, and Basic Interactivity with Buttons 217

exercise 1

ADDING SOUND TO AN ANIMATION

1. Open Ch4Ex04.
2. Save the document with Save As and name it Ch5Ex01. Make sure the Properties panel is collapsed and set the magnification to 70%. If necessary, center the stage within the Flash window.
3. Import and play an audio recording in *wav* format of waves rolling on the beach and seagulls squawking by completing the following steps:
    a. Click File and then click Import.
    b. Click the down arrow next to Files of type in the Import dialog box and then click WAV Sound (*.wav) at the pop-up list.

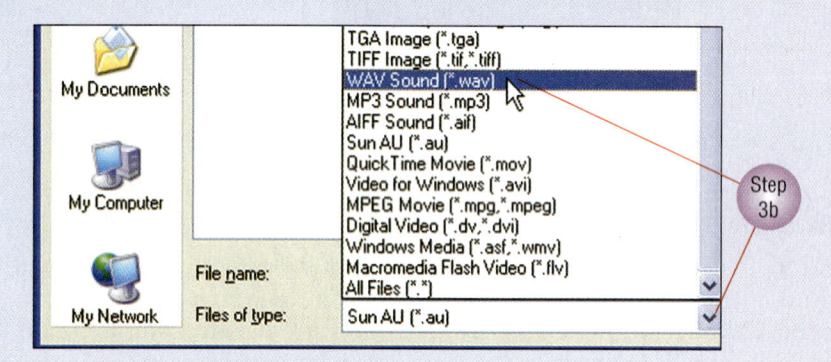

    Step 3b

    c. If necessary, change the Look in location to the drive and/or folder where the data files are stored for Chapter 5.
    d. Double-click the file named seashore.wav. The sound is added to the movie's library and the Import dialog box closes.
    e. Click Window and then click Library.
    f. If necessary, drag the Library panel to the right side of the stage.
    g. Click seashore.wav in the Library panel and then click the Play button in the Preview pane to listen to the recording.

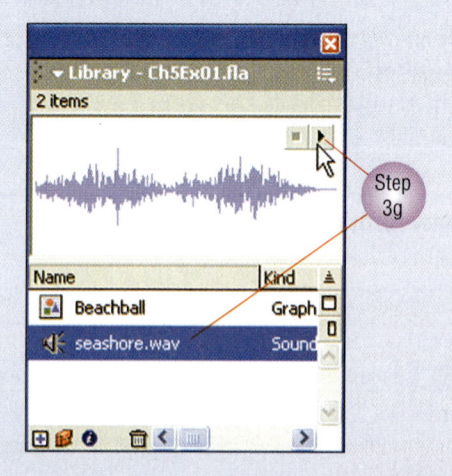

    Step 3g

4. Insert the seashore.wav file in the animation by completing the following steps:
    a. Insert a new layer above *Guide: Beachball* and name it *Sound*.

b. With *Sound* the active layer, click frame 1, position the mouse pointer over seashore.wav in the Library panel and then drag an instance of the sound to the stage. Flash displays a dotted box with the pointer on the stage which disappears when you release the mouse. The sound waveform is displayed in frames 1–45 but is not visible on the stage.

c. Close the Library panel.
d. With frame 1 active, press Enter to preview the animation. Notice the sound continues playing after the playhead has reached the end of the animation until the end of the sound file is reached. By default, the Sync sound option in the Properties panel is set to Event which starts playing the sound in the beginning keyframe and then plays the recording until completion even if the other animation in the movie ends.

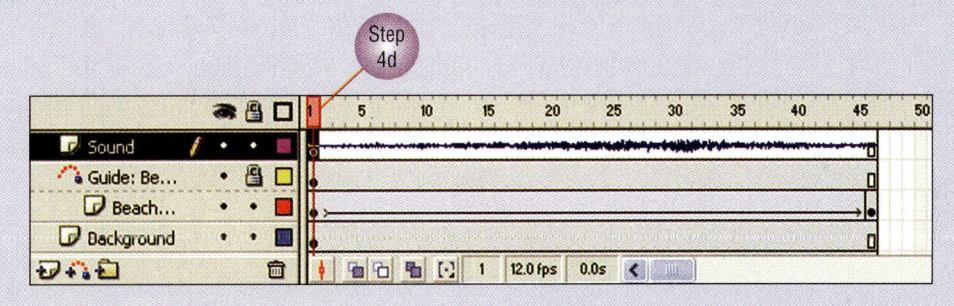

5. Save the revised document using the same name (Ch5Ex01).

Synchronizing Sound to the Animation

A keyframe with a sound instance has properties which can be changed to alter the sound effect, edit the sound envelope, and set the synchronization as shown in Figure 5.3 which displays the properties for seashore.wav added to Ch5Ex01. By default, a sound is inserted as an Event with no sound effect and does not loop.

FIGURE 5.3 **Properties Panel for Keyframe with Sound**

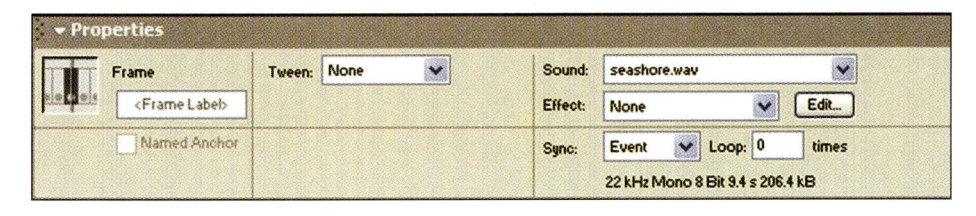

In Exercise 1, the sound continued to play after the end of the animation until the recording was finished. Sound is connected to the animation through the Sync property. Click the down arrow next to the Sync sound list box to choose from the following options:

- **Event.** As you saw in Exercise 1, an event sound starts playing when the playhead reaches the keyframe in which the sound is inserted and the sound plays until the recording is complete regardless of when the animation finishes. For this option, you need only insert the sound in the beginning keyframe since the recording will play until completion regardless of the timeline.
- **Start.** A sound synchronized with the Start option is the same as a sound synchronized with the Event option with the exception that if the sound is already playing through some other instance in the movie, Flash will not reinitiate the recording by starting another instance of the same sound—the other instance will be stopped and this instance started.
- **Stop.** Use this option to stop the playing of a sound instance. Flash will stop playing the sound that is shown in the Sound name list box.
- **Stream.** Streaming sound is synchronized with the Timeline and will stop playing when the playhead reaches the end of the frames for the sound instance. With this option you must ensure that you have inserted the number of frames in the Timeline for the length of time in which you want the sound to play. The Flash player may skip other animated frames that cannot be drawn quickly enough in order to keep streaming sound synchronized with the rest of the animation.

Event sounds must be completely downloaded before the recording starts to play while streaming sounds can begin almost immediately while the remainder of the sound is downloaded in the background.

exercise 2
STARTING AND STOPPING A SOUND INSTANCE

1. With Ch5Ex01 open, edit the sound properties for seashore.wav to end the playing of the recording when the animation ends by completing the following steps:
   a. Expand the Properties panel.
   b. Click frame 1 in the *Sound* layer.
   c. Click the down arrow next to the Sync sound list box and then click Start at the drop-down list.
   d. Right-click frame 45 in the *Sound* layer and then click Insert Keyframe at the shortcut menu.
   e. With frame 45 of the *Sound* layer active, click the down arrow next to the Sound name list box and then click seashore.wav at the drop-down list.
   f. Click the down arrow next to the Sync sound list box and then click Stop at the drop-down list.
   g. Collapse the Properties panel.
2. Press Enter to preview the animation. The sound will play until the playhead reaches frame 45 and then stop.
3. Save the revised document using the same name (Ch5Ex01).
4. Close Ch5Ex01.

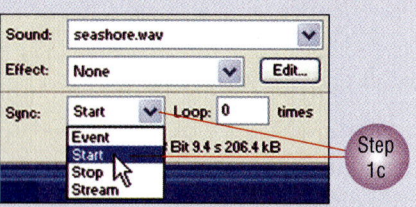

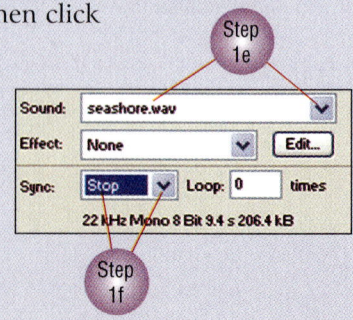

In Exercise 2, you could have achieved the same outcome by setting the Sync sound property to Stream. A keyframe with the stop Sync sound property would not have been required in frame 45 since the sound would have stopped playing when it ran out of frames at frame 45. Streaming sound causes Flash to force the other frames in the animation to keep up with the sound file. If necessary, some frames will be dropped from the movie if, for example, a graphic cannot be drawn on the screen quickly enough. This can sometimes result in a disjointed appearance in a movie. For this reason, it is recommended that streaming be used for large sound files so that you do not have to wait for the entire file to be downloaded before the sound begins playing, or in animations where synchronization to a graphic is essential such as a voice recording being matched to a character's movements.

Looping a Sound Instance

Key a value in the Loop text box in the Properties panel for a sound instance to specify the number of times in which the sound should be replayed in the movie. Looping sound allows you to import a smaller sound file and provide continuous music or other sound effect without negatively impacting the movie's file size.

It is not recommended to loop a sound synchronized as streaming since this will add frames by the number of times the sound is looped within the movie, causing an increased file size. Event or Start sounds do not have this problem since their duration is not dependent on the number of frames within the Timeline.

Applying Sound Effects

The Effect drop-down list in the Properties panel provides preset options for controlling the volume level or moving the sound from one channel to another as it plays. A brief description of each effect follows. Experiment with different effect options to see which is best suited for the movie.

- **Left Channel.** Sound plays in the left channel only.
- **Right Channel.** Sound plays in the right channel only.
- **Fade Left to Right.** Sound volume pans from the left channel to the right channel.
- **Fade Right to Left.** Sound volume pans from the right channel to the left channel.
- **Fade In.** Sound volume gradually increases as the sound is played.
- **Fade Out.** Sound volume gradually decreases as the sound is played.
- **Custom.** Opens the Edit Envelope dialog box in which you can customize the volume or define the starting and ending points for the sound.

Editing the Sound Envelope

Flash provides the ability to edit the sound's volume, starting point, and ending point of a sound instance. Click the Edit button next to the Effect list box in the Properties panel to open the Edit Envelope dialog box shown in Figure 5.4. Use this dialog box to customize a preset effect such as Fade In or create your own effects.

FIGURE 5.4 Edit Envelope Dialog Box

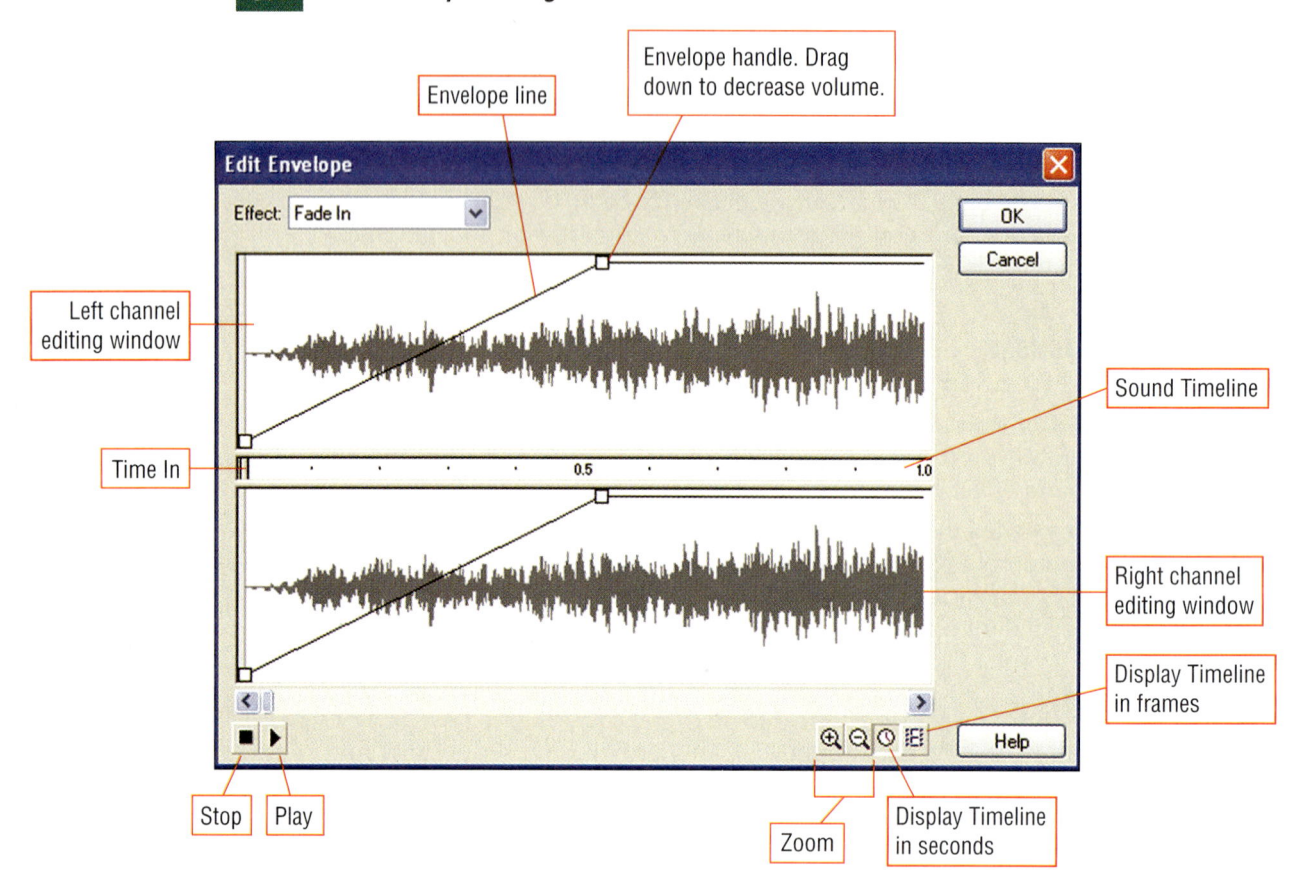

- Envelope line
- Envelope handle. Drag down to decrease volume.
- Left channel editing window
- Time In
- Sound Timeline
- Right channel editing window
- Display Timeline in frames
- Stop
- Play
- Zoom
- Display Timeline in seconds

The top waveform is the editing window for the left channel and the bottom window is for editing the right channel's waveform. Stereo sound files will show two different waveforms while a mono sound displays the same waveform in both channels since the same sounds play in each speaker. Separating the left channel editing window from the right channel editing window is the Timeline. The Timeline can be displayed in either seconds or frames. Use the buttons identified in Figure 5.4 at the bottom of the dialog box to change the Timeline display units.

To change the sound instance's starting point drag the Time In control to the right to the point in the Timeline at which you want the sound to begin. Do not confuse this Timeline with the Timeline in the movie that is controlling the animation; you are not changing the sound's keyframe in the movie, but instead changing the point in the sound file at which the sound will start. For example, if a sound file has two seconds of silence at the beginning, you can cut this portion out of the sound by dragging the Time In control to the right until the Timeline displays 2.0. The ending point of a sound can be changed by dragging the Time Out marker to the left to end a sound sooner than the end of the sound file.

Within each channel editing window, up to eight *envelope handles* display as hollow squares along the volume line, referred to as the *envelope line*. The line displayed along the top of the editing window indicates the volume is playing at 100%. Drag the envelope handles up or down to increase or decrease the volume of the sound. Add an envelope handle by clicking the line.

Click the Play button at the bottom left of the Edit Envelope dialog box to listen to the edited sound.

exercise 3

ADDING SOUND, CUSTOMIZING A SOUND EFFECT, AND DECREASING THE VOLUME

1. Open Ch4SA5.
2. Save the document with Save As and name it Ch5Ex03.
3. Rename Layer 1 *StopSign*.
4. Remove frames from the animation so that it ends at frame 45.
5. Add a screeching tires sound effect to the animation by completing the following steps:
    a. Click File and then Import to open the Import dialog box.
    b. Double-click the sound file named carscreech.wav.
    c. Insert a new layer above *StopSign* and name it *ScreechingTires*.
    d. With frame 1 in the *ScreechingTires* layer active, expand the Properties panel.
    e. Click the down arrow next to the Sound name list box and then click carscreech.wav at the drop-down list.
    f. Click the down arrow next to the Sync sound list box and then click Event at the drop-down list.
    g. Collapse the Properties panel and then press Enter to preview the animation.
6. Edit the sound effect and decrease the volume level for the sound by completing the following steps:
    a. Click frame 1 in the *ScreechingTires* layer and then expand the Properties panel.
    b. Click the down arrow next to the Effect list box and then click Fade In at the pop-up list.
    c. Click the Edit button.
    d. Scroll the Timeline right to view the waveform in the channel editing windows. The sound ends at 2.1 seconds on the Timeline.
    e. Scroll the Timeline back to the beginning of the sound.
    f. The Fade In effect is shown by the envelope line starting at the bottom (0% volume) and rising until the volume is at 100% near 0.5 seconds on the Timeline. Position the mouse pointer on the envelope handle near 0.5 seconds in the left channel editing window and then drag the envelope handle to the right to 1.0 on the Timeline. This will extend the Fade In effect to 1 second. The envelope handle in the right channel window will move to the same position automatically.

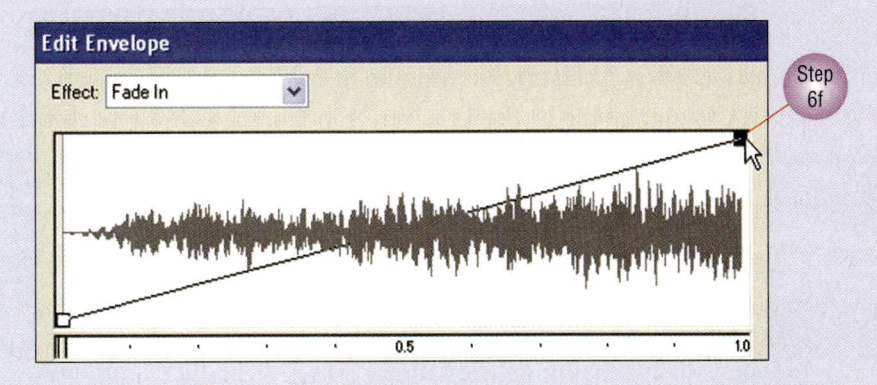

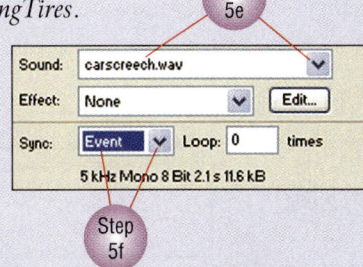

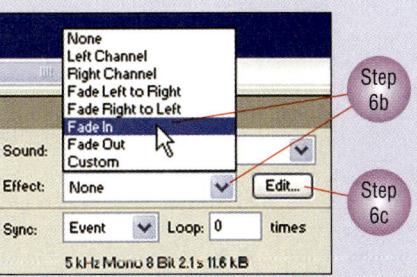

Adding Sound, Video, and Basic Interactivity with Buttons — 223

g. Click the Play button to hear the revised sound effect.
h. Click the Zoom Out button at the bottom of the Edit Envelope dialog box (displays with a minus symbol in a magnifying glass) and then scroll right until you can see the end of the sound in the Timeline.
i. Position the mouse pointer on the envelope handle at 1.0 seconds in the left channel editing window and then drag the envelope down to the position shown. Repeat this step for the envelope marker in the right channel editing window. This will decrease the volume of the sound.
j. Click the Play button to hear the revised sound effect.
k. Click OK to close the Edit Envelope dialog box. Notice the sound effect has changed from Fade In to Custom.

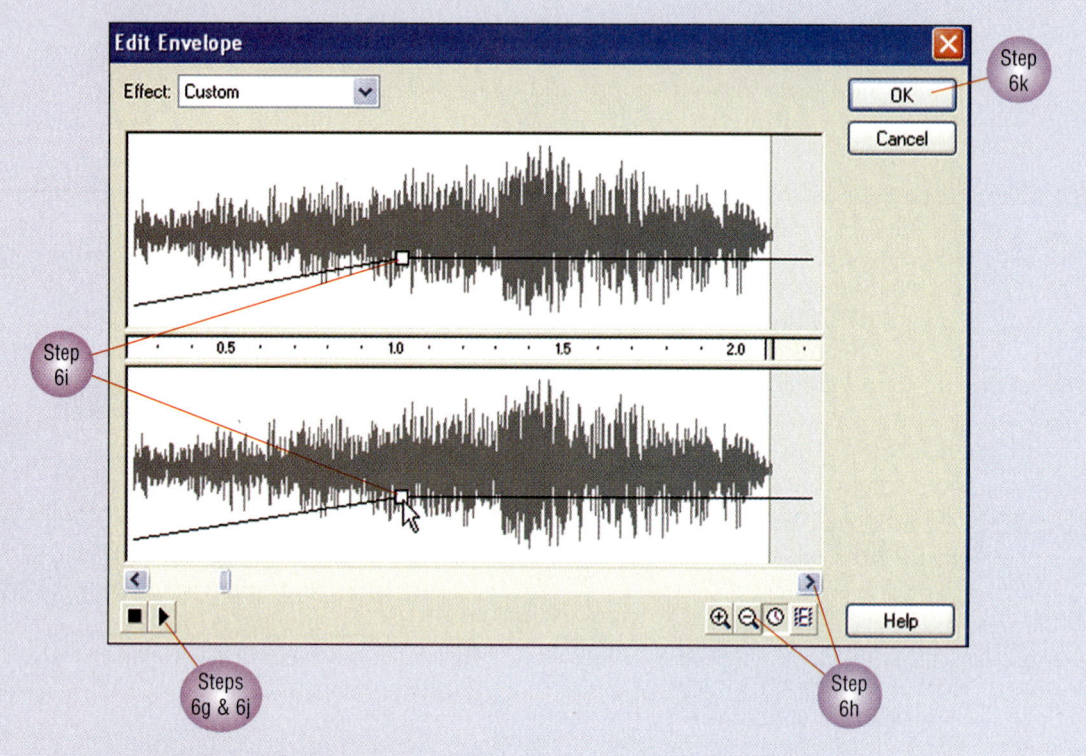

l. Collapse the Properties panel.
7. Press Enter to preview the animation.
8. Save the revised document using the same name (Ch5Ex03).

With a stereo sound file, editing the left and right channel in the Edit Envelope dialog box can be used to create panning effects by decreasing the volume in one channel while increasing the volume in the other at the same point in the Timeline.

Changes made in the Edit Envelope dialog box apply to the selected sound instance only. If the sound is used again in the movie at another point in the Timeline, the original settings from the library sound file will be in effect.

Defining Sound Properties

Just as you learned in Chapter 3 that each imported graphic has a set of properties associated with it, so does each imported sound file. Display the properties for a sound file by displaying the Library panel, right-clicking the sound file name, and then clicking Properties at the shortcut menu, or click the Properties button at the bottom of the Library panel. Figure 5.5 displays the sound properties for the sound inserted in Exercise 1.

FIGURE 5.5 Sound Properties for seashore.wav Inserted in Exercise 1

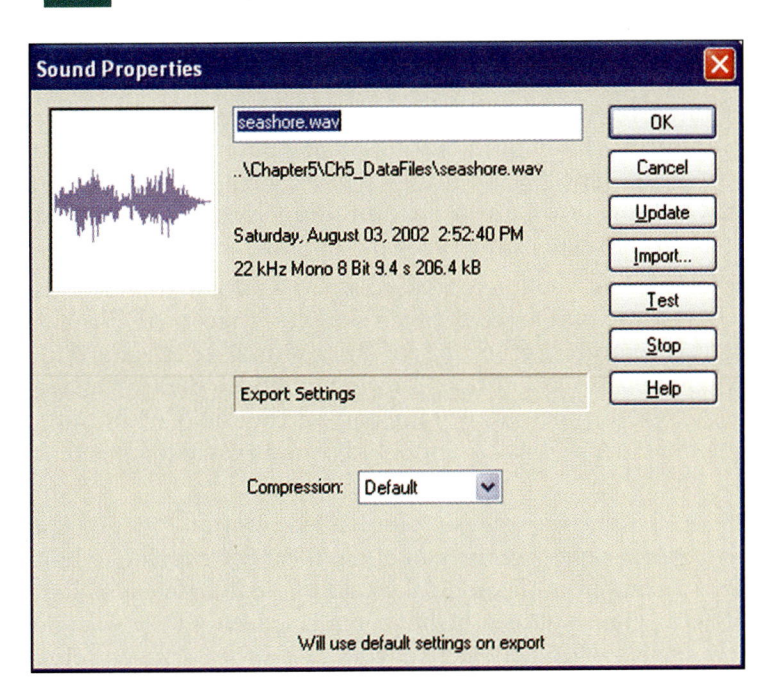

The Preview window displays the waveform for the sound. A stereo sound file will display both the left and right channel waveforms. The name text box displays the current file name of the sound and the path from which the file was imported displays below the sound name text box. Below the sound name and path Flash displays information about the sound file such as the date and time the sound was last modified, the sample rate (also called the *frequency rate*), whether the sound is in mono or stereo, sample size (also called *bit depth*; usually 8-bit or 16-bit), duration of the file in seconds, and the original sound file size when it was imported.

Audio is recorded digitally for use on a computer through a process called *sampling*. A device attached to the computer digitizes sound by taking samples of the continuous waveform at regular intervals and converting the sample to binary data. The number of times per second this measurement is recorded is called the *sampling rate*. The *sample size* is the amount of information stored for each waveform sample. The sample rate and the sample size are independent from one another, meaning a sound can be sampled at a high rate but have a low sample size. A high sampling rate and a high sample size represent very high quality sound. Higher sample rate and size, however, also mean a larger file size.

The seashore.wav file information shown in Figure 5.5 shows that the sound was digitized with a sampling rate of 22 kHz and a sample size of 8-bit. To put this information into perspective, consider that an audio CD uses a sampling rate of 44.1 kHz and a 16-bit sample size. This means that there are 44,100 16-bit samples of the audio per second with two waveforms for stereo sound. The seashore.wav sound was sampled at half the rate at which an audio CD would be sampled. If the seashore.wav was sampled at the same settings as an audio CD, the file size would double.

Compressing Sound Files

Just as you learned to test a graphic file with different compression quality settings to find the right compromise between picture quality and file size, you can also test a sound file using a different file compression option prior to exporting a movie. By default, the Compression option in the Sound Properties dialog box for a selected sound is Default. This means the sound will be exported with the movie using the compression option in the Publish Settings dialog box. Sound events and sound streams can have different global settings. These global options will be discussed in Chapter 6. Click the down arrow next to Compression in the Sound Properties dialog box to change to one of the following options:

- **ADPCM.** *Adaptive Differential Pulse Code Modulation* is a technology in which only the difference between samples is recorded. Flash recommends using this compression setting for short sounds or effects. With ADPCM active, Flash displays options in which you can convert a stereo sound to mono, choose the sample rate, and set the ADPCM bit rate. Available sample rates are 5, 11, 22, and 44 kHz and available bit rates are 2, 3, 4, and 5 bit.

- **MP3.** MP3 is the file extension for MPEG (*Motion Picture Experts Group*), audio *Layer 3* which compresses audio files by removing redundant and irrelevant parts from the original sound that a human ear would not be able to discern. The result is a highly compressed sound file with no noticeable loss in quality. With MP3 active, you can convert a stereo sound to mono, set the bit rate from a range of 8 kbps to 160 kbps, and select a quality setting of Fast, Medium, or Best.

- **Raw.** This option exports the sound with no compression but allows you to resample the sound at a new rate. You can convert a stereo sound to mono and set the new sample rate at 5, 11, 22, or 44 kHz.

- **Speech.** Use this option to export a sound file using compression specific for voice data. You can choose to sample at 5, 11, 22, or 44 kHz.

As with imported graphic files, you need to experiment with sound compression settings to find the right balance of sound quality with the smallest possible file size. Change to the compression options that you want to export and Flash displays the new file size along with the percent of the original file size at the bottom of the Sound Properties dialog box. Click Test to hear the quality of the compressed sound file.

The Sound Properties dialog box also contains an Update button to update the sound file if you have edited the original file outside Flash, an Import button to change all instances of the sound to a different file, and a Stop button to discontinue playing a sound after clicking the test button.

exercise 4
COMPRESSING SOUND FILES

1. With Ch5Ex03 open, test and compress the carscreech.wav sound file by completing the following steps:
    a. Press F11 to open the Library panel.
    b. Click carscreech.wav in the Name list and then click the Properties button at the bottom of the Library panel.
    c. Read the current file information displayed below the sound file date and time.
    d. Click the down arrow next to Compression and then click ADPCM at the drop-down list.
    e. With the Sample Rate set to 22kHz and the ADPCM Bits set to 4 bit, click Test to preview the sound. Notice the file size at these settings has been reduced to 5.8 kB, which is 50% of the imported file size.  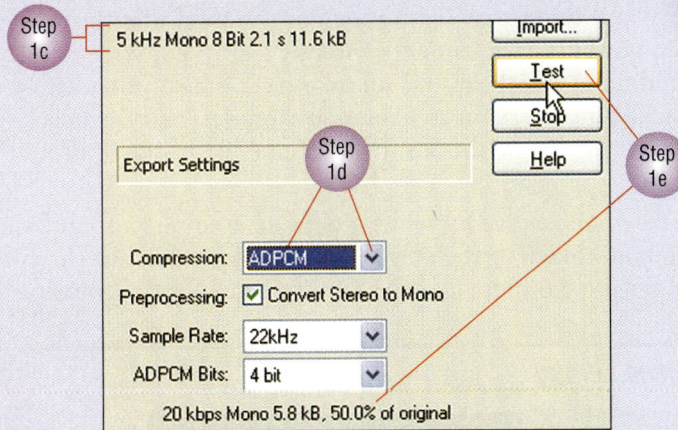
    f. Click the down arrow next to ADPCM Bits and then click 2 bit at the drop-down list. Notice the file size has decreased to 2.9 kB, 25% of the original.
    g. Click Test to preview the sound.
    h. Click the down arrow next to Compression and then click MP3.
    i. With the Bit Rate set to 16 kbps and the Quality set to Fast, notice the file is compressed to 4.2 kB, 36.3% of the original file size. 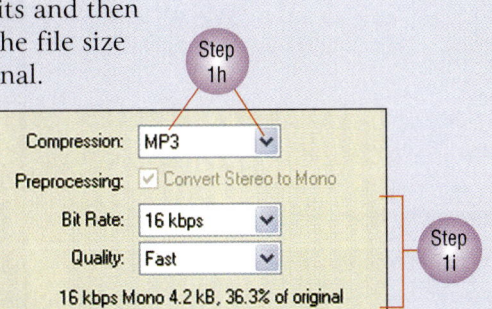
    j. Click Test to preview the sound.
    k. Click OK to close the Sound Properties dialog box.
    l. Close the Library panel.
    m. Close Ch5Ex03. Click Yes when prompted to save changes.
2. Test and compress the seashore.wav sound in the Ch5Ex01 file by completing the following steps:
    a. Open Ch5Ex01.
    b. Press F11 to open the Library panel.
    c. Right-click seashore.wav in the Name list and then click Properties at the shortcut menu.

d. Change the Compression option to ADPCM. With Sample Rate at 22kHz and the ADPCM Bits at 4 bit, notice the compressed file size is 103.2 kB, 50% of the original.
e. Test the sound.
f. Change the Compression option to MP3.
g. With the Bit Rate set to 16 kbps and the Quality set to Fast, notice the file is compressed to 18.7 kB, 9.1% of the original file size.
h. Test the sound.
i. Click OK to close the Sound Properties dialog box.
j. Close the Library panel.
3. Save the revised document using the same name (Ch5Ex01).
4. Close Ch5Ex01.

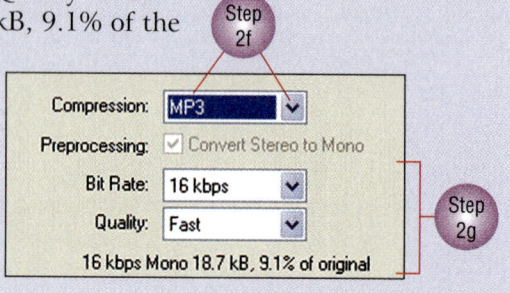

Using Sounds from the Common Library

In Chapter 3 you learned that Flash provides common libraries with symbols that can be used in your Flash documents without fear of copyright infringement. A common sound library with several sound effects is also provided. Within a Flash document, click Window, point to Common Libraries, and then click Sounds at the side menu. Scroll the list of sounds in the Name list to see if a sound is provided that you can use.

With the keyframe active for which you want to insert a sound, drag the sound from the common library to the stage. The sound is added to the current movie's Library panel. Figure 5.6 illustrates the Library panel for the common sound library.

FIGURE 5.6 Common Sound Library

exercise 5
USING SOUND FROM THE COMMON LIBRARY, AND SYNCHRONIZING AND LOOPING SOUND

1. Open Ch4Ex05. If necessary, collapse the Properties panel.
2. Save the document with Save As and name it Ch5Ex05.
3. Preview sounds in the common library by completing the following steps:
    a. Click <u>W</u>indow, point to Common Li<u>b</u>raries, and then click Sounds.
    b. Click Beam Scan in the Name list and then click Play in the Preview pane to listen to the sound.
    c. Scroll down the list of sounds in the Name list. Click and play at least three other sounds.
4. Add and loop a sound from the common library by completing the following steps:
    a. Insert a new layer above *WormHole* and name it *Sound*.
    b. Scroll to the bottom of the Sounds Library panel and then click the sound named Visor Hum Loop.
    c. Play the sound in the Preview pane.
    d. Click frame 1 in the *Sound* layer.
    e. Drag an instance of Visor Hum Loop from the Sounds library to the stage.
    f. Close the Sounds Library panel.
    g. Expand the Properties panel.
    h. Click frame 1 in the *Sound* layer and then view the settings in the Properties panel.
    i. Drag across the value 0 in the Number of times to loop text box and then key **4**.
    j. Collapse the Properties panel.
5. Press Enter to preview the animation. Notice the event sound plays for a second or two longer after the animation is complete.
6. Synchronize the sound to end at the same time as the apple has completed turning red by completing the following steps:
    a. Click frame 1 in the *Sound* layer and then expand the Properties panel.
    b. Change the Sync sound to Start.
    c. Insert a keyframe at frame 40.
    d. With frame 40 active, change the sound name to Visor Hum Loop and the Sync sound to Stop.
    e. Collapse the Properties panel.
7. Press Enter to preview the animation.
8. Press F11 to open the movie's library file. Notice the sound Visor Hum Loop has been added to the library for Ch5Ex05.
9. Close the Library panel.
10. Save the revised document using the same name (Ch5Ex05).
11. Close Ch5Ex05.

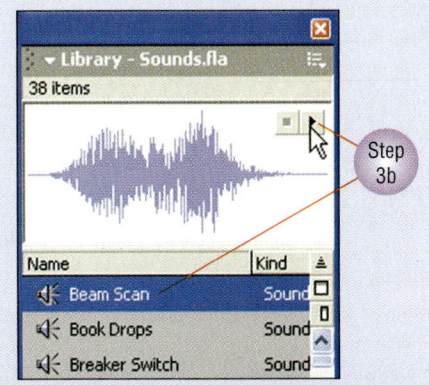

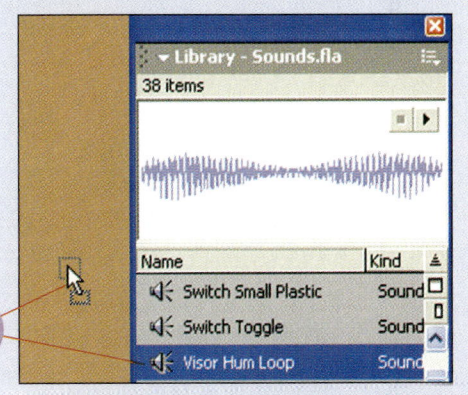

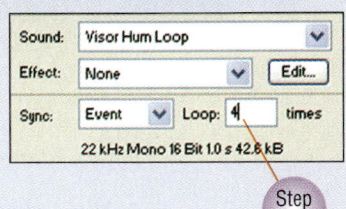

Increasing Layer Height to Display Sound in Frames

Waveforms displayed in the Timeline can be enlarged by changing the layer height. By default, layers in the Timeline display at 100%. This setting can be increased to 200% or 300% in the Layer Properties dialog box. Click the layer containing the waveform, click <u>M</u>odify, and then click <u>L</u>ayer. Click the down arrow next to Layer Height in the Layer Properties dialog box, click 200% or 300%, and then click OK.

Layer Properties can also be displayed by right-clicking the layer and then choosing Properties at the shortcut menu. Figure 5.7 displays the seashore.wav waveform inserted in Exercise 1 at all three height settings.

FIGURE 5.7 **Layer Height at Three Height Settings**

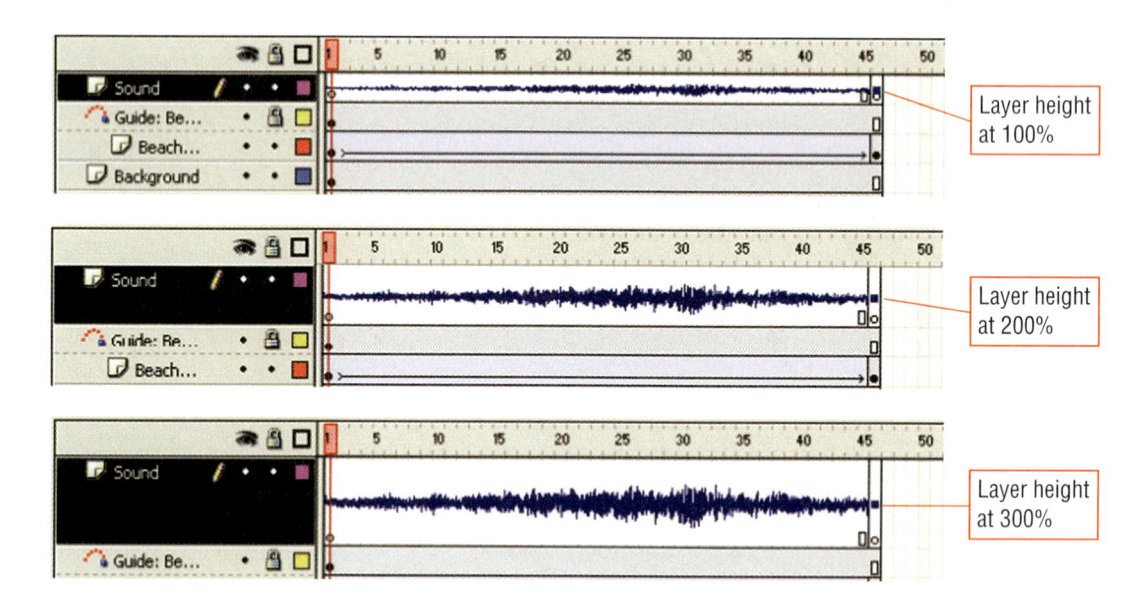

Finding Sound on the Internet

As with graphics, there are many resources for sound files on the Internet. If you would like to add sound to a movie but do not have a sound resource, use the Web to see if you can download a sound file. Several sites offer free sound effects or have sound files available for download for a small fee. CDs are available for purchase on the Web which contain several sound effects for all types of categories. Launch your favorite search engine and then use the keywords "free sound" or "free sound effects."

Some sites require that you register before downloading a sound file. Be sure to read the privacy policy of the site carefully before providing any personal information in the registration form. If you find a sound that you want to use, be sure to check for its permitted terms of use or look for some other restriction policy. These policies can vary widely from site to site. If you are in doubt as to the usability of a sound file, do not download and use it in your Flash movie. Be extra careful when downloading music soundtracks from the Internet that you are not in violation of copyright laws.

230 Chapter Five

Importing Video

Using a process similar to adding graphics and sound to a movie, you can also add video. Flash can import digitized video clips in the following file formats provided QuickTime 4 or later is installed on the computer you are using:

- *avi*
- *dv, dvi*
- *mpg, mpeg*
- *mov*
- *flv*

A Windows-based computer with DirectX 7 or higher installed can also import a Windows Media file in the *wmv* or *asf* file format. Flash imports video using the Sorenson Spark codec which controls how the video is compressed (encoded) and decompressed (decoded) during the import and export process. Sorenson Spark lowers the bandwidth required to use video within Flash while maintaining the highest quality possible. Users will need Flash Player Version 6 which includes the Sorenson Spark decoder that decompresses the video to enable users to view movies with video.

In some cases Flash can import the video but not the audio. A warning message is displayed informing you that the audio will not be imported. If audio is imported with the video it will be published with the movie as streaming audio.

Video source files are usually very large and even when compressed can add greatly to the download time for a Flash movie. Make sure the use of video within Flash is warranted and strive to keep video clips short.

Import video to Flash using the Import dialog box with the Files of type set to the file format that matches the source video. Double-click the name of the video source file in the file list box. When you open a QuickTime movie file as the source video in the Import dialog box, Flash displays the Import Video dialog box shown in Figure 5.8.

FIGURE 5.8 *Import Video Dialog Box for QuickTime Movie File*

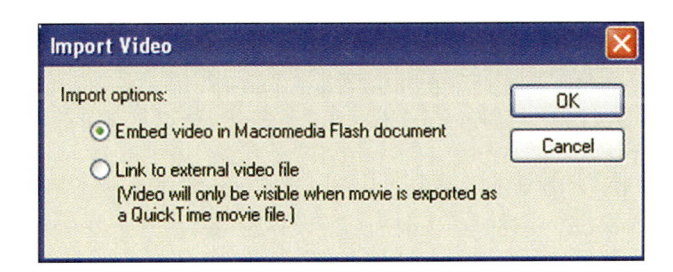

You can choose to import the QuickTime video as an embedded video clip in the Flash document or as a link to an external video file. Choosing to link to an external video file means that you intend to publish your Flash document as a QuickTime movie. Flash includes the message in the dialog box indicating that choosing the link option means that the video clip will only be visible when the movie is exported in QuickTime format.

Choosing the Import Video Settings

When a video source file has been opened in the Import dialog box, the Import Video Settings dialog box shown in Figure 5.9 displays in which you choose the compression settings that you want Flash to use to import the video. In the case of video, compression occurs as the source file is imported to the movie's library as opposed to setting the compression method later as you do with sound and picture files. At the top of the dialog box the video source file name and path display as well as information about the video's pixel size, file size, video length, and number of frames per second.

FIGURE 5.9 Import Video Settings Dialog Box

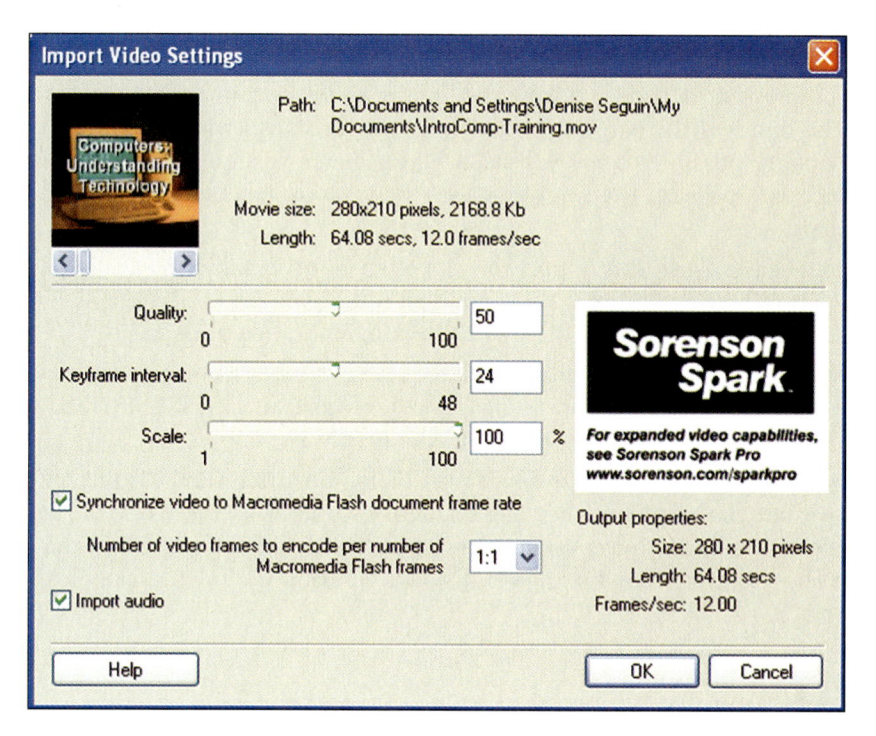

Drag the Quality slider or key a value between 0 and 100 in the Quality text box to specify the compression level for the video. A higher value will cause Flash to maintain the quality of the video by compressing the file at a lower rate. Low values achieve high compression rates but do so by sacrificing quality. Unlike pictures and sound compression properties, there is no Test button in the Import Video Settings dialog box with which you can preview various compression levels.

Drag the Keyframe interval slider or key a value between 0 and 48 to set the number of video keyframes in the imported video clip. A video keyframe stores complete data about the clip. Frames between video keyframes store only the change in the clip from the previous keyframe. Do not confuse the keyframe interval setting with the keyframes in your movie's Timeline; these video keyframes are created by the Sorenson Spark encoder as the video is compressed upon importing. The default keyframe interval of 24 means that a keyframe is stored every 24 frames when the video is imported. A smaller value means more keyframes are created which results in a larger file size.

Drag the Scale slider or key a value between 1 and 100 in the Scale percentage text box to specify the percentage of pixel dimensions in the video. The 100% default setting means that Sorenson Spark maintains the original video's dimensions. Reducing this percentage will reduce the file size and make the video smaller in the Flash document.

By default the Synchronize video to Macromedia Flash document frame rate is selected. This option matches the speed of the imported video with the number of frames per second in the current movie. Click the down arrow next to Number of video frames to encode per number of Macromedia Flash frames to change the number of frames that are created for the video in the Flash Timeline. The default ratio of 1:1 means that one frame is created in the Timeline for each one frame in the video clip. Other frame ratios available are 1:2, 1:3, 1:4, 1:8, 2:3, and 3:4.

If audio is included in the video clip you can choose whether to include or omit the audio segment. If you choose to include audio and Flash cannot convert the audio track, a warning message is displayed with options to continue without importing the sound or to cancel the operation.

Click OK after choosing the appropriate settings. An Importing dialog box displays with a progress bar and a Cancel button. When the encoding process is complete, the Macromedia Flash dialog box shown in Figure 5.10 appears. This dialog box indicates the number of frames that are required in the movie Timeline to play the video and offer you the option to expand the Timeline to include the requisite number of frames in the current layer. Choosing No at this dialog box means that frames in the video that exceed the Timeline span will not be displayed.

FIGURE 5.10 *Macromedia Flash Dialog Box to Expand the Timeline Span for Imported Video*

The imported video is inserted on the stage and the frames are added to the current layer. The video clip is also added to the movie's library as an embedded video clip.

exercise 6

EMBEDDING A QUICKTIME VIDEO INTO FLASH

1. Open the Flash document named IntrotoComputers.
2. Save the document with Save As and name it Ch5Ex06.
3. Make sure the Properties panel is collapsed and set the magnification to 65%. If necessary, center the stage within the Flash window.
4. Assume this document will be the opening movie of an online training course being developed to teach new users about the computer. The opening Flash movie will show a video that has been captured and digitized. This document contains the title of the company and a placeholder in which the video will be inserted. Import and position the video clip by completing the following steps:
    a. Insert a new layer at the top of the Timeline and name it *VideoClip*.
    b. With *VideoClip* the active layer, click File and then click Import.
    c. Click the down arrow next to Files of type and then click QuickTime Movie (*.mov).

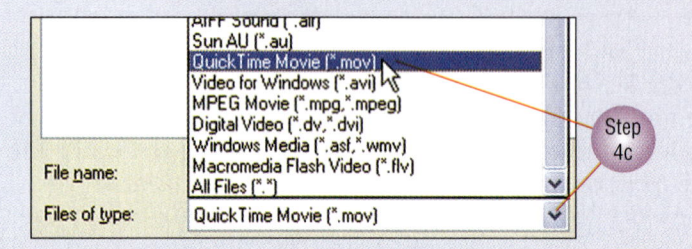

    d. Double-click the file named IntroComp-Training.mov.
    e. Click OK in the Import Video dialog box with *Embed video in Macromedia Flash document* selected.

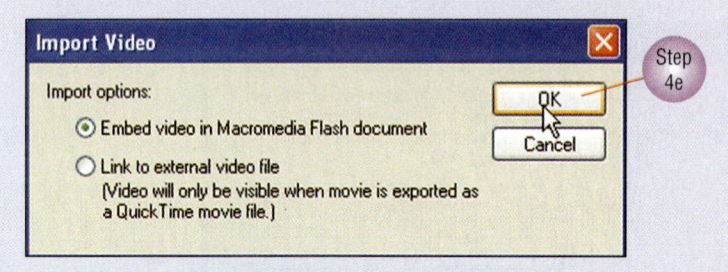

    f. Make sure the following settings are active in the Import Video Settings dialog box, changing any options as necessary:
        1) Quality is 50.
        2) Keyframe interval is 24.
        3) Scale percentage is 100.
        4) Check Synchronize video to Macromedia Flash document frame rate.
        5) Number of video frames to encode per number of Macromedia Flash frames is 1:1.
        6) Check Import audio.

234 Chapter Five

g. Click OK. Flash displays a progress bar indicating the import process until completed. The amount of time required to complete encoding the video will vary depending on the system resources on the computer you are using.

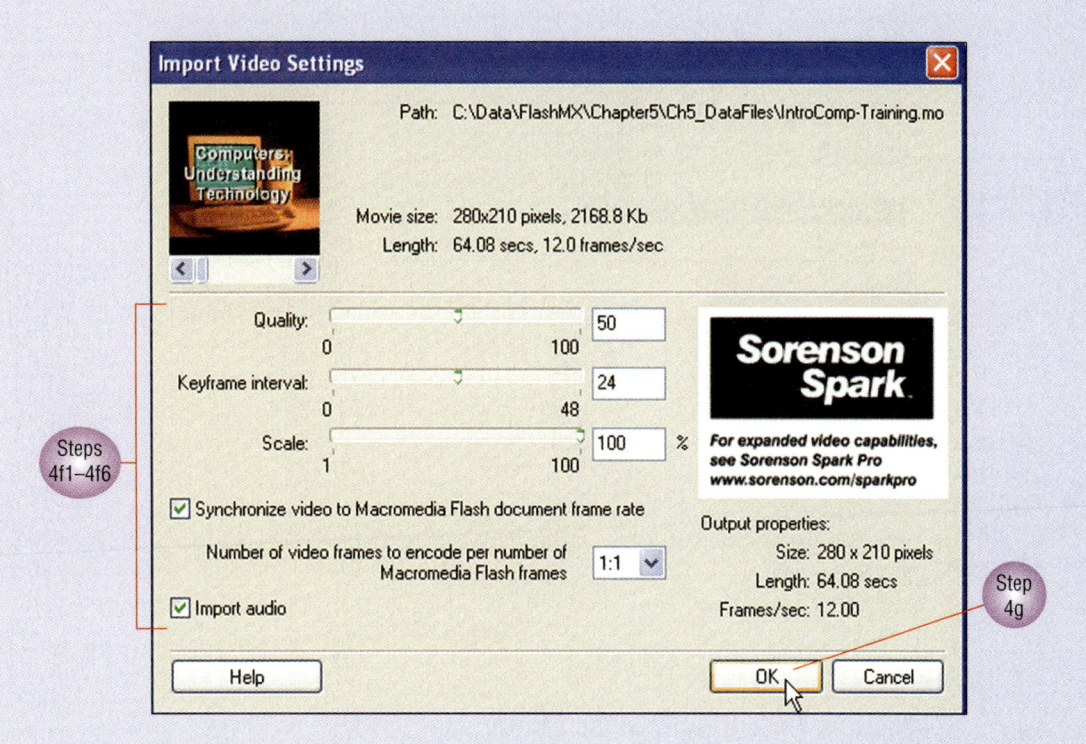

h. Click Yes at the Macromedia Flash dialog box indicating that 769 frames are required in the Timeline and asking if you want the frames automatically inserted. Flash inserts the frames and places an instance of the video on the stage. The video is automatically added to the library.

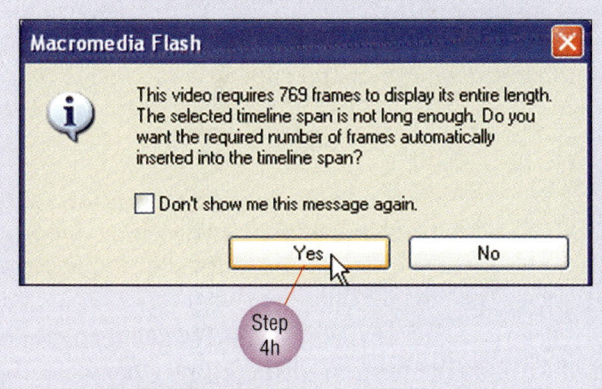

i. Drag the video instance until it is positioned in the center over the yellow box as shown.

Adding Sound, Video, and Basic Interactivity with Buttons 235

5. Animate the other three layers in the movie by completing the following steps:
   a. Click frame 2 in the *VideoPlaceholder* layer.
   b. Scroll the Timeline right until you can see the end of the frames in the *VideoClip* layer.
   c. Hold down the Shift key and then click frame 769 in the *Background* layer.

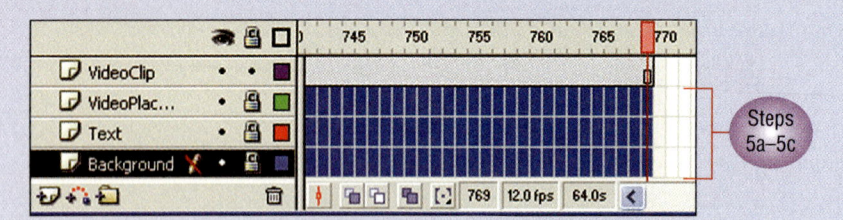

   Steps 5a–5c

   d. Click Insert and then click Frame. Frames 2–769 are added in the remaining layers in the movie.
   e. Scroll the Timeline left back to frame 1.
6. Click Control and then click Test Movie. The animation has to be exported in the Flash Player format and previewed in the Flash Player window in order to hear the audio portion of the imported video.
7. Close the Flash Player window when the video is complete.
8. Save the revised document using the same name (Ch5Ex06).
9. Close Ch5Ex06.

Importing Video Directly to the Library

In Exercise 6, the imported video clip was added to the stage in the active frame when the video encoding was complete. To import video directly to the library, use the File, Import to Library command. When you are ready to insert the video clip in the movie, make active the frame in which you want the video to begin, open the Library panel, and then drag an instance of the video to the stage. Flash will display the message shown in Figure 5.10 (on page 233) advising you about the number of frames required to display the entire length of the clip.

Embedded Video Properties

Open the Properties dialog box for an embedded video clip to view information about the video such as the name and path from which the video was imported, the date the video clip was last modified, the size of the video clip in pixels, the duration of the clip, and the size of the encoded file.

Display the Library panel, click the name of the video clip in the Name list box, and then click the Properties button at the bottom of the Library panel, or right-click the name of the video clip and then click Properties at the shortcut menu. The Embedded Video Properties dialog box for the selected embedded video displays as shown in Figure 5.11, which displays the properties for the video clip inserted in Exercise 6. You can assign a new name to the video clip by selecting the current name in the name text box and then keying a new name. Click Update if you have modified the source video in an external application. Use the Import button to replace the encoded video clip with a new source and click Export to export the video as a Macromedia Flash file in *flv* format.

FIGURE 5.11 Embedded Video Properties Dialog Box

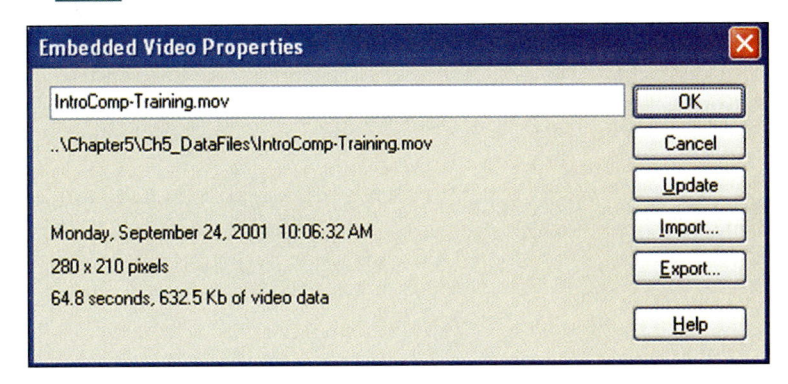

Modifying a Video Instance

An instance of a video can be scaled, rotated, or skewed using the Free Transform tool or moved to a new location on the stage using the Arrow tool. Display the Properties panel for a selected video instance to change the dimensions of the clip by keying new height and width values or change the position on the stage by keying new X and Y coordinates as shown in Figure 5.12.

FIGURE 5.12 Properties Panel for Video Instance

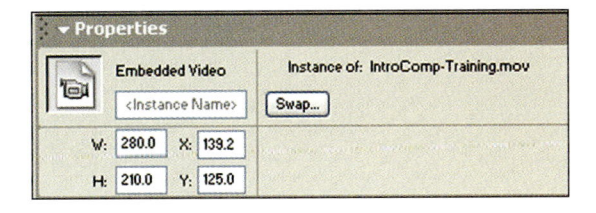

Importing Video in a Movie Clip Symbol

A video clip imported into a movie clip symbol gains the advantage of having its own independent Timeline and the ability to control the clip's brightness, tint, and alpha properties. To add video to a movie within a movie clips symbol, complete the following steps:

1. Click Insert and then click New Symbol to open the Create New Symbol dialog box.
2. Key a name for the video in the Name text box, click Movie Clip in the Behavior section of the Create New Symbol dialog box, and then click OK.
3. In the symbol editing window, click File and then click Import.
4. Change the Files of type to the video file format, navigate to the drive and or folder where the video resides, and then double-click the video file name.
5. Change video import settings as necessary.
6. When the video has completed the import process, click the Back button on the Information bar to return to the Flash document.

7. Insert a layer and/or create frames as required to place the video in the desired location in the movie.
8. With the frame active in which you want to insert the movie, open the Library panel and then drag an instance of the movie clip symbol to the stage.
9. Position, scale, rotate, or otherwise modify the movie clip symbol instance.

exercise 7

IMPORTING VIDEO TO A MOVIE CLIP SYMBOL AND MODIFYING AN INSTANCE OF THE MOVIE CLIP SYMBOL

1. Open the Flash document named IntrotoComputers.
2. Save the document with Save As and name it Ch5Ex07.
3. Make sure the Properties panel is collapsed and set the magnification to 65%. If necessary, center the stage within the Flash window.
4. Assume that this document is a template in which short video clips are being produced for later patching into an online training course. A video clip describing supercomputers has been captured and digitized. Import the video source file into a movie clip symbol by completing the following steps:
   a. Click Insert and then click New Symbol.
   b. Key **Supercomputer video** in the Name text box.
   c. If necessary, click Movie Clip in the Behavior section of the Create New Symbol dialog box.
   d. Click OK.

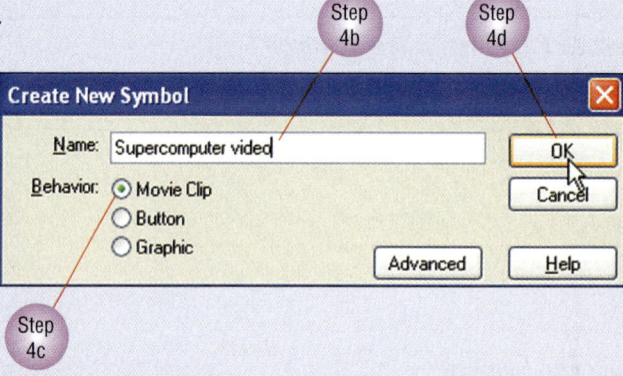

   e. At the symbol editing window, click File and then click Import.
   f. With the Files of type set to QuickTime Movie (*.mov), double-click the file named Supercomputer.mov.
   g. Click OK in the Import Video dialog box with *Embed video in Macromedia Flash document* selected.
   h. Click OK at the Import Video Settings dialog box with the following options active:
      1) Quality is 50.
      2) Keyframe interval is 24.
      3) Scale percentage is 100.
      4) Check Synchronize video to Macromedia Flash document frame rate.
      5) Number of video frames to encode per number of Macromedia Flash frames is 1:1.
      6) Check Import audio.
   i. Click Yes at the message indicating that the video requires 923 frames in the Timeline and asking if you want the frames automatically inserted.

238 Chapter Five

j. With the video displayed in the middle of the stage, click the Back button on the Information bar to exit symbol editing mode.

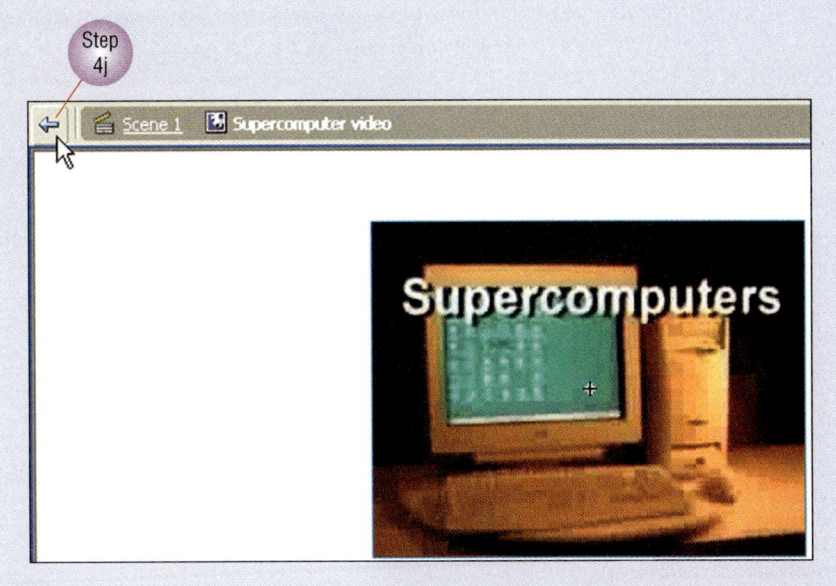

Step 4j

5. Insert an instance of the Supercomputer video movie clip symbol in the movie by completing the following steps:
   a. Insert a new layer at the top of the Timeline and name it *SupercomputerVideo*.
   b. Make active frame 1 of the *SupercomputerVideo* layer.
   c. Press F11 to open the Library panel. Notice the imported video is shown as a separate item in the Library panel in addition to the Supercomputer video movie clip symbol.
   d. Click Supercomputer video in the Name list in the Library panel.
   e. Position the pointer over the video in the Preview pane of the Library panel and then drag an instance of the symbol to the stage as shown.

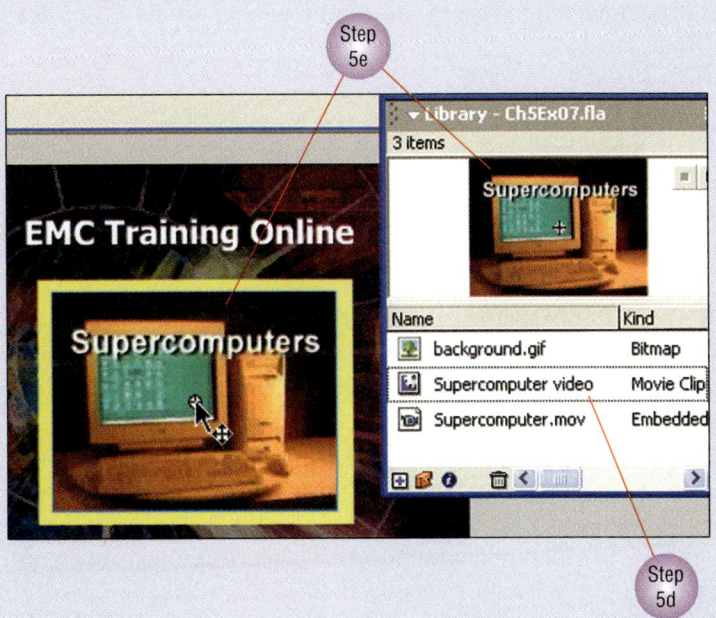

   Step 5e

   Step 5d

   f. Close the Library panel.

6. Modify the instance of the Supercomputer video movie clip symbol by completing the following steps:
    a. Expand the Properties panel.
    b. With the Supercomputer video instance active, click the down arrow next to the Color list box and then click Brightness at the drop-down list.
    c. Drag across the current value in the Brightness percentage text box, key **35**, and then press Enter. The color in the video on the stage is lightened.
    d. Collapse the Properties panel.
7. Click <u>C</u>ontrol and then click Test <u>M</u>ovie to export the video and preview the movie in the Flash Player window.
8. Close the Flash Player window when the video is complete.
9. Save the revised document using the same name (Ch5Ex07).
10. Close Ch5Ex07.

Step 6b

Step 6c

In Exercise 7, since the video was imported to a movie clip symbol, which plays independent of the main movie Timeline, you did not need to insert frames in the other layers of the movie to match the video's 923 frames. Movie clip symbols are created when you want to reuse sections of an animation. Each movie clip has its own Timeline that plays independent of the main movie's Timeline. Think of a movie clip symbol as a submovie inside the main Flash movie. Importing video inside a movie clip symbol means the video can be reused over and over again during a movie.

Creating Buttons

Adding buttons to a movie is a simple method in which you can add interactivity with the user. For example, a button could be added that would turn off sound for those users who do not like to hear the background music that you have added to a movie. A button added to a movie with an embedded video could provide an opportunity for the user to stop or replay the movie. In more complex movies, clicking a button could provide a user with the ability to branch to another section allowing him or her to skip an introduction or section that he or she does not wish to view.

Creating a button in Flash is accomplished by creating a button symbol in the library that has three states: how the button looks when it appears on the screen with no mouse action over it (called the *Up* state), how the button appears when the mouse is rolled over the button (called the *Over* state), and how the button appears when the button has been clicked (called the *Down* state). A fourth state, called the *Hit* state, defines the boundaries for the button which will make the button active.

Click Insert and then click New Symbol to open the Create New Symbol dialog box. Key a name for the button symbol in the Name text box, click Button in the Behavior section of the Create New Symbol dialog box, and then click OK as shown in Figure 5.13.

FIGURE 5.13 Create New Symbol Dialog Box for a Button Symbol

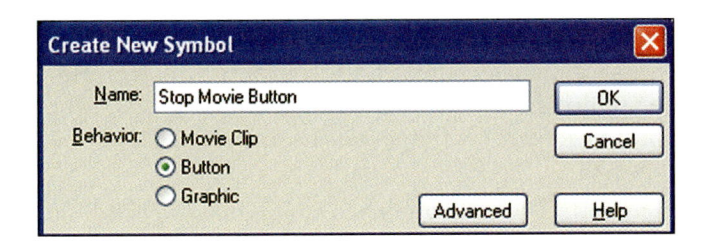

Flash displays the stage in symbol editing mode with a Timeline for the button that includes only four frames: Up, Over, Down, and Hit as shown in Figure 5.14. With Up the active keyframe, use the drawing tools to draw a button as you want it to appear on the stage in the movie with the symbol registration point in the center of the shape. Flash creates a keyframe in Up for you just as the first frame in a new movie is already a keyframe.

FIGURE 5.14 Button Symbol Editing Window

Define the button's appearance for each of the four button states.

Button name

Draw the button around the registration point on the stage.

FLASH MX
Adding Sound, Video, and Basic Interactivity with Buttons — 241

Insert a keyframe in the Over frame and then change the button's appearance to the way in which you want the button to look when a user rolls the mouse over it during the movie. For example, you could change the fill color of the button or text.

Insert a keyframe in the Down frame and then change the button's appearance to the way in which you want the button to look when the user clicks the mouse on it.

Insert a keyframe in the Hit frame and then define the button's boundaries for which the button will become active if the user rolls the mouse over it. If you have maintained the same dimensions for a button in the Up, Over, and Down frames, you will not need to do any further action after inserting the keyframe since the button's shape in the Down keyframe will be automatically copied to the Hit keyframe.

Click the Back button to exit symbol editing mode or click Edit and then Edit Document.

exercise 8

CREATING A BUTTON SYMBOL

1. Open Ch5Ex01.
2. Create a button symbol to stop the sound from playing that will change color when the user rolls the mouse over the button or clicks the button by completing the following steps:
   a. Click Insert and then click New Symbol.
   b. Key **Stop sound button** in the Name text box in the Create New Symbol dialog box.
   c. Click Button in the Behavior section.
   d. Click OK. 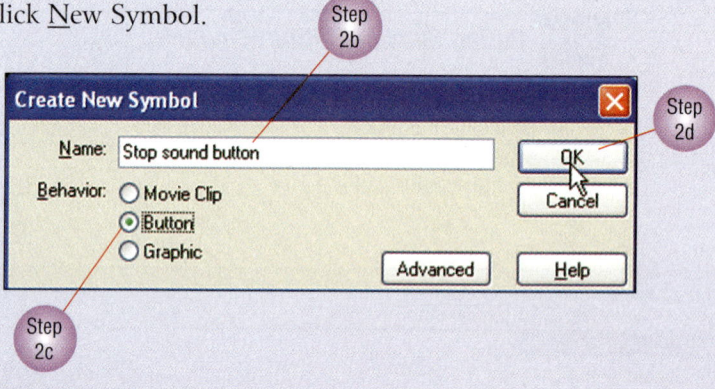
   e. With Up the active keyframe, draw a rounded corner rectangle the approximate size shown around the registration point in the center of the stage with the following properties:
      1) With the rectangle tool active, click Round Rectangle Radius in the Options section, key 8 in the Corner Radius text box, and then click OK.
      2) Choose a medium gray color swatch for the Stroke Color.
      3) Choose the same medium gray color swatch for the Fill Color. 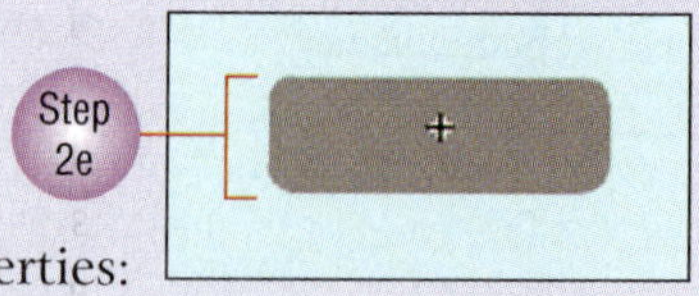
   f. Click the Text tool and then set the following text properties:
      1) Change the Font to Arial.
      2) Change the Font Size to 14.
      3) Change the Text (fill) color to white.
      4) Turn on bold.
   g. Create and position a text block containing the text *Sound Off* as shown.

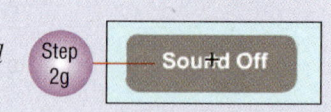

242 Chapter Five   FLASH MX

h. Click the Over frame in the Timeline, click Insert, and then click Keyframe. 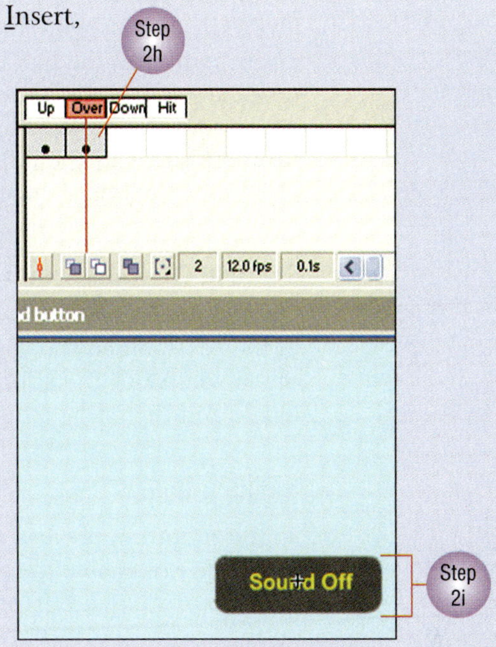
i. With the Arrow tool active in the Over keyframe, make the following changes to the appearance of the button:
   1) Change the Text (fill) color to bright yellow.
   2) Change the fill color for the rectangle to dark gray.
j. Click the Down frame in the Timeline, insert a keyframe, and then make the following changes to the appearance of the button:
   1) Change the Text (fill) color to bright red.
   2) Change the fill color for the rectangle to light gray. 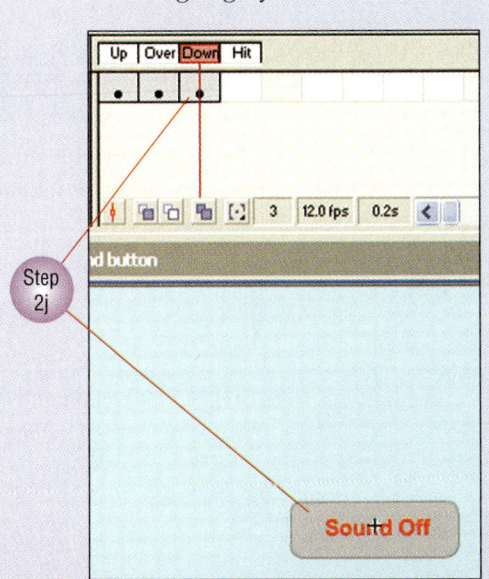 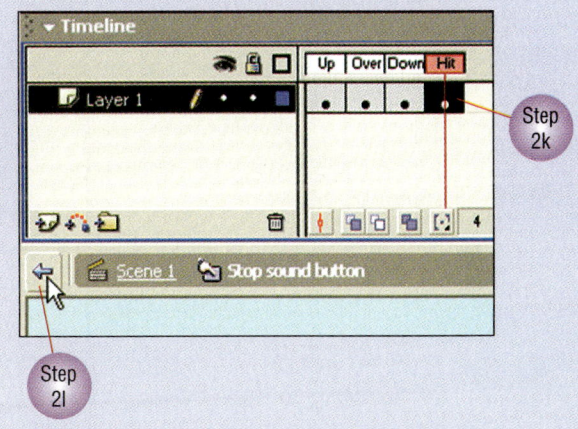
k. Click the Hit frame in the Timeline and then insert a keyframe. Since Flash copies the content of the Down frame to the Hit frame when you insert the keyframe, you do not need to define any further action. The shape in the Hit frame defines the area that is activated by mouse movement. The size of the button has not changed in all three previous frames so the Hit area does not need to be expanded.
l. Click the Back button on the Information bar to exit symbol editing mode.
3. Save the revised document using the same name (Ch5Ex01).

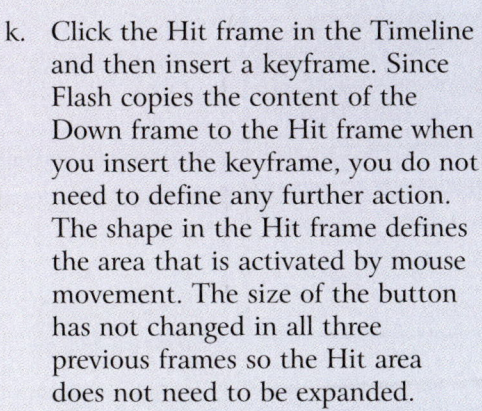

In Exercise 8 you changed the button's appearance for each of the states Up, Over, Hit, and Down. Since the appearance of the mouse pointer changes from the arrow pointer to the hand pointer when positioned over a button symbol, it is not necessary to insert keyframes and change the button's appearance in each state. If no keyframes are created in Over and Down, Flash uses the same button image for these states as the image drawn in the Up state. If no Hit keyframe is created, Flash uses the image created in the Up state.

Inserting an Instance of a Button

Once a button symbol has been created you can insert an instance of the button in the keyframe in the Timeline at which you want the button to appear within the movie. With the appropriate keyframe active, open the Library panel for the movie and then drag a button instance to the desired location on the stage.

Testing a Button

To test a button, preview the animation in the Flash Player using Control and then Test Movie or enable the buttons and then test them on the stage. By default, Flash does not display a button's attributes during movement of the mouse over the button within the authoring environment since you would not be able to edit the button's position, size, shape, and so on if it was active.

To test a button on the stage, click Control and then click Enable Simple Buttons. Enable Simple Buttons is a toggle feature. Click the menu sequence to activate the buttons, test the rollover effects and actions, and then click the menu sequence again to turn off the buttons in order to edit them.

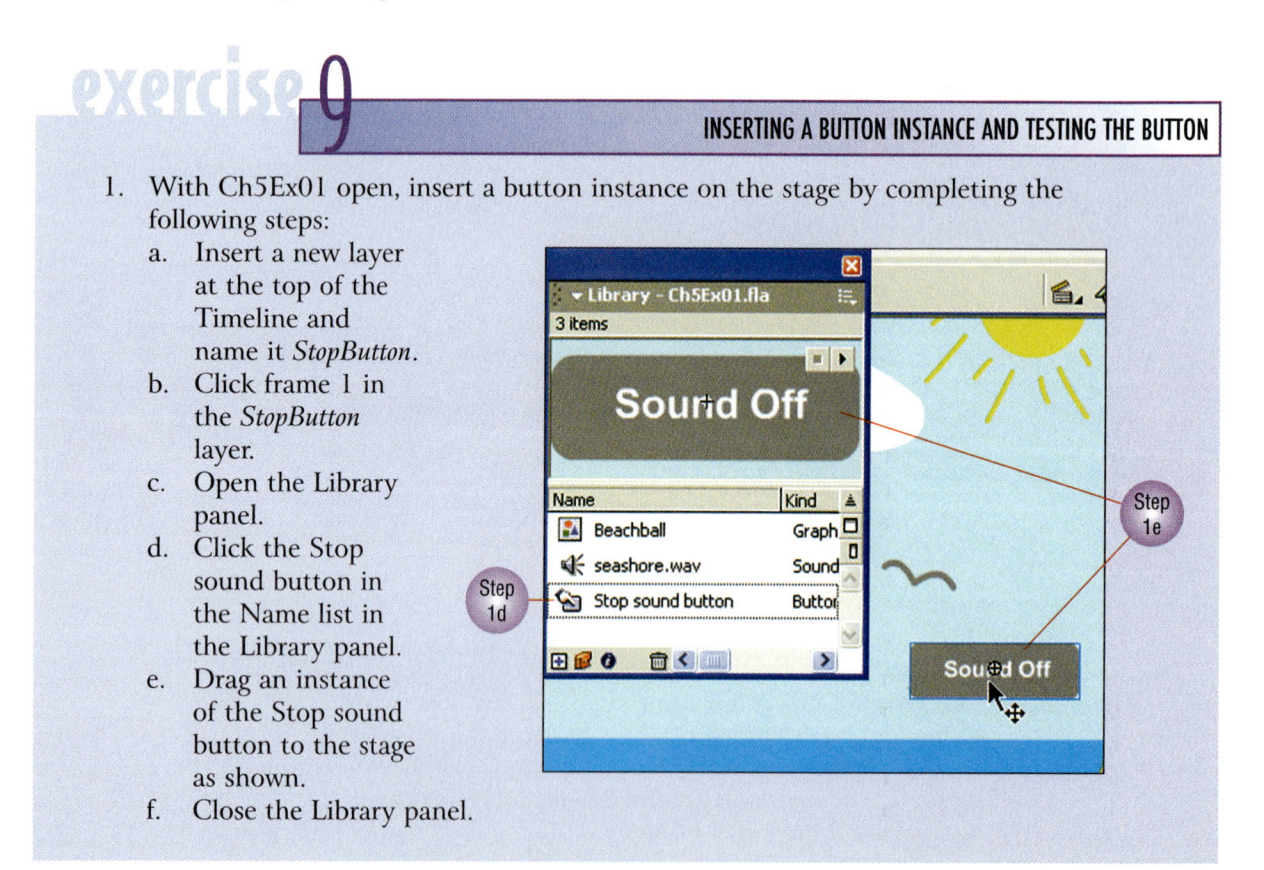

exercise 9

INSERTING A BUTTON INSTANCE AND TESTING THE BUTTON

1. With Ch5Ex01 open, insert a button instance on the stage by completing the following steps:
   a. Insert a new layer at the top of the Timeline and name it *StopButton*.
   b. Click frame 1 in the *StopButton* layer.
   c. Open the Library panel.
   d. Click the Stop sound button in the Name list in the Library panel.
   e. Drag an instance of the Stop sound button to the stage as shown.
   f. Close the Library panel.

244 Chapter Five   FLASH MX

g. Click the Free Transform tool, scale the button instance smaller until it is approximately one-half its current size as shown, and then deselect the button.
2. Press Enter to preview the animation on the stage. During the movie, roll the mouse over the button. Notice that the button does not change its appearance.
3. Click Control and then click Enable Simple Buttons.

4. Change the magnification to 70%.
5. Roll the mouse over the Sound Off button. The button text changes to yellow, the background changes to dark gray, and the pointer displays as the hand with the finger pointing upwards.
6. Click the mouse over the Sound Off button. The button text changes to red and the background changes to light gray.
7. Click Control and then click Enable Simple Buttons to turn off the feature.
8. Save the revised document using the same name (Ch5Ex01).

The button created in Exercise 8 was a simple rounded rectangle with text overlay drawn using the drawing tools. Recall from Chapter 3 that Flash includes a common library of button symbols. Open the common button library and drag one of the Flash-created buttons to the stage to copy the button to the current movie's library. Open the button in symbol editing mode to make changes to the symbol such as adding a sound effect. You can also import a graphic in symbol editing mode and use the graphic as an icon for the button or insert a movie clip symbol.

Adding Sound to a Button

Add sound to a button by importing the sound file containing the sound effect that you want to use and then specify the sound name in the Properties panel for the Up, Over, and/or Down frame in symbol editing mode. You can import different sounds for different states of the button. Since the sound is stored in the master copy of the button in the library, the sound effect will occur for all instances of the button in the movie.

exercise 10
ADDING A SOUND EFFECT TO A BUTTON

1. With Ch5Ex01 open, edit the button symbol to add a sound effect when the button is clicked by completing the following steps:
   a. Click File and then click Import.
   b. Change the Files of type to WAV Sound (*.wav) in the Import dialog box and then double-click the file named click.wav.
   c. Double-click the button instance on the stage. Recall from Chapter 3 that double-clicking a symbol instance causes Flash to go into symbol editing mode. The other objects on the stage are dimmed as you edit the symbol.
   d. With the button in symbol editing mode, rename Layer 1 in the Timeline *Button*.
   e. Insert a new layer above *Button* and name it *ButtonSound*.
   f. Click the Down frame in the *ButtonSound* layer and then insert a keyframe.
   g. Expand the Properties panel.
   h. Click the down arrow next to the Sound name list box and then click click.wav at the drop-down list.
   i. Collapse the Properties panel.
   j. Click the Back button on the Information bar to exit symbol editing mode.
2. Click in the workspace to deselect the button instance.
3. Click Control and then click Enable Simple Buttons.
4. Position the mouse pointer over the Sound Off button and then click the mouse button. The sound effect in the click.wav sound file plays as the button is clicked and goes into the Down state.
5. Click Control and then click Enable Simple Buttons to turn off the feature.
6. Save the revised document using the same name (Ch5Ex01).

In Exercise 10, the imported sound click.wav could have been added to the existing keyframe in *Layer 1* of the Down state for the button symbol by selecting the sound file name in the Properties panel for the keyframe. As you learned when adding sound to a movie, inserting sound in a separate layer makes the sound visible for editing purposes. In the future when you open the symbol in the editing window, seeing the waveform in a separate layer immediately tells you at a glance that a sound is active for the Down button state.

Adding an Action to a Button

At this point you have created a button that has a rollover effect and a sound effect but does not do anything when clicked other than play the sound in the click.wav sound file. The instruction that tells Flash to stop the sound from playing in the movie has yet to be added. A programming language called *ActionScript* is included with Flash that provides the tools with which you instruct Flash on what to do when the user interacts with your movie by clicking a button. As its name implies ActionScript is a scripting language.

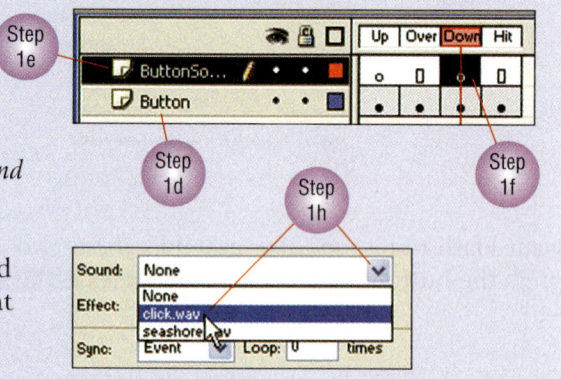

Learning ActionScript statements is like learning how to write in a new language. You have to learn the words that will convey what you mean, the grammar which is the correct placement of the words in order for the meaning of the statement to be understood, and the required punctuation. Grammar and punctuation in programming is referred to as *syntax*. A collection of related ActionScript statements is called a *script*.

Flash provides the Actions panel which allows you to add ActionScript statements to the movie using a point and click approach. Depending on the statement you are inserting, additional parameters may be needed. Using the Actions panel whenever possible is advantageous since Flash takes care of the syntax for you. In Chapter 7 you will learn more about ActionScript statements.

Using the Actions Panel

Actions can be added to keyframes, instances of buttons, and instances of movie clips. An action added to a keyframe will be executed when the playhead reaches the frame during playback of the movie. An action added to a button is executed when the user interacts with the button in the movie. Since the user can interact with a button in a number of ways, you have to specify to which user action you want Flash to respond. For example, the user could roll the mouse over the button, press the button, or press and then release the button. When creating the action statements in the Actions panel you specify to which *mouse event* you want the action performed. *Mouse event* is the term used to describe the action that occurs when the user interacts with the button instance in the movie. The mouse event triggers Flash to perform the action statement associated with the event. The three most common mouse events are:

- **Press.** The user moves the mouse pointer over the button in the movie and presses the mouse button.
- **Release.** The user moves the mouse pointer over the button in the movie, presses, and then releases the mouse button.
- **Roll Over.** The user moves the mouse pointer over the button in the movie.

The Actions panel shown in Figure 5.15 is displayed by clicking Window and then Actions with a button instance selected on the stage. The ActionScript area, where the ActionScript statements are entered, can be scrolled using the up and down scroll bars. If you are entering several statements, you may prefer to work with the Actions panel as a floating window by undocking the panel. Undocking the panel will allow you to resize the window and view a larger script area.

FIGURE 5.15 Actions Panel for Selected Button Instance

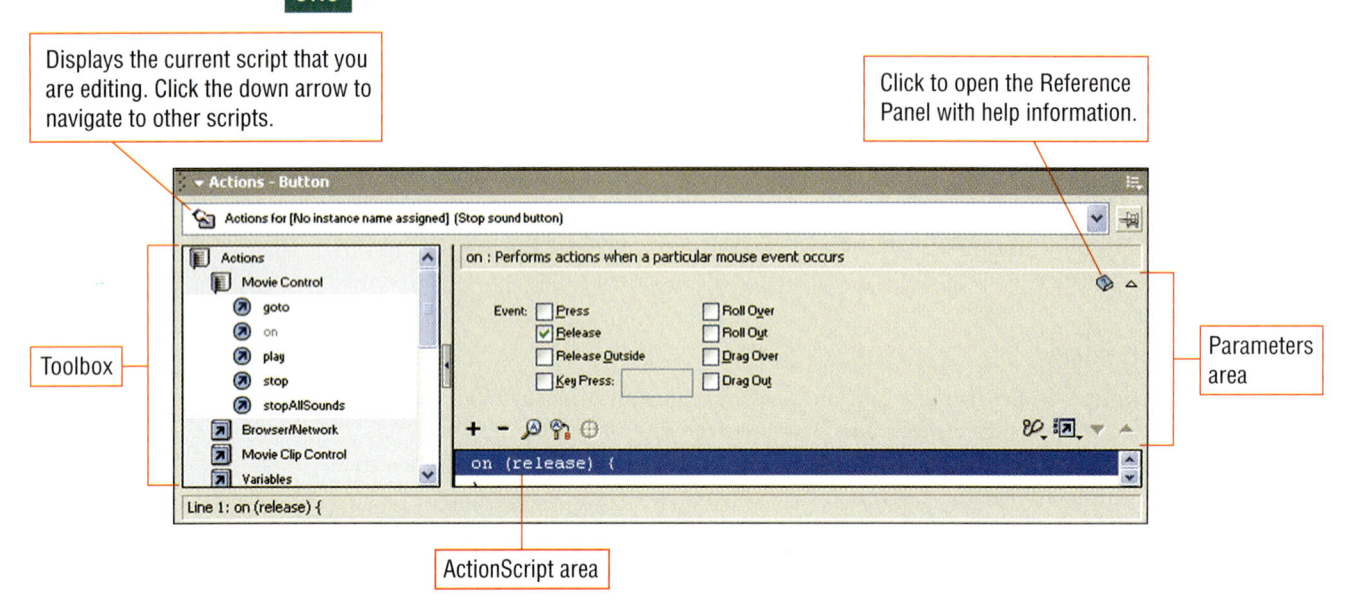

- Displays the current script that you are editing. Click the down arrow to navigate to other scripts.
- Click to open the Reference Panel with help information.
- Toolbox
- Parameters area
- ActionScript area

Flash inserts the script shown in Figure 5.16 for a selected button instance when the on action has been applied. The word *on* is referred to as an *event handler* and is required at the beginning of any ActionScript statement associated with a button. Following the event handler is the mouse event to which the action is associated *(release)*. The action that you want Flash to perform is inserted between the left and right curly braces. The left curly brace indicates the beginning of a list of actions to be performed, and the right curly brace indicates to Flash the end of the actions.

FIGURE 5.16 Default Script Created by Flash for a Selected Button Instance

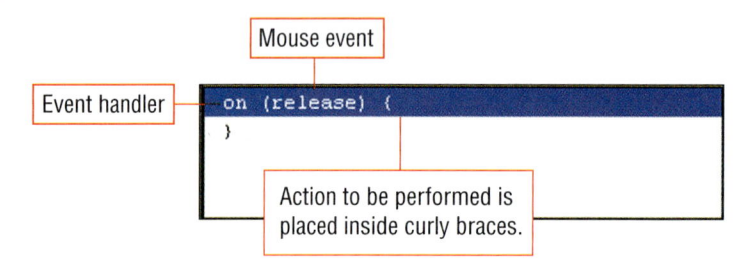

- Event handler
- Mouse event
- Action to be performed is placed inside curly braces.

```
on (release) {
}
```

Using the Actions panel involves selecting the action you want Flash to perform from the toolbox. Actions are listed in the toolbox in a hierarchical fashion similar to how folders and files are displayed in a file list. Related actions are grouped by categories; click the category name to expand the list of actions. Double-clicking the action in the toolbox places the statement in the ActionScript area. More than one action can be performed when the mouse event occurs. Each action statement is placed on a separate line and is executed in the order in which they appear from top to bottom.

In the next exercise you will learn how to use the Actions panel to insert the ActionScript statement that will turn off all sounds in the movie when the user clicks the Sound Off button.

exercise 11

USING THE ACTIONS PANEL TO ADD ACTIONSCRIPT STATEMENTS TO A BUTTON

1. With Ch5Ex01 open, add the ActionScript statement that will cause Flash to turn off the sound during the movie when the user presses and releases the mouse button over the Sound Off button by completing the following steps:
    a. Click the Sound Off button instance on the stage.
    b. Click Window and then click Actions to open the Actions panel.
    c. Click Actions in the toolbox to expand the Actions list if it is not already expanded. Click Movie Control in the Actions list if Movie Control is not already expanded and then double-click *on*.
    d. With the Release check box selected in the Event section of the Parameters area, click the Press check box. Flash adds *press* within the round brackets before *release* in the Script area. The same actions can be assigned to multiple mouse events. Clicking event check boxes in the Parameters area causes Flash to insert each selected mouse event separated by a comma and a space within the ActionScript area.
    e. Click the Roll Over check box. Flash adds *, rollOver* after *release* within the round brackets.
    f. Deselect the Press and Roll Over check boxes in the Event section of the Parameters area. Flash removes the mouse events from the ActionScript area.
    g. Point to the action stopAllSounds in the toolbox. Flash displays the tooltip *Stop playing all sounds*. The action stopAllSounds is within the category Movie Control.
    h. Click stopAllSounds in the toolbox. Flash displays information in the Parameters area on how to add the action to the ActionScript area.
    i. Click the Reference button in the Parameters area. Flash opens the Reference panel with information about the selected action.

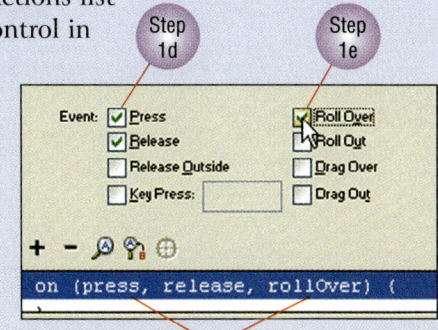

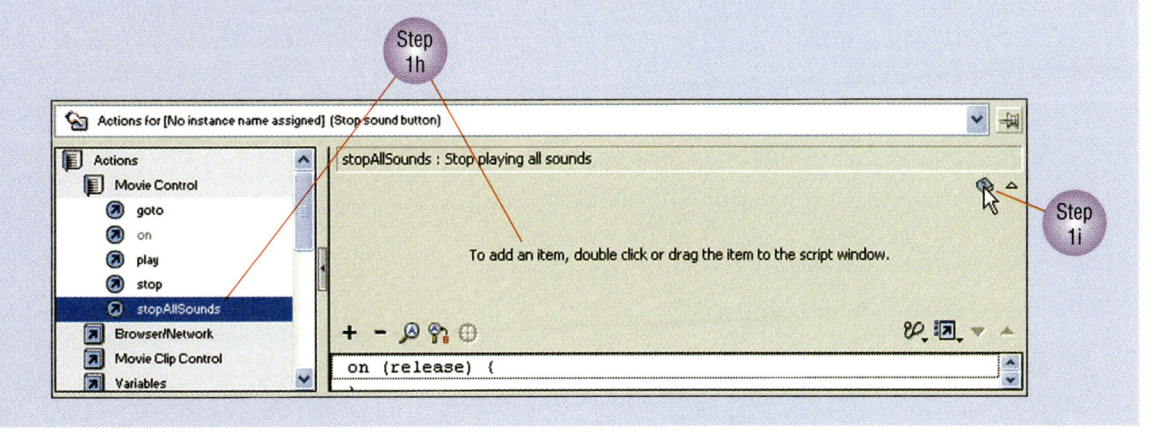

Mouse events are added to script area as check boxes are selected in Parameters area.

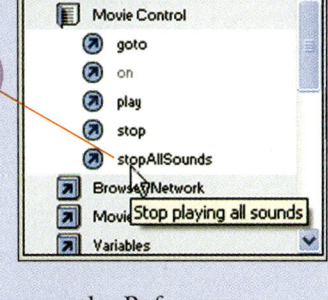

Adding Sound, Video, and Basic Interactivity with Buttons 249

j. Read the information in the Reference panel about the stopAllSounds statement. Scroll to the bottom of the window and read the description and example code.
k. Close the Reference panel.

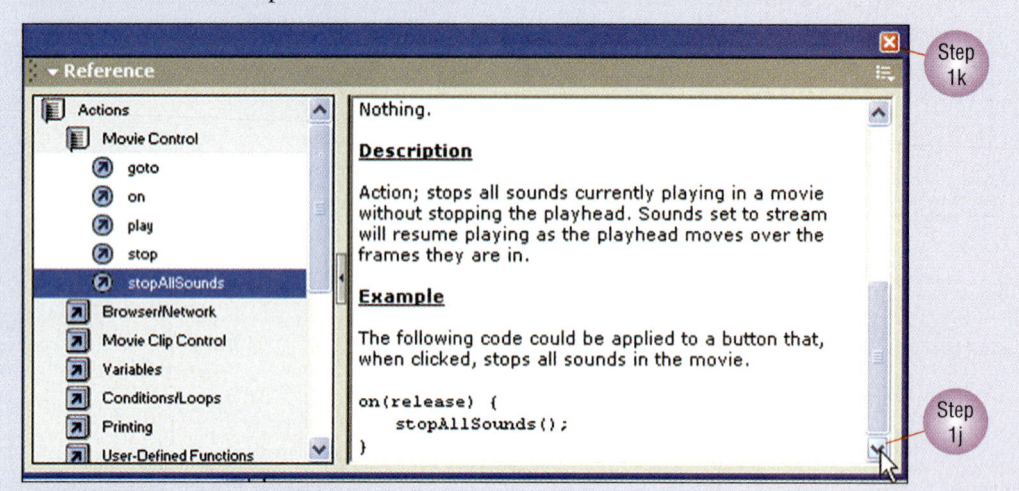

Step 1k

Step 1j

l. Double-click stopAllSounds in the toolbox. Flash adds the statement *stopAllSounds ();* in a new line in the ActionScript area below *on (release) {*.

Step 1l

m. Collapse the Actions panel.
2. Click <u>C</u>ontrol and then click Test <u>M</u>ovie to preview the animation in the Flash Player window. During the movie click the mouse over the Sound Off button. You should hear the sound effect when the mouse is clicked and then the sound will discontinue when you release the mouse button.
3. Close the Flash Player window and then save the revised document using the same name (Ch5Ex01).
4. Close Ch5Ex01.

exercise 12

ADDING BUTTONS FROM THE COMMON LIBRARY AND ADDING ACTIONS TO THE BUTTONS

1. Open Ch5Ex06.
2. Add buttons from the common library to stop, rewind, and play the movie by completing the following steps:
   a. Insert a new layer above *VideoClip* and name it *Buttons*.
   b. With frame 1 in the *Buttons* layer active, click <u>W</u>indow, point to Common Li<u>b</u>raries, and then click Buttons.
   c. If necessary, drag the Library panel for the common library over the imported video clip in the center of the stage.
   d. Scroll down the Name list in the Library panel and then double-click the folder icon next to *Playback* to expand the folder list.

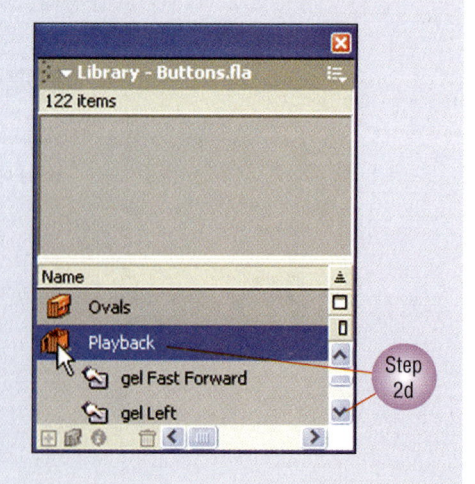

Step 2d

250 Chapter Five

e. Scroll down the expanded list of playback buttons and then click the button named *playback - stop* to view the button in the Preview pane.
f. Drag the *playback - stop* symbol to the right side of the stage next to the video clip as shown.

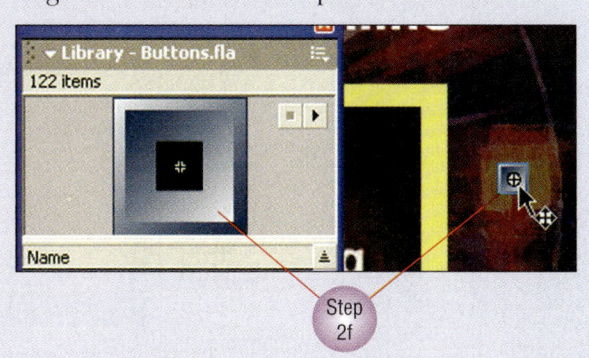

Step 2f

Step 2e

g. Scroll up the list of playback buttons and then drag the *playback - play* button to right side of the stage below the stop button.
h. Drag the *playback - rewind* button to the right side of the stage below the play button.
i. Close the Buttons library panel. The buttons inserted from the common library are automatically copied to the library for Ch5Ex06.
j. Use the Free Transform tool to scale and position the buttons as shown.

Step 2j

3. Lighten the button instances copied from the common library by completing the following steps:
    a. Click the stop button instance on the stage.
    b. Hold down the Shift key and then click the play and rewind button instances.
    c. Expand the Properties panel.
    d. Click the down arrow next to the Color list box and then click Brightness at the drop-down list.
    e. Drag across the current value in the Brightness percentage text box, key **35**, and then press Enter.
    f. Collapse the Properties panel and then click in the workspace to deselect the three button instances.

Step 3a

Step 3b

Step 3d

Step 3e

4. Add movie control actions to the buttons by completing the following steps:
    a. Click the stop button instance on the stage.
    b. Expand the Actions panel. If the Actions panel is not currently visible, click <u>W</u>indow and then click <u>A</u>ctions.

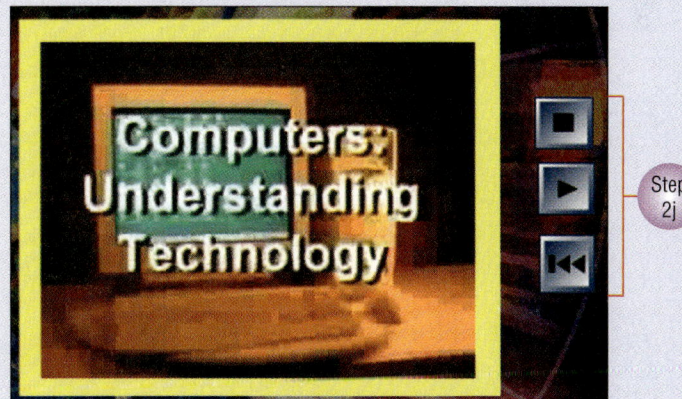

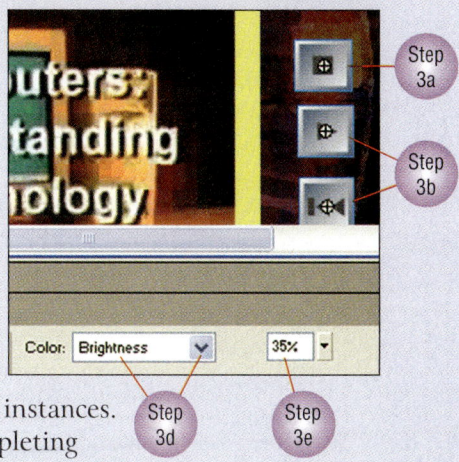

Adding Sound, Video, and Basic Interactivity with Buttons

c. Make sure the Current script/Navigate to other scripts text box displays *Actions for [No instance name assigned] (playback - stop)*. If this entry does not display in the text box, collapse the Actions panel and return to Step 4a.

d. Double-click stop in the expanded Movie Control Actions list in the toolbox. The ActionScript statement *stop ();* is added to a new line in the ActionScript area. Notice the status bar in the Actions panel displays *Line 2: stop();*.

e. Scroll up the ActionScript area to read the first ActionScript line *on (release)* {. Scroll down the ActionScript area to read the third ActionScript line }.

f. Collapse the Actions panel.

g. Click the play button instance on the stage.

h. Expand the Actions panel, make sure *Actions for [No instance name assigned] (playback - play)* displays as the current script, double-click play in the toolbox, and then collapse the Actions panel.

i. Click the rewind button on the stage.

j. Expand the Actions panel and make sure *Actions for [No instance name assigned] (playback - rewind)* displays as the current script.

k. Double-click goto in the toolbox.

l. Click Go to and Stop in the Parameters area. Flash adds the ActionScript statement *gotoAndStop(1);*. This statement instructs Flash to return to the first frame in the movie and then stop the movie. With the goto action, the desired destination frame can be specified by its number or a name if the frame has been assigned a name, and then the movie can either be resumed starting from the destination frame (gotoAndPlay) or stopped at the destination frame (gotoAndStop).

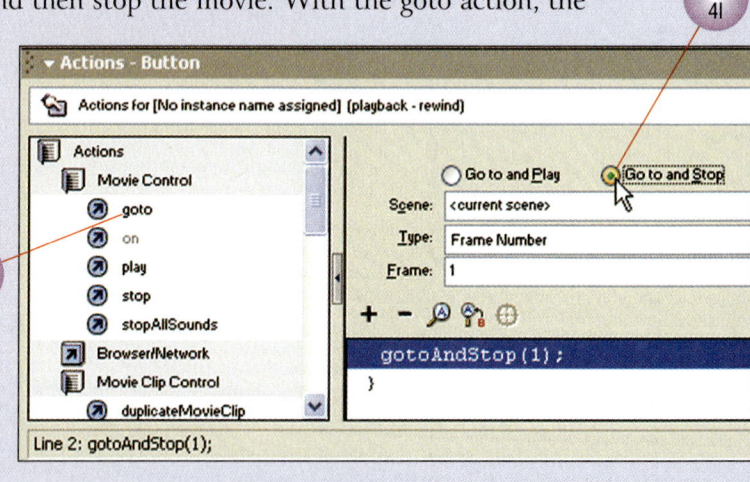

m. Collapse the Actions panel and then click in the workspace to deselect the rewind button.

5. Click Control and then click Test Movie to preview the animation in the Flash Player window. During the movie click the stop, play, and rewind buttons to test the actions.

6. Close the Flash Player window and then save the revised document using the same name (Ch5Ex06).

7. Close Ch5Ex06.

Creating Animated Buttons

Animated buttons are created by inserting movie clip symbols into the keyframes of the button's Up, Over, or Down states. Since movie clip symbols play back within their own independent Timeline, a button containing a movie clip continues playing while the button is onstage during the movie. In the next exercise you will create an animated stop button.

exercise 13

CREATING A MOVIE CLIP SYMBOL AND AN ANIMATED BUTTON USING THE MOVIE CLIP

1. Open Ch5Ex01 and set the magnification to 70%. If necessary, center the stage within the Flash window.
2. Save the document with Save As and name it Ch5Ex13.
3. Open the Library panel, right-click the symbol named Stop sound button, and then click Delete at the shortcut menu. Click the Delete symbol instances check box in the Delete dialog box and then click Delete. The Stop sound button is deleted from the library and the instance of the symbol on the stage is deleted from the document. Close the Library panel. 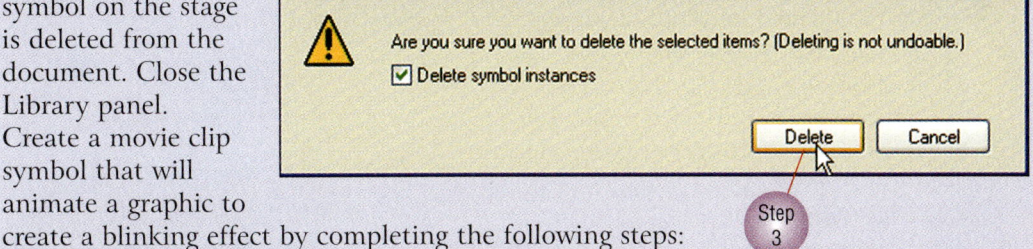
4. Create a movie clip symbol that will animate a graphic to create a blinking effect by completing the following steps:
   a. Click Insert and then click New Symbol.
   b. Key **AnimatedSound** in the Name text box, click Movie Clip in the Behavior section of the Create New Symbol dialog box, and then click OK.
   c. With the stage in symbol editing mode, click File and then click Import.
   d. Change the Files of type in the Import dialog box to JPEG Image (*.jpg) and then double-click the file named Sound.jpg. Flash imports the graphic to the library and places an instance of the graphic on the stage.
   e. Select frames 2–15 in the Timeline.
   f. Right-click the selected block of frames and then click Convert to Keyframes at the shortcut menu.
   g. Click frame 2, hold down the Ctrl key, and then click frames 4, 6, 8, 10, 12, and 14.
   h. Right-click any of the selected frames and then click Clear Frames at the shortcut menu. Clearing the stage of the graphic every other frame will create a blinking effect when an instance of the movie clip is onstage.

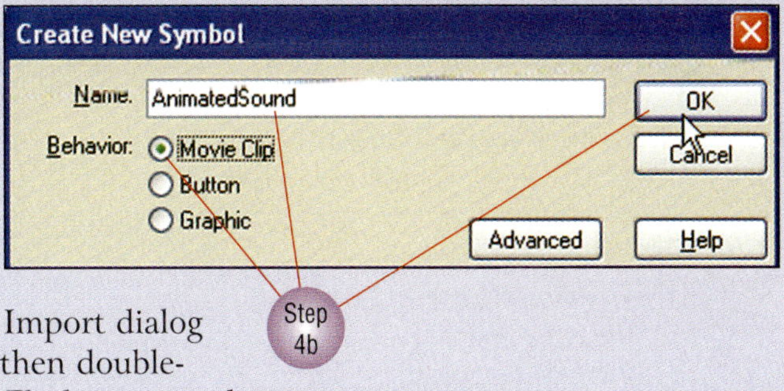

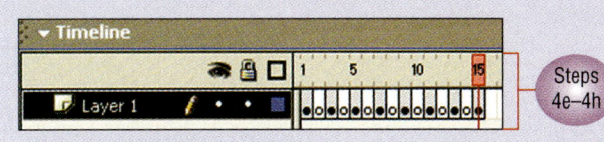

FLASH MX

Adding Sound, Video, and Basic Interactivity with Buttons 253

      i. Press Enter to play the animation.
      j. Click the Back button on the Information bar to exit symbol editing mode.
5. Create a button that uses the movie clip created in Step 4 when the button is in the Up state by completing the following steps:
   a. Click Insert and then click New Symbol.
   b. Key **AnimatedSoundButton** in the Name text box, click Button in the Behavior section, and then click OK.
   c. With the Up keyframe active, press F11 to open the Library panel.
   d. Drag an instance of the AnimatedSound movie clip to the center of the stage.
   e. Insert a keyframe in the Over frame.
   f. With the AnimatedSound instance selected on the stage, expand the Properties panel.
   g. Change the Color Style to Brightness, set the Brightness Amount to –20%, and then collapse the Properties panel.
   h. Insert a blank keyframe in the Down frame.
   i. Drag an instance of Sound.jpg to the center of the stage and then close the Library panel. By inserting a blank keyframe and placing the graphic only in the Down state, the movie clip's blinking effect will appear to have stopped when the mouse is being pressed down over the button symbol.
   j. Exit symbol editing mode.
6. Click frame 1 in the *StopButton* layer. Open the Library panel and then drag an instance of AnimatedSoundButton to the stage in the location shown.
7. Close the Library panel.
8. Click the instance of AnimatedSoundButton and then expand the Actions panel.
9. Double-click stopAllSounds in the toolbox and then collapse the Actions panel.
10. Click Control and then click Test Movie to preview the animation in the Flash Player window. Move the mouse over the blinking graphic and notice the change in brightness as the button is now in the Over state. Hold down the left mouse button over the graphic to see the blinking effect stop and then release the mouse to stop the sound.
11. Close the Flash Player window and then save the revised document using the same name (Ch5Ex13).
12. Close Ch5Ex13.

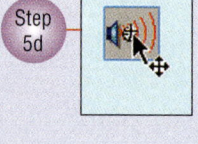

CHAPTER summary

- Sound is added to a movie by importing the sound file to the library and then adding an instance of the sound to the frame in the Timeline in which you want the sound to start playing.
- Flash can import sound files in the following file formats with QuickTime 4 or later installed: *wav*, *aif*, *au*, and *mp3*.
- A Windows-based computer without QuickTime 4 installed cannot import *au* files.
- A Macintosh-based computer without QuickTime 4 installed cannot import *wav* files.
- Open the Import dialog box and change the Files of type to the sound file format to import a sound file.
- Play a sound file from the Preview pane in the library to hear the sound effect or music.
- Insert sound in a separate layer in the Timeline to facilitate editing tasks.
- Insert sound in a keyframe by dragging an instance of the sound from the library to the stage with the keyframe active. The sound will not appear on the stage; however, the waveform appears in the Timeline.
- Pointing at the waveform in the Timeline displays a tooltip with the name of the sound file.
- A sound can also be added to a keyframe by choosing the sound file name from the Sound name drop-down list in the Properties panel.
- Sync sound properties Event, Start, Stop, and Stream can be applied to the keyframe from the Properties panel to synchronize the sound with the other elements in an animation.
- An event sound starts playing when the playhead reaches the keyframe and continues playing the sound to completion.
- An event sound is completely downloaded before it begins to play.
- A start sound is the same as an event sound with the exception that any existing instances of the same sound will be stopped when the start sound plays.
- Use a stop sound to discontinue playing a sound.
- A stream sound is synchronized with the Timeline and will stop playing when the playhead reaches the end of the frames.
- Streaming sound can begin playing almost immediately while the remainder of the data is downloaded in the background.
- Key a value in the Loop text box in the Properties panel for a sound keyframe to specify the number of times in which the sound should be replayed.
- The Effect drop-down list in the Properties panel for a sound keyframe provides preset options to control the volume level or channel from which the sound plays.
- Click Custom at the Effect drop-down list or click the Edit button in the Properties panel to edit the sound envelope by dragging envelope handles to control the volume.
- Drag the Time In or Time Out markers in the Edit Envelope dialog box to change the point in the sound file at which the sound will start or finish.
- Changes made in the Edit Envelope dialog box apply to the selected sound instance only.
- Display the Sound Properties dialog box for a sound file to specify the compression setting to use when the movie is exported.
- Sound is recorded digitally through a process called *sampling* in which a device attached to the computer measures the waveform at regular intervals.

- The *sampling rate* is the number of times per second a sample of the waveform is recorded.
- *Sample size* refers to the amount of information stored for each sampled waveform.
- High sample rate and sample sizes provide high quality sound; however, they also require a larger sound file size to store the information.
- Flash compresses sound using the ADPCM, MP3, Raw, or Speech compression settings.
- Depending on the active compression option, you can test the level at which a sound file will be compressed using various sample rates and bit rates to achieve a balance between quality of sound and file size.
- Flash provides a common sound library containing various sound effects that can be copied to the current movie's library.
- The layer height can be increased to 200% or 300% to enlarge the display of waveforms in the Timeline.
- Sound effects can be downloaded from the Web for free or for a small fee for use in a Flash movie.
- Flash can import video clips in the following file formats with QuickTime 4 or later installed: *avi, dv, dvi, mpg, mpeg, mov,* and *flv.*
- A Windows-based computer with DirectX 7 or later installed can also import a *wmv* (Windows Media File) file format.
- Flash imports and exports video using the Sorenson Spark codec which controls the compression in Flash and the decompression in the Flash Player.
- Users will require Flash Player Version 6 to view a movie with embedded video.
- Import a QuickTime video clip as an embedded movie clip or as a link to an external video file.
- Choosing to link a QuickTime video externally requires that the movie be published as a QuickTime movie.
- Import settings Quality, Keyframe interval, and scale percentage that control the compression level of a video clip are set before the video is imported.
- You can choose to synchronize the video with the Flash document's timeline in the Import Settings dialog box.
- Audio may or may not be able to be imported with a video clip depending on the program used to record the video and audio tracks. Flash displays a message box when the audio cannot be encoded with the video.
- Video is imported to the library for the current movie.
- An instance of a video clip can be scaled, rotated, or skewed.
- Import a video clip to a movie clip symbol in order to change the clip's brightness, tint, or alpha properties, or to maintain the video within its own Timeline.
- Create buttons to add simple interactivity with the user in which the user can control the movie's playback.
- A button is created as a symbol with four states: Up, Over, Down, and Hit.
- Draw the button in the Up state according to how the button should look when no mouse action is occurring over the symbol.
- Change the appearance of the button in the Over keyframe to the way in which you want the button to display when the user rolls the mouse over the button.
- The Down state refers to the appearance of the button when the user clicks the mouse on the button.
- Define the boundaries within which a button will react to mouse movement in the Hit keyframe.

- Flash will use the button's Up state as the Hit property if no image is created in the Hit keyframe.
- Click Control and then Enable Simple Buttons to test a button on the stage.
- Use the Buttons common library to copy button symbols to the current movie.
- Sound can be attached to a button by importing the sound file and then selecting the sound name in the Properties panel for the button state's keyframe.
- A programming language called *ActionScript* is used to instruct Flash on what actions to perform when a button is clicked by the user.
- Learning ActionScript is like learning a new language of words and syntax to convey instructions to the computer.
- Flash provides the Actions panel with which you can create ActionScript using a point-and-click approach.
- Creating an action statement for a button involves associating ActionScript statements with a mouse event.
- A mouse event occurs when the user interacts with the button. The three most common mouse events are Press, Release, and Roll Over.
- An event handler beginning with the keyword *on* is required at the beginning of any ActionScript statement for a button and is created automatically when you add actions using the Actions panel.
- Double-click an action in the Toolbox of the Actions panel to add the action to the ActionScript area for the selected button instance.
- The Movie Control actions Stop, Play, Goto, and stopAllSounds in the Actions panel toolbox are used to allow the user to control the playback of the movie when assigned to a button.
- Create a movie clip symbol with animation and then insert the movie clip symbol within a button's Up, Over, or Down keyframes to create a button that animates.

COMMANDS review

Command or Feature	Mouse/Keyboard	Shortcut Keys
Actions panel	Window, Actions	F9
Common button or sound library	Window, Common Libraries	
Create new symbol	Insert, New Symbol	Ctrl + F8
Enable buttons on stage	Control, Enable Simple Buttons	Ctrl + Alt + B
Import sound or video	File, Import	Ctrl + R
Import to library	File, Import to Library	
Layer properties	Modify, Layer	
Library panel	Window, Library	F11

CONCEPTS check

Indicate the correct term or command for each item.

1. Listen to an imported sound in this panel.
2. Sound can be added to a keyframe using either of these two panels.
3. This visual indicator displays in the Timeline for a sound.
4. This Sync property means the sound will play until completion regardless of the number of frames in the Timeline.
5. Use this Sync property to coordinate the sound with the other elements of the animation and stop playing the sound when the frames have ended.
6. A smaller sound file can be repeated as often as necessary by keying the number of times to repeat in this text box.
7. Use this sound effect to gradually increase the volume of the sound as it is played.
8. Open this dialog box to customize the volume level for the sound.
9. Display this dialog box to choose the compression option for exporting the sound.
10. This sound compression option is popular because it compresses audio files by removing redundant or unnoticeable irrelevant parts without degrading quality.
11. Increase layer height in this dialog box.
12. This is the name of the codec Flash uses to import and export video clips.
13. Selecting a QuickTime video file causes Flash to display these two Import options.
14. This slider in the Import Video Settings dialog box specifies the compression level between 0 and 100.
15. Import video in this type of symbol to have the ability to change the brightness, tint, or alpha property of the video instance.
16. These are the four states for a button symbol.
17. Create a rollover effect for a button in this keyframe in the symbol editing window.
18. This keyframe in symbol editing mode defines the boundaries for the button which will make the button respond to user interaction with the mouse.
19. Buttons cannot be tested on the stage unless this feature is toggled on.
20. This is the name of the programming language included with Flash.
21. Use this panel to add instructions to Flash on what to do when the user clicks a button instance.
22. This is the term for the trigger that causes Flash to do something when a button is activated.
23. Double-click this action to instruct Flash to turn off all sound in the movie.
24. Use this action to rewind the movie back to the first frame.
25. Insert this type of symbol in a keyframe in symbol editing mode to create an animated button.

SKILLS check

Assessment 1

1. Open Ch4SA3.
2. Save the document with Save As and name it Ch5SA1.
3. Import the sound file named bee.wav.
4. Insert a new layer at the top of the Timeline named *Sound*.
5. Insert the bee.wav sound in the first keyframe in the *Sound* layer and repeat its playback three times.
6. Test the movie in the Flash Player window.
7. Save the revised document using the same name (Ch5SA1).
8. Close Ch5SA1.

Assessment 2

1. Open the Flash document named AnimatedSailboats.
2. Save the Flash document with Save As and name it Ch5SA2.
3. Import the sound file named waves.wav.
4. Insert a new layer at the top of the Timeline in the Sailboats scene and name it *WaveSound*.
5. Insert the waves.wav sound in the first keyframe in the *WaveSound* layer and set the sound properties so that sound stops when the Sailboats scene animation is finished.
6. Test the movie in the Flash Player window.
7. Save the revised document using the same name (Ch5SA2).
8. Close Ch5SA2.

Assessment 3

FIGURE 5.17 *Assessment 3*

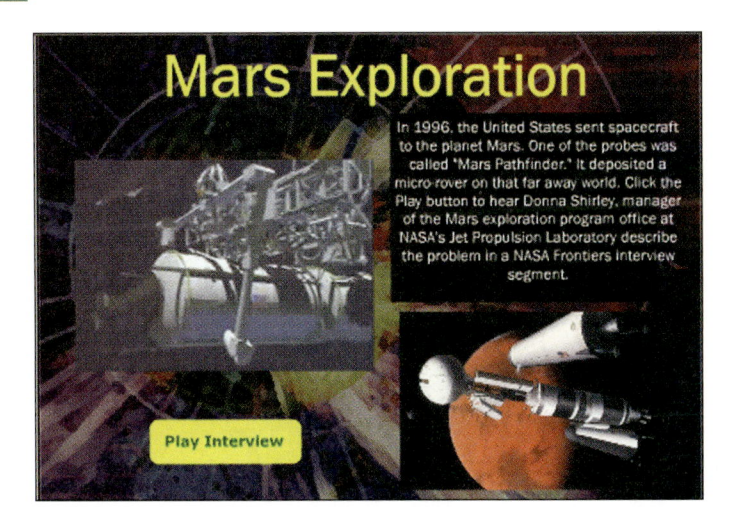

1. Open the Flash document named Mars-Nasa.
2. Save the document with Save As and name it Ch5SA3.
3. Create a new movie clip symbol named MarsVideo.
4. Import the video file named spacearm-NASA.mpeg into the MarsVideo movie clip symbol. Use all of the default video import settings and allow Flash to insert the required number of frames in the movie clip symbol.
5. Insert an instance of the MarsVideo movie clip symbol in frame 1 of the *Video* layer. Scale and position the movie clip at the middle left side of the stage as shown in Figure 5.17.
6. Adjust the brightness amount for the MarsVideo movie clip to 25%.
7. Test the movie in the FlashPlayer window.
8. Save the revised document using the same name (Ch5SA3).

Assessment 4

1. With Ch5SA3 open, create a button that will play an audio clip of an interview with a NASA manager using the following information:
   - Use the drawing tools to create the Play Interview button in the first frame of the *Button* layer as shown in Figure 5.17.
   - Select the button and then convert it to a button symbol named PlayInterview.
   - Edit the button symbol to change the color of the text to red when the mouse rolls over it.
   - Edit the button symbol to change the color of the text to black when the button is clicked.
   - Import the sound file named Mars-NASA.au and then add the sound in a new layer to the Down state for the PlayInterview button. Make sure that only one instance of the sound can be playing at any time.
2. Enable simple buttons and then test the Play Interview button on the stage.
3. Disable simple buttons.
4. Test the movie in the FlashPlayer window.
5. Save the revised document using the same name (Ch5SA3).
6. Close Ch5SA3.

Assessment 5

FIGURE 5.18 Assessment 5

1. Start a new Flash document.
2. Change the background color for the document to pale yellow.
3. Create a new movie clip symbol named Clown.
4. Import the QuickTime movie named clown.mov into the movie clip symbol and then exit symbol editing mode. *(Note: The graphic will appear very large on the stage—do not resize it.)*
5. Rename Layer 1 *Clown*.
6. Insert an instance of the Clown movie clip symbol to the stage. Scale and position the movie clip as shown in Figure 5.18.
7. Create the three text blocks shown in Figure 5.18 in a new layer named *Text*. You determine the text properties.
8. Import the sound file named OpeningMusic.wav and then insert the sound in the first keyframe of a new layer in the Timeline. Set the sound to repeat 99 times.
9. Test the movie in the Flash Player window.
10. Save the document and name it Ch5SA5.

Assessment 6

1. With Ch5SA5 open, expand the Properties panel for the sound keyframe and then edit the sound as follows:
   - Choose the Fade In sound effect.
   - Edit the sound envelope to decrease the volume level by at least half of its current volume.
2. Create a new button symbol named StopSound that is a drawn shape with a text overlay that reads *Stop Sound*. You determine the shapes and colors in the Up, Over, Down, and Hit states.
3. Insert an instance of the StopSound button at the bottom right of the stage below the text block.
4. Enable simple buttons and then test the Stop Sound button on the stage.
5. Disable simple buttons.
6. Add the stopAllSounds action to the button instance.
7. Test the movie in the Flash Player window. Click the Stop Sound button during the movie to make sure the playing of the music discontinues.
8. Save the revised document using the same name (Ch5SA5).
9. Close Ch5SA5.

Assessment 7

1. Open Ch5Ex01.
2. Save the document with Save As and name it Ch5SA7.
3. Create three buttons to allow the user to stop, play, and rewind the movie during playback. Draw your own buttons or use some from the common button library.
4. Position the buttons at the bottom right corner of the stage.
5. Add the required action statements to the buttons.
6. Extend the duration of the movie by 20 frames for all layers.
7. Test the movie in the Flash Player window. Make sure each button performs the correct action.
8. Save the revised document using the same name (Ch5SA7).

CHAPTER 6

ANIMATING USING SYMBOLS AND MASKS AND PUBLISHING FLASH MOVIES

PERFORMANCE OBJECTIVES

Upon successful completion of Chapter 6, you will be able to:
- Create and use an animation in a movie clip symbol.
- Edit instances of a movie clip symbol.
- Create and use an animation in a graphic symbol.
- Describe the differences between animating using movie clip symbols and animating using graphic symbols.
- Duplicate and edit a symbol to reuse existing objects.
- Assign a name to an instance of a symbol.
- Stop a movie clip playback using ActionScript.
- Convert an existing animation to a movie clip symbol.
- Create an animation using a mask layer.
- Understand the test environment within Flash.
- Simulate download performance for various bandwidths.
- Optimize a movie before publishing.
- Choose appropriate Flash Player options in which to publish a movie.
- Choose appropriate HTML options in which to publish a movie.
- Use Publish Preview to view the published movie within a browser window.
- Publish a movie.
- Describe the HTML tags that instruct the browser to display a Flash movie.
- Publish and export a movie in formats other than Flash Player format.
- Publish a document as a self-running standalone movie.

Flash MX Chapter 06

There are four student data files to copy for this chapter.

In the last chapter you learned how to create movie clip symbols in a Flash document for playing a video and for animating a button. Now that you have seen movie clips in action you will further explore their use as a powerful tool for building animations within animations. In Chapter 3 you learned how to use a mask layer to provide a window to objects in the layer below the mask. Animating masks creates interesting movie effects such as moving a spotlight or eyeglass, or scrolling text in a marquee-like fashion.

When you are ready to show the world your Flash creation, Flash provides tools with which you can optimize, preview, and test the movie prior to publishing. Two points to consider before publishing your movie include deciding in which formats the movie should be made available to reach a broad audience, and which options you should use to minimize file size and provide the desired image quality and playback settings.

Creating Animations Using Symbols

In Chapter 5, Exercise 7, you imported video inside a movie clip symbol which allowed you to add the video to the main movie's Timeline using only one frame. In Exercise 13 of the same chapter, you created a blinking effect for a button symbol using a movie clip and saw that the button continued to animate after the beach ball had completed its movement. Movie clips provide the Flash author with the following advantages:

- Main movie Timeline becomes less cluttered with layers and frames.
- Movie clips provide continuous movement during the main movie and can continue after the main movie has completely played back.
- Movie clips can be reused within the same movie or reused in other movies.
- Reused symbols within a movie minimize file size.

As you learned in Chapter 5, movies containing animated movie clip symbols must be exported and previewed in the Flash Player window since only the first frame of the movie clip displays on the stage. Creating a movie clip symbol animation involves the same process as creating animations on the main movie Timeline with the exception that you are doing so in symbol editing mode. In Chapter 5 you created movie clip symbols from scratch in symbol editing mode. You can also create movie clips by converting an existing animation to a symbol by copying and pasting frames from the main movie Timeline to a movie clip symbol Timeline.

exercise 1

CREATING A GRAPHIC SYMBOL AND ANIMATED MOVIE CLIP SYMBOL

1. Open the Flash document named ChristmasTraditions.
2. Save the document with Save As and name it Ch6Ex01.
3. To review creating and using library symbols, create a light bulb socket and a light bulb including an animation on the bulb that produces a blinking effect using a graphic symbol and a movie clip symbol by completing the following steps:
   a. Click Insert and then click New Symbol.
   b. Key **LightSocket** in the Name text box of the Create New Symbol dialog box.
   c. Click Graphic in the Behavior section and then click OK.

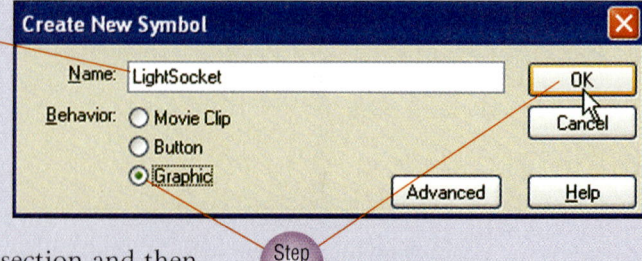

264 Chapter Six

d. Using the drawing tools, draw a socket for a light bulb similar to the one shown.
e. Click the Back button on the Information bar to exit symbol editing mode.
f. Click Insert and then click New Symbol.
g. Key **LightBulb** in the Name text box of the Create New Symbol dialog box, click Movie Clip, and then click OK.

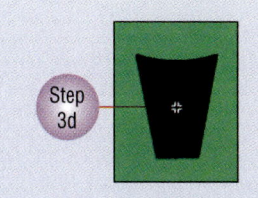

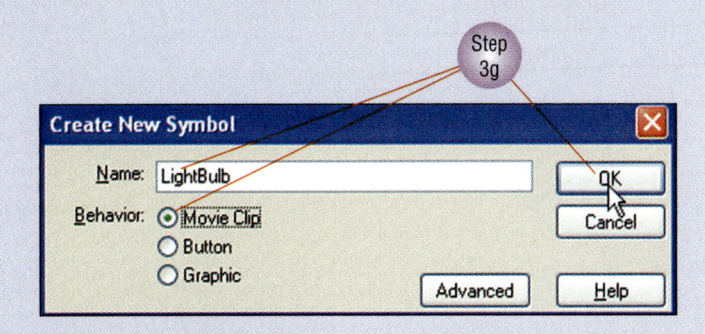

h. Click Window and then click Library to open the Library panel.
i. Drag an instance of the LightSocket graphic symbol to the stage as shown. *(Note: The location of the symbol on the stage is irrelevant at this point. You are using the socket only as a reference to draw the light bulb in proportion to the socket.)*
j. Close the Library panel.
k. Using the drawing tools, draw a light bulb that is sized in proportion to the size of the socket similar to the one shown. *(Note: You will be deleting the socket in the next step so be careful not to overlap the bulb over the socket.)*
l. Select and then delete the LightSocket graphic symbol from the stage.
m. Drag the bulb shape so that the symbol's registration point is in the middle of the bulb.
n. Insert a keyframe at frame 15.
o. Select frames 3, 6, 9, and 12 and then clear the frames.
p. Click frame 1 and then press Enter to view the blinking effect animation.
q. Click the Back button on the Information bar to exit symbol editing mode.

4. Use the LightSocket graphic symbol and LightBulb movie clip symbol to animate the cord around the stage by completing the following steps:
    a. Change the magnification to 150% and scroll the stage so that the top center of the document is in the center of the Flash window.
    b. Insert a new layer at the top of the Timeline and name it *LightBulbs*.
    c. Insert a new layer above *LightBulbs* and name it *LightSockets*.
    d. Open the Library panel.

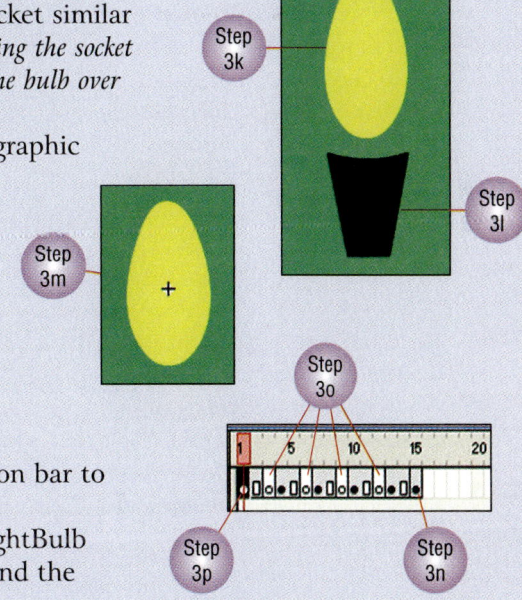

Animating Using Symbols and Masks and Publishing Flash Movies — 265

e. With frame 1 of the *LightBulbs* layer active, drag an instance of the LightBulb movie clip symbol to the stage.
f. With frame 1 of the *LightSockets* layer active, drag an instance of the LightSocket graphic symbol to the stage.
g. Drag the LightBulb object into the LightSocket object so that the socket is slightly overlapping the bulb. This makes the bulb appear inside the socket.
h. Scale, rotate, and position the symbol instances as shown. *(Note: You can select both symbols in order to scale, rotate, and move as one object.)*
i. Repeat steps 4e–4h to place another light bulb to the left of the first light bulb as shown.
j. Select the LightBulb instance, expand the Properties panel, and then change the tint to red and the tint amount to 100%.
k. Complete the remaining light bulbs as shown changing the tint color of bulbs as necessary. *(Note: Select a LightSocket and LightBulb instance and then use the Ctrl key while dragging to create copies of the instances.)*
l. Lock the *LightSockets* layer.
m. Lock the *LightBulbs* layer.
n. Close the Library panel.

5. Click Control and then click Test Movie to export the movie and preview the animation in the Flash Player window.
6. Close the Flash Player window and then save the revised document using the same name (Ch6Ex01).

Animating Using a Graphic Symbol

A graphic symbol contains a Timeline in which you can create animation in the same manner as a movie clip symbol. The main difference between animating using a graphic symbol and animating using a movie clip symbol resides in the way in which Flash treats the symbol's Timeline during movie playback. A movie clip's Timeline is independent of the main movie and uses only one frame in the main movie whereas a graphic symbol's Timeline must be synchronized with the main movie Timeline with respect to the number of frames that must be inserted.

For example, if a graphic symbol that contains 20 frames of animation is inserted into a movie, the main movie must also contain 20 frames in the layer at the point at which the graphic symbol is inserted in order for a user to view the entire animation sequence.

The strategy you decide to use for animating symbols will depend on whether you want to tie the animated object to the Timeline of the main movie or instead animate the object in its own independent Timeline.

Another issue for consideration is whether you want the animated symbol to include sound and interactivity. Animated objects within movie clips can include a soundtrack and interactive capability while graphic symbols cannot include these additional elements.

exercise 2

CREATING AN ANIMATED GRAPHIC SYMBOL

1. With Ch6Ex01 open, create an animated graphic symbol for the telephone number that will shape tween the object by completing the following steps:
   a. Make active the *Background* layer and then unlock the layer.
   b. If necessary, click in the workspace to deselect the text blocks if all of the objects on the *Background* layer are selected. 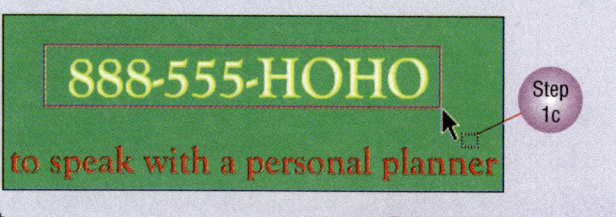
   c. With the Arrow tool active, draw a selection box around the telephone number to select the individual characters as one object.
   d. Click Edit and then click Cut to remove the text from the *Background* layer.
   e. Lock the *Background* layer.
   f. Click Insert and then click New Symbol.
   g. Key **AnimatedPhone** in the Name text box, click Graphic in the Behavior section, and then click OK. 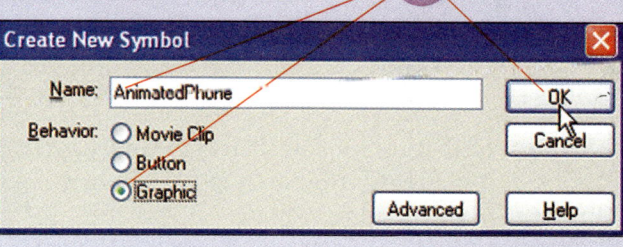
   h. Click Edit and then click Paste to paste the telephone number to the stage in symbol editing mode.
   i. Insert a keyframe at frame 20.
   j. Click frame 1 in the Timeline.
   k. Using the Free Transform tool and the Scale modifier, resize the telephone number to the approximate size shown and then click in the stage to deselect the object. 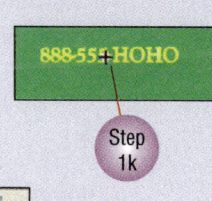
   l. Expand the Properties panel and click frame 1 in the Timeline.
   m. Click the down arrow next to the Tween list box and then click Shape at the drop-down list. 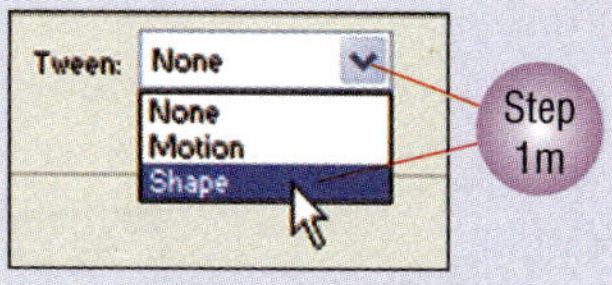
   n. Collapse the Properties panel.
   o. Press Enter to play the animation in symbol editing mode.
   p. Click the Back button on the Information bar to return to the document.

2. Insert an instance of the animated telephone number in the document by completing the following steps:
   a. Insert a new layer at the top of the Timeline and name it *Telephone*.
   b. Open the Library panel.
   c. With frame 1 in the *Telephone* layer active, drag an instance of the AnimatedPhone graphic symbol to the stage as shown. 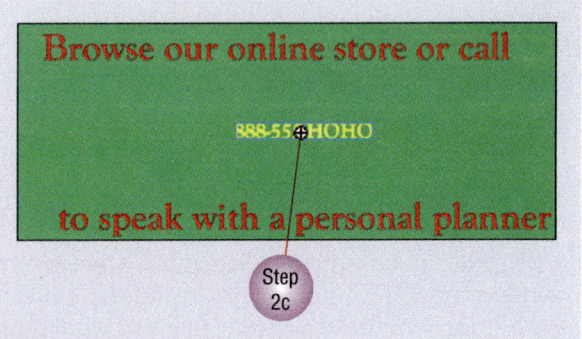
   d. Lock the *Telephone* layer, and then close the Library panel.
3. Click Control and then click Test Movie to export the movie and preview the animation in the Flash Player window. Notice the telephone number does not draw the shape tween you created in the AnimatedPhone graphic symbol. Since the animation resides inside a graphic symbol with 20 frames, the main movie must also contain 20 frames in order to play the graphic symbol's animation.
4. Close the Flash Player window to return to the document.
5. Insert the frames required for the graphic symbol animation and then test the animation by completing the following steps:
   a. Resize the Timeline panel if necessary in order to view all five layers.
   b. Click frame 2 in the *Telephone* layer.
   c. Hold down the Shift key and then click frame 20 in the *Background* layer.
   d. Click Insert and then click Frame. Frames 2–20 are added to the five layers in the document. 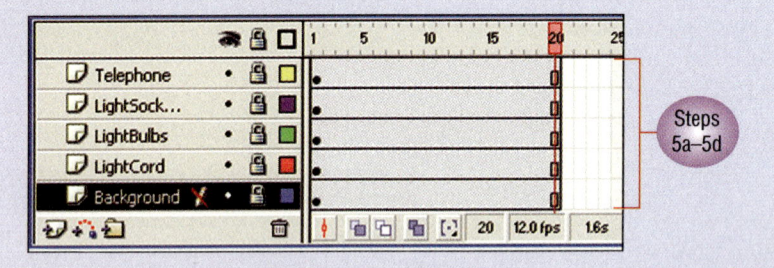
   e. Click Control and then click Test Movie. The shape tween on the telephone number plays back now that the main movie contains the same number of frames as the graphic symbol.
6. Close the Flash Player window to return to the document.
7. Click frame 1 in the Timeline and then press Enter to play the animation. Notice that the graphic symbol's animation can be viewed on the stage while the movie clip animation cannot.
8. Save the revised document using the same name (Ch6Ex01).

Since adding frames to the Timeline of the main movie is required to view animation within a graphic symbol, it follows that animating using graphic symbols creates larger movie files. For complex movies where download time will be a critical factor, it is advisable to create animations in symbols using movie clips.

Duplicating Symbols

A new symbol can be created by duplicating an existing symbol and then editing the content of the copied symbol in symbol editing mode. Use this method to create a new symbol when you want to reuse an object within an existing symbol. Open the Library panel, right-click the existing symbol that you want to reuse, and then click Duplicate at the shortcut menu. Flash opens the Duplicate Symbol dialog box with the name of the selected symbol entered in the Name text box and the word *copy* as shown in Figure 6.1.

FIGURE

6.1 *Duplicate Symbol Dialog Box*

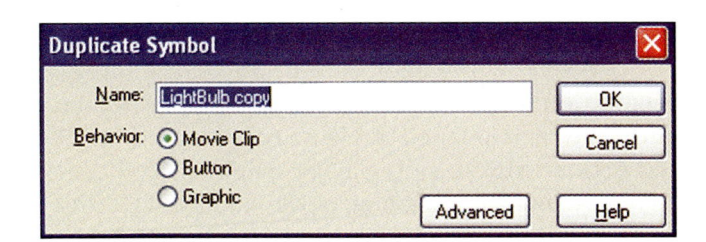

Key a new name for the symbol, change the Behavior if necessary, and then click OK. Edit the symbol to change the content. To do this, right-click the duplicated symbol name in the Name list and then click Edit at the shortcut menu or click the duplicated symbol name, click the Properties button at the bottom of the Library panel, and then click the Edit button in the Symbol Properties dialog box.

If the Library panel is not currently open, you can duplicate a symbol by right-clicking an instance of the symbol on the stage and then clicking Duplicate Symbol at the shortcut menu. Flash displays the Symbol Name dialog box where you can assign a name to the duplicate copy and then click OK.

Stopping Playback of a Movie Clip Symbol Animation

While previewing the Ch6Ex01 animation in the first two exercises, you have seen that the LightBulb movie clip animation continues to replay over and over again after the main movie animation is complete. Movie clips continue in looped playback unless a frame within the main movie contains ActionScript statements to instruct Flash to stop the movie clip, or the playhead reaches either a blank keyframe or a keyframe containing new content in the same layer as the movie clip.

Using ActionScript you can control the Timeline for each movie clip separately as well as the Timeline for the entire movie. To do this, assign a name in the Properties panel to each instance of the movie clip that you want to control. This allows you to create actions directed at a specific *target object*. For example, each individual light bulb instance created in the Ch6Ex01 document can be named and then the playback for each light bulb can be controlled separately.

To stop a named instance of the LightBulb symbol from playing, insert a keyframe in the main movie Timeline at the point at which you want the instance to stop blinking, open the Actions panel, and then click the following sequence in the toolbox: Objects, Movie, Movie Clip, Methods. Double-click Stop in the Methods list. A *method* is an action that the object (in this case a movie clip), can do such as play, stop, or goto. Flash inserts the following statement in the ActionScript area:

<not set yet>.stop( );

Insert a target path

In the Parameters area, with the insertion point positioned in the Object text box, click the Insert a target path button located just above the ActionScript area at the bottom of Parameters. Flash opens the Insert Target Path dialog box. Click the instance name in the target list and then click OK.

Flash replaces <not set yet> with the instance name entered in the Insert Target Path dialog box. Close the Actions panel and then preview the animation. For example, assume you have named an instance of the LightBulb symbol in the Ch6Ex01 document RightBulb. When you choose RightBulb in the target list box of the Insert Target Path dialog box, Flash creates the statement *RightBulb.stop( );*. The instance of the LightBulb symbol that was named RightBulb would be stopped when the playhead reaches the keyframe.

An example of ActionScript entered by Flash using the Actions panel to stop two movie clip instances is illustrated in Figure 6.2. Recall from Chapter 5 that when you created ActionScript to stop playing sound, an event handler for the mouse event was required at the beginning of the statement. In this case, the event handler *onClipEvent (load) {* is required for the stop action to be performed on the movie clip. By working within the Actions panel, these event handlers are created automatically, making the task of using ActionScript easier. You will learn more ActionScript in the next chapter.

FIGURE

6.2 ActionScript to Stop Playing Movie Clip Instances Named LeftBulb and RightBulb

```
onClipEvent (load) {
    LeftBulb.stop();
    RightBulb.stop();
}
```

Two movie clips are the target objects for the stop action.

exercise 3

DUPLICATING AN EXISTING SYMBOL, NAMING SYMBOL INSTANCES, AND STOPPING A MOVIE CLIP USING ACTIONSCRIPT

1. With Ch6Ex01 open, create a new movie clip symbol for the title of the company by completing the following steps:
    a. Make active the *Background* layer and then unlock the layer.
    b. If necessary, click in the workspace to deselect the text blocks if all of the objects on the *Background* layer are selected.
    c. With the Arrow tool active, click the text block for *Christmas Traditions*.
    d. Click Edit and then click Cut to remove the grouped text block from the *Background* layer.
    e. Lock the *Background* layer.
    f. Click Insert and then click New Symbol.
    g. Key **AnimatedTitle** in the Name text box in the Create New Symbol dialog box, click Movie Clip in the Behavior section, and then click OK.
    h. Click Edit and then click Paste to paste the grouped text block to the stage in symbol editing mode.

i. Rename Layer 1 *Text*.
j. Insert a new layer above *Text* and name it *LightBulbs*.
k. Drag the *LightBulbs* layer below the *Text* layer.
l. With *LightBulbs* the active layer, open the Library panel, drag two instances of the LightBulb movie clip symbol to the stage, and then close the Library panel.
m. Rotate, resize, and position the light bulbs behind the text as shown.
n. Click the Back button on the Information bar to exit symbol editing mode.
2. Insert an instance of the AnimatedTitle movie clip symbol in the document by completing the following steps:
   a. Insert a new layer at the top of the Timeline and name it *Title*.
   b. Open the Library panel.
   c. With frame 1 in the *Title* layer active, drag an instance of the AnimatedTitle movie clip symbol to the stage as shown.
   d. Close the Library panel.
3. Click <u>C</u>ontrol and then click Test <u>M</u>ovie to export the movie and preview the animation in the Flash Player window. Since the AnimatedTitle movie clip contained an instance of the LightBulb movie clip, the light bulbs behind the title animate just like the other light bulbs in the movie. The AnimatedTitle movie clip is an example of a nested movie clip symbol—a movie clip within a movie clip.
4. Close the Flash Player window to return to the document. Save the document using the same name (Ch6Ex01).
5. Assume that you have decided the continuous animation of the light bulbs behind the *Christmas Traditions* title is too much movement in the movie. You would like the light bulbs behind the title to stop blinking when the telephone number has completed the shape tween. To do this, insert a keyframe, duplicate the AnimatedTitle symbol, assign a name to each LightBulb instance, insert an instance of the duplicated symbol, and then use the Actions panel to stop the instances from playing by completing the following steps:
   a. Insert a keyframe at frame 20 in the *Title* layer.
   b. Right-click the instance of the AnimatedTitle symbol on the stage and then click Duplicate Symbol at the shortcut menu.

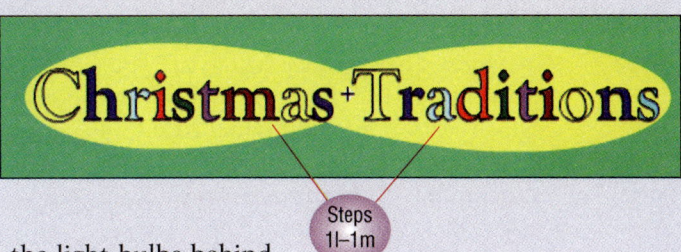

c. Click OK with *AnimatedTitle copy* inserted in the Symbol Name text box in the Symbol Name dialog box. 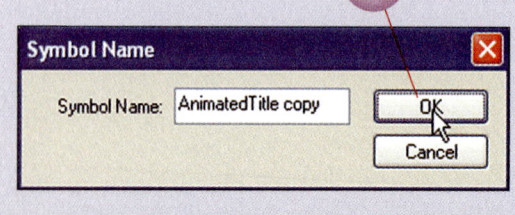
d. Display the rulers and then drag a horizontal and a vertical guide line to the top and left edges of the AnimatedTitle instance. These guides will assist you with placing the duplicate symbol in the same location as the original title in a later step. 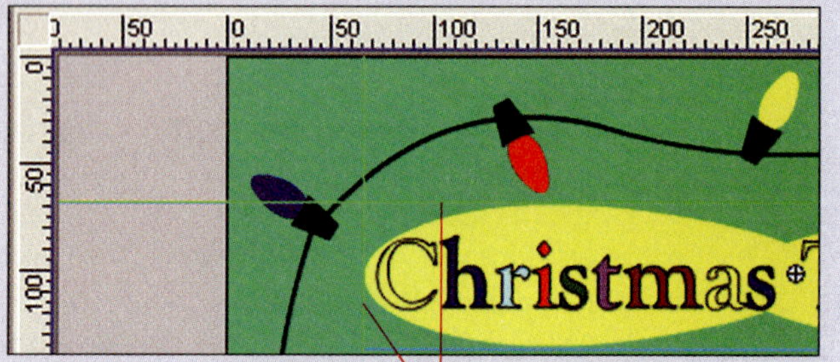
e. With frame 20 in the *Title* layer active, delete the instance of AnimatedTitle.
f. Open the Library panel, right-click AnimatedTitle copy in the Name list, and then click Edit at the shortcut menu.
g. In symbol editing mode, name each instance of the LightBulb symbol by completing the following steps:
   1) Click the instance of LightBulb at the left side of the stage.
   2) Expand the Properties panel.
   3) Click in the <Instance Name> text box and then key **LeftBulb**.
   4) Click the instance of LightBulb at the right side of the stage.
   5) Click in the <Instance Name> text box and then key **RightBulb**.
   6) Collapse the Properties panel.
h. Click the Back button on the Information bar to exit symbol editing mode. The two instances of the LightBulb symbol have now been assigned a name with which you can target an action on each object.
i. Drag an instance of AnimatedTitle copy to the stage using the guides to position the duplicated symbol in the exact same location as the original title.

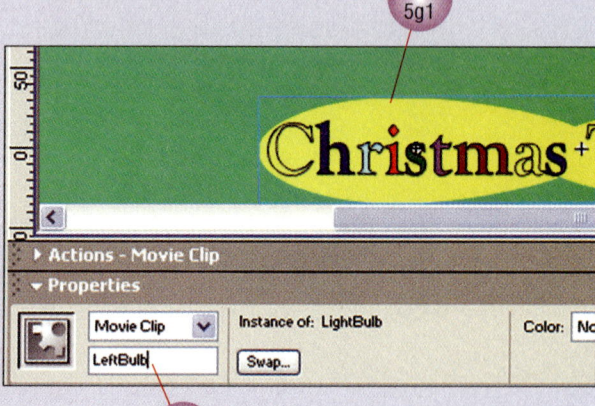

272 Chapter Six

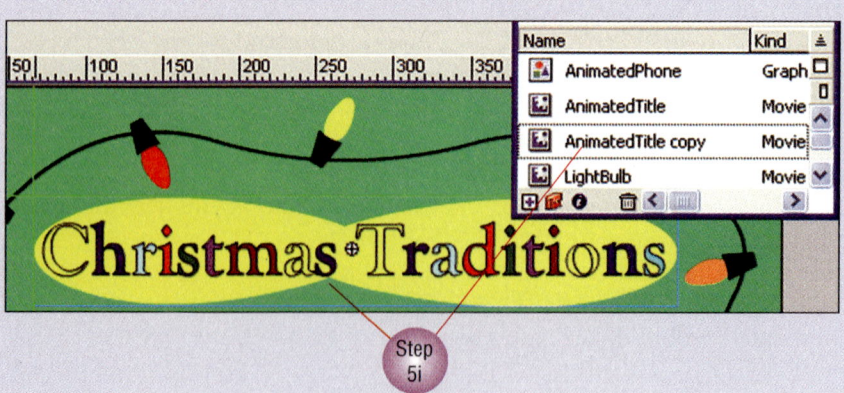

j. Turn off the display of the rulers, drag the guides off the stage and then close the Library panel.
k. With frame 20 in the *Title* layer active, expand the Actions panel. *(Note: Click Window and then click Actions if the Actions panel is not currently visible.)*
l. If necessary, scroll down the toolbox until you can see Objects.
m. Click Objects to expand the Objects list.
n. Click Movie to expand the Objects/Movie list.
o. Scroll down the Objects/Movie toolbox list and then click MovieClip.
p. Click Methods in the Objects/Movie/MovieClip toolbox list.

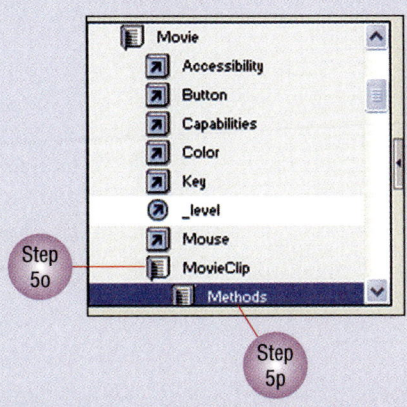

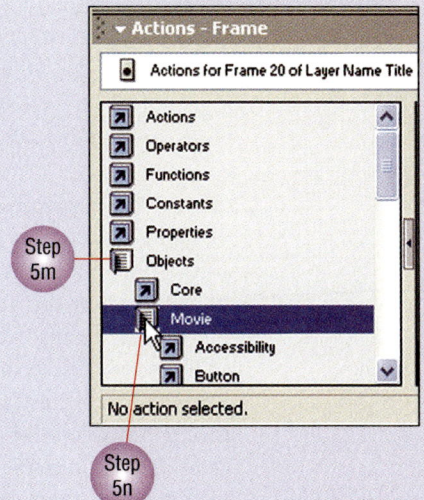

q. Scroll down the Objects/Movie/MovieClip/Methods toolbox list and then double-click stop. Flash adds the statement *<not set yet>.stop( );* to the ActionScript area. Add the names of the two symbol instances to the ActionScript area by completing the following steps:
1) With the insertion point positioned in the Object text box in the Parameters area, click the Insert a target path button at the bottom of the Parameters area.

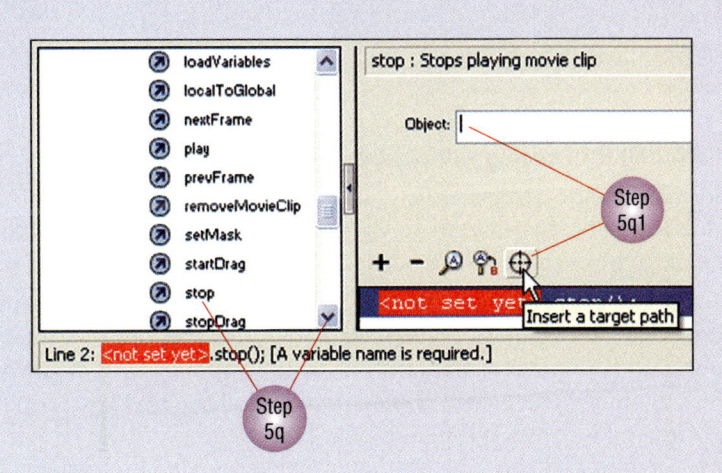

Animating Using Symbols and Masks and Publishing Flash Movies 273

2) With Notation set to Dots and Mode set to Relative, click LeftBulb in the target list and then click OK. *(Note: Click the symbol instance on the stage if the Insert Target Path dialog box does not display LeftBulb and RightBulb.)* Dots notation means Flash inserts dots (periods) between nested movie clip names. Relative mode means that Flash will look for the target object relative to its current location when the statement is encountered. For example, Flash will encounter the statement in frame 20. In frame 20 you will load the duplicated symbol AnimatedTitle copy. Flash looks within the current symbol for the named instance *LeftBulb*.

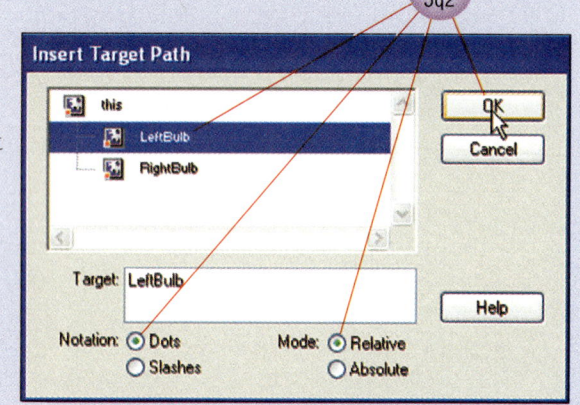

3) Double-click stop in the toolbox. With the insertion point positioned in the Object text box, click Insert a target path.

4) Click RightBulb in the target list and then click OK.

5) View the statements entered in the ActionScript area. If necessary, scroll up and down the ActionScript area to see all 4 lines.

    onClipEvent (load) {
        LeftBulb.stop( );
        RightBulb.stop( );
    }

  r. Collapse the Actions panel.

6. Click Control and then click Test Movie to export the movie and preview the animation in the Flash Player window. The animation will loop by default. Click Control and then click Loop to disable looped playback. Click Control and then click Rewind to rewind the playhead back to the beginning. Click Control and then click Play to restart the animation. The movie will play to frame 20 and then stop. The light bulbs behind the title *Christmas Traditions* stop blinking; however, the remaining light bulbs along the cord continue blinking. Rewind and play the animation a few times.
7. Close the Flash Player window to return to the document.
8. Save the revised document using the same name (Ch6Ex01).

Converting an Existing Animation to a Movie Clip Symbol

You may decide after creating an animation within the main movie Timeline of a document that you want to convert the entire sequence to a movie clip symbol. The animation can then be reused within the same movie or in another movie.

    To convert existing frames to a movie clip symbol, select the frames in the layers that you want to convert and then use the Copy Frames or Cut Frames command to duplicate the content in the clipboard. Click Insert, New Symbol, key a name for the movie clip symbol and choose Movie Clip as the Behavior in the Create New Symbol dialog box, and then click OK. In symbol editing mode, click the first frame in the first layer in the movie clip Timeline and click Edit, and then Paste Frames. If you are converting the entire movie you can easily select all of the frames in the Timeline with the Select All Frames option on the Edit menu.

exercise 4

CONVERTING AN ANIMATION TO A MOVIE CLIP SYMBOL

1. With Ch6Ex01 open, select and then cut the frames to convert the animation to a movie clip by completing the following steps:
   a. Click any frame in the Timeline to activate the Timeline panel.
   b. Click Edit and then click Select All Frames. All frames within all layers in the Timeline are selected.
   c. Click Edit and then click Cut Frames. The frames are removed from the Timeline and inserted in the clipboard. The stage becomes blank since all content has been removed; however, notice that the layers remain in the Timeline.

2. Create a new symbol using the frames in the clipboard by completing the following steps:
   a. Click Insert and then click New Symbol.
   b. Key **Opening-ChristmasTraditions** in the Name text box in the Create New Symbol dialog box.
   c. Click Movie Clip in the Behavior section and then click OK.
   d. Click frame 1 in *Layer 1* for the Opening-ChristmasTraditions symbol.
   e. Click Edit and then click Paste Frames.
   f. Click the Back button on the Information bar to exit symbol editing mode.

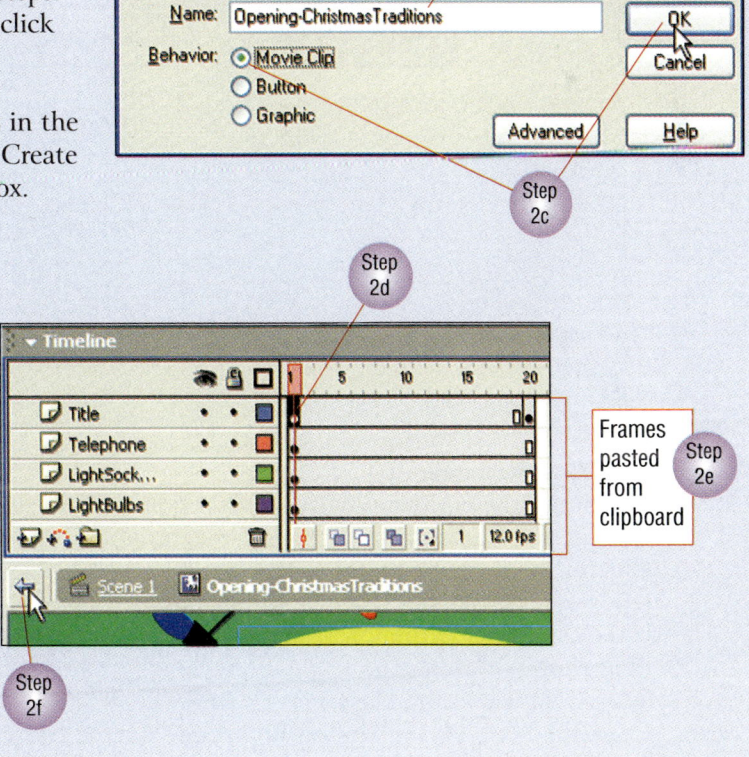

Animating Using Symbols and Masks and Publishing Flash Movies   275

3. Insert an instance of the animation converted to the movie clip symbol in the document by completing the following steps:
   a. Click the *Telephone* layer in the Timeline.
   b. Hold down the Shift key and then click the *Background* layer in the Timeline. *(Note: You may need to scroll down the Timeline to see the* Background *layer.)*
   c. Click the Delete Layer button.

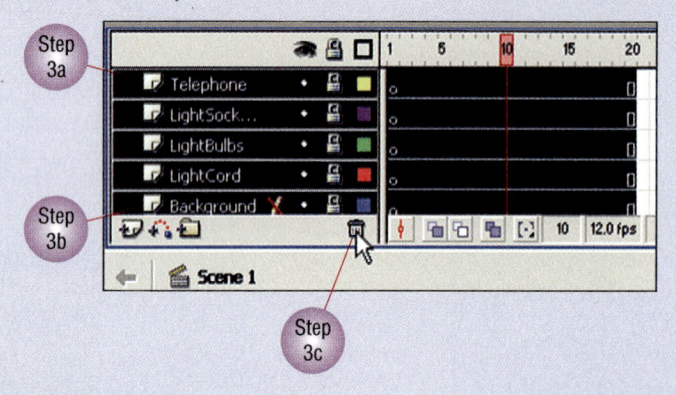

   d. Rename the Title layer *Opening*.
   e. Select frames 2–20 in the *Opening* layer, click Insert, and then click Remove Frames.
   f. Click frame 1 in the *Opening* layer and then open the Library panel.
   g. If necessary, scroll down the Name list in the Library panel, click the Opening-ChristmasTraditions movie clip symbol, and then drag an instance of the symbol to the stage.

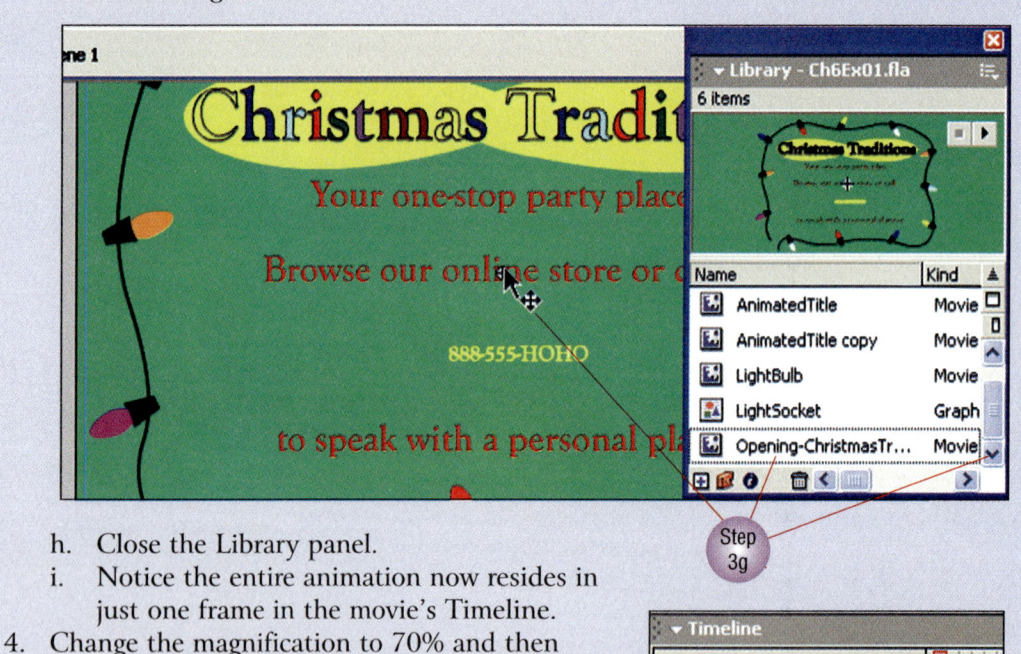

   h. Close the Library panel.
   i. Notice the entire animation now resides in just one frame in the movie's Timeline.
4. Change the magnification to 70% and then reposition the symbol instance if necessary to make sure it fits entirely within the stage boundaries.
5. Test the movie in the Flash Player window.
6. Close the Flash Player window and then save the revised document using the same name (Ch6Ex01).
7. Close Ch6Ex01.

Animating Using a Mask Layer

In Chapter 3 you learned how to create a masked layer to partially conceal the layer immediately below the mask by creating filled objects on a separate layer that overlap content in the linked layer. The areas below the filled objects filter through the stage when the mask is created. All content outside filled objects on the mask layer is concealed.

Animating the filled objects on the mask layer can simulate effects during a movie such as an eyeglass spanning an ocean view or a spotlight lighting a stage. To do this, create a tween or frame-by-frame animation using the objects on the mask layer and then define the layer as a mask.

exercise 5

ANIMATING USING A MASK

1. Open the Flash document named DanceArt.
2. Save the document with Save As and name it Ch6Ex05.
3. Create objects for a mask that will resemble binoculars by completing the following steps:
   a. Insert a new layer above *Picture* named *Binoculars*.
   b. Click frame 1 in the *Binoculars* layer.
   c. Click the Oval tool in the toolbox.
   d. Change the Fill Color to white.
   e. Click the Stroke Color button (not the color swatch) and then click No Color in the Colors section of the toolbox.
   f. Draw two circles the approximate size as shown near the bottom right of the picture overlapping the audience members.
4. Create four motion tweens for the circles that will simulate someone moving a pair of binoculars around the stage by completing the following steps:
   a. Insert frames in all three layers in frames 2–50.
   b. Insert a keyframe in the *Binoculars* layer at frame 12.
   c. With frame 12 in the *Binoculars* layer active, move the two circles near the top left of the picture with the right circle covering the ballerina's face as shown.
   d. Insert a keyframe at frame 25 in the *Binoculars* layer and then move the two circles near the middle center of the picture overlapping the musicians.
   e. Insert a keyframe at frame 37 in the *Binoculars* layer and then move the two circles near the top center of the picture with the left circle covering the ballerina's face.
   f. Insert a keyframe at frame 50 in the *Binoculars* layer and then move the two circles to the same location where the circles started in frame 1.

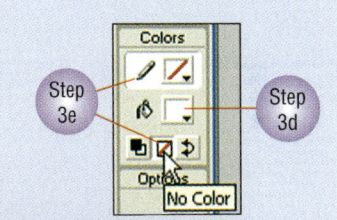

g. Right-click frame 1 in the *Binoculars* layer and then click Create Motion Tween at the shortcut menu.
h. Repeat Step 4g for frames 12, 25, 37, and 50 in the *Binoculars* layer.

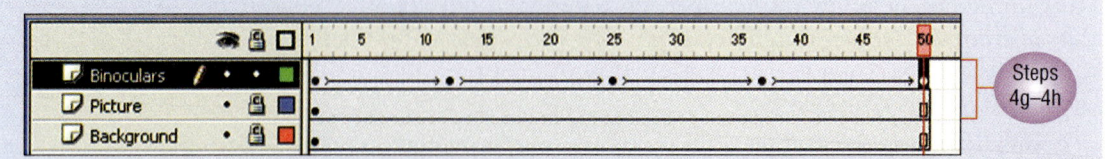

Steps 4g–4h

i. Press Enter to preview the animation of the circle objects moving over the picture.
5. Right-click the *Binoculars* layer in the Timeline and then click Mask at the shortcut menu. The picture in the layer immediately below *Binoculars* is concealed with only the portion overlapping the circles visible.
6. Press Enter to preview the animation.
7. Edit the masked animation by enlarging the size of the circles by completing the following steps:
    a. Unlock the *Binoculars* layer.
    b. Click frame 1 in the *Binoculars* layer.
    c. Double-click the tweened symbol instance near the bottom right of the picture.
    d. Using the Free Transform tool and the Scale modifier, enlarge the instance of the circles to a size that you feel would best allow the picture to show through in the animation.
    e. Click the Back button on the Information bar to exit symbol editing mode.
    f. Click each keyframe in the *Binoculars* layer and then move the tweened symbol instance to adjust its position since the larger circles will now be overlapping different areas of the picture.
    g. Lock the *Binoculars* layer.
8. Press Enter to preview the animation.
9. Test the movie in the Flash Player window so that you can see the effect when the animation is in looped playback mode.
10. Close the Flash Player window and then save the revised document using the same name (Ch6Ex05).

Using the Test Environment Before Publishing a Movie

Preparing a Flash movie prior to publishing the final output involves testing the movie to make sure all elements are animating as expected and determining the download performance by simulating various download speeds. If a performance issue is recognized you can go back to the movie and attempt to correct the error and bottlenecks using various strategies before publishing.

Testing is a critical component of Flash development that should be performed on a regular basis as you build the frames and animations. It is quicker and easier to correct errors as you go along rather than to remember how everything was assembled later when a complex movie is completed.

Throughout this textbook you have been previewing animations in one or both of the following two environments:

- The authoring environment using the Play command by pressing Enter or by clicking <u>C</u>ontrol and then <u>P</u>lay.
- The testing environment using the Test Movie command by clicking <u>C</u>ontrol and then Test <u>M</u>ovie.

Within the authoring environment you have already learned that you cannot view a movie clip animation. Many ActionScript statements cannot be tested in the authoring environment and the speed at which the movie plays will be deceptive since the final exported movie will play back at a faster speed once the file has been optimized and compressed. Finally, within the authoring environment you cannot simulate various download speeds to test the file's performance over the Web.

Viewing the Movie in the Testing Environment

You already have experience previewing the movie in the Flash Player window within Flash to test the animations you have been creating. The <u>C</u>ontrol menu in Flash contains two options to move into the testing environment: Test <u>M</u>ovie and Test <u>S</u>cene. Clicking one of these options causes Flash to either export the entire movie or just the current scene using the default options in the Publish Settings dialog box. A file with the same name as the authoring file and with the extension *.swf* is created and stored in the same drive and folder as the source Flash document. If you choose the Test <u>S</u>cene option, Flash names the file with the same name and adds _Scene # where # is the number of the exported scene.

The Flash Player window that opens to test the movie within Flash provides additional menu options not shown in the normal Flash Player window. In addition to providing <u>E</u>dit, <u>D</u>ebug, and <u>W</u>indow on the menu bar, the <u>F</u>ile, <u>V</u>iew, and <u>C</u>ontrol menus contain additional options.

Testing a movie requires frequent playbacks in which you will need to stop, rewind, step forward, or step backward as you move through the process of making sure each button, interaction, or segment functions correctly. The same Controller toolbar you have used in the authoring environment is available in the testing environment. Within the Flash Player window, click <u>W</u>indow, point to T<u>o</u>olbars, and then click C<u>o</u>ntroller as shown in Figure 6.3.

FIGURE 6.3 *Turning on the Display of the Controller*

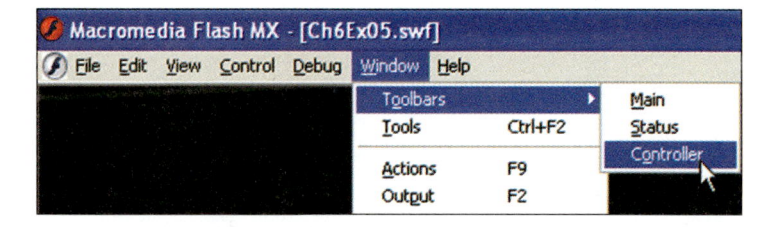

Using the Bandwidth Profiler

Most movies created in Flash are intended for viewing on a Web site. Knowing how the movie will download and play from the Web prior to publishing the movie will afford you the opportunity to correct problem frames if they exist. Flash provides tools within the testing environment with which you can view how the movie will perform.

Bandwidth is the term used to describe the amount of data that can be transferred from a server to a user's computer within a fixed period of time, also called the *transmission rate*. Bandwidth is usually measured and expressed as the number of bits per second (bps) that can be transmitted. Data travels from a Web server to a user's computer via a medium such as a telephone line or a cable line. A medium capable of transmitting a large amount of data in a short period of time is called *broadband*. A user who is connected to the Internet using a cable modem or digital subscriber line (DSL) is said to be using a broadband connection. A medium carrying a smaller amount of data that transmits at a slower speed is called *narrowband*.

A person with a high-speed connection to the Internet can send and receive more data at a faster rate than a person with a low-speed connection. This is accomplished using a broadband medium.

As a Flash developer you have to be concerned with bandwidth since the movie you have created will be viewed by a large audience. Some users will have a broadband connection but most users will have a narrowband connection. Within the testing environment Flash provides the Bandwidth Profiler with which you can view statistics about the movie's download performance at a specific speed. Click View and then click Bandwidth Profiler to toggle on or off the display of these statistics. Figure 6.4 illustrates a movie in the testing environment showing the bandwidth profiler statistics for downloading a movie at 56K, a common modem speed for users with a narrowband connection.

FIGURE 6.4 **Bandwidth Profiler Statistics Using 56K as the Download Speed**

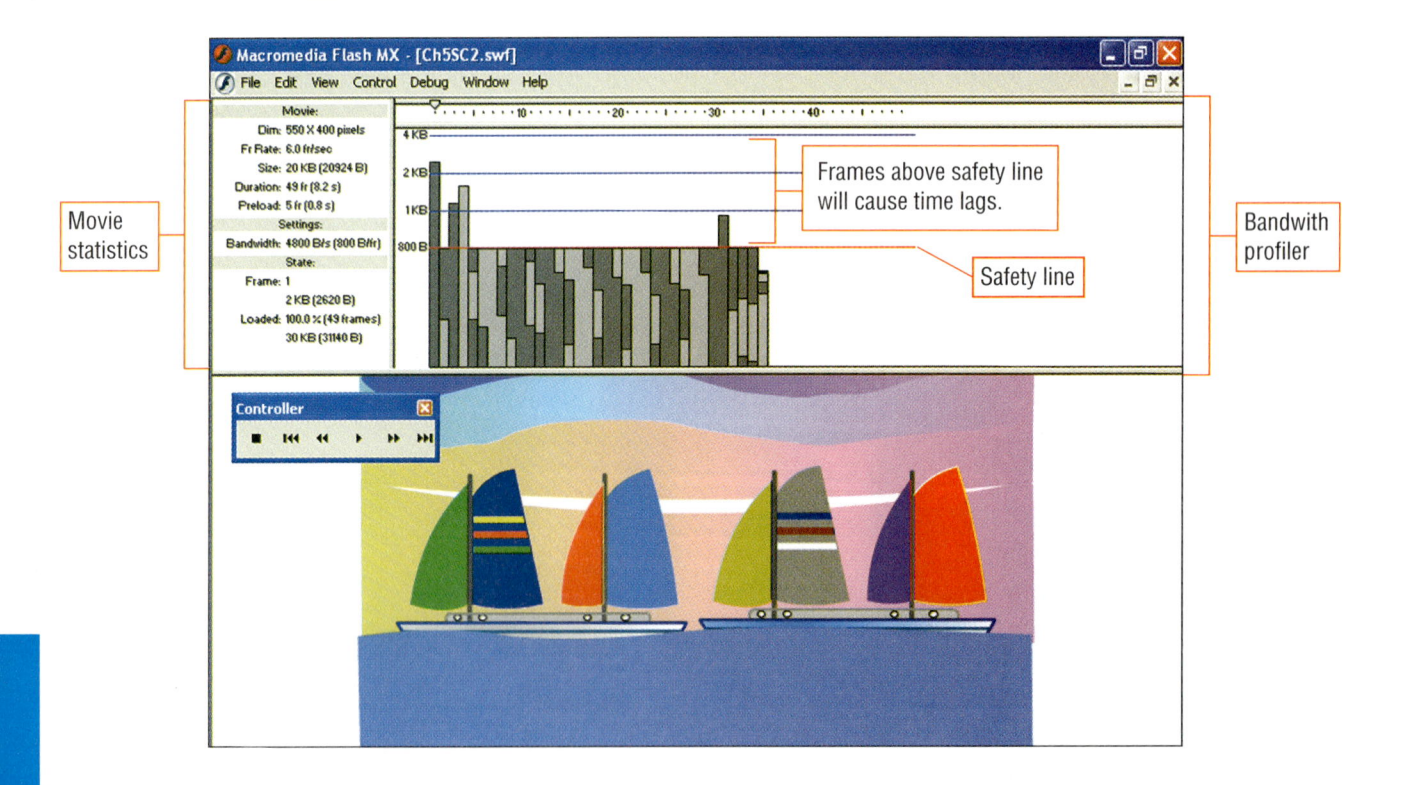

280 Chapter Six

The left pane of the Bandwidth Profiler displays the movie statistics and the settings at which the movie is being tested. The bar graph in the right pane of the Bandwidth Profiler displays the amount of data that is being transmitted in each frame over a Timeline. The height of the bar is scaled to show the frame size in number of bytes of data. The graph shown in Figure 6.4 is a streaming graph depicting how the movie will stream with the number of bytes to be transmitted by frame in order to play the content. The red line denotes the safety zone; bars below the red line will download quickly enough to keep up with the movie and bars above the red line cause the player to pause while data is downloaded. The graph shown in Figure 6.4 illustrates that the movie will encounter problems at streaming frames 1, 3, 4, and 31.

In a streaming graph, clicking a bar on the graph will display the individual frame statistics below *State* in the left pane and stop the movie playback. You can also choose to view the bar graph frame by frame by clicking View and then Frame By Frame at the drop-down menu.

Testing Using Download Speed Statistics

To test the download performance at different bandwidths, click Debug in the Flash Player window and then click a preset speed at the drop-down menu or click Customize to enter your own settings. Figure 6.5 illustrates the Debug menu with a current speed selected of 56K (4.7 KB/s). Flash simulates a 56K modem speed using a transmission rate of 4800 bytes per second (also expressed as 4.7 KB/s), based on estimates of speed during a typical Internet session. The actual download time will vary depending on the volume of Internet traffic at the time the movie is played.

FIGURE 6.5 Debug Menu in Flash Player Window

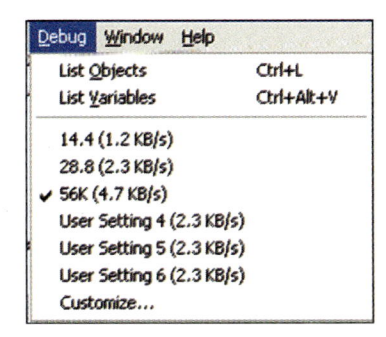

The statistics for the same movie shown in Figure 6.4 show a huge difference in performance when tested at a modem speed of 28.8 (2.3 KB/s) as shown in Figure 6.6. At this download speed, the Bandwidth Profiler is showing that Flash will encounter several time lags as the player waits for data at points in the movie illustrated at frames 1, 3, 4, 8, 11, 15, 18, 21, 24, 27, 30, and 31.

FIGURE 6.6 Bandwidth Profiler Statistics for Same Movie Shown in Figure 6.4 Tested Using 28.8 as the Download Speed

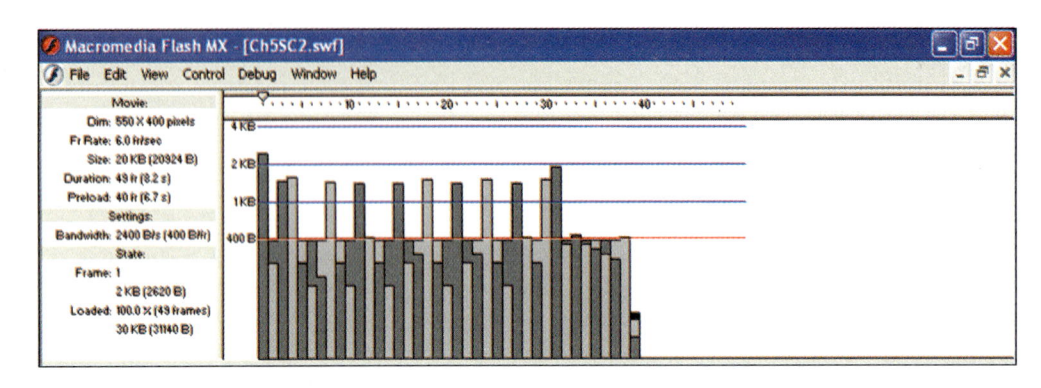

The number of U.S. households with broadband Internet service in 2001 was estimated at slightly over 10 million. Predictions about the growth of broadband vary with some estimates proposing the number of households with high-speed service in 2005 will be well over 40 million. Although these estimates indicate that the number of broadband users will increase at a steady rate, present research indicates that 80 percent of Americans with Internet access use a dial up connection. This means testing a movie using the 56K and 28.8 options is a minimum testing standard.

The National Telecommunications and Information Administration (NTIA), an agency of the U.S. Department of Commerce, maintains a Web site with current information and statistics on information technology issues. Access their Web site at **www.ntia.doc.gov** for updated information on American households and Internet use.

exercise 6 — USING THE BANDWIDTH PROFILER

1. With Ch6Ex05 open, display the Bandwidth Profiler statistics for downloading the movie at a modem speed of 28.8 and at 56K in the testing environment by completing the following steps:
    a. Click Control and then click Test Movie to export the movie and view the animation in the Flash Player window.
    b. Click View and then click Bandwidth Profiler to open the Bandwidth Profiler with the statistics for the current movie.
    c. Click View and then click Streaming Graph. *(Note: Skip this step if a check mark displays next to Streaming Graph since the option is already active.)*
    d. Click Debug and then click 28.8 (2.3 KB/s) at the drop-down menu.

e. Look at the statistics for the movie in the left pane of the Bandwidth Profiler. The Preload time of *263 fr (21.9 s)* indicates that 263 frames or 21.9 seconds will elapse between the point at which the movie begins to download to the user's computer and the point at which the movie can begin to play. The bar graph shows that all of the time lag is occurring at the first frame. *(Note: Your numbers may vary slightly depending on the system you are using.)*

f. Click <u>D</u>ebug and then click 56K (4.7 KB/s) at the drop-down menu.

g. Look at the statistics for the movie in the left pane of the Bandwidth Profiler. The Preload time has been reduced to *131 fr (10.9 s)*. Also notice in the streaming bar graph that streaming is completed in three frames as opposed to four.

2. Close the Flash Player window and then close Ch6Ex05.

3. Open Ch5Ex06. This document created in Chapter 5 contains an imported video clip and movie control buttons.

4. Click <u>C</u>ontrol and then click Test <u>M</u>ovie. Look at the statistics for the movie in the Bandwidth Profiler with the speed still at 56K. The Preload time indicates a user would be waiting 140.1 seconds before the movie would begin to play. *(Note: Your numbers may vary slightly.)*

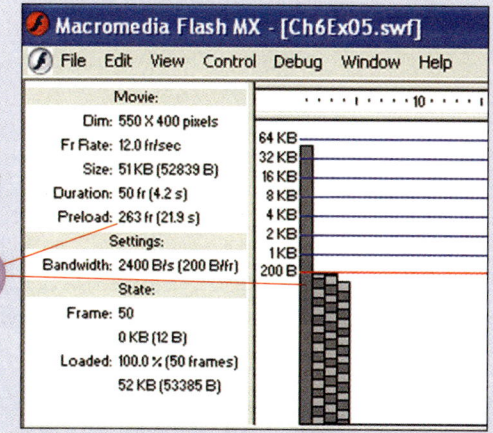

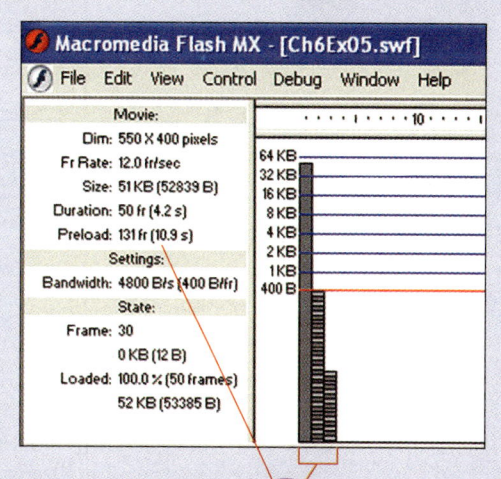

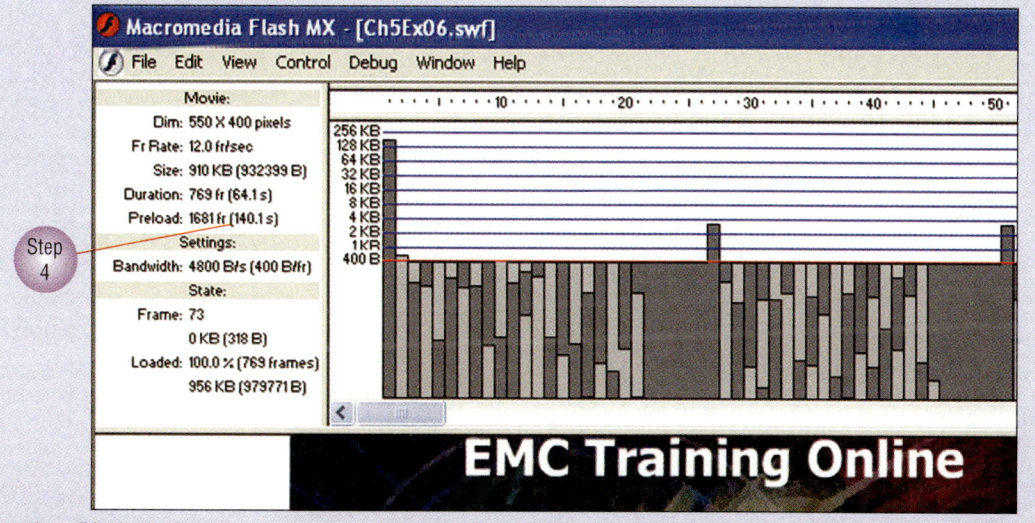

5. Click <u>D</u>ebug and then click 28.8 (2.3 KB/s). The Preload time increases.

6. Click <u>D</u>ebug and then click 14.4 (1.2 KB/s). The Preload time increases even more. A user might be waiting over 12 minutes for this video to start if it was delivered over the Web with a 14.4 modem speed (1200 bytes per second).

7. Close the Flash Player window and then close Ch5Ex06.

To simulate the download performance of a movie at a speed other than the preset speeds of 14.4, 28.8, and 56K, click Customize at the Debug drop-down menu. The Custom Modem Settings dialog box shown in Figure 6.7 opens. Key the text that you want displayed on the Debug menu in the Menu text: text box that currently displays *User Setting 4* and then key the number of bytes per second with which you want the movie simulated in the adjacent Bit rate text box. Click OK to close the dialog box when you have finished adding the custom settings. You can create up to three settings.

FIGURE 6.7 **Custom Modem Settings Dialog Box**

Optimizing the Movie

Even though Flash uses streaming technology in which a movie begins playing as soon as enough information to start the movie has been downloaded, it is still possible as you saw in Exercise 6 for a user to experience time lags. These lags occur when the streaming data cannot keep up with the movie playback. This was especially evident when you viewed the bar graph for the Ch5Ex06 movie containing the imported video. The preload time was very long and then at various points along the Timeline, the streaming bar graph indicated points in the movie above the red safety line.

Use the following strategies to review a movie and then edit frames and/or objects in which the Bandwidth Profiler has indicated poor download performance:

- **Bitmap Graphics.** Avoid animating bitmaps. Open the Bitmap Properties dialog box for an imported graphic and then test various compression settings to reduce the imported graphic's file size as much as possible. If a bitmap is causing a large increase in the file size even when compressed, consider an alternative to using the bitmap such as drawing your own object or finding another source that uses less space. Delete any bitmaps and imported files that you consider dispensable.

- **Vector Graphics.** Draw solid pencil lines whenever possible instead of drawing using the Brush tool since these require less space. Minimize the use of line types other than solid such as dashed or dotted since special line types use more space. Group drawn objects whenever possible since grouped objects use less space than ungrouped objects. Select drawn objects and then reduce the curves using the Optimize Curves dialog box. Be aware that optimizing curves may not produce acceptable results since the object may be unsatisfactorily reshaped.

- **Gradients and Transparency.** Make use of gradient fills and alter an object's alpha property to create a transparency effect sparingly. Gradients use more space and an object with an alpha effect plays back at a slower rate since extra processing is required to create the transparent image.
- **Symbols.** If an object within the movie has been duplicated by copying and pasting, convert the object to a symbol and then place symbol instances where it needs to be duplicated.
- **Animated Symbols.** Create animated symbols in movie clips whenever possible instead of graphic symbols.
- **Sounds.** Open the Sound Properties dialog box for the imported sound and then test various compression settings to reduce the file size as much as possible. In most cases MP3 is the best compression choice. Although sound adds to the rich content of a movie, if the impact on the movie download time is considerable, the benefit does not warrant the use of the sound. Delete unnecessary sound effects and files.
- **Keyframes.** Review the keyframes in the movie and look for any that can be removed without adversely affecting the animation. The more keyframes in the movie the larger the file. Motion tweened frames use less space than frame-by-frame animations. Consider changing a frame-by-frame animation to a motion tween if it is appropriate.

After maximizing the efficiency of the file by reducing its size using the strategies in the above list, if you still note a high preload time or streaming lag, consider using the following solutions:

- Before a frame that requires a bulk download of content, create an animation sequence that includes text. This will provide the user with something to read while the content is being downloaded in the background.
- Lengthen the duration of an animation prior to a frame that requires a lot of content to be downloaded provided the prior animation sequence contains simple objects or uses symbols that do not add greatly to the file size. This will allow more time for the larger content to be downloaded in the background.
- If a large bitmap, sound, or video that is being downloaded at the beginning of the movie is causing a long preload time, add a simple animation to the beginning of the movie to provide a buffer. This is called a *preloader* and generally involves using simple text or other graphical content to amuse the user while the movie is being downloaded. Preloaders sometimes simply display a message to the user such as *Loading....* A better use of a preloader would be a creative animation that provides information or otherwise entertains so that the user does not feel that his or her time is being wasted.

exercise 7

TESTING AND OPTIMIZING A MOVIE

1. Open Ch6Ex05. Recall from Exercise 6 that this movie tested with a preload time of 21.9 seconds when downloaded with a modem speed of 28.8. The front end of this movie is where the time lag occurs because of the bitmap graphic used for the animated mask. Test the movie with a modem speed of 14.4 by completing the following steps:
    a. Click Control and then click Test Movie.

  b. Click Debug and then click 14.4 (1.2 KB/s) at the drop-down menu.
  c. Look at the statistics in the left pane of the Bandwidth Profiler. Flash has calculated that 43.9 seconds are required to preload the movie.
  d. Close the Flash Player window to return to the document.
2. Decrease the file size by increasing the compression level for the bitmap graphic by completing the following steps:
  a. Open the Library panel.
  b. Right-click Ballerina.jpg and then click Properties at the shortcut menu to open the Bitmap Properties dialog box.
  c. Using the hand pointer, drag the image inside the Preview window in the Bitmap Properties dialog box until you can see the ballerina. 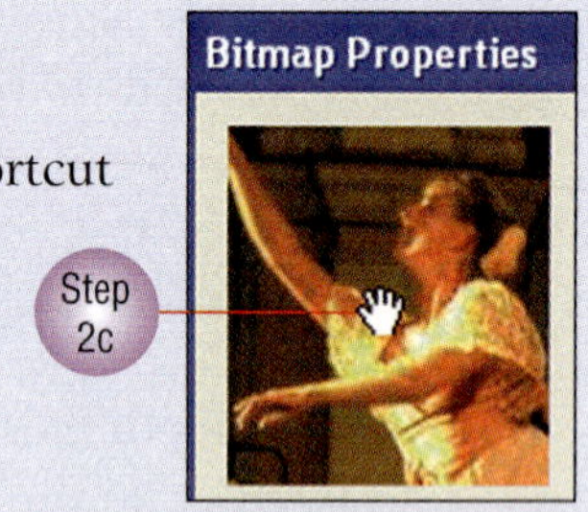
  d. Click the Use imported JPEG data check box to deselect it.
  e. With the Quality value at the default setting of 50, click the Test button to view the file compression values. The file size is compressed to 35.0 kilobytes—3% of the original imported size. 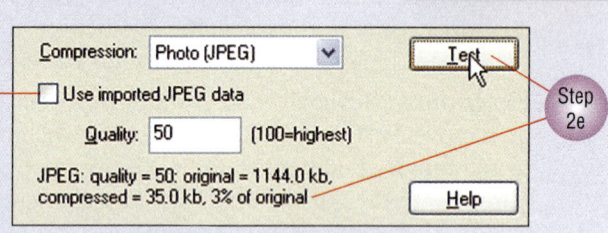
  f. Look at the image in the Preview window to see if any change in the quality of the image is noticeable.
  g. Drag across the value 50 in the Quality text box, key **35**, and then click Test. The file size is reduced to 2% of its original size.
  h. Look at the image in the Preview window to see if any change in the quality is noticeable. *(Note: If necessary, change the quality value back to 50, look at the image and then change the quality value again while watching the Preview window to see the change in the graphic image.)*
  i. Test the file compression with a Quality value of 30 and then 25 by completing steps similar to those in Steps 2g–2h.
  j. Considering that the image is used below a mask layer and is only partially visible throughout the animation, you decide a lower image quality is acceptable for the movie. With the Quality value set to 25 and the file compressed to 20.6 kilobytes, which represents only 1% of its original size, click OK to close the Bitmap Properties dialog box.

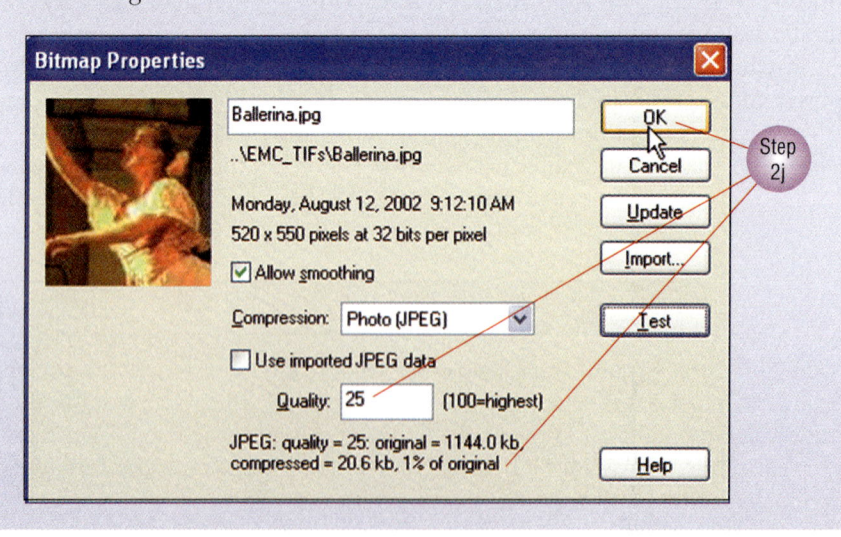

k. Close the Library panel.
3. Click <u>C</u>ontrol and then click Test <u>M</u>ovie. Look at the statistics for the movie in the Bandwidth Profiler with the speed still at 14.4. The Preload time has dropped by half from its initial 43.9 seconds down to 20.7 seconds. The bar graph shows that streaming is complete in 7 frames. Watch the animation play for a few seconds to satisfy yourself that the lower-quality JPEG image is not detracting from the movie.
4. Click <u>D</u>ebug and then click 28.8. The Preload time drops and the number of streaming frames drops to 4.
5. Click <u>D</u>ebug and then click 56K. The Preload time drops even more and the number of streaming frames drops to 3.
6. Close the Flash Player window and then save the revised document using the same name (Ch6Ex05).
7. Close Ch6Ex05.

Simulating the Internet Connection Speed

Viewing a preload time statistic of 20.7 seconds may not be enough to put the movie into its proper perspective from the vantage point of a typical user. While 20.7 seconds can be rationalized as only one-third of a minute by a developer, actually waiting out the 20.7 seconds before the movie starts to play will give you a better insight into the user's experience. You may find that after a download simulation you will have a different viewpoint on acceptable wait times. It is also a good idea to simulate the speed with a variety of users within the target audience to receive feedback.

Click <u>V</u>iew and then click <u>S</u>how Streaming to begin a simulation of a Web connection at the current speed as shown in Figure 6.8. Flash replays the movie simulating the actual Web connection. The streaming progress statistics are displayed in the Loaded section below State in the left pane of the Bandwidth Profiler. A green progress bar in the Timeline of the right pane shows the movie's progress during playback.

FIGURE 6.8 *Turning on Show Streaming to Simulate the Web Connection Speed*

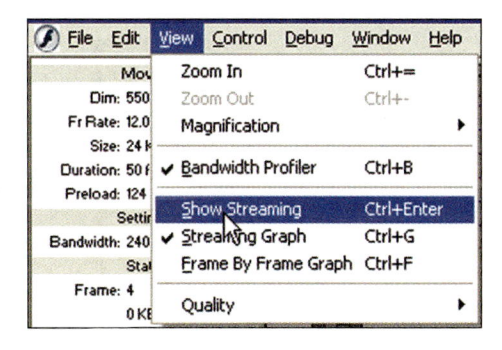

Publishing a Movie

After a movie has been tested, optimized, and then retested, it is ready to be exported from the authoring environment. Exporting the file makes a copy of the movie in the default drive and folder in Flash Player file format *(swf)* and any other formats that you specify. Flash also automatically creates the HTML page that will launch the player and open the player file. The exported files are then copied to a Web server where the movie is then linked to a Web page. This process is referred to as publishing the movie. Publishing in Flash involves the following two steps:

1. Select the file formats and options in which you want the movie exported in the Publish Settings dialog box.
2. Use the Publish command to create the files.

Choosing Publish Settings for a Flash Player File

Click File and then click Publish Settings to open the Publish Settings dialog box with the default options shown in Figure 6.9. If necessary, click the Flash tab to display options for publishing the Flash Player file. A description of each option and the impact on the *swf* file is given in Table 6.1.

Make the changes as required to the options in the Publish Settings dialog box and then click OK to close the dialog box and save the current settings with the file.

FIGURE 6.9 *Default Options for Publish Settings Dialog Box with Flash Tab Selected*

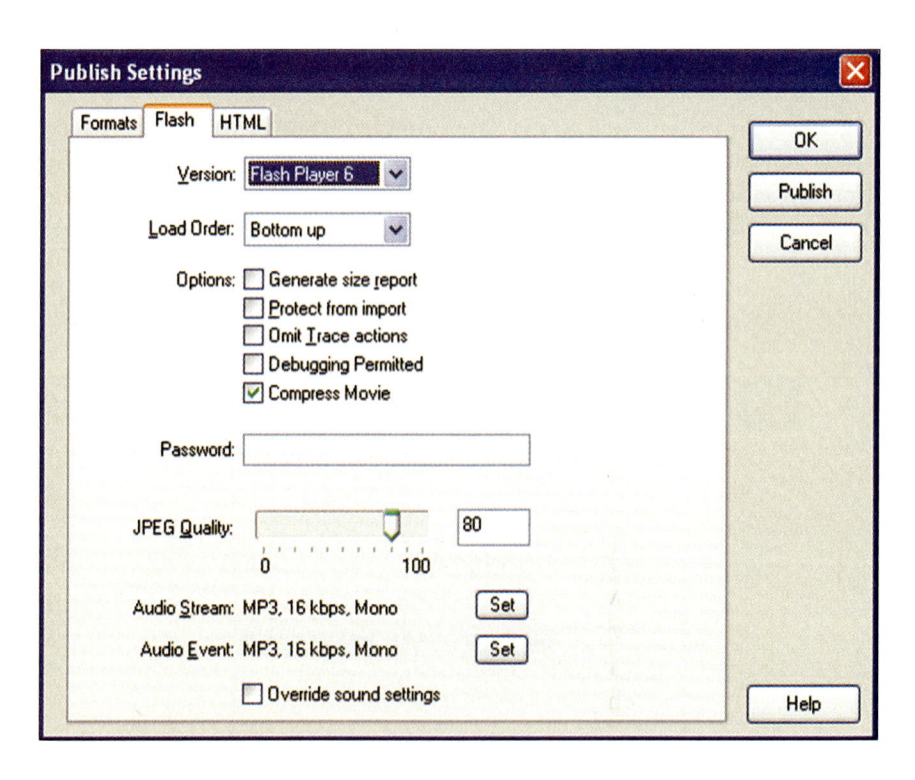

TABLE 6.1 Flash Player Publish Settings Options

Option	Description and Available Settings
Version	Click the down arrow to publish using an earlier version of the Flash Player. You can choose to publish using Flash Player 1 through to Flash Player 6. Features in Flash MX used within the movie that are not available in earlier versions will not work if published in an earlier version. If you used features not available in Flash 5 or lower, consider adding a link to your Web page in which the user can download the latest Flash Player.
Load Order	Set the order in which layers within the first frame are loaded as the data is streamed to the user's computer. The default Bottom up option means the bottom layer loads first. This can be changed to Top down. Loading the first frame starting at the bottom layer is usually preferable since background objects are usually placed in a bottom layer. You would normally want the user to see the objects drawn on the screen in the same stacking order as the movie.
Generate size report	Click this check box to have Flash generate a text file with information about the movie. The text file serves as documentation about each individual frame size, embedded object, bitmap, sound, font, and so on.
Protect from import	Click this check box to make sure other people cannot import the *swf* file back into Flash. Clicking this check box activates the Password text box in which you can assign a password to the movie. This option protects your work from being duplicated and manipulated by others since other people are prevented from importing the file and creating an *fla* file unless they have the password.
Omit Trace actions	Click this check box to prevent Flash displaying the information from trace actions in an Output window. This option only applies if you have added the ActionScript Trace command to a keyframe in the movie to assist with debugging a movie.
Debugging Permitted	Click this check box to allow remote debugging of a movie while it plays over the Web. Clicking this check box activates the Password text box in which you can assign a password to the movie. It is a good idea to password protect the file to prevent unauthorized access to the file while you are in the process of debugging.
Compress Movie	This check box is selected by default when Flash Player 6 is the version option. Flash reduces the file size, which reduces download time; however, the compressed file is only readable with Version 6 of the Flash Player.

Continued on next page

Option	Description and Available Settings
Password	This text box is only active if Protect from import or Debugging Permitted is turned on.
JPEG Quality	Drag the slider or key a value between 0 and 100 in the text box to set the default value for compressing bitmaps upon export.
Audio Stream	Click the Set button to change the default compression options in the Sound Settings dialog box that are used when exporting sounds defined as streamed sounds.
Audio Event	Click the Set button to change the default compression options in the Sound Settings dialog box that are used when exporting sounds defined as event sounds.
Override sound settings	Click this check box to cause Flash to override any individual compression options you may have set for sounds through a Sound Properties dialog box.

Choosing HTML Settings for a Flash Player File

Flash automatically creates the HTML page in addition to the *swf* file when a movie is published. The HTML page is required for users to view a movie over the Web since this page includes the instructions that tell the Web browser to open the Flash Player application and load the movie. The page is created based on the options in effect on the HTML tab of the Publish Settings dialog box shown in Figure 6.10. A description of each option and the impact on the HTML code is given in Table 6.2.

Make the changes as required to the options in the Publish Settings dialog box and then click OK to close the dialog box and save the current settings with the file.

FIGURE

6.10 *Default Options for Publish Settings Dialog Box with HTML Tab Selected*

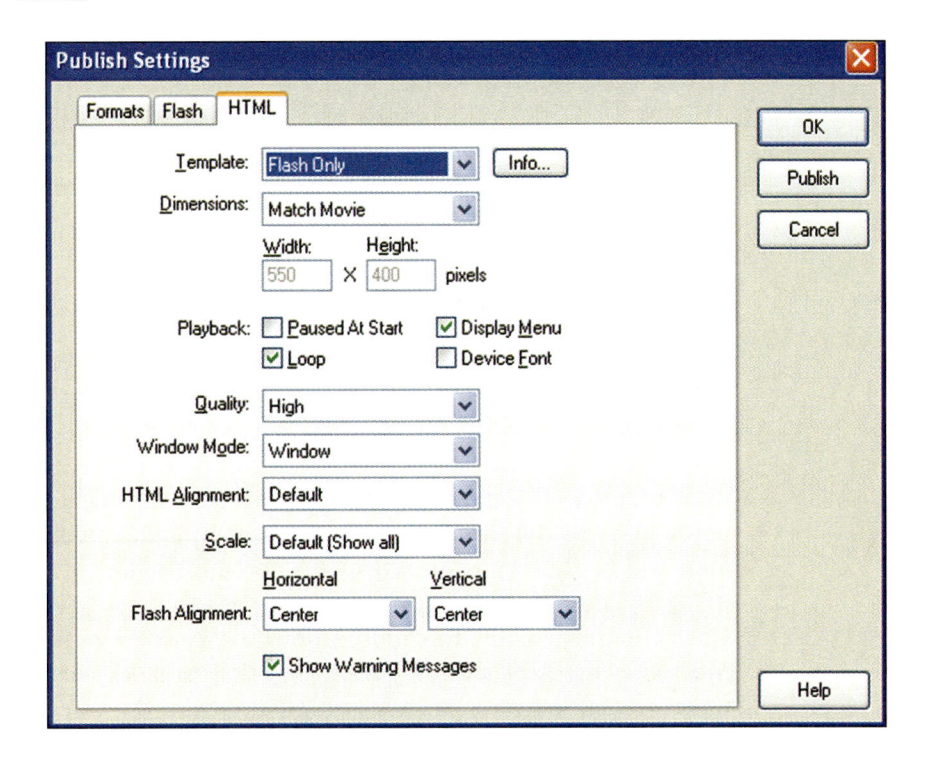

TABLE

6.2 *HTML Publish Settings Options*

Option	Description and Available Settings
Template	Click the down arrow to choose the template upon which to base the HTML code. Flash provides several templates that provide different functions. Choose a template option at the drop-down list and then click the Info button to display a dialog box containing a description of the template. Figure 6.11 displays the Html Template Info dialog box for the file DetectVersion6.html when Detect for Flash 6 is the selected template.
Dimensions	Click the down arrow to choose Match Movie, Pixels, or Percent to specify the values for the width and height of the movie within the HTML page. Match Movie uses the movie's height and width in the Document Properties dialog box. Choose Pixels to key different pixel values in the Width and Height text boxes, or choose Percent to key values in the text boxes that represent the percentage of the movie window relative to the browser window's width and height.

Continued on next page

Option	Description and Available Settings
Paused At Start	Click this check box if you do not want the movie to begin playing until the user clicks a button within the movie or uses the Play option on the Flash Player's shortcut menu.
Loop	By default the movie will repeat playback when it reaches the last frame. Deselect this check box if you want the movie to stop after the last frame is played.
Display Menu	By default a shortcut menu with options to play, stop, and rewind the movie is displayed if the user right-clicks (Windows) or Control-clicks (Macintosh) in the Flash Player window. Deselect this check box to have the shortcut menu display only two options: Settings and About Macromedia Flash Player 6.
Device Font	Applies only to Windows-based computers. If a font that you have used in the movie is not installed on the user's computer, anti-aliased system fonts will be substituted in text that is not animated.
Quality	Click the down arrow to choose from Low, Auto Low, Auto High, Medium, High, and Best. These settings determine the compromise you want to make between the movie's playback speed (Low being the fastest speed) and quality of images (Best providing the highest quality images). The default option is High which emphasizes appearance over playback speed.
Window Mode	Applies only to Windows-based computers using Internet Explorer 4.0 or later and the Flash ActiveX control. Click the down arrow to choose from Window, Opaque Windowless, and Transparent Windowless. The default Window option means the movie plays within its own window on a Web page. Opaque Windowless means other elements on the Web page move behind the Flash movie and do not show through. Transparent Windowless moves other elements on the Web page behind the Flash movie with those objects showing through any transparent areas within the movie.
HTML Alignment	Choose the alignment with which to position the movie within the browser window. Available options are Default, Left, Right, Top, and Bottom. Portions of the movie that extend beyond the browser's window will be cropped.

Continued on next page

Option	Description and Available Settings
Scale	The Scale option determines how the movie is displayed within the boundaries of the browser window if you have keyed height and width dimensions that do not match the movie. Available options are Default (Show All), No border, Exact fit, and No scale. The default option means the movie's aspect ratio is maintained to display all elements without distortion. No border will scale the movie and crop if necessary. Exact fit displays the entire movie without maintaining the original aspect ratio, which can cause distortion. No scale prevents the movie from being scaled when the window is resized.
Flash Alignment	Choose the Horizontal and Vertical alignment options for positioning the movie within the Flash Player window. Horizontal options include Left, Center, and Right. Vertical options include Top, Center, and Bottom.
Show Warning Messages	By default the Show Warning Messages check box is selected meaning that if you choose settings that conflict, a warning message will display providing you with the opportunity to correct the problem.

FIGURE 6.11 **Html Template Info Dialog Box for Detect for Flash 6 Template Option**

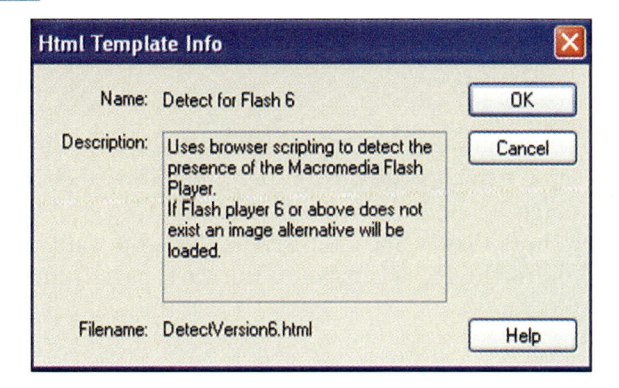

Previewing the Movie in the Browser Window

Click File, point to Publish Preview, and then click the format in which you wish to preview the movie at the side menu shown in Figure 6.12.

FIGURE 6.12 **Publish Preview Options**

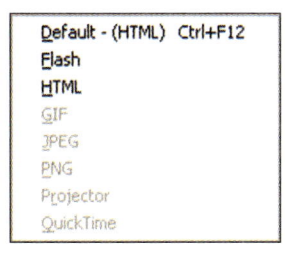

Click Default to publish and preview using the current options in the Publish Settings dialog box. The option displayed next to Default will vary depending on the active options in Publish Settings. Click Flash to publish the movie and open it within the Flash Player window within Flash (same window as using Control and then Test Movie) using the active options in the Flash tab of Publish Settings. Click HTML to publish and then open the movie in the default browser window using the active options in the HTML tab of the Publish Settings dialog box. Other options on the menu are active or dimmed according to the active options in the Formats tab of the Publish Settings dialog box.

Publishing the Movie

Once the appropriate Flash and HTML options have been chosen, you are ready for Flash to create the required *swf* and *html* files. Click File and then click Publish or click the Publish button in the Publish Settings dialog box to export the movie using the current settings. Flash displays a Publishing dialog box similar to the one shown in Figure 6.13 with a progress bar to indicate the status of the publishing process. The dialog box contains a Cancel button should you wish to terminate the publishing process before it is completed.

FIGURE

6.13 *Publishing Dialog Box*

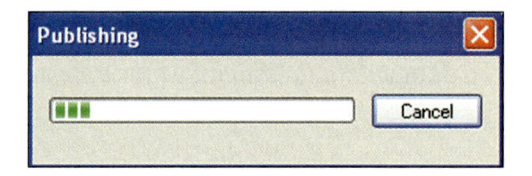

When the publishing process is completed the Publishing dialog box closes. Two files with the same name as the movie's *fla* file and with the extensions *.swf* and *.html* will be created in the same drive and folder from which you opened the source movie. Copy these files to the Web server that you want to host the movie and then create a link to the HTML page on the Web page from which the movie will originate.

exercise 8

CHOOSING PUBLISH SETTINGS, PREVIEWING, AND THEN PUBLISHING A MOVIE

1. Open Ch6Ex01.
2. Choose Publish Settings for the Flash Player file that will generate a text file with documentation about the movie, protect the movie from being imported by others, and password protect the *swf* file by completing the following steps:
    a. Click File and then click Publish Settings.

b. If necessary, click the Flash tab in the Publish Settings dialog box.
c. Click the Generate size report check box.
d. Click the Protect from import check box.
e. Click in the Password text box and then key a password for the file. You determine an appropriate password for the file. 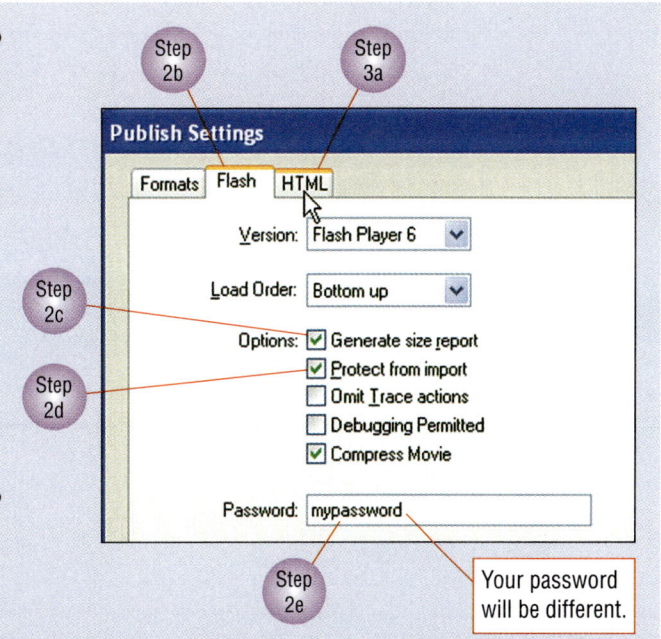
3. Choose Publish Settings for the HTML page that will scale the movie's height and width by 100% relative to the size of the browser window and disable the playback controls on the shortcut menu by completing the following steps:
   a. With the Publish Settings dialog box still open, click the HTML tab.
   b. Click the down arrow next to the Dimensions list box and then click Percent at the drop-down list. The values in the Width and Height text boxes will default to 100. Setting this option is often done as a method to ensure the Flash movie is sized at the full height and width of the browser window.
   c. Click the Display Menu check box to deselect it. 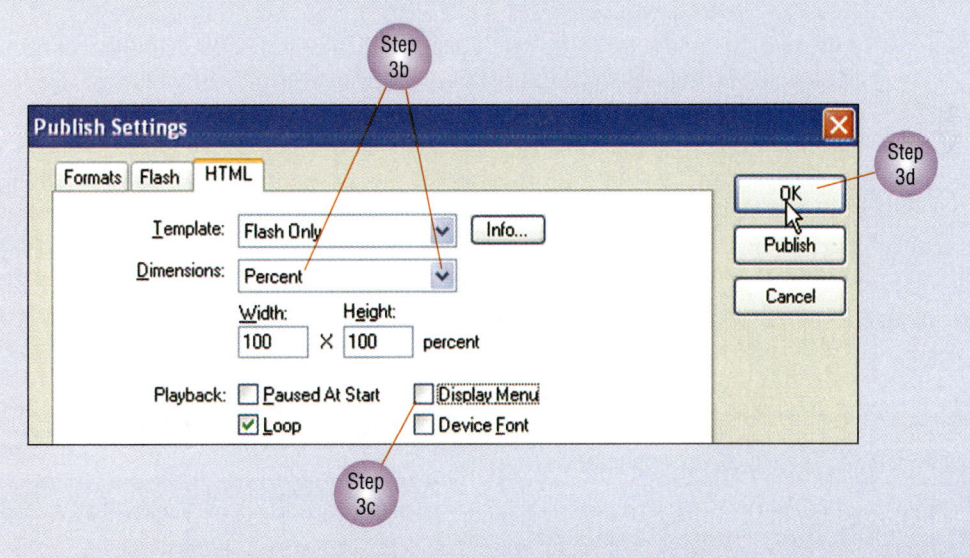
   d. Click OK to close the Publish Settings dialog box. The current settings are saved with the Flash document.
4. Preview the published Flash movie within the default browser window by completing the following steps:
   a. Click File, point to Publish Preview, and then click Default - (HTML). Flash publishes the movie using the current options in the Publish Settings dialog box and then opens the movie in the default browser window. The image shown displays the movie in Internet Explorer Version 6.

Animating Using Symbols and Masks and Publishing Flash Movies   **295**

b. Right-click over the movie to view the shortcut menu. Only two options are available on the menu since the Display Menu option was deselected in the Publish Settings dialog box.

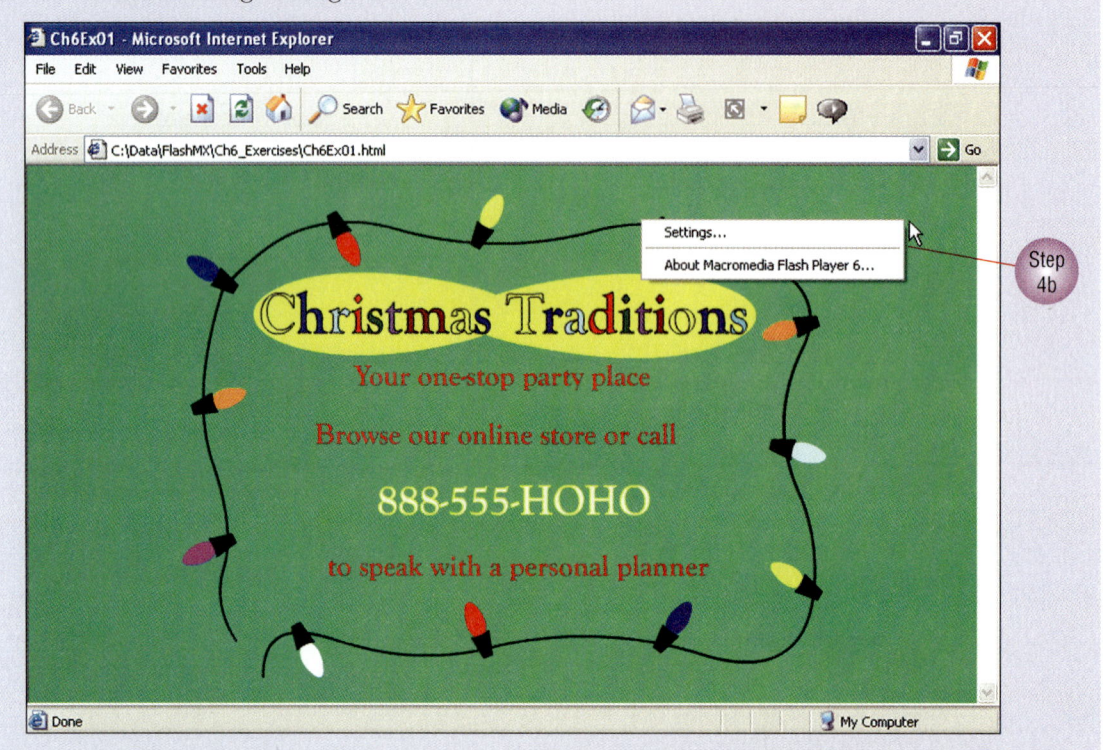

Step 4b

c. Close the browser window.
5. Click File and then click Publish. The Flash movie is published using the current options in the Publish Settings dialog box. Flash does not prompt you when an *swf* and *html* file already exist in the current drive and folder. Existing files with the same name will be overwritten.
6. Open and print the text file in Notepad that was created with the Generate size report option in the Publish Settings dialog box by completing the following steps:
   a. Click Start, point to *Programs* or *All Programs*, point to *Accessories*, and then click *Notepad*. If you do not have Notepad on the computer you are using, open any other word processing program.
   b. Click File and then click Open.
   c. Click the down arrow next to the Look in list box and then navigate to the drive and folder in which the data files for Chapter 6 are stored.
   d. Double-click the file named Ch6Ex01 Report.txt. *(Note: If you are using an application other than Notepad, you will have to change the Files of type option to Text Files (*.txt) before you will see the report file in the file list.)*
   e. Scroll through and read the report text in the Notepad window.
   f. Click File, click Print, and then click Print in the Print dialog box to print the report.
   g. Exit Notepad to return to Flash MX.
7. Close Ch6Ex01. Click Yes when prompted to save changes.

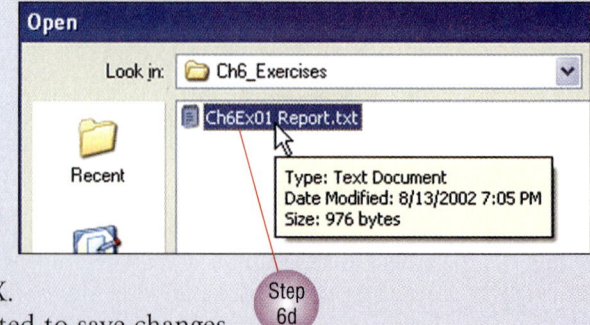

Step 6d

Viewing the HTML Code

Figure 6.14 illustrates the HTML code that was generated by Flash when the Ch6Ex01 document was published. The entries in Figure 6.14 include line breaks in order to display the entire code within the left and right margins of the textbook. HTML is an acronym for *HyperText Markup Language*, a page description language that uses tags to describe to the browser how to display a page. In Figure 6.14, the tags are identified between angle brackets (< >). Tags have a beginning and an ending tag. The ending tag includes a slash in front of the tag. For example, <TITLE> indicates to the browser the beginning of the page title and </TITLE> indicates the end of the page title.

FIGURE 6.14 *HTML Code Created in Exercise 8*

```
<HTML>
<HEAD>
<meta http-equiv=Content-Type content="text/html; charset=ISO-8859-1">
<TITLE>Ch6Ex01</TITLE>
</HEAD>
<BODY bgcolor="#00CC66">
<!-- URL's used in the movie-->
<!-- text used in the movie-->
<!--Your one-stop party placeBrowse our online store or callto speak with a
personal planner-->
<OBJECT classid="clsid:D27CDB6E-AE6D-11cf-96B8-444553540000"
codebase="http://download.macromedia.com/pub/shockwave/cabs/flash/swflash.cab#ve
rsion=6,0,0,0"
 WIDTH="100%" HEIGHT="100%" id="Ch6Ex01" ALIGN="">
 <PARAM NAME=movie VALUE="Ch6Ex01.swf"> <PARAM NAME=menu VALUE=false>
 <PARAM NAME=quality VALUE=high> <PARAM NAME=bgcolor VALUE=#00CC66>
 <EMBED src="Ch6Ex01.swf" menu=false quality=high bgcolor=#00CC66 WIDTH="100%"
  HEIGHT="100%" NAME="Ch6Ex01" ALIGN="" TYPE="application/x-shockwave-flash"
 PLUGINSPAGE="http://www.macromedia.com/go/getflashplayer">
 </EMBED>
</OBJECT>
</BODY>
</HTML>
```

Labels: *Beginning tag* → `<TITLE>`; *Ending tag* → `</TITLE>`

For purposes of displaying the Flash movie, the crucial information resides between the opening and closing <OBJECT> and <EMBED> tags. The code highlighted with yellow in Figure 6.14 is the <OBJECT> tag used to instruct Internet Explorer how to display the Flash movie. The code highlighted with green is the <EMBED> tag used to instruct Netscape Navigator how to display the movie.

The code highlighted in aqua in both the <OBJECT> and <EMBED> tags points out the options that were selected on the HTML tab of the Publish Settings dialog box in Exercise 8. This HTML code tells the browser the movie's width and height dimensions are at 100% and the display menu option is turned off.

You can open the HTML page in any text editor program such as Notepad to view and/or modify the code.

Using HTML Templates

As described in Table 6.2, Flash provides several HTML templates with which you can publish the Flash movie. In Exercise 8, the movie was published using the default Flash Only template. Figure 6.15 displays the other available templates in the Template drop-down list in the Publish Settings dialog box.

FIGURE 6.15 HTML Templates Available for Publishing Flash

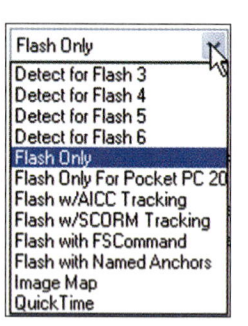

Choosing a template name and then clicking the Info button displays a dialog box similar to the one shown in Figure 6.11 that describes what the template will do. In Exercise 8 the Flash Only template creates HTML code that only displays the movie for users with Version 6 of the Flash Player installed. Other templates provide alternative options for users that do not have the appropriate player. A better choice would probably be the Detect for Flash 6 template which provides the user with the option of viewing an alternative image or getting the Flash Player if the Version 6 Flash Player does not exist.

If you are proficient with HTML you can edit the existing templates or create your own templates for publishing Flash movies. The HTML template files reside in the path C:\Program Files\Macromedia\Flash MX\First Run\HTML for a default Flash MX installation on a Windows-based computer.

Publishing in Other Formats

To accommodate users on the Web who might not have the Flash Player installed you can choose to publish the movie in several alternative formats. Flash will add the required code in the HTML page that will display these alternate images if the Flash Player is not detected provided you choose the appropriate HTML template and the appropriate file formats. Figure 6.16 displays the default file format options in the Publish Settings dialog box with the Formats tab selected. Table 6.3 describes each of the file formats available.

FIGURE 6.16 Default Options in Publish Settings Dialog Box with Formats Tabs Selected

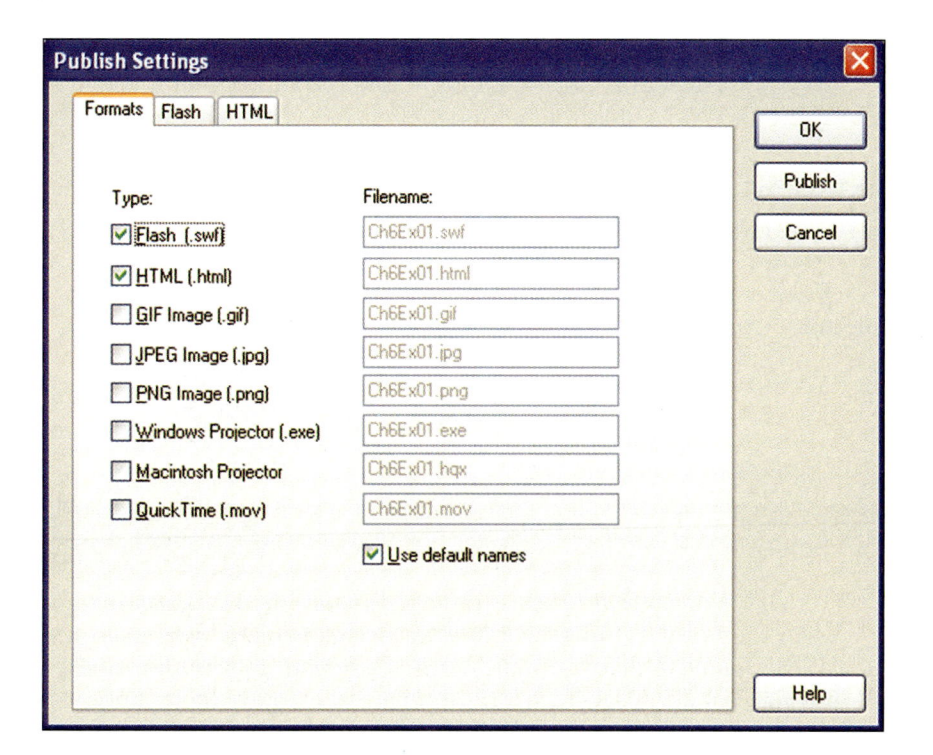

TABLE 6.3 Formats for Publishing Flash Movies

Option	Description
Flash (.swf)	By default, the Flash Player file format is selected to create the *swf* file that opens in the Flash Player application.
HTML (.html)	By default, the HTML file format is selected to generate the code that the browser will use to load the Flash Player and launch the movie.
GIF Image (.gif)	Generates a GIF file as an alternative for the user who does not have the Flash Player installed. Use the GIF tab when this option is active to choose the GIF publish options such as whether to produce a static or animated image.
JPEG Image (.jpg)	Produces the movie as a compressed bitmap without animation or interactive features. Click the JPEG tab when this option is active to set the dimensions of the image and choose the quality level for compression.

Continued on next page

Option	Description
PNG Image (.png)	Choose this option to create a cross-platform bitmap that can include an alpha property for transparency or to create a file for use in Macromedia Fireworks. Click the PNG tab when this option is active to choose the PNG publishing options.
Windows Projector (.exe)	Create a standalone copy of the movie for use on a Windows-based computer without the Flash Player. The Flash Player is embedded within the *exe* file along with the movie.
Macintosh Projector	Creates a standalone copy for a Macintosh computer.
QuickTime (.mov)	Generates a QuickTime version of the movie for viewing with the QuickTime player. Click the QuickTime tab when this option is active to choose the QuickTime publishing options.

Click the check box next to the additional file format that you want to include when the movie is published. You can select as many options as required for the HTML template that you want to use. Flash adds tabs to the Publish Settings dialog box for each format with which you have the ability to set options. For example, clicking the GIF Image (.gif) check box adds the GIF tab to the Publish Settings dialog box shown in Figure 6.17. Using this tab you can set options such as creating a static or an animated GIF.

FIGURE 6.17 GIF Tab Added to Publish Settings Dialog Box When GIF Image Selected on Formats Tab

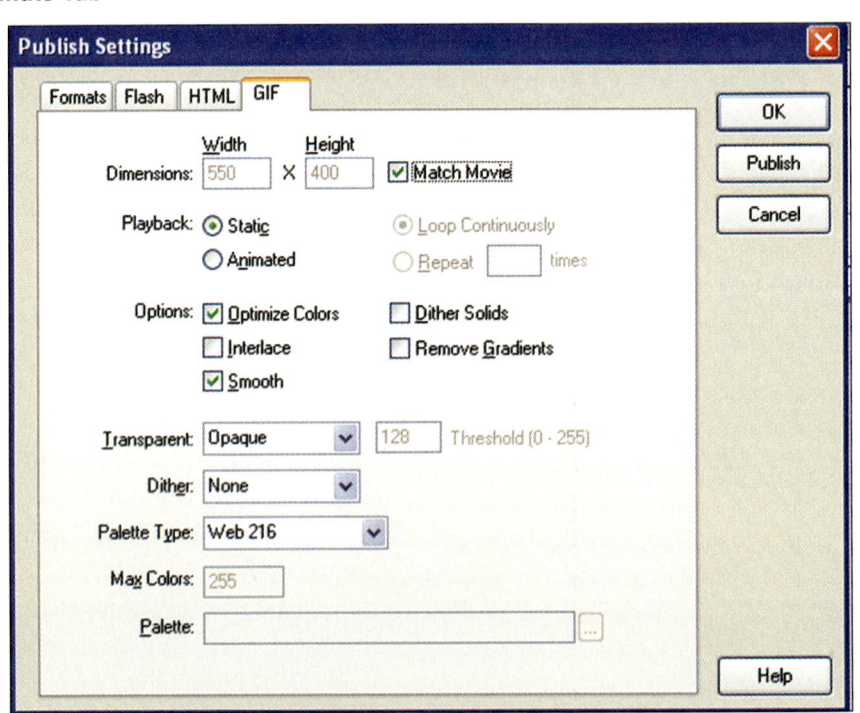

exercise 9
PUBLISHING A WINDOWS PROJECTOR FILE

1. Open Ch6Ex05.
2. Publish the movie as a self-running projector file that can be copied to any Windows-based computer by completing the following steps:
   a. Click File and then click Publish Settings.
   b. Click the Formats tab in the Publish Settings dialog box.
   c. Click the Windows Projector (.exe) check box.
   d. Click any other check boxes that are currently active to deselect them. The only tab remaining in the Publish Settings dialog box is the Formats tab when the Flash and HTML check boxes are inactive.
   e. Click Publish. Flash generates the projector file in the same drive and folder in which the source movie resides.

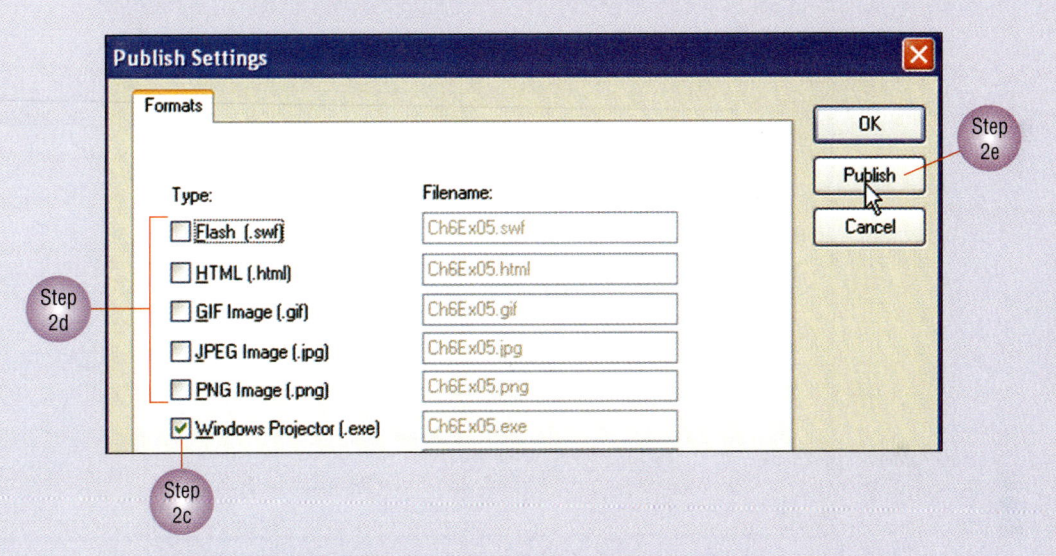

   f. Click OK to close the Publish Settings dialog box.
3. View the movie in the projector file by completing the following steps:
   a. Open Windows Explorer.
   b. Navigate to the drive and folder in which the data files for Chapter 6 are stored.
   c. Double-click the file named Ch6Ex05.exe.
   d. Close the Flash Player window after viewing the movie and then close Windows Explorer.
4. Close Ch6Ex05. Click Yes when prompted to save changes.

FLASH MX
Animating Using Symbols and Masks and Publishing Flash Movies   301

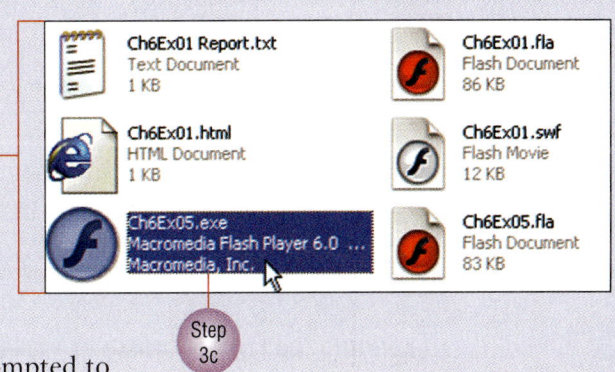

Exporting in Other Formats

In addition to creating files in other formats using the Publish Settings dialog box, the Export Movie option on the File menu can be used to create a file in a format other than Flash. The Export Movie dialog box shown in Figure 6.18 opens where you navigate to the drive and folder in which to save the exported file, assign a file name for the exported file, and choose the format in which to export. Figure 6.18 displays the Save as type pop-up list with the available export file formats.

FIGURE 6.18 *Export Movie Dialog Box with Save as type Pop-Up List*

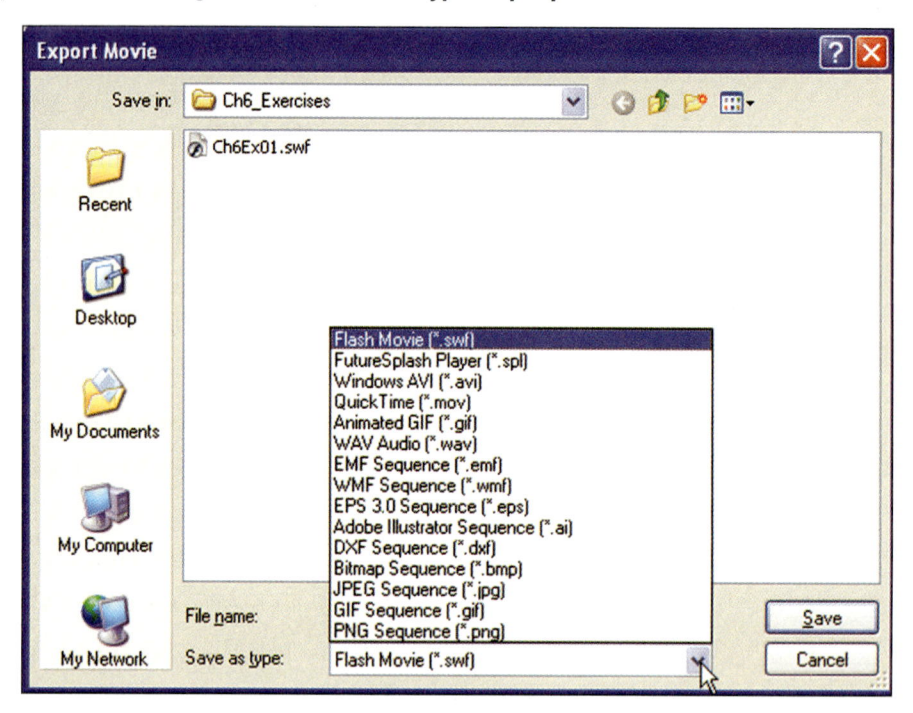

Exporting a movie using any of the sequence options such as GIF Sequence or JPEG Sequence creates a series of files that begin with the assigned file name and end with a sequential number representing the frame number in the movie animation. For example, if a Flash movie containing six frames is exported using GIF Sequence with a file name of DanceArt, the export command would create six files named DanceArt1.gif, DanceArt2.gif, DanceArt3.gif, DanceArt4.gif, DanceArt5.gif, and DanceArt6.gif.

Use the Publish command in the Publish Settings dialog box to export a movie in a format other than Flash and generate the HTML code required to view the alternative format. Use the Export movie feature to create a file to use in another application where you do not need the HTML code created.

Exporting the Current Frame as an Image

Click File and then click Export Image to create an image file for the current frame using the Export Image dialog box shown in Figure 6.19. Navigate to the drive and folder in which to save the exported image, assign a file name for the image, and choose the format in which to export using the Save as type pop-up list shown in Figure 6.19.

FIGURE

6.19 *Export Image Dialog Box with Save as type Pop-Up List*

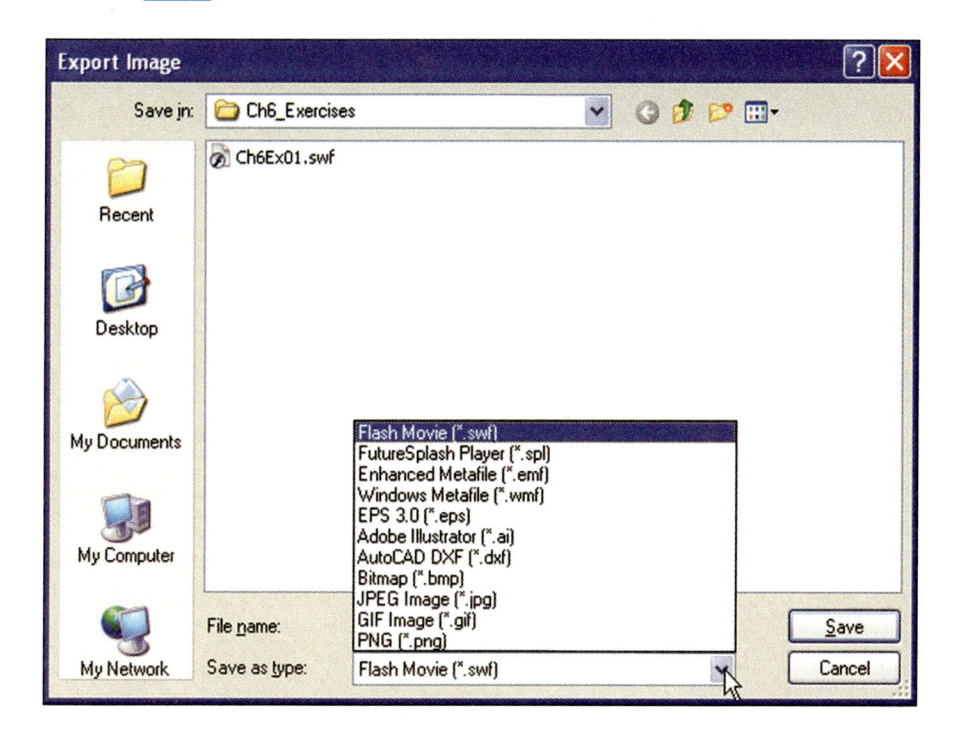

An example of when you would use this feature is to create a bitmap file with an image of the first frame in a movie. The bitmap can then be placed on a Web page and linked to the HTML file that launches the Flash movie from which the image was generated. Visitors to your Web site would click the image to play the movie.

CHAPTER summary

- The main movie Timeline is less cluttered with layers and frames when animations are created in movie clip symbols.
- Move clip Timelines are independent and continue to play after the main movie's Timeline has been played back.
- Animations in movie clips can be reused and require less disk space.
- Animations that include movie clip symbols must be previewed in the Flash Player.
- A graphic symbol animation is synchronized with the main movie's Timeline, meaning enough frames must exist in the layer in which the symbol instance is inserted in order for the entire animation to play back.
- Graphic symbol animations cannot include sound or interactivity.
- A new symbol can be created by duplicating an existing symbol and then editing the duplicated symbol's content in symbol editing mode.
- Stop a movie clip playback by inserting in the same layer as the movie clip symbol a blank keyframe, a keyframe with new content, or a keyframe with ActionScript statements that stop the movie clip.
- Assign a name to each instance of a movie clip symbol in the Properties panel to use as the target object in the ActionScript statement to stop a movie clip playback.
- Follow the sequence Objects, Movie, MovieClip, and then Methods in the Actions Panel toolbox to locate the stop command to halt playing of a movie clip.
- Click the Insert a target path button in the Parameters area of the Actions panel after double-clicking stop to choose the instance name in the Target Path dialog box for the movie clip that you want stopped.
- The event handler *onClipEvent (load)* is required at the beginning of the ActionScript to stop a movie clip.
- An existing animation in the main movie Timeline can be converted to a movie clip symbol by selecting and cutting or copying the frames and then pasting them in symbol editing mode.
- Animate objects on a mask layer to create special effects such as binoculars panning a stage performance or an eyeglass spanning an ocean view.
- Testing within the authoring environment is limited since you cannot view movie clips or test many ActionScript commands.
- Clicking Control and then Test Movie or Test Scene exports the current movie or scene using the default options in the Publish Settings dialog box.
- The Flash Player window that opens within Flash contains additional options for testing purposes that the regular Flash Player window does not contain.
- Display the Controller toolbar within the Flash Player for easy access to playback controls while conducting frequent tests.
- *Bandwidth* is the term used to describe the amount of data that can be transmitted from a server to a user's computer within a fixed time interval and is usually expressed in terms of bits per second (bps).

➤ *Broadband* is the term used for a connection that is capable of transmitting a large amount of data within a short period of time and *narrowband* means the connection transmits a smaller amount of data at a slower speed.

➤ Turn on the display of the Bandwidth Profiler to view statistics about the download performance of a movie and to view a streaming or frame-by-frame bar graph that depicts frames at which the player will have to pause and wait for data.

➤ Click Debug and then choose a download speed at the drop-down menu with which to test the movie.

➤ You can add up to three of your own customized download speed settings for testing.

➤ Flash tests download speed using estimates based on a typical Internet connection. The actual download time will vary depending on the volume of Internet traffic at the time the user requests movie playback.

➤ Present research indicates 80 percent of American households are connected to the Internet using a dial up connection.

➤ Optimize a movie prior to publishing by editing objects, frames, or imported file properties to reduce file size when testing indicates the download performance is unacceptable.

➤ If an optimized file is still experiencing a time lag, consider adding a simple animation before the problem frame to provide a time buffer in which the content can be downloaded in the background.

➤ A *preloader* is an animation at the beginning of a movie that keeps a user amused while content is downloaded.

➤ Click Show Streaming on the View menu in the Flash Player window to simulate a Web connection download at the specified modem speed.

➤ Publishing a movie is a two-step process where the settings for which the movie should be exported are defined and then the publish command is executed.

➤ Use the Flash tab in the Publish Settings dialog box to choose the options in which to publish the Flash Player format file.

➤ Use the HTML tab in the Publish Settings dialog box to choose the options for displaying the movie within the browser window.

➤ Flash automatically generates the HTML page with the tags and code necessary to display the movie according to the options defined in the Publish Settings dialog box.

➤ Use the Publish Preview option on the File menu to publish the movie using the current options in the Publish Settings dialog box and then open the movie in the default browser window.

➤ Click File and then click Publish or click the Publish button in the Publish Settings dialog box to export the movie using the current settings.

➤ When publishing is complete, copy the *swf* and *html* files to the Web server and create a link to the HTML page to make the movie accessible from the Web.

➤ The HTML generated code created by Flash includes the commands necessary for the browser to open the Flash Player and launch the movie.

➤ Internet Explorer uses the <OBJECT> tags in the HTML page and Netscape Navigator uses the <EMBED> tags.

➤ Flash provides several HTML templates with the necessary code to display movies using a variety of options including detecting an earlier version of the Flash Player and providing alternative images if the Flash Player is not found.

➤ The Formats tab in the Publish Settings dialog box is used to specify additional file formats to create when publishing the movie to accommodate users without the Flash Player.

- A projector file is an exported movie with the Flash Player embedded in the file for use when displaying a movie without a browser.
- Use the Export Movie option on the File menu to export a movie to another file format without creating the HTML page.
- Click File and then click Export Image to create an image file in another format for the current frame.

COMMANDS review

Command or Feature	Mouse/Keyboard	Shortcut Keys
Actions panel	Window, Actions	F9
Bandwidth profiler	View, Bandwidth Profiler	Ctrl + B
Controller	Window, Toolbars, Controller	
Copy frames	Edit, Copy Frames	Ctrl + Alt + C
Cut frames	Edit, Cut Frames	Ctrl + Alt + X
Create movie clip or graphic symbol	Insert, New Symbol	Ctrl + F8
Export current frame as image	File, Export Image	
Export movie in another format	File, Export Movie	Ctrl + Alt + Shift + S
Paste frames	Edit, Paste Frames	Ctrl + Alt + V
Preview a published movie	File, Publish Preview	
Publish movie	File, Publish	Shift + F12
Publish settings	File, Publish Settings	Ctrl + Shift + F12
Select all frames	Edit, Select All Frames	Ctrl + Alt + A
Simulate download speed	View, Show Streaming	Ctrl + Enter
Test download speed	Debug, click desired speed	
Test movie	Control, Test Movie	Ctrl + Enter
Test scene	Control, Test Scene	Ctrl + Alt + Enter

CONCEPTS check

Indicate the correct term or command for each item.

1. A move clip's Timeline has this relationship to the main movie's Timeline.
2. Preview an animation that includes a movie clip using this menu sequence.
3. Animated graphic symbols cannot include these elements.
4. Click this option at the shortcut menu for a selected symbol to create a copy of the symbol.
5. Stop playback of a movie clip using any of these three alternatives.
6. Do this with each instance of a movie clip that you want to stop before opening the Actions panel to create the ActionScript statements.
7. Use this menu sequence to easily select all frames in the Timeline.
8. You must do this action in the Timeline before a mask layer can be edited.
9. This is the term that describes a high speed connection to the Internet.
10. Bars above the red line in the Bandwidth Profiler's bar graph indicate this will occur during the movie playback.
11. Click this menu option in the Flash Player window to choose the download speed with which you want to test the movie performance.
12. This time statistic in the left pane of the Bandwidth Profiler indicates how long the user will have to wait after downloading starts and before the movie begins playing.
13. This is the number of user-defined speed settings you can create in the Custom Modem Settings dialog box.
14. Optimizing a movie involves editing frames and objects in order to accomplish this result.
15. This is the term for an animation that is added at the beginning of a movie to provide a time buffer while content is downloaded in the background.
16. Click this option on the View menu in the Flash Player window to begin a simulation of the download time at the current speed setting.
17. These are the file extensions of the two files that are created when a movie is published using the default Publish Settings options.
18. Click this check box in the Publish Settings dialog box with the Flash tab selected to have Flash create a text file with documentation about the file size and embedded objects.
19. This option in the Publish Settings dialog box with the Flash tab selected prevents unauthorized users from importing the player file back into Flash.
20. Click this button in the Publish Settings dialog box with the HTML tab selected to view a description of the type of code in the currently selected HTML template.
21. HTML tags are identified between these brackets.
22. Click this option in the Publish Settings dialog box with the Formats tab selected to create a self-running standalone file.
23. Exporting a movie from the Export Movie dialog box does not generate this additional document.
24. Open this dialog box to export the current frame as an image in another file format.

SKILLS check

Assessment 1

FIGURE 6.20 Assessment 1

1. Start a new Flash document.
2. Create an animated movie clip symbol named FlickeringSun using the following information:
   a. In symbol editing mode, draw a sun similar to the one shown in Figure 6.20 alternating short and long rays along the sun's perimeter.
   b. Create a frame-by-frame animation in frames 1–12 as follows:
      - Copy frame 1 and then paste it individually into frames 2–12.
      - Delete the short rays in frame 2.
      - Delete the long rays in frame 3.
      - Repeat the sequence of first deleting short rays and then deleting long rays in the remaining frames in the Timeline.
3. Save the document and name it Ch6SA1-MovieClip.
4. Close Ch6SA1-MovieClip.
5. Open Ch5Ex01.
6. Save the document with Save As and name it Ch6SA1.
7. Edit Ch6SA1 as follows:
   a. Select and delete the sun on the *Background* layer.
   b. Insert a new layer at the top of the Timeline named *Sun*.
   c. Open the Library panel for Ch6SA1-MovieClip.
   d. With frame 1 of the *Sun* layer active, insert an instance of the FlickeringSun movie clip at the top right of the stage and then scale the instance as necessary.
   e. Close the Library panel for Ch6SA1-MovieClip.
   f. Lock all layers.
8. Test the movie in the Flash Player window.
9. Save the document using the same name (Ch6SA1).

Assessment 2

1. With Ch6SA1 open, stop the FlickeringSun movie clip playback at the last frame using a graphic symbol by completing the following steps:
    a. Unlock the *Sun* layer.
    b. Insert a keyframe in the last frame of the movie in the *Sun* layer.
    c. Duplicate the FlickeringSun symbol instance in the last frame of the *Sun* layer. Accept the default name of FlickeringSun copy. Close the Library panel.
    d. Place horizontal and vertical guides on the stage at the sun's position to assist with placing a new instance of a sun in a later step.
    e. Delete the FlickeringSun instance in the last frame of the *Sun* layer.
    f. Open the Library panel and then display the Symbol Properties for FlickeringSun copy. Change the symbol's behavior to Graphic.
    g. Place an instance of FlickeringSun copy in the last frame of the *Sun* layer. Position and scale it using the guides created in Step 1d.
    h. Remove the display of the guides and rulers.
    i. Lock the *Sun* layer.. Close the Library panel.
2. Save the document using the same name (Ch6SA1).
3. Test the movie in the Flash Player window.
4. Stop the movie playback from looping and then display the Controller toolbar. Remove the Bandwidth Profiler if it is visible.
5. Rewind and play the movie a few times.
6. Close the Flash Player window and then save the document using the same name (Ch6SA1).
7. Close Ch6SA1.

Assessment 3

1. Open Ch5SA1.
2. Save the document with Save As and name it Ch6SA3.
3. Select and copy all of the frames in the Timeline.
4. Create a new move clip symbol named BI-org by pasting the frames from the clipboard and then exiting symbol editing mode.
5. Delete all of the layers in the Timeline except the layer named *Background*. Delete the text blocks on the *Background* layer so that the stage is empty.
6. Rename the *Background* layer *BI-org*.
7. Delete all frames in *BI-org* except frame 1.
8. Open the Library panel and then place an instance of the BI-org movie clip in the center of the stage.
9. Test the movie in the Flash Player window to view the animation.
10. Close the Flash Player window and then save the revised document using the same name (Ch6SA3).
11. Close Ch6SA3.

Assessment 4

1. Open TravelSki.
2. Save the document with Save As and name it Ch6SA4.
3. Create a scrolling text banner for the URL using an animated mask by completing the following steps:
    a. Add a new layer at the top of the Timeline named *URL*.
    b. Cut and paste the text block containing the URL www.emcp.net/fctravel/march/ski from the *Text* layer to frame 1 of the *URL* layer. *(Note: Delete the URL in the ending keyframe in the* Text *layer.)*

c. Move the text block in frame 1 of the *URL* layer so that the first half of the text block is offstage as shown in Figure 6.21. *(Hint: Hold down the Shift key while dragging to stay at the same horizontal position.)*
d. Insert a keyframe in the last frame of the *URL* layer.

FIGURE 6.21 *Assessment 4 Step 3d*

e. Move the text block in the last frame of the *URL* layer so that only the letters *www.emcp* are visible at the right edge of the stage.
f. Create a motion tween on the *URL* layer.
g. Insert a new layer above *URL* named *Banner*.
h. Draw a rectangle in frame 1 of the *Banner* layer similar to the one shown in Figure 6.22 at the same horizontal position as the text block on the *URL* layer.

FIGURE 6.22 *Assessment 4 Step 3h*

i. Mask the *Banner* layer.
4. Preview the animation.
5. Save the document using the same name (Ch6SA4).

Assessment 5

1. With Ch6SA4 open, test the movie in the Flash Player window.
2. Display the Bandwidth Profiler.
3. Test at all three modem speeds and note the Preload time statistics.
4. Use Show Streaming to simulate a Web connection download at a modem speed of 28.8.
5. Optimize the document by compressing the two bitmap files as much as possible.
6. Retest at all three modem speeds and note the revised Preload time statistics.
7. Reduce the file size using other optimization strategies and retest until you believe the file size is reduced as much as possible.
8. Save the revised document using the same name (Ch6SA4).

Assessment 6

1. With Ch6SA4 open, change the following Publish settings:
    - Generate a size report.
    - Protect the Flash Player file from being imported by others.
    - Assign a password to the file.
    - Use the Detect for Flash 6 HTML template.
    - Set the dimensions to 100% of the browser window's width and height.
    - Select GIF Image as the alternative file format. Leave all of the options on the GIF tab at the default settings.
2. Preview the movie in the browser window. Notice the text at the end of the animation does not stay on the screen long enough to be read comfortably.
3. Add frames to the end of the movie so that the text block on the *RestrictText* layer stays on the screen longer.
4. Make any other changes to the movie that you think would improve the animation.
5. Publish the movie.
6. Save the document using the same name (Ch6SA4).
7. Close Ch6SA4.
8. Open, print, and then close the text file for the size report in Notepad or another word processing program.

Assessment 7

1. Open Sailboats.
2. Save the document with Save As and name it Ch6SA7.
3. Test the movie at all three modem speeds. All three speeds will experience several time lags during the movie.
4. Optimize and retest at all three modem speeds using as many strategies as possible to reduce the number of time lags. Work with another student in the class to discuss various solutions.
5. Save the revised document using the same name (Ch6SA7).
6. Create a self-running projector file for the movie.
7. With the playhead at frame 1 export the current frame to a JPEG image named Sailboats. Accept all of the default settings in the Export JPEG dialog box.
8. Exit Flash MX. Click Yes when prompted to save changes.
9. Open Windows Explorer and then navigate to the drive and folder in which the data files are stored.
10. Double-click the file named Ch6SA7.exe to view the movie.
11. Close the Flash Player window.
12. Double-click the file named Sailboats.jpg. The image should open in a browser window or a Windows Picture Viewer window. If it does not, open Internet Explorer or Netscape, display the Open dialog box, and then browse to Sailboats.jpg to open it.
13. Close the browser and then close Windows Explorer.

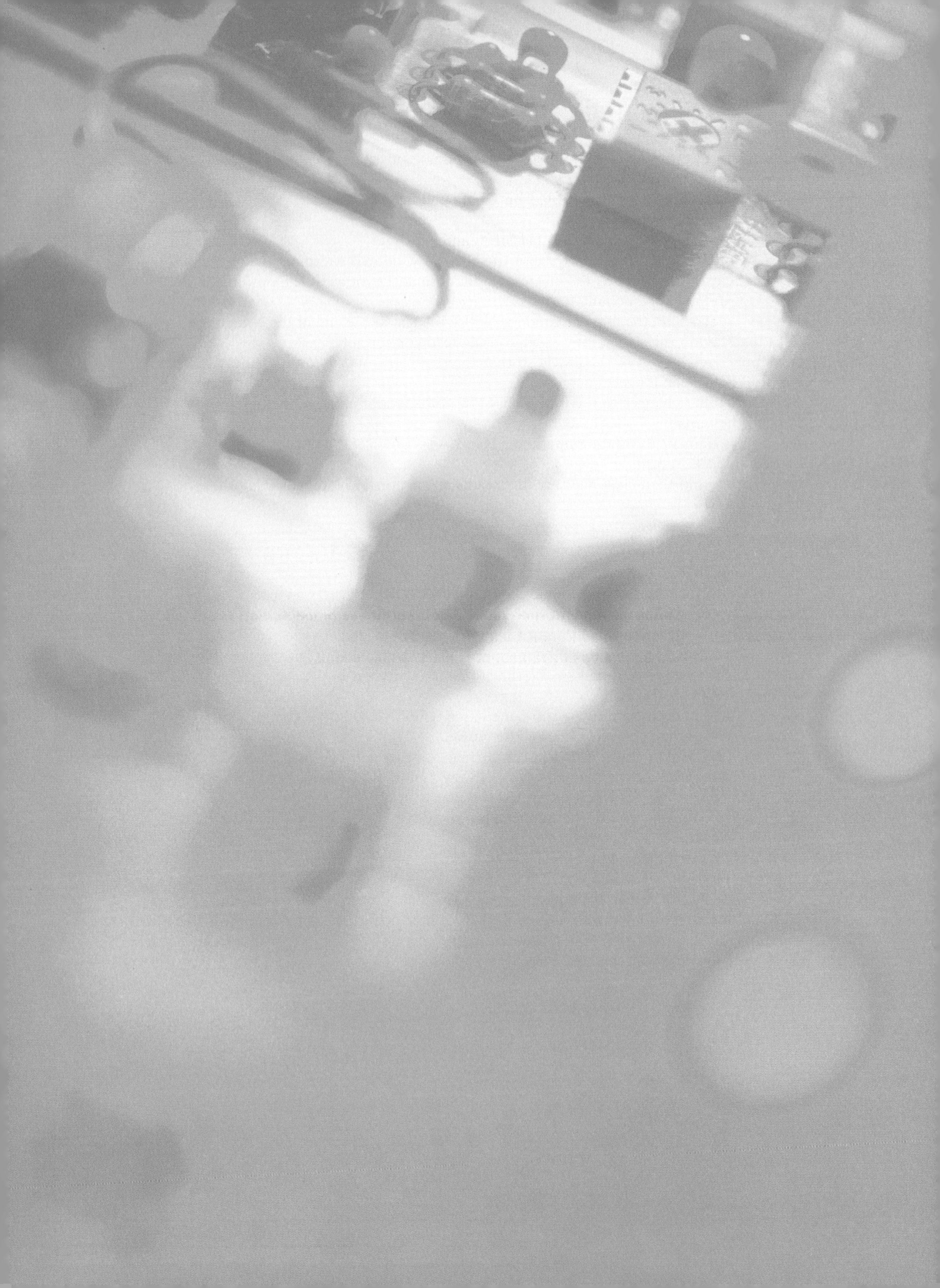

CHAPTER 7

USING ACTIONSCRIPT AND CREATING TEMPLATES

PERFORMANCE OBJECTIVES

Upon successful completion of Chapter 7, you will be able to:
- Define the terms *object-oriented programming*, *object*, *method*, *action*, *event*, and *parameters*.
- List general guidelines for creating ActionScript in movies.
- Switch between Normal mode and Expert mode in the Actions panel and describe the difference between the two modes.
- Add actions to keyframes, buttons, and movie clips.
- Use the goto and stop actions to control movie playback.
- Add labels and comments to frames.
- Create a preloader animation.
- Perform a conditional test on a movie property.
- Create buttons to toggle the playback of a stream soundtrack on and off.
- Use the with action to target start and stop actions at a movie clip instance.
- Use the getURL action to open a Web page during a movie.
- Use the fscommand action to control a projector window.
- Create and use a Flash template.
- Use the Movie Explorer.
- List Web resources for learning more about Flash.

Flash MX Chapter 07

There are eight student data files and two folders with Web files to copy for this chapter.

In Chapters 5 and 6 you were introduced to ActionScript statements applied to a button instance and a movie clip instance to control movie playback. ActionScript is a powerful tool for creating more complex interactivity with a user. In this chapter you will further explore ActionScript for activities such as performing conditional tests, loading other documents during a movie, and controlling the host movie window elements. Creating and using a template in Flash can save time and promote a consistent look and feel to Web sites.

Understanding ActionScript Concepts and Terms

The exercises in Chapters 5 and 6 were designed to introduce ActionScript using the basic movie control actions. As you learned in Exercises 11 and 12 in Chapter 5, creating these basic statements involves a simple point-and-click approach in the Actions panel. You added statements without having to know the nuts and bolts of programming in ActionScript. To use ActionScript for more complex interactive elements, an understanding of basic ActionScript concepts, terms, and organizational structure is beneficial.

As stated in Chapter 5, ActionScript is a scripting language. Scripts are a series of commands that provide instruction to the computer. The commands are generally carried out in sequence with the first instruction in the script performed first, then the second, and so on until the end of the script. As you have already seen with the basic stop, play, and goto commands, scripts are generally easy to understand since they use statements that closely resemble how we would communicate in English.

Learning ActionScript involves learning the keywords that will tell the computer what you want it to do and learning how to write the statement using the proper syntax. Recall from Chapter 5 that syntax is the term used to describe the rules of grammar and punctuation as applied to programming. In this chapter you will add to this knowledge a general understanding of how ActionScript organizes information and the rules with which it operates through the use of examples.

Object-Oriented Programming

ActionScript is similar to JavaScript which is often used to add interactivity to Web pages. ActionScript, like its JavaScript counterpart, is an *object-oriented language*. In object-oriented languages, classes are defined with a set of characteristics and behaviors. In ActionScript terminology a characteristic is a *property* and a behavior is a *method*. Instances of a class are referred to as *objects*. Object-oriented programmers can create relationships between objects so that one object can inherit the properties of another object thereby allowing existing code to be reused. Since modules of code can be reused, object-oriented programs are considered more efficient, easier to maintain, and easier to modify.

As an example, assume a class is created called *player*. Each player is defined with properties such as gender, age, and skill level. Each player also has methods defined such as hit, shoot, and score. Each individual player becomes an object or an instance of the player class. Adding a new player object does not require you to define its properties and methods because it inherits these from the player class.

In Chapter 6 you used ActionScript to stop (method) a named instance of a movie clip (object). All movie clips in Flash are instances of the MovieClip class and each movie clip instance inherits the properties and the methods of the MovieClip class. Each button that you create in Flash is an instance of the Button class with all of the Button class properties and methods.

Actions

An *action* is a statement that tells Flash what to do with the target object. The toolbox in the Actions panel lists the actions in the ActionScript language. The actions are grouped into eight main categories with an Index at the bottom of the categories that alphabetically lists all actions. Expanding a main category in the toolbox will reveal subcategories which can be further expanded in a hierarchical fashion.

The Flash help system provides a comprehensive dictionary with a description, the usage, and an example of how to apply each action. Tutorials are also available within help to provide step-by-step instruction on ActionScript.

Events

Using the Actions panel, you apply ActionScript to a keyframe, to a button instance, or to a movie clip instance. Actions applied to a keyframe are executed when the playhead reaches the keyframe in which the statements reside. Actions applied to button or movie clip instance execute when an event occurs. An event can be a mouse movement, a key pressed on the keyboard, or the loading of a movie clip. The event triggers the action.

As you learned in Chapters 5 and 6 when you added actions to a button and movie clip instance, actions targeted to a button or movie clip are preceded by *event handlers*.

Parameters

Parameters, also called arguments, provide variable information allowing you to perform different actions based on the parameter you provide. For example, the gotoAndPlay action has the frame parameter in which you specify which frame you want the movie to advance to. In one statement the parameter can have a different value than in another statement. Some actions do not provide for a parameter, which means the action functions the same way each time. For example, the stopAllSounds action that you used in Chapter 5 to mute the soundtrack had no parameters, meaning all sounds in the movie would be stopped when the action was executed.

General Guidelines for Writing ActionScript

This chapter will introduce you to some common uses of ActionScript using hands-on examples. You will finish the chapter by learning how to find more information on your own about Flash and ActionScript. As you gain more experience creating animations, you will want to branch out and expand your knowledge base of ActionScript since this is where the power of Flash resides for creating interactive movies. Before you begin a new project in Flash with the intent of adding ActionScript, use the following guidelines to plan the project:

- Define the goal of the movie and how ActionScript will help you to achieve the goal.
- Draw a flow chart of the movie so that you can see each interaction and the action required for each event.
- Decide the objects to which you will apply ActionScript in order to provide for each interaction.

Once the frames and objects are created and you are ready to start creating the ActionScript statements, use the following strategies to make the best use of your time:

- Document the ActionScript using comments that briefly explain what is happening at key points in the script. Statements preceded with two forward slashes (//) are ignored by Flash when the script is run. Key your comment text after //.
- Creating ActionScript statements that will cause the movie to respond according to your plan often takes many cycles of coding, testing, and then debugging. Work on one section at a time. When a section of the movie is performing correctly, save the movie as a separate version before starting the next segment.
- Use Normal mode in the Actions panel whenever possible. Normal mode, as you will learn in the next section, provides the syntax for you.
- Assign descriptive names for objects and variables. Avoid using cryptic names that a few months from now will mean nothing to you when you are trying to modify the movie.

Using Normal Mode and Expert Mode in the Actions Panel

The exercises in Chapters 5 and 6 in which you used the Actions panel made use of the panel in the default *Normal mode* option. In Normal mode, statements are created by double-clicking actions in the toolbox and then choosing variables in the parameters area. Flash built each statement based on the selection you made from the toolbox and parameters area including adding the required syntax as shown in Figure 7.1. Think of Normal mode as *Assisted mode* where Flash assists you with the programming.

FIGURE 7.1 The Actions Panel in Normal Mode

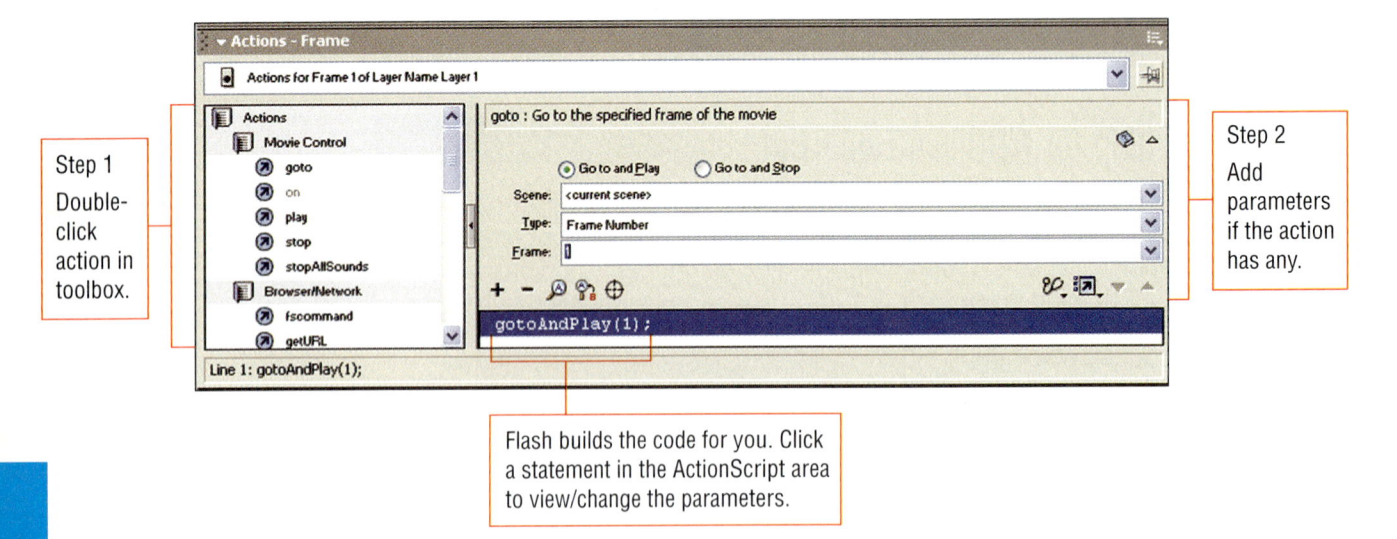

Step 1 Double-click action in toolbox.

Step 2 Add parameters if the action has any.

Flash builds the code for you. Click a statement in the ActionScript area to view/change the parameters.

In *Expert mode* the parameters area is replaced with a larger ActionScript area. The available parameters for an action are not presented in a way in which you can point and click. You can add actions from the toolbox and then complete the statements by keying the required parameters, or by keying the entire action and its parameters yourself directly into the ActionScript area. In this mode you are required to key the syntax correctly. Flash does not automatically check the syntax of the statements as you key them. A Check Syntax button is located above the ActionScript area which you can use periodically to check the statements. Code hints are tooltips that provide the available parameters for an action. Figure 7.2 displays the Actions panel in Expert mode with a code hint for the current action in the ActionScript area.

FIGURE 7.2 **The Actions Panel in Expert Mode**

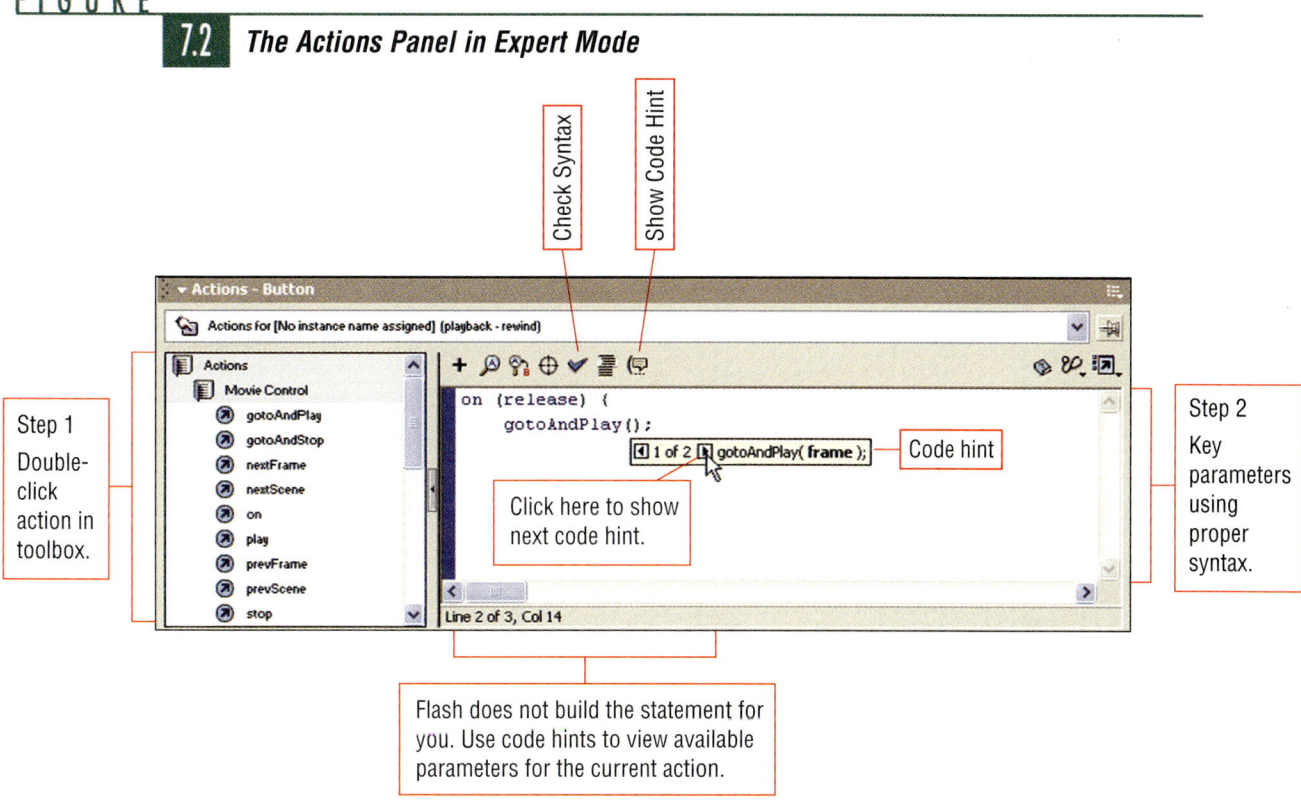

Switching from Expert mode back to Normal mode causes Flash to check syntax at the time of the switch. If errors exist, the message shown in Figure 7.3 is displayed informing you that you must edit the statements in Expert mode.

FIGURE 7.3 **Message Displayed when Switching to Normal Mode from Expert Mode with Errors in Statements**

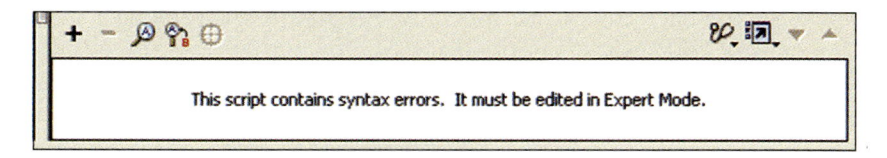

If you leave the Actions panel in Expert mode and then proceed to test or publish a movie in which errors exist in statements, Flash displays an Output window with messages informing you of the existence of these errors.

Using ActionScript and Creating Templates 317

exercise 1

USING THE ACTIONS PANEL IN EXPERT MODE AND SWITCHING BETWEEN EXPERT AND NORMAL MODES

1. Open Ch5Ex01.
2. Expand and undock the Actions panel and then switch between Normal mode and Expert mode by completing the following steps:
   a. Expand the Actions panel. *(Note: If the Actions panel is not visible, click Window and then click Actions.)*
   b. Click the move handle (displays as five dots next to the expand/collapse arrow) and then drag the panel to the middle of the stage as shown.

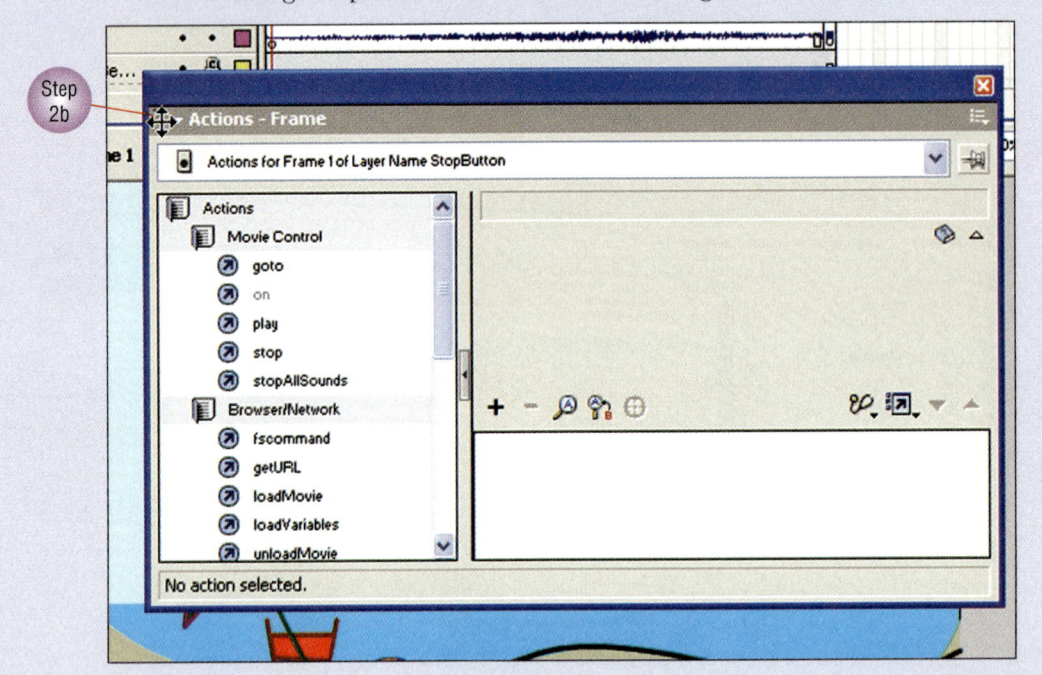

   Step 2b

   c. Click the Options menu button and then click Expert Mode at the drop-down menu.

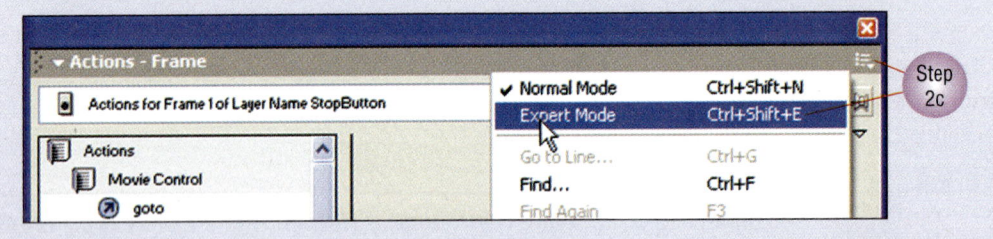

   Step 2c

3. View existing code for the button instance, key additional text in the ActionScript area, and then attempt to switch back to Normal mode by completing the following steps:
   a. Drag the Actions panel title bar left in the Flash window until you can see the Sound Off button on the stage next to the panel.

b. Click the Sound Off button instance. Flash displays the ActionScript applied to the button instance in the ActionScript area of the Actions panel.

c. Assume that you think that the stopAllSounds statement requires a parameter naming the sound that you want to stop. The sound file added to the movie is named seashore.wav. Add the sound file name to the statement by completing the following steps:
   1) Position the mouse pointer between the left and right bracket next to stopAllSounds in the ActionScript area (the pointer displays as the I-beam) and then click the left mouse button.
   2) Key **seashore.wav**.

d. Click the Options menu button and then click Normal Mode at the drop-down menu. Flash displays the error message *This script contains syntax errors. It must be edited in Expert Mode.* in the ActionScript area.

e. Click the Options menu button and then click Expert Mode.

f. Drag across the text *seashore.wav* and then press Delete.

g. Click the Options menu button and then click Normal Mode.

4. Click the Close button on the Actions panel title bar.
5. Close Ch5Ex01. Click <u>N</u>o when prompted to save changes.

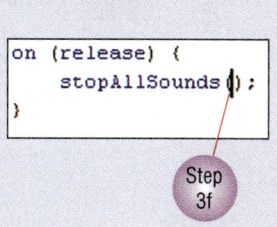

Controlling Movie Playback

In Chapter 5 you learned how to apply the play, stop, goto, and stopAllSounds actions to a button instance to provide the user with control over movie playback. In this chapter, you will learn how to make use of frame labels and variables to improve and expand the functionality of these actions. Click the Movie Control subcategory of the Actions category in the Actions panel toolbox to access the playback actions.

Goto

Goto is used to move the playhead to a different frame in the movie's Timeline. The goto destination and action depends on the specified parameters as shown in Figure 7.4.

FIGURE 7.4 *Parameters Area for Goto Action*

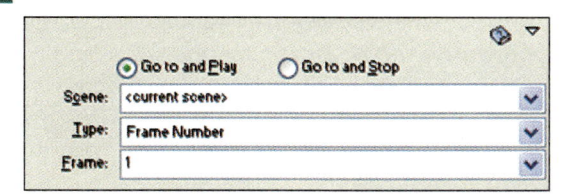

Using ActionScript and Creating Templates 319

Click the down arrow next to the S<u>c</u>ene list box to choose a different scene number or name at the drop-down list or by selecting <next scene> or <previous scene>. Click the down arrow next to the <u>T</u>ype list box to change the method in which you specify the destination frame from Frame Number to Frame Label, Expression, Next Frame, or Previous Frame. The entry in the <u>F</u>rame text box is dependent on the current option in the <u>T</u>ype list box.

Along with specifying the location to move to, the parameters area includes two choices for the goto action when it reaches the destination. Choose *Go to and <u>P</u>lay* or *Go to and <u>S</u>top* to instruct Flash on whether the movie should resume playing or stop at the destination.

On

On is dimmed in the Actions/Movie Control list unless a button instance is active. Use on to create the event handler that specifies to which mouse event (shown in Figure 7.5) you want the action to respond. As you learned in Chapter 5, multiple events can be selected in the parameters area.

FIGURE 7.5 **Mouse Events for On Event Handler**

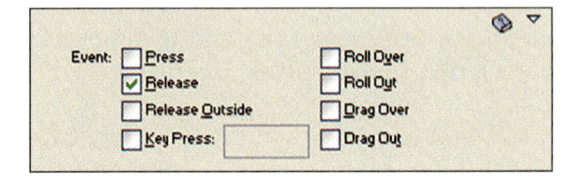

Play

The play action uses no parameters and simply instructs Flash to begin playing the movie at the point in the Timeline at which the action is executed. In most cases, as you did in Chapter 5, this action is applied to a button instance.

Stop

The stop action, like play, uses no parameters and instructs Flash to stop playing the movie. While this action is also often applied to a button instance, you will use the action in a keyframe in the next exercise to stop a movie from replaying as it does in Looped Playback mode.

Another example for adding a stop action would be to prevent the movie playback from starting automatically when the *swf* file is launched in the player window. In this case, a play button inserted at the beginning of the movie would provide the user with the ability to start playback at his or her convenience.

StopAllSounds

As you learned in Chapter 5, the stopAllSounds action stops sounds that are currently playing. However, when you read the Reference information in Chapter 5 for stopAllSounds, you learned that stream sounds will resume playing when the playhead reaches the frame in which it has been associated.

Assigning Labels and Comments to a Keyframe

Actions such as goto have a parameter in which a frame is the target destination. Frames can be referenced by their number as you did in Chapter 5 with the Rewind button. The statement *gotoAndStop(1);* told Flash to go to the first frame in the Timeline and then stop. Using frame numbers to define the destination is not always the best approach. For example, assume you have a movie with several buttons that appear throughout the playback in which the user response sends the playhead to a different location. If you use frame numbers for the goto statements and then subsequently edit the movie by adding frames to the timeline, you will then have to edit each goto statement. Adding the frames will cause the frame numbers of the destination to change. Updating the statements would be time consuming as well as increase the potential for errors.

By adding a frame label to a frame, you can reference the destination by its label name instead of its number in any ActionScript parameter. If frames are added, moved, or removed from the Timeline, no change is required to the ActionScript since the frame's label is part of the frame properties. To add a frame label to a frame, select the frame in the Timeline, expand the Properties panel, click in the Frame text box, and then key a name as shown in Figure 7.6.

FIGURE 7.6 *Frame Text Box in Properties Panel*

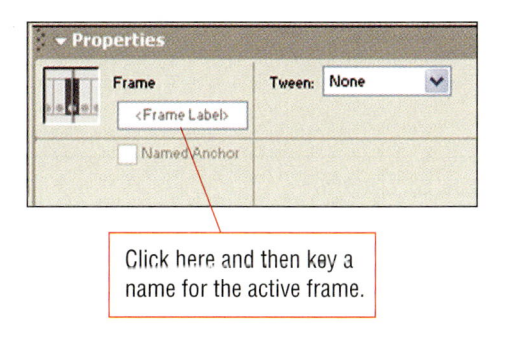

Click here and then key a name for the active frame.

Flash inserts a red flag in a keyframe in the Timeline, indicating a frame label exists and displays the name next to the flag if space permits, as shown in Figure 7.7.

FIGURE 7.7 *Frame Label Displayed in Timeline*

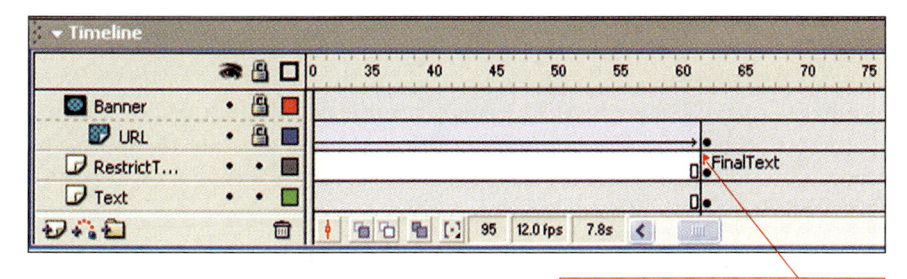

A red flag indicates a frame label has been added and the label name displays if space permits.

Using ActionScript and Creating Templates **321**

Adding a Comment to a Keyframe

The Frame text box in the Properties panel can be used instead as a placeholder for comments within a movie. Adding comments to keyframes in a complex movie helps you to identify what is happening in segments of the Timeline. Editing the movie is then made easier for you or someone else if the comments describe a section of frames as you scroll the Timeline. Often, Flash movies are created by development teams. A good practice for documenting to others what a span of frames is doing is to place a brief description in a comment keyframe within a comment layer. To do this, precede the comment text with two forward slashes (//) in the Frame text box in the Properties panel for the active keyframe. Figure 7.8 displays a comment being entered in the Properties panel and Figure 7.9 displays the comment text in the Timeline.

FIGURE 7.8 *Keying a Comment in the Frame Text Box in the Properties Panel*

Precede comment text with two forward slashes.

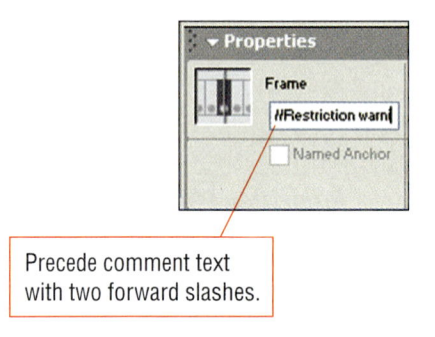

FIGURE 7.9 *Comment Text Displayed in Timeline*

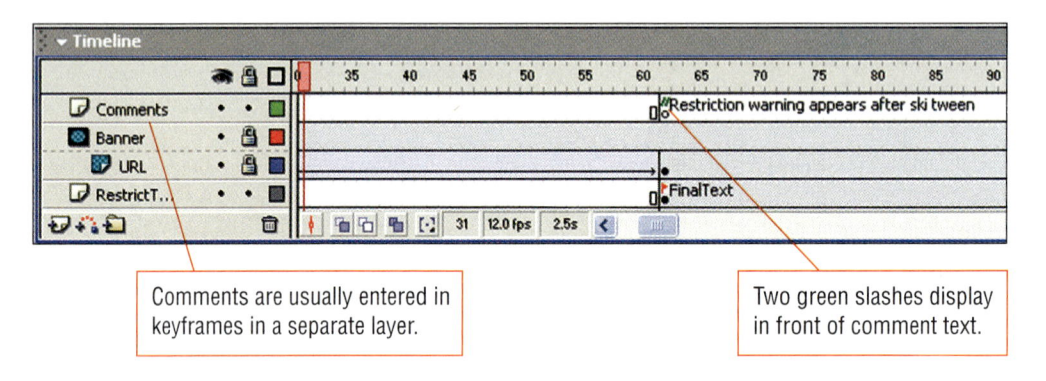

Comments are usually entered in keyframes in a separate layer.

Two green slashes display in front of comment text.

Comments can also be added in long or complex ActionScript code segments using the same technique. For example, in the middle of a group of ActionScript statements, keying two forward slashes in front of text allows you to insert comments. Flash ignores lines beginning with //.

exercise 2

ADDING ACTIONS, FRAME LABELS, AND COMMENTS TO KEYFRAMES

1. Open the Flash document named SunsetVacations.
2. Save the document with Save As and name it Ch7Ex02.
3. The movie contains three scenes and is not yet complete. Click Control and then click Test Movie to preview the animation in the Flash Player window. Turn off the display of the Bandwidth Profiler if it is active as the movie plays. After watching the animation a few times, close the Flash Player window to return to the document.
4. Add a stop action to a keyframe that will stop the movie from playing at the end of the second scene so that the user can decide whether he or she wants to view the island destinations by completing the following steps:
   a. Click the Edit Scene button on the Information bar and then click Main at the drop-down list of scenes. 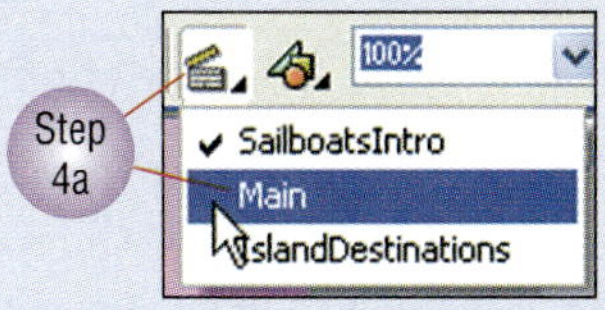
   b. Insert a new layer at the top of the Timeline and name it *Actions*. Organizing actions for keyframes in a separate layer is a good idea for purposes of finding and editing ActionScript at a later time.
   c. Insert a keyframe at frame 30 in the *Actions* layer.
   d. Click Window and then click Actions to open the Actions panel.
   e. Make sure the Current script/Navigate to other scripts text box displays *Actions for Frame 30 of Layer Name Actions*. If it does not display the correct frame, click frame 30 in the *Actions* layer in the Timeline.
   f. With the Movie Control category expanded in the Actions category of the toolbox, double-click stop. The statement *stop ( );* is added to the ActionScript area. Notice also that Flash inserts an *a* at the top of the frame box for frame 30 to indicate that the keyframe contains ActionScript.

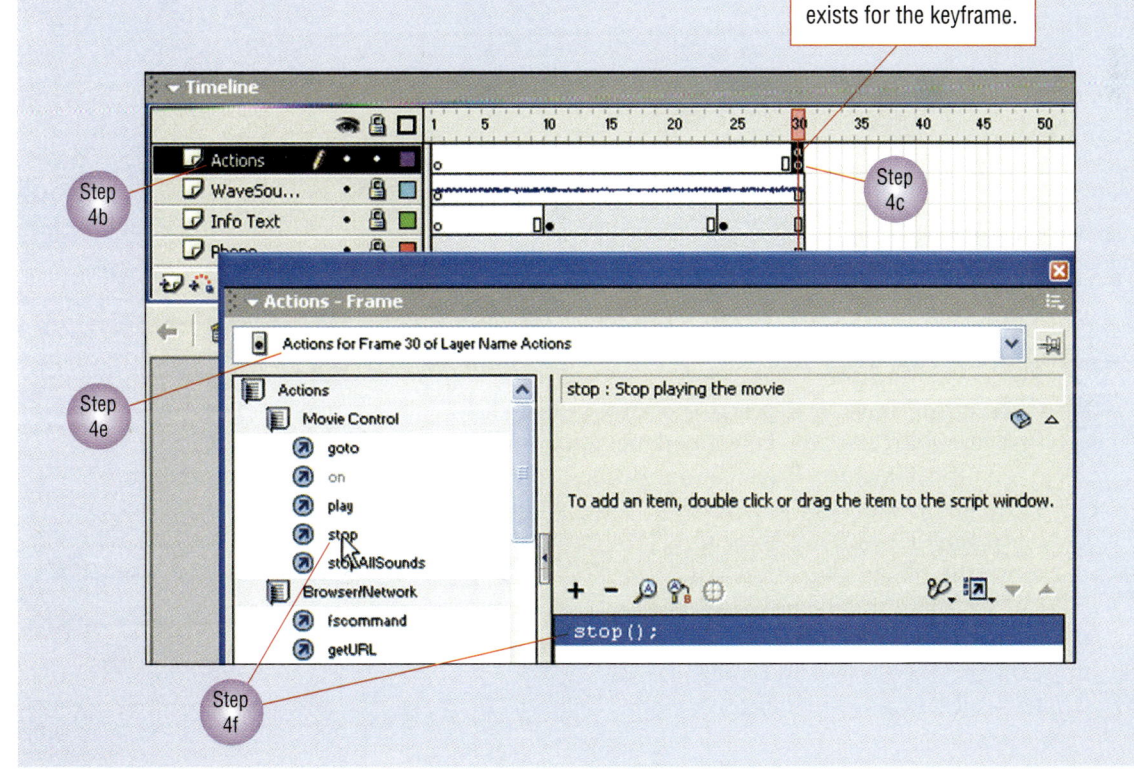

a indicates ActionScript exists for the keyframe.

FLASH MX   Using ActionScript and Creating Templates   **323**

g. Close the Actions panel.
h. Click <u>C</u>ontrol and then click Test <u>M</u>ovie to see the effect of the ActionScript statement. Notice the movie now stops at the end of the second scene. Close the Flash Player window to return to the document.

5. Add a frame label to the keyframe that will be used in the goto statement for the button instance and add comments to keyframes to describe the movie's animation by completing the following steps:
   a. With the Main scene active, insert a new layer at the top of the Timeline and name it *Comments*.
   b. Click frame 1 in the *Comments* layer and then expand the Properties panel.
   c. Click in the Frame text box and then key the following text:

   //Movie stops at frame 30

   d. Click in the stage to deselect the Properties panel. The comment text appears in the Timeline with two green slashes at the beginning of the text. 
   e. Click Edit Scene and then click IslandDestinations.
   f. Insert a new layer at the top of the Timeline and name it *Actions*.
   g. Insert a new layer above *Actions* and name it *Comments*.
   h. Insert a keyframe at frame 33 in the *Actions* layer, open the Actions panel, insert a stop statement, and then close the Actions panel.
   i. Insert the following text as a comment in frame 1 of the *Comments* layer.

   //Movie stops at frame 33

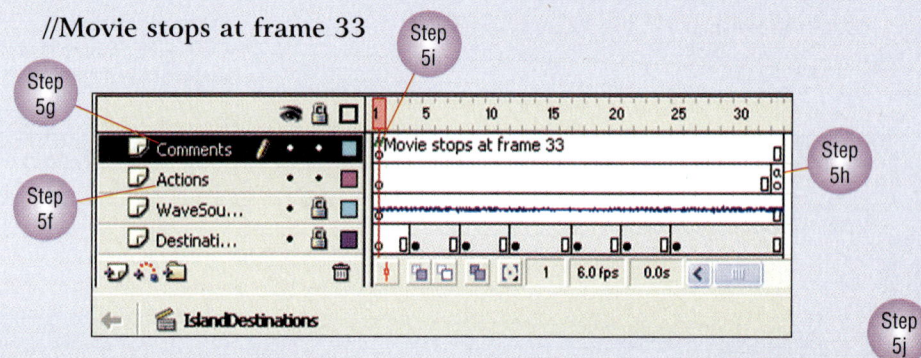

   j. Click frame 1 in the *Destinations* layer, click in the Frame text box in the Properties panel and then key **StartDestinations**. 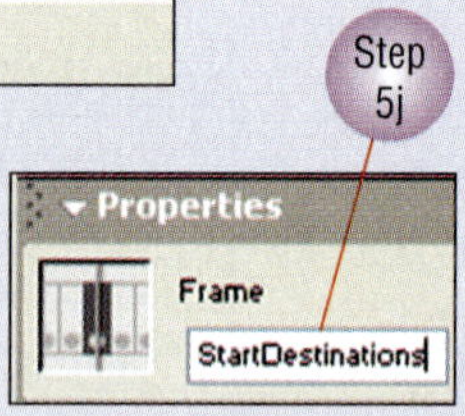
   k. Click in the stage to deselect the Properties panel. The first few characters of the frame label appear next to a red flag in the Timeline. Flash cannot display the entire label since there is not enough space before the next keyframe.
   l. Click frame 20 in any layer to move the playhead so that you can see the frame label in frame 1 of the *Destinations* layer.
   m. Collapse the Properties panel.
   n. Lock all layers in the current scene.

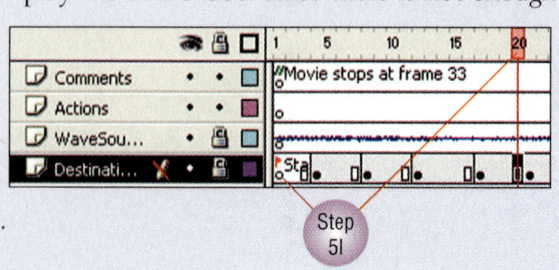

324 Chapter Seven

6. Add the goto statement to the button instance in the Main scene that will move the playhead to the frame label StartDestinations by completing the following steps:
   a. Click Edit Scene and then click Main.
   b. If necessary, scroll down the Timeline until you can see the *Button* layer and then unlock the layer.
   c. Click frame 6 in the *Button* layer to display the button instance.
   d. Open the Actions panel.
   e. If necessary, drag the Actions panel to the top of the window so that you can see the button instance on the stage and then click the button instance. Flash displays *Actions for [No instance name assigned] (IslandButton)* in the Current script/Navigate to other scripts text box.
   f. Double-click goto in the toolbox.
   g. With Go to and Play already active in the Parameters area, click the down arrow next to the Scene list box and then click IslandDestinations at the drop-down list.
   h. Click the down arrow next to the Type list box and then click Frame Label at the drop-down list.
   i. Click the down arrow next to the Frame text box and then click StartDestinations at the drop-down list.
   j. Click the right scroll arrow at the bottom of the ActionScript area to view the entire ActionScript that has been entered and compare it with the following ActionScript. *(Note: The current line is also displayed in the status bar of the Actions panel.)* Scene names and label names are entered in ActionScript between double quotation symbols.

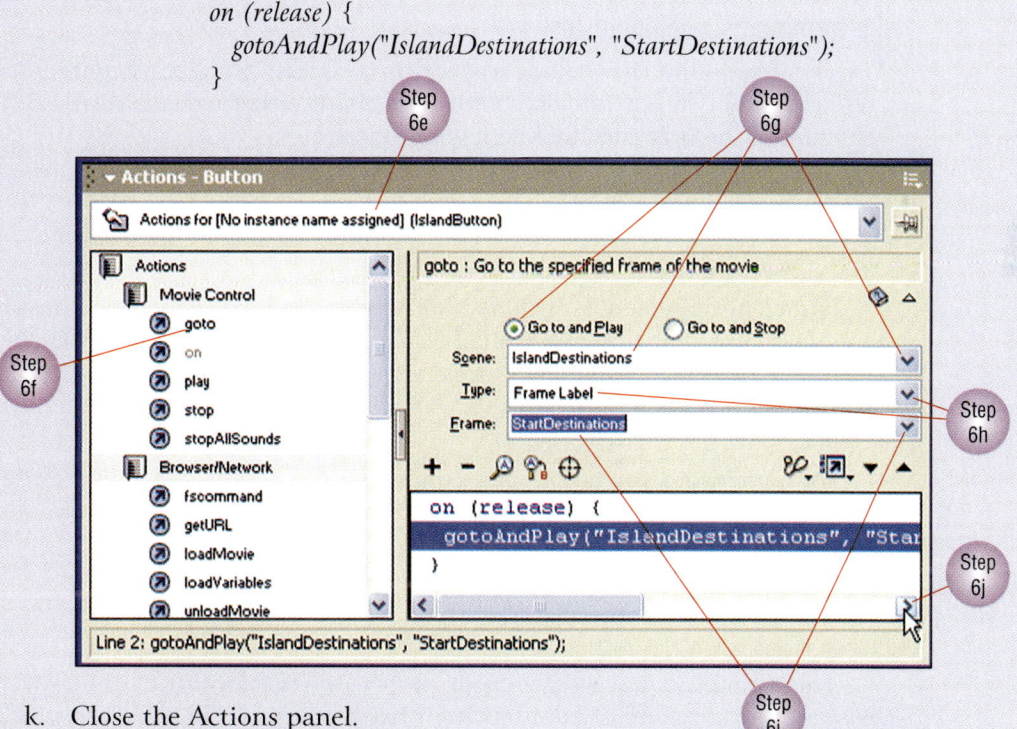

   ```
   on (release) {
       gotoAndPlay("IslandDestinations", "StartDestinations");
   }
   ```

   k. Close the Actions panel.
   l. Lock all layers in the scene.
7. Test the movie in the Flash Player window. When the movie stops at the end of the second scene, click the View Destinations button. Close the Flash Player window when the animation is complete.
8. Save the revised document using the same name (Ch7Ex02).
9. Close Ch7Ex02.

Creating a Preloader Animation

In the last chapter you learned how to test a movie's download performance at various speeds and to simulate a Web connection download. If, after testing and optimizing a movie, you still have several seconds of preload time in which the user would be waiting for frames to download, a solution that is often used is to add a preloader. A *preloader* is a simple animation that includes a small number of frames with minimal content at the beginning of a movie that loops until the remainder of the movie is downloaded. In Exercise 3 you will complete all of the steps to create a preloader. The key concepts of a preloader include:

- A small animation exists at the beginning of a movie that contains simple text such as a Loading message.
- ActionScript is added at the end of the preload animation that causes Flash to return to the first frame and replay the preloader. This creates a loop.
- ActionScript is added at the first frame in the preloader that performs a conditional test. The test checks if all of the frames have been downloaded. If the test returns a true result (meaning all frames have been downloaded), the playhead moves to the frame after the preloader animation frames. If the test is false, the preloader animation continues playing. The conditional test in frame 1 causes Flash to check the status of the download at the beginning of each looped preload animation.

Performing a Conditional Test

Use the if action in the toolbox to perform a conditional test. A conditional test can have only two possible outcomes—the test is either true or it is false. The structure of the if action statement is as follows:

```
if (conditional test) {
    action to be performed if test is true
}
```

Notice no statement is included for what to do if the conditional test result is false. Flash executes the statements between the left and right curly braces only if the test proves true. If the test proves false, Flash ignores the actions inside the curly braces and then moves to the next action statement if one exists beyond the if block.

For a preloader animation, an example of an if action that would cause Flash to check if all of the frames have been downloaded written in words would be:

```
if (frames loaded = all frames) {
    gotoAndPlay(main movie);
}
```

This example is not written using proper ActionScript. It does however illustrate the structure of an if block. In Exercise 3 you will use a proper if action.

Adding an Else Statement

The basic if action does not provide for a place to tell Flash what to do if the test proves false. Flash simply ignores everything within the if action if the conditional test is false and moves to the next action statement outside of the if block. In some cases, this might not be satisfactory and you will want to specify an action to perform if the test is false. For example, if the line of code following the if block is a statement you want executed regardless of the results of the conditional test, you will need to specify the false operation within the if block. To do this, add an else action immediately after the if action. Following is an example of if/else actions for a preloader written in words:

> *if (frames loaded = all frames) {*
>   *gotoAndPlay(main movie);*
> *} else {*
>   *gotoAndPlay(preloader animation);*
> *}*

Nesting If Statements

If you need to perform a test that has more than two possible outcomes, add an else if action after the initial if block. This is referred to as *nesting if actions*. For example, suppose you want one preloader animation to play while the first 10 frames are downloaded and then another animation to play while the remainder of the frames are downloaded. In this example, you need to test and then execute actions using the following logic (assume the preload animation for the first 10 frames is called *A* and the second preload animation is called *B*):

- Have all frames been downloaded? If yes, play the main movie.
- If no, have frames 1–10 been downloaded? If yes, play preload animation *B*.
- If no, play preload animation *A*.

Following is an example of if/else if actions for the preloader written in words:

> *if (frames loaded = all frames) {*
>   *gotoAndPlay(main movie);*
> *} else if (frames loaded > 10) {*
>   *gotoAndPlay(preloader animation B);*
> *} else {*
>   *gotoAndPlay(preloader animation A);*
> *}*

When you are building nested if blocks it is always wise to test the logic using different scenarios and see if the appropriate action will be performed. For example, assume that the number of frames loaded is 15 when Flash encounters the beginning of the if block. In this scenario Flash would return a false result for the first conditional test *if (frames loaded = all frames)*. Since the test is false Flash moves to the next statement after the right curly brace in the first if block. Here Flash would encounter the else if block that tells Flash to perform another conditional test *else if (frames loaded > 10)*. This test would return a true result which causes Flash to execute the action after the else if left curly brace which is *gotoAndPlay(preloader animation B)*.

Testing for Status of Frames Loaded

Each movie Timeline has a group of properties that can be checked or changed while the movie is playing. In a preloader, you need Flash to check if all of the frames in the Timeline have been downloaded. To enable you to perform this conditional test Flash maintains the following two properties for each Timeline:

- *framesloaded*. This property returns a value representing the number of frames that have been loaded.
- *totalframes*. This property returns a value representing the total number of frames within the movie or movie clip.

A conditional test using these two properties that would check if all of the frames have been downloaded would be:

(_framesloaded == _totalframes)

In ActionScript, properties are identified with an underscore character at the beginning of the property name and two equals symbols (called the *equality operator*) are required to tell Flash to check if the value for the property on the left equals the value for the property on the right. If only one equals sign is used, Flash thinks you are trying to update the value on the left.

exercise 3

CREATING A PRELOADER ANIMATION AND PERFORMING A CONDITIONAL TEST

1. Open the Flash document named ClownNRound.
2. Save the document with Save As and name it Ch7Ex03.
3. Change the magnification to 80%. If necessary, scroll so that the stage is centered within the Flash window.
4. The movie's animation resides in a movie clip symbol containing 259 frames inserted in the keyframe in the *Clown* layer. Simulate a Web connection to see if downloading the movie clip is long enough that a preloader should be created by completing the following steps:
   a. Click Control and then click Test Movie.
   b. Click Debug and then click 14.4 (1.2KB/s) at the drop-down menu. Testing at the slowest modem speed will let you experience the worst possible download performance.
   c. Click View and then click Bandwidth Profiler. The left pane of the Bandwidth Profiler indicates a user would be waiting 21.7 seconds before the movie clip starts to play.
   d. Click View and then click Show Streaming to complete a simulation of a Web download at the current 14.4 modem speed. You decide after the simulation that a simple preloader animation would add value to the movie for the end user.
   e. Close the Flash Player window to return to the document.
5. Create the preloader animation frames by completing the following steps:
   a. Insert a new layer at the top of the Timeline and name it *Preloader*.
   b. Insert frames in frame boxes 2–12 for all three layers.
   c. Cut and paste the content in frame 1 of the *Text* layer to frame 12 of the *Text* layer.
   d. Select frames 2–11 in the *Text* layer and then clear the frames.
   e. Repeat Steps 5c–5d for the *Clown* layer. When you are finished this step, frames 1–11 in the *Text* and *Clown* layers are empty, and frames 1–12 in the *Preloader* layer are empty.

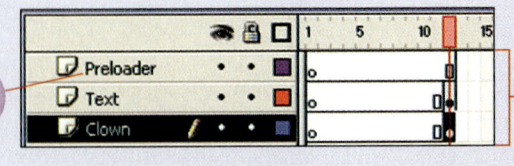

f. Click frame 12 in the *Text* layer.
g. With all three text blocks selected, click <u>E</u>dit and then click <u>C</u>opy.
h. Click frame 1 in the *Preloader* layer, click <u>E</u>dit, and then click Paste <u>i</u>n Place.
i. Click in the workspace to deselect the text blocks.
j. Use the drawing tools to create the text and rectangle on the stage as shown. The font name is Verdana and the font size is 16. You determine any other text properties to use.
k. Insert a keyframe in frame 12 of the *Preloader* layer.
l. Delete the text and rectangle created in Step 5j in frame 12 of the *Preloader* layer.
m. Press Enter to play the preloader animation on the stage.

6. Add ActionScript to loop the preloader animation until all of the movie's frames have downloaded and document the preloader using comment text by completing the following steps:
   a. Insert a new layer at the top of the Timeline and name it *Actions*.
   b. Insert a new layer above *Actions* and name it *Comments*.
   c. Click frame 1 in the *Comments* layer, expand the Properties panel, and then key //**Preloader - 1s** in the Frame text box.
   d. Collapse the Properties panel.
   e. Insert a keyframe at frame 11 in the *Actions* layer
   f. Open the Actions panel.
   g. With the Movie Control action list expanded below Actions, double-click goto in the toolbox with *Actions for Frame 11 of Layer Name Actions* in the Current script/Navigate to other scripts text box, Go to and <u>P</u>lay active and 1 in the <u>F</u>rame text box in the Parameters area. This action will create a loop in which frames 1–11 will continually replay.
   h. Click frame 1 in the *Actions* layer. Flash changes the entry in the Current script/Navigate to other scripts text box to *Actions for Frame 1 of Layer Name Actions*. Create a conditional test that will move the playhead to frame 12 when all of the frames have been downloaded by completing the following steps:

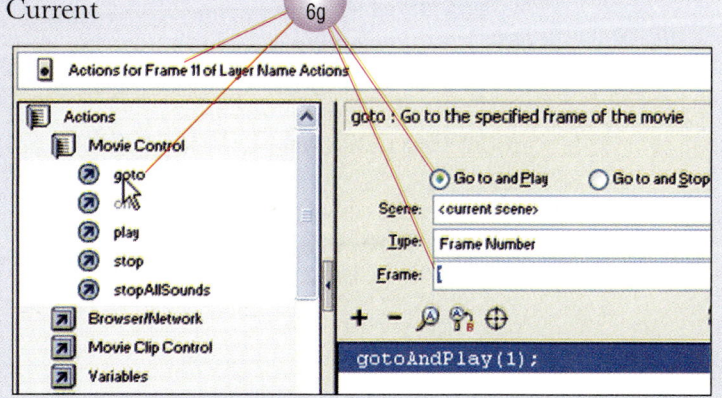

1) Click Conditions/Loops in the Actions category list in the toolbox to expand the subcategory list.
2) If necessary, scroll down the toolbox and then double-click if. Flash inserts *if (<not set yet>) {* in the ActionScript area and displays the Condition text box in the Parameters area. Flash highlights in red code that is not complete—<not set yet> is in red because you have not entered the conditional test.
3) With an insertion point positioned in the Condition text box, scroll down the toolbox and then click Properties to expand the Properties category list.
4) Double-click _framesloaded in the toolbox. Flash adds _framesloaded to the Condition text box.
5) Click in the Condition text box after _framesloaded, key a space, and then key two equals signs (==).
6) If necessary, scroll down the toolbox and then double-click _totalframes. The entry in the Condition text box now reads as follows:

    _framesloaded == _totalframes

7) Scroll up the toolbox, expand the Actions category, expand the Movie Control category, and then double-click goto.
8) Key **12** in the Frame text box in the Parameters area with Go to and Play active. Compare the if statement in the ActionScript area with the image shown.

i. Click frame 12 in the *Actions* layer.

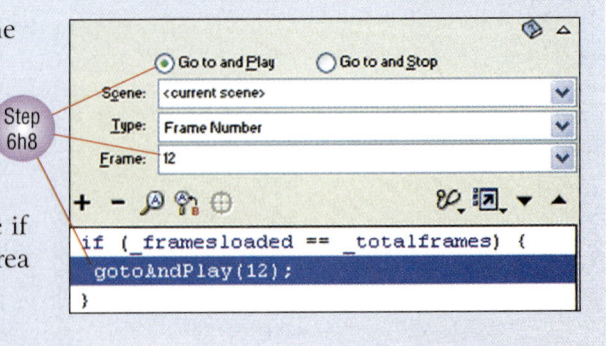

> j. Double-click stop in the toolbox. Flash adds the statement *stop( );* to the ActionScript area. The movie's animation resides entirely within the Clown movie clip inserted in frame 12 of the *Clown* layer. This step causes Flash to stop playing the main movie Timeline which contains only the preloader animation and the move clip instance. As you learned in Chapter 6, a movie clip timeline is independent of the main movie Timeline and continues to play after the main movie Timeline is complete.
> k. Close the Actions panel.
> 7. Test the movie by simulating a Web connection at all three modem speeds to view the preload animation by completing steps similar to those in Step 4.
> 8. Save the revised document using the same name (Ch7Ex03).
> 9. Close Ch7Ex03.

The preloader animation created in Exercise 3 is based on checking if all frames have been downloaded. More sophisticated preloaders display a progress bar showing the download status or a countdown counter. Additionally, in most cases you do not have to wait for the entire movie to download before playback can begin and continue smoothly without time lags. In those instances, you could use the _framesloaded property to test for a value that represents the number of frames that have been downloaded that you know means the bulk of the content. is now available for playback. If the test is true then you can stop the preload and move the playhead to the main movie animation. For example, assume through testing a movie you know that after the first 125 frames are downloaded, the playback does not encounter any time lags. The conditional test *if (_framesloaded >= 125)* would allow you to end the preload and start playing the main movie while the remaining frames are streamed.

Using Buttons to Toggle the Playing of a Soundtrack On and Off

You learned how to add sound to a movie and how to apply the stopAllSounds action to a button in Chapter 5. A sound effect may not always be best treated as an on/off option. In addition, the stopAllSounds action will not prevent the playback of streamed sounds positioned later in a movie's Timeline. This means the user would have to click the stop sound button a second time to mute a sound that occurs later.

In some cases you might want the user to have the ability to temporarily stop sound and then turn it back on. For example, someone watching a movie may want the sound to stop while they answer a telephone call but then be able to turn the sound back on when the call is finished.

A solution to these situations is to create buttons that will toggle the sound on or off as the user desires. In order for this technique to work, the soundtrack must be created with synchronization as stream. As you learned in Chapter 5, event sounds play when started until they are complete regardless of the movie Timeline. Secondly, the soundtrack has to be added to the movie using a movie clip symbol with the movie clip playback controlled using ActionScript.

Inserting the soundtrack in a movie clip allows the Timeline for the soundtrack to be controlled independent of the main movie. The ActionScript statement *with* is required to direct Flash to the target object of the stop and play actions. Since stop and play would stop and play the main movie, you need a method in which to tell Flash to stop and play a movie clip Timeline.

With Statement

Naming an instance of a movie clip symbol allows the movie clip to be treated as a separate object which can be the target of movie control actions such as stop and play. The structure of a with ActionScript statement using words to describe each segment is as follows:

with (name of movie clip symbol instance) {
    action to be performed ( );
}

As an example of how this applies to our sound solution, assume you have inserted a stream sound file in a movie clip symbol, assigned the name *soundtrack* to the instance you placed on the stage, and have inserted two button instances on the stage, one of which will start the sound and the other which will stop the sound. With the start button selected, the following ActionScript would tell Flash to start playing the sound upon pressing and releasing the mouse over the button:

on (release) {
    with (soundtrack) {
        play ( );
    }
}

Notice two sets of curly braces are required in the ActionScript. The first set of braces define the beginning and ending actions for the mouse event *on release*. The inner set of curly braces define the beginning and ending of the with action.

exercise 4
CREATING A SOUNDTRACK IN A MOVIE CLIP SYMBOL AND ADDING A STOP SOUND AND START SOUND BUTTON

1. Open the Flash document named DanceArt.
2. Save the document with Save As and name it Ch7Ex04.
3. This document uses the same masked animation created in Chapter 6, however, it also has a streaming soundtrack added. Click Control then Test Movie to play the animation and listen to the soundtrack. Close the Flash Player window to return to the document.
4. Edit the movie to remove the sound track from the existing frames and insert a streamed sound in a movie clip symbol with ActionScript statements to control the playback by completing the following steps:
    a. Click frame 1 in the *Soundtrack* layer and then expand the Properties panel.
    b. Click the down arrow next to the Sound list box and then click None at the drop-down list.
    c. Select frames 2–50 in the *Soundtrack* layer and then remove the frames.
    d. Click Insert and then click New Symbol.

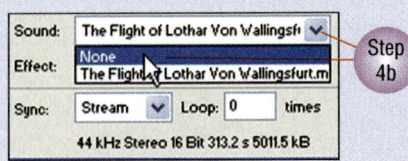

e. Key **Soundtrack** in the Name text box, make sure Movie Clip is active in the Behavior section of the Create New Symbol dialog box, and then click OK.
f. Open the Actions panel with the stage in symbol editing mode for the Soundtrack movie clip.
g. Click frame 1 in the movie clip's timeline and then double-click the stop action in the toolbox. This will prevent the soundtrack from playing unless the user clicks the start sound button to be added later.
h. Collapse the Actions panel, click frame 2 in the Timeline, and then insert a blank keyframe.
i. Open the Library panel, drag an instance of *The Flight of Lothar Von Wallingsfurt.mp3* to the stage as shown, and then close the Library panel.

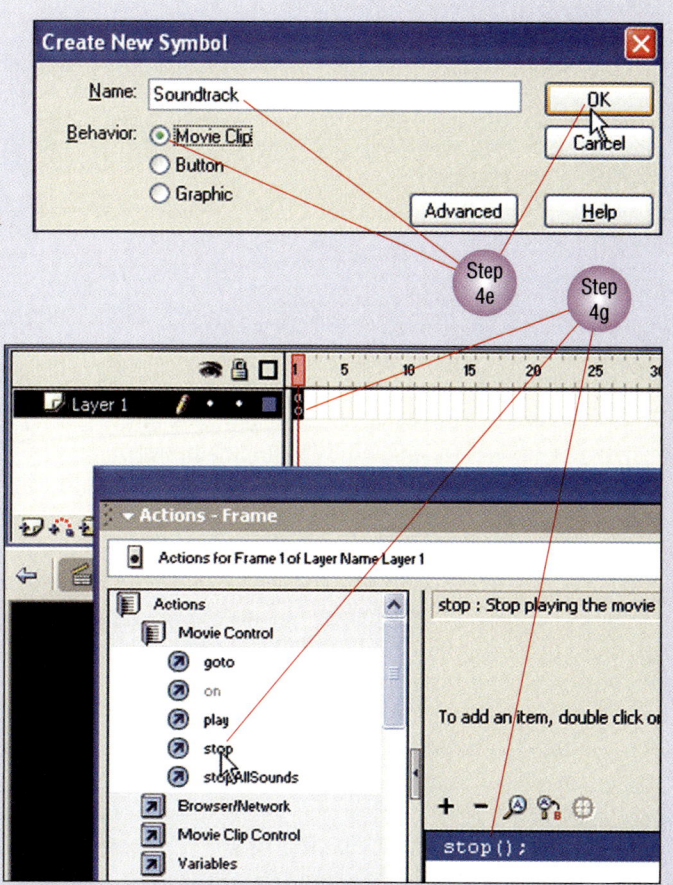

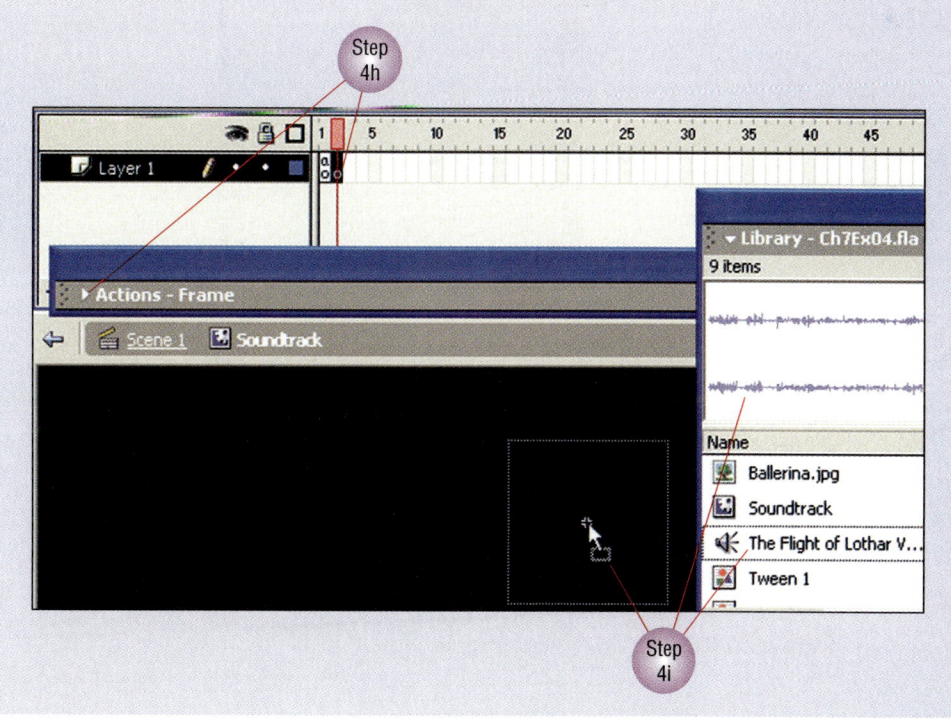

Using ActionScript and Creating Templates   333

j. Expand the Properties panel and then complete the following steps:
   1) Click frame 2 and then assign a frame label with the text *Start*.
   2) Make sure Sync sound is set to Stream.

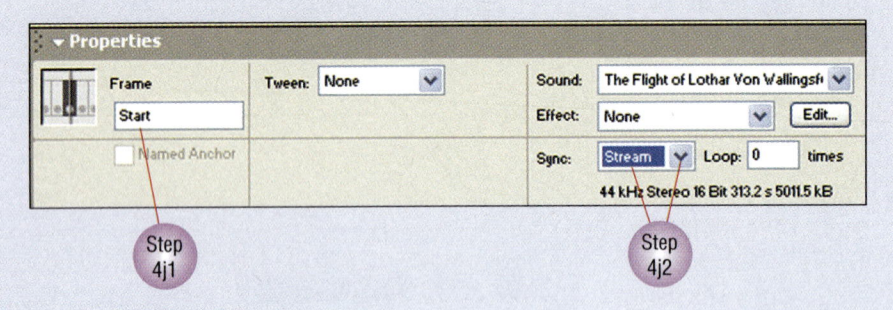

   Step 4j1
   Step 4j2

   3) Collapse the Properties panel.
k. Right-click frame 300 in the Timeline and then click Insert frame. This will add enough frames in the Timeline to play the soundtrack for 25 seconds.
l. Insert a keyframe at frame 300, expand the Actions panel, and then double-click goto. With Go to and Play active, click the down arrow next to Type and then click Frame Label. Click the down arrow next to Frame and then click Start. The statement *gotoAndPlay ("Start");* will cause the soundtrack to loop back to the beginning if the user watches the movie for more than 25 seconds with the sound playing.
m. Collapse the Actions panel.
n. Exit symbol editing mode.

5. Create buttons that the user can click to toggle the soundtrack playback on and off by completing the following steps:
   a. Unlock the *Soundtrack* layer in the Timeline and then click frame 1.
   b. Display the Buttons common library panel.
   c. Expand the Arcade buttons folder, drag an instance of *arcade button – red* and *arcade button – green* to the stage, and then close the Buttons common library panel.
   d. Move and scale the button instances to the approximate size and location shown.
   e. Use the text tool to create two text blocks that overlay the buttons containing the text shown. *(Hint: You will need to use a small font size and decrease line spacing to 0 points to fit the text within the area over the top of the button.)*

   Step 5d
   Step 5e

6. Insert an instance of the Soundtrack movie clip symbol to the stage, assign a name to the instance, and then add stop and play actions to the buttons that will target the soundtrack movie clip object by completing the following steps:
   a. With frame 1 in the *Soundtrack* layer active, open the Library panel.
   b. Drag an instance of the *Soundtrack* movie clip symbol to stage.

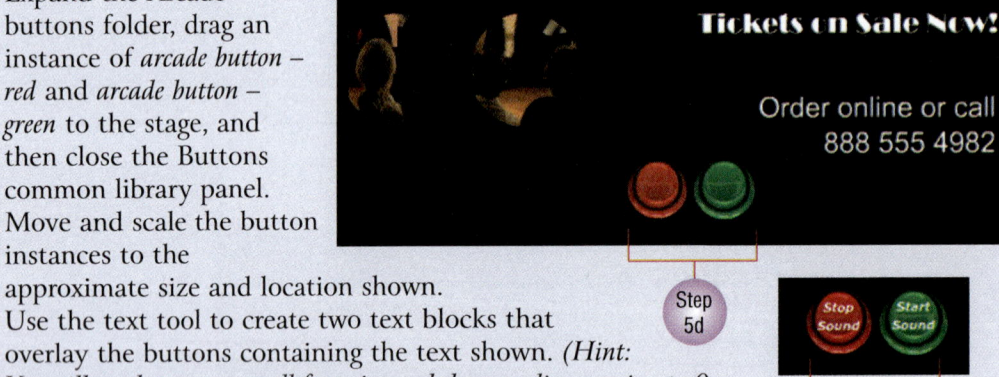

334 Chapter Seven

c. Expand the Properties panel. Click in the Instance Name text box and then key **Soundclip**. Recall from Chapter 6 that a movie clip instance has to be assigned a name in order to become the target object in ActionScript. 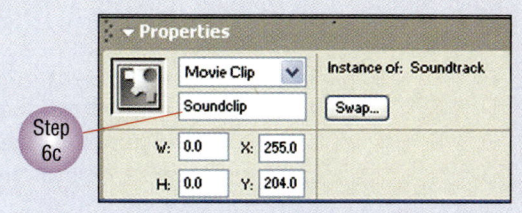
d. Close the Library panel and collapse the Properties panel.
e. Expand the Actions panel.
f. Click the button instance for the green button symbol. Make sure you activate the button instance and not the text overlay.
g. Expand the Variables subcategory list in the Actions category of the toolbox.
h. Double-click with in the Variables list in the toolbox.
i. With the insertion point positioned in the Object text box, key **Soundclip**. 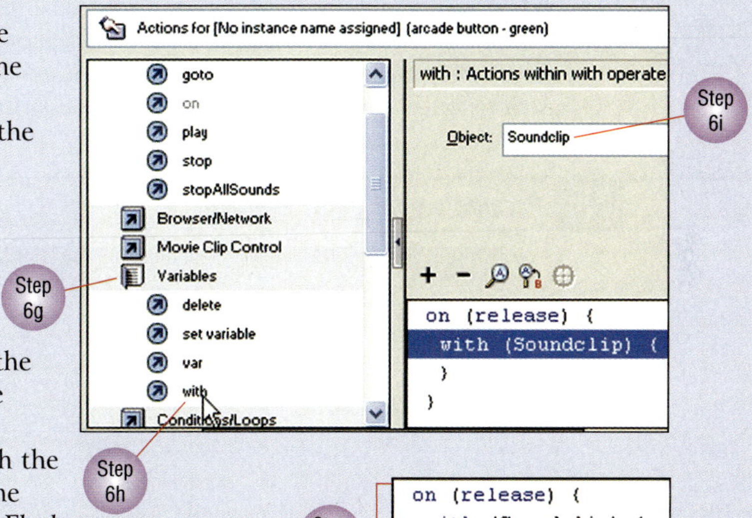
j. Double-click play in the toolbox. Compare the statements in the ActionScript area with the statements shown. The statements will cause Flash to start playing the Soundclip movie clip when the user clicks the green button. With statements allow you to specify to which object the next action in the script is targeted. 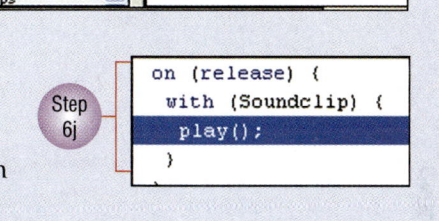
k. Click the button instance for the red button symbol.
l. Double-click with in the toolbox.
m. With the insertion point positioned in the Object text box, key **Soundclip**.
n. Double-click stop in the toolbox. Compare the statements in the ActionScript area with the statements shown. The statements will cause Flash to stop playing the movie clip when the user clicks the red button.
o. Close the Actions panel.
p. Insert a keyframe at frame 50 in the *Soundtrack* layer. This step ensures the two buttons created in Step 5 display during the movie's duration.
q. Lock the *Soundtrack* layer.

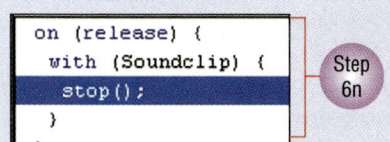

7. Test the movie in the Flash Player window. If necessary, turn off the display of the Bandwidth Profiler to view more of the stage in order to see the buttons. Click the Start Sound button and Stop Sound button a few times to test the actions.
8. Close the Flash Player window to return to the document.
9. Save the revised document using the same name (Ch7Ex04).
10. Close Ch7Ex04.

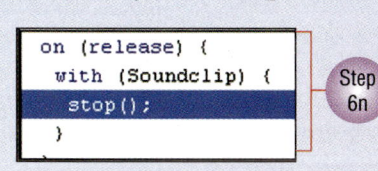

Using the getURL Action to Open a Web Page During a Movie

The getURL action within the Browser/Network category of Actions in the toolbox can be used to load a new document from a Web address while playing a Flash movie. The document loaded can be a Web page, another Flash movie file, an ftp site, or any other document. Using getURL to load a Web page during a movie is like creating a hyperlink.

The document loaded can replace the movie in the current browser window or open in a separate window. The URL (Uniform Resource Locator) used to define the location of the document to be loaded can be specified using an absolute address such as **http://www.macromedia.com** or a relative address such as NewPage.htm. When using a relative address you must ensure that the Web page is stored within the same location as the Flash movie on the Web server hosting the movie so that the page will be found when requested. Double-clicking getURL in the Actions panel displays the parameters shown in Figure 7.10.

FIGURE 7.10 *Parameters for getURL Action*

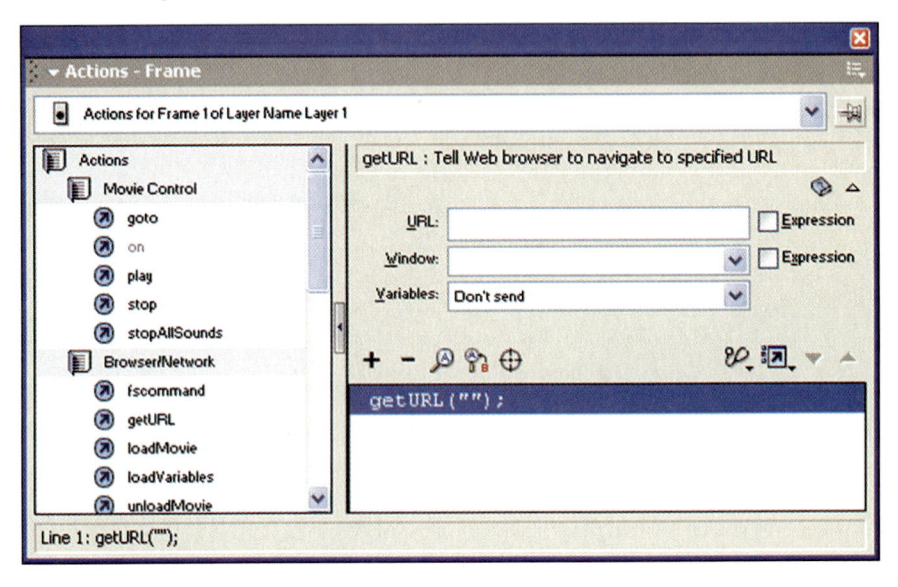

Key the absolute or relative document address in the URL text box. Leave the Expression check box next to the URL text box unchecked in order for Flash to treat the entry as a text string. Click the down arrow next to Window to choose from the following options that specify how the document will be launched from the movie's window:

- _self. The document opens within the current window replacing the movie from which it originated.
- _blank. The document opens in a new browser window.
- _parent. The document opens in the browser in the parent of the current frame.
- _top. The document opens in the top-level frame of the current browser window.

The default option for the Variables parameter is Don't send. The getURL action can be used to make a movie function like a submission form in which information is sent from a Flash movie to a Web server. In this case, Flash provides the Send using GET or Send using POST methods in which the variables can be transmitted.

Assume you are creating a Flash movie in which the user will be able to click a button to browse to an external Web site with the URL **http://www.emcp.com/online**. The getURL attached to the button instance would contain the following ActionScript if you wanted the Web site opened in a window separate from the Flash movie so that the user could close the window after browsing the Web site and return to where they left off:

getURL("http://www.emcp.com/online", "_blank");

exercise 5

USING GETURL TO OPEN A WEB PAGE

1. Open Ch7Ex02.
2. Convert the first island destination text to a button symbol and then edit the symbol including defining a hit state and adding a click sound effect by completing the following steps:
    a. If necessary, change the current scene to IslandDestinations.
    b. Unlock the layer named *Destinations*.
    c. Click frame 33 in the *Destinations* layer and then click in the workspace to deselect the text blocks.
    d. With the Arrow tool active, click the first text block on the stage.
    e. Click Insert and then click Convert to Symbol.
    f. Key **OceanView** in the Name text box in the Convert to Symbol dialog box, click Button in the Behavior section, and then click OK.
    g. Double-click *7 days at OceanView Resort, Dominican Republic* to edit the button in symbol editing mode. 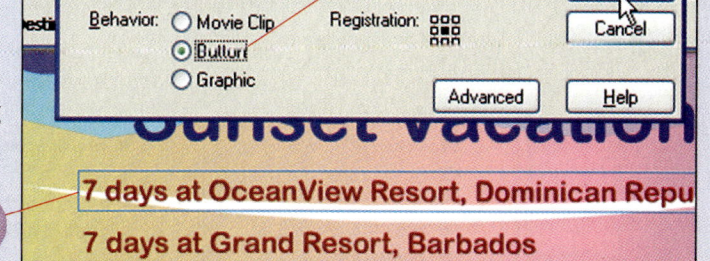 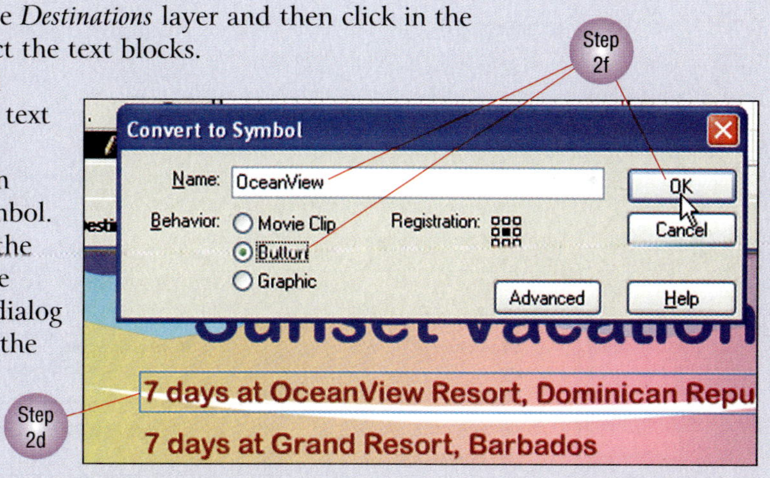
    h. Insert a keyframe in the Over state in the button symbol Timeline.
    i. With the text block selected, change the fill color to a dark blue color swatch similar to the one shown. 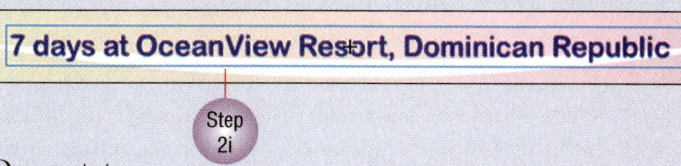
    j. Insert a keyframe in the Down state.
    k. With the text block selected, change the fill color to a bright orange color swatch.
    l. Insert a new layer at the top of the Timeline and name it *Sound*.
    m. Open the Library panel.
    n. Insert a keyframe in the Down state of the *Sound* layer. Drag an instance of *CLICK12A.wav* to the stage and then close the Library panel.

Using ActionScript and Creating Templates 337

o. Insert a keyframe in the Hit state.
p. Click the Rectangle tool and then draw a rectangle covering the text block as shown. Drawing a rectangle over the text block means the mouse pointer will respond as a link when pointing anywhere within the area of the rectangle. In other words, the mouse does not have to be directly over a character in the block. *(Hint: You may have to turn off the snap to grid feature if you have difficulty placing the rectangle over the text as shown.)*
q. Exit symbol editing mode.
3. Attach the getURL ActionScript to the button instance by completing the following steps:
    a. Open the Actions panel.
    b. If necessary, drag the Actions panel up or down until you can see the button instance on the stage and then click the button instance. This inserts *Actions for [No instance name assigned] (OceanView)* in the Current script/Navigate to other scripts text box.
    c. Expand the Browser/Network subcategory list in the Actions category list in the toolbox.
    d. Double-click getURL.
    e. With the insertion point positioned in the URL text box key **OceanView.htm**.
    f. Click the down arrow next to the Window list box and then click _blank at the drop-down list. The statements in the ActionScript area appear as follows:

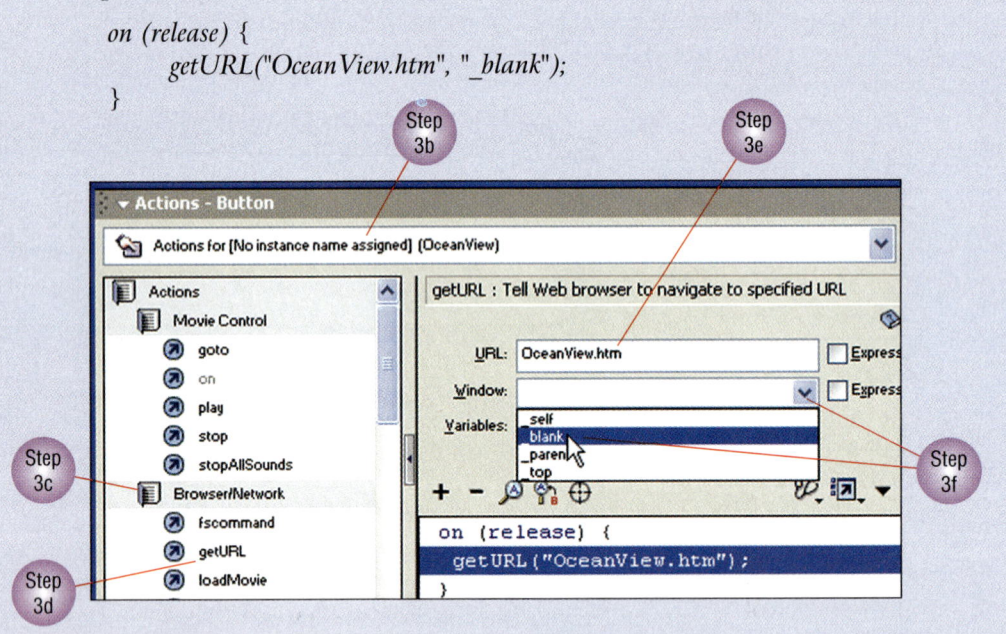

    on (release) {
        getURL("OceanView.htm", "_blank");
    }

    g. Close the Actions panel.
4. Save the revised document using the same name (Ch7Ex02).
5. Test the movie including clicking the View Island Destinations button and then the first destination to view the Web page in a separate browser window. Close the browser window and then close the Flash Player window.
6. Publish the movie as HTML and as a projector file and then test the link in both files by completing the following steps:
    a. Click File and then click Publish Settings.

b. If necessary, click the Formats tab in the Publish Settings dialog box.
c. Click the Windows Projecter (.exe) check box.
d. Click the Publish button.

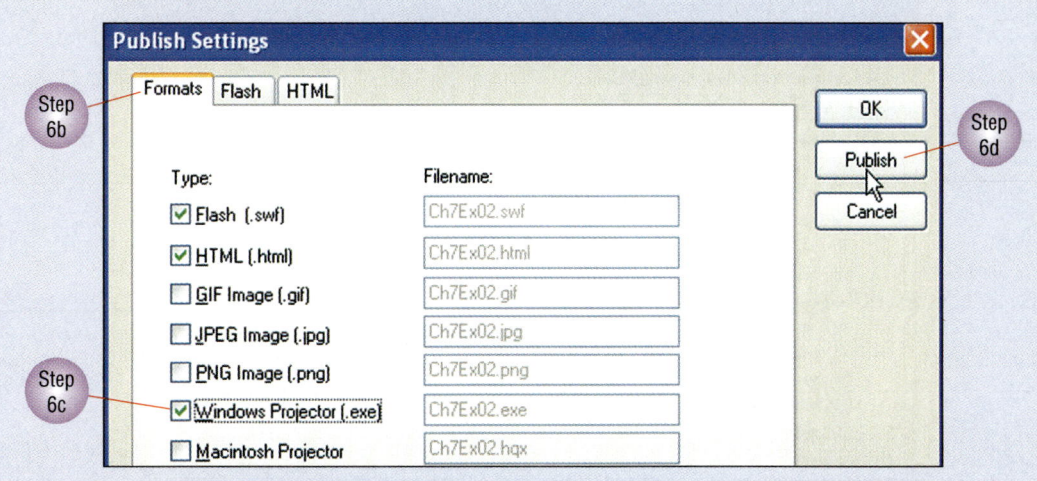

Step 6b → Formats tab
Step 6d → Publish button
Step 6c → Windows Projector (.exe)

e. Click OK when the Publishing dialog box closes to close the Publish Settings dialog box.
f. Open Windows Explorer.
g. Navigate to the drive and folder in which the data files for Chapter 7 are stored.
h. Double-click the file named Ch7Ex02.html. Click the View Island Destinations button and then the first destination to view the Web page in a separate browser window. Close the browser window for OceanView.htm and then close the browser window for Ch7Ex02.
i. Double-click the file named Ch7Ex02.exe. Test the movie in the projector file. Close the browser window for OceanView.htm and then close the Flash Player window.
j. Exit Windows Explorer.
7. Close Ch7Ex02. Click Yes when prompted to save changes.

Using the fscommand to Control the Player Window

The fscommand action within the Browser/Network category of Actions in the toolbox can be used to control the environment in which the movie is being played. These actions send commands to the browser or standalone projector. Another common technique is to use fscommand to relay information to JavaScript on Web pages by sending to the browser text strings that represent commands or variables.

If the intended output of your Flash movie is to run it as a standalone projector in the Flash Player window, six commands available by clicking the down arrow next to the Commands for standalone player list box in the Parameters area shown in Figure 7.11 allow you control over the Flash Player application. Table 7.1 lists each command and describes how it can be used to control the player window.

Using ActionScript and Creating Templates 339

FIGURE 7.11 **Parameters for fscommand Action**

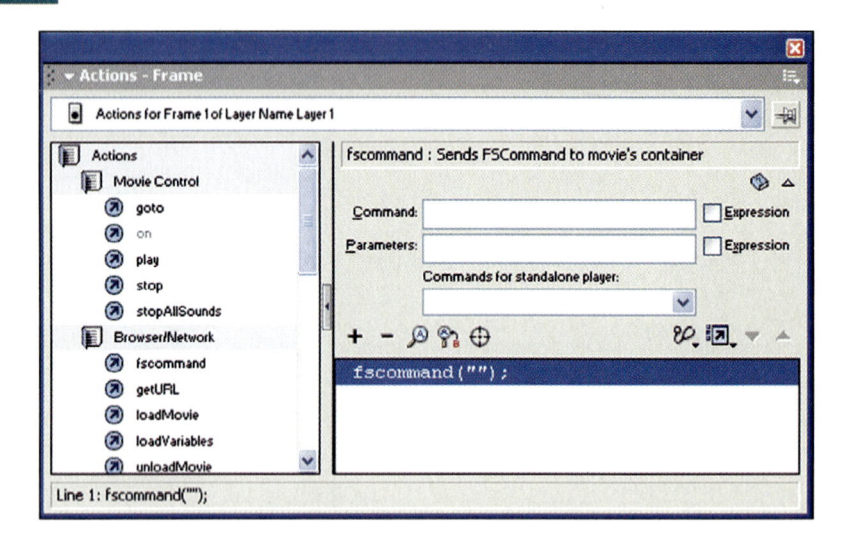

TABLE 7.1 *fscommands for Projector Files*

fscommand	Parameters	Description
fullscreen	true or false	Use true to scale the Flash Player window to a full screen or false to leave the window at its normal size.
allowscale	true or false	Controls scaling of the movie within the player window. Use true to always scale the movie to 100% of the player window size. If a user resizes the player window, the movie within the player window will resize proportionately. Specifying false tells the player that the movie should always be drawn at its original size and never scaled.
showmenu	true or false	True enables the full set of options on the Menu bar to be active by right-clicking in the player window while false dims all of the items except About Flash Player.
trapallkeys	true or false	A true parameter means keys pressed on the keyboard are passed to the movie instead of the player application while false sends the keystrokes to the player window.
exec	provide path to *exe* or *com* file	Opens an executable file within the player window.
quit	n/a	Quits the projector. Use this if you have disabled the menus by inserting the quit command at the end of the movie.

Insert the desired fscommands in a keyframe at the beginning of the movie to specify the environment in which the movie is contained. To use the quit command, insert the fscommand at the end of the movie to close the player window at the last frame. Clicking one of the predefined commands using the down arrow next to Commands for standalone player will insert the command name in the Command text box and the default setting of true or false in the Parameters text box. Click in the Parameters text box to change a true value to false or vice versa.

exercise 6 — SENDING FSCOMMANDS TO CONTROL THE FLASH PLAYER WINDOW

1. Open Ch7Ex04.
2. Save the document with Save As and name it Ch7Ex06.
3. Increase the duration of the movie by adding frames to prepare the movie for playback in a standalone player window by completing the following steps:
   a. Click frame 2 in the *SoundTrack* layer, hold down the Shift key, and then click frame 10 in the *Background* layer.
   b. Click Insert and then click Frame.
   c. Click frame 23 in the *SoundTrack* layer, hold down the Shift key, and then click frame 32 in the *Background* layer.
   d. Press F5. (F5 is the shortcut key for Insert Frame.)
   e. Insert frames in frames 46 through 54 by completing steps similar to those in either 3a–3b or 3c–3d.
   f. Insert frames in frames 66 through 76 by completing steps similar to those in either 3a–3b or 3c–3d.
4. Add comments for documentation purposes and fscommands to set the size of the movie to full screen, disable the menus in the Flash Player window, and then quit the player application at the end of the movie by completing the following steps:
   a. Insert a new layer at the top of the Timeline and name it *Actions*.
   b. Insert a new layer above *Actions* and name it *Comments*.
   c. Key the following text in a comment in frame 1 of the *Comments* layer.

      //Player-FullScreen-No Menus

   d. Open the Actions panel.
   e. Click frame 1 in the *Actions* layer.
   f. With the Browser/Network subcategory list already expanded in the toolbox, double-click fscommand. Flash adds *fscommand("");* to the ActionScript area.

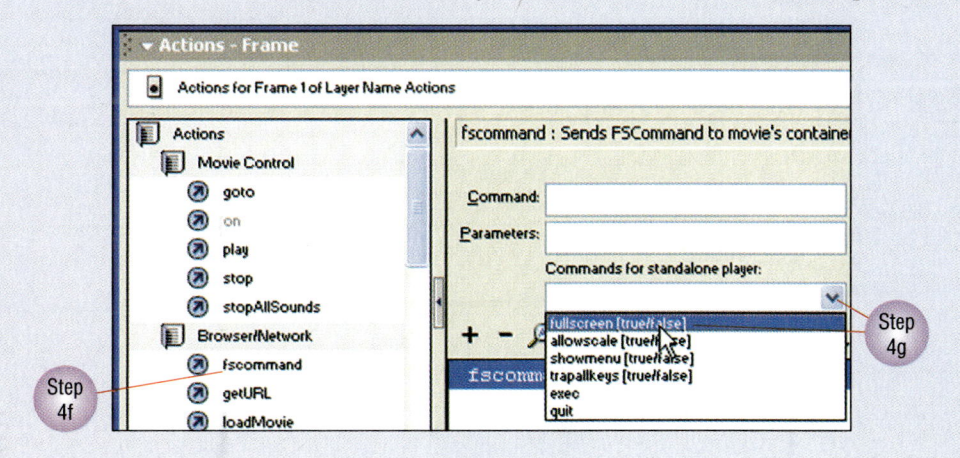

Using ActionScript and Creating Templates 341

g. Click the down arrow next to the Commands for standalone player list box and then click *fullscreen[true/false]* at the drop-down list. Flash adds the text strings *fullscreen* to the Command text box and *true* to the Parameters text box. The statement in the ActionScript area now reads *fscommand("fullscreen", "true");* as shown. 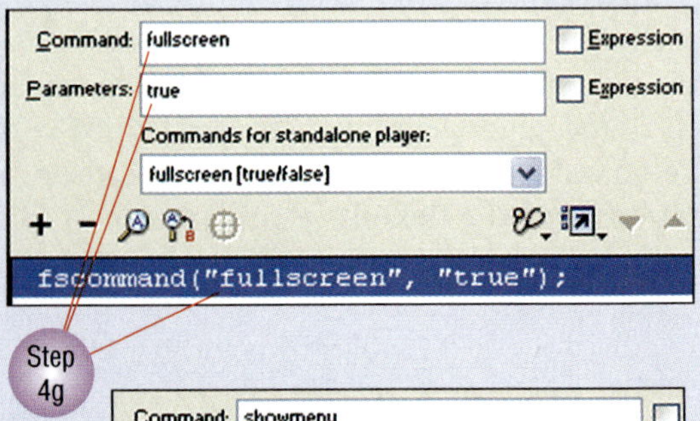
h. Double-click fscommand in the toolbox.
i. Click the down arrow next to the Commands for standalone player list box and then click showmenu[true/false] at the drop-down list.
j. Drag across the text *true* in the Parameters text box and then key **false**. The second statement in the ActionScript area reads *fscommand("showmenu", "false");*. 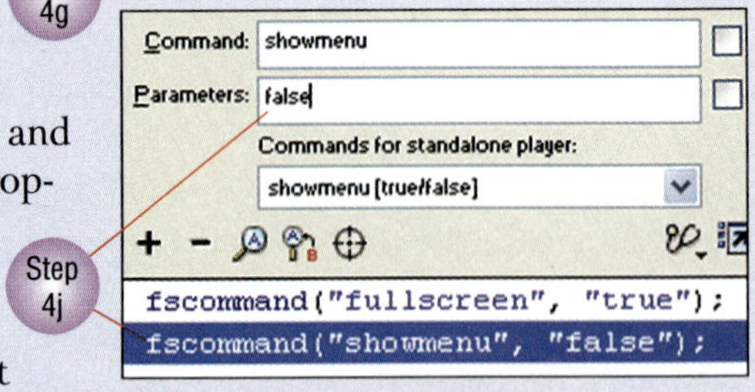
k. Scroll the Timeline right and then insert a keyframe in the last frame in the Actions layer.
l. Double-click fscommand in the toolbox.
m. Click in the Command text box and then key **quit**. The statement *fscommand("quit");* is added to the ActionScript area. 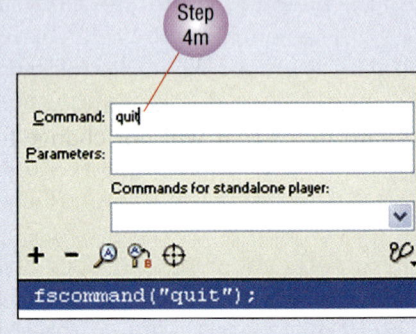
n. Close the Actions panel.
o. Insert a keyframe in frame 75 of the *Comments* layer and then add the comment text **//Quit action in last frame**.

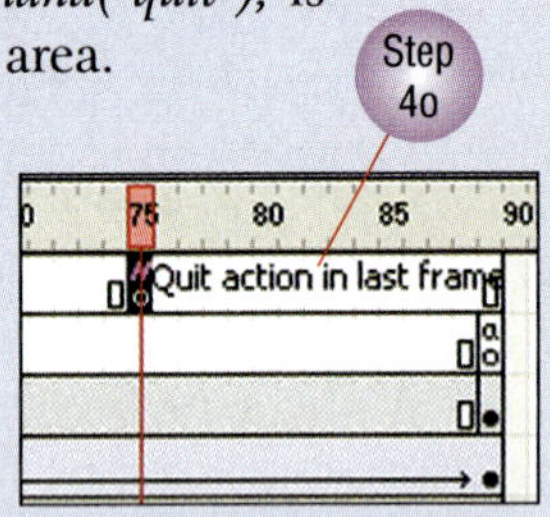

5. Publish the movie as a standalone projector file and then view the movie in the Flash Player window to test the fscommand actions by completing the following steps:
a. Click File and then click Publish Settings.
b. With the Formats tab active, deselect the Flash (.swf) and HTML (.html) check boxes.
c. Click the Windows Projector (.exe) check box.
d. Click the Publish button.

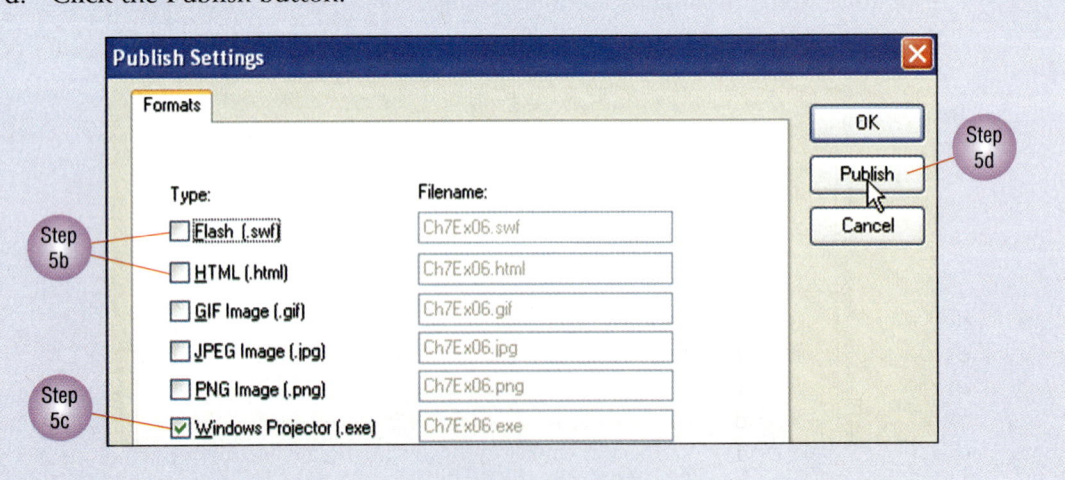

> e. Click OK to close the Publish Settings dialog box.
> f. Open Windows Explorer.
> g. Navigate to the drive and folder in which the data files for Chapter 7 are stored.
> h. Double-click the file named Ch7Ex06.exe. The movie will play in full screen mode and the player application automatically closes when the movie is complete. The movie's duration is only approximately seven seconds, so click Start Sound quickly if you want to hear the soundtrack play before the player application closes.
> i. Exit Windows Explorer.
> 6. Close Ch7Ex06. Click Yes when prompted to save changes.

Creating and Using a Template

A corporation's image is a vital marketing tool. A consistent look to a corporate Web site or other marketing media is important for brand recognition and for establishing a level of comfort with a user. A Flash movie that contains the corporate logo, colors, and interface can be saved as a template. Future movies can be created based on the template ensuring consistency and saving you the time of recreating these elements.

To create a Flash template, start a new Flash document and then create the standard items that will not change for each Flash movie. For example, create the background layer containing the company logo, contact information, interface elements, and so on. You can also set standard compression options or other Publish settings that are used in each movie. When you are ready to save the document as a template, click File and then click Save As Template. The Save As Template dialog box shown in Figure 7.12 opens.

FIGURE 7.12 **Save As Template Dialog Box**

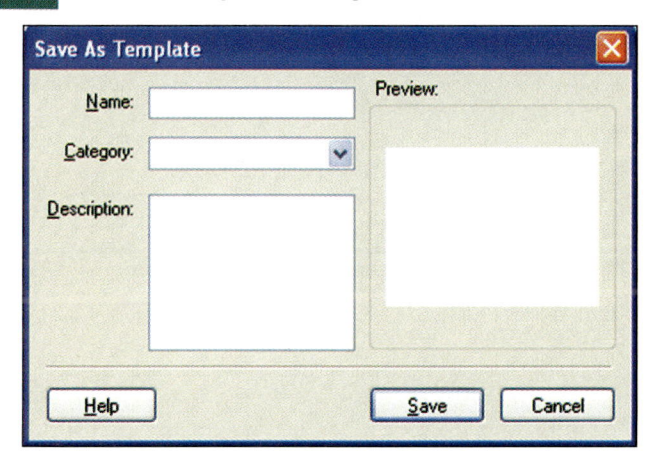

Key a descriptive name for the template in the Name text box. Choose from one of the predefined category lists in which to place the template in the Category drop-down list or key a new category name in the Category text box. Key a brief description of the standardized elements contained in the template in the Description text box. A preview of the document appears in the Preview window. Click Save to close the dialog box when all of the settings have been entered.

Using ActionScript and Creating Templates 343

Using a Template

To start a new movie based on a template that you have created, click File and then click New From Template. Flash opens the New Document dialog box shown in Figure 7.13. By default Flash displays *<Blank Document>* as the active template when the dialog box is opened. Click the category name to which you assigned the template in the Category list and then click the template name in the Category Items list. A preview of the template displays in the Preview window and the description associated with the template shows in the Description text box. Click Create to open a new document with the template items.

Figure 7.13 shows the Presentation_style1 template in the Preview window. Flash ships with several predefined templates that you are free to explore and use to build movies.

FIGURE 7.13 *New Document Dialog Box with Presentation_style1 Template in the Presentation Category Previewed*

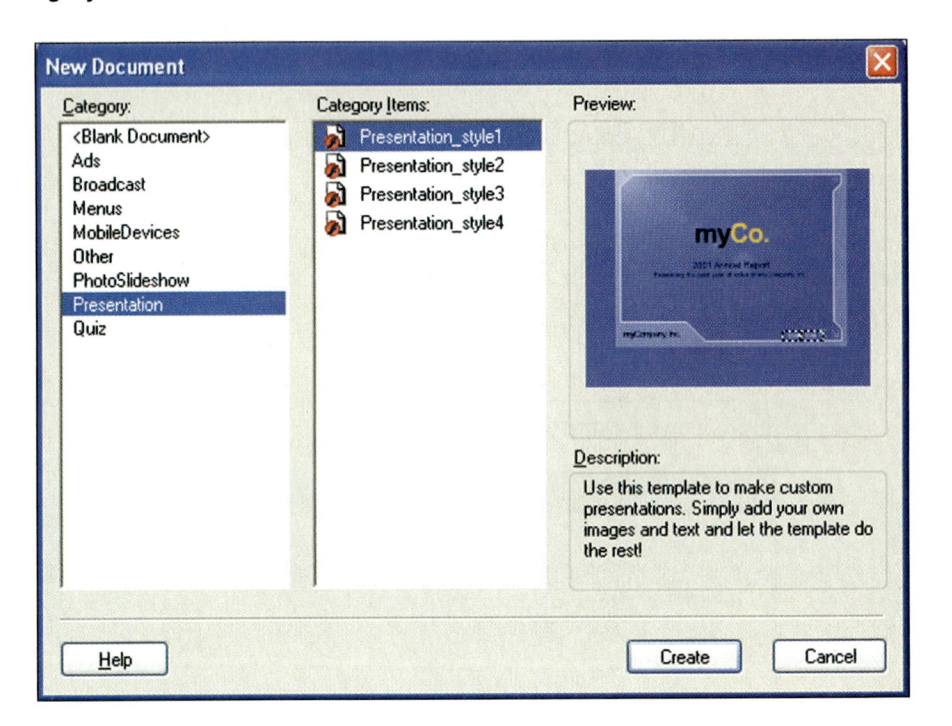

exercise 7

CREATING AND USING A TEMPLATE

1. Start a new Flash document.
2. Create a background layer changing the document color and size, import and place a logo, create a play button including ActionScript, and set publish options as standard items in a template by completing the following steps:
   a. Click Modify and then click Document.

344 Chapter Seven

b. Key **500** in the Dimensions width text box and **375** in the height text box.
c. Click the Background Color color swatch and then choose a pale blue color swatch.
d. Click OK to close the Document Properties dialog box.
e. Click File and then click Import.
f. Change the Files of type to JPEG Image (*.jpg).
g. If necessary, navigate to the drive and folder in which the student data files are stored and then double-click the file named FirstChoiceLogo.jpg in the list box. 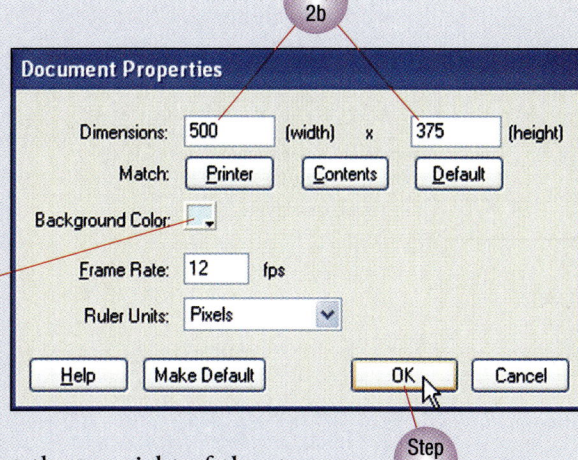
h. Scale and position the logo bitmap at the top right of the stage as shown.
i. Create two text blocks containing the text shown at the top left of the stage using the following Text Properties:
   1) Font name is Tahoma.
   2) Font size is 24-point.
   3) Text (fill) color is dark blue and bold is turned on.

j. Open the common buttons library panel and then drag an instance of the *playback-play* button to the bottom right of the stage as shown. You will need to expand the Playback folder list in the buttons library panel.
k. Close the Buttons library panel.
l. Scale and position the play button as shown.
m. Open the Actions panel.
n. Click the playback-play button instance on the stage and then double-click play in the toolbox.
o. Close the Actions panel.
p. Click File, click Publish Settings, and then click the HTML tab in the Publish Settings dialog box. Make the following changes to the publish options:
   1) Change the Template to Detect for Flash 6. 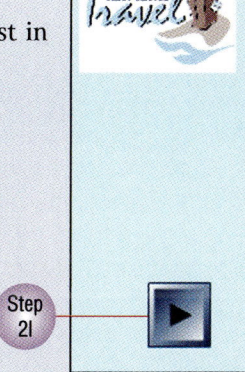
   2) Click the Paused At Start check box.
   3) Click the Formats tab and then click the JPEG Image (.jpg) check box.
   4) Click OK to close the Publish Settings dialog box.
q. Rename Layer 1 *Background* and then lock the *Background* layer.
3. Save the document as a template by completing the following steps:
   a. Click File and then click Save As Template.

b. Key **fctravel** in the Name text box.
c. Key **Other** in the Category text box.
d. Key **Logo, URL, phone, play button and publish settings** in the Description text box.
e. Click Save.
f. Click File and then click Close to close the current document.
4. Use the template saved in step 3 to start a new movie by completing the following steps:
   a. Click File and then click New From Template.
   b. Click Other in the Category list box.
   c. With fctravel selected in the Category Items list box, click Create.
   d. Insert a new layer at the top of the Timeline and name it *Picture*.
   e. Click File, click Import, and then import the file named Sailing.jpg.
   f. Position the bitmap on the stage as shown.
5. Save the document and name it Ch7Ex07.
6. Close Ch7Ex07.

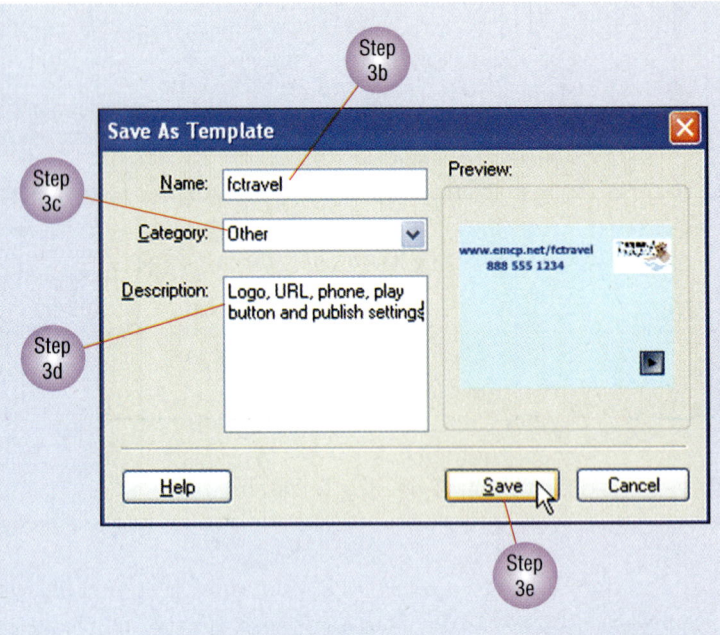

Using the Movie Explorer Panel

As you begin to create more complex movies in Flash, the task of finding and editing objects for editing purposes also grows more complex. Objects can exist in different scenes, keyframes can be spread along a long timeline, and multiple layers all contribute to the difficult and sometimes time consuming task of finding something.

The Movie Explorer is a tool with which you can locate an item and then edit it. Click Window and then click Movie Explorer to open the panel shown in Figure 7.14.

FIGURE 7.14 Movie Explorer Panel

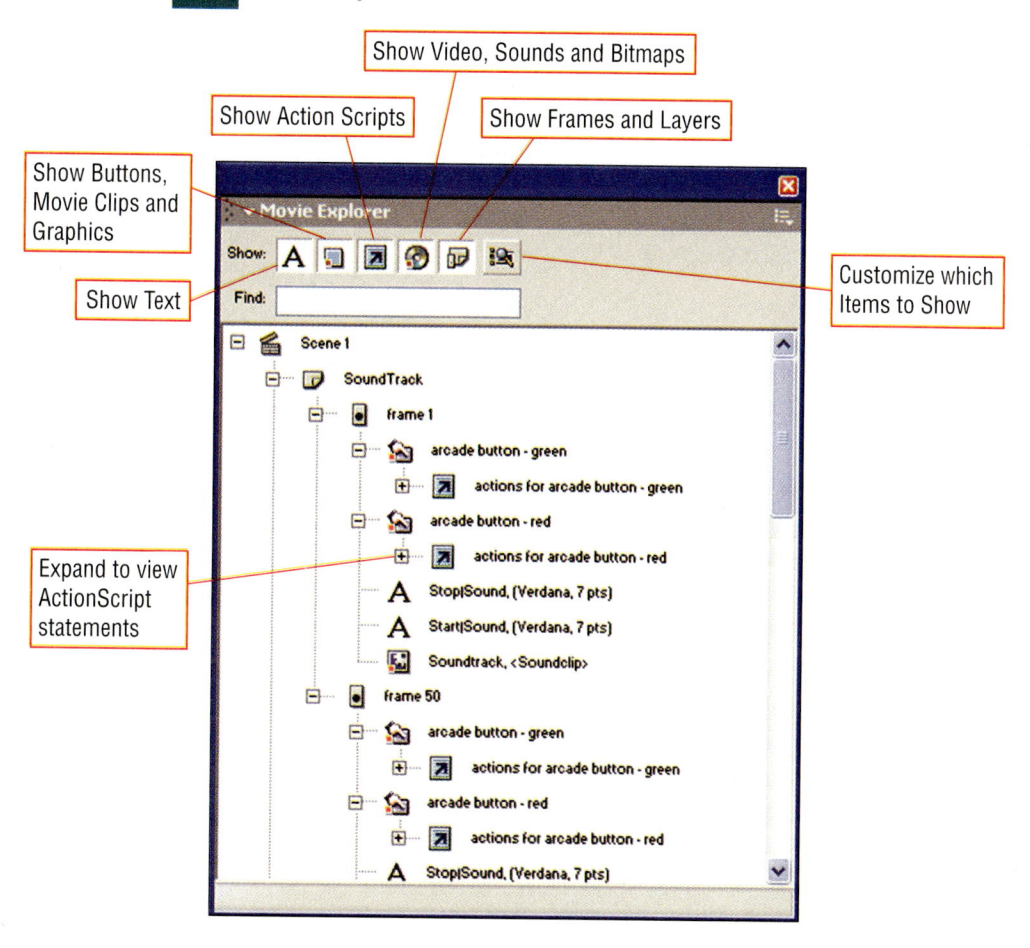

- Show Video, Sounds and Bitmaps
- Show Action Scripts
- Show Frames and Layers
- Show Buttons, Movie Clips and Graphics
- Show Text
- Customize which Items to Show
- Expand to view ActionScript statements

Use the Show buttons at the top of the panel to toggle the display of elements within the movie on or off. For example, if you are only concerned with ActionScript, you can turn off all of the Show buttons except Show Action Scripts to reduce the items in the panel. Key the first few characters of an object you want to locate in the Find text box, such as a movie clip instance name, and Flash starts searching for matches and displaying items in the list box. Expand and collapse levels in the list in a similar manner as you would browse folders and files on a disk drive.

As long as layers are not locked, you can edit text directly in the Movie Explorer panel by double-clicking the text block entry and then inserting and deleting text as required. Clicking an item in the list box selects the item on the stage and moves the playhead to the frame in which it is stored in the Timeline. Double-clicking a symbol opens the symbol in symbol editing mode.

Finally, printing with all items showing is a good method with which to generate a hard copy record of the structure of the movie. To do this, make sure all items are displayed and all levels are expanded in the list box. Click the Options menu and then click Print at the drop-down menu. You could also print individual lists such as a listing by frame of all of the ActionScript code in the movie.

exercise 8
USING MOVIE EXPLORER

1. Open Ch7Ex04.
2. Use the Movie Explorer panel to view and then print all of the ActionScript code in the movie by completing the following steps:
   a. Click Window and then click Movie Explorer.
   b. Click the Show Text button at the top of the panel to turn off the display of text items.
   c. Click the Show Buttons, Movie Clips, and Graphics button to turn off the display of symbols.
   d. If any other Show buttons are active besides Show Action Scripts, click the button to turn off the feature.
   e. Click the expand button (plus symbol) next to *actions for arcade button - green* in the list.
   f. Click the expand button next to each other entry in the list to expand each item and display the ActionScript code below it.
   g. Click the Options menu button and then click Print at the drop-down menu. Within the panel and on the printout you will notice the ActionScript for the green and red arcade buttons appears twice. This is because the buttons reside in two keyframes.
   h. Click the Show Frames and Layers button at the top of the panel.
   i. Scroll the list and review the items.
3. Close the Movie Explorer panel.
4. Close Ch7Ex04.

The Movie Explorer panel automatically updates as you add new content or edit existing content in the movie. Leaving the panel open when you are not using it causes the system to slow down somewhat as resources are used to update the items in the list. For this reason it is recommended that you open the panel only when needed and then close it when finished the task for which you needed Movie Explorer.

Finding Information About Flash on the Web

Now that you have learned the fundamentals of Flash, the possibilities for creating powerful, rich content for Web sites or other multimedia devices such as CD-ROMs is only limited by your imagination or the imagination of others on your development team. Explore new ways to create interactivity or animate special effects. As you broaden your experience, you may find from time to time that you need to find out how to accomplish a task. While the online help can provide task-specific instructions sometimes you need to find out if something is even possible. The Web is resource-rich for Flash developers. Here are three places which you can use to find information. These sites will get you started and then you can use your favorite search engine to find more.

Go to the Source

Macromedia maintains an excellent support site for Flash including tech notes containing articles with step-by-step instructions on how to complete a task. To go directly to the Flash Support Center, use **www.macromedia.com/support/flash** as your URL.

Key a word or phrase describing the feature you need assistance with in the Keyword(s) text box shown in Figure 7.15 and then click Search to search the tech notes and tutorials for related articles.

FIGURE 7.15 Search Utility on Macromedia Flash Support Center

Flashkit.com Flash Developer Resource Site

The first time you visit **www.flashkit.com** you may be overwhelmed by the quantity of information and resources. Start by reading the introduction page shown in Figure 7.16 which describes the various components on the site by clicking *First time here?* on the home page. Flash kit provides articles, tutorials, and forums in which you can ask questions, obtain free downloads for movie resources, open source movies for download, and much more. Download an open source movie and then analyze how the movie was put together to learn new techniques for graphics and animations.

FIGURE 7.16 Flash Kit Introduction Page

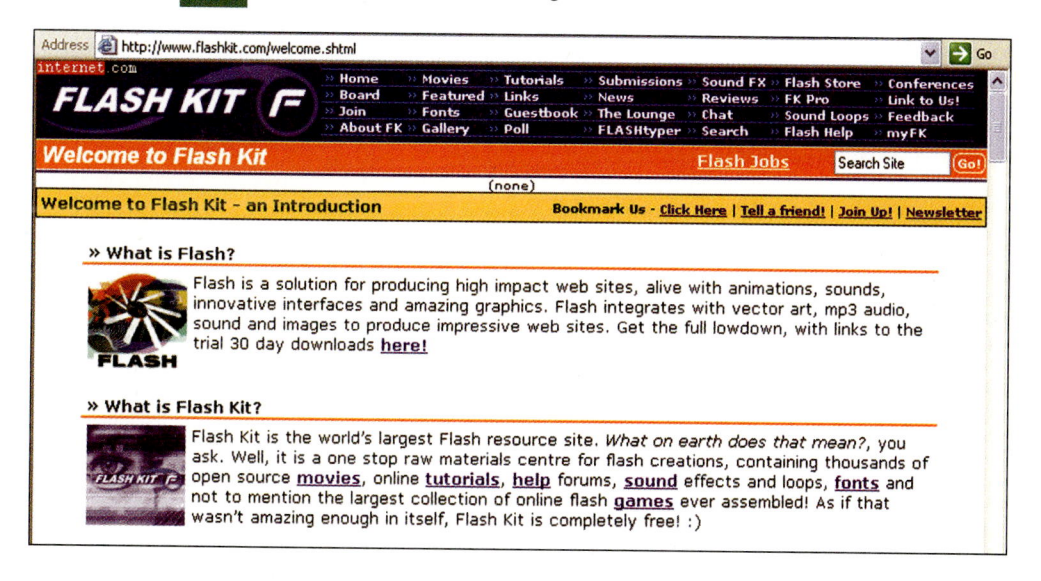

Using ActionScript and Creating Templates **349**

Flash Magazine

Visit **www.flashmagazine.com** for news, articles, tutorials, application articles, and much more. Flash magazine is maintained by Flash developers from around the world who volunteer their time and expertise. Figure 7.17 displays the Web site with the Tutorials page loaded.

FIGURE 7.17 Flash Magazine Tutorial Page

CHAPTER summary

- ActionScript is an object-oriented scripting language similar to JavaScript.
- In object-oriented programming languages, classes are defined with a set of properties and methods that define the object's characteristics and behaviors.
- Instances of a class are referred to as objects in ActionScript.
- With object-oriented programming, existing code can be reused making the program more efficient and easier to maintain.
- Actions are statements that instruct Flash on what to do with a target object.
- Actions applied to a button or movie clip instance execute when an event occurs.
- Parameters are also known as arguments and provide the variable information for the action statement such as which frame to go to.
- Before starting to write ActionScript code you should have a clear definition of the goal of the movie, a flow chart diagramming the movie's actions, and have a plan as to which objects will require ActionScript statements.
- Documenting what is happening in a movie at key points using comments is considered good practice.
- When writing code you should focus on one section at a time until it is working correctly and then save the movie as a separate version as a backup.
- Object and variable names should be descriptive labels that easily identify the element.
- In Normal mode, the Actions panel inserts the proper syntax for each statement for you.
- In Expert mode, the parameters area is replaced with a larger ActionScript area.
- In Expert mode, code hints display which identify the available parameters for an action.
- Flash includes a Check Syntax button in Expert mode which you can use to periodically check the syntax in the statements you have created.
- Switching from Expert mode to Normal mode causes Flash to automatically check the syntax of the existing statements. If errors exist, Flash displays a message indicating editing must be done in Expert mode.
- Goto moves the playhead to a different frame in the Timeline.
- The goto destination parameter can be specified using a frame number or a frame label.
- Using frame labels in goto statements is preferable since the label stays with the frame when editing, causing a frame's location to move.
- The on movie control action is dimmed unless a button instance is active.
- The stop and play movie control actions use no parameters.
- Using stopAllSounds does not prevent playback of stream sounds that occur later in the movie timeline.
- Key a label for a frame in the Frame text box in the Properties panel.
- Frame labels display in the timeline next to a red flag if space permits.
- Key a comment in the Frame Label text box preceded by two forward slashes.
- Comment text appears in the Timeline next to two green forward slashes.
- A preloader is a simple animation at the beginning of a movie that loops until the download is completed.

- The if action is used to perform a conditional test.
- A conditional test can have only two possible outcomes—true or false.
- Place the true action to be performed within a left and right curly brace after the conditional test.
- A false action is not required since Flash will simply skip the actions in the curly braces and move to the next line of code if the conditional test proves false.
- Add an else statement if you want to specify a false action.
- Nesting if actions is accomplished by adding an else if action as the next line of code following the initial if test.
- Each movie Timeline has a set of properties identified with an underscore character in front of the property name that can be checked or modified.
- The _framesloaded property returns the number of frames that have been downloaded.
- The _totalframes property returns a value representing the total number of frames within a movie.
- A stream soundtrack created in a movie clip symbol can be the target action for start and stop sound buttons that provide the user with the ability to turn sound on or off during the movie playback.
- Buttons that toggle the playing of a stream soundtrack on or off require ActionScript using the with statement to target a named instance of a movie clip.
- Use the getURL action to open a new document in a browser window.
- The URL parameter can be an absolute or relative address for a Web page or document.
- The Window parameters _self, _blank, _parent, and _top for the getURL statement specify how the window for the new document should be opened.
- The Browser/Network category of actions in the Actions panel toolbox includes the fscommand action, which is used to control the environment in the window hosting the movie.
- Fscommand actions fullscreen, allowscale, showmenu, trapallkeys, exec, and quit allow you to control the Flash Player window in a standalone projector file.
- Create a template with standard elements such as a company logo and publishing options in a new Flash document and then save the document using the Save As Template option on the File menu.
- A new document based on a template is started by clicking File and then New from Template.
- The Movie Explorer panel is a tool with which you can locate or view objects in a movie in a hierarchical display.
- Use the Show buttons at the top of the Movie Explorer panel to turn on or off the display of elements within the movie.
- Use the Web to find help when working on complex movies in Flash.
- Macromedia maintains tech notes and tutorials on the Flash support center that provide articles on Flash features including step-by-step instructions.
- Flashkit.com is a Web site for developers that includes several resources including forums and free downloads to assist with building Flash movies.
- Flashmagazine.com is a Web site maintained by volunteer Flash developers from around the world with articles and tutorials on using Flash.

COMMANDS review

Command or Feature	Mouse/Keyboard	Shortcut Keys
Actions panel	Window, Actions	F9
Movie Explorer panel	Window, Movie Explorer	Alt + F3
New document based on template	File, New From Template	
Publish settings	File, Publish Settings	Ctrl + Shift + F12
Save document as template	File, Save As Template	

CONCEPTS check

Indicate the correct term or command for each item.

1. ActionScript is an object-oriented scripting language that is very similar to this other language used to add interactivity to Web sites.
2. A class in an object-oriented language has a defined set of characteristics referred to by this term.
3. An instance of a class is referred to by this term in ActionScript.
4. A parameter is also referred to by this term.
5. Draw this diagram before attempting to write ActionScript code so that you can see each interaction and required action in the movie.
6. With the Actions panel in Expert mode, tooltips display this hint for you when writing a statement.
7. Stop, play, and goto actions are part of this category list in the Actions panel toolbox.
8. Use this list box in the parameters area for a goto action to specify the destination using a frame label instead of a frame number.
9. A label or this other element can be assigned to a frame using the Frame text box in the Properties panel.
10. A frame label displays in the Timeline if space permits with this symbol in front of the label text.
11. What encloses the conditional test in an if action?
12. What encloses the action to be performed if the test proves true in an if statement?
13. Add this action to nest another if statement at the end of the initial if action.
14. In ActionScript, properties are identified by this character.
15. This action is added in the last frame of a preloader to create a loop.
16. Do this with an instance of a movie clip symbol so that it can become the target of an action.
17. Use this ActionScript action with an instance of a movie clip to control the movie clip's playback with start and stop instructions.
18. This Window parameter for getURL instructs the browser to open a new document in a separate window from the host movie.

19. This fscommand instructs the Flash Player window to close.
20. Create a template from the current document by accessing this menu sequence.
21. Click this menu sequence to start a new document based on an existing template.
22. Open this panel to display all of the elements in a movie in a list similar to the structure of a Windows file and folder list.
23. This Web site is maintained by Flash developers who volunteer their time and expertise to share articles and tutorials on using Flash.
24. This Web site provides open source movies which can be downloaded and analyzed for learning new techniques to build animations.

SKILLS check

Assessment 1

1. Open SunsetBeachWear.
2. Save the document with Save As and name it Ch7SA1.
3. The movie contains three scenes. View the movie in the Flash Player window to become familiar with the document.
4. Add a stop action at the end of the second scene so that the movie will not play the third scene unless the user clicks the button using the following information:
   - Insert a new layer for actions at the top of the Main scene Timeline.
   - Insert a new layer above the actions layer for comments in the Main scene.
   - Insert a stop action in the last frame of the Main scene.
   - Insert a comment in the first frame of the comments layer that describes where the movie will stop.
5. Assign a stop action and assign a frame label to keyframes in the third scene using the following information:
   - Insert a new layer for actions at the top of the CatalogPage scene Timeline.
   - Insert a new layer above the actions layer for comments in the CatalogPage scene.
   - Insert a stop action in the last frame of the CatalogPage scene.
   - Insert a comment in the first frame of the comments layer that describes where the movie will stop.
   - Assign a frame label to the first frame in the *CatalogList* layer with the text **StartList**.
6. Add a goto action to the button instance in the Main scene that will cause the playhead to move to the frame labeled *StartList* when the user clicks the button.
7. Lock all layers in all scenes.
8. Test the movie.
9. Save the revised document using the same name (Ch7SA1).

Assessment 2

1. With Ch7SA1 open, save the document with Save As and name it Ch7SA2.
2. Test the movie to determine the preload time under all three modem speeds.
3. Add a scene named *Preloader* at the beginning of the movie.
4. Create a short animation in the Preloader scene using the following information:
   - The title *Sunset Beach Wear* should appear near the top center of the stage in the same font, size, and color as the CatalogPage scene.

- A text block containing the text **Loading . . . Please Wait** should blink on and off in the center of the stage. You determine the text properties.
- You determine how many frames to use.
- Add a *Comments and Actions* layer to the preloader scene.
- Add goto and if action statements to the preloader frames that will cause the animation to loop until the total frames for the movie have downloaded.
- Add a comment in the first frame of the preloader scene documenting the length of the preloader animation.

5. Test the preloader by simulating a Web connection at all three modem speeds.
6. Save the revised document using the same name (Ch7SA2).
7. Close Ch7SA2.

Assessment 3

1. Open Ch7SA1.
2. Edit the movie to remove the *Sound* layer in all three scenes.
3. Create a new movie clip symbol named Sound in the opening scene that will play the sound file seashore.wav as a stream sound in frames 2–110. Add a stop action to frame 1. Assign and use a frame label in frame 2 and add a gotoAndPlay action to frame 110 that will cause the sound to loop back to the beginning of the soundtrack.
4. Create buttons that will toggle the playing of the Sound movie clip on and off in a new layer in the Opening scene. Use button symbols from the common library and use text blocks to overlay Start Sound and Stop Sound text. Position the button instances at the bottom right of the stage.
5. Insert an instance of the Sound movie clip on the stage and name the instance SoundMC.
6. Add action statements to the Start Sound and Stop Sound buttons that will play and stop the SoundMC movie clip.
7. Make sure the two buttons created in Step 4 display during the entire animation in the Opening scene.
8. Test the movie with the Bandwidth Profiler turned off.
9. Copy the start and stop sound buttons to the Main and CatalogPage scenes so that a user can hear the sound during the entire movie.
10. Test the movie.
11. Save the revised document using the same name (Ch7SA1).

Assessment 4

1. With Ch7SA1 open, edit the CatalogPage scene to load a new document using the following information:
   - Convert the first text block on the CatalogPage scene to a button symbol named BWButton.
   - Edit the BWButton to change the color of the text to dark blue in the Over state and orange in the Down state. Draw a rectangle that covers all of the text in the text block in the Hit state.
   - Add a getURL action statement to the BWButton instance that will load the Web page named BeachWear.htm in a separate window when the user clicks the button.
2. Test the movie.
3. Close the browser window and close the player window and then save the revised document using the same name (Ch7SA1).

Assessment 5

1. With Ch7SA1 open, add frames to all three scenes to lengthen the duration of the animation by a few seconds. Edit the comments as necessary to reflect this change.
2. Add an *Actions* layer and a *Comments* layer to the top of the Opening scene Timeline.
3. Add two fscommands to the first frame in the *Actions* layer that will display the movie in the Flash Player window in full screen mode and turn on the display of the menu bar.
4. Add a comment in the first frame of the *Comments* layer that documents the action statements added in Step 3.
5. Publish the movie as a Windows projector file only.
6. Launch the projector file created in Step 5 and play the movie to the end of the third scene. Click the <u>Beach Wear Catalog</u> link on the last scene.
7. Close the browser window and then Exit the Flash Player.
8. Save the revised document using the same name (Ch7SA1).

Assessment 6

1. With Ch7SA1 open create a template from the document using the following information:
   - Delete the CatalogPage scene.
   - Delete the layer containing the Browse Catalog button on the Main scene.
   - Save the document as a template named **SunsetBeachWear**. Assign the template to the Other category and include an appropriate description.
2. Close the document.
3. Create a new document based on the SunsetBeachWear template.
4. Create a new layer above the *Title* layer in the Main scene. Add a text block to the layer that will display your name and student number in the middle of the stage. You decide how to animate the text.
5. Save the document and name it Ch7SA6.
6. Close Ch7SA6.

Assessment 7

1. Open Ch7SA1.
2. Open the Movie Explorer panel.
3. Show all elements in the movie.
4. Expand actions for all frames and buttons.
5. Print the list.
6. Close the Movie Explorer panel.
7. Close Ch7SA1. Click <u>Y</u>es if prompted to save changes.

Assessment 8

1. Open Internet Explorer or Netscape and go to the URL **www.macromedia.com/support/flash**.
2. Click the <u>Tutorial and Article Index</u> link.
3. Scroll through the list of articles and then click a link to an article or tutorial that interests you.
4. Read the article or tutorial and print the pages.
5. Go to the URL **www.flashkit.com**.
6. Click the <u>Tutorials</u> link at the top of the page.
7. Scroll the list of tutorials and then click the link to the Special Effects tutorials.
8. Scroll the list of Special Effects tutorials and then click a link to a tutorial that interests you.
9. Read the tutorial. If desired, download the files used in the tutorial for future reference.
10. Close Internet Explorer or Netscape.

INDEX

A

Actions, 315
  else, 327
  else if, 327
  fscommand, 339–343
  getURL, 336–339
  goto, 319–320, 321, 325
  if, 326
  on, 320
  play, 320
  stop, 320, 323–324, 333
  stopAllSounds, 320, 331
  with, 331–332
ActionScript. *See also specific applications, actions*
  actions, 315
  adding actions to a button with, 246–252
  conditional test, 326–328, 330
  events, 315
  guidelines for writing, 315–316
  object-oriented programming, 314
  parameters, 315
  preloader animation, 326–331
Actions panel
  accessing, 247
  Expert mode, 316–319
  Normal mode, 316
  playback actions, control of, 319
  switching from Expert to Normal mode, 317–319
  undocking, 247
  using, 247–250
Add Motion Guide command, 169, 170
Add Shape Hint command, 185, 186, 187
Add to Custom Colors option, 24
Adobe Illustrator, 132, 148
ADPCM (Adaptive Differential Pulse Code Modulation), 226–228
Advanced Effect dialog box, 173
aif format, 216
Alignment, text, 57–58
Allowscale command, 340
Allow smoothing check box, 135
Alpha, 173
Anchor points, 71, 72
Angular blend mode, 182–183, 186
Animation
  adding sound to, 217–219
  of buttons, 253–254
  definition, 32
  duration, 174, 178, 285
  frame rate, adjusting, 187–189
  with frames, 32–36
  with mask layer, 277–278
  motion path, creating, 169–171
  organizing using scenes, 198–201
  playback, stopping, 269–274
  preloader, 326–331
  previewing, 179–181
  scrubbing, 179–181
  with symbols, 264–276
  converting an existing animation to movie clip symbol, 274–276
  graphic symbol, 266–268
  movie clip symbol, 264–266
  synchronizing sound to, 219–221, 229
Antialiasing, 135
Arrow tool
  editing stroke lines with, 79–81, 85
  selecting objects with, 28
  uses, 28, 30–31
Artwork, 153. *See also* Graphics
Audience, determining, 203
Audio. *See* Sound
Audio Event option, 290
Audio Stream option, 290
au format, 216
Authoring, 3
AutoKern, 59
avi format, 231

B

Background color, changing, 69
Bandwidth, 280
Bandwidth Profiler, 171, 279–283
Bézier curves, 13, 19–20, 71, 72
Bit depth, 225
Bitmap graphics
  breaking apart, 138–139
  converting to vector, 142–144
  download performance, 284
  editing colors, 138
  file size, 6
  formats, 132
  importing, 131–134
  overview, 6
  properties, 134–137
  renaming, 135
  using as fill, 140–141
Bitmap Properties dialog box, 132, 134–135
Blank Keyframe, 35
Blend properties, 182–183
bmp format, 132
Break Apart command, 60–61
Breaking apart bitmaps, 138, 139
Brightness, 90, 173
Bring Forward command, 87
Bring to Front command, 87
Broadband, 280, 282
Brush tool
  Brush Mode, 18, 25
  Brush Shape, 19
  Brush Size, 19, 25
  fill color, custom, 24
  icon and function, 14
  use, 17
Buttons
  action addition to, 246–252
  animated, 253–254
  creating, 240–243
  definition, 121
  Down state, 240–244, 246, 254
  editing, 241–242
  Hit state, 240–244
  inserting an instance of, 244–245
  Over state, 240–244, 254
  panel, 10
  sound addition to, 245–246
  testing, 244–245
  to toggle the playing of a soundtrack on and off, 331–335
  Up state, 240–244, 254

C

Category list box, 16
Center Frame button, 198
Center Justify button, 57
Change direction of text button, 55–56
Character position list box, 59
Character space, 59
Check Syntax button, 317
Clear, 30
Clear Frames command, 175
Clipart, 153. *See also* Graphics
Clipboard
  copying and pasting images using, 144
  moving and copying objects to a Layer using, 106–107
Closing panels, 12
Collapse arrow, 11
Color
  alpha, 173
  brightness, 173
  changing with a motion tween, 172–174
  gradient fill, 91–95
  palette, displaying, 14
  text, 54, 55
Color dialog box
  Basic colors section, 24
  Custom colors section, 24
  font color, custom, 54
Color Mixer panel
  changing stroke or fill color, 89
  creating custom color, 90
  gradient creation, 92–93
  luminosity slider, 90
  opening, 89
  red, green, and blue composition, adjusting, 90–91
Color Picker, 91
Color Swatches panel, 91
Color Threshold text box, Trace Bitmap, 142
Comment, adding to a keyframe, 322, 324
Common libraries
  creating your own, 128
  inserting symbols from, 127–128
  sound, 228–229
  viewing symbols in, 129–130
Compressing sound files, 215, 226–228
Compression drop-down list, 135
Compress Movie check box, 289
Conditional test, 326–328, 330
Controller toolbar, 179–181, 279
Control menu
  Enable Simple Buttons, 244, 245
  Loop Playback, 179
  Play, 179
  Stop, 179
  Test Movie, 171, 172, 179, 244, 279
  Test Scene, 279
Convert to Blank Keyframe command, 190
Convert to Keyframe command, 190
Convert to Symbol command, 128
Convert to Symbol dialog box, 125–126
Copy command, 30, 51, 144
Copy Frames command, 176, 177, 274
Copying
  frames, 176–177
  objects with Arrow tool, 28, 30
  text block, 51
Create button, 16
Create Motion Tween command, 167
Create New Symbol dialog box, 121, 123, 237, 241
Curves
  Bézier, 19–20, 71, 72
  drawing, 71–74
  editing, 72, 74
  optimizing, 151–152
Cut command, 106
Cut Frames command, 274–275

D

Debugging Permitted check box, 289
Debug menu, 281–284
Delete Layer button, 108
Delete Scene button, 196
Delete Scene Confirmation dialog box, 199
Deleting
  a layer, 108
  objects with Arrow tool, 28, 30
  text, 51
  text block, 51
Design guidelines, 201–204
  audience, 203
  communication, 202
  flow chart, 203
  goals, defining, 202
  limiting factors, determining, 202
  researching best practices, 203
  storyboard, 203–204
Device Font check box, 292
Dimensions option, 291
Display Menu check box, 292, 295
Distorting a shape, 76, 78, 84
Distribute to Layers feature, 112
Distributive blend property, 182–183
Document Properties dialog box
  displaying, 62–63
  frame rate, changing, 187–189
  measurement units, changing, 20, 62
  overview, 62–63
Dots notation, 274
Download performance, testing, 281–284
Drawing
  basic shapes, 12–15

Brush tool, 17–19
Line tool, 17
Pencil tool, 17
Pen tool, 19–20
process, 13
tools, 13–14
Duplicate Scene button, 199
Duplicate Symbol dialog box, 269
dv format, 231
dvi format, 231

E

Ease values, 168–169, 182–183
Edit button, Symbol Properties dialog box, 269
Edit Document command, 122
Edit Envelope dialog box, 221–224
Edit Grid command, 21, 26
Edit Guides command, 20
Editing
curved line, 72, 74
fills, 82–86
with Free Transform tool, 75–78
grouping shapes, 86
sound envelope, 221–224
Stroke lines, 79–81
with Subselection tool, 72, 74
Editing tab, Preferences dialog box, 79
Edit menu
Clear, 30
Clear Frames, 175
Copy, 30, 107, 144
Copy Frames, 176, 177
Cut, 106
Cut Frames, 274–275
Edit Document, 122
Paste, 30, 106–107, 144
Paste Frames, 176, 177, 274–275
Paste in Place, 183, 200
Preferences, 79
Select All Frames, 274–275
Undo, 81
Edit Multiple Frames command, 194, 195–196
Edit Scene button, 199, 200, 323
Else action, 327
Else if action, 327
Embedded Video Properties dialog box, 236–237
Enable Simple Buttons command, 244–245
Enlarge modifier button, 67, 69
Envelope, modifying a shape's, 76–77, 78
Envelope handles, 222
Envelope line, 222
Erase Fills mode, 67–68
Erase Inside mode, 67–68
Erase Lines mode, 67–68
Erase Normal mode, 67–68
Eraser tool
Eraser modes, 67–69
Eraser Shape, 67, 68, 71
Faucet button, 67, 68
uses, 67
Erase Selected Fills mode, 67–68
Event handler, 248, 270, 315
Events, 315

Exec command, 340
exe format, 301
Export button, Embedded Video Properties dialog box, 236
Export Image dialog box, 302–303
Export Movie dialog box, 302
Eye Dropper tool, 64, 66
Eye icon, 109

F

Fading sounds, 221
Faucet button, 67
File menu
Export Image, 302
Export Movie, 302
Import, 131, 133, 144, 216, 237, 238
Import to Library, 144, 236
New, 14, 15
New from Template, 16, 344, 346
Open as Library, 127, 128
Print, 296
Publish Preview, 293, 294, 295, 296
Publish Settings, 288
Revert, 16
Save, 16
Save As option, 15, 16
Save As Template, 343, 345
Files of type list box, 131, 133, 146, 216, 218, 231
Fill
changing with Eye Dropper tool, 64, 66
changing with Paint Bucket tool, 63–64, 65
color swatch, 89
editing, 82–86
erasing, 68, 71
gradient color, applying, 91–92
gradient color, creating, 92–93
segmenting within shapes, 83
selecting with Lasso tool, 84
style, 92, 93
using bitmap as, 140–141
Fill Color button, 14, 15, 24, 90, 91, 92, 94
Fill Transform tool, 93–95
Fireworks, importing drawings into Flash, 148–150
Fireworks PNG Import Settings dialog box, 148–150
fla file, 16
Flash
advantages of, 5
ease of use, 7
starting, 7–8, 11
swf format, 299
uses of, 4
Flash Alignment options, 293
Flashkit.com, 349
Flashmagazine.com, 350
Flash Player
downloading, 4
launch, automatic, 4
Flash screen, 8–12
panels, 10–12
property inspector, 10

stage, 9
Timeline, 10
toolbox, 9
workspace, 9
Flash Support Center, 38–39, 349
Flow chart, creating, 203
flv format, 231
Font
attributes, 54
color, 54
list, 53
size, 54–55
Font list box, 53
Font Preview window, 53
Font Size text box, 54, 55
Format Options dialog box, 57–58
Frame-by-frame animation, 164
clearing frame from, 175
creating, 189–192
Onion Skin view, 192–196
Frame by Frame option, 281
Frame rate
adjusting, 187–189
default, 33
Frames. *See also* Keyframes
animation creation using, 32–36
centering within the Timeline, 198
clearing, 175
converting to keyframe, 190
copying, 176
dimmed, 193
inserting, 174, 178
interpolated, 164
labeling, 321
moving, 175–177
ordinary, 33
overview, 10
removing, 174, 178
selecting, 174
view options, 196–198
Framesloaded property, 328, 331
Frame View feature, 196–197
FreeHand, importing graphic from, 145–148
FreeHand Import dialog box, 146–147
Free Transform tool
Distort option, 76, 78, 84
Envelope option, 76–77, 78
modifying an instance of a symbol, 122, 124
Rotate and Skew option, 75–76, 77, 85
Scale option, 76, 77
selecting object with, 76
Frequency rate, 225
fscommand action, 339–343
Full Justify button, 57
Fullscreen command, 340, 342

G

Gap Size options, for Paint Bucket, 63
Generate size report check box, 289, 295
GET method, 337
getURL action, 336–339
gif format, 132, 299, 300
goto action, 319–320, 321, 325

Go to and Play action, 320, 325, 334
Go to and Stop action, 320, 321
Gradient fill
applying, 91–92
creating, 92–93
download performance and, 285
transforming, 93–95
Graphics. *See also* Bitmap graphics; Vector graphics
bitmap as fill, 140–141
breaking apart, 138–139
converting bitmap to graphic, 142–144
copying and pasting using Clipboard, 144
definition, 121
download performance, 284
importing, 131–134
Adobe Illustrator graphic, 148
Fireworks drawing, 148–150
FreeHand vector graphic, 145–148
importing bitmaps directly to the Library, 144
optimizing, 151–152
raster, 6
sources of, 153
Graphic symbol, animating using a, 266–268
Grid
editing, 21, 26
showing, 21, 26
snapping to, 22, 26, 27
Grid dialog box, 21
Grouping shapes, 86–89
Guide layer
creating, 116–118
definition, 104
Guidelines. *See* Design guidelines
Guides (guidelines)
color, 20
dragging from ruler, 20, 21, 22–23
removing, 24
showing, 20
snapping to, 22

H

Hand tool, 67, 69, 70
Help menu
Flash Support Center, 38
Using Flash, 36, 39
Help system, 36–40
CONTENTS, 37, 39–40
INDEX, 37, 40
SEARCH, 38, 40
HTML
code, viewing, 297
format, 299
settings for Flash Player file, choosing, 290–293
tags, 297
templates, 298
HTML Alignment options, 292
HTML Template Info dialog box, 291, 293

I

If action, 326

Illustrator Import Settings dialog box, 148
Import Bitmap dialog box, 136
Import button
    Bitmap Properties dialog box, 136
    Embedded Video Properties dialog box, 236
    Sound Properties dialog box, 226
Import dialog box, 131–132, 133, 146, 216, 218, 231
Importing
    bitmaps directly to the library, 144
    Fireworks drawing into Flash, 148–150
    FreeHand vector graphic, 145–148
    a Sound file, 216–217
Import to Library command, 144, 236
Import Video dialog box, 231, 234
Import Video Settings dialog box, 232–235, 238
Include Background Layer check box, 147
Indent value, 57
Index, Flash Help, 37, 40
Information resources, Web, 348–350
Ink Bottle tool, 64, 65
Ink mode, 17, 27
Insert Blank Keyframe command, 189, 201
Insert Frame command, 174, 192
Insert Keyframe command, 189, 191
Insert Layer button, 106, 107, 114
Insert Layer Folder button, 120
Insert menu
    Blank Keyframe, 35
    Convert to Symbol, 125–126
    Create Motion Tween, 167
    Frame, 174, 190
    Keyframe, 34, 35, 166
    Layer, 106
    Layer Folder, 120
    New Symbol, 121, 123, 237, 238, 241
    Remove Frames, 174, 276
    Remove Scene, 199
    Scene, 198
Insert Target Path dialog box, 270
Instance
    creating a tween to change the color of, 172–174
    definition, 104
    inserting and modifying, 122
    overview, 120–121
Instance Name text box, 272
Interpolated frames, 164
Interpolate drop-down list, 181, 182

J

jpeg format, 132, 299
JPEG Quality value, 290

K

Kerning, 59
Keyframe interval slider, 232
Keyframes
    action addition to, 247
    clearing, 190
    comments, adding, 321, 324
    converting regular frame to, 190
    copying, 176–177
    defined, 33
    download performance and, 285
    in frame-by-frame animation, 164
    inserting, 33, 34, 35, 189, 191–192
    inserting blank, 189
    inserting in a motion tween, 174
    labels, assigning, 3321
    moving, 175–177
    sound insertion, 217
Keyframe span, 190

L

Labeling frames, 321
Lasso tool
    for fill selection, 84
    Magic Wand modifier, 138
    Polygon modifier, 84
    selecting with, 28–29, 84
Layer Height option, 119, 230
Layer Properties dialog box, 118–119, 230
Layers
    copying objects to, 107
    deleting, 108
    distributing objects to, 112–113
    guide layer, creating, 116–118
    height, 119, 230
    hiding, 109–110
    inserting, 106, 114
    locking, 109–110
    mask layer, creating, 116–118
    motion guides, 116
    moving, 108, 109
    moving objects to, 106
    moving to Layer folder, 120
    overview, 10, 104–105
    renaming, 106
    stacking order, 105
    tools, 106
Left Margin value, 57
Left/Top Justify button, 57
Library, 120–121
    importing sound to, 236
    management, 130–131
Library panel
    of another movie, 127
    editing a symbol, 124
    opening, 121, 122, 123
    Preview pane, 122, 123–124, 134
    sound previewing, 216, 218
Linear fill style, 92, 93
Lines
    drawing curved, 71–74
    editing, 79–81
    erasing, 68, 71
    intersecting to create segments, 85–86
    smoothing, 79, 81, 85
    straightening, 79, 81
Line segments
    creating with intersecting lines, 85–86
    lengthening, 80
    shortening, 80, 81
Line Spacing value, 57, 58
Line tool
    icon and function, 13
    using, 23, 27
Load Order option, 289
Lock/Unlock All Layers button, 109, 111
Loop check box, 292
Looping a sound instance, 221, 229
Loop Playback command, 179
Lossless (PNG/GIF) option, 135
Luminosity slider, 90

M

Macintosh Projector format, 300
Macromedia
    Flash Support Center, 38–39, 349
    FreeHand, 132, 145–148
    Web site, 4–5
Magic Wand Settings dialog box, 138–139
Magnification
    changing with Zoom text box, 66
    changing with Zoom tool, 67
Magnifying glass, 67, 69
Mapping, 185
Mask, animating using a, 277–278
Mask layer
    creating, 113–116
    definition, 104
Master copy, 120, 121, 124
Menu Bar, Flash window, 9
Menus, accessing, 9
Method, 270, 314
Modify menu
    Arrange
        Bring Forward, 87
        Bring to Front, 87
        Send Backward, 87
        Send to Back, 87
    Break Apart, 60, 61, 138, 139, 140
    Distribute to Layers, 112
    Document, 20, 62, 187, 188
    Group, 87, 88
    Layer, 119, 230
    Optimize, 151–152
    Shape
        Add Shape Hint, 185, 186, 187
        Remove All Hints, 185
    Trace Bitmap, 142
    Transform, 78
        Distort, 78
        Scale and Rotate, 76
    Ungroup, 87
Modify Onion Markers feature, 194–196
Morphing, 165
Motion guides, 116, 169–171
Motion tweened animation
    color change of an instance, 172–174
    combining shape tweened animation with, 183–184
    creating, 165–167
    duration, 174, 178
    keyframe, inserting, 174
    motion guide layer, adding, 169–171
    moving frames, 175–177
    orienting an object to the path, 172–171
    overview, 165
    rotating, 167–168
    scaling, 167–168
    speed, changing, 168–169
Mouse events, 247–249, 320, 332
mov format, 231
Movie, definition, 4
Movie clip, definition, 121
Movie clip symbol
    advantages of, 264
    button animation, 253
    converting existing animation to, 274–276
    creating, 264–266
    importing video in a, 237–240
    stopping playback of animation, 269–274
Movie Explorer panel, 346–348
Moving
    frames, 175–177
    a layer, 108, 109
    objects with Arrow tool, 28, 30
mp3 format, 216, 226, 285
mpeg format, 231
mpg format, 231

N

Naming layers, 106
Narrowband, 280
National Telecommunications and Information Administration (NTIA), 282
Nesting if statements, 327
New Document dialog box, 10, 344
New From Template command, 16, 344, 346
New Symbol command, 123, 237, 238, 241, 242
Notepad, 297

O

Object-oriented programming, 314
Omit Trace actions check box, 289
On action, 320
Onion Skin Outlines button, 193, 195–196
Onion Skin view, 192–196
    accessing, 192
    advantages of, 193
    dimmed frames, 193
    editing in, 194–196
    Modify Onion Markers feature, 194–196
    outlines, 193, 195–196
On release event, 332
Open as Library dialog box, 127
Optimize Curves dialog box, 151
Optimizing the movie, 284–287
Ordinary frames, 33
Orient to path check box, 172

Outline
> viewing objects as, 110
> viewing onion skinned frames as, 193

Ovals, drawing, 14–15
Oval tool
> icon and function, 14
> using, 14–15

Override sound settings check box, 290

P

Padlock icon, 109, 115
Paint Behind brush mode, 18
Paint Bucket tool
> Gap Size options, 63
> uses of, 34, 63–64, 65

Paint Fills brush mode, 18
Paint Inside brush mode, 18, 25
Paint Normal brush mode, 18
Paint Selection brush mode, 18
Panels
> buttons, 10
> closing, 12
> collapsing, 11
> description, 10
> expanding, 11
> moving, 11
> opening, 11

Panning effects, 224
Parameters, 315
Password text box, 290, 295
Paste command, 30, 51, 106–107, 144
Paste Frames command, 176, 177, 274–275
Paste in Place feature, 183, 200
Paused At Start check box, 292
Pencil tool
> icon and function, 14
> Pencil Mode, 17, 27
> using, 27

Pen tool
> drawing curves with, 71–74
> icon and function, 13
> uses, 19–20, 26–27

Photo (JPEG) option, 135
Pixels
> definition, 6
> ruler measurements, 20

Play action, 320
Play button
> Controller toolbar, 180
> Edit Envelope dialog box, 223–224

Playhead, 33
png format, 132, 148–150, 300
Polygon modifier, of Lasso tool, 84
POST method, 337
Preferences dialog box
> Editing tab, 79
> tolerance settings, 79

Preloader, 285, 326–331
Preload time, 283, 287
Press mouse event, 247, 249
Preview frame view, 197
Preview in Context frame view, 197
Previewing
> animations, 179–181
> movie in the browser window, 293–294, 295–296
> sound file, 216, 218

Print command, 296
Progress bar, 331
Properties panel
> Change direction of text button, 55–56
> Character position list box, 59
> description, 10
> Effects drop-down list, 221
> Fill color button, 14, 15
> Font list box, 53
> Font Size text box, 54, 55
> Format button, 57, 58
> Frame text box, 321–322, 324
> for motion tween, 167–168
> Orient to path check box, 172
> Size button, 20
> Stroke color button, 14, 15
> Stroke height text box, 15, 23
> Stroke style list box, 15, 23
> text alignment buttons, 57, 58

Property inspector, 10, 314. *See also* Properties panel
Protect from import check box, 289, 295
Publishing a movie, 287–303
> in alternate formats, 298–301
> exporting, 302–303
> HTML code, viewing, 297
> HTML templates, using, 298
> previewing in browser window, 293–294, 295–296
> Publish Settings, 288–293, 294–295
> steps, 288

Publishing dialog box, 294
Publish Preview command, 293, 295
Publish Settings dialog box
> Flash tab, 288–290
> Formats tab, 298–301
> GIF tab, 300
> HTML tab, 290–293

Q

Quality options, 292
Quality slider, Import Video Settings dialog box, 232
Quality text box, 135–137
QuickTime, 216, 231, 300
Quit command, 340, 342

R

Radial fill style, 92
Rectangles, drawing, 15
Rectangle tool
> icon and function, 14
> using, 15

Reduce modifier button, 67, 69
Reference panel, 249–250
Registration point, 121–122
Release mouse event, 247, 249
Remove All Hints command, 185
Remove Frames command, 174, 178, 276
Remove Scene command, 199

Remove Tween command, 184
Resizing
> text block, 51–53
> Timeline panel, 120

Revert feature, 16
Rewind, Controller toolbar, 180
Right/Bottom Justify button, 57, 58
Right Margin value, 57, 58
Roll Over mouse event, 247, 249
Rotating
> motion tween, 167–168
> objects, 75–76, 77, 85

Rotation button, 56
Ruler
> dragging guides from, 20, 21, 22–23
> measurement units, 20, 21
> removing, 24
> viewing, 20, 22

Ruler units drop-down menu, 62–63

S

Sampling, 225
Sampling rate, 225–226
Save As option, 15, 16
Save As Template dialog box, 343, 346
Save button, 15
Save command, 16
Scale and Rotate dialog box, 76
Scale option, Publish Settings dialog box, 293
Scaling
> motion tween, 167–168
> video, 233

Scene panel, 198–201
> accessing, 11
> Options menu button, 12

Scenes
> adding, 198
> deleting, 199
> duplication, 199
> navigating, 199
> numbering, 198–199
> reordering, 199

Scroll bars, 67, 69
Scrubbing, 179–181
Search applet, Flash Help, 38, 40
Select All Frames command, 274–275
Selecting
> with Arrow tool, 28
> frames, 174
> with Lasso tool, 228–229
> multiple objects, 28
> with Subselection tool, 29, 31

Send Backward command, 87
Send to Back command, 87
Shapes
> adjusting, 80–81
> breaking apart, 83
> grouping, 86–89
> segmenting fills within, 83

Shape tweened animation
> combining with a motion tweened animation, 183–184
> creating, 181–183
> description, 165
> shape hints, 184–187
> adding, 185, 186–187
> removing, 185
> viewing, 185

Show Action Scripts button, 347, 348
Show All command, 66
Show All Layers as Outlines button, 110
Show Buttons, Movie Clips, and Graphics button, 348
Show Frame command, 66
Show Frames and Layers button, 348
Show Grid command, 21, 26
Show Guides command, 20
Show/Hide All Layers button, 109, 111
Show menu command, 340, 342
Show Shape Hints command, 185
Show Streaming command, 287
Show Text button, 348
Show totals message check box, 151
Show Warning Messages check box, 293
Size button, 20
Skewing objects, 75, 85
Smoothing, bitmapped graphics, 135
Smoothing, Magic Wand, 138, 139
Smooth mode, 17, 27
Smooth modifier, 79, 81, 85
Snap to Grid, 22, 26
Snap to Guides, 22
Snap to Objects, 22, 31–32
Sorenson Spark codec, 215, 231–233
Sound
> adding to a button, 245–246
> adding to a movie, 216–230
> from Common Library, 228–229
> compression, 215, 226–228
> download performance and, 285
> effects, applying, 221
> envelope, editing, 221–224
> fading, 221
> file formats, 216
> finding on the Internet, 230
> importing sound file, 216
> looping an instance, 221, 229
> panning, 224
> previewing, 216, 218, 226–227
> properties, defining, 224–226
> sampling rate, 225–226
> streaming, 220, 221
> synchronizing to an animation, 219–221, 229
> toggling soundtrack on and off, 331–335
> waveform display, 217, 222, 230

Spacing
> character, 59
> line, 57, 58

Speed, changing motion tween, 168–169
Spell checking, 51
Square, drawing, 15

Stacking order, 87, 105
Stage, 9
  magnification, 66
  moving with Hand tool, 67, 69, 70
  size, 62
  symbol editing mode, 121
Start Sound button, 335
Step Back button, 179
Step Forward button, 179, 180
Stop action, 320, 323–324, 333
stopAllSounds action, 249–250, 320, 331
Stop button
  Controller toolbar, 180
  Sound Properties dialog box, 226
Stop Sound button, 335
Storyboard, creating, 203–204
Straighten mode, 17
Straighten modifier, 79, 81
Streaming Graph option, 282
Streaming technology, 7, 220, 221, 284
Stroke color
  changing with Eye Dropper tool, 64
  changing with Ink Bottle tool, 64, 65
Stroke color button, 14, 15, 90, 91
Stroke color swatch, 89
Stroke height, changing with Ink Bottle tool, 64
Stroke height text box, 15, 23
Stroke lines, editing, 79–81
Stroke style list box, 15, 23
Subscripts, 59–60
Subselection tool
  curve modification, 20
  editing curved lines with, 72, 74
  modifying objects with, 29, 31–32
  selecting with, 29, 31
Superscripts, 59–60
swf format, 16, 299
Symbol Name dialog box, 269
Symbol Properties dialog box, 131, 269
Symbols
  advantages, 120–121
  animation creation using, 264–276
  behaviors, 121
  changing color with a motion tween, 172–174
  converting existing object to, 125–126
  creating, 121–122, 123
  definition, 104, 120
  download performance and, 285
  duplicating, 269, 271–272
  editing, 121–122, 124–125, 272
  inserting from another movie's library file, 127, 128
  inserting from common libraries, 127–128
  instance, 120, 122
  managing, 130–131
  master copy, 120, 121, 124

viewing symbols in common library, 129–130
Synchronize video to Macromedia Flash document frame rate option, 233, 235
Sync sound option, 219–221

T

Template option, 291
Templates, using, 16, 343–346
Test button, 134, 136–137
Testing
  authoring environment compared to testing environment, 279
  Bandwidth Profiler, using, 279–283
  importance of, 278
  optimizing the movie, 284–287
  simulating Internet connection speed, 287
  using download speed statistics, 281–282
  viewing the movie, 279
Test Movie command, 171, 172, 179
Text. *See also* Text block
  alignment, 57, 58
  character spacing, 59
  color, 54
  default settings, 53
  deleting, 51
  editing, 51
  font, 53–54
  font attributes, 54
  font size, 54–55
  formatting, 57–58
  kerning, 59
  rotating, 56
  subscripts, 59–60
  superscripts, 59–60
  wrapping, 50
Text block
  breaking apart, 60–61
  copying, 51
  deleting, 51
  distorting, 77
  extending, 50–51
  fixed, 50–51
  height, 50
  moving, 51
  positioning, 50
  resizing, 51–53
  vertical, 55–57
Text (fill) color button, 54, 55
Text menu
  Align, 60
  Font, 60
  Size, 60
  Style, 60
  Tracking, 60
Text tool
  converting extending text block to fixed text block, 51
  extending text block, creating, 50
  fixed text block, creating, 50
Threshold text box, Magic Wand, 138, 139
Time In control, 222
Timeline
  description, 32

frames, 33
overview, 10
sound waveform displayed in, 217
Timeline panel
  Center Frame button, 198
  Edit Multiple Frames button, 194, 195, 196
  Layer folder, 119–120
  layer management, 104–105
  Lock/Unlock All Layers button, 109, 111
  Modify Onion Markers button, 195
  Onion Skin button, 192
  resizing, 120
  Show All Layers as Outlines button, 110
  Show/Hide All Layers button, 109, 111
  tools, 105–106
Time Out marker, 222
Tint color options, 172–173
Tinted Frames option, 197
Title Bar, Flash window, 9
Toggle Sorting Order button, 131
Toolbox
  Colors section, 14, 24
  drawing tools, 12–14
  moving, 9
Tooltip, 12
Totalframes property, 328
Trace Bitmap dialog box, 142
Tracking, 59
Transformational point, 75
Transmission rate, 280
Transparency, 173, 285
trapallkeys command, 340
Tweened animation
  advantages, 164
  types, 165

U

Ungroup command, 87
Update button
  Bitmap Properties dialog box, 136
  Embedded Video Properties dialog box, 236
  Sound Properties dialog box, 226
URL text box, 336, 338
Use imported JPEG data check box, 135, 136
Use multiple passes (slower) check box, 151

V

Vector graphics
  converting bitmap to, 142–144
  download performance, 284
  file size, 5
  importing FreeHand, 145–148
  overview, 5
Version option, 289
Video
  audio tract, 233
  compression, 215, 231, 232

embedded video properties, 236–237
embedding a QuickTime video, 234–236
file formats, 231
importing, 231–240
  directly to the library, 236
  Import Video Settings, 232–235
  in a movie clip symbol, 237–240
modifying a video instance, 237
Viewing Flash content on the Web, 4–5
View menu
  Bandwidth Profiler, 171, 280, 282
  Frame By Frame, 281
  Go To, 199, 200
  Grid
    Edit Grid, 21, 26
    Show Grid, 21, 26
    Snap to Grid, 22, 26, 27
  Guides
    Edit Guides, 20
    Show Guides, 20
    Snap to Guides, 22
  Magnification, 14
  Rulers, 20, 22
  Show Streaming, 287
  Snap to Objects, 22, 31–32
  Streaming Graph, 282

W

wav format, 216, 218
Web page, opening during a movie, 336–339
White space, 59
Wide Library View button, 129
Window menu
  Actions, 247, 249, 251
  Color Mixer, 89
  Color Swatches, 91, 94
  Common Libraries, 127–129
    Sounds, 228, 229
  Library, 121, 122, 123, 218
  Movie Explorer, 346, 348
  open documents, 16
  Scene, 198, 199
  Toolbars
    Controller, 179–181, 279
Window Mode options, 292
Windows Projector (*exe*) format, 300, 301
With action, 331–332
Workspace, 9

Z

Zoom Out button, Edit Envelope dialog box, 224
Zoom text box, 66, 70
Zoom tool, 67, 69